I0885204

Gender Gaps and the Social Inclusion Movement in ICT

Idongesit Williams
Aalborg University, Denmark

Olga Millward
Aalborg University, Denmark

Roslyn Layton
Aalborg University, Denmark

A volume in the Advances in Human and Social Aspects of Technology (AHSAT) Book Series

IGI Global
DISSEMINATOR OF KNOWLEDGE

Published in the United States of America by
IGI Global
Information Science Reference (an imprint of IGI Global)
701 E. Chocolate Avenue
Hershey PA, USA 17033
Tel: 717-533-8845
Fax: 717-533-8661
E-mail: cust@igi-global.com
Web site: http://www.igi-global.com

Library of Congress Cataloging-in-Publication Data

Names: Williams, Idongesit, editor. | Millward, Olga, 1972- editor. | Layton, Roslyn, 1974- editor.
Title: Gender gaps and the social inclusion movement in ICT / Idongesit Williams, Olga Millward, and Roslyn Layton, editors.
Description: Hershey, PA : Information Science Reference, [2019] | Includes bibliographical references.
Identifiers: LCCN 2018014731| ISBN 9781522570684 (hardcover) | ISBN 9781522570691 (ebook)
Subjects: LCSH: Computers and women. | Information technology. | Sex discrimination. | Digital divide. | Social inclusion.
Classification: LCC QA76.9.W65 G464 2019 | DDC 303.48/33--dc23 LC record available at https://lccn.loc.gov/2018014731

This book is published in the IGI Global book series Advances in Human and Social Aspects of Technology (AHSAT) (ISSN: 2328-1316; eISSN: 2328-1324)

British Cataloguing in Publication Data
A Cataloguing in Publication record for this book is available from the British Library.

For electronic access to this publication, please contact: eresources@igi-global.com.

Advances in Human and Social Aspects of Technology (AHSAT) Book Series

Ashish Dwivedi
The University of Hull, UK

ISSN:2328-1316
EISSN:2328-1324

Mission

In recent years, the societal impact of technology has been noted as we become increasingly more connected and are presented with more digital tools and devices. With the popularity of digital devices such as cell phones and tablets, it is crucial to consider the implications of our digital dependence and the presence of technology in our everyday lives.

The **Advances in Human and Social Aspects of Technology (AHSAT) Book Series** seeks to explore the ways in which society and human beings have been affected by technology and how the technological revolution has changed the way we conduct our lives as well as our behavior. The AHSAT book series aims to publish the most cutting-edge research on human behavior and interaction with technology and the ways in which the digital age is changing society.

Coverage

- Technology Adoption
- Technology Dependence
- End-User Computing
- Gender and Technology
- Activism and ICTs
- Computer-Mediated Communication
- ICTs and social change
- Digital Identity
- Human-Computer Interaction
- Technoself

IGI Global is currently accepting manuscripts for publication within this series. To submit a proposal for a volume in this series, please contact our Acquisition Editors at Acquisitions@igi-global.com or visit: http://www.igi-global.com/publish/.

The Advances in Human and Social Aspects of Technology (AHSAT) Book Series (ISSN 2328-1316) is published by IGI Global, 701 E. Chocolate Avenue, Hershey, PA 17033-1240, USA, www.igi-global.com. This series is composed of titles available for purchase individually; each title is edited to be contextually exclusive from any other title within the series. For pricing and ordering information please visit http://www.igi-global.com/book-series/advances-human-social-aspects-technology/37145. Postmaster: Send all address changes to above address.

Titles in this Series

For a list of additional titles in this series, please visit: www.igi-global.com/book-series

Analytical Frameworks, Applications, and Impacts of ICT and Actor-Network Theory
Markus Spöhrer (University of Konstanz, Germany)
Information Science Reference • copyright 2019 • 327pp • H/C (ISBN: 9781522570271) • US $175.00 (our price)

Analyzing Human Behavior in Cyberspace
Zheng Yan (University at Albany (SUNY), USA)
Information Science Reference • copyright 2019 • 333pp • H/C (ISBN: 9781522571285) • US $175.00 (our price)

Handbook of Research on Technology Integration in the Global World
Efosa C. Idemudia (Arkansas Tech University, USA)
Information Science Reference • copyright 2019 • 535pp • H/C (ISBN: 9781522563679) • US $195.00 (our price)

Returning to Interpersonal Dialogue and Understanding Human Communication in the Digital Age
Michael A. Brown Sr. (Florida International University, USA) and Leigh Hersey (University of Louisiana at Monroe, USA)
Information Science Reference • copyright 2019 • 299pp • H/C (ISBN: 9781522541684) • US $180.00 (our price)

Intimacy and Developing Personal Relationships in the Virtual World
Rejani Thudalikunnil Gopalan (Gujarat Forensic Sciences University, India)
Information Science Reference • copyright 2019 • 355pp • H/C (ISBN: 9781522540472) • US $175.00 (our price)

Handbook of Research on Children's Consumption of Digital Media
Gülşah Sarı (Abant Izzet Baysal University, Turkey)
Information Science Reference • copyright 2019 • 423pp • H/C (ISBN: 9781522557333) • US $225.00 (our price)

Handbook of Research on Multicultural Perspectives on Gender and Aging
Rekha Pande (University of Hyderabad, India) and Theo van der Weide (Radboud University Nijmegen, The Netherlands)
Information Science Reference • copyright 2018 • 361pp • H/C (ISBN: 9781522547723) • US $225.00 (our price)

Narratives and the Role of Philosophy in Cross-Disciplinary Studies Emerging Research and Opportunities
Ana-Maria Pascal (Regent's University London, UK)
Information Science Reference • copyright 2018 • 198pp • H/C (ISBN: 9781522555728) • US $135.00 (our price)

IGI Global
DISSEMINATOR OF KNOWLEDGE

701 East Chocolate Avenue, Hershey, PA 17033, USA
Tel: 717-533-8845 x100 • Fax: 717-533-8661
E-Mail: cust@igi-global.com • www.igi-global.com

This book is dedicated to:

Nkoyo Uko, Norah Williams, and Dr. Itoro Ndoh
Women who inspire as STEM graduates and promoters of STEM based education for women.

Silvia Elaluf Calderwood and Bronwyn Howell
Women engineers who exemplify the Western tradition of inquiry and scientific method and have offered valuable insights to the topic of gender and ICT.

Karin Kalda
An Estonian woman who transformed her life through self-directed study to become a top ICT practitioner.

We hope that this book helps girls and women improve their quality of life and for academics and policymakers to uplift their knowledge of the field.

Editorial Advisory Board

Table of Contents

Detailed Table of Contents

The USA and Denmark are leading information communications technologies (ICT)-enabled economies and have a variety of policies to promote women in ICT occupations, but both report that just roughly 25% of math and computing jobs in their respective countries are held by women, a number that continues to decline. The trend is odd given that the ICT industry globally notes a growing shortage of workers as well as a potential for lost revenue if positions go unfilled. Given the situation and a significant evidence that women's participation in companies is associated with greater profitability, one would assume ICT companies to be profit-maximizing and thus do more to attract and retain women. The trends are also odd given that the participation of women in scientific occupations in the life, physical, and social sciences are increasing overall. This chapter briefly reviews the situation and recommendations to address it, including increasing mentorship for women and recognizing and addressing bias in the workplace.

Women constitute one of the risk groups vulnerable to poverty; therefore, enabling their participation in the labor force is crucial to promoting social inclusion in a society. Employment in the information and communication technology (ICT) sector is widely known for being male-dominated, and recently women's participation has become an important subject. This chapter aims to examine women's employment in Turkey's ICT sector from 2009 to 2016, from a social inclusion perspective, by using various indicators. Comparisons with European Union (EU) countries provide perspective on tracking the progress of employment structure and education choices for ICT by gender. All indicators signify the existence of a gender gap resulting in low rates of inclusion of women in Turkey's ICT employment during the period. Examination of the reasons leads to making some policy recommendations to promote social inclusion of women in Turkey's ICT employment.

Gender essentialism is often used to excuse gender-based biases in the use of ICT tools and online services encouraging gender inequalities in opportunities for both males and females. This chapter aims at exploring ICT tools and online services currently being used by university students. The chapter investigates gender differences in preferences and proclivities for ICT tools and online services. Data collected from 618 university students were analyzed. The results show that males significantly differ in the use and preferences of ICT tools and devices (smart phones and tablets) from females. Conversely, females significantly differ in the use and preferences for online services (WhatsApp, text messaging, and library search engines) from males. The study also finds that smartphone and laptop computers are

study findings are anchored on existing literature, relevant theoretical positions, and data from statistical analyses. It concludes that equal opportunities in ICT studies for male and female students will empower all groups to contribute maximally to science and technology revolution for achieving needed economic and national development in the country.

There is no single field that is unaffected by the developments experienced in information and communication technologies today. However, the questions, Have women been affected by these intensive technological developments and technology utilization—which are efficient in every field—as much as men have? If not, how may this be reversed? and how may technology be made effective in making women economic? arouse curiosity. Therefore, the study was shaped by answering these questions. Another reason why the study took these questions as the basis is that women and technology are of profound importance in the sustainable development and growth of societies. Women's efficient use of technology is a must to turn the changes and developments experienced in information and communication technologies into opportunities and to reach the standards of the information society. Women's economic empowerment and technology were examined, the importance of the subject was emphasized, and recommendations were made within the scope of the study.

The discussion on the digital gender divide is often focused on the women who are yet to adopt ICT. The focus on women who adopt and reject ICT is rare. Women who adopt and reject ICT also account for women who do not access ICT. They often reject ICT because they are unsatisfied with the ICT technology or service adopted. To shed light on this discussion, a small scaled deductive exploratory research was conducted to understand the role of post-adoption satisfaction on the adoption of functionalities provided via mobile Facebook. The theoretical approach was the expectation and confirmation theory. The outcome indicated that post-adoption satisfaction did affect how much of the functionalities on mobile Facebook the female respondents were interested in exploring. Based on this outcome, this chapter presents a postulation in the form of a discussion to indicate that post-adoption satisfaction could be one of the reasons for the global digital gender divide.

This chapter will bridge theories such as ICT, creativity, learning, and gender in one framework, and particularly focuses on how to meet gender gaps in learning contexts by using ICT and the strategies of developing gender sensitive creativity training programs in developing contexts. In this sense, this chapter contributes to imply both how to encourage more women users and how women can better use

Foreword

The fact that women are still underrepresented studying and working in science, technology, engineering and mathematics (STEM) creates a need to understand the challenges and problems. This book presents a unique view and learning possibility on gender differences and possibilities within engineering, ICT policies, creativity, e-government, social inclusion and social networks. The book is divided into a number of ICT relevant studies on visualizing and studying the gender divide.

The book visualizes various ways women can experience exclusion in production, adoption and usage of ICT and how the problems can be addressed. Papers present the gender gap in ICT both in learning contexts, with respect to accessibility of Internet and mobile technologies in country studies, as well as processing of information online and preferences in ICT tools and ICT services. Additionally, the book presents papers on gender differences with respect to e-government services, employment in ICT sectors and secondary schools with respect to attitude and perception towards ICT. Also, the perspectives of personality and social media adoption as well as politicization in the ICT workforce is a theme in the book.

The book is edited by young researchers who daily experience the gender divide and exclusion within ICT adoption and usage. On top of this, they represent a difference in culture and nationality which challenge the discussion on the gender divide in ICT today. This perspective is found to be central in the book and the book, therefore, provides insights and possibility for comparison and discussions beyond single gender studies.

The book presents an interesting and relevant contribution to setting the scene and supporting discussions on the gender divide experienced in a multiplicity of places within the ICT era. The book contributes to a better understanding of the problem and points to new ways of dealing with the gender divide through research covering an array of areas within ICT production, adoption and usage.

Lene Tolstrup Sørensen
Aalborg University, Denmark

Preface

OVERVIEW OF THE BOOK

The Greek Philosopher, Heraclitus of Ephesus indicated that "the only constant thing is change". This idea holds true for Information and Communication Technologies (ICT) as well. In the early parts of the last two decades in the twentieth century, ICT technologies and services enabled communication between people and machines. It also served as a supporting system for information dissemination, decision- making and the conducting of transactions in organizations. In the later years of the twentieth century to the early parts of the twenty first century, ICT evolved into an enabler in society. It enabled different sectors of the economy such as education, health, commerce etc. As we progressed into the twenty first century, ICT has also evolved into a being a pervasive technology which does not just serve as a means of support or as an enabler. But it now an integral part of society enabled by the Internet.

However, the digital gender divide does not diminish as ICT evolve. Largely, from a global perspective, the digital gender divide affects women more than men. As a result most women become marginalized and socially excluded in the new and emerging ICT driven society. Initially the marginalization was evident in their access to ICTs. But now, women are additionally marginalized when it comes to the production of ICTs. Globally there are very few women who, either use ICTs, utilize ICT as entrepreneurs, study to become an ICT engineer, work in ICT firms as developers or research into new possibilities that could be made possible by ICT. Hence in one way, one could say that Heraclitus' assumption is false and in another way it could be seen as true when discussing the gender divide. It can be deemed false because the gender divide is constant in the face of evolving ICTs. It can be deemed true because, as ICTs evolve, so the gender divide evolve in different ways.

Now if change is a constant, then it is imperative that the byproduct of change is a positive. If the byproduct of change is a negative, then something has to be done about it. So far, the byproduct of the change with respect to the gender divide has been more negative than positive. The positives can be identified in the west with respect to the adoption of ICT. This positive outcome is driven greatly the appeal of social media platforms to women (see Poushter, Bishop, & Chwe, 2018). The negatives are much more than the positives. A few of the negatives are as follows,

1. The digital gender gap with respect to the adoption of ICT, globally, is not decreasing but increasing. The International Telecommunications Union reports and increase from 11% to 12% between 2011 and 2016 respectively (ITU, 2016). The gender gaps are larger in developing countries than in developed countries (ibid).

2. The number of women employed as ICT specialist in the EU decreased by 5% than the number employed as ICT specialist in 2006 (see Eurostats, 2018). And fewer women are in leadership position in the ICT sector (see European Commission, 2013)
3. Globally, the as the number of women studying for computer degrees decreased from 14% in 2010 to 13% in 2014 (see WES, 2018)

These negative outcomes further marginalize women as the world moves into the 4th industrial revolution. It also further entrenched the social exclusion of women in a world that is driven by ICT. It is important to note that the vision of an ICT driven world was conceived in the 1970s (see Kay, 1972; Isaacson, 1978). The vision of this future world was not that of a male dominated ICT driven world. It also involved women and men becoming producers and users of ICT services (Isaacson, 1978). The vision took into consideration the fact that the present world as we know it will change because of ICT. And to survive in that world, adopting ICT will not be sufficient but gaining the competences that will aid in the delivery of these services will be of great importance. So far, the negative outcomes indicates that there was no plan on how to facilitate the holistic view of this vision globally. Hence the gender divide is likely to persist in the 4th Industrial revolution.

Be that as it may, it not too late to steer the wheel of the outcome from the negative to the positive. Now that we are at the verge of the 4th industrial revolution, it is important to identify the existing challenges that produce these negative outcomes. And furthermore find out ways by which social inclusion of can be facilitated for the 4th industrial age. These solutions could either be incremental or full blown. It is against this back ground that this book was conceived.

In this book, some these problems, the effects of these problems and solutions to these problems are highlighted. The problems are highlighted in the form of comparative studies, country studies, individual centric studies, the theoretical perspective, and from the organizational perspective. The effect is evident in the usage of online services, women empowerment and economic development, the low employment of women in the ICT sector, the existence of few women in management positions in the ICT sector and the fewer number of women educated within Science, Technology, Engineering and Mathematics (STEM) disciplines. The proposed solutions highlighted includes a human rights-based approach, adopting creativity, diversifying research, enhancing STEM competences in Women, and from a policy based perspective.

This book is relevant for head of Governments agencies, policy makers, researchers, academics, students, consultants, International Development Agencies, Non-governmental organizations, ICT associations, Industry Associations, and any agency or organization. The reason for the audience divergence is because, the ICT gender divide is not a sector specific issue. As we move towards a new world driven by ICT, bridging the gender divide in ICT is the responsibility of everyone. In this way social inclusion can be promoted and no gender would be marginalized in anyway. Another reason is because, the greater the level of social inclusion, the greater the promotion of democracy. Else, as we move into the 4th and future industrial ages, the less democratic the world might become.

Therefore in order to cater for the divergence in the scope of our audience, the different authors have adopted different styles for the presentation of their work. This was done to facilitate effective communication with our readers. Therefore some of the chapters are descriptive while others are expository and there are chapters that are aimed at initiating conversations that hitherto has been avoided.

As this book is not designed purely for academics, what was not an aim in the development of this book was the proving of hypotheses or scientific theories. This does not imply that the book is devoid of scientific theories and hypotheses. The aim rather was to paint the picture of the problem and proffer solutions to these problems. This aim is achieved obviously with the support of empirical work. The empirical work in this book either identifies the problem, present a solution or serve as a basis for discussion.

OVERVIEW OF THE CHAPTERS

There are 13 chapters in this book. The chapters are as follows:

Chapter 1 is a comparative study between Australia and Chile. It identifies and explain the discrimination women engineers and ICT professional face in their career. The chapter identifies that the discrimination is experienced in developed and developing countries. This chapter will be of interest not only to policy makers but to employers in the ICT section.

Chapter 2 is a country study on India. The study explains the influence of social norms on the digital gender divide in India. It is explained that these social norms perpetuate the economic disadvantage of women in India. These norms are seen as infringing the fundamental human rights of the Indian woman. Therefore if there has to be gender equality, the chapter proposes that it has to be from a human rights perspective.

Chapter 3 provides an analysis on the increasing trend in the decline in the participation of women in math and computering jobs. The context of the analysis are 2 digital economies, Denmark and the USA. The chapter enumerates challenges faced by women when applying to join the labor force in math and computering jobs as well as challenges that lead to the exit of women from these jobs. Solutions to these challenges are present in the chapter. These solutions aim at employers and policy makers. The solutions also provide a basis for discussion and debate in the academia.

Chapter 4 examines the level of inclusiveness with respect to the employment of women in the ICT sector. This is a country studies on Turkey. Turkey's performance is rated based on its comparison with countries in the EU. The outcome indicates that the level of inclusion of women in the ICT sector in Turkey is low. Policy recommendations are provided as solutions to this problem. This chapter will be of interest not only to policy makers but to employers in the ICT section.

Chapter 5 is an empirically based chapter. The authors adopt an exploratory approach to identify gender differences and proclivities when they use online services. The empirical analysis supported the existing notion that women are prone to adopting online services while men are also interested in the devices and tools provided by an ICT service.

Chapter 6 is a discussion on the effect of personality and ICT adoption. This chapter argues that the gender divide could also exist because the female user is averse to the service delivered by the ICT. The aversion could be as a result of her personality.

Chapter 7 examines how the gender pattern in the usage of e-government services in Turkey. The investigation is moderated by factors such as household income, education level, employment status and frequency of use of the Internet. Based on the findings, the chapter provides insights that will be relevant for policy makers which will enable them deal with the gender divide in the adoption of e-government service.

Chapter 8 is a country study on the gender difference in the enrolment in STEM in secondary school (high school) student in Nigeria. This chapter describes gender differences in terms of students' attitude, perception and choice of ICT subjects. It further highlights the influence of parental influence, age, and religion on their choice of going for an IT subject or otherwise.

Chapter 9 is a review making the case for empowering the digital competences of women. The forms of empowerment include educating more female students using the STEM curriculum, facilitating capacity building by training women to become ICT entrepreneurs and employing more women in the ICT sector. The argument in this chapter is that such an empowerment will lead to the adoption of ICTs by women, the production of ICT services by women and the development of women centric ICT services.

Chapter 10 is a discussion on the effect of Post-adoption and the digital gender divide. The context of the discussion is on the adoption of ICT by women. The authors bemoan the fact that research on ICT adoption focuses on the adoption process and not on the post- adoption process. They posit that it is possible that the gender divide could also be as a result of the rejection of ICT by women who were not satisfied with the ICT after adopting it.

Chapter 11 provides a review of how women could be encouraged to use ICT to develop context aimed at enhancing a creative society. The framework of the review is anchored on the conceptual framework relating ICT, creativity, learning and gender. The chapter highlights the gender gaps in ICT and how it affects creativity and further provides strategies on how to empower women to become part of the creative society.

Chapter 12 provide proposals for bridging the gender divide based on theories related to online consumer behavior. The proposals are solutions to the gender gap in online information processing. The focus of these proposals is in the modification of consumer behavior, In this case the behavior of female online users. This chapter provides a great deal of insight to ICT service companies developing product for the mass market. This is because being able to generate interest from the end user is also crucial to the adoption of ICT.

Chapter 13 is an interesting chapter and a country study on Ghana which does not deal with another aspect on the gender divide and social inclusion. The context of the chapter is on male and female students who already adopt ICTs, not because the ICT is useful but they are plagued with the fear of missing out. But the inquiry is to understand which gender is experiencing a downturn in their studies as a result of using the Internet for social activities. The chapter identifies that the dip in academic performance is greater in women than men. This chapter was necessary because it was important to present a balance on the impact of ICT on women and men.

CONCLUSION

This book covers theories and literature on marketing, public policy, psychology, education, economics, and a bit of political science. It also covers theories and literature from an interdisciplinary perspectives such as Information and Communication Technology, development studies and gender studies. Therefore one could describe the book as both Inter disciplinary and cross-disciplinary. Hence this book contributes to theory and literature. However on the practical side, initiatives embarked upon by public agencies,

International Development Agencies, Non-governmental organizations, etc. have been mentioned and analyzed. Hence this book provides an insight into the outcome of some of their initiatives as well as provide the way forward as we transition into the 4th Industrial revolution. Since "the only constant thing is change as" Heraclitus declared many years ago. Let us ensure that the outcome of this change, with respect to dealing with the gender divide, is positive.

Idongesit Williams
Aalborg University, Denmark

Olga Millward
Aalborg University, Denmark

Roslyn Layton
Aalborg University, Denmark

REFERENCES

European Commission. (2013, October 3). *Digital Agenda: Bringing more women into EU digital sector would bring €9 billion annual GDP boost, EU Study show*. Retrieved from European Commission: http://europa.eu/rapid/press-release_IP-13-905_en.htm

Eurostats. (2018). *ICT specialists in employment*. European Commission. Retrieved from http://ec.europa.eu/eurostat/statistics-explained/index.php/ICT_specialists_in_employment

Isaacson, P. (1978). Personal Computing Position paper. *ACM SIGPC*, *1*(2), 5–9. doi:10.1145/1164917.1164919

ITU. (2016). *ICT facts and figures 2016*. Retrieved 9 16, 2016, from ITU: http://www.itu.int/en/ITU-D/Statistics/Documents/facts/ICTFactsFigures2016.pdf

Kay, C. K. (1972). A personal Computer for Children of all Ages. In ACM '72 proceedings of the ACM annual conference (Vol. 1). Boston: ACM.

Poushter, J., Bishop, C., & Chwe, H. (2018, June 19). *Social network adoption varies widely by country*. Retrieved from Pew Research Center: http://www.pewglobal.org/2018/06/19/3-social-network-adoption-varies-widely-by-country/

WES. (2018, January). *Statistics on women in Engineering*. Retrieved from Womwn in Engineering Statistics: https://www.wes.org.uk/sites/default/files/2018-01/Women%20in%20Engineering%20Statistics%20-%20January%202018%20-%20created%20by%20Sarah%20Peers_0.pdf

Acknowledgment

We the editors want to specially thank the contributors to this book: Selda Gorkey, Ching Luk, Andrea Aranda, Marjorie Jerrard, Tekin Kose, Winfred Yaokumah, Fred Totimeh, Peace Kumah, Chunfang Zhou, Tijen Ozcelik, Ceyda Tanrikulu, Daniel Adjin, Hannah Muat, Tayo George, Anthony Onwumah, Michael Fagbohun, Michael Adebayo, Olawale Olonade, and Joseph Wireko for their immeasurable contribution to make this book a success. We were privileged to have worked with you on the dissemination of knowledge in this area of research.

We are also grateful to the Editorial Advisory Board, the team of peer reviewers and the Editorial Team from IGI for their assistance in making this book a reality. We are grateful to the assistant development editor from IGI and the project manager for the book, Ms. Jordan Tepper for her immense contribution, guidance and supervision in the course of this project.

Finally, we want to also extend special thanks to Assoc. Prof. Lene Sørensen of CMI, Aalborg University for writing the forward for the book and to Assoc. Prof. Reza Tadayoni, Director of CMI, and Aalborg University for his support and motivation towards this project.

We owe you all a deep sense of gratitude.

Introduction

As we approach the 4th Industrial revolution, sadly the digital gender divide still exist. This divide exists with respect to the adoption of ICTs, the usage of ICTs, the development of ICT services, and the gender disparity in the pursuance of STEM related educational courses and career. The divide has resulted in women being marginalized and socially excluded in the emerging ICT driven world. In the 4th industrial revolution and beyond, the adoption of ICTs would be imperative. However, developing the competences needed to exist in such a world will also be of great necessity. Therefore the digital gender divide is bound to increase if concrete steps are not taken to address these problems.

As a way of addressing the aforementioned problems, the editors deliberated on the problem and decided on a book that will highlight the problem as they are today as well as offer solutions for these problems. In the development of the book, a group academics with interdisciplinary and multidisciplinary backgrounds from diverse parts of the world were invited. Their task was to analyze the problem and propound solutions that will be useful to, industry players, policy makers, academics, International Development Agencies and a host of other players working on bridging the digital gender divide. The authors are from Australia, Singapore, Denmark, Ukraine, Turkey, Ghana, and Nigeria. To facilitate quality assurance for the book, distinguished academic experts from USA, Singapore, Denmark, Lithuania, New Zealand, Vietnam, Ghana and Nigeria were invited as members of the editorial board. The members of the editorial board are researchers into different aspects of the digital gender divide.

The diversity in research approach, country cases addressed, topics, and countries represented by the authors has enabled the delivery of rich content in this book. Whoever reads this book will benefit greatly from the rich insights on the issues addressed, both from developed and developing country perspectives. We, the editors, owe every member of the team our immense gratitude.

The production of this book was made possible by the Editorial Team at IGI who, in the last 30 years, have published highly rated books. In this book, our audience will not only learn about well-known issues, but also lesser known issues about the digital gender divide and how these issues could be solved as we transit into the 4th Industrial revolution. We believe the book has fulfilled the purpose it was written. And we sincerely thank everyone, who contributed in making this book possible.

Idongesit Williams
Aalborg University, Denmark

Olga Millward
Aalborg University, Denmark

Roslyn Layton
Aalborg University, Denmark

Chapter 1
A Comparison Between Australia and Chile of Factors Facing Women Engineers and ICT Professionals in Their Careers

Andrea Soledad Díaz Aranda
Monash University, Australia

Marjorie A. Jerrard
Monash University, Australia

ABSTRACT

Is this a man's world? Surprisingly the 21st century is still struggling with gender discrimination issues in many countries and in many professions. This chapter presents an analysis of the situation facing women professionals working in a developed country, Australia, and in a developing country, Chile, in the engineering/ICT sectors. The approach taken emphasizes the continued existence of inequality in these male-dominated professions based on existing research that shows what continues to be an underrepresentation of women in engineering/ICT. It is expected that the overview of this significant problem of underrepresentation will identify a number of factors at play here and that solutions to the problem will be similar in different countries.

INTRODUCTION

The chapter offers a literature review on issues focusing on women engineers and ICT professionals in two countries, Australia and Chile. It critiques the construction of the engineering and ICT profession from a gendered perspective to establish if the 'image' of the profession adds to the difficulties in overcoming the underrepresentation of women within its ranks (Comunidad Mujer, 2016; Hitschfeld & Martinez, 2016; Puri, 2017). It also examines how the various traditional factors such as harassment,

DOI: 10.4018/978-1-5225-7068-4.ch001

gender discrimination, managing long hours and trying to balance family commitments, a lack of support and mentoring from male managers, and the lack of transparency regarding their careers paths and pay, when combined, give rise to a lack of role confidence for women as engineers and ICT professionals. Existing research appears to include an individual's lack of role confidence as a separate factor contributing to women leaving the engineering profession; however, it is argued that this can arise from the traditional deterrents women face when entering the profession.

Gender equity is lacking at all stages of an engineering career and there are moves internationally to rectify this issue because of the loss of talent to the profession and to society and, specific to Australia and Chile, a shortage of mining engineers. Both the inequality and the moves to rectify it begin with tertiary education engineering degree programs (Global Engineering Deans Council (GEDC), 2017). In comparing possible disadvantage for female engineers and ICT professionals in Australia and Chile, factors common to both countries have emerged from the literature. This chapter identifies these factors and analyzes possible solutions for overcoming the disadvantage which shapes and limits career opportunities for women in these professions. A simple comparison shows that both countries have economies with a heavy dependence on mining (Banco Central de Chile, 2017), both are southern hemisphere countries, and both have a similar population size. In terms of differences, there are obviously cultural and language differences. Similarities in the engineering and ICT professions can be found in the knowledge and skills within the professions, including hard skills such as advanced mathematics, and the challenges faced in educating girls from a young age on how engineering is about problem-solving and being creative and innovative and that technology is easy to use and easy to develop; for example, writing computer code, building a 3D printer to design 3D objects, and building apps should be seen as something interesting, useful, creative, and fairly easy to do irrespective of gender. Therefore, it is worth considering the image of the profession and how this is constructed, and in doing so, recognize that any study of gender in these professions may perhaps be divisive along gender lines but will raise necessary public debate which can alter attitudes and professions to achieve greater equality. The authors relied on published research from the last three decades, which includes academic sources and industry and government reports to support our arguments.

BACKGROUND

Gender stereotyping evolving from long held perception and biases means that possible future career paths in STEM are jeopardized for women from childhood (Broadley, 2015; Mills, 2011). When high school students are in their last years, it is essential to decide what career path they will follow; however, often female students have already made choices about math and science subjects in primary school which will limit their subsequent tertiary study and career choices (Heaverlo, 2011; Puri, 2017). Where female students want to pursue careers in engineering or ICT, they soon realize that most of their colleagues will be males. Pursuing a career in engineering or ICT can be considered an excellent choice for students due to employment possibilities after graduation and further opportunities for career progression. Additionally, these jobs are well remunerated and considered prestigious right from entry into university because of the high tertiary entrance marks required (Cipriano, 2008; Hoerning, 1940).

However, once women graduate and become the new professional engineers, their career paths to gain full professional acknowledgement from their male peers will not always be uniform and nor will they be co-operative (Edwards, Pearce, Perkins, & Brown, 2014). Further, women graduates have found that their university education has not prepared them properly for performing in the real work environment and they lack professional role confidence which is an individual's confidence to fulfil the various features of a profession (Cech, Rubineau, Silbey, & Seron, 2011). Consequently, each of them has to alter their career projections and be 'realistic' about the way they could suitably perform their roles to obtain better career outcomes and professional respect, irrespective of sub-disciplines such as ICT, chemical, civil, electrical, environmental, metallurgy, mining and others (Gill, Sharp, Mills, & Franzway, 2008).

Once employed, women start to notice different types of discrimination – both direct and systemic, with the latter being the most difficult to identify and therefore eradicate - perpetrated in their workplace and they have to cope with many issues such as harassment, discrimination, long hours, often remote sites, balancing family commitments, a lack of support and mentoring from male managers, a lack of women role models, and the non-existence of transparency regarding their careers paths and pay (Edwards et al., 2014; McGregor, Davies, Giddings, & Pringle, 2017; Roberts & Ayre, 2002). These issues are common to women engineers and ICT professionals in both Australia and Chile. When considering the history of the two countries, it could be assumed that the former would have made considerable progress in the area of gender equity and equality as it has had a stable political, military, economic and social history throughout the twentieth century in comparison with Chile. Chile had experienced political suppression, military unrest, and economic collapse (Undurraga, 2015) and it has only been over the last three decades that the country has restructured and recovered to take a place in the international arena (French-Davies, 2014) and to become noted for its institutional stability, economic growth, and its high level of educational attainment by women (Parrado Herrera, 2017). Chile, like Australia, has a resources-driven economy which means that there is a demand for mining engineers and civil engineers in both countries and that both countries are experiencing a shortage of mining engineers which could be partly alleviated by attracting more women to this profession (Monash University, 2018). In Australia, undergraduate degrees are four years in length and in Chile, they may be four years or six years for execution and civil engineers respectively. Both countries have high levels of secondary and tertiary education achievement for women, albeit not necessarily in traditionally male degrees and professions. Both countries now have gender agencies to address inequality. A difference is found in Chile being a Catholic country with the strong socially conservative legacy of motherhood stereotypes which conflict with Chile's feminist movement (Power, 2004) while Australia still has one of the most gender-segmented labor markets in the world (Healy, 2015; Pocock, 1998) which seems to have arisen from the centralized industrial relations system that legally undervalued women's skill definitions and wages when compared to those of men. The outcome for both countries is, ironically, virtually the same, with under-representation of women in what have come to be male-dominated occupations with higher remuneration levels and which have come to also be referred to in the organization studies literature as 'extreme jobs', a term which applies to the work of highly paid (usually male) professionals and managers who work long hours in demanding decision-making roles (Gascoigne, Parry, & Buchanan, 2015)

In Australia, the Federal Government has established the Workplace Gender Equality Agency (WGEA) (2018b) under the *Workplace Gender Equality Act 2012*. This Agency is to work collaboratively with employers across Australia to assist them in achieving all aspects of gender equality through offering industry-specific advice, practical assistance, and education and training. The WGEA (2018c) has a reporting system around gender equality for non-public sector employers with 100 or more employees to track the outcomes of their gender policies and programs. Some current recipients of gender equality awards where women engineers are found include St Barbara Limited (mining), Alcoa of Australia Limited, Caltex Australia Limited, Dow Chemical (Australia) Pty. Ltd., GM Holden (manufacturing), and Mirvac Limited (construction) (WGEA, 2018a). In contrast with Australia, despite the fact that Chile is considered 'the tiger of Latin America', there is still much to be done regarding eliminating gender discrimination. In June 2016, Chilean President Michelle Bachelet created the Ministry of Women and Gender Equality – Ministerio de la Mujer y la Equidad de Género – led by Claudia Pascual (2017), former leader of the National Women's Service. The Ministry is tasked with raising awareness of gender issues and perspectives in public policy-making.

WOMEN ENGINEERS AND ICT PROFESSIONALS: A COMPARISON OF CAREER CHALLENGES BETWEEN AUSTRALIA AND CHILE

1. Women ICT Professionals/Engineers are Challenged At All Stages of Their Careers

The Australian Department of Education Employment and Workplace Relations identified that Australia's National Career Development Strategy must advise and prepare Australians for their career choices from primary school, not just high school. There is a clear tendency for girls to compromise their studies in mathematics and science by choosing alternative subjects while still at primary school or lower grades of high school and this derives from the teaching methods in the STEM disciplines (Education Council, 2015) which means that, from the beginning, their possible future career paths in STEM are jeopardized (Broadley, 2015; Mills, 2011). Therefore, young women when in their final years of high school have already blocked off the study and career path leading to engineering and ICT. However, for the few – usually between 15 percent and 20 percent of the first year intake – they will soon experience the reality of being in a male-dominated environment: total undergraduate and postgraduate enrolments of women in Australian universities in 2017 in engineering and related technologies was 15.8 percent and in ICT, 18.9 percent (University Rankings Australia, 2018, Table 2), with a drop-out rate of 25 percent (Mills, 2011). However, many institutions or universities are providing specially tailored programs for gender equity to incentivize women to choose these degrees and occupations with traditionally lower numbers of female enrolments (Mills, 2011; Monash University, 2017; Professionals Australia, 2014). Examples of such programs include Griffith University's Supporting Women Scholarships to enable women from across the Australian state of Queensland to study and work in under-represented or non-traditional disciplines and occupations and the University of Technology Sydney established the Women in Engineering and IT Program to specifically augment numbers of women in these degree programs (University Rankings Australia, 2018). It is worth noting that women's numbers in postgraduate courses in Australia is higher than undergraduate – engineering and related technologies 14.4 percent for the latter and 21 percent for the former and for ICT 16.1 percent and 25 percent respectively (University Rankings Australia, 2018, Table 2). These figures indicate that women who have an undergraduate degree and usually some employment experience in the field will seek additional qualifications to progress their careers and improve their rates of pay. This appears encouraging but when the actual employment figures for engineering occupations are examined by gender and only 6.7 percent of those employed in Australia as industrial, mechanical, or production engineers are women (Australian Government, 2018d), a more realistic picture of the profession and its sub-disciplines emerges. For civil engineers, 10.1 percent are women (Australian Government, 2018b), for electronics engineers, nine percent are women (Australian Government, 2018c), for electrical engineers, 4.2 percent (Australian Government, 2018e), for chemical engineers, 12.1 percent (Australian Government, 2018a), and for mining and petroleum engineers, 7.9 percent

(Australian Government, 2018f); which portrays a rather bleak set of figures for women's employment in this profession. Thus in total, less than 10 percent of engineers in Australia are women (Gill et al., 2008) and in Chile, the figure is even lower at 5.8 percent as is shown in the Appendix (Meller, 2010).

A similar path is being followed by Chile in terms of programs to incentivize women to study engineering and ICT, as Chilean universities have a major role developing gender parity programs to encourage young women to study and take up these careers. For instance, from 2013 onwards, the Pontificia Universidad Católica de Chile (UC) and the Universidad de Chile have implemented inventive programs which support access, knowledge and permanence of talented women in STEM courses. Mujeres Ingeniería (Women Engineers) UC has focused on school students as potential tertiary students in order to increase their numbers in civil engineering careers through generating adequate cultural and material conditions to directly encourage and promote their motivation to study and work in these disciplines. Likewise, the program, More Women for Engineering and Science at the Universidad de Chile, through the initiative Priority Gender Equality, has finalized plans to publicize information about these study programs and careers in secondary schools. These plans consist of openings to increase women's participation in the Faculty of Physical and Mathematical Sciences aimed at abolishing cultural biases pertaining to women (Soto, Etchegaray, Guzmán, Soto, & Calderón, 2016). Chile in terms of women's educational attainment ranks 39 out of 144 countries but this is not reflected in the labor market participation of women nor in the pay rates received by women (Parrado Herrera, 2017).

On entering the labor market in both countries, especially in non-traditional labor market professions such as engineering and ICT, women notice differences in how they are perceived and treated in relation to their male colleagues (McGregor et al., 2017; Roberts & Ayre, 2002). This differential treatment results in reduced career outcomes for women, starting with discriminatory hiring practices and different remuneration levels at the entry level to the profession (Weiss, Parkinson, & Duncan, 2015) which widen as they continue working. Reduced opportunities for taking on projects - often but not always, associated with travel being required – and reduced career development and promotion opportunities continue (McGregor et al., 2017). Specifically, when women have families to care for, they face greater barriers than men who have families; the perception at the workplace is that the woman will be devoted to her family, rather than her career, and she may be more easily moved into casual work, short term contracts, and part-time work against her will. The final outcome of this in Australia is that a woman retires with an average of AUD112, 000 in superannuation compared to men with an average of AUD198, 000 which results in an increased likelihood of older women living in poverty, and for longer (Weiss et al., 2015).

Gill et al. (2008) used a survey to gather information in three Australian engineering companies about age, years of experience and gender which revealed that there were clear dissimilarities within the companies between male and female engineers. The profession remains dominated by men with women appearing only as a minority group with less than five years of experience within that company (Gill et al., 2008). In keeping with generational research, this could be attributed to the fact that younger employees are prepared to move more between organizations to further their careers; however, in the case of engineers, it seems that men stay with the same company from entry point and work their way up the career hierarchy in that company until they dominate the senior positions (Gill et al., 2008). This blocks opportunities for both young men and women. All three firms in the study were facing change and restructuring in a competitive global market and this was a challenge for the older established male engineers but regarded as an opportunity by young women and man. These older male engineers in the study offered comments such as 'it's not a job for a girl!' (Gill et al., 2008) - 'a girl' and not even a 'woman' demonstrates the paternalistic and chauvinistic view in that company and it is easy to extrapolate this treatment across the profession where women might "be allowed into a man's world" (Watts, 2009). The women in the study lacked opportunities for achieving managerial positions and observed that men had the opportunity to attend sophisticated courses, networking opportunities, and to attend important professional reunions, thus making women extremely dissatisfied at not having the possibility for career advancement (Gill et al., 2008). This may also explain why women engineers do not remain with the same company for longer time periods and why women are more likely to forgo their engineering careers for another occupation. Twenty-five percent of women who enroll into undergraduate engineering courses at university abandon their studies while fifty percent of the graduated women engineers abandon their career paths ten years after graduation (Mills, 2011). This means that the number of experienced women engineers available is reduced by half for Australian companies such as GM Holden (Francese, 2017; Thorpe & Delaney, 2014) which have WGEA reporting responsibilities for gender equity achievements.

In contrast to the Australian situation, in Chile's financial sector which has been growing over recent years, there has been transformation with increasing numbers of women - from 25,000 to 58,000 – entering its labor market (Mauro, 2004) and 29,000 of these are professionals, including ICT professionals and engineers. However, they still experience gender discrimination when it comes to promotion and therefore have limited career paths (Mauro, 2004) which in turn negatively impacts on their earning capacity. This financial sector is a white collar industry so if gender stereotyping is applied, this industry may be more appealing to women engineers than blue collar industries with traditional male dominance.

Existing research such as that by Mauro (2004) about gender discrimination has identified a company's culture, a company's representations of gender and work organization, demography, the role of women in social activities, and family responsibilities (including being part of the 'sandwich' generation with caring responsibilities for children and older parents) as barriers to women's career progression. One of the women interviewed by Mauro, Marcela – 33 years old, recently married, no children and the Manager of Security and IT - stated that as her duties were performed in night shifts, it was very complicated to maintain relationships because:

Working more hours than what is usual is not acceptable for women. Additionally, not all men would like it that a woman has an important role, as a manager. (…) it's not very accepted that women can earn money, decide to live alone and be independent.

Marcela's husband has a similar job so is more empathetic to her career commitments; however, she admits not knowing what to do when deciding to have children (Mauro, 2004) and the influence of the Catholic Church in Chilean society may have an impact on her decision and thus on Marcela's career options.

This is why in the same study by Mauro (2004), Eugenia stated:

With our development process within the companies. When we have more responsibilities, we need to work harder, sometimes staying longer hours; when, for example, we are in charge of a project, we need to get this to its end, one has to sacrifice one way or another our family lives; that is the reason many of us say no, I'm good this way, I can continue in this role so I can make my family responsibilities compatible with my work duties. I don't want to go any further than this.

This is a clear example of the constrained gender choices that women are forced to make in relation to balancing careers and family roles and which perpetuates gender inequality (Gascoigne et al., 2015).

One senior male manager told Mauro (2004) that the reason for the absence of women in training courses was because it was their decision to stay at home and manage their family responsibilities. Even if the company wants to include women it is not possible because the company perceives women as regarding their family responsibilities as more important than their careers (Mauro, 2004). However, women in the same study identified that flexibility and support during pregnancy and afterwards would assist them to cope with pressures of work and family responsibilities (Mauro, 2004). These women believed this would assist in eliminating gender segregation in the workplace and would encourage women into the workforce and retain them as engineers and ICT professionals (Seron, Silbey, Cech, & Rubineau, 2016; Soto et al., 2016). There is also the unfounded belief that engineering, particularly civil engineering, precludes shorter working hours and flexible working (Gascoigne et al., 2015; Watts, 2009). However, evidence from Australia where negotiated workplace flexibility and limited paid maternity leave are available by law, the situation of women in the workplace has not necessarily improved and these work-life balance arrangements have served to reinforce the stereotype that women are not prepared to work the same hours as men and therefore continue to be overlooked for promotions and paid less than men doing the equivalent job (Gascoigne et al., 2015).

2. The Impact of Gender on Leadership Opportunities and Remuneration in Australia and Chile

A second critical aspect of women's career development is learning through working experience and determining how they can put into practice their leadership skills. This can be formally achieved when they can move into management positions because the organization allows this to occur. However, there are still discussions about gender differences in managerial preferences within organizations and the public arena, despite decades of research that has found there to be no such differences between male and female management styles (Konrad, Waryszak, & Hartmann, 1997; White & Özkanlı, 2010). Furthermore, is has been proven that female leadership is more people-oriented since women can be more egalitarian (Konrad et al., 1997). It would appear that if women have ambition to take on a managerial role within engineering or ICT, then this could have a positive outcome through a people-oriented leadership. However, systemic or institutionalized discrimination in promoting or hiring into the most senior levels continues to occur and has done for generations as evidenced in research (Snizek & Neil, 1992; Strachan, 2010).

The IT industry does not attract the same number of women and men, again because of perceptions and biases that women are not suited to this type of work and therefore are less well paid than men performing similar roles (Lang & Craig, 2010). The perceptions held generally are that men have a 'special' aptitude for positions such as Software Engineer, Data Business Administration, Business Analyst, Programmers and CIO just as in the engineering profession, they have an aptitude to be a Process Analyst, Project Manager, and many other such jobs, including managerial positions (Lang & Craig, 2010). This perception is clearly illustrated in Google's 2017 experience when a software engineer, James Damore voiced the stereotypical view that women are not suited to being software engineers and Google's response was to terminate his employment (Damore, 2017). Against this context though, Google has only 20 percent women employed in the Information Technology Department but 80 percent men. Additionally, 25 percent of the women have a leadership role within the company against the 75 percent of men (Google Diversity, 2017).

Salignac, Galea, and Powell (2017) identified that networking opportunities for graduates are many fewer for women because of the limited numbers already in the profession to whom they can turn. This is in contrast to the continuation of 'the old boys' network' which continues to assist men with opportunities for promotions and new jobs, meaning women have fewer employability and promotion opportunities (Salignac et al., 2017). The same situation occurs in both Australia and Chile (Godoy & Mladinic, 2009).

Chile, as an emerging economy, faces the same issues around leadership and pay disparities still being faced by Australian women engineers and ICT professionals. A survey conducted by the College of Engineers of Chile in 2014 revealed that male engineers earn more than their female colleagues in the same role and with the same level of education. The average fluctuates between 10 percent in the lowest salaries to 33 percent in the highest ones (Flores, 2016). Engineering has been a profession traditionally considered 'only for men' but the growing presence of women in engineering in Chile is evidence that soon there would be no profession or university course to which women would not be admitted (Meller, 2010). According to Meller (2010), the Study of Wages of Engineers and Labor Market shows that Chilean women have less access to promotion to managerial positions in engineering and only about 10 percent of managers are women in contrast to more than 20 percent who perform analysts' roles. The salary disparities mentioned in this study are very similar for all industries and occur globally. The cases where gender inequality is smaller are considered an exception. Conexion Ingenieros (2016) observed that women negotiate lower incomes compared with men and tended to easily settle for what the company offered. This could be because of a cultural bias against themselves (Conexion Ingenieros, 2016) or a lack of negotiations skills.

In another study of the drivers of unequal status between female engineers compared with male engineers, the interviewees indicated that some of the pressures they encountered as professionals included that working in a traditionally male-dominated field such as engineering made them feel more aware of the continual need to validate themselves and their abilities when they were leading a research or project team (Godoy & Mladinic, 2009). They had to make major efforts to be respected and treated as leaders because they were responsible for managing a team of men. In order to be accepted as front-runners over and above validating their professional skills, women had to assume certain personalities, such as a strong character, fierceness and authority, characteristics traditionally associated with men (Godoy & Mladinic, 2009). Put simply, if women are not able to access leadership and managerial roles, the gender pay gap that they experience on the lower rungs of their career will be exacerbated which is an issue of growing economic concern both for individual women and governments.

3. Women in Engineering and ICT Continue to be Underrepresented in Australia and Chile

The consequences of under-representation of women in STEM fields can be seen for those already in the labor market. Gender inequality in Australia and Chile in these fields is complex (Broadley, 2015; Soto et al., 2016). Sectors experiencing growth in Australia and Chile have included mining and resources and construction; but due to a lack of STEM education, qualifications, and experience, women remain largely precluded from these industries (Mayes & Pini, 2014) which reinforces the lifetime earnings gap because jobs in these industries are usually highly paid.

Efforts have been made in the Australian construction industry to introduce training and skills programs but little has been done to increase women's access to jobs in the industry. Research by Salignac et al. (2017) demonstrates that men and women perceive gender issues in the construction industry differently from one another. For men, it appears that they do not see an under-representation of women as problematic and do not realize that some of their behavior towards the few women at the workplace is inappropriate. For example, Salignac et al. (2017) found that gender discrimination was quite "intense and obvious, right through to harassment, possibly segregating [women] through language". In the same study, Julie (female, operational, Company A) said that "there isn't any [gender diversity] to measure" because there are so few women employed across the company. The fact that there are so few women engineering graduates and that many of them leave the profession within five to ten years of starting means that all industries requiring engineers are in the same situation as GM Holden in Australia (Francese, 2017) which was unable to attract experienced women engineers for these same reasons.

Salignac et al. (2017) also found that once men were made aware by senior managers of the issues women colleagues were facing in the construction industry, that behavioral and attitudinal changes may be made. Zac (male, operational, Company A) realized it was very difficult as a man to understand the gender gap and it was only after it was brought to his attention by a senior manager responsible for managing a female employee that he began to understand that he could be part of the problem but also part of the solution (Salignac et al., 2017). The drivers of gender equality in the workplace are then the senior managers who set examples and create the culture of the workplace so that gender inequality can be reduced with benefits for all (Huppatz & Goodwin, 2013). In Australia since 2010, the Male Champions of Change Institute (2018), now consisting of 130 senior men across a range of industries, focuses on strategies to achieve gender equality and supports women to move to leadership roles, particularly in male-dominated fields. Given Australia's fairly extensive range of legislation to protect against harassment, bullying and discrimination and the government agencies tasked with overseeing the operation of the various Acts at state and federal levels, the findings in these studies clearly show that it takes more than law to change behaviors and attitudes, and that the support of men in leadership positions is essential to achieving gender equality.

The Australian federal Department of Employment, Science and Training (DEST) collects data on male and female participation in tertiary study and also academic employment in universities. Using DEST data, Austen (2004) identified gender differences in academic rank in Australian universities. Major disparities were found to occur between men and women academics and men were more likely to be employed in senior classifications in all fields, but especially in IT and Engineering. The data in Appendix 2, shows that 15 percent of males are in IT are in senior academic positions as against 8.5 percent of females; 21.5 percent of males are in senior academic positions in engineering versus 3.9 percent of females (Austen, 2004).

One of the biggest IT outsourcing companies in Chile, Kibernum (2011), identified that ICT careers are being perceived as only for 'geeks' and that this image, when combined with the belief that it is a difficult academic area to study and the need for 'hard skills' with performance being based on computer coding, make it an unattractive profession to women. Consequently, the company and the industry in Chile are missing out on a large source of untapped talent and the demands of the industry are not being met (Kibernum, 2011). According to Hernán Astudillo, Deputy Director of the Information Technology Department of the Federico Santa María Technical University (UTFSM) Santiago Campus, this situation has created great concern for his University because presently just one in ten computer science students is female (Kibernum, 2011). He believes this can be attributed to the fact that "in general the concept that computer engineering is a more masculine place is very deeply rooted, and possibly that also affects the fact that the computer science career is not attractive for women" (Kibernum, 2011). Faced with this conclusion, Hernán Astudillo believes that the solution should not come only from the academic world because he recognises that in Chile "there is little promotion directed at women in computer careers, contrasting with countries such as the United States where there are measures aimed at interesting more women in IT careers" (Kibernum, 2011); however the success of the American promotion strategy is questionable given the statistics reported by Google Diversity (2017) earlier in this chapter.

In Chile, engineering represented 27.4 percent of the total first-year enrolment in 2017 but remains a male-dominated field (Comunidad Mujer, 2017). Within the OECD countries, it is observed that Chile's female participation in STEM professions in higher education is one of the lowest. That is why Comunidad Mujer since 2014 has promoted two versions of the campaign 'LasNiñasPueden (The girls can)', which seeks to make visible and deconstruct the practices that reinforce the stereotypes that are the barriers for the development of women, promoting measures that help correct their low participation (Comunidad Mujer, 2017).

Definitively, with the evidence provided, the objective should be oriented towards a greater scientific development in general from an earlier age and a rethinking of the way STEM is taught in schools and then at universities. Further, it is estimated that female engineers are still abandoning their professions more so than men, meaning that their underrepresentation in these occupations continues (Gill et al., 2008) until something is done about the image of engineering as difficult, hard, and non-welcoming for women. The negatives associated with the engineering and ICT professions undermine a woman's confidence in her role as an engineer, making it difficult to continue with the profession (Cech et al., 2011; Comunidad Mujer, 2017).

4. Analysis of Similarities and Differences Between the Countries

The similarities and differences between Australia and Chile are presented in Table 1.

SOLUTIONS AND RECOMMENDATIONS

Some of the approaches that produce positive results in Australia are the enforcement of policies and legislation about employment parity and diversity guidelines. For example, in the engineering and ICT fields, employment parity must be monitored; it must take into consideration an holistic approach to evaluate the complex factors: flexible and part-time schedules, motherhood, staffing and retaining talent based on performance, training for all employees, and maternal support services (Orser, Riding, & Stanley, 2012). Moreover, certain industry associations and online sites and symposia provide guidance to women who seek knowledge in maths and language programming wants to grow their sense of professional belonging. Also, mentoring and programmes aiming to notify females about career openings and lessons to develop essential abilities should be offered (Orser et al., 2012) and of course, the changes in school curricula and teaching recommended in the Education Council (2015) National STEM School Strategy (2016-2026) (Orser et al., 2012).

In Chile, modifications concerning educational, social and cultural dimensions of society could occur which might begin from primary school, to encourage girls to play games in order to develop their creativity and inquisitiveness. Another alternative might be inspiring girls to 'love math'. Also, teachers need to be trained to eliminate biases between female and male students in their classrooms, especially when it comes to teaching mathematics and science (Hitschfeld & Martinez, 2016). Recently, Chilean companies are recognizing the contributions made by female's engineers. This is facilitating an increased number of women being hired. According to Hitschfeld and Martinez (2016), the director of Engineers in

Table 1. Analyzis of similarities and differences between Australia and Chile

Similarities	Differences
Both are southern hemisphere countries, and both have a similar population size. • Australia: 24,770,700 (Australian Bureau of Statistics, 2017) • Chile: 17,574,003 (Instituto Nacional de Estadísticas de Chile (INE), 2017)	• Cultural and language differences.
Both countries have economies with a heavy dependency on mining although Australia is a developed country and Chile is a developing country. • Chile, like Australia, has a resources-driven economy which means that there is a demand for mining engineers and civil engineers in both countries.	• Australia has more initiatives to encourage women in engineering and ICT careers compared with Chile. More Australian universities are implementing programs for women, incentivizing them to enroll in STEM degrees.
• Similarities in the engineering and ICT professions can be found in the knowledge and skills within the professions, including hard skills such as advanced mathematics, and the challenges faced in educating girls from a young age on how engineering is about problem-solving and being creative and innovative and that technology is easy to use and easy to develop.	• Australia has a 4-year course for its sub-disciplines in the field of engineering. • Chile has a 4-year course (execution engineering, a more technical degree) or 6-year course (civil engineering which includes an engineering sciences degree and more possibilities for future managerial roles).
• Both countries now have gender agencies to address inequality. • Australia passed the *Workplace Gender Equality Act 2012* creating the WGEA, while Chile created the Ministry of Women and Gender Equality in mid-2016.	• Though both countries still have much work to do regarding gender discrimination, Australia is ahead of Chile in terms of dealing with discrimination against women.
• Both countries demonstrate that the influence of family has a fundamental impact on women's career.	• Chile is a Catholic country with the strong socially conservative legacy of motherhood stereotypes which conflict with Chile's feminist movement. • Australia still has one of the most gender-segmented labor markets in the world.
• Pursuing a career in engineering or ICT can be considered an excellent choice for students due to employment possibilities after graduation and opportunities for career progression. These jobs are well remunerated and considered prestigious right from entry into university because of the high tertiary entrance scores required.	Considering the history of the two countries: • It could be presumed that Australia would have made considerable progress in gender equity and equality as is has had a stable political, military, economic and social history throughout the twentieth century in comparison with Chile. Chile experienced political suppression, military unrest, and economic collapse and it has only been over the last three decades that the country has restructured and recovered its institutional stability, economic growth, and its high level of educational attainment by women.

Source: (Díaz & Jerrard, 2018)

Ireland, Caroline Spillane, highlighted the importance of women's inclusion in the engineer labor force in Chile. She stated that "to deliver the best creative solutions to satisfy the societies' needs, it is required to reduce the gender gap and create a balance inside these careers." Randstad (2017) also supports this with findings from Chile showing the importance of reducing gender imbalances in engineering and ICT. Hence, a new program called Diversidad en la Ingeniería (Diversity in Engineering) for STEM occupations has been created.

Engineering and ICT need a change of professional image. The GEDC (2017) recognized that these careers have the potential to solve a wide range of societal problems and contribute to a range of areas from sustainability, to safeguarding communities against natural disasters, to prosthetics, to more traditional engineering such as designing and building infrastructure and logistics. If these disciplines are portrayed as a way of finding a solution in a creative and innovative way by using STEM knowledge and skills, STEM will become more appealing for all students and from a younger age. This will also boost role confidence for women from early in their careers. The GEDC's ambitions for greater co-operation across engineering faculties worldwide may result in better outcomes for women students as all students have opportunities to experience studying and living in countries with more gender-neutral policies and approaches (GEDC, 2017).

Table 2 provides an overview of issues and solutions in both countries as identified from the literature.

FUTURE RESEARCH DIRECTIONS

It is obvious that the introduction of STEM into primary school curricula will have a significant impact on how girls gain knowledge about these subjects and develop an interest in them. There is a need for research into pedagogy and curriculum development in both countries. There is also an opportunity for multi-disciplinary research teams drawn from education, engineering, ICT, and other sciences to work together on large scale projects that can track educational and career outcomes of student cohorts from the initial introduction of curriculum changes.

There is much work that could be done on professional identity and role confidence for women in engineering and ICT and this could be supported by the GEDC which reflects the changing perceptions of engineering at the senior levels of university faculties, although these organizations remain male-dominated at the moment.

Government policy and legislation aimed at improving outcomes for women in all aspects of life could be analyzed from a comparative standpoint to identify best practice approaches and degrees of transferability of these approaches to other countries.

CONCLUSION

The perception of women as homemakers, nurturers, non-leaders lacking the skills to perform roles in engineering and ICT, and as not part of these professions has to be changed to achieve parity between genders in both Australia and Chile. It was also determined that the number of solutions currently provided are still surpassed by the number of issues identified from this literate review. While Australia is a developed and multicultural country, Chile is still a developing country due to its historical political suppression, military unrest, and economic collapse; nevertheless, both countries have similar sized population and high dependency on the mining and resources sector.

Australia, in order to solve the problem of gender discrimination, promoted a reliance on government agencies and legislation to protect and further women's rights. Also there is the possibility to promote several customized programs for gender equity to incentivize women to choose engineering and ICT careers by increasing the numbers of female enrolments. The idea was to change the professional image that women have about STEM careers with the use of creative and innovative knowledge and abilities, so these professions can become more attractive for many and from a young age. All these initiatives have the potential to enhance women's confidence when performing their roles. However, this has been shown to not necessarily overcome long held prejudices and stereotypes that come into a woman's life from early childhood causing many problems to persist.

Table 2. Issues and Solutions identified in Australia and Chile

Australia		Chile	
Issues	**Solutions**	**Issues**	**Solutions**
• Gender stereotyping evolving from long held perceptions and prejudice means that possible future STEM careers are endangered for women from childhood. • Engineering and related technologies 14.4% for the latter and 21% for the former and for ICT 16.1% and 25% respectively. • Only 10.1% of civil engineers are women. • Only 9% of electronic engineers are women. • Only 4.2% of electrical engineers are women. • Only 12.1% of chemical engineers are women. • Only 7.9% of mining and petroleum engineers are women. • In total, less than 10% of engineers are women.	• Many organizations and universities are providing specially-tailored programs for gender equity. • The programs are incentivizing women to opt for engineering or ICT careers and degrees with traditionally lower numbers of female enrolments. • If engineering and ICT professionals emphasize their creativity and inventive STEM knowledge and skills, STEM will become more appealing for all students and from a younger age. • Role models could be helpful, particularly from within the family. • Boost role confidence for women from early in their careers.	• ICT careers are perceived as only for 'geeks'. • The 'geek' image when combined with the belief that it is a difficult academic area to study makes it unattractive profession to women. • Chile's female participation in STEM professions in higher education is one of the lowest. • Engineering represented 27.4% of the total first-year enrolment in 2017, remaining a male-dominated field. • In total, less than 5.8% of engineers in Chile are women and in Chile.	• Creation of more programs as the one promoted by the Randstad company, Diversity in Engineering for STEM occupations. • Comunidad Mujer since 2014 has initiated two versions of the campaign 'LasNiñasPueden (The girls can)' to increase visibility and deconstruct the practices reinforcing the stereotypes that are the barriers for the development of women. • Promote measures that help correct the low participation of women in the STEM careers. • Teachers should not promote gender biases in the classroom. • Schools must not create differences in the teaching of mathematics between boys and girls. • Modifications regarding educational, social and cultural dimensions of society should occur from primary school. • Role models could be helpful, particularly from within the family. • Encourage girls to play games and inspire girls to 'love math' in order to develop their creativity and inquisitiveness.
• Gender equity is lacking at all stages of an engineering career. • After becoming the new professional engineers, women's career paths to obtain full professional acknowledgement from their male peers will not be uniform and neither will it be co-operative. • Individual's lack of role confidence as a separate factor contributes to women leaving the engineering profession. • 25% of women who enroll into undergraduate engineering courses at university abandon their studies. • 50% of the graduated women engineers abandon their career paths between 5 and 10 years after graduation.	• Greater cooperation across engineering and ICT faculties worldwide may result in better outcomes for women students. • With this cooperation, all students will have opportunities to experience studying and living in countries with more gender-neutral policies and approaches. • There are moves internationally to rectify this issue because of the loss of talent to the profession and to society. • Engineering and ICT need a change of professional image. • Engineering and ICT careers have the potential to solve a wide range of societal problems.	• Gender equity is lacking at all stages of an engineering career. • Women negotiate lower incomes compared with men. • Women tend to easily settle for what the company offered. • Reasons for that are cultural bias against themselves or an absence of negotiations skills.	• Greater cooperation across engineering and ICT faculties worldwide may result in better outcomes for women students. • With this cooperation, all students will have opportunities to experience studying and living in countries with more gender-neutral policies and approaches. • There are moves internationally to rectify this issue because of the loss of talent to the profession and to society. • Engineering and ICT need a change of professional image. • The engineering and ICT careers have the potential to solve a wide range of societal problems. • Women's contributions in many areas ranging from sustainability, to safeguarding communities against natural disasters, to prosthesis development, to more traditional engineering such as designing and building infrastructure and logistics. • Contributions made by women engineers are increasing the number of women being hired.
• Managing long hours and trying to balance family commitments. • When women have families to care for, they face greater barriers than men who have families. • The perception at the workplace is that the woman will be devoted to her family, rather than her career, and she may be more easily moved into casual work, short term contracts, and part-time work against her will.	• Negotiated workplace flexibility and limited paid maternity leave are available by law, but the situation facing women in the workplace has not necessarily improved nor have the work-life balance arrangements.	• Managing long hours and trying to balance family commitments. • Even if a company wants to include women, it is not possible because the company perceives women as prioritizing their family responsibilities over their careers.	• Women pointed out that flexibility and support during pregnancy and after would assist them to meet the pressures of work and family responsibilities.
• Reduced career opportunities for women, starting with discriminatory hiring practices and different remuneration levels at the entry point to the profession and widening as they continue working. • The IT industry does not attract the same number of women and men, again due to the perceptions and biases, that women are not suited to this type of work and therefore are less well paid than men performing similar roles.	• Australia have gender agencies to address inequality although much remains to be done. • Australia has the Male Champions of Change program to encourage women into leadership roles and non-traditional careers.	• Women's educational attainment in Chile ranks 39 out of 144 countries but this is not reflected in the labor market participation of women nor in the pay rates received by women. • Networking opportunities for graduates are fewer for women because of the limited numbers already in the profession to whom they can turn.	• Chile now has gender agencies to address inequality although much remains to be done as this agency has just begun its duties two years ago (June 2016).

continued on following page

Table 2. Continued

Australia		Chile	
Issues	**Solutions**	**Issues**	**Solutions**
• Women lack opportunities for achieving managerial positions. • Women observed that men had the opportunity to attend sophisticated courses, networking opportunities, and were invited to important professional reunions. • Absence of support and mentoring from male managers. • Lack of women role models, and the absence of clarity related to their careers paths and salaries. • Systematic or institutionalized discrimination in promoting women to or hiring into the most senior levels continues to occur and has done for generations as evidenced in research.	• Some of the approaches that produce positive results in Australia are the enforcement of policies and legislation about employment parity and diversity guidelines. • In the engineering and ICT fields, employment parity must be monitored. It must take into consideration an holistic approach to evaluate the complex factors: ○ Flexible and part-time schedules, motherhood and maternal support services, staffing and retaining talent based on performance, training for all employees.	• Women have less employability and promotion opportunities. • Male engineers earn more than their female engineers in the same role and with the same level of education. • Women have limited career paths which in turn negatively impact on their earning capacity in the financial sector. • Women have less access to promotion to managerial positions in engineering. • Only about 10% of managers are women in contrast to more than 20% who perform in analysts' roles. • Men engineers earn more than women colleagues in the same role and with the same level of education. The average fluctuates between 10% in the lowest salaries to 33% in the highest ones.	• Chile could adopt a program similar to the Male Champions of Change to provide role models for women and to support them in their careers.
• Sectors experiencing growth have included mining and resources and construction. • Due to a lack of STEM education, qualifications, and experience, women remain largely precluded from these professions which reinforces the lifetime earnings gap because these professions are usually highly paid. • Men, appear to not see an under-representation of women as problematic and do not realize that some of their behavior towards the few women at the workplace is inappropriate.	• The construction industry introduced training and skills programs although little has been done to increase women's access to jobs in the industry. • The drivers of gender equality in the workplace are the senior managers who set examples and create the culture of the workplace so that gender inequality can be reduced with benefits for all. • Given Australia's fairly extensive range of legislation to protect against harassment, bullying and discrimination and the government agencies tasked with overseeing the operation of the various Acts, it is concluded that it takes more than law to change behaviors and attitudes.	• Sectors experiencing growth have included mining and resources and construction. • Due to a lack of STEM education, qualifications, and experience, women remain largely precluded from these professions which reinforces the lifetime earnings gap because these professions are usually highly paid.	• The drivers of gender equality in the workplace are the senior managers who set examples and create the culture of the workplace so that gender inequality can be reduced with benefits for all.

Source: (Díaz & Jerrard, 2018)

On the other hand, Chile recently legislated to protect women's rights and may face the same outcome as Australia; namely, that the law does not change deeply embedded attitudes but forces people to become better at hiding them. This will not result in gender parity and will do nothing to further the opportunities for women in engineering and ICT. Notwithstanding the above, Chile still needs to take many steps to reach Australia's actual level and it needs to create more programs at universities or institutions and within companies to increase the number of enrolments and the number of occupations to close the gender gap. Furthermore, Chile needs to train teachers at primary schools to avoid gender prejudice in their schoolrooms. This means that all schools need to adapt teaching methods to avoid gender biases in STEM subjects. Therefore, adjustments concerning educational, social and cultural factors of society must occur and must begin from primary school to reach universities, institutions and employing organizations.

Overall, gender equality initiatives are taking place inside schools, universities and workplaces in order to alternate women's under-representation in engineering and ICT careers but the results will be slow in coming and must be tracked to identify which initiatives are successful and the reasons for the success. In the 21st century, women should be able to obtain the same rights, opportunities and support to perform their careers as men, otherwise it will continue to be 'a man's world' because women will not have the role confidence to succeed in traditionally male-dominated fields such as engineering and ICT.

ACKNOWLEDGMENT

The authors would like to thank the anonymous reviewers for the detailed and helpful suggestions and the editor, Dr. Idongesit Williams, for this opportunity to publish with IGI Global. This research received no specific grant from any funding agency in the public, commercial, or not-for-profit sectors. I, Andrea Díaz would like to acknowledge Dr Marjorie Jerrard BA MA PhD, Senior Lecturer in Employment Relations from the Department of Management at Monash Business School, Monash University. She was the one who assisted and encouraged me to write this book chapter. It was a pleasure working under her guidance.

REFERENCES

Austen, S. (2004). Gender differences in academic rank in Australian universities. *Australian Bulletin of Labour*, *30*, 113–133.

Australian Bureau of Statistics. (2017). *Australian Demographic Statistics, Dec 2017*. Retrieved from http://www.abs.gov.au/AUSSTATS/abs@.nsf/mf/3101.0

Australian Government. (2018a). *Department of Education and Training Occupational Summary Sheets, 2331 Chemical and Materials Engineers*. Retrieved from https://docs.education.gov.au/system/files/doc/other/2331_chemical_and_materials_engineers.pdf

Australian Government. (2018b). *Department of Education and Training Occupational Summary Sheets, 2332 Civil Engineering Professionals*. Retrieved from https://docs.education.gov.au/system/files/doc/other/2332_civil_engineering_professionals_0.pdf

Australian Government. (2018c). *Department of Education and Training Occupational Summary Sheets, 2334 Electronics Engineers*. Retrieved from https://docs.education.gov.au/system/files/doc/other/2334_electronics_engineers.pdf

Australian Government. (2018d). *Department of Education and Training Occupational Summary Sheets, 2335 Industrial, Mechanical and Production Engineers*. Retrieved from https://docs.education.gov.au/system/files/doc/other/2335_industrial_mechanical_and_production_engineers.pdf

Australian Government. (2018e). *Department of Education and Training Occupational Summary Sheets, 2336 Electrical Engineers*. Retrieved from https://docs.education.gov.au/system/files/doc/other/2336_mining_engineers.pdf

Australian Government. (2018f). *Department of Education and Training Occupational Summary Sheets, 2336 Mining Engineers*. Retrieved from https://docs.education.gov.au/system/files/doc/other/2336_mining_engineers.pdf

Banco Central de Chile. (2017). *Statistics Database: National Accounts*. Retrieved from http://si3.bcentral.cl/Siete/secure/cuadros/arboles.aspx

Broadley, K. (2015). Entrenched gendered pathways in science, technology, engineering and mathematics: Engaging girls through collaborative career development. *Australian Journal of Career Development, 24*(1), 27–38. doi:10.1177/1038416214559548

Cech, E., Rubineau, B., Silbey, S., & Seron, C. (2011). Professional role confidence and gendered persistence in engineering. *American Sociological Review, 76*(5), 641–666. doi:10.1177/0003122411420815

Cipriano, A. (2008). Jerarquización Académica en Ingeniería, Pontificia Universidad Católica de Chile. *Theoria, 17*(2), 15–25.

Comunidad Mujer. (2016). *Informe GET: Género, Educación y Trabajo. La brecha persistente. Primer estudio sobre la desigualdad de género en el ciclo de vida. Una revisión de los últimos 25 años*. Retrieved from http://www.informeget.cl/wp-content/uploads/2016/08/Informe-GET-Final.pdf

Comunidad Mujer. (2017). *Mujer y trabajo: Brecha de género en STEM, la ausencia de mujeres en Ingeniería y Matemáticas*. Retrieved from http://www.comunidadmujer.cl/biblioteca-publicaciones/wp-content/uploads/2017/12/BOLETIN-42-DIC-2017-url_vf.pdf

Conexion Ingenieros. (2016). *Estudio de Sueldos de Ingenieros 2016 y Mercado Laboral*. Retrieved from http://conexioningenieros.com/wp-content/uploads/2016/11/Estudio-de-Sueldos-Conexi%C3%B3n-Ingenieros-2016.pdf

Damore, J. (2017). *Google's Ideological Echo Chamber*. Retrieved from https://assets.documentcloud.org/documents/3914586/Googles-Ideological-Echo-Chamber.pdf

Education Council. (2015). *National STEM School Strategy, 2016-2026: A comprehensive plan for Science, Technology, Engineering and Mathematics education for Australians*. Retrieved from http://www.educationcouncil.edu.au/site/DefaultSite/filesystem/documents/National STEM School Education Strategy.pdf

Edwards, D., Pearce, J., Perkins, K., & Brown, J. (2014). *Final Report, Focus Groups for the Engineering Workforce Study, ACER*. Retrieved from http://research.acer.edu.au.ezproxy.lib.monash.edu.au/cgi/viewcontent.cgi?article=1039&context=higher_education

Flores, S. B. (2016). *¿Por qué las mujeres no quieren ser ingenieras? Caso: alumnas de Ingeniería de Tecnología Industrial en la UPCT*. UPCT. Retrieved from http://repositorio.upct.es/bitstream/handle/10317/5786/tfg-flo-por .pdf?sequence=1&isAllowed=y

Francese, M. (2017, August). *Wage Determination, Modern Awards, and Salary Setting*. Paper session presented at the meeting of Work and Employment Relations, Melbourne, Australia.

French-Davies, R. (2014). Is Chile a Model for Economic Development? Santiago de Chile: Departamento de Economía de la Universidad de Chile.

Gascoigne, C., Parry, E., & Buchanan, D. (2015). Extreme work, gendered work? How extreme jobs and the discourse of 'personal choice' perpetuate gender inequality. *Organization, 22*(4), 457–475. doi:10.1177/1350508415572511

Gill, J., Sharp, R., Mills, J., & Franzway, S. (2008). I still wanna be an engineer! Women, education and the engineering profession. *European Journal of Engineering Education, 33*(4), 391–402. doi:10.1080/03043790802253459

Global Engineering Deans Council (GEDC). (2017). *Global Engineering Deans Council Conference.* Niagara Falls, Canada: Author.

Godoy, L., & Mladinic, A. (2009). Estereotipos y roles de género en la evaluación laboral y personal de hombres y mujeres en cargos de dirección. *Psykhe (Santiago), 18*(2), 51–64. doi:10.4067/S0718-22282009000200004

Google Diversity. (2017). *Google diversity annual report 2018.* Retrieved from https://diversity.google/annual-report

Healy, J. (2015). The Australian labour market in 2014: Still ill? *The Journal of Industrial Relations, 57*(3), 348–365. doi:10.1177/0022185615571981

Heaverlo, C. A. (2011). *'STEM Development: A Study of 6th-12th Grade Girls' Interest in Mathematics and Science'* (Graduate Theses and Dissertations). Iowa State University. Retrieved from www://lib.dr.iastate.edu/etd/10056

Hitschfeld, K. N., & Martinez, S. (2016). *En búsqueda de la equidad de género en ingeniería: Estudio de la participación femenina en la FCFM y los 40 cupos de equidad. Conversatorio: "Más emprendedoras de alto impacto para Chile".* Girls In Tech. Retrieved from http://www.girlsintechchile.com/wp-content/uploads/2016/08/Conversatorio2016.pdf

Hoerning, C. (1940). *Preparación de los ingenieros y la admiración de empresas industriales y comerciales.* Paper presented at the Anales del Instituto de Ingenieros de Chile.

Huppatz, K., & Goodwin, S. (2013). Masculinised jobs, feminised jobs and men's 'gender capital' experiences: Understanding occupational segregation in Australia. *Journal of Sociology (Melbourne, Vic.), 49*(2-3), 291–308. doi:10.1177/1440783313481743

Instituto Nacional de Estadísticas de Chile (INE). (2017). *Compendio Estadístico.* Retrieved from http://www.censo2017.cl/descargas/home/sintesis-de-resultados-censo2017.pdf

Kibernum. (2011). *Sólo el 10% de los estudiantes son mujeres: ¿Por qué no ingresan más mujeres a estudiar carreras informáticas?* Retrieved from http://www.kibernum.com/noticias/solo-el-10-de-los-estudiantes-son-mujeres-por-que-no-ingresan-mas-mujeres-a-estudiar-carreras-informaticas/

Konrad, A. M., Waryszak, R., & Hartmann, L. (1997). What do managers like to do? Comparing women and men in Australia and the US. *Australian Journal of Management, 22*(1), 71–97. doi:10.1177/031289629702200104

Lang, A., & Craig, C. (2010). International collaboration for women in IT: How to avoid reinventing the wheel. *Information in Motion: The Journal Issues in Informing Science and Information Technology, 7*, 329.

Male Champions of Change Institute. (2018). *About the Male Champions of Change: A Strategy Focused on Gender Equality*. Retrieved from http://malechampionsofchange.com/about-us/

Mauro, A. (2004). *Trayectorias Laborales en el Sector Financiero. Recorridos de las Mujeres*. Unidad Mujer y Desarrollo. Retrieved from https://books.google.com.au/books?id=bdkXxgx0kncC&pg=PA49&lpg=PA49&dq=trayectoria+laboral+de+la+mujer+ingeniero+en+chile&source=bl&ots=bwZU-gk4V4&sig=RFV2AIf00JM09RCmPFF2jVNoS6o&hl=es-419&sa=X&ved=0ahUKEwiWppLB0tnZAhVDwrwKHd82CxcQ6AEIcTAL-v=onepage&q&f=false

Mayes, R., & Pini, B. (2014). The Australian mining industry and the ideal mining woman: Mobilizing a public business case for gender equality. *The Journal of Industrial Relations*, *56*(4), 527–546. doi:10.1177/0022185613514206

McGregor, J., Davies, S. G., Giddings, L. S., & Pringle, J. (2017). Pursuing equal pay: The perspectives of female engineers and potential policy interventions. *The Journal of Industrial Relations*, *59*(1), 3–21. doi:10.1177/0022185616659677

Meller, P. (2010). Perspectiva histórica de la discriminación femenina a nivel profesional. In *Carreras universitarias. Rentabilidad, selectividad y discriminación*. Santiago de Chile: UQBAR-editores.

Mills, J. E. (2011). Reflections on the past, present and future of women in engineering. *Australasian Journal of Engineering Education*, *17*(3), 139–146. doi:10.1080/22054952.2011.11464065

Monash University. (2017). *Women's Mentoring Program*. Retrieved from https://www.monash.edu/gender-equity/programs/mentoring

Monash University. (2018). *Severe shortage of mining engineers looming*. Retrieved from https://www.monash.edu/engineering/about-us/news-events/latest-news/articles/2018/severe-shortage-of-mining-engineers-looming2

Orser, B., Riding, A., & Stanley, J. (2012). Perceived career challenges and response strategies of women in the advanced technology sector. *Entrepreneurship and Regional Development*, *24*(1-2), 73–93. doi:10.1080/08985626.2012.637355

Parrado Herrera, E. (2017). *Can behavioural science 'nudge' Chilean women towards equality?* World Economic Forum. Retrieved from https://www.weforum.org/agenda/2017/11/chile-women-equality-nudge-gender-gap-report-2017/.Harvard

Pascual, C. (2017). *Q&A: 3 questions for Chile's minister of gender equity. Devex Inside Development/Gender Equality/Interviewer: K.* Rogers.

Pocock, B. (1998). All change, still gendered: The Australian labour market in the 1990s. *The Journal of Industrial Relations*, *40*(4), 580–604. doi:10.1177/002218569804000405

Power, M. (2004, Spring). Gender and Chile's split culture. *Harvard Review of Latin America*.

Professionals Australia. (2014). *Women in IT scholarship – Continuing Professional Development as a way to help address barriers to advancement*. Retrieved from http://www.professionalsaustralia.org.au/support/career-progression/scholarships/-tab-1433426140677-3-5

Puri, I. K. (2017). *Why Engineering Schools Globally Need More Creative Women*. Retrieved from http://theconversation.com/au

Randstad. (2017). *Diversidad en ingeniería en 2017*. Retrieved from https://www.randstad.cl/tendencias360/archivo/diversidad-en-ingenieria-en-2017_1365/

Roberts, P., & Ayre, M. (2002). Did she jump or was she pushed? A study of women's retention in the engineering workforce. *International Journal of Engineering Education*, *18*(4), 415–421.

Salignac, F., Galea, N., & Powell, A. (2017). Institutional entrepreneurs driving change: The case of gender equality in the Australian construction industry. *Australian Journal of Management*, *43*(1), 152–169. doi:10.1177/0312896217705179

Seron, C., Silbey, S. S., Cech, E., & Rubineau, B. (2016). Persistence is cultural: Professional socialization and the reproduction of sex segregation. *Work and Occupations*, *43*(2), 178–214. doi:10.1177/0730888415618728

Snizek, W. E., & Neil, C. C. (1992). Job characteristics, gender stereotypes and perceived gender discrimination in the workplace. *Organization Studies*, *13*(3), 403–427. doi:10.1177/017084069201300305

Soto, J. A. F., Etchegaray, M. V. S., Guzmán, S. A. C., Soto, P. A. G., & Calderón. (2016). *Mujeres Ingeniería UC y más Mujeres para la Ingeniería y las Ciencias de la U. de Chile: Una Mirada al Impulso del Acceso, Experiencia y Permanencia de las Mujeres en las Carreras Ingenieriles y Científicas en Chile* (Magíster en Gestión de Obras Públicas). Universidad de Chile, Santiago de Chile.

Strachan, G. (2010). Still working for the man? Women's employment experiences in Australia since 1950. *The Australian Journal of Social Issues*, *45*(1), 117–130. doi:10.1002/j.1839-4655.2010.tb00167.x

Thorpe, D., & Delaney, B. (2014). *Enhancing the role of women in engineering*. Paper presented at the 25th Annual Conference of the Australasian Association for Engineering Education: Engineering the Knowledge Economy: Collaboration, Engagement & Employability.

Undurraga, T. (2015). Neoliberalism in Argentina and Chile: Common antecedents, divergent paths. *Revista de Sociologia e Politica*, *23*(55), 11–34. doi:10.1590/1678-987315235502

University Rankings Australia. (2018). *Male-Female Ratios by University*. Retrieved from http://www.universityrankings.com.au/gender-balance-ratio.html

Watts, J. H. (2009). 'Allowed into a man's world' meanings of work–life balance: Perspectives of women civil engineers as 'minority'workers in construction. *Gender, Work and Organization*, *16*(1), 37–57. doi:10.1111/j.1468-0432.2007.00352.x

Weiss, C., Parkinson, D., & Duncan, A. (2015). Living longer on less: Women, paid work, and superannuation in Victoria, Australia. *SAGE Open*, *5*(3). doi:10.1177/2158244015597966

White, K., & Özkanlı, Ö. (2010). A comparative study of perceptions of gender and leadership in Australian and Turkish universities. *Journal of Higher Education Policy and Management*, *33*(1), 3–16. doi:10.1080/1360080X.2011.536976

Workplace Gender Equality Agency (WGEA). (2018a). *2017-2018 WGEA EOCGE citation holders by industry*. Retrieved from https://www.wgea.gov.au/sites/default/files/WGEA-Employer-of-Choice-citation-holders-by-industry-2017-18.pdf

Workplace Gender Equality Agency (WGEA). (2018b). *Our Role*. Retrieved from https://www.wgea.gov.au/about-wgea/our-role-0

Workplace Gender Equality Agency (WGEA). (2018c). *Relevant Employers*. Retrieved from https://www.wgea.gov.au/who-needs-report/relevant-employers

ADDITIONAL READING

Anker, R. (1997). Theories of occupational segregation by sex: An overview. *International Labour Review*, *136*(3), 315–339.

Cardoso, P., & Marques, J. F. (2008). Perception of career barriers: The importance of gender and ethnic variables. *International Journal for Educational and Vocational Guidance*, *8*(1), 49–61. doi:10.100710775-008-9135-y

CIO. (2015). Reports and Revelations: The Latest Research and Industry Findings on IT Use and Management (15 September). Retrieved from https://www.cio.com.au

Fort, L., John-Abraham, I., Orlando, M., & Piras, C. (2007). Chile: Reconciling the Gender Paradox. En Breve. No 105.

Girls in Tech Chile. (2016). Archivos de la categoría: Escolares. Recuperado el 10 de Septiembre de 2015. Retrieved from http://www.girlsintechchile.com/

Ingeniería 2030. (2 de Junio de 2016). USM inaugura programa que fortalecerá inclusión femenina en el área de la ingeniería. Retrieved from https://www.ingenieria2030.org/

Lingard, H., & Lin, J. (2004). Career, family and work environment determinants of organizational commitment among women in the Australian construction industry. *Construction Management and Economics*, *22*(4), 409–420. doi:10.1080/0144619032000122186

Poblete, B., & Hitschfeld, N. (23 de Septiembre de 2013). La discriminación (positiva) en Ingeniería de la Chile: ¿por qué las académicas apoyamos los cupos de equidad de género? Retrieved from http://ingenieria.uchile.cl/noticias/94805/la-discriminacion-positiva-en-ingenieria-de-la-chile

Roberts, P., & Ayre, M. (2002). Did she jump or was she pushed? A study of women's retention in the engineering workforce. *International Journal of Engineering Education*, *18*(4), 415–421.

Timms, C., Lankshear, C., Anderson, N., & Courtney, L. (2008). Riding a hydra: Women ICT professionals' perceptions of working in the Australian ICT industry. *Information Technology & People*, *21*(2), 155–177. doi:10.1108/09593840810881060

KEY TERMS AND DEFINITIONS

Chief Information Officer (CIO): It is a role normally assumed by the most senior executive in a business, responsible for the information technology and computer systems that contribute to the enterprise's goals.

Civil Engineering Course: Six-year program to study engineering. It could be in any discipline: industrial, mechanics, electronics, and many others. The main reason it is called "civil" is due to its professionals being capable of creating or designing. Civil engineers are particularly suitable for managerial positions.

Department of Education Employment and Workplace Relations (DEWR): Provides assistance to the Australian government and administers programs, aiming to accomplish government goals for schooling, employment, and workplace relations. The department works in partnership with the states and territories, non-government authorities, providers, and industry in Australia.

Department of Employment, Science, and Training (DEST): Australian government department that is responsible for the policies and programs of the primary and secondary schools to incentivize students towards STEM careers.

Execution Engineering Course: Four-year program to study engineering. It could be in any discipline: industrial, mechanics, electronics, and many others. The main reason it is called "execution" is due to its professionals being capable of interpreting the designs and executing them. It is more technical than the civil course.

Gender Gap: The differences between women and men with regard to social, political, intellectual, cultural, or economic outcomes.

Global Engineering Deans Council Conference (GEDC): International forum constituted by 20 leaders from engineering education institutions and corporate associates. The main goal of the GEDC is to offer engineering deans and rectors ideas, tools, and "best" practices necessary to become innovative leaders of engineering education.

Information and Communications Technology (ICT): It is an extension of information technology (IT) integrating the field of communications. It is a broad concept that involves any outcome that will store, manipulate, transmit, retrieve, or receive information automatically in a digital form (e.g., personal computers, digital television, emails).

Science, Technology, Engineering, and Math (STEM): It is a scholastic program established to instruct primary and secondary students for university and graduate study in the fields of science, technology, engineering, and mathematics.

APPENDIX

Figure 1.

	2000			2006		
University Professions	**Number of Women**	**Women's % in the Career**	**Women's % in Career in Total of Professional**	**Number of Women**	**Women's % in the Career**	**Women's % in Career in Total of Professional**
Teachers	1,996	76,8%	22,7%	6,432	78,2%	34,3%
Commercial Engineering	961	43.0%	10.9%	1.283	45.5%	6.9%
Accountant and Auditor	703	50.0%	8.0%	926	56.7%	4.9%
Psychology	581	71.9%	6.6%	1.468	73.5%	7.8%
Engineers	522	19,6%	5,9%	1,084	25,8%	5,8%
Journalism	477	61.5%	5.4%	649	59.7%	3.5%
Nursing	470	94.2%	5.3%	833	86.6%	4.4%
Social Work	410	88.4%	4.7%	944	87.7%	5.0%
Law	375	42.6%	4.3%	622	47.3%	3.3%
Medicine	261	42.4%	3.0%	331	44.7%	1.8%
Architecture	206	39.0%	2.3%	419	41.7%	2.2%
Agronomists	155	34.3%	1.8%	264	41.5%	1.4%
Obstetrics	138	88.5%	1.6%	327	86.7%	1.7%
odontology	116	56.0%	1.3%	189	51.8%	1.0%
Veterinarians	93	49.2%	1.1%	225	56.4%	1.2%
Chemicals and	92	60.1%	1.0%	205	56.9%	1.1%
Psychopedagogy	20	87.0%	0.2%	110	96.5%	0.6%
Other Professions	1.214	55.2%	13.8%	2.417	58.9%	12.9%
Women's Total	8.790	52.1%	100.0%	18.728	59.6%	100.0%
% University Professional Women in the total number of Professionals	52,1%			59,6%		

Figure 2.

		MALE		FEMALE	
		Level A to C	Level D or E	Level A to C	Level D or E
Variable	**Definition**	**% of sample population**			
Age	Age in years				
*Less than 40		22.6	3.5	22.5	4.0
40-49		36.3	27.3	40.8	32.7
50-59		33.7	52.0	32.0	50.4
60+		7.3	17.3	4.6	12.9
Qualification	Highest qualification				
Doctorate		50.0	82.4	39.0	84.3
Masters		29.3	8.3	37.1	11.3
Bachelor's		12.2	2.6	15.6	2.9
*Other qualification/don't know		8.5	3.5	8.3	4.8
Discipline	Academic Organisational Group				
Natural & physical science*		15.1	23.4	9.7	13.2
Information technology		9.8	5.2	4.7	3.8
Engineering & related technologies		9.2	12.3	1.6	2.3
Architecture & building		1.8	1.8	3.5	1.4
Agriculture, environmental & related studies		2.5	2.7	1.2	1.1
Health		7.5	12.0	17.7	20.2
Education		5.6	4.1	11.8	10.0
Management & commerce		12.2	9.9	14.3	11.0
Society and culture		23.3	25.0	30.0	33.2
Creative Arts		9.0	4.9	9.1	2.6
Post Graduate Enrolment in Institution	% of students who are postgrad.				
High	>20%	48.7	56.2	49.5	55.2
Medium	20-25%	27.1	26.9	26.7	27.8
*Low	<20%	24.1	16.0	23.8	17.9
Fee Paying Student Enrolment in Institution	% of students who are fee paying				
High	>25%	39.2	43.3	37.1	40.2
Medium	15-25%	42.9	40.5	43.3	44.1
*Low	<15%	17.7	16.2	19.7	15.7

Chapter 2
A Human Rights-Based Approach to Bridge Gender Digital Divide:
The Case Study of India

Ching Yuen Luk
Nanyang Technological University, Singapore

ABSTRACT

Using India as a case study, this chapter examines four elements of gender digital divide, the causes of gender digital divide, and ways to bridge gender digital divide. It finds that girls and women do not have equal access to the internet and mobile technologies like men do. This is due to social norms favoring men in the distribution of resources and opportunities, women's lack of the economic means, and ineffective law enforcement. This study calls for a human rights-based approach to bridge gender digital divide, which emphasizes women's rights to ICT-related education and training, internet privacy and freedom of expression, and mobile phone ownership.

INTRODUCTION

India, which is the world's second-most populous country, has transformed government's way of working through information and communications technologies (ICTs) since the 1980s. In 2015, the government launched the Digital India programme with a vision to transform the nation into knowledge economy and a digitally empowered economy (Ministry of Electronics & Information Technology, 2017). However, the problems of digital divide between urban and rural areas and between men and women are serious in the nation. A review of previous literature shows that there is a lack of study on gender digital divide and ways to bridge gender digital divide in India. In order to fill the research gaps, this study examines four elements of gender digital divide, the causes of gender digital divide, and ways to bridge gender digital divide using a human rights based approach.

DOI: 10.4018/978-1-5225-7068-4.ch002

BACKGROUND

Gender digital divide refers to the inequalities between men and women in terms of access to ICTs. According to Van Dijk (2004), digital divide can be understood as inequalities in four types of access: (a) mental access which refers to lack of elementary digital experience due to anxiety or lack of interest; (b) material access which refers to no possession of computers and network connections; (c) skills access which refers to inadequate education or social support; and (d) usage access which refers to lack of significant usage opportunities (p.160). Gender digital divide is a serious problem in developing countries where girls and women lack access to computers, the Internet and mobile technologies. The exclusion of women from ICTs adversely affect their self-confidence, social and economic status and capacity-building opportunities. The problem of gender digital divide continues to capture worldwide attention. According to a recently published report, less than one third of India's Internet users were female (UNICEF, 2017). There are some social, cultural and economic reasons attributed to gender digital divide in India, such as social norms favouring men in the distribution of resources and opportunities and women's lack of the economic means. Gender digital divide has put women in a very disadvantageous position in terms of educational opportunity, economic opportunity, earnings potentials and peer connections. For married women, gender digital divide may also adversely affect their children's welfare and development outcomes due to limited employment opportunities and lower income level. Gender digital divide has been a long-standing problem in India that deserves an in-depth analysis.

GENDER DIGITAL DIVIDE IN INDIA

Mental Access

In India, mental barrier is one of the main reasons why many females do not have Internet or mobile access. A comparative study on the Internet gender gap found that the rate of female Internet access was the lowest in India, which accounted for only 8 percent, compared with that of Uganda (9 percent), Egypt (32 percent) and Mexico (34 percent) (Intel Corporation and Dalberg Global Development Advisors, 2012, pp. 23-4). While the study cited larger rural population (69 percent) and lower Gross National Income (GNI) per capita (USD 3,620) as two macro barriers to women's access to the Internet in India (Intel Corporation and Dalberg Global Development Advisors, 2012, p. 24), it cited discomfort with technology (38 percent) and lack of interest (31 percent) as two mental barriers to Indian women's access to the Internet (Intel Corporation and Dalberg Global Development Advisors, 2012, pp.48-9). Women's perception that using the Internet was inappropriate (12 percent) and disapproval from family and friends (8 percent) also created psychological pressure on women's access to the Internet (Intel Corporation and Dalberg Global Development Advisors, 2012, p. 52). The study found that women in India were six times more than women in Uganda to report that using the Internet was inappropriate (Intel Corporation and Dalberg Global Development Advisors, 2012, p. 52). Through the interviews, the study found that the fear of watching wrong things online (Intel Corporation and Dalberg Global Development Advisors, 2012, p. 46), doing household work and looking after children were reasons why family members opposed women's access to the Internet (Intel Corporation and Dalberg Global Development Advisors, 2012, p. 53). The study showed that "barriers related to cultural and gender norms play[ed] a significant role in limiting women's use of the Internet" (Intel Corporation and Dalberg Global Development Advisors, 2012, p. 52). In 2015, a survey conducted by Google revealed that almost half of the Indian female respondents did not see any reasons to access the Internet while some respondents feared angering their in-laws for spending too much time online (The Indian Express, 2015 May 26). Another survey which examined women's mobile access and usage in 10 low- and middle-income countries (hereafter the 2015 survey) found that the fear of making mistake with their mobile phone and losing money was a barrier to women using mobile phone or using a mobile phone more often or for more varied usages (GSMA, 2015b, p. 54). In rural India, most of the female respondents in selected villages in Eastern Uttar Pradesh did not have confidence in using mobile financial service (MFS) on their own because of "a lack of literacy and numeracy skills, or fear of making a mistake" (Grameen Foundation, 2013, p.6). Although the majority of them were trained by a mobile money agent or another person, their hesitancy and lack of confidence in their abilities to use MFS continued to exist (Grameen Foundation, 2013, p.6). Fear of technology led to women relying on assistance from a male household member or an agent to transact for them (Grameen Foundation, 2013, p.20).

Material Access

In India, there is gender gap in Internet access in the nation due to women's lack of economic means. The 2012 survey showed that "a woman in India is 27 percent less likely to have internet access than a man" (Intel Corporation and Dalberg Global Development Advisors, 2012, p. 98). 19 percent of Indian female respondents said that they could not easily access a computer or mobile phone with Internet (Intel Corporation and Dalberg Global Development Advisors, 2012, p. 57). Cost was cited by 13 percent of Indian female respondents as a significant barrier to their access to the Internet (Intel Corporation and Dalberg Global Development Advisors, 2012, p. 54). In India, desktop or laptop was the most expensive Internet platform, which cost USD 275 (Intel Corporation and Dalberg Global Development Advisors, 2012, p. 62). The less expensive Internet platform was tablet (USD 80), which was followed by smartphone (USD 40) and Internet enabled feature phone (USD 20) (Intel Corporation and Dalberg Global Development Advisors, 2012, p. 62). Those who could not afford a desktop or laptop at their homes may use public and shared facilities to access the Internet, including public libraries, rural village telecenters and information kiosks, and cybercafés (Haseloff, 2005). The statistics provided by Cyber Café Association of India showed that India had 72,000 cybercafés in 2016 (Sharma, 2016 July 31). Cybercafés offered "a low-cost alternative to the otherwise expensive model of in home-ownership and access" (Haseloff, 2005). The hourly surfing charge was about 11 rupees (Sharma, 2016 July 31). However, most of the women did not go there because of the perception that cybercafés were not safe (Intel Corporation and Dalberg Global Development Advisors, 2012, p. 54) and "cultural norms that discourage[d] the mingling of men and women" (Intel Corporation and Dalberg Global Development Advisors, 2012, p. 54).

Meanwhile, Indian women have difficulty in owning a mobile phone although the price of it is less expensive. Gender gap in mobile phone ownership, which referred to "how less likely a female is to own a mobile phone than a male" (GSMA, 2015b, p.19), was high in India. The 2015 survey found that gender gap in mobile phone ownership in India was 36 percent (GSMA, 2015b, p.74), which was higher than the average gender gap in mobile phone ownership in low- and middle-income countries, which only accounted for 14 percent (GSMA, 2015b, p.24). Besides, there was a sharp difference in mobile phone ownership between urban and rural women in India. The National Family Health Survey 2015-16 showed that about 62 percent of urban women had a mobile phone that they themselves used compared with about 37 percent of rural women (Ministry of Health and Family Welfare, 2017, p.6). According to the 2015 survey, half of the Indian female respondents reported that handset cost and credit recharge was the greatest barrier to mobile phone ownership and usage (GSMA, 2015b, p.44). It is because earning less income or being less likely to earn an income made Indian women less financially independent (GSMA, 2015b, p.45). "India has amongst the lowest women's labour force participation rates (LFPR) in the world" (International Labour Organization Country Office for India, 2017, p.2). In 2012, India's female LFPR was about 33 percent, which was well below the global average of about 50 percent (Das et al., 2015, pp.4-5). "Traditional social norms regarding women's mobility and their primary role as family caretakers limit women's participation in paid economic work" (Malhotra et al., 2012, p.13). The husband and in-laws imposed restrictions on women's movements outside the household (Chaudhary and Verick, 2014, p.16). For example, "[i]n villages in Rajasthan and Gujurat, in northwest India, women do not step out of their houses" (Intel Corporation and Dalberg Global Development Advisors, 2012, p.65). In India, most women need permission from family members to "undertake a job or start a business, usually prioritizing their responsibilities as daughters, wives, and mothers" (Malhotra et al., 2012, p.13). For women who can work outside the home, "structural constraints make it difficult for them to break into better paying and more stable jobs" (Surie, 2016). "[M]oney is often scarce for the millions of Indian women" (The GSMA Development Fund et al., 2010, p.39) because most of them are employed in "the informal, semi-or unskilled sector such as domestic work, where incomes are low and there are limited benefits or job security" (Surie, 2016). The National Sample Survey Organization report (2011-2012) found that about 64 percent of urban women and 60 percent of rural women in India engaged in domestic work (Singh, 2014 October 13). Rural women had a less stable income than urban women. The share of regular wage or salaried employees for rural women was 7.6 times less than that of urban women (Ministry of Statistics and Programme Implementation, 2017, p.60). Besides, the average per day wage/salary earned by a female was less than that by a male, irrespective of education level and residence (Ministry of Statistics and Programme Implementation, 2017, p.60). For example, the average per day wage/salary earned by a rural female and urban female was respectively about 202 rupees and 366 rupees while the average per day wage/salary earned by a rural male and urban male was respectively about 322 rupees and 470 rupees (Ministry of Statistics and Programme Implementation, 2017, p.75).

Due to the lack of economic means, most of Indian female respondents said that they used their husband's money to buy their mobile phone (48 percent) and refill credit balance or pay a monthly bill (50 percent) (GSMA, 2015b, pp.121-2). Women had low level of decision-making power in India (GSMA, 2015b p.75) because fathers, husbands and brothers were the main decision makers of households (Bhattacharya, 2017 April 26). Since men played a dominant role in making decisions about general household expenses, women who earned an income could hardly control how that income was spent, including on mobile-related expenses (GSMA, 2015b, p.45). According to the 2015 survey, of the 44 percent of Indian female respondents who used their own money or the household budget to pay for their mobile phone, 61 percent of them had to ask for permission to spend this money on a mobile phone (GSMA, 2015b, p.60). Besides, 41 percent of Indian female respondents reported that they had no role at all in choosing a mobile phone while only 19 percent of Indian female respondents could make the mobile phone purchasing decision themselves compared with 72 percent of male respondents (GSMA, 2015b, p.60). For women who did not own a mobile phone, it was common practice for them to borrow a mobile phone from other people. The 2015 survey found that Indian women had the highest mobile borrowing rate, which accounted for 29 percent (GSMA, 2015b, p.34). In India, borrowing was more common among women with lower education level (39 percent) and in rural areas (34 percent) (GSMA,

2015b, pp. 34-5). Most of them borrowed a mobile phone from household members (GSMA, 2015b, p.35), which unavoidably limited their privacy (Bhattacharya, 2017 April 26). Unfortunately, 49 percent of Indian female respondents reported in the 2015 survey that they never had the opportunity to try a mobile phone (GSMA, 2015b, p.35). However, about 66 percent of these non-mobile phone users said that they would use a mobile phone if they were given one (GSMA, 2015b, p.35).

Skills Access

In India, girls and women are not provided with equal access to education. The male-female gap in literacy rates is still very high although India has achieved substantial progress in improving women's literacy rate (Nair, 2010, p.100). The female literacy rate steadily increased from 8.9 percent in 1951 (Nair, 2010, p.100) to 59 percent in 2016 (Ministry of Statistics and Programme Implementation, 2017, p.39). But it was still lower than the male literacy rate, which accounted for 79 percent in 2016 (Ministry of Statistics and Programme Implementation, 2017, p.39). Besides, there is a great disparity in adult literacy rate between urban and rural women. In 2016, adult literacy rate for women in urban areas was about 77 percent while adult literacy rate for women in rural areas was only about 51 percent (Ministry of Statistics and Programme Implementation, 2017, p.39). Gender inequality in education is largely attributed to parents' reluctance to educate girls (Nair, 2010, p.103). Parents think that it is unnecessary for women to receive education because women will end up becoming child bearers and rearers (Nair, 2010, p.103). The importance of education of girls is also downplayed by domestic responsibilities and lack of mobility (United Nations, 2005, p.16). Engaging in domestic activities was one of the main reasons why Indian females aged 5 to 29 years never enrolled in schools (Ministry of Statistics and Programme Implementation, 2017, p.48). In rural areas, parents cannot afford to pay tuition fees for their children and most of the girls are kept at home to do household chores and serve as free labour in the farms (Nair, 2010, p.104). Meanwhile, inadequate toilet facilities (Nair, 2010, p.103) and "discriminatory stances, such as women's education having lower economic utility or at best being a secondary wage earner" (Nair, 2010, p.103) are other factors inhibiting women's access to education. Without literacy or having poor literacy, girls and women are unable to develop the cognitive skills of reading and writing and numeracy skills to process and interpret mathematical information (UNESCO, 2006, pp.149-150). "Literacy is often a pre-requisite for the acquisition of many other skills" (Kapur and Murthi, 2009, p.4) and "an indispensable instrument for access to further learning and training opportunities" (Gunawardena, 1997, p.596).

Without literacy or having poor literacy, girls and women are unable to possess skills related to the use of new technologies such as digital media. In India, many girls and women are digitally illiterate that they lack "the skills, understandings and practices required to successfully navigate the ever-changing digital landscape" (Meyers et al., 2013, p.356). They are unable to make effective use of the Internet and may encounter informational obstacles on the Internet because they are unable to access or understand information online (Birru et al., 2004). For example, a government survey in 2014 found that only 9 percent of female respondents knew how to do an Internet search or use either a computer or a mobile phone to send emails, compared with over 16 percent of male respondents (Bellman and Malhotra, 2016 October 13). According to the 2012 survey, 19 percent of Indian female respondents cited 'There is no one to show me how to use it' as one of the reasons for not accessing the Internet (Intel Corporation and Dalberg Global Development Advisors, 2012, p. 49). During the survey interviews, female respondents "called for classes to educate females about the Internet and free training in computer education" (Intel Corporation and Dalberg Global Development Advisors, 2012, p. 50). In rural areas, women have very low awareness of the Internet. A survey which examined the use of mobile Internet among urban and rural women in Kenya, India, and Indonesia found that rural non-users in India had the lowest awareness of the Internet (GSMA, 2015a, p.30). Many admitted in the interviews that "they were not completely sure what the internet was, or what it could be used for" (GSMA, 2015a, p.30). Although some rural women enquired about the Internet, they failed to receive any positive responses from friends and family members. They were told that "there was no point in them learning it because 'a woman's place was in the household'" (GSMA, 2015a, p.34). This discouraged women from learning the Internet when family members and friends refrained from teaching them how to use it (GSMA, 2015a, p.34). Meanwhile, lack of economic independence was a barrier to women's digital literacy (GSMA, 2015a, p.31). For rural women who were users of mobile Internet, their reliance on men to recharge their mobile phones "inhibited them from freely spending money on learning" (GSMA, 2015a, p.31).

While computers demand high skill sets, mobile phones are user friendly (United Nations Development Programme, 2012, p.13) and "only require basic literacy" (United Nations Development Programme, 2012, p.13). Nevertheless, many Indian women still lack the related knowledge and skills to use mobile phones. The 2015 survey showed that technical literacy was cited by Indian women from both wealthier and poorer households as a barrier to mobile phone ownership and usage (GSMA, 2015b, p.28). The survey found that 34 percent of Indian female respondents said that they did not know how to use a mobile phone or how to use the more complex features of their mobile phone (GSMA, 2015b, p.54). Besides, 32 percent of Indian female respondents said that they had trouble reading and/or understanding handsets and/or content language (GSMA, 2015b, p.54). Another survey found that language was a barrier to women's use of mobile phone. Smartphones and apps that were in English or Hindi prevented rural, low-educated women in India from using mobile phones (GSMA, 2015b, p.56). Due to "low mobile literacy and a lack of digital skills" (GSMA, 2015a, p.11), many Indian women have to seek assistance from other people in order to use a mobile phone. Compared with women in other low- and middle-income countries, more women in India needed help when using mobile Internet. While over 70 percent of women in Turkey, Mexico, Columbia, Jordan and Egypt reported that they could use mobile Internet without any help, only 24 percent of Indian female respondents said that they could use mobile Internet without any help (GSMA, 2015b, p.55). According to the 2015 survey, many Indian female respondents needed help to use mobile Internet (76 percent) and send SMS (50 percent) while some of them needed help to make a call (5 percent) (GSMA, 2015b, p.123). Most of the female respondents (39 percent) reported that their husband was the first person who taught them how to use a mobile phone while 33 percent of female respondents reported that they worked it out on their own (GSMA, 2015b, p.124). It means that some women learnt to use many features on their mobile phones independently by experimenting with various buttons and icons (GSMA, 2015a, p.30). In rural area, many women experienced difficulties in using voice calling feature on their mobile phones. A survey found that many uneducated rural female respondents relied on their household members to make calls for them due to the lack of numeracy skills (Grameen Foundation, 2013, p.6; Grameen Foundation, 2013, p.15). All of them "could use the phone only if somebody else dialled the number for them or if they were on the receiving end" (Grameen Foundation, 2013, p.15). Some of them could only use mobile phones to watch videos or listen to music unless their husbands or other household members assisted them to download content in advance (Grameen Foundation, 2013, p.15). About 70 percent of female respondents said that they did not use other non-voice features such as SMS because "they did not know how" (Grameen Foundation, 2013, p.16). Recently, a report has revealed that village women are only taught to press the green button to pick up phone calls and the red button to disconnect the mobile phone (Khan, 2017).

Usage Access

For many women in India, especially those in rural areas, "the hurdles to Internet access are too high for regular use" (Intel Corporation and Dalberg Global Development Advisors, 2012, p.65). There is gender disparity in Internet access due to various reasons. According to the 2012 survey, women's access to the Internet was much less than men's because of less formal schooling, less physical mobility, and less employment outside the home (Intel Corporation and Dalberg Global Development Advisors, 2012, p. 50). The heavy burden of unpaid family and household responsibilities, such as cooking, cleaning and child care, also leads to women having little free time to access and use the Internet (The International Center for Research on Women, 2010, p.7). However, it is the lack of freedom greatly limiting women's opportunities to use the Internet. Osama Manzar, head of India's Digital Empowerment Foundation, said that a woman needed to first give her family a reason why she wanted to use the Internet (Intel Corporation and Dalberg Global Development Advisors, 2012, p.65). Even though a woman got approval from family members to use the Internet, she could only use the Internet in a very limited way. For example, a 16-year-old Indian girl whose brother kept an eye on which website she was accessing was allowed to use online dictionaries for help with homework, but was not allowed to use social media sites such as Facebook (Subramanian, 2017 May 29). Besides, she was not allowed to own a mobile phone because her parents wanted to prevent her from chatting with boys (Subramanian, 2017 May 29). In rural India, young women can only use mobile phones in a limited way because they had "their access and use of mobile monitored and controlled by their families" (GSMA, 2015b, p. 60) to reduce their contact with men outside the immediate family or protect them from harassment from untoward admirers (GSMA, 2015b, p. 60). These examples show that social norms limit women's access to social media sites and ownership of mobile phones. In fact, "Facebook has a massive gender divide in India" (Bhattacharya, 2016 September 7). In 2015, there were "roughly 3 men for every woman on Facebook in India" (GSMA, 2015b, p. 30). Moral panic of family members is a barrier to girls' and women's access to mobile and Internet technology (Subramanian, 2017 May 29). Another situation faced by women in India is that they can hardly use the Internet to express their views or participate in political debates because men dislike them posting their views online. A study which examined whether the democratic nature of Twitter allows Indian women to be more free and vocal about politics found that women were significantly underrepresented in Twitter's political conversations (Anderson, 2015, p.1). Only 7.72 percent out of 23,250 tweets under political trending topics were by women, compared to 46.15 percent by men (Anderson, 2015, p.4). The finding mirrored "an under representation of women in actual processes of electoral politics in India" (Anderson, 2015, pp.5-6). Women were discouraged to express their political views online because women who took up space online were regarded as trespassers in a male dominated Internet structure (Anderson, 2015, p. 6). Most of them faced cyber abuse that they were forced offline. This will be explained in detail in the next section.

THE CAUSES OF GENDER DIGITAL DIVIDE IN INDIA

In India, "the gender gap in [ICT] access is often symptomatic of underlying structural inequalities – especially in education and income – between women and men" (Gurumurthy and Chami, 2014, p.12). India is a patrifocal society that "women are subordinate to the welfare of the family" (Varma, 2010, p.258). The appropriate female behaviour emphasizes "obedience to family rules and authority, fondness for simplicity and home life" (Varma, 2010, p.258). Due to patrifocality, women "fall far behind men in almost all spheres of life" (Katiyar, 2016, p.47). They are not treated at par with men politically, economically and socially (Katiyar, 2016, p.47). The Global Gender Gap Index, which measures the relative gaps between women and men across the key areas of politics, economy, education, and health in 144 countries (World Economic Forum, 2017, p. v), showed that India experienced a decline in its overall Global Gender Gap Index ranking from 87th in 2016 to 108th in 2017 (World Economic Forum, 2016, p.11; World Economic Forum, 2017, p.11). Its decline was attributed to a widening of its gender gaps in political empowerment, economic participation and opportunity, and healthy life expectancy (World Economic Forum, 2017, p.176). While it "rank[ed] fourth-lowest in the world on Health and Survival" (World Economic Forum, 2017, p.22), it dropped to sixth-lowest in the world on Economic Participation and Opportunity (World Economic Forum, 2017, p.176). In the previous section, some economic, social and cultural reasons that attributed to four types of gender digital divide have been examined. In this section, two more reasons that affect females' use and access of the Internet and mobile phones would be examined in detail.

Khap Panchayats' Ban on the Use of Mobile Phones Among Girls and Women

Over the past few years, informal village councils known as khap panchayats have issued orders prohibiting girls and women from using mobile phones and imposed fines on violators (The Express Tribute, 2017 May 3). "The word 'Khap' connotes village area inhabited by a clan" (Gurtoo, 2016, p. 46). "*Panchayat* literally means assembly (*yat*) of five (*panch*) prudent and respected elders chosen and accepted by the village community" (Kachhwaha, 2011, p. 298). Khap panchayats are dominated by men and have a patriarchal ideology (Singh and Pawar, 2016, p.240). They are "being acknowledged and supported by powerful male elements of the society" (Thakur et al., 2015, p.10). They "believe themselves to be autonomous from the state and claim to represent all members of that particular community" (Sadiq and Khan, 2015, p.11753). They "have been declared illegal and unconstitutional bodies by the Supreme Court for their alleged encouragement of honour killings" (Rajpurohit and Kaur, 2017, p.291). But they have considerable influence in rural India (The Express Tribute, 2017 May 3) and "even big politicians are dominated by them (Rajpurohit and Kaur, 2017, p.291). They "impose self-created norms backed by sanction in the name of preserving morals and values of the society" (Rajpurohit and Prakash, 2015, p.81). They "are known for issuing diktats aimed at upholding the socially conservative traditions that have long held sway and resisting modernisation" (The Express Tribute, 2017 May 3). "The question of rights for women does not exist anywhere in the territories ruled by Khap panchayats" (Sunita and Yudhvir, 2013, p.16). It is because Khap panchayats "uphold the dictum of Manu that women should be protected by men in every stage of life" (Ameera, 2017, p.156) and girls are brought up with the notion that they are submissive to men and have to bear all suppression (Ameera, 2017, p.157). Khap panchayats "override any notion of gender equality or gender empowerment that the Indian legal system provides" (Gurtoo, 2016, p. 48). They sustain control over female members of the community and instil fear in minds of girls by issuing various orders that are degrading and mortifying to the women (Ameera, 2017, pp.156-7).

In December 2012, a panchayat in Bihar village in Northeast India banned girls and women from using mobile phones (Firstpost, 2012 December 3). A girl who was found using a mobile phone would face fines of 10,000 rupees while a married woman who was found using a mobile phone outside her house would face fines of 2,000 rupees (Firstpost, 2012 December 3). The financial penalty was heavy because the average daily wage in India was only 193 rupees and 250 million people living below the poverty line could only earn 86 rupees per day (Lewis, 2016 February 22). Most of the village elders favoured such ban because they thought that mobile phone was the cause of all evils leading to an increase in love affairs and the incidents of elopement (Firstpost, 2012 December 3). In 2014, Muzaffarnagar village in Northern India banned young girls from using mobile phones (Chauhan, 2016 February 19). In 2015, Barmer village in the north western Indian state of Rajasthan also imposed such ban on girls (Chauhan, 2016 February 19). In February 2016, Basauli village in Northern India completely banned unmarried girls from using mobile phones or social media (Chauhan, 2016 February 19). Those who broke the rule would face hefty penalties of up to 1,000 rupees or their parents would be punished by sweeping 500 metres of village roads for five days (Chauhan, 2016 February 19). According to the khap panchayat coordinator, the reason behind such ban was that the use of mobile phone led to girls getting spoiled and getting involved in relationships with boys at a young age (Chauhan, 2016 February 19). Village elders and other men decided in a meeting that several teams would be formed to keep a tab on girls carrying mobile phones (Chauhan, 2016 February 19). In the same month, Gujarat village in Western India banned unmarried women from using mobile phones because community leaders thought that unmarried women' use of mobile phones created a nuisance in society (Dave, 2016 February 18). Village sarpanch claimed that the move could help girls "better utilise their time for study and other works" (Dave, 2016 February 18). According to the diktat, women who possessed or used a mobile phone would face fines of 2,100 rupees while informers could get 200 rupees as reward (Dave, 2016 February 18). The only exception to the ban was that women were allowed to use their parents' mobile phone if their relatives wanted to talk to them (Dave, 2016 February 18). In May 2017, Mathura village in Northern India banned girls from using mobile phones in public or while walking through the village lanes (Chaturvedi, 2017 May 3). Any girls who violated the diktat would face fines of 2,100 rupees (The Hindu, 2017 May 3). According to Head of the panchayat, such ban was due to the fact that girls were not much educated and the use of mobile phones was an 'evil' that may lead girls to a 'wrong path' (Chaturvedi, 2017 May 3). Former head of the village said that girls' use of mobile phones encouraged elopement (Financial Express Online, 2017 May 3) and elopement could sometimes lead to violence (The Hindu, 2017 May 3). Hence, the all-male panchayat decided that "girls should use mobile phones only within the boundaries of their homes" (The Hindu, 2017 May 3). Local police said that the ban on the use of mobile phones among women were against the constitution because of curbing the freedom of women and they would take action (The Express Tribute, 2017 May 3). But no concrete action has been taken by the police so far.

Ineffective Law Enforcement

Due to the pervasiveness of patriarchal mindset on the online spaces, women's use of Twitter, Facebook or other social media platforms to express their views are often met with cyber stalking, bullying, sexual harassment, the threat of violence (Arya, 2013 May 8), gender-based hate speech (Padte and Kovacs, 2013), disturbing emails (Krishnani, 2015) and harassing phone calls from unknown men (Dutt, 2017 May 12). Their personal information or their family members' personal and related information are also leaked onto the Internet (Arya, 2013 May 8; Halder and Jaishankar, 2011, p. 394) that lead to repeated acts of harassment in real life. Online trolling has been used to create a hostile culture in which sexism and woman-hating is expressed (Kovacs et al., 2013) and this works to "control, intimidate and eventually silence women" (Dutt, 2017 May 12). In 2010, a survey which examined 60 Indian female respondents' cyber victimization experiences found that 85 percent of them received abusive mails with sexual images and dirty messages and 75 percent of them received sexually teasing remarks in their social networking profiles or associated email (Halder and Jaishankar, 2010, p.17). Besides, the survey found that 45 percent of the respondents had been targeted because of her sexuality or feministic ideologies while about 42 percent of them received hate messages and 40 percent of them had been victim of cyber stalking (Halder and Jaishankar, 2010, p.17). The survey result showed that women could be victims of different types of cyber abuse. Many women facing cyber bullying did not go to the police "in fear of defamation of her profile as well as her family's name" (Saha and Srivastava, 2014, p.62). They were "taught to shun their voice for the fear of being stigmatized" (Saha and Srivastava, 2014, p.61). That is one of the reasons why many cyber abuse cases go unreported. For women who went to the police, their complaints were dismissed as trivial and they were even told by the police that it was unnecessary for women to express their views online (Arya, 2013 May 8). When women tried to approach their friends to ask for help, most of their friends told them to 'let it go' (Krishnani, 2015). Secondary victimization of women due to the unmotivated attitude of police to pursue proper investigations and the unempathetic attitude of their friends (Halder and Jaishankar, 2011, pp. 387-8) put women into a very disadvantageous, helpless and vulnerable situation. Most of the women ended up handling cyber bullying on their own. They responded to cyber bullying in different ways, which included getting the abusive content removed (Arya, 2013 May 8), blocking abusers (Krishnani, 2015), refraining from expressing their views online (Arya, 2013 May 8), shutting down their social media accounts temporarily (Walia, 2016 March 3), deleting their social media accounts (Hindustan Times, 2017 May 12) or withdrawing from online spaces (Subramanian, 2017 May 29). According to the 2015 survey, 33 percent of Indian female respondents said that harassment from strangers was a barrier to their use of mobile phones (GSMA, 2015b, p. 50). Cyber abuse adversely affects "the exercise of and advocacy for free speech and other human rights" (The United Nations Broadband Commission for Digital Development, 2015, p.2).

A HUMAN RIGHTS BASED APPROACH TO BRIDGE GENDER DIGITAL DIVIDE

Gender equality is a human right critical for advancing development. It is also an important value that the United Nations has made unremitting efforts to promote in different conferences and documents. It is important to inform, educate and empower women through ICTs so that women have the ability to make informed decisions that shape their lives, make their voices heard, improve their economic and social status, have political participation, and contribute to the nation's economy. At present, gender digital divide is a pervasive problem in India. There is an urgent need to address this gender divide. Otherwise, there might be "a risk that ICT may exacerbate existing inequalities between women and men and create new forms of inequality" (United Nations, 2005, p.3). The adoption of a human rights based approach to bridge gender digital divide is to encourage rights holders to claim their rights as well as developing the capacity of duty-bearers to meet their obligations (United Nations Population Fund, 2014). Women being rights holders have the rights to receive ICT education, obtain online information and services, have freedom of expression online, participate in decision-making processes, and privacy. Meanwhile, the adoption of a human rights based approach recognizes that duty bearers which are usually governments have the obligations to respect, protect and guarantee these rights (United Nations Population Fund, 2014). "Gender sensitivity is the prerequisite that must prevail and be strengthened at all levels" (Parihar, 2017, p.29). The government, private organizations and non-government organizations should foster a gender-responsive culture and environment to realize the rights of women through ICT and facilitate women's empowerment.

Women's Right to ICT-Related Education and Training

The Internet can bring both tangible and intangible benefits to women in developing countries (Intel Corporation and Dalberg Global Development Advisors, 2012, p.29). Tangible benefits include finding more education and job opportunities, having greater access to information ranging from government services to health and other needs (Intel Corporation and Dalberg Global Development Advisors, 2012, p.29), and improving their networking capabilities (Gallup, Inc. and the International Labour Organization, 2017, p.55). For example, female respondents in India reported in the 2012 survey that tangible benefits brought by Internet use included improving their education/studies (77 percent), searching and applying for jobs (59 percent), expanding their networks to improve job prospects (59 percent) and earning additional income (39 percent) (Intel Corporation and Dalberg Global Development Advisors, 2012, pp.32-3). Meanwhile, intangible benefits brought by the Internet include greater confidence, higher self-esteem, a sense of connection and participation, empowerment, and even a feeling of liberation (Intel Corporation and Dalberg Global Development Advisors, 2012, pp. 29-30). In order to absorb and exploit the benefits of Internet use, the government, local communities or non-governmental organization (NGO) should provide girls and women with ICT-related education and training so that their knowledge and skills can be developed and enhanced. Different training programmes should be available and learner-centred to suit different needs, such as beginners computer class, advanced computer class, career developing trainin, and career enhancement training (Women Centre of Peel, 2018). For example, Feminist Approach to Technology (FAT) was established in 2007 in New Delhi, India with an aim to increase women's access to technical resources so that they had broader career choices (Intel Corporation and Dalberg Global Development Advisors, 2012, p. 38). FAT hosts a community tech center that has female-only staff to provide underprivileged girls with training and guidance when they learn and experiment with computers and the Internet (Intel Corporation and Dalberg Global Development Advisors, 2012, p. 38). Another example was that a new Women's Resource Center was established by Rural Education and Development (READ) Global in Bihar to provide a 6-month computer training for women to acquire basic computer skills that could help them find higher paying jobs (Greene, 2016). Also, telecentre is a public access point where people have access to computers and the Internet that enable them to get information and receive training and education (Mukerji, 2008, pp.1-2). For example, women reported that the acquisition of computer skills at the Baduria ICT Centre in West Bengal helped increase their confidence in approaching the job market and gain more respect at both the family and community levels (United Nations, 2005, p.8). The availability of basic ICT infrastructure, a stable electricity supply, a convenient location, competent teachers and trainers, and regular computer maintenance can ensure smooth and efficient operation of telecentres. Telecentres can facilitate women's participation more effectively by having women-trainers and providing women-only training environments (United Nations, 2005, p.8). Meanwhile, they can enhance women's learning experience by simplifying and adapting training materials into local contexts and translating the materials into local languages (United Nations, 2005, p.8). Capacity building through ICT can enable the ability of girls and women to use computers, the Internet and mobile technologies at their own pace and in whatever manner they see fit. It can also enable girls and women to integrate into their daily lives and even create positive impacts to local communities and economic development such as driving Gross Domestic Product (GDP) and income growth

(Intel Corporation and Dalberg Global Development Advisors, 2012, p.30). In recent years, Google has partnered with local philanthropy Tata Trusts to launch a campaign known as Helping Women Get Online (Purnell, 2016 October 3). The campaign sends thousands of bicycle-riding female tutors to their own and neighbouring villages in order to provide rural women with free access to Internet-enabled devices like tablets and smartphones and basic Internet skills training (Parbat, 2016 June 8). Over 2 million rural women have benefited from the campaign (Parbat, 2016 June 8) and their lives have been improved by learning to "search online for information about government benefits, crop prices, health tips, recipes, agricultural techniques, cattle deworming and how to keep animals healthy" (Dhillon, 2016 December 5).

Women's Right to Internet Privacy and Freedom of Expression

"Rights of women in cyber space are as important as rights of women in physical space" (Halder and Jaishankar, 2012, p.55). Women have the right to safe and protected cyber life (Halder and Jaishankar, 2012, p.62) and this can be achieved by protecting their rights to digital privacy and freedom of expression. Right to privacy is "universal and applicable to both women and men on an equal basis" (Mendel et al., 2012, p.10). Freedom of expression is also "a fundamental right, and its preservation requires vigilance by everyone" (The United Nations Broadband Commission for Digital Development, 2015, p.3). The rights to privacy and freedom of expression are closely linked (Mendel et al., 2012, p.95). Respect for privacy of online communications is a prerequisite for trust by those who engage in communicative activities (Mendel et al., 2012, p.95), "which is in turn a prerequisite for the exercise of the right to freedom of expression" (Mendel et al., 2012, p.95). At present, "online gender-based abuse and violence assaults basic principles of equality under international law and freedom of expression" (DigitalWatch Observatory, 2017). It also jeopardizes women's right to privacy. The large-scale cyber abuses faced by girls and women must be addressed with sufficient legal recourse (Padte and Kovacs, 2013). Women deserve to have "equal treatment for legal protection against cyber crimes" (Halder and Jaishankar, 2012, p.62). Both the Indian Penal Code (IPC) and the Information Technology (Amendment) Act, 2008 (hereafter the 2008 IT Act) provide sections that protect women against online harassment. Section 503 of IPC protects women against criminal intimidation such as rape threats online whereas Section 509 of IPC protects women against acts of sexual harassment that intend to insult the modesty of a woman (Padte, 2012). For example, a male student in 2001 "was convicted under section 509 for making vulgar remarks about female classmates on a website called Amazing.com" (Padte and Kovacs, 2013). As regards the 2008 IT Act, Section 67 punishes those who publish or transmit obscene material in electronic form with an imprisonment of up to three years and a fine of up to five lakh rupees whereas (Padte and Kovacs, 2013). Section 66A of the 2008 IT Act punishes those who send any information or message by means of a computer resource or a communication device for the purpose of causing annoyance, insult, enmity, ill will, criminal intimidation, inconvenience, obstruction, danger, or injury with imprisonment for a term which may extend to three years and with fine (Padte and Kovacs, 2013). For example, two men were arrested under Section 66A for making vulgar remarks to sexually harass singer Chinmayi Sripada on Twitter (Roy, 2012 November 6). However, these laws have not been widely applied to protect women who experience online abuse due to several reasons. Firstly, many women lack the knowledge of these provisions and hence they seldom resort to legal sanctions (Padte and Kovacs, 2013). Secondly, women's access to justice was negated by the "prevailing attitudes in society and of the duty bearers characterised by gender bias and discrimination" (The United Nations Broadband Commission for Digital Development, 2015, p.42). The problem of 'victim blaming' leads to some women being reluctant to engage with law enforcement because "such engagements often result in women being disbelieved or, worse, blamed for the harassment they face, both online and offline" (Padte and Kovacs, 2013).Thirdly, there is opposition to Section 66A of the 2008 IT Act because its vague framing leaves huge scope for interpretation and thereby potentially creating situations where the powerful are protected and a higher degree of censorship is enforced by the state to protect its interests (Padte and Kovacs, 2013).

The legal sanctions of the IPC and the 2008 IT Act have a deterrent effect and the courts have the ability to "enforce compliance and punitive consequences for perpetrators" (The United Nations Broadband Commission for Digital Development, 2015, p.3). But the introduction and implementation of legislation alone is not enough to protect women's rights to privacy and freedom of expression. It also "requires a broad-based societal action, engaging all stakeholders" (The United Nations Broadband Commission for Digital Development, 2015, p.3). Firstly, to ensure that women can get protection under the IPC and the 2008 IT Act, the government needs to raise awareness of girls and women on these laws through advertising campaigns and media coverage. Secondly, the government, the private sector, NGOs or women's groups can provide legal assistance for women who experience cyber abuse through 24/7 helpline, legal awareness training, workshops and legal aid centres. Thirdly, the government can consider amending the 2008 IT Act in order to make it clearer to use. Fourthly, prevention is important to eliminate cyber abuses (The United Nations Broadband Commission for Digital Development, 2015, p.3). The government can learn from international experience in launching public awareness campaign to educate citizens about combating and preventing cyber abuse. This can help "[b]ring visibility and positive public consciousness to the issue" (The United Nations Broadband Commission for Digital Development, 2015, p.28) and eliminate prejudices and other practices that are based on stereotyped roles for men and women or the idea of the superiority or the inferiority of either of the sexes (The United Nations Broadband Commission for Digital Development, 2015, p.27). For example, the Canadian government launched anti-cyberbullying public awareness campaign called Stop Hating Online to "raise awareness among Canadians of the impact of cyberbullying and how this behaviour amounts to criminal activity" (Government of Canada, 2014) and provide citizens with a comprehensive resource that included "information, advice and tools needed to identify, prevent and stop cyberbullying" (Government of Canada, 2014). Fifthly, active participation of industry as digital gatekeepers is also important to combat cyber abuses (The United Nations Broadband Commission for Digital Development, 2015, p.3). Providers of social media sites should develop clear guidelines that take sufficient action to address cyber abuses against women. Due diligence and duty to report abuse should be promoted (The United Nations Broadband Commission for Digital Development, 2015, p. 28). Staff should be trained to be more responsive to complaints on cyber abuses (The United Nations Broadband Commission for Digital Development, 2015, p. 31). Different types of tools should be developed to make online abuse and harassment easier and prevent unwanted communications (Strickland and Dent, 2017, p.21). These can include establishing a report link that let users directly report online abuse to the platform, block or mute the person who has uploaded abusive content, and unsubscribing accounts which produce or share offensive material (Strickland and Dent, 2017, p.21). Takedown procedures should be established for harmful materials that include violence against women content (The United Nations Broadband Commission for Digital Development, 2015).

Women's Right to Mobile Phone Ownership

Social norms are an underlying barrier to girls' and women's access to and use of mobile phones in India (GSMA, 2015b, p.58). But studies have shown that mobile phone ownership can empower women in different ways. A previous study found that women's mobile phone ownership in India "significantly decrease[d] tolerance for wife beating and husband's control issues, and increase[d] women's autonomy in mobility and economic independence" (Lee, 2009, p.18), which reflected "higher women's status or greater gender equality" (Lee, 2009, p.11). Another study showed that the use of low-costs mobile phones as learning and business tools by 325 illiterate and semiliterate women farmers in Tamil Nadu, Theni District, Southern India could enhance their literacy levels through sending cost-free text messages (UNESCO, 2015, pp.107-8), facilitate continuous self-directed and collective learning among farmers (UNESCO, 2015, p.53) and "vertical and horizontal knowledge transfers related to the women's goat-rearing enterprises" (UNESCO, 2015, p.38) that consequently "enhance[d] their livelihood opportunities and skills" (UNESCO, 2015, p.94) and increased their voice and participation in their households and communities (UNESCO, 2015, p.75). The Self Employed Women's Association (SEWA), which was a trade union comprised over 1 million women members working in the informal sector in India, enhanced agricultural workers' ability to do crop planning, make informed harvesting decisions, and increased their incomes by sending them SMS messages with up-to-date spot and future commodity prices for each market (The GSMA Development Fund et al., 2010, p.39). Over the past few years, some creative methods have been adopted as solutions to overcome the social norm barrier that limits women's mobile phone ownership (UNESCO, 2015, p.89). For example, women in the goat-rearing project in Theni District "carried their mobile phone in a small pouch called a surukku pai, which is associated with women's identity and objects in the Indian culture" (UNESCO, 2015, p.89). The piloted combo SIM plan introduced by Uninor, which was the youngest telecom operators in India, was another example to increase SIM ownership among rural women (GSMA, 2015b, p.61). The marketing campaign promoted the idea that when two paired SIMs were sold together, one of the SIMs would be used by a woman while the other would be used by her husband or another male household member (GSMA, 2015b, p.61). Uninor offered various talktime benefits to incentivize local people to subscribe the combo SIM plan (GSMA, 2015b, p.61). One of the benefits was that "if the 'male' SIM [was] refilled then the 'female' SIM automatically receive[d] an equivalent free refill (and vice versa)" (GSMA, 2015b, p.61).

FUTURE RESEARCH DIRECTIONS

At present, the problem of gender digital divide is serious in India. However, actions to bridge gender digital divide are insufficient and a human right based approach to bridge gender digital divide has not been strongly advocated in the nation. This may be due to the fact that the status of females is undermined in this male-dominant society. In recent years, the government has made effort to bridge gender digital divide. But there is still much room for improvement. Future research directions can examine whether the adoption a human right based approach can effectively bridge gender digital divide or whether best practices for bridging gender digital divide overseas can be applied into India.

CONCLUSION

In conclusion, gender digital divide is a serious problem that deserves an in-depth investigation. The adoption of a human rights based approach to bridge gender digital divide requires strong political will and the government's long-term commitment to implement gender-responsive ICT policy. Besides, it requires an elimination of prejudice in society and an increased public awareness regarding the benefits of empowering women through the use of ICT. Looking forward, it is anticipated that more females can access the Internet and mobile technologies and hence their status and livelihoods can be improved.

REFERENCES

Ameera, V. U. (2017). Wails Unheard: The Women under Khap Panchayats. *Social Sciences International Research Journal, 3*(2), 156–158.

Anderson, S. (2015). *India's Gender Digital Divide: Women and Politics on Twitter*. Retrieved December 31, 2017 from http://cf.orfonline.org/wp-content/uploads/2015/12/ORFIssueBrief_108.pdf

Arya, D. (2013, May 8). *Why Are Indian Women Being Attacked on Social Media?* Retrieved December 25, 2017 from http://www.bbc.com/news/world-asia-india-22378366

Bellman, E., & Malhotra, A. (2016, October 13). *Why the Vast Majority of Women in India Will Never Own a Smartphone*. Retrieved January 1, 2018 from https://www.wsj.com/articles/why-the-vast-majority-of-women-in-india-will-never-own-a-smartphone-1476351001

Bhattacharya, A. (2016, September 7). *Facebook has a massive gender divide in India*. Retrieved January 1, 2018 from https://qz.com/775470/facebook-fb-has-a-massive-gender-divide-in-india/

Bhattacharya, A. (2017, April 26). *Rural Indian Women Are Lagging Far behind Their Urban Counterparts in Mobile Phone Usage*. Retrieved December 28, 2017 from https://qz.com/969565/rural-indian-women-are-lagging-far-behind-their-urban-counterparts-in-mobile-phone-usage/

Birru, M. S., Monaco, V. M., Charles, L., Drew, H., Njie, V., Bierria, T., ... Steinman, R. A. (2004). Internet Usage by Low-Literacy Adults Seeking Health Information: An Observational Analysis. *Journal of Medical Internet Research, 6*(3), e25. doi:10.2196/jmir.6.3.e25 PMID:15471751

Chaturvedi, H. (2017, May 3). *Mathura Village to Fine Girls Using Cell Phones*. Retrieved December 24, 2017 from http://www.hindustantimes.com/india-news/mathura-village-to-fine-girls-using-cell-phones/story-6xmL3kYEKqEEAFG0YNbp8M.html

Chaudhary, R., & Verick, S. (2014). *Female Labour Force Participation in India and Beyond*. Retrieved December 29, 2017 from http://www.ilo.org/wcmsp5/groups/public/@asia/@ro-bangkok/@sro-new_delhi/documents/publication/wcms_324621.pdf

Chauhan, A. (2016, February 19). *Panchayat Bans Mobile Phones Among Girls*. Retrieved December 24, 2017 from https://timesofindia.indiatimes.com/city/agra/Panchayat-bans-mobile-phones-among-girls/articleshow/51060339.cms

Das, S., Jain-Chandra, S., Kochhar, K., & Kumar, N. (2015). *Women Workers in India: Why So Few Among So Many?* Retrieved December 29, 2017 from https://www.imf.org/external/pubs/ft/wp/2015/wp1555.pdf

Dave, H. (2016, February 18). *Gujarat Village Bans Mobile Phones for Unmarried Women*. Retrieved December 24, 2017 from http://www.hindustantimes.com/india/gujarat-village-bans-mobile-phones-for-unmarried-women/story-iziKwjYckgmOOP8ZRBNn3K.html

Dhillon, A. (2016, December 5). *Women Tap into New Roles as Mobile Internet Scheme Targets Rural India*. Retrieved June 20, 2018 from https://www.theguardian.com/global-development/2016/dec/05/india-women-mobile-internet-scheme-rural-digital-literacy

DigitalWatch Observatory. (2017). *Fighting Online Gender-based Violence Supports Freedom of Expression*. Retrieved January 20, 2018 from https://dig.watch/updates/fighting-online-gender-based-violence-supports-freedom-expression

Dutt, B. (2017, May 12). *Let's Talk About Trolls: Online Abuse A Weapon to Silence Women*. Retrieved December 25, 2017 from http://www.hindustantimes.com/india-news/let-s-talk-about-trolls-trolling-is-a-weapon-to-silence-women-barkha-dutt/story-A9X3fAuRwZiwVrhYQnKbYL.html

Financial Express Online. (2017, May 3). *Village Panchayat Bans Mobile Phones for Girls; Threatens to Impose Rs 2,100 Fine on Violators*. Retrieved December 24, 2017 from http://www.financialexpress.com/india-news/village-panchayat-bans-mobile-phones-for-girls-threatens-to-impose-rs-2100-fine-on-violators/652483/

Firstpost. (2012, December 3). *Bihar Panchayat's Diktat: Girls Using Mobiles to be Fined!* Retrieved December 24, 2017 from http://www.firstpost.com/india/bihar-panchayats-diktat-girls-using-mobiles-to-be-fined-543124.html

Gallup, Inc., & International Labour Organization (2017). *Towards A Better Future for Women and Work: Voices of Women and Men*. Retrieved December 29, 2017 from http://www.ilo.org/wcmsp5/groups/public/---dgreports/---dcomm/---publ/documents/publication/wcms_546256.pdf

Government of Canada. (2014). *Harper Government Launches the Next Phase of Stop Hating Online to Combat Cyberbullying*. Retrieved January 3, 2018 from https://www.canada.ca/en/news/archive/2014/09/harper-government-launches-next-phase-stop-hating-online-combat-cyberbullying.html

Grameen Foundation. (2013). *Use of Mobile Financial Services Among Poor Women in Rural India and The Philippines*. Retrieved December 30, 2017 from https://www.gsma.com/mobilefordevelopment/wp-content/uploads/2014/07/Use-of-Mobile-Financial-Services-Among-Poor-Women-in-Rural-India-and-the-Philippines.pdf

Greene, H. (2016). *Job Skills Training to Empower Women in India*. Retrieved January 2, 2018 from http://www.readglobal.org/blog/161-job-skills-training

GSMA. (2015a). *Accelerating Digital Literacy: Empowering Women to Use the Mobile Internet*. Retrieved January 1, 2018 from https://www.gsma.com/mobilefordevelopment/wp-content/uploads/2015/06/DigitalLiteracy_v6_WEB_Singles.pdf

GSMA. (2015b). *Bridging the Gender Gap: Mobile Access and Usage in Low- and Middle-Income Countries*. Retrieved December 27, 2017 from https://www.gsma.com/mobilefordevelopment/wp-content/uploads/2016/02/GSM0001_03232015_GSMAReport_NEWGRAYS-Web.pdf

Gunawardena, C. (1997). Problems of Illiteracy in a Literate Developing Society: Sri Lanka. *International Review of Education, 43*(5-6), 595–609. doi:10.1023/A:1003010726149

Gurtoo, R. (2016). Khap Panchayats in Relation to Women's Human Rights: Indian Perspective. *Journal of Legal Studies and Research, 2*(2), 46–59.

Gurumurthy, A., & Chami, N. (2014). *Digital Technologies and Gender Justice in India: An Analysis of Key Policy and Programming Concerns*. Retrieved December 30, 2017 from http://www.itforchange.net/sites/default/files/IT%20for%20Change%20-%20HLPC%20Submission%20-%2016%20April%202014-1.pdf

Halder, D., & Jaishankar, K. (2010). *Cyber Victimization in India: A Baseline Survey Report*. Retrieved December 25, 2017 from http://www.cybervictims.org/CCVCresearchreport2010.pdf

Halder, D., & Jaishankar, K. (2011). Cyber Gender Harassment and Secondary Victimization: A Comparative Analysis of the United States, the UK, and India. *Victims & Offenders, 6*(4), 386–398. doi:10.1080/15564886.2011.607402

Halder, D., & Jaishankar, K. (2012). *Cyber Crime and the Victimization of Women: Laws, Rights, and Regulations*. Hershey, PA: IGI Global. doi:10.4018/978-1-60960-830-9

Haseloff, A. M. (2005). Cybercafes and Their Potential as Community Development Tools in India. *The Journal of Community Informatics, 1*(3). Retrieved from http://ci-journal.net/index.php/ciej/article/view/226/181

Hindustan Times. (2017, May 12). *Gurmehar Kaur Deletes Her Facebook Account*. Retrieved December 25, 2017 from http://www.hindustantimes.com/delhi-news/gurmehar-kaur-deletes-her-facebook-account/story-dnLz9leGiQ2gWmF9YGrwEM.html

Intel Corporation and Dalberg Global Development Advisors. (2012). *Women and the Web*. Retrieved December 26, 2017 from https://www.intel.com/content/www/us/en/technology-in-education/women-in-the-web.html

International Labour Organization Country Office for India. (2017). *India Labour Market Update*. Retrieved December 29, 2017 from http://www.ilo.org/wcmsp5/groups/public/---asia/---ro-bangkok/---sro-new_delhi/documents/publication/wcms_568701.pdf

Kachhwaha, K. (2011). Khap Adjudication in India: Honouring the Culture with Crimes. *International Journal of Criminal Justice Sciences, 6*(1&2), 297–308.

Kapur, S., & Murthi, M. (2009). *Literacy in India*. Retrieved December 31, 2017 from http://www.bbk.ac.uk/ems/faculty/kapur/personal/literacy

Katiyar, S. P. (2016). Gender Disparity in Literacy in India. *Social Change, 46*(1), 46–69. doi:10.1177/0049085715618558

Khan, Z. (2017). *The Internet is Bad for Indian Women*. Retrieved June 20, 2018 from https://internet-democracy.in/media/the-internet-is-bad-for-indian-women/

Kovacs, A., Padte, R. K., & Shobha, S. V. (2013). *'Don't Let It Stand!' An Exploratory Study of Women and Verbal Online Abuse in India*. Retrieved December 25, 2017 from https://internetdemocracy.in/wp-content/uploads/2013/12/Internet-Democracy-Project-Women-and-Online-Abuse.pdf

Krishnani, R. (2015). Indian Women: No Friends Online. *World Policy Journal*, *32*(2), 85–91. doi:10.1177/0740277515591546

Lee, D. (2009). *The Impact of Mobile Phones on the Status of Women in India*. Retrieved January 21, 2018 from https://pdfs.semanticscholar.org/e9fc/09860814f607f84c2f33b4db274dc48435dc.pdf

Lewis, K. (2016, February 22). *Girls and Unmarried Women in India Banned from Using Mobile Phones to Prevent 'Disturbance in Society'*. Retrieved December 24, 2017 from http://www.independent.co.uk/news/world/asia/girls-and-unmarried-women-in-india-forbidden-from-using-mobile-phones-to-prevent-disturbance-in-a6888911.html

Malhotra, A., Kanesathasan, A., & Patel, P. (2012). *Connectivity: How Mobile Phones, Computers and the Internet Can Catalyze Women's Entrepreneurship. India: A Case Study*. Retrieved December 30, 2017 from https://www.icrw.org/wp-content/uploads/2016/10/Connectivity-how-mobile-phones-computers-and-the-internet-can-catalyze-womens-entrepreneurship.pdf

Mendel, T., Puddephatt, A., Wagner, B., Hawtin, D., & Torres, N. (2012). *Global Survey on Internet Privacy and Freedom of Expression*. Retrieved January 3, 2018 from http://unesdoc.unesco.org/images/0021/002182/218273e.pdf

Meyers, E. M., Erickson, I., & Small, R. V. (2013). Digital Literacy and Informal Learning Environments: An Introduction. *Learning, Media and Technology*, *38*(4), 355–367. doi:10.1080/17439884.2013.783597

Ministry of Electronics & Information Technology. (2017). *About Digital India: Introduction*. Retrieved December 13, 2017 from http://www.digitalindia.gov.in/content/introduction

Ministry of Health and Family Welfare. (2017). *National Family Health Survey 4: 2015-16*. Retrieved December 28, 2017 from http://rchiips.org/nfhs/pdf/NFHS4/India.pdf

Ministry of Statistics and Programme Implementation. (2017). *Women and Men in India-2016*. Retrieved December 29, 2017 from http://www.mospi.gov.in/publication/women-and-men-india-2016

Mukerji, M. (2008). Telecentres in Rural India: Emergence and A Typology. *The Electronic Journal on Information Systems in Developing Countries*, *35*(5), 1–13. doi:10.1002/j.1681-4835.2008.tb00242.x

Nair, N. (2010). Women's Education in India: A Situational Analysis. *IMJ*, *1*(4), 100–114. PMID:20486309

Padte, R. K. (2012). *Section 66A, Sexual Harassment and Women's Rights*. Retrieved January 3, 2018 from https://internetdemocracy.in/2012/12/section-66a-sexual-harassment-and-womens-rights-2/

Padte, R. K., & Kovacs, A. (2013). *Keeping Women Safe? Gender, Online Harassment and Indian Law*. Retrieved January 3, 2018 from https://internetdemocracy.in/reports/keeping-women-safe-gender-online-harassment-and-indian-law/

Parbat, K. (2016, June 8). *Google, Tata Trusts launch 'Internet Sathi' in West Bengal to Empower Rural Women*. Retrieved June 20, 2018 from https://economictimes.indiatimes.com/tech/internet/google-tata-trusts-launch-internet-sathi-in-west-bengal-to-empower-rural-women/articleshow/52651338.cms

Parihar, J. (2017). How Digital India Minimised the Great Gender Divide? *IOSR Journal Of Humanities And Social Science*, *22*(11), 29-33.

Purnell, N. (2016, October 3). *How Google's Bicycle-Riding Internet Tutors Are Getting Rural Indian Women Online*. Retrieved June 20, 2018 from https://blogs.wsj.com/indiarealtime/2016/10/03/how-googles-bicycle-riding-internet-tutors-are-getting-rural-indian-women-online/

Rajpurohit, G. S., & Kaur, A. (2017). An Appraisal of Khap Panchayat: Issues and Concerns. *International Journal of Science and Research*, *6*(4), 290–295.

Rajpurohit, G. S., & Prakash, A. (2015). Khap Panchayat in India: Legitimacy, Reality and Reforms. *International Journal of Allied Practice. Research and Review*, *2*(3), 81–90.

Roy, P. K. (2012 November 6). *Why Was An Indian Man Held for Sending A Tweet?* Retrieved January 3, 2018 from http://www.bbc.com/news/world-asia-india-20202275

Sadiq, S., & Khan, A. (2015). Khap Panchayats in India: Precepts and Practices. *International Journal of Current Research*, *7*(1), 11753–11757.

Saha, T., & Srivastava, A. (2014). Indian Women at Risk in the Cyber Space: A Conceptual Model of Reasons of Victimization. *International Journal of Cyber Criminology*, *8*(1), 57–67.

Sharma, M. (2016, July 31). *20 Years On: India's Cyber Cafes Disappearing as Pocket Internet Takes Over*. Retrieved December 28, 2017 from http://www.hindustantimes.com/india-news/20-years-on-india-s-cyber-cafes-disappearing-as-pocket-internet-takes-over/story-vszaWMYND6Mm2lqOxkx5SK.html

Singh, M. (2014, October 13). *64% of Urban Indian Women Busy with Housework, Study Reveals*. Retrieved December 28, 2017 from https://timesofindia.indiatimes.com/india/64-of-urban-Indian-women-busy-with-housework-study-reveals/articleshow/44796358.cms

Singh, S., & Pawar, G. S. (2016). Khap Panchayat: Analysis in Light of Jurisprudence. *Bharati Law Review*, *5*(3), 240–251.

Strickland, P., & Dent, J. (2017). *Online Harassment and Cyber Bullying*. Retrieved January 20, 2018 from http://www.parliament.uk/commons-library

Subramanian, S. (2017, May 29). *Why Are There So Few Women on the Internet in India?* Retrieved December 25, 2017 from http://www.hindustantimes.com/opinion/locating-gender-in-the-digital-divide/story-zt10VjNAwnOqcChjkYCLfN.html

Sunita, & Yudhvir. (2013). Khap Panchayat: Changing Perspectives. *Asian Journal of Multidimensional Research*, *2*(7), 14-20.

Surie, M. D. (2016). *Where Are India's Working Women?* Retrieved December 29, 2017 from https://asiafoundation.org/2016/03/09/where-are-indias-working-women/

Thakur, R., Sinha, A. K., & Pathak, R. K. (2015). *Khap* Panchayats in Transition with Contemporary Times: An Anthropological Evaluation. *South Asian Anthropologist, 15*(1), 9–14.

The Express Tribute. (2017, May 3). *Indian Village Bans Women from Using Mobile Phones*. Retrieved December 24, 2017 from https://tribune.com.pk/story/1399963/indian-village-bans-women-using-mobile-phones/

The GSMA Development Fund, The Cherie Blair Foundation for Women, & Vital Wave Consulting. (2010). *Women & Mobile: A Global Opportunity A Study on the Mobile Phone Gender Gap in Low and Middle-Income Countries*. Retrieved December 28, 2017 from http://www.cherieblairfoundation.org/wp-content/uploads/2012/07/women_and_mobile_a_global_opportunity.pdf

The Hindu. (2017, May 3). *₹2,100 Fine on Women Using Mobile Phones in Public in U.P. Village*. Retrieved December 24, 2017 from http://www.thehindu.com/news/national/2100-rupees-fine-on-women-using-mobile-phones-in-public-in-up-village/article18377318.ece

The Indian Express. (2015, May 26). *Almost Half of Indian Women Find No Reason to Use Internet, Says Google*. Retrieved June 20, 2018 from https://indianexpress.com/article/technology/technology-others/49-indian-women-find-no-reason-to-use-internet-google/

The International Center for Research on Women. (2010). *Bridging the Gender Divide: How Technology Can Advance Women Economically*. Retrieved January 1, 2018 from https://www.icrw.org/wp-content/uploads/2016/10/Bridging-the-Gender-Divide-How-Technology-can-Advance-Women-Economically.pdf

The United Nations Broadband Commission for Digital Development. (2015). *Cyber Violence Against Women and Girls: A World-wide Wake-up Call*. Retrieved January 3, 2018 from http://www.unesco.org/fileadmin/MULTIMEDIA/HQ/CI/CI/images/wsis/GenderReport2015FINAL.pdf

UNESCO. (2006). *Education for All Global Monitoring Report*. Retrieved December 31, 2017 from http://www.unesco.org/education/GMR2006/full/chapt6_eng.pdf

UNESCO. (2015). *Mobile Phones & Literacy: Empowerment in Women's Hands - A Cross-Case Analysis of Nine Experiences*. Retrieved January 21, 2018 from http://unesdoc.unesco.org/images/0023/002343/234325E.pdf

UNICEF. (2017). *The State of the World's Children 2017: Children in a Digital World*. Retrieved December 13, 2017 from https://www.unicef.org/publications/index_101992.html

United Nations. (2005). *Gender Equality and Empowerment of Women through ICT*. Retrieved January 2, 2018 from http://www.un.org/womenwatch/daw/public/w2000-09.05-ict-e.pdf

United Nations Development Programme. (2012). *Mobile Technologies and Empowerment: Enhancing Human Development through Participation and Innovation*. Retrieved January 1, 2018 from http://www.undp.org/content/dam/undp/library/Democratic%20Governance/Access%20to%20Information%20and%20E-governance/Mobile%20Technologies%20and%20Empowerment_EN.pdf

United Nations Population Fund. (2014). *The Human Rights-Based Approach*. Retrieved December 13, 2017 from http://www.unfpa.org/human-rights-based-approach

Van Dijk, J. (2004). Digital Media. In J. D. H. Downing, D. McQuail, P. Schlesinger, & E. Wartella (Eds.), *The SAGE Handbook of Media Studies* (pp. 145–164). Thousand Oaks, CA: SAGE. doi:10.4135/9781412976077.n8

Varma, R. (2010). Computing Self-Efficacy Among Women in India. *Journal of Women and Minorities in Science and Engineering*, *16*(3), 257–274. doi:10.1615/JWomenMinorScienEng.v16.i3.40

Walia, S. (2016, March 3). *From Rape Threats to Twitter Trolls: Being A Woman Journalist in India is Tough*. Retrieved December 25, 2017 from https://qz.com/629423/from-rape-threats-to-twitter-trolls-being-a-woman-journalist-in-india-is-tough/

Women Centre of Peel. (2018). *IT Computer Training*. Retrieved January 2, 2017 from http://www.womencentreofpeel.org/it-computer-training/

World Economic Forum. (2016). *The Global Gender Gap Report 2016*. Retrieved December 29, 2017 from http://www3.weforum.org/docs/GGGR16/WEF_Global_Gender_Gap_Report_2016.pdf

World Economic Forum. (2017). *The Global Gender Gap Report 2017*. Retrieved December 29, 2017 from http://www3.weforum.org/docs/WEF_GGGR_2017.pdf

KEY TERMS AND DEFINITIONS

Cyber Abuse: Any harassment that is carried out using the internet, mobile technologies, or other digital devices.

Diktat: A harsh decree imposed on society without popular consent.

Gender Digital Divide: The inequalities between men and women in terms of access to information and communications technologies.

Literacy Rate: The percentage of the population that is able to read and write.

Moral Panic: Public fear in response to a condition or an issue which is perceived as a threat to societal values.

Social Norms: Unspoken rules of behaviors that are considered acceptable in a group or society.

Telecentre: A public access point where people have access to computers and the internet.

Chapter 3
The Conundrum of Falling Participation of Women in Math and Computing Jobs:
Observations From the USA and Denmark

Roslyn Layton
Aalborg University, Denmark

ABSTRACT

The USA and Denmark are leading information communications technologies (ICT)-enabled economies and have a variety of policies to promote women in ICT occupations, but both report that just roughly 25% of math and computing jobs in their respective countries are held by women, a number that continues to decline. The trend is odd given that the ICT industry globally notes a growing shortage of workers as well as a potential for lost revenue if positions go unfilled. Given the situation and a significant evidence that women's participation in companies is associated with greater profitability, one would assume ICT companies to be profit-maximizing and thus do more to attract and retain women. The trends are also odd given that the participation of women in scientific occupations in the life, physical, and social sciences are increasing overall. This chapter briefly reviews the situation and recommendations to address it, including increasing mentorship for women and recognizing and addressing bias in the workplace.

INTRODUCTION

The USA and Denmark are leading information communications technologies (ICT)-enabled economies and have a variety of policies to promote women in ICT occupations, but both report that just roughly 25% of math and computing jobs in their respective countries are held by women, a number that has declined or stagnated since 1990. Moreover, Nordic countries, noted for their advanced gender equality policies, also lag in the percentage of women in math and computing jobs. This defies the conventional wisdom that countries with a set of gender equality policies should have a higher, if not equal rate of women's participation in such jobs. The trend is odd given that the ICT industry globally notes a growing

DOI: 10.4018/978-1-5225-7068-4.ch003

shortage of workers as well as a potential for lost revenue if positions go unfilled. Given the situation and a significant evidence that women's participation and employment in companies is associated with greater profitability, one would assume ICT companies to be profit-maximizing and thus would do more to attract and retain women. The trends are also odd given that the participation of women in other scientific occupations, such as the life, social sciences, and many areas of natural science--are increasing overall. The debate also emerges as a critique of the Silicon Valley culture of high-tech powerhouses, billionaires, and geeks (Accenture, 2018) with its underside of exploitation of women, people of color, and public policy (Griffith, 2018). While there is one view that there is systematic sexism related to math and computer jobs which can only be fixed by top-down national policy, another view is that there cultural and behavioral differences which are better addressed within the university and firm through mentorship of women. This paper offers a modest overview of the the multiple perspectives on the problem and the conundrum that national gender policies purported to create "equality" in employment have not improved women's participation in math and computer jobs, some possible explanations, and solutions.

COMPARING THE US AND DENMARK

Globally, the ICT industry topped $4.5 trillion in revenue in 2017 and is expected to reach $4.8 trillion in 2018 (CompTIA, 2018) The US is the single-largest ICT market in the world and accounts for 31 percent of the global ICT market (CompTIA, 2018). The US ICT economy was $1.6 trillion in 2018, 9.2 percent of America's gross domestic product (GDP) (CompTIA, 2018). The numbers are even more staggering from an equities perspective; the American tech industry accounts for a quarter of the value of the US stock market, some $34 trillion (Nasdaq, n.d.). There are half a million tech companies in the US, with 34,000 new startups in 2017 alone (Cyberstates, n.d.). While women have increasing representation in a variety of roles in the ICT industry, but not in math and computing, a key policy research question would be whether the inclusion of women in said roles, would make ICT firms even more profitable and innovative.

Denmark, while a small country by population, is perhaps the world's leading digital nation. The country is rated as one of the top digital nations by the International Telecommunication Union's *Measuring the Information Society Report*, which has measured countries' access to, use of, and skills in information communications technologies (ICT) since 2007 (International Telecommunications Union, n.d.). Denmark is also celebrated for performance of broadband networks across a range of measures including competition, availability, speed, and price (Layton & Kane, 2017).

The groundbreaking book *TechnoFeminism* questioned whether technology creates utopia or dystopia for women, or both (Wajcman, 2004). There is no doubt that technological innovation has improved the human condition through the printing press, electricity, penicillin, semiconductors, and optical lenses among others, (Fallows, 2013) that it has drastically reduced the work burden and time poverty of women in agriculture in emerging countries (Food and Agriculture Organization of the United Nations, 2018), and that the advent of refrigerators and washing machines allowed women to reduce the amount of time they spent on housekeeping and enter the workforce in developed countries (Science Daily, 2009). On the one hand Wacjman celebrates how the Internet offers women unprecedented opportunities for their own social and political purposes while at the same time, its enabling of dehumanizing behaviors including pornography, harassment, the international sex trade, and pedophilia (Wajcman, 2004). While digital technologies and economies have allowed women the means to learn and work in information-related industries, she laments that many women may be relegated to contingent employment with simple, routine and predictable tasks (only to be replaced by robots) and that so-called family friendly telecommuting options may exacerbate women's domestic burden and the intensification of work (Wajcman, 2004).

The USA and Denmark have robust ICT sectors, and ICTs are integrated in a variety of industries and jobs. However, the ratio of women in specific functions in math and computing is disproportionately low compared to men. While women may comprise 57% of the US workforce and slight majority in all management and professional occupations, they account for just a quarter of the jobs in math and computing (Bureau of Labor Statistics, 2018). Moreover, while women have been gaining representation in economy and leadership overall, the number of women in pure math/computing jobs in the US has declined from a high of 35% in 1990 to just 25% today, the same rate as 1960 (Bureau of Labor Statistics, 2018). In Denmark women make up about 24% of ICT workforce, down from 28% in 2010 (Andersen, 2018).

The statistic is interesting because Denmark has even higher labor workforce participation rate of women than men (The Global Economy, 2018) and is perceived to have superior policies to support women in the workplace, such as one year of paid family leave whereas there is no standard policy in the US. A US News and World Report survey of 9000 women concludes that Denmark is best nation in the world for women (Radu, 2018). More broadly the gender policies across the Nordic region have long been described as superior to promote women's employment and are credited with driving 10-20% of gross domestic product growth (GDP) for the last 40-50 years. But the Nordic region does not display a higher rate of women's participation in math and computing. Indeed, across the 28 European Union countries, a region with a variety of official policies to promote women in the workplace, no country has a greater participation of women in the ICT sector than 25%, with the exceptions of Bulgaria (30.2%) and Romania (26.3%) (European Data Journalism Network, 2018).

Explanations for Bulgaria's superior performance include the early development of its ICT industry and social norm started in high school that girls should expect to enter the ICT industry (OECD, n.d.). A 2006 report on the history of its software industry, the Bulgarian government observes that while a competitive ICT industry never developed in Bulgaria, the country developed a competency in producing computer professionals along with its role to supply other communist countries (COMECOM) with computers since the 1960s (Vatchkov, n.d.). At its height, the country had almost 5000 computer scientists and accounted for more than half of the production of computers (notably the Pravec) in the COMECOM region, producing 10 times as much as the Soviet Union (Vatchkov, n.d.). The computers were mainly used by governments in other communist countries; there was not a corporate or consumer market for ICT as such.

With the fall of communism in 1989, the COMECOM countries realized that their computer industry was far behind the West. Bulgaria responded by privatizing state-owned computer production facilities, promoting its ICT workforce for coding projects internationally, and partnering with American ICT firms. Today the Bulgarian ICT industry drives over $USD 1 billion in annual revenue (about 2% of its gross domestic product) and 22,000 workers, including its relatively high percentage of women (Invest Sophia, 2017; Statista, 2018). However internet penetration and consumer use of ICT lags considerably in Bulgaria today; less than 60% of adults go online (Statista, 2018). The story illustrates the holistic, evolving view of ICT in society. Frequently called the "national innovation system (NIS)," a vibrant digital economy requires more than just the ability to produce one input well, whether ICT professionals or computers (Organization For Economic Co-Operation and Development, 1997). It requires multiple inputs, continuous learning, the ability to market ICT products and services, and the diffusion of innovation into society (Rogers, 2003). The NIS view has given way to a global system of innovation mediated by multinational firms (Narula & Zanfei, 2006).

The debate in the US is arguably more complex because the notion of diversity incorporates not just gender, but race and age whereas in Denmark, the discussion focuses on the ratio of men and women in math and computing jobs.

Possible Theories to Explain the Discrepancy

The Nordic countries also launched their ICT industries in the late 1950s and early 1960s, notably through the commercialization of university and academic projects for industrial applications which were marketed internationally (Gram et al., 2005). The story of the development of the modern ICT industry is interesting from a gender perspective. In many countries women occupied math and computing jobs in the 1960s and increased in subsequent decades, only to fall in the last 10-20 years. A leading theoretical explanation is the systematic devaluation of work performed by women (England, 1992). The "devaluation" theory holds that the math and computing jobs with mainframes, punchcards, and the like of the 1960s were seen as repetitive and secretarial, and therefore suitable for women. As the ICT industry became more complex, women either exited or were pushed out and men came to dominate the math and computing roles. Scholars have found statistical support for this theory, and they suggest that social processes exclude women from highly rewarded roles historically dominated by men and that cultural devalues and lowers the rewards associated with roles historically held by women (Levanon et al., 2009). However this theory does not explain that in any given ICT enterprise, women have advanced to other roles which may be equally or better paying, for exaple in sales, management, or finance. Proponents of the devaluation theory suggest that employers simply prefer men, and desire men even though they could theoretically get a woman to do the same job for less (Sommers, 2015). If this is the case, then firms, at least on this dimension, are not rational profit-maximizers.

Both the US and Denmark have a variety of policies to women in the ICT sector, including specific federal laws prohibiting workplace discrimination (Rets Information, n.d.). policies to encourage women to enter technical fields, and outreach programs to attract and retain women in technical roles (CompTIA, n.d.). Significantly the US is graduating more women with college degrees than ever. Between 1970 and 2010, the number of women with college degrees in the US has tripled in the workplace for women aged 25-64 (Bureau of Labor Statistics, 2011). This suggests that the problem of declining female in the ICT industry is not necessarily a legal one related to national policy and legislation.

It is also curious that there would be a decline because reports of the ICT sector note that it cannot hire enough workers overall (Council of European Professional Informatics Societies, n.d.). Executive search firm Korn Ferry estimates that the US tech firms could lose $160 billion annually in revenue because of a labor shortage (Laouchez et al., 2018). It's not clear why ICT firms don't do more to attract and retain when facing the specter of a labor shortage and lost revenue. Notably, women's representation is growing in jobs in the life, physical, and social sciences (today at 47%) and their share of the degrees awarded in these fields is increasing (Laouchez et al., 2018), but interestingly, women are leaving or never entering pure math or computing fields and fewer women chose these degrees at universities. Could it be that math and computing work environments are systematically sexist?

The trends are even more strange given the greater awareness and support of women's participation as well as research demonstrating the value that women bring to the workplace (National Center For Women and Information Technology, 2014). For example workplace teams in ICT functions with both men and women demonstrate superior team dynamics and productivity, stay on schedule and under budget, report improved individual employee performance (National Center For Women and Information Technology, 2014).

Moreover a number of studies document that firms with higher proportion of women in top management positions and boards of directors perform better financially (National Center For Women and Information Technology, 2014). In 2017 the most profitable industries overall in the US were accounting and bookkeeping firms, real estate leasing companies and legal services, all firms where women have near equal or greater representation than men, according to the US Bureau of Labor Standards (Biery, 2017). This study is performed annually by Sageworks, a leading analyst of the financial performance of private companies (SageWorks, 2017). It does not report on the representation of women as such, but its listing of most profitable industries largely conforms with the numbers reported by the US Bureau of Labor Standards where women have equal or greater representation.

While it does not address the question of the rate of women in math and engineering, a cursory review of leading women in the global ICT industry note some common paths, either being outstanding professionals in other disciplines who bring their skills to the ICT company, or working within the same company over a long period and being promoted (Bradford, 2018). While the number of pure female CEOs of ICT companies may be low, these women lead global multibillion enterprises and their ascension is impressive from any gender perspective. Moreover the increasing number of women in senior management is also important. At least 500 women in senior management in the American ICT industry are on the CEO/executive track (Geek Feminism, n.d.a). An additional 450 women who serve of the board of directors of American ICT companies (Geek Feminism, n.d.b)

Some suggest that the lack of women in math and computing limits the innovative and product development options of ICT products and services. The book *Technically Wrong: Sexist Apps, Biased Algorithms, and Other Threats of Toxic Tech* suggests that male-dominated department of math and computing bring one-sided values, processes, and assumptions into product development which inadvertently or not, create products with oversights, biases, and ethical problems (Wachter-Boettcher & Emmes, 2017).

Before drawing conclusions, it should be noted that while there is much emphasis on women's participation in math/computing jobs (about 5 million total), there is limited outcry about the limited participation of women in the construction and extraction industries which employ some 8 million of which only 3% are women; the installation, maintenance and repair industries of which 4% of its 5 million workers are women; or the transportation and materials moving industries employing some 10 million of which just 17% are women (outside of flight attendants of which women make up 77%). Moreover, women make up just 13% of America's police officers and only 3.5% of its firefighters. Notably math and computer jobs pay higher than these other fields, which could explain why greater emphasis is placed on these jobs.

Similarly, there are certain jobs in which 80% or greater are held by women, and yet there is not an outcry that these need to be diversified to include more men, for example social workers, legal assistants, pre-school and kindergarten teachers, nurses, nutritionists, dental hygienists, veterinarians, bookkeepers, payroll clerks, tellers, restaurant hosts, and maids. Indeed 92% of all health care ICT records managers are women, an important job which incorporates ICT skills, though not purely math or computing. Consider that almost three quarters of America's 10 million teachers and 10 million health care workers are women as well as three quarters of its 6 million workers in hair and personal service occupations; 72% of office support function (some 17 million workers), and 62% of sales force of 34 million workers in sales and office. Women may have a clear majority in a variety of leadership roles in public relations, human resources, education, health services, and community services. These fields increasingly incorporate ICT, both in firms themselves and their consumers (Farhadi et al., 2012)

One view is that certain fields lend themselves to employment by gender, though that is changing, particularly as automation removes perception that a job is associated with gender (Velasco, 2017). The number of male nurses, though still small, has tripled since the 1970s for example (Velasco, 2017).

A key difference between the USA and Denmark emerges on occupation or job prestige. The United States has calculated the relative public opinion about the worthiness of certain jobs to society for decades (Smith & Son, 2014). Computer scientists, physicists, and architects are top scoring positions which happen to have a preponderance of men. This could explain why there is debate and concern about the relative lack of women in the roles. However other top prestige jobs are physicians, lawyers, chemists, and life scientists, which are increasingly held by women. Hofstede suggests that that American cultural dimension of masculinity (score 62) rewards competition, achievement, and success (Hofstede Insights, n.d.).

While these dimensions exist in Denmark, they are less pronounced. In Hofstede's cultural dimension, Denmark is a "feminine" society (score 16) where work/life balance is valued as is social inclusion. Managers are expected to help their people and decision making is achieved through employee involvement (Hofstede Insights, 2018). Moreover, the notion of the Law of Jante ("you are not to think that you are special") pervades Danish society (Sandemose, 1936). Whereas Americans, particularly tech workers, may boast about their salaries, status, or achievements (Ungerleider, 2013), this is gauche is Denmark. On the flip side, Denmark (18) scores low in power distances versus the US (40). This explains the Danish egalitarian mindset, predilection for decentralization of power, and employee autonomy (Ungerleider, 2013). This suggests that Danes have a greater respect for all roles in organizations and don't believe that some jobs are "more important" to society than others.

These trends in women's declining employment in math and computing jobs have been documented for some time. A variety of culprits are suggested. One view is that men are more likely to use informal networking than women to further their careers (McDonald, 2011), whereas many women believe they must prove themselves on pure merit (Carmichael, 2015).

Another view is that Silicon Valley ICT success prevails not in spite of masculinity, but because of it, that it is predicated on a "bro culture" that creates an unfriendly workplace for women on purpose (Chang, 2018). However this view should be tempered by the reality that most of America's tech workers are outside of Silicon Valley. Moreover, the Best Places to Work in Technology 2018 finds that of the top 20 best places to work, half are not in Silicon Valley (Great Place to Work, 2018). While Google, Facebook, and Twitter account for a large share of the media coverage of the tech industry, their Silicon Valley employees number less than 100,000. According to the study, the top companies aggressively recruit diverse staff and successfully allow them to "be themselves" regardless of their age, gender, race, or what they do within the organization (Great Place to Work, 2018). Up to 30 percent of tech workers feel they can't be themselves at work, reducing employee innovation, effort, and retention. Employee recommendations and lower turnover help nurture a diverse workplace., Employees at companies with winning cultures are six times more likely to recruit their friends on behalf of their company and see half the voluntary turnover of peer companies (Great Place to Work, 2018).

Great Places to Work performs an additional survey specifically on women's employment (Great Place to Work, 2017). While this survey does not report on the parity of men and women in math/computing jobs, it does report on the total employment of women overall as well as women in management and leadership, and workplace satisfaction of all employees across a variety of measures. In the best places for women survey, just 2 pure ICT companies appear in the top ten (Ultimate Software and Intuit) but the other companies incorporate ICTs with medicine, finance, and so on.

Women in math and computers jobs report a range of workplace experiences, some with gender bias, frequently unintentional, to unlawful discrimination and harassment (Hill, 2018). Uber is an extreme example of a sexist and racist ICT workplace between 2014 to 2017in which women were subjected to "degrading marginalizing, discriminatory and sexually harassing conduct (Shu, 2018). The firm was subsequently challenged by class action lawsuits and litigation by female Latina engineers which lead to multiple firings of executives and the resignation of the CEO (Shu, 2018).

However, the more likely and common reason for a lack of women in ICT roles is a lack of mentors. The Women in Technology Survey by the Information Systems Audit and Control Association note that the three biggest barriers to both greater and longer female participation are a lack of female mentors (48 percent), a lack of female role models (42 percent), and limited networking opportunities (27 percent) (ISACA, n.d.). Women are leaving the field and it seems to be creating a negative feedback loop in that fewer women are on hand to mentor new female recruits.

The Center for Talent Innovation reveals that female attrition rates among ICT professionals are substantially higher than those observed in other STEM (Science, Technology, Engineering and Mathematics) occupations. After 12 years, 56 percent of those entering the workforce following graduation will have quit the profession. This compares to 47 percent of women in science occupations, 39 percent in engineering, and only around 10 percent for non-STEM occupations (Howell, 2017).

The research finds that women are not leaving for "family reasons" but rather to use their technical skills in other industries (frequently with the interest to be self-employed, run a startup, or work in government or a non-profit), or to work in the same company or industry but not in a technical role.

The National Center for Women and Information Technology (NCWIT) provides a valuable overview of the research and suggestions to remedy the situation (Ashcraft et al., 2016). They note as well that the problem is concerning not only for women overall, but even more so when women are categorized by race, as representation falls further when describing the figures for black, Hispanic and Asian women in the US (Ross & Goodwin, 2016). It notes the poor workplace experience for women in math and computing jobs and lack of access to creative technical roles, even though the women employed display the same degrees, skills, and ambition as men.

It notes that the rate of female-only patenting accounts for only 2% of all ICT patents and mixed male-female teams taking about 10% of ICT patents, and the remaining being all male patenting. However, the rate of women-only patenting can differ significantly by firm (between 0-30%), depending on how "transparent" the process is and that men tend to occupy the creative and innovative roles related to patents while women are in the roles of execution.

NCWIT describes that there is implicit bias, which plays out either in unintentional but subtle ways, or even institutional barriers. They note that addressing bias is not about assigning blame or "fixing people", but rather "fixing the environment", taking mindful steps to recognize bias and address the practices that may potentially hinder women.

One issue noted was that some physical office environments resemble a stereotypically "geeky" or "male" domain with action figures, sci-fi posters, stacked soda cans and so on could be deterrents to women. What is not clear, however is to what degree that those kinds of "geeky" environments are important for existing male employees to succeed, and whether changing them would make men less effective. The ideal workplace should bring out the best in both men and women. The question is whether what is optimal for men is not optimal for women, and whether a compromise or even another model, would improve outcomes for both (Roelofsen, 2002). The evolution of the office environment includes the paradigms of the open plan, the cubicle farm, the action office, and the activity based work in which the employee has no dedicated personal workspace but moves around to a variety of locations (K2 Space, n.d.). These designs can be evaluated between a continuum of conformity vs. autonomy, the combination of which informs a company's culture.

The research notes further that some hiring managers may have "fixed binary mindsets" that candidates either "have it or they don't", which may reinforce hiring candidates of whom implicitly reflect themselves. Bias could also emerge when an applicant's gender is made an issue during the application, interview, or other evaluation process. Alternatively there can be tokenism, for example encouraging women or minorities to apply, as if the matter is merely one of "body count" rather than a commitment to build and grow the competency of the organization; or hiring women and minorities merely to "check the box", as if to appear as being a diverse organization; also to ask women and minorities to take disproportionate responsibility for "diversity" initiatives. On the other hand, could such initiatives be authentic reflections of a company's desire to attract women? Moreover, while corporate diversity efforts should be open to all (Zurer, 2018) there can be an implicit bias that diversity does not apply to white men, and some suits have been filed against ICT employers as a result (Weber, 2018).

Another explanation is that problem is not necessarily gender bias but political and ideological bias. This was highlighted by the firing not of a woman, but a man, who described his perception of workplace hypocrisy, propaganda, and indoctrination at Google. Called the "Ideological Echo Chamber Memo," (Conger, 2017) engineer James Damore penned the memo as a reaction to a company diversity program, explaining that any critique of the prevailing workplace culture is shamed and considered sexist. Reportedly the memo was a response to an employer request to solicit feedback from the program.

Damore rejects the company's view that discrimination can be ascribed to systematic oppression and calls its authoritarian to address gender disparities through "reverse discrimination." He writes that the disparities between men and women at Google could partly be explained by biology and gender preferences, that women prefer people to things and that they may be more social, artistic, and prone to neuroticism. He suggests that disparities between men and women could be improved by adapting the workplace to be more receptive to women.

Damore was fired by Google for the memo and is suing the company for wrongful termination. He has found a new employment, a job which is not made public to protect Damore's safety following an intense media backlash. An "all-hands" meeting for Google's staff and its CEO to discuss the memo for Google staff was scheduled and then cancelled due to safety concerns (Feldman, 2017).

SOLUTIONS

While advances have been made in public policy to improve opportunities for women, it may be unrealistic, if not undesirable, to expect that a society can achieve perfect equality in all professions. Indeed social engineering efforts to indoctrinate men or women to enter certain occupations (or to systematically discourage them from certain choices) amounts to coercion and violation of human rights, not just in the right to work, but notably the right to marriage and family, right to own property, freedom of belief and region, and freedom of opinion and information (United Nations, 2015). Indeed there are inherent limits to social policy which attempt to achieve outcomes through top-down policy instruments such quotas and regulations which could be more effectively realized through bottom-up solutions incorporating family, community, and university and company-driven improvements (Glazer, 1988).

A more workable solution to improve women's participation in math and computing may be mentorship in higher education and in the workplace. Looking at both universities and corporations are important. It is important to address the falling rate of women choosing math and computer majors as well as to arrest the decline in jobs.

Beddoes reviews over 40 years of attempts to improve the rate of women who choose engineering education at universities and offers the following conclusions about where to focus reform efforts at universities (Beddoes, 2016).She notes that most schools have not performed an assessment as to why students leave engineering programs. The assessment needs to be both quantitative and qualitative, allowing students to give candid feedback. She notes that requirement for full-time enrollment adversely affects some students who have to juggle commitments for work and family and suggests that part-time options would increase the diversity of students. She notes further that the retention of female students could be incorporated into tenure and promotion criteria.

Cornell University, University California-Davis, and the University of Washington have implemented dynamic peer advising/mentorship programs. Reported success factors are planning, program oversight, ongoing training, funding, and strategic implementation

Additionally a case study from Montana State University highlights the value of mentorship and improving the number of women in engineering, computer science, and physics majors as well as ensuring that they keep their majors (Clark et al., 2015). The success of the pilot program is even more interesting considering the challenges of geo-demographics of the university which is located in a relatively remote and rural part of the US and which has limited gender and ethnic diversity. The case study notes the research documents peer relationships as part of student satisfaction, integration and retention. The program focused on first and second year college students in the relevant majors and ensured that they felt welcomed, prepared, and connected. This included the hiring and placement of Peer Mentors who received a $1000 stipend per semester, were assigned 20 students, and participated in mentor training. Their tasks included getting the students to become involved in relevant clubs, study groups, and internships and being a source of support. Mentors spent about 1-4 hours per week on the project.

The program assessment by mentees notes that mentors contacted each student about 5-10 times; mentees desired more contact but it wasn't possible because of lack of time. Networking organizations such Engineers Without Borders, Association of Women in Computers and the Alpha Lambda Delta Honor Society, turned out to be more important than study groups. The key takeaways for students appear to be that the mentor helped them access resources on campus and served as a role model, listener, and advisor.

The formalization of a fee to pay the mentor seems particularly compelling. The fee works out to be roughly $15/hour to the mentor, not dissimilar to a college job wae. Moreover, it amounts to an investment of about $50/student, a pittance when considering that student regularly pay between $40-$500 in required student activity fees. This could be a proof point for corporations which desire mentorship program, but all have not formalized a way to compensate managers for their time.

The research suggests that mentorship can be vital to improve women's recruitment and retention in the ICT industry but very few companies have formal mentorship programs (Emrich et al., 2017). Indeed many companies have tried and failed to implement mentorship programs, either because the programs demand too much time of top-performing employees or departments, or they rely on outdated, obsolete models (Jones, 2017). However identifying and overcoming the reasons for failed mentorship could be helpful to address the declining role of women in math/computing roles (DeLong et al., 2008). Importantly both male and female mentors appear to benefit women, so it does not appear to be essential that women necessarily need female mentors. On a more practical level, the issue appears to be giving mentors proper compensation for their time in being a mentor (Minton-Eversole, 2010).

As of this writing, a woman, Donna Strickland, has just been awarded the Nobel Prize in Physics, only the third woman to win the award and the first woman in 55 years (The Nobel Prize, 2018). The award, shared with two male colleagues, reflects pioneering work in the field of lasers including applications for eye surgery. In an interview, Strickland does not seem to express that she experienced systematic discrimination. She notes that she found the recent comment of another Nobel physicist that physics was "built by men", as "silly" and a comment that she did not take "personally" (Rincon, 2018). She also was surprised that only 3 women had won the Nobel prize in physics (National Post, n.d.). Some Nobel winners observe that role models have been important for them to pursue their careers.

An incident following the announcement illustrates one feminist critique that the prevalence of male engineers who embed, whether intentionally or not, gender bias into ICT products and services (Bivens & Haimson, 2016). Some social media brouhaha erupted because Strickland had no Wikipedia page at the time of the Nobel announcement, and an attempt to create a Wikipedia entry for Strickland in May 2018 was denied by a Wikipedia moderator saying, "This submission's references do not show that the subject qualifies for a Wikipedia article" (Koren, 2018). The Wikipedia entry is now live and includes a section on "Coverage of Wikipedia's anti-woman Bias" which notes that just 17% of Wikipedia's biographical entries feature women and that there are few on female scientists (Wikipedia, n.d.a). The thread linked to a longer Criticisms of Wikipedia article that described systemic gender bias of Wikipedia's editors, some 90% of whom are male (Wikipedia, n.d.b). In the section on Gender bias and sexism, the article notes that the Wikimedia Foundation which runs Wikipedia attempted to achieved a goal that 25% of editors would be female by 2015, but the organization gave up because it proved too difficult. Essentially female editors were harassed about their entries by male editors so women tend not to edit (Wikipedia, n.d.b).

Under such circumstances it is understandable that women opt not to fight every math and computing battle and look for opportunities elsewhere. While on the one hand it is lamentable that women don't have higher participation in math and computing jobs, the reality is that women are seeking places where they can go and prosper, notably in other scientific and professional disciplines. Given the coming of 5G, the next generation of mobile wireless connectivity, the internet of things, and bio-driven technology, women are increasingly well-positioned to participate in a new wave of technological innovation that is increasingly less connected to Silicon Valley and its culture.

REFERENCES

K2 Space. (n.d.). *The History of Office Design*. Retrieved October 3, 2018 from https://k2space.co.uk/knowledge/history-of-office-design/

Accenture. (2018). *California Dreaming*. Retrieved from https://www.accenture.com/us-en/insight-outlook-california-dreaming-corporate-culture-silicon-valley

Andersen, M. S. (2018). *IT-branchen hungrer efter kvinder, men de kommer ikke af sig selv*. Retrieved from https://universe.ida.dk/artikel/it-branchen-hungrer-efter-kvinder-men-de-kommer-ikke-af-sig-selv-55868/

Ashcraft, C., McLain, B., & Eger, E. (2016). *Women in Tech: The Facts*. Retrieved from https://www.ncwit.org/sites/default/files/resources/womenintech_facts_fullreport_05132016.pdf

Beddoes, K. (2016). Selling Policy Short? Faculty Perspectives on the Role of Policy in Addressing Women's Underrepresentation in Engineering Education. *Studies in Higher Education*, *43*(9), 1561–1572. doi:10.1080/03075079.2016.1266610

Biery, M. E. (2017). *These Are The 10 Most Profitable Industries in 2017*. Retrieved from https://www.forbes.com/sites/sageworks/2017/08/06/these-are-the-10-most-profitable-industries/

Bivens, R., & Haimson, O. L. (2016). *Baking Gender Into Social Media Design: How Platforms Shape Categories for Users and Advertisers*. Retrieved from http://journals.sagepub.com/doi/pdf/10.1177/2056305116672486

Bradford, L. (2018). *15 of the Most Powerful Women in Tech*. Retrieved October 3, 2018 from https://www.thebalancecareers.com/powerful-women-in-tech-2071172

Bureau of Labor Statistics. (2011). *Educational Attainment of Women in the Labor Force, 1970–2010*. Retrieved September 25, 2018 from https://www.bls.gov/opub/ted/2011/ted_20111229.htm

Bureau of Labor Statistics. (2018). *Employed Persons by Detailed Occupation, Sex, Race, and Hispanic or Latino Ethnicity*. Retrieved from https://www.bls.gov/cps/cpsaat11.htm

Carmichael, S. G. (2015). *Why 'Network More' Is Bad Advice for Women*. Retrieved from https://hbr.org/2015/02/why-network-more-is-bad-advice-for-women

Center for Talent Innovation - Research & Insights. (n.d.). Accessed September 25, 2018, http://www.talentinnovation.org/publication.cfm?publication=1420

Chang, E. (2018). *Brotopia: Breaking Up the Boys' Club of Silicon Valley*. New York, NY: Portfolio.

Clark, J., Codd, S. L., Des Jardins, A. C., Foreman, C. M., Gunnink, B. W., Plumb, C., & Stocker, K. R. (2015). *Peer Mentoring Program: Providing Early Intervention and Support to Improve Retention and Success of Women in Engineering, Computer Science, and Physics: American Society for Engineering Education*. Retrieved from https://www.asee.org/public/conferences/56/papers/12642/view

CompTIA. (2018). *IT Industry Outlook 2018*. Retrieved from https://www.comptia.org/resources/it-industry-trends-analysis#section5

CompTIA. (n.d.). *Advancing Women in Technology*. Retrieved from https://www.comptia.org/communities/advancing-women-in-it

Conger, K. (2017). *Exclusive: Here's The Full 10-Page Anti-Diversity Screed Circulating Internally at Google* [Updated]. Retrieved September 25, 2018 from https://gizmodo.com/exclusive-heres-the-full-10-page-anti-diversity-screed-1797564320

Council of Euproean Professional Informatics Societies. (n.d.). *Europe's Widening ICT Skills Gap*. Retrieved from https://www.cepis.org/media/CEPISe-CFBackgrounder1.pdf

Cyberstates. (n.d.). *Data Appendix*. Retrieved from https://www.cyberstates.org/

DeLong, T. J., Gabarro, J. J., & Lees, R. J. (2008). *Why Mentoring Matters in a Hypercompetitive World*. Retrieved from https://hbr.org/2008/01/why-mentoring-matters-in-a-hypercompetitive-world

Emrich, C., Livingston, M. H., & Pruner, D. (2017). *Creating a Culture of Mentorship*. Retrieved September 25, 2018 from https://www.heidrick.com/Knowledge-Center/Publication/Creating_a_culture_of_mentorship

England, P. (1992). *Comparable Worth: Theories and Evidence* (1st ed.). New Brunswick, NJ: Aldine Transaction.

European Data Journalism Network. (2018). *The ICT Sector Is Booming. But Are Women Missing Out?* Retrieved from https://www.europeandatajournalism.eu/eng/News/Data-news/The-ICT-sector-is-booming.-But-are-women-missing-out

Fallows, J. (2013). *The 50 Greatest Breakthroughs Since the Wheel*. Retrieved from https://www.theatlantic.com/magazine/archive/2013/11/innovations-list/309536/

Farhadi, M., Ismail, R., & Fooladi, M. (2012). *Information and Communication Technology Use and Economic Growth*. Retrieved September 25, 2018 from https://www.ncbi.nlm.nih.gov/pmc/articles/PMC3495961/

Feldman, B. (2017). *Google Cancels Meeting on Memo After Employees Fear for Safety*. Retrieved from http://nymag.com/selectall/2017/08/google-cancels-meeting-on-bad-memo.html

Food and Agriculture Organization of the United Nations. (2018). *Lightening the Load: Addressing Rural Women's Work Burden and Time Poverty*. Retrieved from http://www.fao.org/gender/insights/detail/en/c/424537/

Geek Feminism. (n.d.a). *List of Women Executives at Tech Companies*. Retrieved October 3, 2018 from http://geekfeminism.wikia.com/wiki/List_of_women_executives_at_tech_companies

Geek Feminism. (n.d.b). *Women on Boards of Directors of Tech Companies*. Retrieved October 3, 2018 from http://geekfeminism.wikia.com/wiki/Women_on_boards_of_directors_of_tech_companies

Glazer, N. (1988). *The Limits of Social Policy* (1st ed.). Cambridge, MA: Harvard University.

Gram, C., Laaksonen, T., Ohlin, T., Lawson, H., Skår, R., & Stangegaard, O. (2005). History of the Nordic Computer Industry. In J. Bubenko, J. Impagliazzo, & A. Sølvberg (Eds.), *History of Nordic Computing. HiNC 2003. IFIP International Federation for Information Processing* (Vol. 174). Boston, MA: Springer.

Great Place to Work. (2017). *Best Workplaces for Women 2017*. Retrieved October 3, 2018 from https://www.greatplacetowork.com/best-workplaces/women/2017

Great Place to Work. (2018). *Best workplaces in Technology 2018*. Retrieved from https://www.greatplacetowork.com/best-workplaces/technology/2018?utm_source=online&utm_medium=press-release&utm_content=website&utm_campaign=2018-technology-list

Griffith, E. (2018). *Everyone Hates Silicon Valley, Except Its imitators*. Retrieved from https://www.wired.com/story/everyone-hates-silicon-valley-except-its-imitators/

Hill, C. (2018). *Solving the Equation: The Variables for Women's Success in Engineering and Computing*. Retrieved from https://www.aauw.org/research/solving-the-equation/

Hofstede Insights. (2018). *Country Comparison - Denmark*. Retrieved October 3, 2018 from https://www.hofstede-insights.com/country-comparison/Denmark

Hofstede Insights. (n.d.). *Country Comparison USA*. Retrieved October 3, 2018 from https://www.hofstede-insights.com/country-comparison/USA

Howell, B. (2017). *Can Smart Policies Alter the Lot of Women in the ICT Workforce?* Retrieved from http://www.aei.org/publication/can-smart-policies-alter-lot-women-ict-workforce/

International Telecommunication Union. (n.d.). *Measuring the Information Society Report 2017*. Retrieved from https://www.itu.int/pub/D-IND-ICTOI

Invest Siophia. (2017). *ICT Sector in Bulgaria Is The Best Performing Industry - 600% Income Growth for 10 Years*. Retrieved from http://investsofia.com/en/it-sector-in-bulgaria-is-the-best-performing-industry-600-income-growth-for-10-years/

ISACA. (n.d.). *2017 Women In Technology Survey: Breaking Down Gender Barriers to Build the Future Tech Workforce*. Retrieved from http://www.isaca.org/info/2017-women-in-technology-survey/index.html

Jones, M. (2017). *Why Can't Companies Get Mentorship Programs Right?* Retrieved from https://www.theatlantic.com/business/archive/2017/06/corporate-mentorship-programs/528927/

Koren, M. (2018). *One Wikipedia Page Is a Metaphor for the Nobel Prize's Record With Women*. Retrieved from https://www.theatlantic.com/science/archive/2018/10/nobel-prize-physics-donna-strickland-gerard-mourou-arthur-ashkin/571909/

Laouchez, J. M., Penk, W., Binvel, Y., Guarino, A., & Franzino, M. (2018). *The $8.5 Trillion Talent Shortage*. Retrieved from https://www.kornferry.com/institute/talent-crunch-future-of-work

Layton, R., & Kane, J. (2017). *Alternative Approaches to Broadband Policy: Lessons on Deregulation from Denmark*. Retrieved from https://www.mercatus.org/publications/broadband-policy-deregulation-denmark

Levanon, A., England, P., & Allison, P. (2009). Occupational Feminization and Pay: Assessing Causal Dynamics Using 1950–2000 U.S. Census Data. *Social Forces*, *88*(2), 865–891. doi:10.1353of.0.0264

McDonald, S. (2011). What You Know or Who You Know? Occupation-Specific Work Experience and Job Matching through Social Networks. *Social Science Research*, *40*(6), 1664–1675. doi:10.1016/j.ssresearch.2011.06.003

Minton-Eversole, T. (2010). *Mentoring: Make It Pay*. Retrieved from https://www.shrm.org/resourcesandtools/hr-topics/organizational-and-employee-development/pages/makementoringpay.aspx

Narula, R., & Zanfei, A. (2006). *Globalization of Innovation: The Role of Multinational Enterprises*. The Oxford Handbook of Innovation. doi:10.1093/oxfordhb/9780199286805.003.0012

Nasdaq. (n.d.). *Technology Companies*. Retrieved September 25, 2018 from https://www.nasdaq.com/screening/companies-by industry.aspx?industry=Technology&sortname=marketcap&sorttype=1

National Center For Women and Information Technology. (2014). *What Is the Impact of Gender Diversity on Technology Business Performance? Research Summary*. Retrieved from https://www.ncwit.org/sites/default/files/resources/impactgenderdiversitytechbusinessperformance_print.pdf

National Post. (n.d.). *Who is Donna Strickland and Why is She One of the Few Women to Win a Nobel Prize?* Retrieved from https://nationalpost.com/news/world/donna-strickland-nobel-prize

OECD. (n.d.). *Where Are Tomorrow's Female Scientists?* Retrieved October 3, 2018 from http://www.oecd.org/gender/data/wherearetomorrowsfemalescientists.htm

Organization For Economic Co-Operation and Development. (1997). *National Innovation Systems*. Retrieved from https://www.oecd.org/science/inno/2101733.pdf

Radu, S. (2018). *These Are the 5 Best Countries for Women*. Retrieved from https://www.usnews.com/news/best-countries/best-women

Rets Information. (n.d.). *Bekendtgørelse af lov om ligestilling af kvinder og mænd*. Retrieved from https://www.retsinformation.dk/forms/r0710.aspx?id=160578

Rincon, P. (2018). *First Woman Physics Nobel Winner in 55 Years*. Retrieved from https://www.bbc.com/news/science-environment-45655151

Roelofsen, P. (2002). The impact of office environments on employee performance: The design of the workplace as a strategy for productivity enhancement. *Journal of Facilities Management*, *1*(3), 247-264.

Rogers, E. M. (2003). *Diffusion of Innovations* (5th ed.). New York, NY: Simon and Schuster.

Ross, M. S., & Godwin, A. (2016). *Engineering Identity Implications on the Retention of Black Women in the Engineering Industry*. Retrieved from https://peer.asee.org/engineering-identity-implications-on-the-retention-of-black-women-in-the-engineering-industry

SageWorks. (2017). *Most Profitable Industries over Past Year*. Retrieved from https://www.sageworks.com/most-profitable-industries-over-past-year/

Sandemose, A. (1936). A Fugitive Crosses His Tracks [En flyktning krysser sitt spor]. New York, NY: Alfred A. Knopf.

Science Daily. (2009). *Fridges And Washing Machines Liberated Women, Study Suggests*. Retrieved from 1. https://www.accenture.com/us-en/insight-outlook-california-dreaming-corporate-culture-silicon-valley

Shu, C. (2018). *Former Software Engineer Accuses Uber of 'Degrading Conduct' toward Women in New Lawsuit*. Retrieved October 3, 2018 from http://social.techcrunch.com/2018/05/21/former-software-engineer-accuses-uber-of-degrading-conduct-toward-women-in-new-lawsuit/

Smith, T. W., & Son, J. (2014). *Measuring Occupational Prestige on the 2012 General Social Survey*. Retrieved from http://gss.norc.org/Documents/reports/methodological-reports/MR122%20Occupational%20Prestige.pdf

Sommers, C. H. (2015). *The Gender Gap: What the World Economic Forum Got Wrong*. Retrieved from http://www.aei.org/multimedia/the-gender-gap-what-the-world-economic-forum-got-wrong/

Statista. (2018). *Forecast of the Internet User Penetration Rate in Bulgaria from 2015-2020*. Retrieved from https://www.statista.com/statistics/567448/predicted-internet-user-penetration-rate-in-bulgaria/

The Global Economy. (2018). *Female Labor Force Participation by Country, around the World*. Retrieved from https://www.theglobaleconomy.com/rankings/Female_labor_force_participation/

The Nobel Prize. (2018). *The Nobel Prize in Physics 2018*. Retrieved from https://www.nobelprize.org/prizes/physics/2018/summary/

Ungerleider, N. (2013). *What It Really Takes To Succeed In Silicon Valley: Money And Status*. Retrieved from https://www.fastcompany.com/3017402/what-it-really-takes-to-succeed-in-silicon-valley-money-and-status

United Nations. (2015). *Universal Declaration of Human Rights*. Retrieved from http://www.un.org/en/universal-declaration-human-rights/

Vatchkov, P. (n.d.). *Bulgarian Software Industry*. Retrieved from http://www.daits.government.bg/gallery/BSI/BulgarianSoftwareIndustry.pdf

Velasco, S. (2017). *Male Nurses? Female Firefighters? Yes, as Career Boundaries Erode*. Retrieved from https://www.csmonitor.com/Business/2017/0713/Male-nurses-Female-firefighters-Yes-as-career-boundaries-erode

Wachter-Boettcher, S., & Emmes, A. (2017). *Technically Wrong: Sexist Apps, Biased Algorithms, and Other Threats of Toxic Tech, Unabridged edition*. Prince Frederick, MD: HighBridge Audio.

Wajcman, J. (2004). *Echnofeminism*. Malden, MA: Polity.

Weber, L. (2018). *White Men Challenge Workplace Diversity Efforts*. Retrieved from https://www.wsj.com/articles/white-men-challenge-workplace-diversity-efforts-1521036001

Wikipedia. (n.d.a). *Talk: Donna Strickland.* Retrieved from https://en.wikipedia.org/wiki/Talk:Donna_Strickland#Coverage_of_Wikipedia's_anti-woman_bias

Wikipedia. (n.d.b). *Criticism of Wikipedia.* Retrieved from https://en.wikipedia.org/wiki/Criticism_of_Wikipedia

Zurer, R. (2018). *Diversity Is For White Men Too. Here's How — and Why It Matters.* Retrieved from https://consciouscompanymedia.com/workplace-culture/diversity-inclusion/diversity-is-for-white-men-too/

APPENDIX

Employed persons by detailed occupation and sex, annual averages 2011-2017
United States Bureau of Labor Statistics, accessed September 20, 2018. https://www.bls.gov/cps/demographics.htm

Table 1.

Year	Computer and mathematical occupations	Computer scientists and systems analysts	Computer programmers	Computer software engineers	Computer support specialists	Database administrators	Network and computer systems administrators	Network systems and data communications analysts	Operations research analysts	Statisticians	Computer and mathematical occupations	Computer systems analysts	Information security analysts	Software developers, applications and systems software	Web developers	Computer network architects	Computer occupations, all other
2000	29.70%	34.00%	26.40%	24.50%	35.10%	42.60%	23.40%	24.90%	50.60%								
2001	28.50%	31.70%	26.90%	23.80%	32.70%	47.00%	21.10%	26.90%	39.10%								
2002	28.60%	30.50%	24.90%	22.80%	37.70%	40.50%	20.70%	26.20%	50.50%								
2003	28.80%	30.30%	28.10%	24.40%	37.60%	40.30%	21.60%	23.70%	50.50%								
2004	27.00%	29.40%	26.80%	25.10%	29.80%	34.00%	20.50%	21.80%	43.30%								
2005	27.00%	30.30%	26.00%	21.90%	33.20%	32.60%	18.50%	24.50%	50.00%								
2006	26.60%	31.90%	25.30%	21.70%	29.00%	36.70%	16.70%	25.60%	40.00%								
2007	25.60%	27.20%	24.70%	20.70%	29.80%	35.60%	14.50%	26.40%	47.10%								
2008	24.80%	27.50%	22.30%	20.90%	27.70%	29.00%	21.60%	23.70%	48.00%								
2009	24.80%	26.90%	20.30%	20.30%	26.80%	35.50%	22.20%	24.70%	47.20%								
2010	25.80%	30.50%	22.10%	20.90%	27.60%	36.60%	16.60%	26.20%	45.80%								
2011	25.00%		20.70%		26.20%	37.30%	22.70%		44.80%		25.00%	34.00%		19.00%	38.50%	11.20%	21.60%
2012	25.60%		22.50%		27.10%	36.60%	25.20%		54.60%		25.60%	30.90%	15.40%	19.70%	33.70%	7.90%	24.30%
2013	26.10%		22.90%		29.00%	37.80%	17.10%		51.60%	37.50%	26.10%	34.80%		19.70%	39.60%	7.40%	22.90%
2014	25.60%		21.40%		26.50%	27.80%	19.00%		55.80%	49.40%	25.60%	34.10%	17.60%	19.80%	35.00%	12.20%	23.00%
2015	24.70%		21.00%		26.30%	37.60%	16.10%		50.40%	52.30%	24.70%	34.20%	20.00%	18.00%	34.30%	12.30%	24.30%
2016	25.50%		22.50%		25.40%	45.60%	17.00%		55.80%	52.70%	25.50%	35.70%	21.30%	20.00%	33.70%	9.60%	23.50%
2017	25.50%		21.10%		27.10%	40.60%	23.30%		51.70%	48.30%	25.50%	39.00%	20.00%	18.80%	32.40%	3.80%	22.70%

Chapter 4
Women's Employment in Turkey's ICT Sector:
An Examination From a Social Inclusion Perspective

Selda Gorkey
Istanbul Kultur University, Turkey

ABSTRACT

Women constitute one of the risk groups vulnerable to poverty; therefore, enabling their participation in the labor force is crucial to promoting social inclusion in a society. Employment in the information and communication technology (ICT) sector is widely known for being male-dominated, and recently women's participation has become an important subject. This chapter aims to examine women's employment in Turkey's ICT sector from 2009 to 2016, from a social inclusion perspective, by using various indicators. Comparisons with European Union (EU) countries provide perspective on tracking the progress of employment structure and education choices for ICT by gender. All indicators signify the existence of a gender gap resulting in low rates of inclusion of women in Turkey's ICT employment during the period. Examination of the reasons leads to making some policy recommendations to promote social inclusion of women in Turkey's ICT employment.

INTRODUCTION

Information and Communication Technology (ICT) is a rapidly growing sector throughout the world, and hence its weight and importance in the overall economy is rising. This expansion requires an examination of various aspects of the sector (Palvia, Baqir & Nemati, 2018). Employment represents the use of potential resources in an economy, making it one of the main economic issues, but it is also a social issue. The contribution of women to the labor force is crucial, both economically and socially (Dreze & Sen, 2002; Oxoby, 2009; Atkinson, 1998; Balaban, 2014).

DOI: 10.4018/978-1-5225-7068-4.ch004

The motivation for this study mainly arises from two facts. One is the exclusion of women from social and economic life, even in developed countries. In developing nations or less developed countries, the degree of exclusion of women is even greater. (Daly, 1989; Dedeoglu, 2009; Tezgel & Gokbayrak, 2013). Increasing the well-being of women and fostering economic and social development requires eliminating exclusion through social inclusion policies (Oxoby, 2009). In this context, encouraging women to participate in the labor force is crucial for fostering not only economic, but also social development. The other fact is that perceptions of jobs in ICT sector are generally accepted as men's jobs (Hodgkinson, 2000). Female participation in labor in the relevant sector is significantly low in many countries, signaling the exclusion of female labor. Both of those facts are even more crucial in emerging economies with respect to their dynamism. Indeed, the topic of social inclusion is not limited only to gender, employment, or the ICT sector. It is a broad concept that encompasses the exclusion of any individual or group from access to or participation in any right or institution (Balaban, 2014; Genc & Cat, 2013; Gunduz, 2007). However, this study focuses on ICT-sector employment from the perspective of gender, in the context of social inclusion.

Turkey is an emerging country that experiences high growth rates in the ICT sector, in parallel with the world (Dube, Dube, & Turan, 2015). Hence, the analysis of employment in the sector from the perspective of gender is crucial for such an emerging economy to comprehend the current state of the gender gap in sector employment. Determining the gender gap in the sector can lead to social policy recommendations for increasing the contribution of women to the ICT labor force. If Turkey succeeds in reducing the ICT employment gender gap in the future, its progress can serve as a success story for other emerging or developing countries. Turkey is specifically chosen for examination because of its cultural structure as a patriarchal country in which women are not expected to engage much in economic life. Hence, the cultural structure is another factor that results in exclusion of women from working life, causing women to live in poverty unless they live under the protection of men (Dedeoglu, 2009). This situation makes it even harder for women to engage in working life. In this context, by examining women's participation in Turkey's ICT employment, this study approaches social inclusion from the perspectives of gender, employment, and the ICT sector. Since the literature lacks studies from all these perspectives, to the best of the author's knowledge, focusing on a single emerging country such as Turkey would contribute to the existing literature. In addition, this study would create benefits for practical use by policy designers.

This study aims to analyze the contribution of women in the ICT sector in Turkey from 2009 to 2016, to examine the participation of women in the labor force and the change in female employment in the sector. Since education shapes future employment structure, the study also analyzes female participation in education in the relevant field. After that, Turkey's position is compared with European Union (EU) countries for the period. The proxies used in this study are the share of women in employment and among ICT specialists, the share of women with ICT education, and the share of women in ICT-related education.

The objective of this study is to seek answers to the following research questions:

Research Question 1: How did female employment in ICT in Turkey change from 2009 to 2016?
Research Question 2: How did the position of Turkey change in terms of social inclusion, compared to EU countries in the period analyzed?

The findings show that the sector experiences a clear gender gap, and the female participation in Turkey's ICT sector is lower than that in the EU. Education choices show that ICT-related education is mostly preferred by males; however, that gender gap is even larger in the EU than in Turkey.

The rest of the chapter is organized as follows. The concepts of social and economic inclusion and exclusion, their relationship with women's employment in ICT, and the literature review are presented in the background section. Then, the methodology of the paper is explained. Thereafter, Turkey's ICT-sector employment from the gender perspective is examined, with comparisons to EU countries. Then, some solutions and policy recommendations are offered, along with some future research directions and the conclusion.

BACKGROUND

Women's Employment as the Key to Poverty and Social Exclusion

Some societies alienate or deprive certain individuals or groups of individuals of access to certain activities, rights, or institutions. Such deprivation is regarded as social exclusion. However, the coverage and the scope of this concept are generally vague. The vagueness of the concept stems from determining excluded individuals or groups (e.g., elderly, women, children, the disabled) and the reasons behind such exclusions (Atkinson, 1998; Behera, 2013; Genc & Cat, 2013; Gunduz, 2007; Balaban, 2014).

Oxoby (2009) authored a very detailed literature review on the topic of social inclusion, pointing out the definition of social exclusion by Avramov (2002): *a feeling of not belonging and not having been given a chance to be included in society* (p. 26). This definition emphasizes that exclusion is not solely limited to access of individuals to certain rights and institutions; it also affects the behaviors and decisions of those individuals. If any individual believes that he or she will not be accepted into an activity or an institution, or that he or she will not be able to take advantage of a right, then that individual may choose not to become involved in such an activity, right, or institution, effectively self-excluding. In this regard, exclusion is not only an outcome, but also a reason that shapes individual behaviors. Such beliefs generally stem from cultural aspects or from identities (e.g., gender, age, race, ethnicity) (Akerlof & Kranton, 2015; Oxoby, 2009).

The strict relationship between exclusion, unemployment, and poverty signals that excluded groups generally face obstacles to participating in the labor force. If this process continues in the long run, these groups may be at risk for poverty—in short, exclusion may result in poverty (Atkinson, 1998). Women's exclusion from the social and economic aspects of life is well grounded at this point, because of their identified roles in the society as mothers, wives, and daughters. In some cultures, contributions of females in social life are strictly opposed, which in turn results in their nonparticipation in the labor force. Associated with low participation levels or nonparticipation of women in employment, women are prone to be at-risk for poverty. This situation forces women to live under the protection of another person, generally a father or a spouse. It is also a fact that even if women are not excluded from economic life, they may work in "womanly jobs" with low wages, or they are often paid less than men when they undertake equal jobs to those that men hold (Daly, 1989; Dedeoglu, 2009). These explanations clearly show that exclusion and poverty affect each other. Exclusion may result in poverty, and poverty may result in exclusion of an individual from society, because not only is he or she not able to earn enough income, but also his or her social status and morale are affected. From this perspective, exclusion and poverty create a vicious circle (Gunduz, 2007).

Policies aimed toward reducing social exclusion are regarded as social policy, and efforts to eliminate deprivation of risk groups are referred to as social inclusion. This approach supports protecting excluded groups through the implementation of relevant policies (Oxoby, 2009; Avramov, 2002). Complicating the design and implementation of social inclusion policies is interrelation of the process with many aspects of life, such as sociology, economics, psychology, policy, law, and human rights (Gunduz, 2007). Oxoby (2009) uses the term "economic exclusion," which focuses on poverty, unemployment, nonparticipation in the labor force, low school enrollments, and obstacles to consumption. In this context, employment is the key in the relationship, insofar as it can break the vicious circle of poverty and exclusion. If social inclusion policies succeed perfectly, deprivations in a society will end, and all individuals will have equal access to work and the same right to participate in the labor force. In turn, this will lead to reduction, and possibly elimination of poverty (Atkinson, 1998; Genc & Cat, 2013). In this context, the examination of female employment in a country would contribute to the academic research by analyzing both women and employment to evaluate the current state of gender employment and offer necessary inclusion policies.

The Necessity of Focusing on ICT Sector

ICT is a rapidly growing sector throughout the world, including in Turkey, and hence its weight and importance in the overall economy are rising (Deloitte, 2012). This expansion requires examination of various aspects of the sector. As one of the crucial dimensions of such analysis, employment plays a key role in understanding both the current state and the future dynamics of the sector. When employment in the sector is analyzed from the perspective of gender, it is obvious that ICT is generally accepted as a male dominated field by various disciplines in academia (Hodgkinson, 2000; Huyer & Mitter, 2003; Arun, Heeks & Morgan, 2004; Vodanovich, Urquhart, & Shakir, 2010; UN, 2002). This perception exists not only in usage, but also in creation and production of goods and services. The situation results in lower female participation in labor in the sector, which signals exclusion of female labor. When various studies for different countries examine the issue with respect to the labor side of economics, it is clear that male dominance is more than just a perception. Hence, there are numerous studies that examine the gender perspective on ICT employment in the literature (Arun & Arun, 2002; Arun, Heeks, & Morgan, 2004; Moore, Griffiths, Richardson & Adam, 2008; Kelan, 2008; Mumporeze & Prieler, 2017; Gonzalez, Revelles, Almeda, Bosch & Garcia, 2016; Annabi & Lebovitz, 2018; Yeganehfar, Isfandyari-Mogghadam & Famil-Rouhani, 2018).

Despite numerous studies exploring the gender gap in ICT employment, only a limited number of studies analyze the gender gap in Turkey's ICT employment. In Turkey, the examination of the subject of ICT usage and its spread—i.e., the digital divide—occurs from the perspective of gender (Torenli, 2006; Aypay, 2010; Yildiz, 2010; Kilinc-Savrul, & Kilic, 2011; Karakaya Polat, 2012; Bilgel-Asici & Kocak-Usluel, 2013; Erdogdu & Erdogdu, 2015). In other words, the literature lacks a sufficient number of studies that focus on the gender gap in Turkey's ICT sector from an employment perspective, to the best of the author's knowledge. Since Turkey is an emerging country, the current state of the subject and any prospective progress could function as a case study for other emerging countries. Hence, this study aims to fill this gap in the literature by examining social inclusion from the perspectives of women, employment, and the ICT sector at once.

The studies that examine female employment in Turkey's ICT sector are Torenli (2010), Atik and Altiparmak (2011), and Dube et al. (2015). Torenli (2010) examines the impact of ICT and internet usage on female employees. This study specifically focuses on home-based workers from the gender perspective, and finds that the use of ICT does not significantly bring any advantage to women home-based workers in Turkey. Atik and Altiparmak (2011) examine the employment structure of the ICT sector in Turkey in comparison to the 27 countries of the EU from 1990 to 2008. This study aims to analyze the share in overall employment of information-sector employment, and examines the weight of female employment in the sector. The study finds that female employment in the relevant sector in Turkey is remarkably lower than that in EU-27. Dube et al. (2015) examine the relationship between the growth of the ICT sector and the unemployment rates by various aspects in Turkey, such as gender, age, and educational levels, from 1990 to 2013. Among many results of the mentioned study, those from the perspective of gender show a positive correlation between female unemployment rates and growth of domestic production.

WOMEN'S EMPLOYMENT IN TURKEY'S ICT SECTOR

Methodology

This study aims to analyze the progress of female participation in Turkey's ICT-sector employment. Using annual data collected from 2009 to 2016, the study seeks answers to the following research questions:

Research Question 1: How did female employment in ICT in Turkey change from 2009 to 2016?
Research Question 2: How did the position of Turkey change in terms of social inclusion, compared to EU countries in the period analyzed?

This study answers these questions by using various measures. Those measures are the share of females in ICT employment, the share of women as ICT specialists, the share of female employees with ICT education, and the share of women with ICT-related education. The first three measures are generated by the author's own calculations from the European Union Labor Force Statistics (EU-LFS) Household Survey. This is micro data collected from households in 33 countries, 28 of which are EU countries, two candidate countries (Macedonia, and Turkey), and European Free Trade Association (EFTA) countries (Iceland, Norway, and Switzerland). The EU-LFS dataset includes employment, unemployment, and inactivity statistics by economic activity, sex, age, and educational attainment (Eurostat, 2018a). The last measure is author's own calculations from Organization for Economic Cooperation and Development (OECD) Statistics (OECD, 2018b). The relevant subsections present details of those measures and their method of calculation.

To evaluate the progress of Turkey and its position, comparisons with EU countries are made. EU countries were selected for comparison because social policies in Turkey were mainly designed according to European experiences for Turkey's cohesion to EU after 2000, especially during the adjustment process for EU membership (Kilic, 2008). The period is limited to 2009 to 2016, since data before 2009 are not comparable with data after 2009 in the EU-LFS dataset, and the data beyond 2016 are not available for most of the countries analyzed.

Before directly focusing on the female employment in the ICT sector, the employment structure of the country is examined. Hence, the subsequent section examines the overall employment structure from the perspective of gender, using the author's own calculations from the Turkish Statistical Institute (TurkStat; Official Statistical Institute of Turkey) dataset. After that, the chapter's main focus is addressed.

Employment Structure in Turkey from a Gender Perspective

It is necessary to examine the structure of employment in Turkey before focusing on the ICT sector and the gender perspective. In 2016, TurkStat (2018) reported the population older than 15 years old was approximately 58,720,000 persons. The labor force, sum of employed and unemployed, in all the sectors was approximately 30,535,000 in the same year; hence, the labor force participation rate (the proportion of labor force to population over 15 years old) was only 52% in 2016.

OECD (2018b) and Eurostat (2018b) measure labor force statistics slightly differently than that of TurkStat, by limiting both the employment and the population by ages between 15-64. OECD refers to this age group as the "working-age population." Thus, it calculates the labor force participation rate as the proportion of labor force between 15-64 ages to total population within the same age group. OECD (2018b) reports that the labor force participation rate was 57% in Turkey, 71.7% in OECD total, 73.2% in EU-28, and 74.1% in G7 countries, in 2016. These rates clearly show that the relevant measure is remarkably low in Turkey compared to other OECD and EU countries.

Figure 1 depicts the share of women in total employment in Turkey and selected countries in the EU for the years 2009 and 2016. The difference between 100%, and the values in Figure 1 corresponds to the share of men in total employment. The figure shows that the proportion of females in total employment is prominently lower than for men in EU countries, except for Lithuania in 2009 and 2016, and for Estonia in 2009, among the countries examined. However, the gender gap is more viable in Turkey, compared to selected EU countries. Even though there was slight recovery from 27.57% in 2009 to 30.66% in 2016, in Turkey, women's contribution to the work force is remarkably low compared to men, which is indicative of an obvious employment gender gap in Turkey.

Figure 1. The share of women in employment (% in total employment, 2009 and 2016)
Source: (Eurostat, 2018b), own calculations

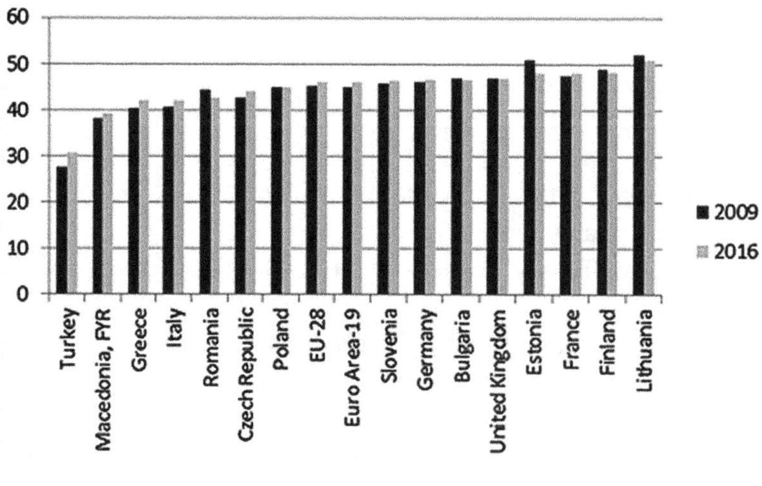

The Share of Women in ICT Employment

The primary and most relevant measure used in this study to analyze the gender gap is the percentage of women in ICT employment, i.e. the percentage of women in the ICT sector in Turkey.

The ICT sector comprises some sub-industries, and it may be measured and announced differently in several databases. For this reason, it is necessary to compile statistics from different sub-industries and take the sum of those in order to accurately quantify the relevant indicator. Before focusing on and interpreting the measures in Turkey and other EU countries, there is a need to make define the ICT sector in order to construct series.

The coverage of the ICT sector has changed throughout time, and it has reached its final and agreed upon definition to the OECD's definitions in 2006 and 2007. OECD (2006, 2007, 2011) defines the ICT as, *The production (goods and services) of a candidate industry must primarily be intended to fulfill or enable the function of information processing and communication by electronic means, including transmission and display*. With the use of this agreed upon definition, data can be gathered in the same way in different countries, thus, comparisons can accurately be made at the international level. In order to fit internationally comparable indicators, data on the ICT sector need to be collected and added together, depending on three sub-categories: ICT manufacturing, ICT trade, and ICT services industries. Different economic variables, such as employment and growth, are measured and reported depending on this industry categorization. Therefore, to properly analyze the ICT sector, ICT-related data must first be obtained from different industries, and then added together to reach a measure that reliably reflects the dynamics of the ICT sector. OECD (2006, 2007, 2011) also mentions these specific sub-industries in terms of ISIC (International Standard Industrial Classification of all Economic Activities), which is an industrial classification system of the United Nation (UN), aimed at grouping goods and services under specific codes, so that international comparisons can be made accurately (UN, 2008). Constituted by EU, statistical classification of economic activities in the European Community (NACE) is another classification system, which groups commodities under specific industry categories (Eurostat, 2008). Both ISIC and NACE announce some revisions when necessary. These two industry classifications are frequently used worldwide, thus correspondence lists between these two classifications are available (Eurostat, 2018c).

Since the percentage of female employment in the ICT sector data is not available for Turkey in terms of ISIC, the relevant indicator is compiled from NACE Revision (Rev.) 2 classification. Depending on the correspondence of economic activity between ISIC Rev. 4 and NACE Rev.2 classifications (UNCTAD, 2015), total employment data is gathered as the sum of the following sub-industries classified according to NACE Rev.2 two-digit level: manufacture of computer, electronic, and optical products; telecommunications; computer programming, consultancy and related activities; and information service activities. The correspondence table of NACE from ISIC is provided in Appendix 1.

The proxy generated from the relevant sectors indicates that total ICT employment has increased remarkably from approximately 140,500 persons in 2009 to approximately 219,200 persons in 2016, resulting in a 56% increase in seven years in Turkey. Among the 140,500 total ICT employees in 2009, 106,900 employed were men, whereas the remaining 33,700 were women. The distribution of 219,200 total employed in the ICT sector between the sexes in 2016 was as follows: 162,900 men and 56,000 women. The share of females in ICT employment in Turkey and some selected EU countries is presented in Table 1, in order to compare Turkey's ICT sector with other EU countries from the gender perspective.

Table 1. The share of women employees in ICT sector (% in total ICT employment)

Country	2009	2010	2011	2012	2013	2014	2015	2016
Turkey	23.99	21.26	19.77	24.16	23.59	23.49	25.57	25.55
EU-28	28.93	28.68	28.75	28.45	28.04	27.87	27.53	27.44
Czech Rep.	34.15	34.56	31.47	32.63	31.37	30.56	30.10	29.09
Germany	28.08	27.71	28.44	27.13	28.45	28.41	28.41	28.43
Spain	31.00	28.40	28.84	30.38	29.64	28.97	27.32	27.39
France	28.47	29.31	31.01	28.07	27.40	28.86	25.00	25.95
Italy	29.86	30.23	29.60	32.44	29.17	28.29	29.26	29.14
Hungary	39.42	-	-	35.41	35.63	36.03	34.05	36.86
Netherlands	20.58	17.49	18.28	19.24	17.83	18.78	18.69	20.44
Poland	34.40	35.39	36.27	35.00	34.20	33.55	32.32	31.24
Romania	36.07	35.52	35.08	37.77	37.50	33.04	38.73	37.68
Slovenia	26.60	32.79	28.42	29.84	27.63	-	32.39	-
Slovakia	-	39.62	40.69	36.29	27.44	29.62	28.15	30.43
Sweden	26.87	25.47	25.38	27.12	26.32	24.22	23.70	24.14
UK	24.37	24.02	22.82	22.97	22.95	23.56	23.43	22.59

Source: (Eurostat, 2018d), own calculations

Table 1 shows the percentage of women's employment in the ICT sector for EU countries and Turkey from 2009 to 2016. The data is constructed by dividing the number of women employees in ICT sector by the total number of employees in the sector. Thus, the difference between 100% and the values presented in the table correspond to the percentage of men's employment in the sector. The percentage of women employees in Turkey did not change much, except for the years 2010 and 2011. The statistics indicate a gender gap in Turkey, showing that approximately only one fourth of employees in the sector are women, except for the years 2010 and 2011. The table clearly shows that the contribution of women to Turkey's ICT sector is remarkably lower than men's, confirming the presence of a gender gap between 2009 and 2016. The contribution of women is even lower in ICT employment than in total employment, which was presented as 30.66% in the previous section. The values of EU-28 also signify that the share of female employees in the sector is remarkably lower than that of males; however, the gender gap is slightly narrower than that of Turkey. The share of women employees is the highest in Hungary and in Romania during the period examined. Female employment in Turkey's ICT sector is slightly below EU-28, which reveals that a gender gap, and therefore female exclusion in the relevant sector's employment is not limited to Turkey's economy.

Figure 2 shows the share of women and men employees in the ICT sector in total employment in the economies of selected EU countries and Turkey for 2009 and 2016. Hence, the sum of men and women's shares in ICT presents total ICT employment in overall employment in economies.

Figure 2 shows that the share of ICT employment is remarkably lower in Turkey than in other selected EU countries. The progress from 2009 to 2016 had been very weak, showing that the gender gap had been viable in the period analyzed. The share of males in total employment had risen from 0.52% in 2009 to 0.62% in 2016; and the same share for females had changed from 0.16% in 2009 to 0.21 in 2016

Figure 2. The percentages of ICT sector's men and women employees in total employment (2009 and 2016)
Source: (Eurostat, 2018d), own calculations
Note: For Romania, 2014 instead of 2009; for Poland, 2010 instead of 2009; for Hungary, 2012 instead of 2009.

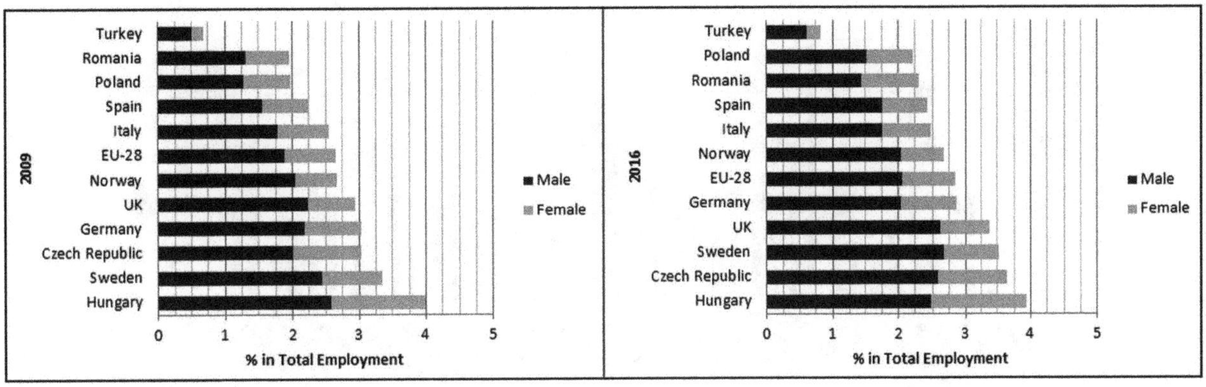

in Turkey. Even the two closest countries to Turkey's ICT sector employment structure, Romania and Poland, have much higher employment shares for women, as well as for total employment of both sexes. Even though total ICT employment is lower than other EU countries, women's share is significantly lower in Turkey, indicative of a gender gap, and hence low social inclusion of women in employment in the relevant sector.

The Share of Women in ICT Specialists

Another important measure is the share of employed female ICT specialists in relationship to the total employment of ICT specialists. The OECD (2004) defines ICT specialists as individuals *who have the ability to develop, operate and maintain ICT systems. ICTs constitute the main part of their job* (p.219). This measure is particularly important since it represents ICT-intensive employment and the capability of using digital skills in an economy. Not only is the analysis of the current situation important, but also examination of indicators throughout time is also crucial to evaluate the trend of relevant employment (European Commission, 2015).

The classification of occupations is built upon a widely known job organization system, the International Standard Classification of Occupations (ISCO), offered by the International Labor Organization (ILO). ISCO classifies ICT specialists by certain groups of occupations, and announces revisions when necessary (ILO, 2012). Detailed information about occupations is provided in Appendix 2.

The data gathered in this study to analyze the share of females in ICT specialist positions is collected from the Eurostat EU-LFS, which collects data depending on OECD (2004) definition in terms of ISCO. A new revision of relevant classification, ISCO-08, was released after 2010, causing a severe change in datasets beginning in 2011. In order to keep the data comparable throughout time, the data used in this study does not start from 2009 as the other data. Figure 3 shows the percentages of females in all ICT specialist positions for the years 2012, 2014, and 2016.

The number of ICT specialists for both sexes in Turkey was 245,200 persons, and women constituted only 24,300 of the specialists in 2016, signaling the existence of a gender gap among ICT specialists in Turkey. Figure 3 shows the gap clearly, not only in 2016, but also in 2012, and 2014, by comparing the percentages of female ICT specialists in all ICT specialist positions for Turkey and selected EU countries.

Figure 3. The percentage of women in all ICT specialist positions (2012, 2014, and 2016)
Source: (Eurostat, 2018e)

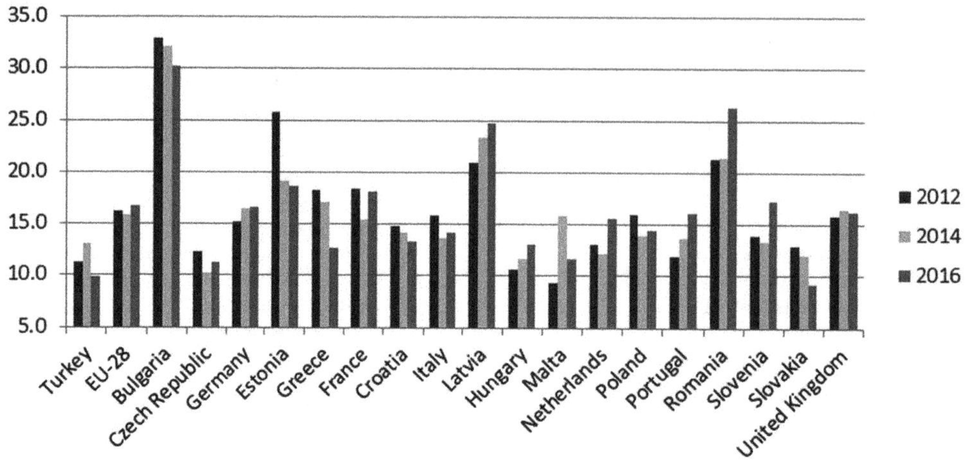

Figure 3 shows that the percentages for 2012, 2014, and 2016 were 11.3%, 13.1%, and 9.9%, respectively, following a fluctuating trend between approximately 10% and 13% in Turkey. The percentages reported for EU countries also reflects a gender gap showing that the position of ICT specialist is an occupation that is male dominated in practice. However, the share of female ICT specialists in Turkey is remarkably lower by comparison. These measures reveal that there is a considerable gender gap in the employment of ICT specialists in Turkey, and this disparity is greater than in other selected EU countries. The Czech Republic, Hungary, and Slovakia are the other countries in the analysis that remarkably differentiated from the remaining countries by gender perspective for the years examined.

The Share of Female Employees With ICT Education

Further understanding the gender gap is facilitated by examination of female employees who are equipped with ICT training. The data depicts employed persons with ICT education, focusing not only on the ICT sector, but all sectors, by examining employees who were educated in ICT disciplines. In other words, the data does not differentiate these employees depending on their sector of employment (Eurostat, 2018f).

The classification of the disciplines that correspond to ICT education is made according to United Nations Educational, Scientific and Cultural Organization's (UNESCO) The International Standard Classification of Education (ISCED). UNESCO approved ISCED at the beginning of 1970s by classifying education according to two aspects: level of education and field of education. The classification aims to create comparable statistics both at the international and national levels (UNESCO, 2006).

Figure 4 presents the percentage of female and male employees with ICT education in all employees aged between 15-74 in Turkey and the EU-28 countries. The data is constructed by dividing male and female employed persons with ICT education by total employment. The data was collected from Eurostat, and education classification was based upon UNESCO's ISCED. A new version of ISCED (ISCED-2011) is applied to datasets 2016 onwards. Hence, in order to keep the data comparable throughout time, Figure 4 presents data from 2009 to 2015 according to ISCED-1997. According to ISCED-1997, ICT education corresponds to the highest educational levels attained in the following fields: 48 Computing,

Figure 4. The percentage of male and female employed persons with ICT education in total employment from 2009 to 2015, in Turkey and EU-28
Source: (Eurostat, 2018d; EuroStat, 2018g), own calculations

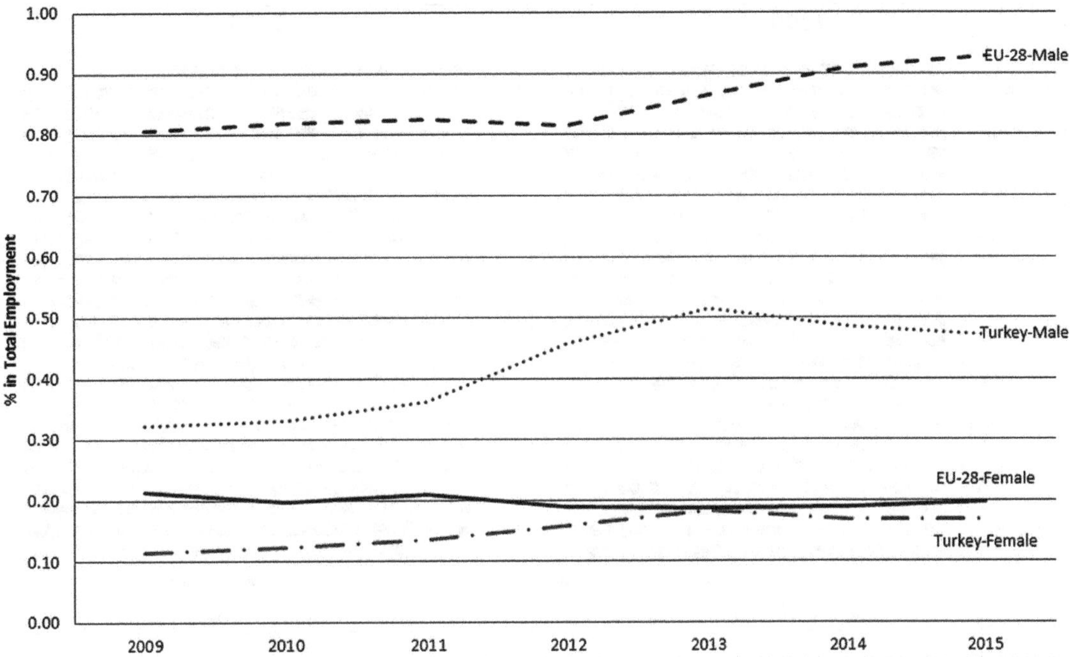

481 Computer Science, and 482 Computer use. The numbers before the fields show the ISCED-1997 codes (Eurostat, 2018f).

Figure 4 shows that the percentage of male employed persons who are equipped with ICT education constituted 0.32% of the total employment in all sectors by both sexes in 2009. The value reached its maximum at 0.51% in 2013, and then decreased slightly to 0.47% in 2015. The relevant measures for female employed persons is remarkably lower than males in Turkey, with 0.12% in 2009, hitting a maximum by 0.18% in 2013, and decreasing slightly to 0.17% in 2015. However, the data for EU signifies an even larger gender gap than that of Turkey. The percentage of male employed persons with ICT education increased from 2009 to 2015, whereas the female percentage decreased slightly. These statistics on employed persons with an ICT education further confirm the gender gap that is more obvious in EU countries than in Turkey.

In order to see the gender gap more clearly in Turkey and the EU countries, the distribution of all employed persons with an ICT education by gender as percentages is presented in the Figure 5. The data is from Eurostat's EU-LFS, and was calculated by the author as the percentages of male and female employed persons with an ICT education, in total employed persons with ICT education. Thereby, the sum of percentages of males and females total 100%.

Among all employed persons with ICT education, women constitute 26.3% and men 73.7% in 2009, in Turkey. The relevant percentages changed to 26.4% for women and 73.6% for men in 2015; the percentages of women for the same indicator for the EU-28 countries were 21.0% in 2009 and 17.5% in 2015, showing a decrease in the period analyzed. The statistics show that the percentages of male employees with an ICT education are higher in EU-28 than in Turkey in both years, and the shares of female em-

Figure 5. The share of women and men employed persons with ICT education in total employed persons with ICT education
Source: (Eurostat, 2018g), own calculations

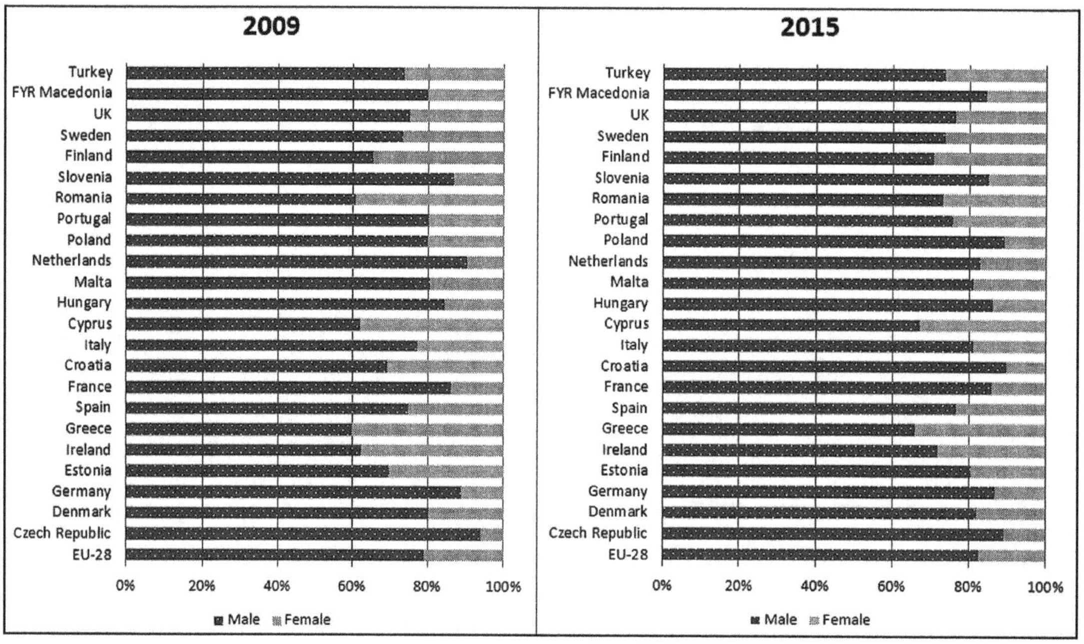

ployees with an ICT education are lower in the EU-28 than that of Turkey. This comparison indicates that a gender gap is more viable in the EU-28 than in Turkey from the point of employed persons with an ICT education. Among the countries examined, the UK, Sweden, Romania, Portugal, Spain, and Ireland have closer female percentages to Turkey. The countries that have made progress in favor of the share of female employed persons with ICT education are Portugal, Netherlands, and the Czech Republic. These countries have made progress in narrowing the gender gap from 2009 to 2015.

The Share of Women in ICT-Related Education

Another measure used in this study is the proportion of women in ICT education, which quantifies the percentages of females currently receiving their ICT education. Since current education choices influence the labor force of the future, education statistics are crucial for analyzing trends in gender employment dynamics. Montagnier and Welsum (2006) emphasized that education in ICT measures also matter, since it represents the individuals acquiring relevant skills to perform ICT-related occupations after graduation. Their study listed computing as a proxy for ICT education, and they revealed that the share of women in computing was lower than that of other fields in 2004 in OECD countries.

In order to analyze the current situation of inclusion of women in ICT education, this study uses data from OECD for 2015. OECD's relevant database currently categorizes ICT education as a specific field that includes the following as sub-fields: computer use, database and network design and administration, software and applications development and analysis, ICT not elsewhere classified, and interdisciplinary programs (OECD, 2018a). Data presents education at the tertiary level. According to the ISCED 2011, tertiary education includes the following degrees: short-cycle tertiary education, bachelor's or equivalent level, master's or equivalent level, and doctoral or equivalent level (UNESCO, 2012). Since the dataset is from OECD database, the comparison is made with OECD member countries (OECD-Total), and European countries that are also members of OECD (OECD-Europe).

Figure 6 shows the percentages of enrolled female students in tertiary education in Turkey, OECD-Total, and OECD-Europe in 2015. In Turkey, female students are of a lower share in the total; education; arts and humanities; social sciences, journalism, and information; business, administration, and law; and engineering, manufacturing, and construction, than OECD-Europe countries. Only ICT; natural sciences, mathematics, and statistics are the fields in which the share of female students are higher in Turkey, compared to OECD-Europe countries. The figure clearly indicates a gender gap in ICT education in all OECD countries; however, the gender gap is much more viable both in OECD-Total and OECD-Europe than in Turkey. These statistics also indicate that the share of female students is higher in total fields, as well as in education, arts and humanities, social sciences, business, and law disciplines in OECD countries. Based on the proxies on current ICT education, the dominance of men in the ICT sector is likely to continue, keeping the gender gap visible in the near future in Turkey, as well as in OECD-Total and OECD-Europe.

Figure 6. The share of women in education by fields (% in both sexes), tertiary education, 2015
Source: (OECD, 2018a), own calculations

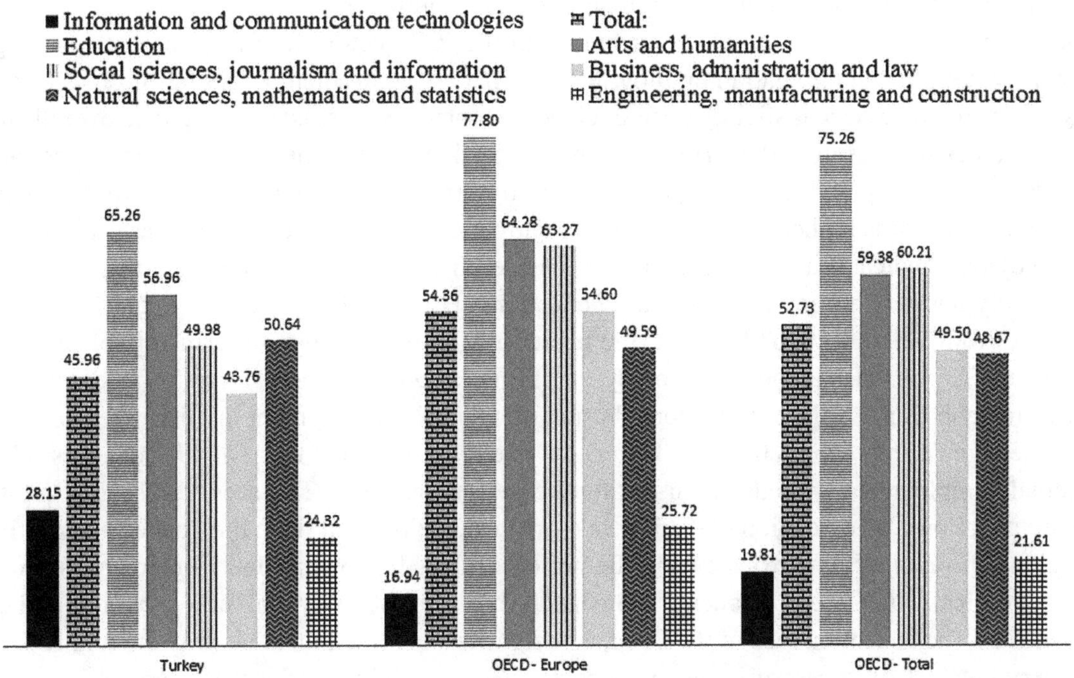

Some Comments on the Employment of Women in Turkey's ICT Sector in Comparison to EU Countries

The share of female employment both in total employment, and in ICT sector, did not change much from 2009 to 2016. The viable gender gap at the beginning of period examined showed only a slight recovery, and it continued up to 2016, signifying that women are weakly included in ICT employment, as well as in total employment. The gender distribution of ICT employment, in which female employees constitute only 25.55% in 2016, shows this gap clearly at the end of the period examined. The share of women ICT employees in total employment in the overall economy is only 0.21% in 2016. In other words, among all employed persons, only 0.21% of those are women employees who worked in the ICT sector in 2016.

From this point, this is the indicator that shows the existence of the gender gap, and hence a low degree of social inclusion of women's employment in ICT sector the most clearly. Women's employment in Turkey's ICT lags behind EU countries significantly, as well. There is a need to place a special emphasis by highlighting the low participation of men in ICT as well, with only 0.62% in total employment. The share of women ICT specialists was very low during the period analyzed in Turkey, reaching approximately 10% in 2016. This indicator, too, confirms the gender gap in the sector clearly, since Turkey lagged behind all selected EU countries. Even though education-related indicators, the share of female employed persons with ICT education in total employment, all employed persons with ICT employment, and the share of women in ICT education, signifies the existence of a gender gap, it is narrower than that of EU-28. However, the low social inclusion of women in ICT education indicates that the gender gap in Turkey's ICT sector is likely to continue in the near future, as well.

The proxies reflecting the female contribution to the ICT sector clearly indicate a gender gap in Turkey. However, the gender gap in employment is a pervasive problem affecting most sectors of the Turkish economy. The issue is slightly different in EU countries where the gender gap in overall employment is not as extreme as in Turkey. However, female participation in the ICT sector in EU countries is remarkably lower compared to female participation in overall employment. In other words, the gender gap in the ICT sector is higher than the overall employment in EU countries, whereas Turkey's female ICT employment indicates a narrower gap with the overall employment in the economy.

This study answers the following research questions: How did female employment in ICT in Turkey change from 2009 to 2016? How did the position of Turkey change in terms of social inclusion, compared to EU countries in the period analyzed? Depending on the indicators, this study answers the first research question as follows: The contribution of women's employment in Turkey's ICT sector did not change significantly from 2009 to 2016. There is only a slight recovery in all indicators related to both female employment and education during the period analyzed. The second research question is answered as follows: The position of Turkey in women's employment from the gender perspective had been behind those of EU countries during the period analyzed, showing that women are not included much economically in ICT employment. There had been a slight recovery in Turkey, but it is still behind EU countries. The education side of the issue, too, signifies that, the inclusion of women in ICT education is very low in Turkey. However, when its position among EU countries was examined, Turkey was ahead of the EU-28, and most of the EU countries in the period examined. This situation shows that, women are socially more included in ICT education in Turkey than that of the EU-28.

SOLUTIONS AND RECOMMENDATIONS

ICT is a rapidly growing sector; therefore the share of its employment in overall employment is expected to increase in economies. Moreover, the employment structure (i.e. by age and gender) of the relevant sector is crucial to track the future growth of the sector. The structure of women's employment in ICT in Turkey has been examined in the previous section, and it is clear that the contribution of women's employment in Turkey's ICT sector is remarkably low; the relevant ICT education statistics did not change significantly from 2009 to 2016.

In order to experience progress in women's participation in ICT employment, there is a need to examine the reasons behind it. In Turkey, the problem starts with women's low participation in the labor force. The main reason may be the *norms* in Turkish society. Pareto (1920, 1980) puts forward that people get utility depending on their tastes, however, usefulness also depends on the view of others in a society. Based on norms, individuals are categorized depending on the types of people from different aspects such as gender, age, race, ethnicity, etc., and different identities arise in societies. The views of others shape the norms in a society, and norms can change by means of formal and informal education, over the course of time (Akerlof & Kranton, 2005). These norms and categorizations build perceptions, and those perceptions may create exclusions in societies. Turkey is a patriarchal country in which most of the population is Muslim. In such countries, women face difficulties in participating in social and economic life, and in entering the labor force (Cherayi & Jose, 2016; Tariq & Syed, 2017; Vodanovich, Urquhart, & Shakir, 2010). In Turkey, the role of women is being mothers, wives, or daughters whose main responsibilities are taking care of housework and members of the family, as well as the older relatives (Gunduz, 2007). Thus, their contribution in the labor force is sparse, confirmed by the statistics provided in the previous section. Moreover, the Social Security Institution (SSI) of the country provides social services to citizens if they are employees or relatives of an employee. The social security system is structured to offer more benefits to wives, and daughters compared to sons (Kilic, 2008). This structure indicates the existence of a vicious cycle of social exclusion in Turkey from the gender perspective. Such that the culture and the perceptions affect exclusion of individuals, and this situation in turn affect the behavior of individuals, as well as the working mechanisms of institutions. Therefore, first of all, there is a need to change the perceptions in Turkey by viewing women's roles differently, so that they should be perceived equal to men. With this regard, priority should be given to women's role as employees and must be given by social policies.

A special emphasis needs to also be placed on the perceptions of the ICT sector, which is widely accepted as a male dominated field in the Turkish economy. Women should be encouraged to work in the ICT sector or in ICT-related jobs. However, the current gender gap cannot be closed suddenly, since it takes time to change the structure of employment in an economy. The current gender gap in the sector can be reduced in the near future by increasing the share of women in ICT education. In order to eliminate perceptions towards ICT employment and education, female students can be encouraged to attain ICT education by social policies. In this manner, Turkey does not only need to provide higher female participation rates of employment in overall economy, but also needs to encourage female students to attain in ICT education. These goals can be achieved by designing coherent social policies, which aim at reducing economic exclusion of women in the society, and implementing such policies in a decisive way.

FUTURE RESEARCH DIRECTIONS

Future research may be directed to ICT education from the gender perspective in Turkey, as parallel to the solutions and recommendations offered in the previous section. Since education statistics signal the structure of employment in the future, an emphasis needs to be placed on the training aspect. The indicators show that even though the ICT employment of women is significantly lower than that of EU countries, the share of female students in ICT disciplines is higher than that of the OECD-European countries. This situation, which can be interpreted as the gender gap between Turkey and the EU countries, is likely to be narrowed in the future. However, this interpretation does not reflect an optimistic view since Turkey remarkably lags behind many European countries with respect to female participation in the ICT sector of employment. In order to close the gender gap in the long run, Turkey must attach importance to encouraging young individuals to be trained in ICT-related disciplines. However, as Akerlof and Kranton (2005) emphasized, expectations about the future shape the current decisions of individuals. If young individuals believe that they will not be able to find jobs in the relevant sector, they will not prefer to be equipped with ICT education. From this point of view, there is a need to change perceptions towards ICT occupations, which is generally accepted as a "man's job." This can be achieved by analyzing the perceptions of individuals at the micro level. Depending on the result of such analysis, appropriate educational policies should be designed and implemented under the leadership of government institutions.

CONCLUSION

This study analyzes women's employment in Turkey's ICT sector with regard to social inclusion from 2009 to 2016, with an attempt to seek answers to the research questions proposed in the previous sections. Depending on the indicators of this study, it is pointed out that participation of women in ICT sector employment is remarkably low. The progress during the period had been little in the relevant sector. Indicators related to the ICT education of women are also remarkably lower than that of men, and the progress in the period analyzed was very weak. This situation confirms the existence of a gender gap, and low social inclusion of women both in ICT sector employment and in ICT education attainment in Turkey from 2009 to 2016.

When Turkey's position in female employment in the ICT sector compared to EU countries is examined, the indicators show that Turkey has been obviously behind those in the relevant sector from 2009 to 2016. However, the position of Turkey compared to EU countries from the points of female employed persons with an ICT education, and females in ICT education attainment, is different. Even though the education indicators confirm the existence of a gender gap, and low inclusion of women in education, Turkey is ahead of most of the EU countries, and this was maintained during the period analyzed.

Turkey is a patriarchal country in which most of the population are Muslim. In such countries, women are not included much in the economic life since their identities in the society are generally based primarily on maternity and housewifery, rather than on their productive role in employment. As a consequence, female employment is significantly low in Turkey, not only in the ICT sector, but also in the overall economy. In addition to this, occupations in ICT sector are widely accepted as being men's jobs in Turkey. When these two situations come together, the degree of women exclusion in Turkey's ICT employment is high. In order to reduce and eliminate the perception, and lower social inclusion, social policies that aim at changing the role of women in society should be designed. Moreover, it is known that education equips individuals with the necessary information for any occupation, and those individuals build up the future's labor force. For this reason, an emphasis should be placed on the encouragement of female students to attain an ICT education. In short, coherent social policies regarding shaping the role of women in society, and encouraging female students to be equipped with an ICT education should be designed and implemented simultaneously. Pursuing these policies will promote the social and economic inclusion of women employment in Turkey. However, the effects of such policies are expected to be apparent in the long run. Therefore, pursuing those policies in a decisive way over the next several years is necessary in order to experience positive, long-term effects both in the society and economy.

REFERENCES

Akerlof, G. A., & Kranton, R. E. (2005). Identity and the economics of organizations. *The Journal of Economic Perspectives*, *19*(1), 9–32. doi:10.1257/0895330053147930

Annabi, H., & Lebovitz, S. (2018). Improving the retention of women in the IT workforce: An investigation of gender diversity interventions in the USA. *Information Systems Journal*, 1–33. doi:10.1111/isj.12182

Arun, S., & Arun, T. (2002). ICTs, gender, and development: Women in software production in Kerala. *Journal of International Development*, *14*(1), 39–50. doi:10.1002/jid.866

Arun, S., Heeks, R., & Morgan, S. (2004). *ICT initiatives, women and work in developing countries: reinforcing or changing gender inequalities in South India?* Development Enformatics Working Paper Series No:20. Institute for Development Policy and Management.

Atik, H., & Altiparmak, A. (2011). Avrupa Birligi ve Turkiye'de Bilgi Sektorunun Istihdama Katkisi. *The Journal of Knowledge Economy & Knowledge Management*, *6*, 117–126.

Atkinson, A. B. (1998). Social Exclusion, poverty and unemployment. In B. A. Atkinson & J. Hills (Eds.), *Exclusion, Employment and Opportunity* (pp. 1–20). London, UK: Centre for Analysis of Social Exclusion, London School of Economics.

Avramov, D. (2002). *People, demography and social exclusion*. Council of Europe.

Aypay, A. (2010). Information and communication technology (ICT) usage and achievement of Turkish students in PISA 2006. *The Turkish Online Journal of Educational Technology*, *9*(2), 116–124.

Balaban, U. (2014). Türkiye ve Avrupa Birliği'nde sosyal içerme uygulamaları: 2000'li yıllara ilişkin karşılaştırmalı bir değerlendirme. *Mülkiye Dergisi*, *38*(1), 103–149.

Behera, D. K. (2013). Dams, development and the exclusion of indigenous groups: a case from Odisha. In U. Skoda, K. B. Nielsen, & M. Q. Fibiger (Eds.), *Navigating social exclusion and inclusion in contemporary India and beyond: structures, agents, practices* (pp. 167–187). London, UK: Anthem Press.

Bilgel-Asici, T., & Kocak-Usluel, Y. (2013). Sayisal ucurumun universite ogrencilerinin demografik ozelliklerine gore incelenmesi. *Hacettepe Universitesi Egitim Fakultesi Dergisi*, *44*, 73–84.

Cherayi, S., & Jose, J. P. (2016). Empowerment and social inclusion of Muslim women: Towards a new conceptual model. *Journal of Rural Studies, 45*, 243–251. doi:10.1016/j.jrurstud.2016.04.003

Daly, M. (1989). *Women and poverty*. Dublin: Attic Press.

Dedeoglu, S. (2009). Eşitlik mi ayrımcılık mı? Türkiye'de sosyal devlet, cinsiyet eşitliği politikaları ve kadın istihdamı. *Çalışma ve Toplum, 2*(21), 41-54.

Deloitte. (2012). *Information and Communication Technologies on the Road to 2023*. Uluslararasi Yatirimcilar Dernegi (YASED).

Dreze, J., & Sen, A. (2002). *India: Development and Participation*. Oxford, UK: Oxford University Press. doi:10.1093/acprof:oso/9780199257492.001.0001

Dube, S., Dube, M., & Turan, A. (2015). Information technology in Turkey: Creating high-skill jobs along with more unemployed highly-educated workers? *Telecommunications Policy, 39*(10), 811–829. doi:10.1016/j.telpol.2015.07.001

Erdogdu, F., & Erdogdu, E. (2015). The impact of access to ICT, student background and school/home environment on academic success of students in Turkey: An international comparative analysis. *Computers & Education, 82*, 26–49. doi:10.1016/j.compedu.2014.10.023

European Comission. (2015). *Monitoring the Digital Economy & Society 2016 – 2021*. European Commission DG Communications Networks, Content & Technology. Retrieved from http://ec.europa.eu/eurostat/documents/341889/725524/Monitoring+the+Digital+Economy+%26+Society+2016-2021/7df02d85-698a-4a87-a6b1-7994df7fbeb7

Eurostat. (2008). *NACE Rev. 2. Statistical classificationof economic activities in the European Community: Methodologies and working papers*. Luxembourg: Eurostat.

Eurostat. (2018a). *Main features of the European Union – Labour Force Survey (EU-LFS) and scope of data*. Retrieved from http://ec.europa.eu/eurostat/web/lfs/overview)

Eurostat. (2018b). *Employment and activity by sex and age: annual data*. European Union Labor Force Survey (EU-LFS). Retrieved from http://appsso.eurostat.ec.europa.eu/nui/submitViewTableAction.do

Eurostat. (2018c). *Correspondence Tables: NACE Rev.2 – ISIC Rev.4*. Retrieved from http://ec.europa.eu/eurostat/ramon/relations/index.cfm?TargetUrl=LST_LINK&StrNomRelCode=NACE%20REV.%202%20-%20ISIC%20REV.%204&StrLanguageCode=EN

Eurostat. (2018d). *Employment by sex, age and detailed economic activity*. European Union Labor Force Survey (EU-LFS). Retrieved from http://appsso.eurostat.ec.europa.eu/nui/show.do?dataset=lfsq_egan22d&lang=en

Eurostat. (2018e). *Employed ICT specialists by sex*. European Union Labor Force Survey (EU-LFS). Retrieved from http://appsso.eurostat.ec.europa.eu/nui/show.do?dataset=isoc_sks_itsps&lang=en

Eurostat. (2018f). *ICT training Reference Metadata in Euro SDMX Metadata Structure*. European Union Labor Force Survey (EU-LFS). Retrieved from http://ec.europa.eu/eurostat/cache/metadata/en/isoc_skt_esms.htm

Eurostat. (2018g). *Employed persons with ICT education by sex*. European Union Labor Force Survey (EU-LFS). Retrieved from http://appsso.eurostat.ec.europa.eu/nui/show.do?dataset=isoc_ski_itsex&lang=en

Eurostat. (2018h). *ICT specialists in employment sex*. European Union Labor Force Survey (EU-LFS). Retrieved from http://ec.europa.eu/eurostat/statistics-explained/index.php/ICT_specialists_in_employment

Genc, Y., & Cat, G. (2013). Engellilerin istihdamı ve sosyal içerme ilişkisi. *Akademik İncelemeler Dergisi*, *8*(1), 363–393.

Gonzalez, A., Revelles, B., Almeda, E., Bosch, N. V., & García, J. (2016). Women in ICT: opportunities for their inclusion in an international labor market. *6th IFIP World Information Technology Forum (WITFOR), IFIP Advances in Information and Communication Technology AICT-481*, 171-177.

Gunduz, G. S. (2007). *Sosyal içerme politikalarının uygulanmasında kamu istihdam kurumlarının rolü (Yayınlanmamış uzmanlık tezi)*. Ankara: T.C. Çalışma ve Sosyal Güvenlik Bakanlığı, Türkiye İş Kurumu Genel Müdürlüğü.

Hodgkinson, L. (2000). Is technology masculine? Theorising the absence of women. In *Technology to Society, IEEE International Symposium on Technology and Society* (pp. 121-126). Rome, Italy: IEEE.

Huyer, S., & Mitter, S. (2003). Poverty reduction, gender, equality and the knowledge society: Digital exclusion or digital opportunity? In *ICTs, Globalisation and Poverty Reduction: Gender Dimensions of the Knowledge Society*. Retrieved from http://unpan1.un.org/intradoc/groups/public/documents/unpan/unpan037351.pdf

International Labour Organization (ILO). (2012). *International Standard Classification of Occupations (ISCO-08): Structure, Group Definitions and Correspondence Tables*. Geneva: International Labour Organization.

Karakaya Polat, R. (2012). Digital exclusion in Turkey: A policy perspective. *Government Information Quarterly*, *29*(4), 589–596. doi:10.1016/j.giq.2012.03.002

Kelan, E. K. (2008). Emotions in a rational profession: The gendering of skills in ICT work. *Gender, Work and Organization*, *15*(1), 49–71.

Kilic, A. (2008). The gender dimension of social policy reform in Turkey: Towards equal citizenship. *Social Policy and Administration*, *42*(5), 487–503. doi:10.1111/j.1467-9515.2008.00620.x

Kilinc-Savrul, A., & Kilic, A. (2011). Küreselleşme sürecinde bilişim sektörünün Türkiye ve Avrupa Birliği ülkelerinin ekonomileri üzerindeki etkileri. *İstanbul Üniversitesi İktisat Fakültesi Mecmuası*, *61*(2), 257-289.

Montagnier, P., & van Welsum, D. (2006). ICTs and gender: Evidence from OECD and non-OECD countries. *UNCTAD Expert Meeting*. In *Support of the Implementation and Follow-Up of WSIS: Using ICTs to Achieve Growth and Development. Jointly organized by UNCTAD*, OECD and ILO.

Moore, K., Griffiths, M., Richardson, H., & Adam, A. (2008). Gendered futures? Women, the ICT workplace and stories of the future. *Gender, Work and Organization*, *15*(5), 523–542. doi:10.1111/j.1468-0432.2008.00416.x

Mumporeze, N., & Prieler, M. (2017). Gender digital divide in Rwanda: A qualitative analysis of socioeconomic factors. *Telematics and Informatics, 34*(7), 1285–1293. doi:10.1016/j.tele.2017.05.014

Organisation for Economic Cooperation and Development. (2004). *Information Technology Outlook 2004*. Paris: OECD Publishing.

Organisation for Economic Cooperation and Development (OECD). (2006). *Classifying Information and Communication Technology (ICT) Services*. Paris: OECD Publishing.

Organisation for Economic Cooperation and Development (OECD). (2007). *Measuring the Impacts of ICT Using Official Statistics*. Paris: OECD Publishing.

Organisation for Economic Cooperation and Development (OECD). (2011). *OECD Guide to Measuring the Information Society 2011*. Paris: OECD Publishing. doi:10.1787/10.1787/9789264113541-e

Organisation for Economic Cooperation and Development (OECD). (2018a). *Education and training: Enrolment by field*. Retrieved from http://stats.oecd.org/Index.aspx?DataSetCode=EDU_ENRL_FIELD

Organisation for Economic Cooperation and Development (OECD). (2018b). *Labour force participation rate*. Retrieved from https://data.oecd.org/emp/labour-force-participation-rate.htm

Oxoby, R. (2009). Understanding social inclusion, social cohesion, and social capital. *International Journal of Social Economics, 36*(12), 1133–1152. doi:10.1108/03068290910996963

Palvia, P., Baqir, N., & Nemati, H. (2018). ICT for socio-economic development: A citizens' perspective. *Information & Management, 55*(2), 160–176. doi:10.1016/j.im.2017.05.003

Tariq, M., & Syed, J. (2017). Intersectionality at work: South Asian muslim women's experiences of employment and leadership in the United Kingdom. *Sex Roles, 77*(7-8), 510–522. doi:10.100711199-017-0741-3 PMID:28979062

Tezgel, O., & Gokbayrak, S. (2013). The effects of gender inequalities in the labor market and the social security system on women's social inclusion in Turkey. *Is. Guc Industrial Relations and Human Resources Journal, 15*(4), 39–59. doi:10.4026/1303-2860.2013.0236.x

Torenli, N. (2006). The 'other' faces of digital exclusion: ICT gender divides in the broader community. *European Journal of Communication, 21*(4), 435–455. doi:10.1177/0267323106070010

Torenli, N. (2010). The potential of ICT to generate 'solidaristic' practices among women home-based workers in Turkey. *New Technology, Work and Employment, 25*(1), 49–62. doi:10.1111/j.1468-005X.2009.00238.x

Turkish Statistical Institute (TurkStat). (2018). *Labour force statistics*. Retrieved from https://biruni.tuik.gov.tr/medas/?kn=72&locale=en

United Nations Conference on Trade and Development (UNCTAD). (2015). *Global assessment of sex-disaggregated ICT employment statistics: Data availability and challenges on measurement and compilation.* UNCTAD Technical Notes on ICT for Development No.4. United Nations.

United Nations Educational, Scientific and Cultural Organization (UNESCO). (2006). *International Standard Classification of Education (ISCED) 1997*. UNESCO Institute for Statistics.

United Nations Educational, Scientific and Cultural Organization (UNESCO). (2012). *International Standard Classification of Education ISCED 2011*. Montreal, Canada: UNESCO Institute for Statistics.

United Nations (UN). (2002). *Information and Communication technologies and their impact on and use as an instrument for the advancement and empowerment of women* (Report of the Expert Group Meeting Seoul, Republic of Korea, 11 – 14 November 2002). United Nations Division for the Advancement of Women (UN DAW), Department of Economic and Social Affairs. Retrieved from http://www.un.org/womenwatch/daw/egm/ict2002/reports/EGMFinalReport.pdf

United Nations (UN). (2008). *International Standard Industrial Classification (ISIC) of All Economic Activities Revision 4*. New York: United Nations Department of Economic and Social Affairs Statistics Division.

Vodanovich, S., Urquhart, C., & Shakir, M. (2010). Same but different: understanding women's experience of ICT in the UAE. *The Electronic Journal on Information Systems in Developing Countries*. Retrieved from https://onlinelibrary.wiley.com/doi/abs/10.1002/j.1681-4835.2010.tb00286.x

Yeganehfar, M., Zarei, A., Isfandyari-Mogghadam, A. R., & Famil-Rouhani, A. A. (2018). Justice in technology policy: A systematic review of gender divide literature and the marginal contribution of women on ICT. *Journal of Information, Communication and Ethics in Society*. doi:10.1108/JICES-06-2017-0038

Yildiz, M. (2010). Digital divide in Turkey: A general assessment. In E. Ferro, Y. K. Dwivedi, J. R. Gil-Garcia, & M. D. Williams (Eds.), *Handbook of research on overcoming digital divides: Constructing an equitable and competitive information society* (pp. I75–I89). Hershey, PA: IGI Global. doi:10.4018/978-1-60566-699-0.ch005

ADDITIONAL READING

Atkinson, A. B., & Marlier, E. (2010). *Analysing and Measuring Social Inclusion in a Global Context*. United Nations.

Howcroft, D., & Richardson, H. (2016). A gendered analysis of IT-enabled service work in the global economy. In H. Peterson (Ed.), *Gender in Transnational Knowledge Work* (pp. 11–30). Switzerland: Springer.

Huyer, S. (2003). Gender equality and poverty reduction in the knowledge society. In *ICTs, Globalisation and Poverty Reduction: Gender Dimensions of the Knowledge Society*. Retrieved from http://gab.wisat.org/PartII.pdf

Huyer, S., & Carr, M. (2002). Information and communication technologies: A priority for women. *Gender, Technology and Development*, *6*(1), 85–100. doi:10.1080/09718524.2002.11910024

Khan, F., & Ghadially, R. (2010). Empowerment through ICT education, access and use: A gender analysis of Muslim youth in India. *Journal of International Development*, *22*(5), 659–673. doi:10.1002/jid.1718

Sen, A. (2001). The many faces of gender inequality. *Frontline, 18*(22). Retrieved from http://www.frontline.in/static/html/fl1822/18220040.htm

Wilson, J., & Gapsiso, N. D. (2016). *Overcoming Gender Inequalities through Technology Integration*. Hershey, PA: IGI Global. doi:10.4018/978-1-4666-9773-7

World Economic Forum. (2017). *Insight Report: The Global Gender Gap Report 2017*. Switzerland: World Economic Forum.

KEY TERMS AND DEFINITIONS

Economic Exclusion: Barriers that limit or block the access or participation of individuals in economic life, more precisely in labor, education, consumption, or economic transactions.

Economic Inclusion: Enabling individuals the right to access and participate in economic life.

Employment: The condition of working, generally emphasizing the paid work.

Gender Gap: Difference between males and females regarding any subject.

ICT Employment: The condition of working in the ICT sector, generally emphasizing the paid work.

ICT Sector: An industry that aims at producing, processing, and transmitting information, as well as creating communication with the use of electronic tools, and technology.

Labor Force: The sum of employed and unemployed persons in an economy.

Social Exclusion: Alienation or deprivation of any groups or individuals from social life.

Social Inclusion: Efforts that aim to eliminate alienation or deprivation of individuals from social life.

Women's Employment: The contribution of women to working life, generally emphasizing paid work.

APPENDIX 1

Depending on OECD's most recent definition of ICT sector (OECD, 2006, 2007, 2011), the sector comprise from three industries: ICT manufacturing, ICT trade, and ICT services industries.
2-digit NACE Rev.2 (corresponds to 3-digit ISIC Rev.4):

- C26 Manufacture of computer, electronic and optical products
- J61 Telecommunications
- J62 Computer programming, consultancy and related activities
- J63 Information service activities

According to United Nations Conference on Trade and Development (UNCTAD) (2015), the most accurate correspondence between ISIC to NACE for the ICT sector is from 4-digit ISIC Rev.4 to 3-digit NACE Rev.2. However, due to lack of data for some countries; this study uses correspondence from 3-digit ISIC Rev.4 to 2-digit NACE Rev.2

APPENDIX 2

A new revision of ISCO, ISCO-08, was released after 2010, and the change was applied to the dataset of Eurostat's EU Labor Force Survey from 2011 to date. According to ISCO-08, ICT specialists are the employees who work in the following occupation fields (Eurostat, 2018h):

- ICT service managers
- Information and communications technology professionals (software and multimedia developers and analysts, and database specialists and systems administrators)
- Information and communications technicians (ICT operations and user support technicians, and communications technicians)
- Electronic engineers; telecommunication engineers
- Graphic and multimedia designers; information technology trainers
- ICT sales professionals
- Electronics engineering technicians
- Electronics mechanics and servicers
- ICT installers and servicers

Chapter 5
Gender Differences in Preferences and Proclivities for ICT Tools and Online Services

Winfred Yaokumah
Pentecost University College, Ghana

Fred Totimeh
Pentecost University College, Ghana

Peace Kumah
Ghana Education Service, Ghana

ABSTRACT

Gender essentialism is often used to excuse gender-based biases in the use of ICT tools and online services encouraging gender inequalities in opportunities for both males and females. This chapter aims at exploring ICT tools and online services currently being used by university students. The chapter investigates gender differences in preferences and proclivities for ICT tools and online services. Data collected from 618 university students were analyzed. The results show that males significantly differ in the use and preferences of ICT tools and devices (smart phones and tablets) from females. Conversely, females significantly differ in the use and preferences for online services (WhatsApp, text messaging, and library search engines) from males. The study also finds that smartphone and laptop computers are the most frequently used ICT tools and WhatsApp and Facebook are the most preferred online services. Gender studies in ICT to understand gender differences and proclivities are importance for policy direction towards an effort to bridge the gender gap.

DOI: 10.4018/978-1-5225-7068-4.ch005

INTRODUCTION

There has been a rapid advancement in information technology platforms, tools, devices and services. Currently, the use of information and communications technology (ICT) tools and services spans almost every area of life. For example, ICT tools and services are used in modern technical and medical devices (Mridha, 2016), in education and for dissemination of scientific knowledge (Hinojosa & Guzman, 2015), for collaborative learning (Rodríguez, 2017), and in bringing communities together for peace building (Vrasidas, Zembylas, Evagorou, Avraamidou, & Aravi, 2007). Information and communications technologies are deployed via different technologies and platforms. For instance, cloud computing enables the deployment of several social media and online services. Also, big data technologies and analytics allow users to obtain salient information of increasing volumes from historical data. The eminence of Internet-of-Things that allow objects to be identified uniquely and the upsurge of mobile computing devices have led to massive deployment of social media platform services. Currently, people tend to use their personal mobile devices at the workplace (Bring-Your-Own-Device or BYOD) and for accessing online social network services.

The use of social network tools and enterprise social networks facilitate collaboration, knowledge sharing, and support business processes to deliver a better experience in communication with the stakeholders (European Commission, 2014). A recent study estimates that in the near future ICT jobs will concentrate on online social media services (Fuciua & Gorski, 2013). Moreover, several organizations will employ teleworks - employees working from home (European Commission, 2014). Thus, the world looks forward to witness increasingly massive technological advancements in the near future. Despite the availability and accessibility of these services, Ilomaki (2011) speculates that there exists a gap between genders and generations in technical ICT competencies. Mendonça, Crespo, and Simões (2015) find that there is a prevalence of inequalities in ICT usage. However, for economic development of a nation, both men and women should be involved in the developments that come with ICT. There are different degrees of social exclusion within different societies, regions and cultures of the world with regards to gender. The term *gender* refers to the different roles men and women play in a society, which are determined by cultural, social and economic factors and differ within and between cultures and countries (Moghaddam, 2009).

There are gender preferences and likings of ICT technologies and services. The nature of gender gaps may differ based on ICT tools, devices, platforms and online social media services being used. Essentially, there are significant differences between genders. For instance, females show more concern than males, develop people-skills, and are more conversant with the people side of ICT (Koppi, Sheard, Naghdy, Edwards, & Brookes, 2010). Accordingly, gender gaps in using different ICT tools and online services may exist. The question as to the role of gender towards embracing, preferring, and liking of ICT tools, platforms, devices, and services is yet to be fully ascertained. Debate is still on-going with respect to gender differences in the use of technology with differing findings. Wiseman et al. (2018) find that female teachers use technology in the classroom more frequently than that of males. On the other hand, in a related study that examines the role of gender in ICT usage, Ilomaki (2011) reports that male teachers are more competent in ICT use than the female teachers. Critical to the increasing developments in technology platforms, tools, and online services is the degree of preferences and likings people attach to them. Of great importance are the gender preferences and proclivities towards the current technology.

While previous studies attempt to establish significant differences in the use of social media services, a study into gender preferences towards particular ICT tools and online services has not received much attention in the literature. The purpose of this chapter is to explore information and communications technology tools, social media and online services currently being used by university students. In particular, the chapter examines gender differences in preferences and proclivities for ICT tools, devices, and online services. In order to ascertain gender preferences and proclivities for ICT platforms, tools, and online services, the following research questions are stated for the study.

1. Which ICT devices and online services do students currently use and which would they prefer to use?
2. Are there gender differences in the preferences and proclivities for ICT tools and devices?
3. Are there gender differences in the preferences and proclivities for online services?

Data was collected through questionnaire from students in five universities in Ghana. These include three large public and two private universities, which have extensively integrated ICT into teaching and learning. The questionnaire was distributed to two thousand students. The data were analyzed using frequency analysis to ascertain students' preferences and proclivities for ICT devices and online services. Further, the T-test of independent samples was employed to ascertain gender differences in the preferences and proclivities for ICT tools and online services.

BACKGROUND

Gender and Information Technology

A gender theory can be used to explain gender differences in the use of ICT services. Gender essentialism theory suggests that there are certain universal, innate, biological or psychological features of genders that form the root of male and female differences in behavior (Hepburn, 2003). Gender essentialism posits that men and women act differently because of intrinsic or essential differences between them and that these characteristics are unchangeable. This theoretical perspective was used to explain the under representation of women in information technology field (Trauth, Nielsen, & von Hellens, 2003). However, gender essentialism is most often used to excuse gender-based biases in society (Arends-Tóth & van de Vijver, 2009). Though gender essentialism does not attempt to claim that the behavior of male and female are the same, there is no reason biological differences should lead to specific expectations for male and female behavior - otherwise, such differences will encourage inequalities in opportunity (Arends-Tóth & van de Vijver, 2009). For example, gender essentialism may be used to justify the idea that the use of ICT tools and online services are fundamentally the male domain, leading to creating gender gap.

ICT Tools and Online Services

Technological advances have brought about numerous ICT tools and devices which are use today by individuals and organizations. The Internet provides the platform for the use of online services. It is the way of life for millions of people across the world (Harcar & Yucelt, 2012) and has transformed the way businesses are conducted (Tshin, Tanakinja, & Sondoh, 2014). Digital mobile devices have greatly impacted higher educational institutions (Sevillano-García & Vázquez-Cano, 2015). In academic environment, there are various computing devices that students use, including laptop computers, desktop computers, tablets, smartphones, eBook readers, and several other devices that can access the Internet. According to Fauville, Lantz-Andersson and Säljö (2014), there is a rich variety of ICT tools in educational environment but there is far less research on their suitability and implications for student learning. Students use these devices to access online services for academic work and for social networking.

Thelwall (2009) classified social networking services (SNS) into three types: a) socializing, b) networking, and c) social navigation. Socializing SNS are primarily designed for recreational social communication with existing friends (e.g., Facebook, Cyworld); networking SNS are primarily for non-social interpersonal communication (e.g., LinkedIn); and social navigation are primarily for helping other users to find a particular information or resources (e.g., dig.com and Goodreads for books). Similarly, White (2014) categorized social networking into seven major types: a) social connections (e.g., Facebook, Google+, and MySpace) for connecting to friends, family members, and acquaintances; b) multimedia sharing (e.g., YouTube, Instagram, and Snapchat) for sharing videos and photos; c) professional social networks (e.g., LinkedIn and Konnects) for career-related goals; d) informational social networks (e.g., Super Green Me, Do-It-Yourself Community) for seeking answers to everyday problems; e) educational networks (e.g., the Student Room, ePALS School Blog) for collaborating with others on academic projects; f) hobby and special interest social networks (e.g., ActionProfiles, FanIQ) for helping individuals to find other people with similar interests; and g) academic social networks (e.g., Academic.edu, Connotea Collaborative Research) for academic researchers to share their research results.

The use of online services and social media is rampant among students. A previous study indicated that the majority of students are heavily using Twitter and Facebook (Hamade, 2013). Fuciua and Gorski (2013) found that 95% of high school students use online social networks and almost all the students use Facebook. Similarly, Tuurosong and Faisal (2014) found Facebook and Whatsapp as the most frequently used social media, followed by Twitter, Skype and YouTube. Likewise, Fuciua and Gorski (2013) presented a marketing research that aimed to identify the main reasons for using online social networks (OSN) by high school students from the counties of Sibiu, Salaj, and Satu Mare. The study examined the main activities undertaken by the students, the average number of connections and the influence of OSN on their lives. The results of the research showed that 95% of the high school students use online social networks while only 5% stated that they do not use or have an online social network account. The results of the analysis also indicated that Facebook.com is known by all the students, followed by Google+ and Hi5 (Fuciua & Gorski, 2013).

In a related study, Hamade (2013) examined the perception and use of social networking sites among university students. This study aimed to explore the perception and use of SNS among university students in the state of Kuwait, a small Arab country in the Gulf and a member of the Gulf Cooperating Council Countries (GCCC). The findings indicated that the majority of students are heavily using Twitter and Facebook. However, Gómez, Roses and Malaga (2012) reported that the frequency of use of online services for academic activities is rather low. Tuurosong and Faisal (2014) ascertained the frequency of social media usage among students, their reasons for using such media and the harmful effects of new media usage on the academic and socio-economic lives of students. The study found that Facebook and Whatsapp are the most frequently used social media, followed by Twitter, Skype and YouTube. However, Taddeo and Floridi (2016) raised serious concerns on the management of these online services regarding information filtering, Internet censorship, circulation of harmful content, and privacy. Kablan, Oulaı and Elliott (2015) suggested that one should consider the legal aspects of accessibility and usability of online public services.

Based on gender essentialism perspective and the empirical literature discussed above, a conceptual framework was developed to investigate gender differences in the use of ICT tools and online services among university students. Figure 1 posited that there will be gender differences in the preferences and proclivities for ICT tools and devices (hypothesis, H1). Moreover, H2 hypothesized that there will be gender differences in the preferences and proclivities for online services.

MAIN FOCUS OF THE CHAPTER

This section begins by presenting the characteristics of the respondents. This is followed by analyzing the ICT devices and online services students currently use and which they would prefer to use by using frequency distribution. Next, the section investigates gender differences in the preferences and proclivities for ICT tools and online services using T-Test of independent samples.

Out of the total of 2000 respondents invited to take part in the study, 618 questionnaires were completed and used in the data analysis. This represented 30.9% response rate. Table 1 shows the distribution of the respondents. About 73.8% of the students were male while 26.2% were female. The majority of the respondents (42.1%) aged between 21 and 25 years. The vast majority of the respondents (80.7%) were local students and 95.5% were undergraduates.

Preferences of ICT Tools and Online Services

The research question 1 investigates the ICT devices and online services the students currently use and which they would prefer to use.

1. **ICT Tools and Devices:** From Table 2, the greatest number of the students (51%) currently uses smartphones. Additionally, 31.6% of the students would like to use Smartphones. Thus, smartphones are the most preferred ICT tool among the students. Also, though currently 30.1% of the students use

Figure 1. Conceptual Model of Gender Differences in the Use and Preferences for ICT Tools and Online Services

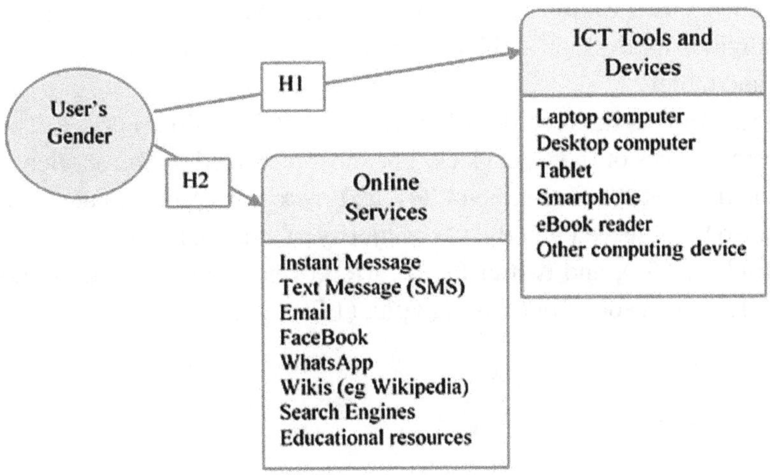

Table 1. Characteristics of the Respondents

Respondents	Frequency	Percentage
Gender		
Male	447	73.8
Female	159	26.2
Age		
18 or less	45	7.7
19-20	129	22.1
21-25	246	42.1
26-30	111	19.0
31-40	51	8.7
41-50	3	.5
International/Local		
International	117	19.3
Local	489	80.7
Level of Education		
Undergraduate	573	95.5
Postgraduate coursework	24	4.0
Postgraduate research	3	3
Year of Study		
First year	250	40.5
Second Year	171	27.7
Third Year	30	4.9
Fourth year	167	27.0

$N = 618$

laptop computers, only 19.9% would prefer to use it. Likewise, 18% currently use tablets, whereas 29.6% would prefer to use it. It can also be observed from the table that even though currently 8.7% of the students use desktop computers, only 7.3% would prefer to use it. This means that the students' proclivities for desktop and laptop computers are dwindling as against the preference for smartphones and tablets.

2. **Online Services:** Table 3 ranks students' preferences of 23 online services. The mean scores show the students' preferences of these services. The most preferred online service is WhatsApp (4.63), followed by the Internet search engine (4.24), text messaging (3.83), FaceBook (3.83), and Email (3.61). It can also be observed that the vast majority of students do not use conference technology (2.92), e-portifolio (2.54), and twitter (2.50). Moreover, many students do not use online multi-player games (1.84) and social booking/tagging (1.70).

Table 2. Students' Preferences for ICT Tools and Devices

ICT Tools and Devices	Currently Use			Prefer to Use		
	Mean	SD	Percent	Mean	SD	Percent*
Laptop computer	1.70	.460	30.1	1.80	.400	19.9
Desktop computer	1.91	.283	8.7	1.92	1.420	7.3
Tablet (eg iPad, Samsung Galaxy or similar)	1.82	.384	18.0	1.70	.4571	29.6
Smartphone (eg iPhone, Android, Blackberry)	1.49	.500	51.0	1.70	.519	31.6
eBook reader (eg Kindle, Nook)	1.97	.181	3.4	1.94	.337	7.3
Other computing device with Internet access (eg games console)	1.96	.193	3.9	1.97	.302	4.9

N = 618; 1 – Use; 2 – Not Used; * - Additional students who want to use the tools

Table 3. Students' Preferences for Online Services

Online Services	N	Mean	Std. Deviation	Rank
1. Instant Message	588	3.12	1.580	11
2. Text Message (SMS)	597	3.83	1.326	3
3. Email	591	3.61	1.229	5
4. Conferencing Technology	594	2.92	1.517	14
5. FaceBook	597	3.83	1.372	3
6. Twitter	588	2.48	1.650	16
7. WhatsApp	603	4.63	.965	1
8. Other Social Network Sites	591	2.36	4.027	19
9. Virtual Worlds	579	1.84	2.531	21
10. Blogs	591	2.37	1.495	18
11. Wikis (eg Wikipedia)	588	3.28	1.468	8
12. Online Multi-player games	603	1.81	1.233	22
13. Social bookmarking/tagging	579	1.69	1.146	23
14. Audio/Video Software	588	2.27	1.435	20
15. Presentation Software	600	3.57	3.103	6
16. Data Analysis Software	591	2.98	1.373	12
17. Google docs or drive	576	2.98	1.503	12
18. e-portfolios	585	2.54	1.507	15
19. Photo or Video share on the web	600	3.40	1.567	7
20. Library Search Engines	579	3.20	1.566	10
21. Internet Search Engines	588	4.24	1.278	2
22. Freely available educational resources	600	3.21	1.472	9
23. RSS Feed Using a Variety of web sources	579	2.45	1.480	17

1 - Never or Rarely; 2 - A few times a SEMESTER; 3 - A few times a MONTH; 4 - A few times a WEEK; 5 - One or more times a DAY

Gender Differences in the Use and Preferences of ICT Tools and Devices

In this section the research question enquires whether there are gender differences in the preferences and proclivities for ICT tools and devices. This section investigates a) gender differences in the use of ICT tools and devices and b) gender differences in preferences for ICT tools and devices.

1. **Gender Differences in the Use of ICT Tools and Devices:** Six hypotheses were tested to determine gender differences in the use of ICT tools and devices. These are:
   H1a$_1$: *There is statistical significant difference between male and female students in the use of desktop computers.*
   H1a$_2$: *There is statistical significant difference between male and female students in the use of laptop computers.*
   H1a$_3$: *There is statistical significant difference between male and female students in the use of tablets.*
   H1a$_4$: *There is statistical significant difference between male and female students in the use of smartphones.*
   H1a$_5$: *There is statistical significant difference between male and female students in the use the of eBook readers.*
   H1a$_6$: *There is statistical significant difference between male and female students in the use of other computing devices.*

The mean and standard deviation of ICT tools and devices are presented in Table 4. The t-test of independents samples was conducted to investigate gender differences in the use of ICT tools and devices. From the analysis (see Table 5), significant differences were found in usage of Desktop Computers, $H1a_1$ (t=1.203, p= .025) and other computing devices, $H1a_6$ (t=-1.562, p=.001). These two hypotheses were supported and hence accepted. Thus, the male students use desktop and other ICT devices more than the female students. However, as can be observed from the table, there were no significant differences between males and females with respect to the use of Laptop Computers (t=.269, p=.592), Tablets (t=-.506, p= .305), Smart Phones (t=1.239, p=.073), and eBook readers (t=.247, p=.622). Therefore, they were not supported and hence rejected. This indicates that males and females do no differ statistically significantly in the use of Laptop Computers, Tablets, Smart Phones, and eBook readers.

2. **Gender Differences in Preferences for ICT Tools and Devices:** The six hypotheses tested to determine gender differences in the in the preferences and proclivities for ICT tools and devices. These are:
   H1b$_1$: *There is statistical significant difference between male and female students in the preferences and proclivities for desktop computers.*
   H1b$_2$: *There is statistical significant difference between male and female students in the preferences and proclivities for laptop computers.*
   H1b$_3$: *There is statistical significant difference between male and female students in the preferences and proclivities for tablets.*
   H1b$_4$: *There is statistical significant difference between male and female students in the preferences and proclivities for smartphones.*
   H1b$_5$: *There is statistical significant difference between male and female students in the preferences and proclivities for f eBook readers.*

Table 4. Mean and SD of Gender Differences in Use of ICT Tools and Devices

ICT Tools and Devices	Gender	N	Mean*	SD
Desktop Computer	Male	447	1.71	.454
	Female	159	1.66	.475
Laptop Computer	Male	447	1.91	.283
	Female	159	1.91	.293
Tablet	Male	447	1.81	.391
	Female	159	1.83	.377
Smart Phones	Male	447	1.51	.500
	Female	159	1.45	.499
eBook reader	Male	447	1.97	.180
	Female	159	1.96	.191
Other computing device with Internet access	Male	447	1.95	.212
	Female	159	1.98	.136

N = 618; 1 – Use; 2 – Not Used; * - Smaller mean values represent more use of the tools and devices

Table 5. T-Test of Gender Differences in the Use of ICT Tools and Devices

Hypotheses	ICT Tools and Devices	Equal Variances	Levene's Test for Equality of Variances		t-Test for Equality of Means		Support/Not Supported
			F	Sig.	t	df	
H1a$_1$	Desktop Computer	Assumed	5.081	.025	1.203	604	Supported
		Not assumed			1.177	267.140	
H1a$_2$	Laptop Computer	Assumed	.287	.592	.269	604	Not Supported
		Not assumed			.264	269.172	
H1a$_3$	Tablet	Assumed	1.054	.305	-.506	604	Not Supported
		Not assumed			-.515	287.442	
H1a$_5$	Smart Phones	Assumed	3.228	.073	1.239	604	Not Supported
		Not assumed			1.241	278.482	
H1a$_5$	eBook reader	Assumed	.243	.622	.247	604	Not Supported
		Not assumed			.240	264.421	
H1a$_6$	Other computing device with Internet access	Assumed	10.202	.001	-1.562	604	Supported
		Not assumed			-1.906	432.312	

H1b$_6$: *There is statistical significant difference between male and female students in the preferences and proclivities for other computing devices.*

The mean and standard deviation of ICT tools and devices are presented in Table 6. The t-test of independents samples was conducted to investigate gender differences in the preferences and proclivities ICT tools and devices. From the analysis (see Table 7), significant differences were found in preferences and proclivities for Tablets, $H1b_3$ (t=-1.815, p<.05) and Smart Phones, $H1b_4$ (t=-1.467, p<.05). These two hypotheses were supported and hence accepted. Therefore, the male students prefer and would like to use tablets and smart phones more than the female students. On the other hand, as can be observed from the Table 6, there were no significant differences between males and females with respect to preferences and proclivities for desktop computer, laptop computers, eBook reader, and other computing devices. These, hypotheses were not supported and therefore rejected. This indicates that males and females do no differ statistically significantly in their preferences and proclivities for desktop computer, laptop computers, eBook reader, and other computing devices.

Gender Differences in the Preferences of Online Services

This research question examines gender differences in the preferences and proclivities for online services. Twelve hypotheses were tested as follows:

H2a: *There is statistical significant difference between male and female students regarding their preferences and proclivities for Instant Message.*
H2b: *There is statistical significant difference between male and female students regarding their preferences and proclivities for Text Message (SMS).*
H2c: *There is statistical significant difference between male and female students regarding their preferences and proclivities for Email.*
H2d: *There is statistical significant difference between male and female students regarding their preferences and proclivities for FaceBook.*
H2e: *There is statistical significant difference between male and female students regarding their preferences and proclivities for WhatsApp.*

Table 6. Mean and SD of Gender Differences in Preferences of ICT Tools and Devices

ICT Tools and Devices	Gender	N	Mean*	Std. Deviation
Desktop Computer	Male	447	1.80	.401
	Female	159	1.81	.392
Laptop Computer	Male	447	2.04	1.668
	Female	159	1.98	.136
Tablet	Male	447	1.68	.468
	Female	159	1.75	.432
Smart Phones	Male	447	1.68	.545
	Female	159	1.75	.432
eBook reader	Male	447	1.94	.371
	Female	159	1.94	.232
Other computing device with Internet access	Male	447	1.97	.336
	Female	159	1.96	.191

N = 618; 1 – Use; 2 – Not Used; * - Smaller mean values represent more use of the tools and devices

Table 7. T-Test of Gender Differences in the Preferences for ICT Tools and Devices

Hypotheses	ICT Tools and Devices	Equal Variances	Levene's Test for Equality of Variances		t-Test for Equality of Means		Support/Not Supported
			F	Sig.	t	df	
$H1b_1$	Desktop Computer	Assumed	.482	.488	-.344	604	Not Supported
		Not assumed			-.347	283.564	
$H1b_2$	Laptop Computer	Assumed	3.116	.078	.446	604	Not Supported
		Not assumed			.742	462.481	
$H1b_3$	Tablet	Assumed	15.671	.000	-1.815	604	Supported
		Not assumed			-1.886	299.138	
$H1b_4$	Smart Phones	Assumed	12.304	.000	-1.467	604	Supported
		Not assumed			-1.637	348.413	
$H1b_5$	eBook reader	Assumed	2.432	.119	-.121	604	Not Supported
		Not assumed			-.149	445.856	
$H1b_6$	Other computing device with Internet access	Assumed	1.358	.244	.148	604	Not Supported
		Not assumed			.190	488.138	

H2f: *There is statistical significant difference between male and female students regarding their preferences and proclivities for Wikis (eg Wikipedia).*

H3g: *There is statistical significant difference between male and female students regarding their preferences and proclivities for Presentation Software*

H3h: *There is statistical significant difference between male and female students regarding their preferences and proclivities for Photo or Video share on the Web.*

H2i: *There is statistical significant difference between male and female students regarding their preferences and proclivities for Library Search Engines.*

H3j: *There is statistical significant difference between male and female students regarding their preferences and proclivities for Internet Search Engines.*

H2k: *There is statistical significant difference between male and female students regarding their preferences and proclivities for freely available educational resources.*

Table 8 shows the mean and the standard deviation of gender preferences of online services. The t-tests of independent samples were conducted to ascertain gender differences in preferences and proclivities for online services. From Table 9, significant differences were found in preferences and proclivities for Text Message, *H2b* (t=-3.569, p<.05), WhatsApp, *H2e* (t= -3.779, p<.05), Presentation Software, *H2g* (t= -1.279, p<.05), and Library Search Engines, *H2i* (t= -1.644, p<.05). These hypotheses were supported and therefore accepted. Therefore, the female students prefer Text Message, WhatsApp, Presentation Software, and Library Search Engines more than the male students. Conversely, no significant differences between the genders were found in the rest of the online services (see Table 8), including for instance Instant Message, *H2a* (t= .709, p= .400), Email, *H2c* (t= .220, p= .639), and FaceBook, *H2d* (t= 1.929, p= .165).

Table 8. Mean and Standard Deviation of Gender Preferences of Online Services

Online Services	Gender of Respondents	N	Mean *	Std. Deviation	Std. Error Mean
Instant Message	Male	426	3.11	1.586	.07683
	Female	150	3.10	1.558	.12718
Text Message (SMS)	Male	432	3.73	1.399	.06733
	Female	153	4.16	1.039	.08404
Email	Male	429	3.60	1.231	.05945
	Female	150	3.58	1.238	.10112
Facebook	Male	438	3.82	1.401	.06695
	Female	150	3.88	1.295	.10573
WhatsApp	Male	438	4.54	1.062	.05074
	Female	153	4.88	.584	.04723
Wikis (eg Wikipedia)	Male	426	3.35	1.446	.07004
	Female	150	3.06	1.494	.12196
Presentation Software	Male	432	3.47	1.355	.06521
	Female	156	3.85	5.649	.45229
Photo or Video share on the web	Male	435	3.43	1.563	.07495
	Female	156	3.38	1.539	.12319
Library Search Engines	Male	423	3.16	1.589	.07727
	Female	147	3.41	1.461	.12048
Internet Search Engines	Male	429	4.30	1.248	.06024
	Female	147	4.04	1.389	.11458
Freely available educational resources	Male	438	3.27	1.446	.06909
	Female	150	3.04	1.541	.12581

* Higher mean values represent higher use of the service

SOLUTIONS AND RECOMMENDATIONS

Exploring the ICT tools and online services students currently use and would prefer to use revealed important findings. The current study found that smart phones and laptop computers are the most ICT tools used by the students whereas WhatsApp, Facebook, and text messaging are the most preferred online services. This finding is consistent with earlier studies. For example, Tuurosong and Faisal (2014) conducted a study among students in Ghana and found that Facebook and WhatsApp were the most frequently used social media, followed by Twitter, Skype and YouTube. Also, more than a quarter of respondents use such media more than once a day while over half of them engaged in social media usage once a day. Moreover, more than half of the respondents used social media mainly to chat with friends and relations while a fifth used it for academic purposes. Respondents admitted that social media usage took time from their academic work. Some respondents indicated that they spent about two United States dollars each day on social media and that they used such media during lectures (Tuurosong & Faisal, 2014). In a study that investigated the use of online social networking services, 25.7 percent used Facebook and 19.8 percent used Twitter (Salehan, Kim, & Kim, 2017).

Table 9. T-Test of Gender Differences in Preferences of Online Services

Hypotheses	Online Services	Variance	Levene's Test for Equality of Variances		t-Test for Equality of Means							Supported/ Not Supported
			F	Sig.	t	df	Sig. (2-tailed)	Mean Diff	Std. Error Diff	95% Confidence Interval of the Difference		
										Lower	Upper	
H2a	Instant Message	Assumed	.709	.400	.085	574	.933	.01268	.14986	-.28167	.30702	Not Supported
		Not Assumed			.085	265.202	.932	.01268	.14858	-.27987	.30523	
H2b	Text Message (SMS)	Assumed	28.038	.000	-3.569	583	.000	-.44158	.12372	-.68457	-.19860	Supported
		Not Assumed			-4.101	357.765	.000	-.44158	.10768	-.65335	-.22982	
H2c	Email	Assumed	.220	.639	.183	577	.855	.02140	.11697	-.20834	.25114	Not Supported
		Not Assumed			.182	259.009	.855	.02140	.11730	-.20958	.25238	
H2d	FaceBook	Assumed	1.929	.165	-.499	586	.618	-.06493	.13008	-.32040	.19054	Not Supported
		Not Assumed			-.519	277.260	.604	-.06493	.12514	-.31129	.18142	
H2e	WhatsApp	Assumed	58.790	.000	-3.779	589	.000	-.34126	.09030	-.51861	-.16390	Supported
		Not Assumed			-4.923	481.976	.000	-.34126	.06932	-.47746	-.20505	
H2f	Wikis (eg Wikipedia)	Assumed	.373	.541	2.059	574	.040	.28507	.13846	.01313	.55701	Not Supported
		Not Assumed			2.027	253.817	.044	.28507	.14065	.00809	.56205	
H2g	Presentation Software	Assumed	8.753	.003	-1.279	586	.201	-.37393	.29229	-.94800	.20013	Supported
		Not Assumed			-.818	161.485	.414	-.37393	.45696	-1.27632	.52846	
H2h	Photo or Video share on the web	Assumed	1.003	.317	.296	589	.768	.04297	.14528	-.24236	.32830	Not Supported
		Not Assumed			.298	277.415	.766	.04297	.14419	-.24088	.32682	
H2i	Library Search Engines	Assumed	10.527	.001	-1.644	568	.101	-.24504	.14909	-.53787	.04779	Supported
		Not Assumed			-1.712	274.731	.088	-.24504	.14313	-.52680	.03672	
H2j	Internet Search Engines	Assumed	1.568	.211	2.116	574	.035	.25988	.12282	.01865	.50111	Not Supported
		Not Assumed			2.008	231.815	.046	.25988	.12945	.00484	.51493	
H2k	Freely available educational resources	Assumed	2.362	.125	1.632	586	.103	.22712	.13913	-.04614	.50038	Not Supported
		Not Assumed			1.582	244.838	.115	.22712	.14353	-.05560	.50984	

On the contrary, twitter did not appear to be a preferred online media for social networks among the students. This is in consonance with Capano et al. (2010), who found that more students use Facebook and YouTube than any other social media platform such as Twitter. Alzouebi and Isakovic (2014) concluded that some social media tools are more preferred than others for students' use in the learning process, whiles others are more effective for social interactions. Compared with other online social network sites, the students' most popular online social network site is Facebook (Wanpena, 2012). Similarly, a Malaysian study found that students make use of social networking services for activities that are common for informal learning i.e. communicating with peers and arranging for meetings (Hamat, Embi & Hassan, 2012). Majority of students in Kuwait heavily use Twitter and Facebook (Hamade, 2013). Social networks usage in the student population is very high, but the use of such networks for academic activities is rather low (Gómez, Roses & Malaga, 2012).

Though gender essentialism theory suggested that there are certain universal, innate, biological or psychological features of gender that forms the root of male and female differences in behavior (Hepburn, 2003), evidence from this study largely found no significant differences in the use and preferences of several ICT tools and online services between the genders. For example, there were no significance differences in the use and preferences between males and females with respect to Facebook, Wikis, Email, desktop computer, and laptop computer.

Exploring further the preferred information and communications technology tools and online services by university students revealed some gender differences in preferences and proclivities in the use of few ICT tools and online services. Significant differences were observed between the genders with regards to the use and preferences for ICT tools. Males differ significantly from females in the use of tablets and smart phones (ICT tools and devices). Conversely, females differ significantly from male in the use of WhatsApp, text messaging, library search engines, and the use of presentation software. Manjunatha (2013) found that male students in India use social networking services more than female students. According to the study, among the total users of social networking services, 71 percent of the users are male and 29 percent are female. This result is rather inconsistent with the findings from the current study. But, Tham and Ahmed (2011) found significant difference between gender and degree of SNS usage. A significant difference was also found between gender and the time spent on studying or revising academic-related materials outside of class sessions (Tham & Ahmed, 2011).

As a whole, the study found that males have more inclination towards ICT tools and devices, whereas females are more inclined to use online services. While inequalities in the use and preferences exists (Mendonça, Crespo, & Simões, 2015), National ICT policies should mediate the concept of digital-divide and gender differences by focussing on equal application of ICT tools and online services between genders in schools and workplaces for accelerated national development.

FUTURE RESEARCH DIRECTIONS

The use and preferences for information and communications technologies (ICT) tools and services spans almost every area of life, involving people of all ages, cultures, races, and academic disciplines. However, the focus of the current study is limited to a particular country that share similar culture and among university students only. However, to gain in-depth understanding of gender differences in the use and preferences for ICT tools, devices, and services, a cross-cultural research would be needed. Moreover, examining age, educational differences and academic program offerings alongside gender differences might provide insightful findings. These would be addressed in future research. Another area that needs further enhancement in the current study is the sample representation and sampling. These issues would be addressed through multiple data collection methods, including interviews and focus groups.

CONCLUSION

Gender studies in ICT to understand gender gaps, differences, and proclivities are important for policy direction, development of services and tools to meet gender needs, and the effort to bridge the gender gap. This current study identified gender preferences and recommended solutions towards gender social inclusion in ICT. While policymakers for tertiary educations might find this study informative, academics and researchers might use it to further gender related research in developing economies. Besides, the study provided data for international non-governmental organizations as to where to focus advocacy and channel funding. Service and platform providers could improve and integrate diverse digital devices and online services to foster learning activities, gender preferences, and gender equality and competencies that would provide opportunities towards bridging gender ICT gaps.

REFERENCES

Alzouebi, K., & Isakovic, A. (2014). Exploring learner perspective of social Media in Higher Education in a UAE Context: Experience beyond Knowledge. *Global Education Journal, 2014*(2).

Arends-Tóth, J., & van de Vijver, F. J. (2009). Cultural differences in family, marital, and gender-role values among immigrants and majority members in the Netherlands. *International Journal of Psychology, 44*(3), 161–169. doi:10.1080/00207590701545676 PMID:22029491

Capano. (2010). *Social Networking Usage and Grades Among College students*. Whittemore School of Business and Economics. Retrieved from http://www.unh.edu/news/docs/UNHsocialmedia.pdf

European Commission. (2014). *ICT TRENDS 2020 - Main Trends for Information and Communication Technologies (ICT) and their Implications for e-LEADERSHIP SKILLS*. Retrieved from http://eskills-lead.eu/fileadmin/lead/reports/lead_-_technology_trends_- _august_2014_rev_sep1.pdf

Fauville, G., Lantz-Andersson, A., & Säljö, R. (2014). ICT tools in environmental education: Reviewing two newcomers to schools. *Environmental Education Research, 20*(2), 248–283. doi:10.1080/13504622.2013.775220

Fuciua, M., & Gorski, H. (2013). Marketing Research regarding the Usage of Online Social Networking Sites by High School Students. *Procedia Economics and Finance, 6*, 482–490. doi:10.1016/S2212-5671(13)00166-4

Gómez M, Roses S & Malaga P. S (2012). The Academic Use of Social Networks among University Students. *Comunicar Scientific Journal of Media Education, 38*(19), 131-138.

Hamade, S. N. (2013). Perception and use of social networking sites among university students. *Library Review, 62*(6/7), 388–397. doi:10.1108/LR-12-2012-0131

Hamat, A., Embi, M. A., & Hassan, H. A. (2012). The use of social networking sites among Malaysian university students. *International Education Studies, 5*(3), 56–66. doi:10.5539/ies.v5n3p56

Harcar, T., & Yucelt, U. (2012). American Consumer's Attitudes Towards Different Airline Companies Channels: A Comparison of Transaction Methods. *Recista De Turismoy Patrimonio Cultural, 10*(2), 59–68. doi:10.25145/j.pasos.2012.10.027

Hepburn, A. (2003). Feminist critics: hetrosexism and lesbian and gay psychology. An introduction to critical social psychology. Thousand Oaks, CA: Sage.

Iglesias Rodríguez, A., García Riaza, B., & Sánchez Gómez, M. C. (2017). Collaborative learning and mobile devices: An educational experience in Primary Education. *Computers in Human Behavior*, 72664–72677. doi:10.1016/j.chb.2016.07.019

Ilomaki, L. (2011). Does Gender Have a Role in ICT Among Finnish Teachers and Students? *Scandinavian Journal of Educational Research*, *55*(3), 325–340. doi:10.1080/00313831.2011.576910

Kablan, S., Oulaı, A., & Elliott, E. (2015). Legal aspects of accessibility and usability of online public services in Quebec and Canada. *Electronic Commerce Research*, *15*(3), 387–406. doi:10.100710660-015-9186-3

Koppi, T., Sheard, J., Naghdy, F., Edwards, S. L., & Brookes, W. (2010). Towards a gender inclusive information and communications technology curriculum: A perspective from graduates in the workforce. *Computer Science Education*, *20*(4), 265–282. doi:10.1080/08993408.2010.527686

Manjunatha, S. (2013). The Usage of Social Networking sites Among the College Students in India, *International Research. Journal of Social Sciences*, *2*(5), 15–21.

Mendonça, S., Crespo, N., & Simões, N. (2015). Inequality in the network society: An integrated approach to ICT access, basic skills, and complex capabilities. *Telecommunications Policy*, *39*(3/4), 192–207. doi:10.1016/j.telpol.2014.12.010

Moghaddam, G. G. (2009). Information technology and gender gap: Toward a global view. *The Electronic Library*, *28*(5), 722–773. doi:10.1108/02640471011081997

Mridha, M., Erlandsson, B. E., Islam, M., & Sultana, N. (2016). To improve rural health care and patient safety by empowering the health workers utilizing the modern medical devices and ICT tools. *Annual Global Healthcare Conference*, 1-4.

Palmero Hinojosa, M. G., & Guzman, M. G. (2015). Application deployment on mobile devices as a useful tool for self-learning in health doctors in training in secondary hospital. *International Journal of Integrated Care*, 1565–1568.

Salehan, M., Kim, D. J., & Kim, C. (2017). Use of Online Social Networking Services from a Theoretical Perspective of the Motivation Participation-Performance Framework. *Journal of the Association for Information Systems*, *18*(2), 141–172. doi:10.17705/1jais.00449

Sevillano-García, M. L., & Vázquez-Cano, E. (2015). The Impact of Digital Mobile Devices in Higher Education. *Journal of Educational Technology & Society*, *18*(1), 106–118.

Taddeo, M., & Floridi, L. (2016). The Debate on the Moral Responsibilities of Online Service Providers. *Science and Engineering Ethics*, *22*(6), 1575–1603. doi:10.100711948-015-9734-1 PMID:26613596

Tham, J., & Ahmed, N. (2011). The Usage and Implications of Social Networking Sites: A Survey of College Students. *Journal of Interpersonal. Intercultural and Mass Communication*, *2*(1), 1–11.

Trauth, E. M., Nielsen, S. H., & von Hellens, L. A. (2003). Explaining the IT gender gap: Australian stories for the new millennium. *Journal of Research and Practice in IT*, *35*(1), 7–20.

Tshin, E. Y. H., Tanakinja, G. H., & Sondoh, S. L. (2014). The Key Dimensions of Online Service Quality: A Study of Consumer Perceptions. *The IUP. Journal of Marketing Management, 13*(2).

Tuurosong, D., & Faisal, M. A. (2014). The Social Media Scourge among University Students: A Study of the University for Development Studies. *Ghana J. Asian Dev. Studium (Roma), 3*(2).

Vrasidas, C., Zembylas, M., Evagorou, M., Avraamidou, L., & Aravi, C. (2007). ICT as a Tool for Environmental Education, Peace, and Reconciliation. *Educational Media International, 44*(2), 129–140. doi:10.1080/09523980701295125

Wanpena, S. (2013). The Relationship between Learning Styles and the Social Network Use of Tertiary Level Students. *Procedia: Social and Behavioral Sciences, 88*, 334–339. doi:10.1016/j.sbspro.2013.08.514

Wiseman, A. W., Al-bakr, F., Davidson, P. M., & Bruce, E. (2018). Using technology to break gender barriers: Gender differences in teachers' information and communication technology use in Saudi Arabian classrooms. *Compare: A Journal of Comparative Education, 48*(2), 224–243. doi:10.1080/03057925.2017.1301200

KEY TERMS AND DEFINITIONS

Gender Essentialism: A theory that posits that men and women have certain attributes that are fixed. These characteristics universally uniquely identify men and women.

Gender Gap: Is a disproportionate difference or disparity between the males and females.

ICT Tools and Devices: Diverse set of technological tools and resources used to communicate, create, disseminate, store, and manage information. This includes laptop computers, smartphone, e-book readers, and desktop computers.

Information and Communications Technologies: Any communication device or application, encompassing radio, television, cellular phones, computer and network hardware and software, satellite systems and so on, as well as the various services and applications associated with them, such as WhatsApp, Facebook, chats, and videoconferencing.

Online Services: Any information and services provided over the Internet, intranet and extranet.

Preference: A greater liking for one thing over others.

Proclivity: An inclination, tendency to choose or do something regularly, a pre-disposition towards using and preferring a particular thing.

Social Media: A platform, most often a website and application, that enables users to create and share content or to participate in social networking.

Chapter 6
Personality and ICT Adoption: The Call for More Research

Idongesit Williams
Aalborg University, Denmark

ABSTRACT

Globally, the gender gap still exists. An interesting reason for this is the passive usage or non-adoption of ICT by women who have access to ICTs and can also afford ICTs. In order to understand this phenomenon, an exploratory research was conducted to identify why women adopt current ICTs. The most used ICTs are social media platforms and mobile internet services. An exploratory study was conducted to observe four women: three from South America and one from the Middle East who subscribe to WhatsApp. The major outcome was the plausible influence of a woman's personality on her usage of WhatsApp. The women with high extroversion used social media and mobile phones more than women at the opposite end of the spectrum. The women with very low extroversion almost rejected social media platforms and recorded low mobile phone usage. This implies that women with very low extroversion may not find ICTs appealing. Based on these outcomes, the chapter advocates for a more concrete research to understanding this trend.

INTRODUCTION

This chapter presents an argument for research into the influence of an individual's personality on their decision to adopt an Information and Communication Technologies (ICT) technology or services. There is a spectral divergence, when one discusses ICT technology and services. So to narrow the scope of discussion in this chapter, social media platform is chosen as a representative ICT service. *This argument is anchored on the idea that the personality of individual female potential ICT users could be enabling the gender divide*. Specifically, the gender divide in the adoption of Internet technologies and services. These ideas are inspired from two sources. The first source being a surprise finding from another study aimed at understanding the motivations for using WhatsApp, social media platform and mobile internet. The surprise finding, which is presented in this chapter indicates the plausibility of a female's personality towards the adoption or rejection of social media platforms. The second source of inspiration for the idea

DOI: 10.4018/978-1-5225-7068-4.ch006

was based on a study from GSM Association (GSMA) which indicated that gender gap in mobile internet adoption exist in urban areas in some urban areas in Asia, Africa and Latin America (Rowntree, 2018). It is common knowledge that Internet networks are available and accessible in urban areas compared to rural areas (See Williams, 2016; Williams, 2015). In most urban areas, more than 50% of the residents can afford mobile telephone and mobile internet services. However, there are men and women in urban areas in developing countries who neither adopt mobile phone nor mobile internet services (see Wanga, 2016). And report from GSMA indicates that this trend exists in developing countries (see Rowntree, 2018). Even in this circumstances, the number of men refraining from adopting these services are less than women. If we juxtapose both inspirations, among other factors, the personality of an individual could be identified as an important influencing variable, which could be enhancing the gender divide.

The global gender divide in the adoption of ICTs still exists. More men adopt ICT globally and specifically, social media than women (see Fatehkia, Kashyap, & Weber, 2018; ITU, 2017). This is one of the reasons, social media was chosen for making the argument in this chapter. It is believed that women are more social than men and are most likely to adopt social media platforms (see Rowntree, 2018). This is evident in developed countries than in developing countries (Pew Research, 2017). However, there is no statistic at the moment that indicates that 100% of females, 18 years and older in developed countries, use social media platforms. This implies that among other factors, personality could influence their adoption or otherwise of social media platforms. This could also be the case with respect to the adoption of other ICT. On the surface, the problem can be thought to be attitudinal. However, attitude can be influenced by a lot of factors including the individual's personality (see Dong & Sivakumar, 2017).

To guide the argument, this chapter is steered by two questions. The first being an overarching question and the second being a chapter specific question. The overarching question is "How does an individual's personality characteristic affect the actual adoption of an ICT technology or service?" The chapter specific question is "How does an individual's personality characteristic affect the actual adoption of a social media platform?" The answers provided in this chapter are based on literature which is supplemented by surprise finding. The surprise finding from the female respondent was explored using thematic analysis, guided by the Five-Factor model. There were 4 female respondents among the numerous responses from male respondents. *This chapter is developed from the interpretivist worldview*. The chapter is divided into 7 sections. The first section is this section, the introduction. The next section provides a background on the existence and reason for the gender gap on social media platform. The section also explains the rationale for investigating the correlation between personality and social media platform adoption. The following section provides the conceptual framework for analysing the relationship between personality and social media adoption. This section is followed by the methodology, findings, discussion and conclusion.

BACKGROUND

This section provides an overview of the problem and reasons why it exists. The section is divided into 2 parts. In the first section, Facebook is used as case to reveal the existing gender gap on social media. The second part presents the possible reason for the gender gap.

Gender Gap Assessment on Social Media Platforms

At first sight is quite difficult to actually pinpoint to a gender divide in the usage of social media. This is because there are lots of social networks and instant messaging services. And users adopt more than one of these social media platforms. That makes it seemingly difficult to quantify unique social media subscription per individual. But the position of Facebook in the social network ecosystem makes it possible to estimate the gender gap on social media platforms. Facebook accounts for 2.167 billion active users (Chaffey, 2018). More data is presented in the appendix section. This number is not up to half of the world's population.

However, there are other statistical insights which work in favour of using Facebook to gauge the gender divide in Social media usage. In order to access any social media platform on any device you need either the Internet or in some cases Unstructured Supplementary Service Data (USSD) (Surman, Gardner, & Ascher, 2014). In the early part of 2018 4.021 billion persons globally were active internet users (Chaffey, 2018). However 3.196 billion persons were active social media users globally. This implies that 825 million Internet users did not subscribe to social media. It further implies that almost three quarters of those who subscribe to social media globally subscribe to Facebook. Numerically that amounts to 238 million social media subscribers. This number is not insignificant, but it can be ignored. This is because in statistics sighted so far, the social media gender gap which is associated with women, mostly in developed countries, is quite small. If this number is added to the existing figures, it will still favour males. Based on this fact the global social media gender gap data from Facebook is actually representative.

Figure 1 provides a representative insight from Facebook into the gender gap on social media.

As seen in Figure 1, in 2018, 56% of men and 43% of women globally use Facebook. The figure does not account for 1% of Facebook users. However, corroborative findings from other sources point to a similar insight. Data extracted for 2017 indicate that 56% of Men and 44% of women globally use Facebook (York, 2017). Durgesh Kaushik, who was head-Online marketing – Asia Pacific for Facebook also confirmed the gender divide on Facebook on his Quora page (Kaushik, 2017). There is also confirmation from literature which confirms that there is a gender gap on Facebook which corroborates with the ICT Gender gap as reported by development agencies (see Fatehkia, Kashyap, & Weber, 2018). The possible reasons for the gender gap are explained in the next sub section.

Reasons for the Social Media Gender Gap

The reasons for the gender gap on social media are socio-economic and socio-cultural. These reasons include the low income level of women compared to men which results in low ownership of mobile phone and the high cost of mobile phones compared to the income level of women (Rowntree, 2018). This point was corroborated by Kaushik. He explained that most women in the world live in rural areas in developing countries where Facebook subscription is low and they cannot afford smart phones and internet subscription compared to men (Kaushik, 2017). Furthermore the GSMA report indicated that women in developing countries are more likely to adopt social media and messaging services when they adopt mobile Internet services. These reasons can be extended to other forms of social media as well. However in western countries, these reasons do not apply. It is a fact that more women use social media than men in the US and some countries in the European Union (EU) (see Pew Research Center, 2018)

Figure 1. Distribution of Facebook users worldwide as of April 2018, by age and gender
Source (Statista, 2018)

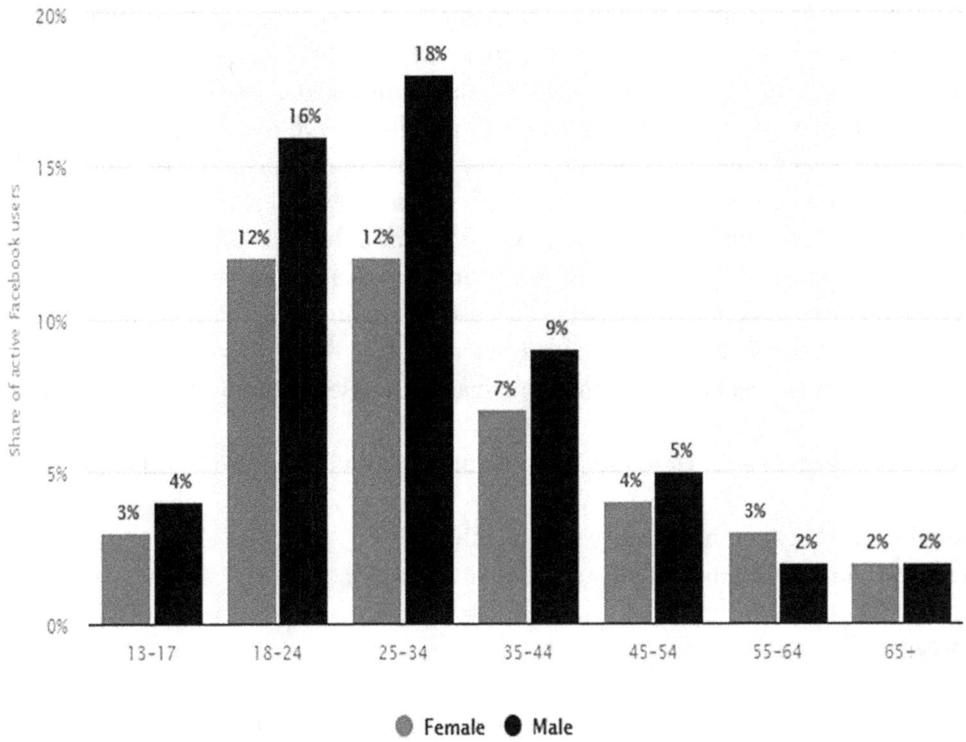

(Statista, 2018; Statista, 2018)). In the west, women can afford mobile phones as well as gain access to social media.

From a socio-cultural perspective, the main reason women who have access to the Internet do not adopt social media is because they do not find the service to be of relevance to them (see Rowntree, 2018; Williams, Siddi, & Kwofie, 2016). Other reasons which does not only affect social media include, lack of awareness, low digital literacy, low level of education, lack of local content, inhibition by social norms, inhibition against female child education because they are women and more inhibition of females by family members to own mobile phones (see Rowntree, 2018; Pew Research, 2017).

These reasons, among others, are very valid reasons for the gender divide on social media and the mobile internet. However, most of these reasons are focused on women who are totally disenfranchised. Furthermore, these reasons are mostly external variable which enable the gender gap. But if focus is shifted to those who have access to social media (and ICTs) but do not adopt it, some of these variables may hold. But there is the likelihood that that an Internal variable such as the individual's personality could be a strong factor. That could be one of the reasons the 825 million internet users, mentioned earlier, do not adopt social media platforms and ICTs in general. That could be the reason, why some females in developing countries living in urban areas do not adopt social media platforms and ICTs in general. However, at this stage, it is a speculation until proven empirically, which this chapter does advocate for. In the next section, the conceptual framework for the argument in this chapter is presented.

CONCEPTUAL FRAMEWORK

The main concepts that make up the theoretical framework of this chapter are personality, sociability and social media platform adoption/usage. The concepts "personality" and "social media adoption/usage" are derived from the research question mentioned earlier in the introduction. Sociability was chosen based on the need to identify a construct that could possibly serve as a moderating variable between "personality" and "social media adoption/usage." Sociability is an aspect of a personality characteristic and a significant reason for social media adoption (see examples Cheek & Buss, 1981; Leung & Wei, 1998; Zolkepli & Kamarulzaman, 2011; Chan, 2011; McCrae & John, 1992). Based on this idea, a person who is not either sociable or willing to socialize, is unlikely to adopt or passively adopt a social media platform. Based on these insights, an individual whose personality constitute a high level of sociability is likely to adopt social media platform and vice-versa.

In this section, each concept and how they relate are discussed. The discussions are on:

1. The concept of personality. Here the Five-Factor Model will be introduced and explained.
2. Sociability
3. The relationship between personality and sociability
4. The relationship between personality and social network adoption.

Personality

The American Psychology Association defines personality as the "individual differences in characteristics of thinking, feeling and behaving" (APA, 2018). This definition is used in this chapter. Over the years, many personality traits have been identified and classified by several psychologists. However, the personality traits of interest to this chapter are the so-called "Five-Factor model" developed by two research teams led by Paul Costa and Robert R. McCrae in the 1970s ((Laher, 2013). These personality characteristics are neuroticism, agreeableness, openness-to-experience, conscientiousness and extraversion (McCrae & John, 1992). Extraversion, Agreeableness and Openness – to – experience are interpersonal traits. Conscientiousness and neuroticism are not, but they indirectly influence interpersonal relationships.

These personality characteristics can also be identified by their personality characteristics that are opposite to those mentioned in the "Five-Factor model." As an example, the opposite of extraversion is introversion, and the opposite of agreeableness is disagreeableness, etc. A person does not possess one personality trait or personality characteristic. Rather they could possess different traits, but obviously one trait will be dominant, while some other traits could exist at different degrees (McCrae & John, 1992).

The Five-Factor model or personality taxonomy serve as a theoretical framework for analysing the personalities of the female respondents presented in this chapter. The description of these traits is as follows:

1. **Neuroticism:** In the Five-Factor model, neuroticism denotes physical characteristics that are expressed by being highly emotionality, impulsiveness, fear and anger (Costa & McCrae, Influence of Extraversion and Neuroticism of Subjective well-Being: Happy and Unhappy People, 1980). Such individuals are easily hurt. They are generally anxious, express self-pity, tensed, touchy, unstable, and always worry (McCrae & John, 1992).

2. **Agreeableness:** Denote the ability to get along with others. Persons with this trait are appreciative, forgiving, generous, kind, sympathetic, and trusting (McCrae & John, 1992).
3. **Openness:** In the Five-Factor model, Openness actually denotes openness-to-experience. This is a personality trait that denotes that the individual is able and willing to explore live outside the confines of routine or social inhibitions. It also denotes individuals who are willing to accept change and adapt to inevitable social changes (McCrae & Costa, Conceptions and correlates of openness to experience, 1997). Persons with this trait exhibit a high level of curiosity, and the desire to explore, be it intellectually or otherwise. The variance in the degree of openness to experience correlates with the level of curiosity and mental independence possessed by an individual. According to McCrae and Costa (1992), people with these personality traits are often artistic, curious, imaginative, insightful, original and enjoy wider interests. The opposite personality characteristics or trait is closeness- to-experience or as McCrae and Costa (1997) puts it - someone who doesn't deviate from laid down rules and not too willing to accept inevitable social changes.
4. **Conscientiousness:** In the Five-Factor model, this concept denotes traits that are related to the degree to which an individual is organized and diligent (Ross, Orr, Sisic, Arseneault, Simmering, & Orr, 2009). They are described in the model as efficient, organised, planful, reliable, responsible and thorough (McCrae & John, 1992). These individuals could sometimes exhibit some level of closeness-to-experience. And some could possess a degree of openness to experience due to the fact that they are open to adapting new forms of social awareness. But they may not push to go beyond the boundaries created by society. They thrive in order.
5. **Extraversion:** Extraversion refers to people who are mostly extroverts. They are very sociable, they possess tempo and vigor (Costa & McCrae, Influence of Extraversion and Neuroticism of Subjective well-Being: Happy and Unhappy People, 1980). In the Five-Factor Model, they are described as active, assertive, energetic, enthusiastic outgoing, and talkative. The opposite personality characteristic is introversion.

The concept "sociability" is described in the next sub-section.

Sociability

In the previous sub-section, an attempt was made to describe the concept of personality from the perspective of psychology. This section provides an overview on the concept "sociability." The concept of sociability is discussed because the primary aim of social media networks, as mentioned earlier, is to promote sociability (See Hughes, Rowe, Batey, & Lee, 2012). The concept of sociability as used in this chapter denotes the tendency to enjoy the company of others (see Cheek & Buss, 1981).

In the Five-Factor model, sociability is an adjective associated with extraversion (McCrae & John, 1992). The concept is not an adjective for extraversion, it also has a strong correlation to extraversion (see Ferrari & Guerrero, 2018; Harari, Thompson, & Viswesvaran, 2018; Hampson, Andrews, & Barckley, 2007). But this does not imply that persons with other personality traits are devoid of sociability. Persons, who are agreeable, conscientious and exhibit openness to experience do possess some level of sociability- though not as high as extraversion (George & Zhou, 2001).

Although conscientiousness and neuroticism are not interpersonal personality characteristics, persons with such traits do possess some level of sociability. As an example, persons with Neuroticism do adopt social media (See Whaite, Shensa, Sidani, Colditz, & Primack, 2018; Ross, Orr, Sisic, Arseneault,

Simmering, & Orr, 2009). But their level of interaction on social media is either very low or passive. However the degrees of sociability exhibited by individuals with these personality traits could be of a high or low but not totally absent. In the next sub-section, an attempt is made to juxtapose the different personality characteristics and their perceived level of sociability. This scale served as the bases for determining the level of sociability based on the personality characteristics exhibited by the respondents.

Personality and the Level of Sociability

Based on the description of each personality characteristic identified in the Five-Factor model by McCrae and John (1992), the level of sociability of persons with each dominant personality characteristics can be determined. The figure below is an attempt at this extraction – determining the level of sociability with persons with each dominant physical characteristic.

As seen in the Figure 2, people with the dominant physical characteristics of extraversion, from a sociability point of view can be termed "social butterflies." They possess little to no inhibition towards being sociable and show no concern for privacy (Junglas, Johnson, & Spitzmuller, 2008). If they possess some level of agreeableness, then the sociability index is bound to go up. Hence, sociability exhibited by such a dominant physical characteristic (extraversion) can be deemed the highest.

Figure 2. Personality - Sociability scale

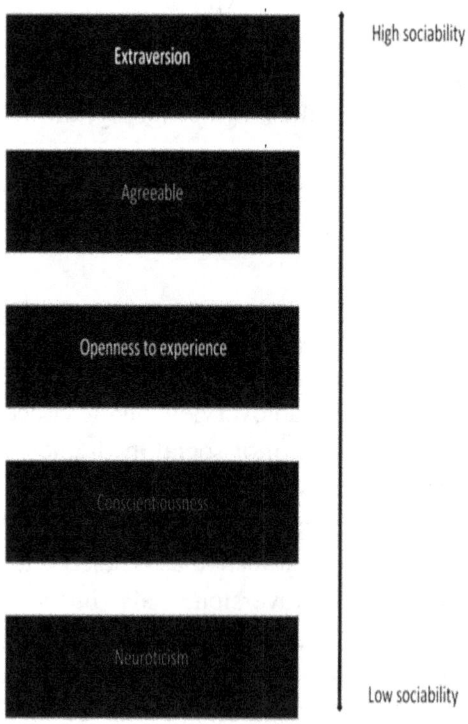

The sociability level below extraversion on the sociability scale as seen in the figure 2 is agreeableness. This characteristic is described as a dimension of interpersonal behaviour (Costa, McCrae, & Dye, 1991). Persons that are possess this characteristic are open to being social. They may not necessarily go out of their way to be social, unless they possess a high degree of extraversion. However, they possess the interpersonal skills towards sustaining a good relationship as opposed to people who are or become disagreeable.

The sociability level below agreeability, as seen in Figure 2, is openness to experience. Openness-to-experience, unlike Extraversion and Agreeability is not a pure interpersonal characteristic. But it points to how such persons can be identified from the exterior (Junglas, Johnson, & Spitzmuller, 2008). The same could be said of conscientiousness and neuroticism. However, one can deduce how these characteristics can influence interpersonal relationships – assuming. The level sociability of persons with high openness to experience cannot be pegged as either very high or very low. They can be termed moderate. This is because such individuals are not only receptive to various forms of experience but their structure of consciousness is highly absorptive (McCrae, 1994). Therefore, persons with a high level of this personality are obviously going to be socially interactive. But their interest will not be in making friends with everybody or working to maintain friendship. Rather their interest will be in socializing with people they can learn from and be inspired. They may maintain few or no close friends but have many acquaintances because they also try to protect their privacy (Junglas, Johnson, & Spitzmuller, 2008). If persons who are open to experience also possess extraversion and agreeableness or both as complementary traits, then their sociability will obviously increase.

The next level of sociability below openness to experience, as seen in Figure 2, is conscientiousness. People who are conscientious are governed by constraints which provide discipline in their life (Costa, McCrae, & Dye, 1991). Conscientious persons are well organized and purposeful. This also plays a role in their level of sociability and who they chose to socialize with. They are able to create a limit as to who they allow into their circle of friendship and who to avoid. They will value privacy to enable them concentrate as well as create time for themselves. This assumption is based on the fact that research shows that people who are conscientious do have concern for privacy (Junglas, Johnson, & Spitzmuller, 2008).

The final level of sociability below conscientiousness, as seen in Figure 2, is neuroticism. The description of this personality trait by McCrae and John (1991) points to people that are prone to emotional wounds. People that lack emotional stability. These persons might naturally want to become a "social butterfly" but are often plagued with the fear of being hurt. On the other hand, the attributes that describes such a character also indicate that few persons would want to tag along with them. This implies that their social circle will be small, and it will consist of those who can accommodate the person's neurotic behaviour.

Based on these characterizations, a person could assume that if a person possesses such any of these traits as a dominant trait, the person's level of sociability can be determined. However, the dominance of these traits could vary in an individual due to the aging process or external influence from the circumstances of life. The variance could be temporal or permanent. This implies that; our level of sociability is not necessarily a constant. It can fluctuate depending on circumstance and context. This obviously could affect our relationship with social media and ICTs in general.

Having established the relationship between personality and context, in the next section, we will identify selected literature that points to the relationship between personality and social media/ICT usage.

Personality and Social Media Usage

Though this chapter advocates for more research on the influence of technology and ICT adoption, it does not overlook existing related research on the issue. Actually, there is a piece of literature advocating for such research (see Devaraj, Easley, & Crant, 2008). There is literature that is indicates that personality is a reason why people accept or reject technology (see Nov & Ye, 2008). In a further research in this light, the Technology Acceptance Model (TAM) has been critiqued for not including personality, based on the Five-Factor model, as a determinant towards technology adoption (See Svendsen, Johnsen, Almås-Sørensen, & Vittersø, 2011). The research indicated that traits such as emotional stability (opposite of neuroticism) has a direct influence on behavioural intentions. It further noted that extraversion has an influence on "perceived ease of use" and "perceived usefulness"; while openness to experience, emotional stability and conscientiousness do have direct influences on "perceived ease of use".

However, within the context of this chapter, some literature makes points to the relationship between personality, based on the Five-Factor model and the different ways in which social media platforms are used. The first example is the correlation between personality traits such as neuroticism, agreeableness and extraversion and self-expression on Facebook (Seidman, 2013). The second example is the correlation between personality and motivation to use Facebook (Ross, Orr, Sisic, Arseneault, Simmering, & Orr, 2009). The research reported that neurotics preferred to post on walls but share nothing intimate; persons who were open to experience were more active in using the tools on Facebook to socialize; and persons with extraversion though very social on Facebook, did not use Facebook as a "substitute for real-world interactions." A third example is the correlation between social media usage, personality and social isolation. The case was among young adults in the United States (Whaite, Shensa, Sidani, Colditz, & Primack, 2018). The social media platforms represented in this study were more than those mentioned in the previous studies (examples 1 and 2). The social media platforms used for the study were Facebook, Twitter, Google+, YouTube, LinkedIn, Instagram, Pinterest, Tumblr, Vine, snapchat, and Reddit. Their sample size was 1768, aged 19-32. The study reported that persons who possess extraversion and agreeableness were at less odds to be socially isolated online. However, persons with neuroticism and low conscientiousness were more likely to become socially isolated online.

The literature cited so far all point to the idea that personality does affect social media and social network adoption, continued usage and the level of socialization on such a platform. Persons with any of the personality traits represented in the Five-Factor model will use social networks differently. These set of literature add a bit of credence to the advocacy made in this chapter. What literature lacks includes how this relationship affects the gender and digital divide. In addition, very few of these studies do focus on the effect on this relationship on the decision to adopt or reject ICT or specifically social media. Hence, there is need for more research. However, the literature examples cited points to the fact there is a relationship between personality and social media and ICT adoption in general; at least within the context and environment where the study was conducted.

METHODOLOGY

Although the ideas promoted on this chapter are not based on empirical research, an exploratory research was adopted for the purpose of identifying practical supporting examples. Before proceeding, it is important to indicate that the data used in this chapter were meant for another research. In the process of analysing that data a surprise finding was made. The surprise finding was further analysed and presented in this chapter. Therefore, the methodology section is divided into 2. The first sub-section provides an overview of the methodology utilized for the original research. The second sub-section provides a description of the methodology used in this chapter.

Methodology of the Original Research

The original aim of the research was to understand the reason more people are adopting WhatsApp. This is because recently WhatsApp has experienced astronomical growth in the number of its subscribers –expanding its user base to 1.5 billion users in the first quarter of 2018 (see Chaffey, 2018; Table 5 in the appendix section). As seen in Table 5 in the appendix section, they are the third largest social media platform globally. In addition, there were questions aimed at understanding their pattern of using mobile Internet and other social media platform.

To facilitate the exploratory research, a semi-structured questionnaire with 26 questions was developed using Google forms and distributed online. In addition to the anonymous online distribution, snowball sampling method was also utilized, as friends were asked to assist in the distribution of the Google form links to their friends.

The structured bit of the original research was a questionnaire designed based on the Technology Acceptance Model (TAM). *TAM is not used as the theoretical approach in this chapter*. However, the Technology Acceptance Model posits that the perceived usefulness and the perceived ease of use of a technology are the variables that influence the behavioural intention of a user to either use or reject a technology (Davis, 1985). The unstructured bit was designed to provide an insight into the personal profile of the respondents, the type of mobile phones they use, the network technology they subscribe to for internet access, their frequency of WhatsApp usage, what they use WhatsApp for, their usage pattern of other social media platform, their usage pattern of other messenger applications, Their usage pattern of mobile telephone, their usage pattern of mobile Internet services, technology savviness and the role of network effect in their adoption of WhatsApp.

Majority of the respondents to the questionnaire were men. However, 4 of the respondents were female. 3 of them from Brazil and one from Jordan. The 3 Brazilians were friends to a colleague who forwarded the questionnaire to the respondents. This was a coincidental even and not planned. This was useful as there was a means of validating the observation, which is explained later. The table below presents the age, country and occupation of the respondents. It was easy to use the middle man to get more information that validated the assessment made on the women.

Table 1. The respondents

Respondent	Occupation	Age	Country
1	Economist	33	Brazil
2	Lawyer/PhD fellow	31	Brazil
3	Economist/PhD fellow	36	Brazil
4	Student	21	Jordan

Source. Field data (Williams, 2018)

The respondent are numbered based on whose answer was received first. The idea of evaluating the responses using the Technology Acceptance Model was postponed till one could gather a sizable sample size.

Methodology Used for Data Analysis Presented in this Chapter

An exploratory qualitative approach was adopted as the methodological basis for this chapter. The worldview used as a foundation for this research is the interpretivist paradigm. The responses from the 4 questionnaires were read thoroughly. Answers to selected questions that denoted sociability were extracted. Notes on impressions that led to the conclusion on their perceived sociability (both online and offline) were documented. The notes are presented in Table 2 in the next section. Before proceeding to the next level of analysis, the friend to the three Brazilians, mentioned earlier, verified the initial (online and offline) assessments of each respondent. These assessments are identified as "second opinion" is seen in Table 2. Based on the assessments, a thematic analysis of the relevant responses was conducted to identify the personality and the level of extraversion in each respondent. This assessment was guided by the "Five-Factor Model". The process was as follows:

Step 1 - The Identification of Implied Meanings of Responses: For each relevant answer which denoted sociability, implied meaning of the answer within the context of the question asked were derived. For example, if a person is a smart phone user, this implied that the person was curious and probably open-to-experience. But it also implied that the person "moving the times technologically". So the phrase "moving with the times" was adopted as an implied meaning. This was an attempt to expand on the answers chosen in the question in order to aid the coding process.

Step 2 - Coding of the Implied Meanings: Personality based adjectives and phrases which embodied the implied meanings were used as codes. And how these codes were derived was also heavily influenced by data on their sociability as expressed in Table 2, their occupation and the second opinion. For example as seen in Table 3, respondent 1 is not a frequent user of WhatsApp. In order to provide a code for that art of the answer, one had to also consider that she is an economist and she uses WhatsApp to communicate with co-workers only. WhatsApp is used for communicating and socializing. But she chose the communication bit. As seen in Table 3, the implied meaning is that "*Able to delay social gratification*", the adjective used as code to embody the implied meaning and personality is that she is "plan full". That presents a nutshell on how the coding process was executed.

Step 3 - Dominant Personality Identification: This is presented in Table 3, the derived codes were matched with the "Five-Factor Model" to determine the dominant personalities. The framework in McCrae and John (1992) was use as the guide.

Step 4 - Determination of the Level of Extraversion: The dominant personality of each respondent was matched to the personality- sociability scale presented in Figure 2. Respondents that possessed one personality type were placed on the scale easily and the level of extraversion determined as explained in the section "personality and the level of sociability". Personalities that possessed no clear dominant personality were assessed in two ways. If the individual possessed a personality that is interpersonal and one which is not, then the emphasis is placed on the non-interpersonal trait and judged using the personality-sociability scale in Figure 2. The person's overall extraversion could be termed low if the person is possesses a bit of neuroticism or introversion. If a person is conscientious or emotionally stable and possess any of the other positive interpersonal traits, the extraversion is termed medium. But the person possessed dominant interpersonal traits. They you have "very high" if the person possess mostly extraversion, Agreeableness and Openness-to-Experience; "High", if the person possesses a Extraversion and Agreeableness or extraversion and openness to experience and "moderately high", if a person possess mostly agreeableness and Openness-to-Experience.

Step 5 - Outline Plausible Relationships: The final step was to summarise the findings in order to identify plausible relationships between personality and social media adoption.

The findings are relayed in the next section.

FINDINGS

Sociability Level of Each Respondent

As seen in Table 2, the first impression on respondent 1 was that, she has some element of self-discipline. The self–discipline she possesses offline is transferred online. Her adoption of social media is based on necessity which is linked to her job, and she is a very passive user. The confirmation from her acquaintance was that she was a private person, and this has been transferred online as well. Respondent 2 is evaluated as being social. She is social offline and online. She is not only social on WhatsApp and Facebook, but also in her usage of the mobile phone. She did not know how WhatsApp worked, but once she knew it will enhance her sociability, she adopted it. The second opinion from her acquaintance is that she is very friendly. This also reflects on her high social engagement on social media. Respondent 3 was also evaluated as being social. However, she is not too engaged on social media. If she was compared to respondent 1 and 2, she would be deemed in between. It seems she occasionally enjoys using social media to keep in touch with her social contacts. Respondent 4 was identified as very social among the 4. She was the youngest of the respondents and she was highly engaged both on social media and online, compared to the other respondents.

Personality and Level of Extraversion of Each Respondent

Based on this outcome represented in Table 2, the thematic analysis was conducted. The results of the thematic analysis are represented in Table 3. In summary, the following plausibility was identified for each respondent.

Respondent 1 was identified as an individual with a low level of extraversion. There could also be elements of conscientiousness, introversion and being disagreeable in her personality traits. However, in another light, assuming there was no second opinion on her personality, one could assume that the respondent was an introvert. It could be assumed further that her introversion offline actually influenced her activities on social media and online in general. But with respect to adopting high speed internet, she is enthusiastic. There could be an element of being open to experience which fuels this enthusiasm. Or it could be that she is generally conscientious and the technology supports her work.

Respondent 2 plausibly possesses a high level of extraversion. There are elements of agreeableness in her which enables her to maintain trusted friendships via WhatsApp chat and the posting on Facebook.

Table 2. Sociability level of each respondent

Respondent	Questions	Responses	First Impression*	Second Opinion	Sociability Scale on Social Media**
1	Country?	Brazil	A self- disciplined person	A private person	Low
	Frequency of WhatsApp usage?	occasionally			
	Why Use WhatsApp?	Communication with co-workers			
	Engagement on Social Media?	Least engaged			
	Did you know how to use WhatsApp before adopting it?	Yes			
	Did you know how to use WhatsApp before adopting it?	Computer savvy			
	What made you subscribe to WhatsApp?	Communication with co-workers			
	Which Features on WhatsApp influenced your adoption?	Non			
	What do you use mobile phone for?	-			
	Mobile Internet usage?	Least engaged			
2	Country?	Brazil	Frequent user	A very friendly person	High
	Frequency of WhatsApp usage?	Uses WhatsApp Multiple times a day			
	Why use WhatsApp?	Primarily to Chat with friends			
	Engagement on social Media?	Very engaged on Facebook and Facebook messenger			
	Did you know how to use WhatsApp before adopting it?	No			
	What made you subscribe to WhatsApp?	• It was easy to communicate with friends • All her friends use WhatsApp • Communication with co-workers • Communication with family • Everybody talks about WhatApp • I can communicate for many hours at no cost			
	Which Features on WhatsApp influenced your adoption?	• Chat			
	What do you use mobile phone for?	• Calling friends, • Reading news online • Viewing postings on Facebook			
	Internet usage?	• Using Whatsapp, • Calling friends • Downloading from the Internet, • Reading news online • Viewing and posting on Facebook • Car bicycle navigation • Traffic information.			

continued on following page

Table 2. Continued

Respondent	Questions	Responses	First Impression*	Second Opinion	Sociability Scale on Social Media**
3	Country?	Brazil	Social but net very active on social media	A social person	Medium
	Frequency of WhatsApp usage?	Multiple times a week			
	Why use WhatsApp?	• Chatting with friends • Voice calling			
	Engagement on social Media?	Not too engaged on Facebook			
	Did you know how to use WhatsApp before adopting it?	Yes			
	What made you subscribe to WhatsApp?	• It is cheaper to communicate on WhatsApp • All my friends use WhatsApp • Communications with family • It is a reliable means of sending messages • I can communicate for many hours at no cost			
	Which Features on WhatsApp influenced your adoption?	• Chat • Video calling • Voice calling			
	What do you use your mobile phone for?	• Calling friends • SMS to friends • Downloading online • Reading news online • Listening to Music • Playing games • Car/cycle navigation			
	Mobile Internet usage?	• Using WhatsApp • Calling friend • Download online • Reading news • Playing games • Car/bicycle navigation			

continued on following page

Table 2. Continued

Respondent	Questions	Responses	First Impression*	Second Opinion	Sociability Scale on Social Media**
4	Country?	Jordan	Very social	-	Very social
	Frequency of WhatsApp usage?	Multiple times a day			
	Why use WhatsApp?	Chat with friends			
	Engagement on social Media?	Very engaged on Facebook, Viber, skype etc			
	Did you know how to use WhatsApp before adopting it?	Yes			
	What made you subscribe to WhatsApp?	I was influenced by the features provided by WhatsApp			
	Which Features on WhatsApp influenced your adoption?	• Chat • Video calling • Voice calling • Sharing pictures • Sharing videos • Broadcasting			
	What do you use your mobile phone for?	• Calling friends • Sending SMS to friends • Reading news online • Listening to music • Viewing and posting on Facebook			
	Mobile Internet usage?	• Using WhatsApp • Calling friends • Sending SMS • Downloading from the internet • Streaming movies • Listening to music • Playing games • Viewing and posting on Facebook • Car/bicycle navigation • Traffic information • Planning trips • Event planning			

Source. Field data (Williams, 2018)

*First impression implies the impression the researcher had when analysing the data

**This scale is with respect to the four respondents and not a general scale measuring sociability on social media

Table 3. Personality and the level of extraversion of each respondent

Respondent	Question	Answer	Implied Meaning	Code	Theme (s) (Personality (s))	Level of Extraversion
1	Country	Brazil				Low Extraversion
	What type of smart phone do you use?	Smart phone	Moving with the times technologically	Enthusiasm		
	What network do you use?	4G	Moving with the times technologically	Enthusiasm		
	How often do you use WhatsApp?	Occasionally	Not very communicative	Low enthusiasm	Introversion/disagreeable	
	What do you use WhatsApp for most?	No answer		No activity	Introversion	
	*Which WhatsApp Services do you consider most useful?	**(All on the not useful scale)** None	Services not useful to her	Impractical	Conscientious	
	What else do you use your mobile phone for?	Other things	Not self-indulgent	Reliable (possibly)	Conscientious	
	How often do you use the following services on WhatsApp? • Chat • Video calling • Voice calling • Sharing pictures • Sharing Videos	• Once a week • Once a week • Once a week • Once a week • Once a week	Able to delay social gratification	Plan full	Conscientious	
2	Country	Brazil				High level of Extraversion
	What type of mobile phone do you use?	Smart phone	Moving with the times technologically	Enthusiasm		
	What network do you use?	3G	Moving with the times technologically	Enthusiasm		
	How often do you use WhatsApp?	Multiple times a day	Very communicative	Highly conversable	Agreeableness/ Extraversion	
	What do you use WhatsApp for most?	Chatting with friends	Values instant/almost instant feedback in communication	Very active	High extraversion	
	*Which WhatsApp Services do you consider most useful?	**(All on the most useful scale)** • Chatting with friends • Sharing pictures • Sharing videos	Adopts some means needed for communication	Moderately active	Moderate Extraversion	
	What else do you use your mobile phone for?	• Calling friends • Reading news on the Internet • Viewing and posting on Facebook • Car/bicycle Navigation	Enjoys socializing, being entertained	Enthusiasm	High Extraversion	
	How often do you use the following services on WhatsApp? • Chat • Video calling • Voice calling • Sharing pictures • Sharing Videos	• Multiple times a day • Once a week • Once a week • Multiple times a day • Once a day	Selectively socially engaged	Active	Extraversion	

continued on following page

Table 3. Continued

Respondent	Question	Answer	Implied Meaning	Code	Theme (s) (Personality (s))	Level of Extraversion
3	Country					Medium level of Extraversion
	What type of smart phone do you use?	Smart phone	Moving with the times technologically	Enthusiasm		
	What network do you use?	3G	Moving with the times technologically	Enthusiasm		
	How often do you use WhatsApp?	Multiple times a week	Communicative	Conversable	Extraversion	
	What do you use WhatsApp for most?	Chatting with friends	Values instant/almost instant feedback in communication	Active	Agreeable/ Extraversion	
	*Which WhatsApp Services do you consider most useful?	(**All on useful scale**) • Chatting with friends • Voice calling • Sharing pictures • Sharing videos • Broadcasting	Adopts some means needed for communication	Moderately active	Extraversion	
	What else do you use your mobile phone for?	• Calling friends • Sending SMS. • Download from the Internet. • Reading news online • Listening to music. • Playing games on my phone. • Car/bicycle navigation	Confident in herself (she can socialize as well as keep herself entertained)	Self esteem	Emotional stability	
	How often do you use the following services on WhatsApp? • Chat • Video calling • Voice calling • Sharing pictures • Sharing Videos	• Multiple times a week • Once a week • Once a week • Once a week • Once a week	Prioritizes her time	Organized (likely)	Conscientious	

continued on following page

Table 3. Continued

Respondent	Question	Answer	Implied Meaning	Code	Theme (s) (Personality (s))	Level of Extraversion
4	Country	Jordan				Very High level of Extraversion
	What type of mobile phone do you use?	Smart phone	Moving with the times technologically	Enthusiasm		
	What network do you use?	4G	Moving with the times technologically	Enthusiasm		
	How often do you use WhatsApp?	Multiple times a day	Very communicative	Highly Conversable	Agreeable/ Extraversion	
	What do you use WhatsApp for most?	Chatting with friends	Values instant/almost instant feedback in communication	Very Active	High Extraversion	
	*Which WhatsApp Services do you consider most useful?	**(All on most useful scale)** • Chatting with friends • Video calling • Voice calling Sharing pictures • Broadcasting events, message etc.	Adopts every means to facilitate communication.	Very Active	High Extraversion	
	What else do you use your mobile phone for?	• Calling friends • Sending SMS • Reading news online • Listening to Music • Viewing and posting on Facebook	Enjoys socializing and being entertained	Enthusiasm	High Extraversion	
	How often do you use the following services on WhatsApp? • Chat • Video calling • Voice calling • Sharing pictures • Sharing Videos	• Multiple times a day • Multiple times a week • Multiple times a week • Multiple times a week • Multiple times a week	High engagement on WhatsApp	Active	Extraversion	

Source. Field data (Williams, 2018)

*Respondents were to choose from a scale of 1-10. 10 being Very useful and 1 being not useful. 1-2 (not useful), 3-4(not very useful), 5-6 (moderately useful), 7-8 (useful), 9-10 (very useful).

However, her level of extraversion is not very high. This could be circumstantial, because as a PhD fellow, she may have to prioritize her time. Or it could be that she prefers ongoing conversations enabled by the chat functionality as opposed to time limited conversation enabled by the voice and video call functionalities. Whatever could be the case, she is quite active and engaged on social media platforms using the chat functionality.

Respondent 3, plausibly possess a medium level of extraversion. She possesses some elements of emotional stability (no self-pity), Extraversion, agreeableness and conscientiousness. She is sociable, but she is also seemed to be content with herself. This led to the belief that she possesses an element of self-esteem and that she knows what she wants per-time. This leads her to keep a select group of friends she could keep in touch with. And just as respondent 2 she prefers chatting with her social contacts using WhatsApp when she has the time to do so.

Respondent 4 plausibly possesses a very high level of extraversion. Although there was no variable that indicated Openness of experience, she could likely possess a great deal of the trait. That is why she is graded "very high" However, she also possesses high levels of extraversion and plausible agreeability. She is very active on social media and very open to exploring the different functionalities on social media as seen in the case of WhatsApp.

However, an interesting part of this finding was that the four respondents were sort of enthusiastic in the adoption of high speed Internet. However, what they use the connectivity for varied, as indicated in Table 3.

The Relationship Between Personality and Social Media Usage and Adoption

Based on the findings made so far, it was evident that respondents who were judged to possess a high level of extraversion adopted, accepted, and used social media. Respondents with low extraversion, adopted, had no interest in social media and became either passive or non-users of social media. It was also evident that this pattern was seen with respect to the adoption pattern for mobile internet services. The reason is likely that mobile Internet services also supports sociability. The summary of the findings is presented in Table 4.

As seen in the table above, based on the observations made, there is a plausible correlation between personality and the adoption of social media and mobile Internet services. However, a more concrete research is needed to prove these hypothesis. Be, that as it may, this is an example supporting the advocacy for research into the relationship between personality and social media adoption.

DISCUSSION

The surprise findings presented in this chapter are suggestive of the possible effect of personality affecting the adoption of social media adoption. But as it has been mentioned in this chapter, there is the need for a concrete research to determine the correlations between personality and social media adoption and similarly for ICTs. Such a research could result in potential contributions to practice, theories on personality and literature on both personality and the adoption of ICTs.

Table 4. Plausible relationship between Personality and social media adoption

Respondent	Level of Sociability	Perceived Personality	Level of Extraversion	Adoption of WhatsApp, Other Social Media and Mobile Internet
1	Low	Conscientious, Introversion, Disagreeable	Low	Passive/non-existent user
2	High	Extraversion, Agreeable	High	Frequent user
3	medium	Medium Extraversion, Agreeable Conscientious, Emotionally stable,	Medium	Moderate user
4	Very high (very social)	High Extraversion, Agreeable, (Possible Openness-to-Experience)	Very high	Always online (Super user)

Source. Field data (Williams, 2018)

However, if the plausibility identified in this chapter were to be proven true, then it could be said that one of the major reasons for women not adopting social media platforms is as a result of their individual dominant personality types. This would then result in a rethink into how initiatives aimed at bridging the digital gender divide is approached. Areas where there is the need for a rethink are in literature and in practice. Currently, in literature, when the digital gender divide is discussed, women are often identified based on their economic, social, cultural, and environmental profiles. These profiles provide insight into the external variables that inhibit women from adopting ICTs. The approach to dealing with the ICT gender divide from the practical point of view is not different from literature. Actually, different agencies such as the UN, OECD, GSMA and developmental agencies such as Plan International and Women ICT Frontier Initiative, etc., also rely on findings from literature. Most of these agencies such as the GSMA do conduct their own assessment but they also arrive at similar conclusions as found in literature. The rethinking will involve accessing the impact of the individual's personality and how it affects her, when selecting ICT services and platforms. The insights from such an investigation could also reveal potential means and ways of solving the problem. Furthermore the results from the rethinking will obviously affect how ICT gender divide policies are crafted; how development agencies handle the diffusion of ICTs; and how ICT companies approach the development of their products to a target market, etc.

Another reason why the rethinking is important is because; as the divergence of ICT technologies and services continue, there will be one of two outcomes. One outcome will be the growing digital gender divide which we experience today (See Plan International, 2018; ITU, 2017) or the shrinking of the gender divide, which we hope for. But if one could look into the future, based on the emerging technologies powered by Artificial Intelligence (AI) and the Internet of Things (IoT), we will still experience a diverging digital gender divide. This is because of the lack of use cases that cater for women in developing countries. This implies that most women will stick to basic communication services, if it does not become extinct. And if the basic communications services do become extinct and there is no relevant use cases which cater for their needs. Then these women are unlikely to adopt AI and IoT services. However by understanding the contextual needs and most importantly, the personality of the women in these region useful use cases can be developed. Use cases could be developed for persons with extraversion, agreeableness, openness-to-experience, conscientiousness and neuroticism/emotional stability. These use cases could be cases that enhance their commercial activities, social life, communal life, culture, etc. As seen in the findings, all the respondents were open to adopting new technologies. Respondent 1 and respondent 4 are 4G subscribers. Respondents 2 and 3 are 3G subscribers. However, respondent 1 did not find the services useful due to her personality. Other respondents had varied assessments of the services. Which means respondent 1 probably would prefer a service that aids her job, as an example. So, these personality factors has to be taken into consideration when developing use cases for AI and IoT services for developing countries. Hence, this rethink is important.

These ideas and implications will only be necessary if the hypothesis proves true. If the hypothesis is ignored, there is the possibility that the missing link towards solving the digital gender divide could also be ignored.

CONCLUSION

This aim of this chapter was to advocate research into the correlation between personality and ICT adoption. In a previous chapter write up, it was identified that most women do not adopt ICTs because they do not find the ICT services useful to them in their circumstances. This chapter takes the issue a step further by advocating that personality could also be the reason why some women do not adopt ICTs. This hypothesis is based on a surprise finding presented in this chapter, using social media (in this case WhatsApp) as a case. The surprise finding indicated that the higher the level of extraversion, the higher the likelihood of an individual to adopt social media platforms. The same hypothesis seemed to emerge with respect to a possible correlation between personality and ICT adoption. The empirical sample was too low to make a definitive case/proposition.

From a research perspective though a definitive case was not made, the emerging hypothesis is indicative of a possible correlation. At best, there is a plausible correlation within the hypothesis based on examples presented in this chapter. The plausible correlation can enable contextual research within various female populations. The Five-Factor model need not be the only framework used. The Five-Factor model could be used with any of the ICT adoption models. Or any other theoretical framework on personality could be used with or without the Five-Factor model.

From a practical perspective, the hypothesis provides the opportunity for agencies involved in the diffusion of ICT to women to provide solutions to the existing gender divide on social media and towards ICTs in general. Identifying the personality factors (hereditary or external) influencing the rejection of ICT could be crucial to closing the gender divide. It will further help in reducing social exclusion. If the personality traits are externally or internally (hereditary) influenced, looking for new approaches of delivering the ICT service to suit the social, cultural, political and even religious context might help. But more purposive studies are needed to get this right.

In conclusion, the answer to the question posed earlier in the introductory part of this chapter is that "There is the plausibility that personality does have an influence on ICT (social media inclusive) adoption and rejection by women".

REFERENCES

APA. (2018, June 22). *Personality*. Retrieved from American Psychological Association: http://www.apa.org/topics/personality/

Chaffey, D. (2018, March 28). *Global social media research summary 2018*. Retrieved from Smart Insight: https://www.smartinsights.com/social-media-marketing/social-media-strategy/new-global-social-media-research/

Chan, M. (2011). Shyness, sociability, and the role of media synchronicity in the use of computer-mediated communication for interpersonal communication. *Asian Journal of Psychology*, *14*(1), 84–90.

Cheek, J. M., & Buss, A. H. (1981). Shyness and Sociability. *Journal of Personality and Social Psychology*, *41*(2), 330–339. doi:10.1037/0022-3514.41.2.330

Correa, T., Hinsley, A. M., Bachmann, I., & Gil de Zuniga, H. (2013). Personality and Social Media Use. In E. Li, S. Loh, C. Evans, & F. Lorenzi (Eds.), *Social Media to Engage Consumers* (pp. 41–61). Hershey, PA: IGI Global.

Costa, P. T., & McCrae, R. R. (1980). Influence of Extraversion and Neuroticism of Subjective well-Being: Happy and Unhappy People. *Journal of Personality and Social Psychology*, *38*(4), 668–678. doi:10.1037/0022-3514.38.4.668 PMID:7381680

Costa, P. T. Jr, McCrae, R. R., & Dye, D. A. (1991). Facet Scales for Agreeableness and Conscientiousness: A Revision of the NEO Personality Inventory. *Personality and Individual Differences*, *12*(9), 887–898. doi:10.1016/0191-8869(91)90177-D

Davis, F. (1985). *A technology Acceptance Model for emperically testing new end-user Information Systems: Theory and results*. Cambridge, MA: MIT Sloan School of Management.

Devaraj, S., Easley, R. F., & Crant, J. M. (2008). ResearcResearch note—How Does Personality Matter? Relating the Five-Factor Model to Technology Acceptance and Use. *Information Systems Research*, *19*(1), 93–105. doi:10.1287/isre.1070.0153

Dong, B., & Sivakumar, K. (2017). Customer participation in services: Domain, scope, and boundaries. *Journal of the Academy of Marketing Science*, *45*(6), 944–965. doi:10.100711747-017-0524-y

Fatehkia, M., Kashyap, R., & Weber, I. (2018). Using Facebook ad Data to track the global digital gender gap. *World Development*, *107*, 189–209. doi:10.1016/j.worlddev.2018.03.007

Ferrari, J. R., & Guerrero, M. (2018). My dad, the deacon:" Assessing the personality of married Catholic clergy fathers as predictor of number and gender of children. *Journal of Spirituality in Mental Health*, *20*(2), 185–197. doi:10.1080/19349637.2017.1374113

George, J. M., & Zhou, J. (2001). When openness to experience and conscientiousness are related to creative behavior: An interactional approach. *The Journal of Applied Psychology*, *86*(3), 513–524. doi:10.1037/0021-9010.86.3.513 PMID:11419810

Hampson, S. E., Andrews, J. A., Barckley, M. P., & Peterson, M. (2007). Trait Stability and Continuity in Childhood: Relating Sociability and Hostility to the Five-Factor Model of Personality. *Journal of Research in Personality*, *41*(3), 507–523. doi:10.1016/j.jrp.2006.06.003 PMID:18488082

Harari, M. B., Thompson, H. A., & Viswesvaran, C. (2018). Extraversion and job satisfaction: The role of trait bandwidth and the moderating effect of status goal attainment. *Personality and Individual Differences*, *123*(1), 14–16. doi:10.1016/j.paid.2017.10.041

Helmers, C. (1980). *The Era of the off-the-shelf personal computers (Byte Magazine)*. Retrieved from Archive.org: https://archive.org/stream/byte-magazine-1980-01#page/n7/mode/2up

Hughes, D. J., Rowe, M., Batey, M., & Lee, A. (2012). A tale of two sites: Twitter vs Facebook and the personality indicators of scial media usage. *Computers in Human Behavior*, *28*(2), 561–569. doi:10.1016/j.chb.2011.11.001

IBM. (2018). *The birth of the IBM PC*. Retrieved from IBM: https://www-03.ibm.com/ibm/history/exhibits/pc25/pc25_birth.html

Isaacson, P. (1978). Personal Computing Position paper. *ACM SIGPC*, *1*(2), 5–9. doi:10.1145/1164917.1164919

ITU. (2017). *ITU Facts and Figures 2017*. Geneva: ITU. Retrieved from https://www.itu.int/en/ITU-D/Statistics/Documents/facts/ICTFactsFigures2017.pdf

Junglas, I. A., Johnson, N. A., & Spitzmuller, C. (2008). Personality traits and concern for privacy: An empirical study in the context of location-based services. *European Journal of Information Systems*, *17*(4), 387–402. doi:10.1057/ejis.2008.29

Kaushik, D. (2017, February 23). *Why are the number of female Facebook users more than male users even if total male users of the internet are more than female?* Retrieved from Quora: https://www.quora.com/Why-are-the-number-of-female-Facebook-users-more-than-male-users-even-if-total-male-users-of-the-internet-are-more-than-female

Kay, C. K. (1972). A personal Computer for Children of all Ages. In ACM '72 proceedings of the ACM annual conference (vol. 1). Boston: ACM.

Laher, S. (2013). Understanding the Five-Factor Model and Five-Factor Theory through a South African cultural lens. *South African journal of psychology = Suid-Afrikaanse tydskrif vir sielkunde, 43*(2), 208-221.

Leung, L., & Wei, R. (1998). The gratifications of pager use: Sociability, information- seeking, entertainment, utility, and fashion and status. *Telematics and Informatics*, *15*(4), 253–264. doi:10.1016/S0736-5853(98)00016-1

McCrae, R. R. (1994). Openness to Experience: Expanding the boundaries of Factor V. *European Journal of Personality*, *8*(4), 251–272. doi:10.1002/per.2410080404

McCrae, R. R., & Costa, P. T. (1997). Conceptions and correlates of openness to experience. In R. Hogan, J. Johnson, & S. Briggs (Eds.), Handbook on Personality Psychology (pp. 825-847). Academic Press.

McCrae, R. R., & John, O. P. (1992). An introduction to the Five-Factor Model and its applications. *Journal of Personality*, *60*(2), 175–216. doi:10.1111/j.1467-6494.1992.tb00970.x PMID:1635039

Neely, C. (2018, Jan 29). *Japan's Top Social Media Networks in 2018*. Retrieved from Humble Bunny: http://www.humblebunny.com/japans-top-social-media-networks-2018/

Nov, O., & Ye, C. (2008). Personality and Technology Acceptance: Personal Innovativeness in IT, Openness and Resistance to Change. In *Proceedings of the 41st Annual Hawaii International Conference on System Sciences (HICSS 2008) 7-10 Jan. 2008*. Waikoloa, HI: IEEE. 10.1109/HICSS.2008.348

Pew Research. (2017). *Pew Global*. Retrieved from Gender divide on social media use tilts toward men in developing economies, women in advanced economies: http://www.pewglobal.org/2018/06/19/3-social-network-adoption-varies-widely-by-country/pg_2018-06-19_global-tech_3-03/

Pew Research Center. (2018, February 5). *Social Media Fact Sheet*. Retrieved from Pew Research Center: http://www.pewinternet.org/fact-sheet/social-media/

Plan International. (2018, April 26). *Digital empowerment of girls*. Retrieved from Plan International: https://plan-international.org/sites/default/files/digital_empowerment_of_girls_-_briefing_paper_26_april_2018_-_final.pdf

Poushter, J., Bishop, C., & Chwe, H. (2018, June 19). *Social network adoption varies widely by country*. Retrieved from Pew Research Center: http://www.pewglobal.org/2018/06/19/3-social-network-adoption-varies-widely-by-country/

Ross, C., Orr, E. S., Sisic, M., Arseneault, J. M., Simmering, M. G., & Orr, R. R. (2009). Personality and mtivation associated with Facebook use. *Computers in Human Behavior*, *25*(2), 578–586. doi:10.1016/j.chb.2008.12.024

Rowntree, O. (2018). *Connected Woman: The mobile gender gap report*. GSMA.

Seidman, G. (2013). Self-presentation and belonging on Facebook: How personality influences social media use and motivations. *Personality and Individual Differences*, *54*(3), 402–407. doi:10.1016/j.paid.2012.10.009

Statista. (2018a). *Distribution of Facebook users worldwide as of April 2018, by age and gender*. Retrieved from Statista: https://www.statista.com/statistics/376128/facebook-global-user-age-distribution/

Statista. (2018b, March). *Percentage distribution of Facebook users in Spain in 2017, by gender*. Retrieved from Statista: https://www.statista.com/statistics/774511/distribution-by-gender-from-the-users-from-facebook-in-spain/

Statista. (2018c, January). *Share of users of selected social networks in the United Kingdom (UK) in January 2018, by gender*. Retrieved from Statista: https://www.statista.com/statistics/611848/penetration-of-social-networks-in-the-united-kingdom-by-gender/

Surman, M., Gardner, C., & Ascher, D. (2014). Local Content, Smartphones, and Digital Inclusion. *Innovations: Technology, Governance, Globalization*, *9*(3-4), 63–74. doi:10.1162/inov_a_00217

Svendsen, G. B., Johnsen, J. K., Almås-Sørensen, L., & Vittersø, J. (2011). Personality and technology acceptance: The influence of personality factors on the core constructs of the Technology Acceptance Model. *Behaviour & Information Technology*, *32*(4), 323–334. doi:10.1080/0144929X.2011.553740

Wanga, J. (2016, July 3). *Men and women who operate without mobile phones*. Retrieved from Daily Nation: https://www.nation.co.ke/lifestyle/lifestyle/1214-3277376-76g2y0/index.html

Whaite, E. O., Shensa, A., Sidani, J. E., Colditz, J. B., & Primack, B. A. (2018). Social media use, personality characteristics, and social isolation among young adults in the United States. *Personality and Individual Differences*, *124*(1), 45–50. doi:10.1016/j.paid.2017.10.030

Williams, I. (2015). *Analysis of Public Private Interplay Frameworks in the Development of Rural Telecommunications Infrastructure: A Multi-Case Study*. Aalborg: Aalborg University Press.

Williams, I. (2016). Co-Financing of Bottom-Up Approaches towards Broadband Infrastructure Development: A New Opportunity for Universal Service Funding. *Journal of NBICT*, *1*, 39–64.

Williams, I., Siddi, F., & Kwofie, B. (2016). Public Demand Aggregation as a means of Bridging the ICT Gender Divide. In J. Wilson & N. N. Gapsiso (Eds.), *Overcoming Gender Inequalities through technology Integration* (pp. 123–143). Hershey, PA: IGI Global. doi:10.4018/978-1-4666-9773-7.ch006

York, A. (2017, March 6). *Social Media Demographics to Inform a Better Segmentation Strategy*. Retrieved from Sprout Social: https://sproutsocial.com/insights/new-social-media-demographics/

Zolkepli, I. A., & Kamarulzaman, Y. (2011). Understanding Social Media Adoption: The Role of Perceived Media Needs And Technology Characteristics. *World Journal of Social Sciences*, *1*(1), 188–199.

APPENDIX

Table 5. Most used social media platforms

Social Network/Instant Messengers	Number of Users in Millions (1st Quarter 2018)
Facebook	2 167
YouTube	1 500
WhatsApp	1 300
Facebook Messenger	1 300
WeChat	980
QQ	843
Instagram	800
Tumblr	794
QZone	568
Sina Weibo	376
Twitter	330
Baidu Tieba	330
Skype	300
LInkedIn	260
Viber	260
Snapchat	255
Reddit	250
Line	203
Pinterest	200

Source (Chaffey, 2018)

Chapter 7
Gender and Use of E-Government Services in Turkey:
E-Government in Turkey

Tekin Kose
TED University, Turkey

ABSTRACT

This chapter investigates the relationship between gender and use of e-government services in Turkey. Based on household surveys, probit regression models are estimated to quantify determinants of e-government use for Turkish citizens. Empirical findings imply that there is a gender gap in use of e-government services. Turkish females are less likely to employ e-government tools compared to Turkish males. Household income, education level, being employed, and frequency of internet use are positively correlated with probability of e-government use for Turkish individuals. Finally, age demonstrates negative association with use of online government services. As the individual gets older, probability of using e-government platforms decreases. Thus, the digital divide prevails among Turkish citizens and should be addressed by policymakers.

INTRODUCTION

Advances in information and communication technologies (ICTs) lead to striking changes in daily of individuals, costs and operations management of firms and structure of government services. As the use of internet widens, decision making processes of economic agents are restructured for the online world. In 2016, 3.5 billion people used the internet around the world (ITU, 2017). Thus, businesses and governments adjust their actions and policies to enhance customer and citizen satisfaction levels as well as reduce costs to increase efficiency through adoption of online services. The use of ICTs for public administration and government services is usually referred as 'e-government' (Taipale, 2013). Implementation of e-government projects has the potential to bring variety of benefits. E-government applications would

DOI: 10.4018/978-1-5225-7068-4.ch007

enable governments to easily set up networks and service delivery; provide less costly interaction with citizens; increase transparency, accountability and efficiency of government platforms (Yildiz, 2007).

Many countries employ e-government services for establishment of various public services such as tax filing, employment and business processes, licensing, provision of policy and voting information, fine payment, procurement and law services, public health care services, etc. (Akman, Yazici, Mishra, & Arifoglu, 2005; Gupta, Singh, & Bhaskar, 2016). Provision of public services by online platforms has crucial implications for citizens as well. The electronic government tools provide easy access and convenience for government services and information systems. However, effectiveness of e-government relies on citizens' acceptance and utilization of corresponding services (Carter & Belanger, 2005). In this chapter, determinants of e-government use are analyzed for Turkish case with a special focus on gender.

Various studies investigate the factors influencing use of e-government services by citizens. The literature provides evidence on the relationship between e-government adoption, demographics and socioeconomic variables such as age, gender, education, income, employment status, marital status, trust in government and technology (Belanger & Carter, 2009; Colesca & Dobrica, 2008; Gupta, Singh, & Bhaskar, 2016; Hung, Chang, & Yu, 2006; Reddick, 2005). The earlier findings for the effect of gender on e-government use are mixed. Some studies report that men are more likely to employ online public services (Akman, Yazici, Mishra, & Arifoglu, 2005; Choudrie & Dwivedi, 2005; Venkatesh, Sykes, & Venkatraman, 2014) whereas many researchers find no significant gender differences in adoption of e-government services by citizens (Belanger & Carter, 2009; Colesca & Dobrica, 2008; Reddick, 2005; Taipale, 2013). Thus, this chapter complements the literature by providing further evidence for the association of gender and employment of online public service tools from a developing country.

The author conducts an empirical analysis in order to investigate covariates of e-government use in Turkey. Multiple waves of Information and Communication Technology (ICT) Usage Survey of the Turkish Statistical Institute (TSI, 2015; TSI, 2016) are used to obtain individual level data. Probit estimation framework is employed for regression analysis. Empirical results exhibit that Turkish females are less likely to use e-government services. Household income, education level, being employed and frequency of internet use demonstrate positive associations with probability of using e-government services. However, age is negatively correlated with e-government use in Turkey.

Rest of the chapter first provides analysis of literature in the background section. The next section describes data and estimation methodology. Fourth section presents and discusses findings of the empirical analysis. The last section describes conclusions with policy implications and raises issues for further research.

BACKGROUND

Definition and Aims of E-Government

There are several definitions of e-government used by researchers, governmental and non-governmental organizations. Although they are significantly similar, these definitions may vary with respect to heterogeneities in purposes of offered services and strategies of adopting institutions. A group of definitions focus on online service provisions whereas others emphasize the use of ICTs in government services and processes (OECD, 2003).

The Organisation for Economic Co-operation Development (OECD, 2003, p.23) defines e-government as follows: "the use of information and communication technologies, and particularly the internet, as a tool to achieve better government." In a similar fashion, European Union (EC, 2003, p.7) refers to e-government as "the use of information and communication technologies in public administrations combined with organizational change and new skills in order to improve public services and democratic processes and strengthen support to public policies."

The introduction of e-government gateways by various countries are aimed at improving the quality and delivery of public services as well as citizen's satisfaction. EC (2003) notes that e-government applications helps in the reduction of time costs; enhances cost efficiency and productivity thereby improving accountability and transparency for government services and processes. The use of ICTs in public administration aims to achieve better public services by using fewer resources in the provision of governmental services to both government and citizens. Similarly, OECD (2003) emphasizes that objectives of e-government applications include "improving efficiency in government", "enhancing quality of services", "supporting more effective outcomes" in policy applications, "promoting economic policy objectives", and "improving the overall trust" between government, public administrators and citizens. From the perspective of citizens, time-saving properties, flexibility and ease of access and use of e-government platforms are crucial. Thus, e-government applications have potential to significantly save costs for government and citizens and decrease administrative burdens.

Adoption of E-Government Services by Citizens

As the use of ICTs extends within society, through applications provided by both private and public organizations, so have researchers investigated trends on the adoption of online services. Related literature explores different factors affecting citizens' use of e-government tools across various countries. A branch of literature focuses on properties of e-government applications whereas others consider individual level characteristics of e-government users. Rana et al. (2013) provide excellent literature review and concluded that "perceived usefulness", "perceived ease of use" "trust", "attitude", "subjective norm", "performance expectancy", "effort expectancy", "social influence", "service quality", and "information quality" are significantly associated with citizen adoption of e-government services. Focusing on the latter group of studies, this section analyzes earlier findings for socio-demographic determinants for e-government usage of citizens with great emphasis on gender.

The first of such socio-demographic determinants can be identified using the Diffusion of Innovation Theory. Based on the "Diffusion of Innovations" theory individuals with higher levels of education and income are more likely to adopt new technologies whereas elderly are less likely to adjust for innovations (Dimitrova, & Chen, 2006; Rogers, 2003; Zhang, Xu & Xiao, 2014). Though these determinants are gender inclusive, empirical studies also reveal that there are gender differences in individual behavior with respect to technology adoption (Ilie, Van Slyke, Green, & Hao, 2005; Sanchez-Franco, 2006). Moreover, Morris, Venkatesh and Ackerman (2005) reports that gender differences in the adoption of technology correlates with age of individuals. Hence, it could be said that the gender effect in acceptance of new technology prevails in older ages whereas no gender gap exists among younger individuals.

Furthermore, previous research demonstrates mixed findings in the association of gender with e-government usage. The emergence of these mixed results may be attributed to differences in data collection methods, data analysis frameworks, sample selection processes and characteristics, and cross-country variations in culture and lifestyles. Most researchers find that males are more likely to use e-government tools in various countries. By analyzing results from a questionnaire, Akman et al. (2005) and Voutinioti (2013) show that the gender factor significantly affects the use of e-government services in Turkey and Greece, respectively. Similarly, Choudrie and Dwivedi (2005) identify that the patterns in citizen awareness and use of e-government services are aligned with gender in the United Kingdom. Venkatesh et al. (2014) provide empirical evidence for the gender gap in e-government use from India. Employing a data set from the United States, some researchers show that males are more likely to use e-government services (Bimber, 1999; McNeal, Hale & Dotterweich, 2008; Nam, 2014). Similar gender differences are also reported for Australia and New Zealand by Goldfinch et al. (2009). Moreover, Rodrigues et al. (2016) show that females are more reluctant to employ e-government services than males in the United Arab Emirates. Finally, considering Dubai case, Sarabdeen and Rodrigues (2010) find that there are both similarities and differences between females and males in willingness to use e-government services. On the other hand, some researchers find no significant gender differences in adoption of e-government services by citizens in different countries such as the United States, Romania and Finland (Belanger & Carter, 2009; Colesca & Dobrica, 2008; Reddick, 2005; Taipale, 2013). Similarly, Gauld et al. (2010) report no gender differences in use of e-government measures for Australia and New Zealand, which contradicts Goldfinch et.al (2009). Moreover, Moreno et al. (2013) use a sample from Spain and Sharma (2015) and employs a data set from Oman to show that there are no correlations between gender and e-government adoption.

Despite the mixed findings with respect to the adoption of e-government services along gender lines, there exist research literature analyzing the interaction between e-government usage and other socio-demographic variables such as age, education, income and employment status (Belanger & Carter, 2009; Colesca & Dobrica, 2008; Gupta, Singh, & Bhaskar, 2016; Hung, Chung, & Yu, 2006; Reddick, 2005).

1. **Age:** Empirical evidence about the relationship between e-government use of citizens and age are mixed. Some researchers report that age negatively influences the likelihood towards adopting e-government tools/services (Akman, Yazici, Mishra, & Arifoglu, 2005; Bimber, 1999; Colesca & Dobrica, 2008; Choudrie & Dwivedi, 2005; Goldfinch, Gauld, & Herbison, 2009; Sharma, 2015). In a similar fashion, Gauld et al. (2010) and McNeal, Hale and Dotterweich (2008) reveal that younger persons are more likely to use e-government platforms. However, some studies find no significant effect of age on e-government use (Nam, 2014; Venkatesh, Sykes, & Venkatraman, 2014).
2. **Education:** Previous research establishes a robust positive relationship between use of e-government services and education level of individuals. Akman et al. (2005) and Choudrie and Dwivedi (2005) do show that better education leads to the likelihood to the usage of e-government. In line with these findings, McNeal, Hale and Dotterweich (2008) find that education enhances adoption of e-government services; which is also supported by empirical evidence from other studies (Colesca & Dobrica, 2008; Gauld, Goldfinch, & Horsburgh, 2010; Goldfinch, Gauld, & Herbison, 2009; Nam, 2014; Sipior, Ward, & Connolly, 2011; Venkatesh, Sykes, & Venkatraman, 2014).
3. **Income:** Although Colesca and Dobrica (2008) and Gauld et al. (2010) find no significant relationship between income level and use of e-government tools, other studies provide evidence for positive association of income with adoption of e-government (McNeal, Hale & Dotterweich, 2008; Sipior, Ward, & Connolly, 2011; Venkatesh, Sykes, & Venkatraman, 2014).
4. **Employment Status:** Moreover, Sipior et al. (2011) indicate that employment status significantly affects access to e-government services.

Finally, familiarity with the internet and usage habits do have an on impact e-government adoption by individuals. Some studies report that the frequency of internet usage has a direct correlation with e-government adoption. Researchers reveal that frequent users of the internet are more likely to show intentions of using e-government services (Belanger & Carter, 2009; Carter & Belanger, 2005). However, another line of research finds no significant relationship between e-government adoption and frequency of internet use (Belanger & Carter, 2008; Urbina & Abe, 2017).

Provision of E-Government Services by Government in Turkey

The initial use of internet in Turkey dates back to 1993 and the first online government platform was established for the tax system in 1998 (Kurfali, Arifoglu, Tokdemir, & Pacin, 2017). In order to conform with the "e-Europe Action Plan" of European Commission, "eTransformation" The Turkish project was launched by the 58th Government of Turkey, which was enhanced by 59th Government (Cayhan, 2008; Kurfali, Arifoglu, Tokdemir, & Pacin, 2017). This project had three key aims which are listed below:

1. "Achieving efficiency and effectiveness in eGovernment projects;"
2. "Coordinate information society activities;"
3. "Align its related policies with EU standards in ICT." (EC, 2017, p.14)

The State Planning Organization for Turkey (currently Ministry of Development) led and coordinated the establishment of the e-government project in Turkey. The Turkish government introduced the "e-Government Gateway" platform in 2006. The officially defined principles and objectives of the Turkish e-government transformation project for 2006-2010 are summarized as follows on 27th of February 2003 by the Prime Minister's office:

1. Policies, laws and regulations regarding ICT are to be re-examined and changed, if necessary, so as to comply with those of the EU;
2. The eEurope+ Action Plan, initiated for candidate countries, to be adopted by Turkey;
3. Mechanisms that facilitate participation of citizens in the decision-making process via ICT are to be developed;
4. Transparency and accountability for public management to be enhanced;
5. Good governance principles to be applied in government services through increased use of ICT;
6. Widespread use of ICT to be supported;
7. Public IT projects to be coordinated, monitored, evaluated and consolidated, if necessary, so as to avoid duplication or overlaps;
8. Private sector guidance to be provided in accordance with those principles. Source: (Cayhan, 2008, p.3; EC, 2017, p.14)

The Turkish government keeps enhancing e-government platforms and integrating these platforms within government institutions, private sector and the society. The "Ninth Development Plan (2007 - 2013)" and "Tenth Development Plan (2014 - 2018)" includes strategies on spreading of e-government tools in Turkey. Similarly, the "2016 – 2019 National eGovernment Strategy and Action Plan" is aimed at achieving "integrated", "technological", "participatory", "innovative", and "qualified" e-government ecosystem (EC, 2017). The official e-government platform of Turkey was introduced by the Prime

Figure 1. Use of e-government in Turkey and European Union
Source: Eurostat, 2018

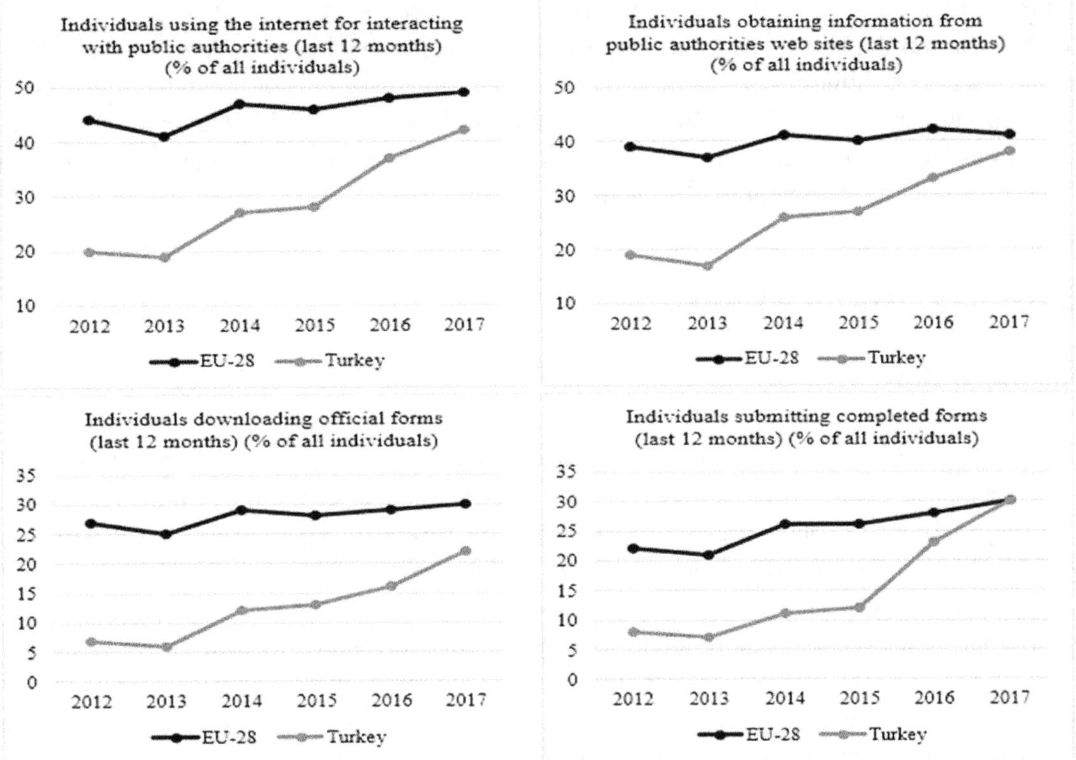

Minister on December 18, 2008. It is currently available through web site: https://www.turkiye.gov.tr/. For citizens, Turkish e-government portal provides variety of services for issues such as health, education, personal information, social security, financial transactions (taxes, fees and fines), traffic and transportation, laws and regulations, etc. Ministry of Transport, Maritime Affairs and Communications manages e-government platforms in Turkey. According to e-Government Gateway of Turkey (2018), there are 36.3 million registered users in e-government system, which provides 2,9828 e-services and 1,161 mobile services.

Figure 1 reveals data indicating the trend of e-government usage in Turkey and European Union (EU) countries. Overall, the e-government adoption rates of e-government by Turkish citizens has an increasing trend and they have been converging towards the EU-28 figures over time. 44% of individuals in Europe interacted with government via online platforms in 2012 whereas this rate for Turkish citizens was only 20%. However, the rate of online interaction with public authorities was 49% for the EU-28 and 42% for Turkey in 2017. Similarly, the rate of online information gathering from public institutions' web sites were 39% and 19% for EU and Turkey in 2012, respectively. The gap between EU and Turkey substantially declined in 2017 as the same figures read 41% and 38%, respectively. In Turkey, only 7% of individuals downloaded official forms whereas that measure for the EU-28 was 27% in 2012. However, the latest data shows that Turkish citizens are adopting e-government fast and the percentage of individuals who downloaded online forms increased to 22% whereas this value for EU-28 was 30% in 2017. Finally, 8% of Turkish citizens uploaded forms on the Turkish e-government platform in 2012 whereas 22% of Europeans performed similar tasks. However, this gap diminished over time and 30% of individuals completed online forms in both Turkey and European Union in the year 2017.

According to United Nations (UN, 2016), Turkey is ranked 68th among 194 countries with respect to e-government development index. Ranging from zero to one, this index is based on measures for the "scope and quality of online services", "status of the development of telecommunication infrastructure" and "inherent human capital" (UN, 2016, p.133). With index value of 0.59, Turkey is classified in the "high" indexed group of countries. Thus, data show that Turkey has made rapid progresses in establishment and spread of e-government platforms in last decade.

DATA AND ESTIMATION FRAMEWORK

Data Description

In order to analyze covariates of e-government use in Turkey, this chapter utilizes data sets from the individual level, nationally representative, surveys. Information and Communication Technology (ICT) Usage Survey of Turkey is conducted by Turkish Statistical Institute (TSI). Two recent waves of the survey (2015 and 2016) are used to provide an empirical analysis for the Turkish case. The data sets include individual level variables such as gender, age, education level, employment status, household income and internet usage habits. With more than 40 questions, the ICT surveys cover approximately 40,000 individuals and almost 14,000 households in Turkey. Since many participants do not use the internet, this chapter uses operating samples, which are restricted by internet users up to 13,000 participants.

Table 1 provides frequency measures for computer, internet and e-government usage with respect to gender. First, males are more likely to use computers. For 2016, 49% of males used a computer within last three months whereas 34% of females reported computer usage. In both 2015 and 2016, 57% of female participants reported that they have never used a computer whereas 40% of males have never used computers. Polat (2012) finds that women tend to use the internet less than men in Turkey. Descriptive results of Table 1 are in line with findings of Polat (2012). 51% of females and 34% of males report that they have never used the internet in a 2016 survey. On the other hand, 63% of male participants employed the internet tools within last-three months in 2016 whereas this measure for females was 46%. Among the internet users, gender differences in the frequency of use are not substantial. 82% of females and 84% of males were daily users of the internet in 2016.

According to Table 1, the use of e-government services displays an increasing trend. During 2015, 50.9% of females did not employ e-government tools whereas that measure for 2016 was 43.47%. Similarly, the percentage of males who did not engage in e-government online platforms decreased from 43.58% to 34.39% between 2015 and 2016. E-government services are mostly used for obtaining information by Turkish citizens. In 2016, 59.94% of males and 48.38% of females report that they used e-government system to obtain information. For the same year, 23.64% of females and 29.65% of males downloaded official forms from online government resources. The share of females and males who uploaded forms to the e-government gateway of Turkey are 37.25% and 38.13%, respectively. Furthermore, literature focusing on the use of the internet in Turkey report on the time spent on internet activities, the type of internet activities and the purposes for internet usage are significantly associated with gender and other sociodemographic variables (Ak, Koruklu, & Yilmaz, 2013; Akman & Mishra, 2010; Tahiroglu, Celik, Uzel, Ozcan, & Avci, 2008).

Table 1. Gender and computer use in Turkey

	2015				2016			
	Females		Males		Females		Males	
	N	%	N	%	N	%	N	%
Latest Computer Use	12,006	100	10,971	100	13,359	100	11,699	100
Never used	6,845	57.01	4,396	40.07	7,621	57.05	4,713	40.29
More than a year ago	527	4.39	539	4.91	813	6.09	798	6.82
3-months to a year ago	356	2.97	368	3.35	389	2.91	414	3.54
Within last 3-months	4,278	35.63	5,668	51.66	4,536	33.95	5,774	49.35
Latest Internet Use	12,006	100	10,971	100	13,359	100	11,699	100
Never used	6,792	56.57	4,202	38.30	6,838	51.19	3,984	34.05
More than a year ago	243	2.02	252	2.30	223	1.67	224	1.91
3-months to a year ago	221	1.84	242	2.21	140	1.05	139	1.19
Within last 3-months	4,750	39.56	6,275	57.20	6,158	46.10	7,352	62.84
Internet Use Frequency	4,683	100	6,235	100	6,158	100	7,352	100
Less than once a week	313	6.68	352	6.65	351	5.70	374	5.09
At least once week	791	16.89	1,041	16.70	781	12.68	830	11.29
Almost every day	3,579	76.43	4,842	77.66	5,026	81.62	6,148	83.62
E-Government Use	4,904	100	6,477	100	6,298	100	7,491	100
None	2,496	50.90	2,823	43.58	2,738	43.47	2,576	34.39
Obtaining Information	2,278	46.45	3,513	54.24	3,047	48.38	4,490	59.94
Download Form	1,026	20.92	1,637	25.27	1,489	23.64	2,221	29.65
Upload Form	1,006	20.51	1,503	23.21	2,346	37.25	2,856	38.13

Source: TSI (2015, 2016)

The main variable of interest for this chapter is e-government usage by Turkish individuals. There were three "Yes/No" questions related to e-government use in the survey: 1) "Did you use the internet for obtaining information from web sites of public organizations in the last 12 months?"; 2) "Did you use the internet for downloading official forms/documents from websites of public organizations in the last 12 months?" and; 3) "Did you use the internet for filling out an online form in the websites of public institutions/organizations in the last 12 months?" By using answers provided by survey participants for the above questions, the author constructs a binary index for e-government use. The variable "e-government use" is coded either as one if the individual used e-government tools for obtaining information or downloading forms or filling out forms in last 12 months and zero otherwise.

As the chapter focuses on gender differences in e-government use in Turkey, the main explanatory variable for the empirical analysis is a dummy variable which indicates the gender of the respondent. The female indicator is constructed as "one" if the participant is a female and "zero" if the participant is a male. Other demographic variables of the empirical estimation framework include age, education level, employment status and household income. Age is measured in years and it ranges from 16 years to 74 years. The education level is constructed as an ordered variable for 8 categories with the lowest level of "No Diploma" coded as zero and highest level of "PhD Degree" coded as seven. Employment level is measured by a dummy variable which indicates whether the respondent is employed or not employed. Monthly household income is continuously measured in Turkish Liras. Finally, internet usage frequency of participants is also included in the regression equation. Frequency of internet use is constructed by the use of following survey question: "What is the internet usage frequency of internet users in last three months?" Participants report one of the following choices: "1- Less than once a week; 2-At least once week; 3-Almost every day." Hence, internet usage frequency ranges from one (lowest frequency) to three (highest frequency). Detailed descriptions of all variables are provided in Appendix Table 3.

The summary statistics for the variables used for empirical analysis are provided in Table 4 (for 2015) and Table 5 (for 2016) in Appendix. According to Table 4 and Table 5, the share of Turkish citizens who used e-government services increased from 53.2% to 61.4% between 2015 and 2016. For both years, half of participants in operating samples of this chapter are females. The averages age for the samples of both years are around 40 years. The mean in the education level almost corresponds to a secondary school (high school) degree in both samples. 40% and 41% of participants are employed in 2015 and 2016, respectively. Average monthly household income corresponds to 2,020 Turkish Liras in 2015 and 2,407 Turkish Liras in 2016. Finally, internet usage frequency of both samples generates an average of 2.7, which implies that participants included in operating samples use the internet almost every day.

Estimation Framework

Dependent variable of empirical analysis is a binary indicator of e-government use. This feature of the data requires estimation of probability models. Since linear probability model has the potential to predict out of range probabilities especially at outliers of the sample, non-linear probability models would be appropriate as an estimation framework. Hence, this chapter employs non-linear probability models with probit methodology to quantify demographic and socioeconomic factors that relates to e-government use in Turkey. Theoretical regression equations are presented by the following equations.

$$Z_i = \gamma_0 + \gamma_1 Female_i + \gamma_2 Age_i + \gamma_3 Education\ Level_i + \gamma_4 Employed_i + \gamma_5 Household\ Income_i + \gamma_6 Internet\ Usage\ Frequency_i + \varepsilon_i \quad (1)$$

$$P(E - Government\ Use_i = 1) = \Phi(Z_i) \quad (2)$$

where $\Phi(Z_i)$ is the cumulative standard normal distribution function and ε_i is a normally distributed error term. It should be noted that due to nature of binary dependent variable, probability models are prone to heteroscedasticity in the error term of regression equation. Therefore, probit model estimations of this chapter are conducted by using heteroscedasticity consistent standard errors (White, 1980) in order to ensure robustness of standard errors for coefficients.

EMPIRICAL RESULTS

Empirical findings of the probit analysis are presented in Table 2. Overall, the findings are robust across two years of survey as the data reflect similar signs and significance for both years. The first regression results indicate that there exists a significant gender gap in the use of e-government platform in Turkey. The marginal effect of being female on the probability of using e-government is significantly negative. Namely, females are less likely to adopt e-government in Turkey during 2015 and 2016. This finding is not surprising given the fact that percentage of females using computers and internet are lower than males in Turkey as discussed above. Empirical findings on gender differences in the usage of e-government in Turkey are in line with earlier findings which reports that females are less likely to adopt e-government tools (Akman, Yazici, Mishra, & Arifoglu, 2005; Bimber, 1999; Choudrie & Dwivedi, 2005; Goldfinch, Gauld, & Herbison, 2009; McNeal, Hale & Dotterweich, 2008; Nam, 2014; Rodrigues, Sarabdeen, & Balasubramanian, 2016; Venkatesh, Sykes, & Venkatraman, 2014; Voutinioti, 2013).

Data analysis reveals that age is negatively associated with use of e-government services in Turkey. Older individuals are less likely to adopt e-government gateway of Turkey. This result provides additional evidence in favor of the literature pointing out the inverse relationship between age and likelihood of e-government adoption of individuals (Akman, Yazici, Mishra, & Arifoglu, 2005; Bimber, 1999; Colesca & Dobrica, 2008; Choudrie & Dwivedi, 2005; Gauld, Goldfinch, & Horsburgh, 2010; Goldfinch, Gauld, & Herbison, 2009; McNeal, Hale & Dotterweich, 2008; Sharma, 2015). Technology adoption and use of online tools are more likely to prevail among the young as suggested by the Diffusion of Innovations framework. According to TSI (2015, 2016) figures, share of internet and computer users both demonstrate declining trends with respect to age groups. The share of internet users and computer users are lower in older age groups. Hence, Turkish data confirm the findings of previous research.

The education level of Turkish citizens is significantly related to e-government adoption in Turkey. Similar to earlier research findings (Akman, Yazici, Mishra, & Arifoglu, 2005; Colesca & Dobrica, 2008; Choudrie & Dwivedi, 2005; Gauld, Goldfinch, & Horsburgh, 2010; Goldfinch, Gauld, & Herbison, 2009; McNeal, Hale & Dotterweich, 2008; Nam, 2014; Sipior, Ward, & Connolly, 2011; Venkatesh, Sykes, & Venkatraman, 2014), citizens with higher level of education are more likely to employ online government platforms. Education level of participants would affect their technology use and adaptation processes for newly introduced information and communication tools. As discussed in descriptive statistics, many participants have never used a computer in Turkey. Anecdotal evidence indicate that most students are to physically touch a computer first time at their school. Thus, schooling resources and educational activities have the potential to transform society's approach to technology use in Turkey.

Consistent with earlier research (Sipior, Ward, & Connolly, 2011), employment status is significantly correlated with the adoption of e-government services at individual level. The employed participants are more likely to use e-government services in Turkey. Government institutions own e-government platforms and they may require employees to conduct certain activities by using e-government tools. Then, participants who are government employees would adopt and use the e-government gateway in their work place. Similarly, private sector firms and organizations also adopt these e-government tools to conduct businesses with the government and other institutions. Moreover, human resources operations and activities for employees may be processed through e-government services in both private and public sector of Turkey. Hence, different mechanisms, and processes in the work place may lead individuals to use e-government services for work related purposes. Using e-government services and getting used to the platform may trigger the use of e-government services for personal level issues by Turkish citizens.

Table 2. Probit regression results for e-government use

	2015		2016	
	Coefficients	**Marginal Effects**	**Coefficients**	**Marginal Effects**
Female	-0.174***	-0.0598***	-0.244***	-0.0776***
	(0.0283)	(0.00966)	(0.0263)	(0.00829)
Age	-0.00575***	-0.00197***	-0.0145***	-0.00460***
	(0.00111)	(0.000380)	(0.000988)	(0.000306)
Education Level	0.285***	0.0978***	0.345***	0.110***
	(0.0107)	(0.00332)	(0.0103)	(0.00291)
Employed	0.155***	0.0532***	0.112***	0.0355***
	(0.0286)	(0.00979)	(0.0268)	(0.00852)
Household Income	0.0590***	0.0202***	0.0310***	0.00987***
	(0.00823)	(0.00281)	(0.00895)	(0.00284)
Internet Usage Frequency	0.308***	0.106***	0.317***	0.101***
	(0.0238)	(0.00797)	(0.0232)	(0.00721)
Constant	-1.4831***		-1.011***	
	(0.0777)		(0.0765)	
Wald: $\chi^2(6)$	1593.29***		2383.86***	
Pseudo R^2	0.126		0.155	
Observations	10,918	10,918	13,510	13,510

Source: TSI (2015, 2016). Robust standard errors in parentheses.*** p<0.01, ** p<0.05, * p<0.1

Household income level demonstrates significantly positive relationship with the probability of e-government usage in Turkey. In a similar vein with previous research (McNeal, Hale & Dotterweich, 2008; Sipior, Ward, & Connolly, 2011; Venkatesh, Sykes, & Venkatraman, 2014), these findings indicate that citizens with higher levels of income are more likely to participate in and use e-government platforms. Individuals with higher income are more likely to access and adapt new technologies and they may have higher interests in following latest improvements – including the usage of these technologies to deliver e-governance.

Empirical results, provided in Table 2, indicates that the frequency of internet usage is a significant covariate of e-government use. Unlike Urbina and Abe (2017), this result supports findings presented by earlier literature (Belanger & Carter, 2009; Carter & Belanger, 2005). More frequent users of internet are more likely to adopt e-government in Turkey. As they are used more to being online and employing internet tools, frequent users would access e-government platforms faster and use them more easily compared to less frequent users.

Overall, the empirical analysis of this chapter indicates that Turkish citizens have similar patterns with other countries in e-government adoption since most findings are in line with earlier research. However, the gender gap in use of information and communication technologies significantly prevails in Turkish case as well. This phenomenon is called "the digital divide" to refer to gaps in use of information and communication technologies among different groups with respect to sociodemographic or regional variables (Chinn & Fairlie, 2007; Cooper, 2006; Cooper & Weaver, 2003; Helbig, Gil-García, & Ferro, 2009; Norris, 2001; Van Dijk, 2005; Van Dijk & Hacker, 2003; Warschauer, 2003).

CONCLUSION

Expansion of information and communication technologies drive substantial changes in daily routines of individuals, government institutions and business processes. The provision of public services through online platforms is a crucial component of e-government adoption projects in many countries from different regions of the world. Participation of citizens in e-government platforms are primary determinants for successful implementation of these policies. Hence, researchers and policy makers should prudently analyze citizens' behavior and adoption processes for new technologies, particularly e-government tools.

Earlier research provide evidence for covariates of e-government use at individual level such as demographics, socioeconomic factors, trust measures and perceptions of technology. Analysis of technology use at micro level indicates that there are inequalities in access and use of technologies as different segments of the society. Specifically, there are research findings revealing that females are less likely to have access to different tools of technology and internet platforms compared to males.

In this chapter, the author investigates determinants of use of e-government platforms in Turkey by focusing on gender differences. By employing individual level representative survey data, probit models are estimated. Empirical findings indicate that the gender gap in adoption of e-government gateways prevails among Turkish citizens. Age, education level, household income, employment status and internet use frequency are significant predictors for e-government use. These results imply that the digital divide extends to Turkey as a developing country, located between Europe and Middle East.

Furthermore, analyzing the Turkish case for the gender gap in e-government use, this chapter provides crucial insights for policy makers. First, there is urgent need for policies addressing inadequacy of women's access to technologies in Turkey. Before considering internet use or e-government use; one should note that most Turkish women have never used a computer in their lifetime. Thus, public policies which engage women with information and communication technologies would significantly help with reduction of the digital divide in Turkey. Empowerment of women for adapting new technologies through training programs would encourage them to be more active in social life and labor market. Higher access to technology would improve inclusion rates of women in e-government platforms as well. However, regional, socioeconomic and cultural variation in Turkey are potential challenges to overcome in implementation of gender specific policies in the country. In order to tackle such potential problems, policies should be flexibly designed and modified with respect to needs of specific groups across different segments of the society. Moreover, policies should be also designed to establish various incentives for citizens and enhance their trust levels. Thus, one-size-fits-all policies would not be able to address the challenges of digital divide.

Reduction of digital divide would have crucial repercussions on inclusion of women for various dimensions of social, political and economic systems of a country. Policies focusing on specific types of gaps in implementation of information and communication technologies should connect multiple perspectives from both supply and demand side with respect to special needs of target groups. Although this chapter contributes to large body of literature on digital divide by exploring current state of e-government adoption in Turkey, identification of mechanisms driving these results is beyond the scope of this chapter. Hence, further research is needed for investigation of channels leading to the gender gap in use of technology in Turkey and other developing countries. Exploration of various links and mechanisms which drive gender differences in technology adoption would significantly contribute to policy formation and implementation as well as robustness and effectiveness of policy outcomes.

REFERENCES

Ak, S., Koruklu, N., & Yilmaz, Y. (2013). A study on Turkish adolescent's Internet use: Possible predictors of Internet addiction. *Cyberpsychology, Behavior, and Social Networking*, *16*(3), 205–209. doi:10.1089/cyber.2012.0255 PMID:23253206

Akman, I., & Mishra, A. (2010). Gender, age and income differences in internet usage among employees in organizations. *Computers in Human Behavior*, *26*(3), 482–490. doi:10.1016/j.chb.2009.12.007

Akman, I., Yazici, A., Mishra, A., & Arifoglu, A. (2005). E-Government: A global view and an empirical evaluation of some attributes of citizens. *Government Information Quarterly*, *22*(2), 239–257. doi:10.1016/j.giq.2004.12.001

Belanger, F., & Carter, L. (2008). Trust and risk in e-government adoption. *The Journal of Strategic Information Systems*, *17*(2), 165–176. doi:10.1016/j.jsis.2007.12.002

Belanger, F., & Carter, L. (2009). The impact of the digital divide on e-government use. *Communications of the ACM*, *52*(4), 132–135. doi:10.1145/1498765.1498801

Bimber, B. (1999). The internet and citizen communication with government: Does the medium matter? *Political Communication*, *16*(4), 409–428. doi:10.1080/105846099198569

Carter, L., & Belanger, F. (2005). The utilization of e-government services: Citizen trust, innovation and acceptance factors. *Information Systems Journal*, *15*(1), 5–25. doi:10.1111/j.1365-2575.2005.00183.x

Cayhan, B. E. (2008). Implementing E-government in Turkey: A Comparison of Online Public Service Delivery in Turkey and the European Union. *The Electronic Journal on Information Systems in Developing Countries*, *35*(1), 1–11. doi:10.1002/j.1681-4835.2008.tb00245.x

Chinn, M. D., & Fairlie, R. W. (2007). The determinants of the global digital divide: A cross-country analysis of computer and internet penetration. *Oxford Economic Papers*, *59*(1), 16–44. doi:10.1093/oep/gpl024

Choudrie, J., & Dwivedi, Y. (2005). A survey of citizens' awareness and adoption of e-government initiatives, the 'Government Gateway': A United Kingdom perspective. eGovernment Workshop'05 (eGOV05).

Colesca, S. E., & Dobrica, L. (2008). Adoption and use of e-government services: The case of Romania. *Journal of Applied Research and Technology*, *6*(3), 204–217.

Cooper, J. (2006). The digital divide: The special case of gender. *Journal of Computer Assisted Learning*, *22*(5), 320–334. doi:10.1111/j.1365-2729.2006.00185.x

Cooper, J., & Weaver, K. D. (2003). *Gender and computers: Understanding the digital divide*. Psychology Press.

Dimitrova, D. V., & Chen, Y. (2006). Profiling the adopters of e-government information and services: The influence of psychological characteristics, civicmindedness, and information channels. *Social Science Computer Review*, *24*(2), 171–188. doi:10.1177/0894439305281517

e-Government Gateway of Turkey. (2018). Retrieved from: https://www.turkiye.gov.tr/

European Commission (EC). (2003). *The Role of eGovernment for Europe's Future: COM (2003)567*. Brussels: European Commission.

European Commission (EC). (2017). eGovernment in Turkey. March 2017, Edition 3.00. European Commission.

Gauld, R., Goldfinch, S., & Horsburgh, S. (2010). Do they want it? Do they use it? The 'Demand-Side'of e-Government in Australia and New Zealand. *Government Information Quarterly*, *27*(2), 177–186. doi:10.1016/j.giq.2009.12.002

Goldfinch, S., Gauld, R., & Herbison, P. (2009). The participation divide? Political participation, trust in government, and e-government in Australia and New Zealand. *Australian Journal of Public Administration*, *68*(3), 333–350. doi:10.1111/j.1467-8500.2009.00643.x

Gupta, K. P., Singh, S., & Bhaskar, P. (2016). Citizen adoption of e-government: a literature review and conceptual framework. *Electronic Government, an International Journal*, *12*(2), 160-185.

Helbig, N., Gil-García, J. R., & Ferro, E. (2009). Understanding the complexity of electronic government: Implications from the digital divide literature. *Government Information Quarterly*, *26*(1), 89–97. doi:10.1016/j.giq.2008.05.004

Hung, S. Y., Chang, C. M., & Yu, T. J. (2006). Determinants of user acceptance of the e-Government services: The case of online tax filing and payment system. *Government Information Quarterly*, *23*(1), 97–122. doi:10.1016/j.giq.2005.11.005

Ilie, V., Van Slyke, C., Green, G., & Hao, L. (2005). Gender differences in perceptions and use of communication technologies: A diffusion of innovation approach. *Information Resources Management Journal*, *18*(3), 13–31. doi:10.4018/irmj.2005070102

International Telecommunication Union (ITU). (2017). *ICT Facts and Figures 2016 Report*. ITU.

Kurfali, M., Arifoglu, A., Tokdemir, G., & Pacin, Y. (2017). Adoption of e-government services in Turkey. *Computers in Human Behavior*, *66*, 168–178. doi:10.1016/j.chb.2016.09.041

McNeal, R. S., Hale, K., & Dotterweich, L. (2008). Citizen-government interaction and the internet: Expectations and accomplishments in contact, quality, and trust. *Journal of Information Technology & Politics*, *5*(2), 213–229. doi:10.1080/19331680802298298

Moreno, R. R., Molina, C. M., Figueroa, J. C. S., & Moreno, M. R. (2013). Gender and E-government adoption in Spain. *International Journal of Electronic Government Research*, *9*(3), 23–42. doi:10.4018/jegr.2013070102

Morris, M. G., Venkatesh, V., & Ackerman, P. L. (2005). Gender and age differences in employee decisions about new technology: An extension to the theory of planned behavior. *IEEE Transactions on Engineering Management*, *52*(1), 69–84. doi:10.1109/TEM.2004.839967

Nam, T. (2014). Determining the type of e-government use. *Government Information Quarterly*, *31*(2), 211–220. doi:10.1016/j.giq.2013.09.006

Norris, P. (2001). *Digital divide: Civic engagement, information poverty, and the Internet worldwide*. Cambridge University Press. doi:10.1017/CBO9781139164887

Organisation for Economic Co-operation Development (OECD). (2003). *The e-Government Imperative*. OECD e-Government Studies.

Polat, R. K. (2012). Digital exclusion in Turkey: A policy perspective. *Government Information Quarterly, 29*(4), 589–596. doi:10.1016/j.giq.2012.03.002

Rana, N. P., Dwivedi, Y. K., & Williams, M. D. (2015). A meta-analysis of existing research on citizen adoption of e-government. *Information Systems Frontiers, 17*(3), 547–563. doi:10.100710796-013-9431-z

Reddick, C. G. (2005). Citizen interaction with e-government: From the streets to servers? *Government Information Quarterly, 22*(1), 38–57. doi:10.1016/j.giq.2004.10.003

Rodrigues, G., Sarabdeen, J., & Balasubramanian, S. (2016). Factors that influence consumer adoption of e-government services in the UAE: A UTAUT model perspective. *Journal of Internet Commerce, 15*(1), 18–39. doi:10.1080/15332861.2015.1121460

Rogers, E. M. (2003). *Diffusion of innovations* (5th ed.). New York: Free Press.

Sanchez-Franco, M. J. (2006). Exploring the influence of gender on the web usage via partial least squares. *Behaviour & Information Technology, 25*(1), 19–36. doi:10.1080/01449290500124536

Sarabdeen, J., & Rodrigues, G. (2010). Gender differences in e-government adoption in Dubai. *The Business Review, Cambridge, 16*(2), 120–126.

Sharma, S. K. (2015). Adoption of e-government services: The role of service quality dimensions and demographic variables. *Transforming Government: People. Process and Policy, 9*(2), 207–222.

Sipior, J. C., Ward, B. T., & Connolly, R. (2011). The digital divide and t-government in the United States: Using the technology acceptance model to understand usage. *European Journal of Information Systems, 20*(3), 308–326. doi:10.1057/ejis.2010.64

Statistical Office of the European Communities (EUROSTAT). (2018). *Eurostat Information Society Indicators*. Luxembourg: Eurostat.

Tahiroglu, A. Y., Celik, G. G., Uzel, M., Ozcan, N., & Avci, A. (2008). Internet use among Turkish adolescents. *Cyberpsychology & Behavior, 11*(5), 537–543. doi:10.1089/cpb.2007.0165 PMID:18785800

Taipale, S. (2013). The use of e-government services and the Internet: The role of sociodemographic, economic and geographical predictors. *Telecommunications Policy, 37*(4), 413–422. doi:10.1016/j.telpol.2012.05.005

Turkish Statistical Institute (TSI). (2015). *Information and Communication Technology (ICT) Usage Survey on Households and Individuals, 2015*. TSI.

Turkish Statistical Institute (TSI). (2016). *Information and Communication Technology (ICT) Usage Survey on Households and Individuals, 2016*. TSI.

United Nations (UN). (2016). *United Nations e-Government survey 2016. E-government in support of sustainable development*. New York: Department of Economic and Social Affairs, United Nations.

Urbina, A. U., & Abe, N. (2017). Citizen-centric Perspective on the Adoption of E-Government in the Philippines. *Electronic. Journal of E-Government, 15*(2).

Van Dijk, J. (2005). *The deepening divide: Inequality in the information society*. London: Sage.

Van Dijk, J., & Hacker, K. (2003). The digital divide as a complex and dynamic phenomenon. *The Information Society, 19*(4), 315–326. doi:10.1080/01972240309487

Venkatesh, V., Sykes, T. A., & Venkatraman, S. (2014). Understanding e-Government portal use in rural India: Role of demographic and personality characteristics. *Information Systems Journal, 24*(3), 249–269. doi:10.1111/isj.12008

Voutinioti, A. (2013). Determinants of user adoption of e-government services in Greece and the role of citizen service centres. *Procedia Technology, 8*, 238–244. doi:10.1016/j.protcy.2013.11.033

Warschauer, M. (2003). *Technology and social inclusion: Rethinking the digital divide*. Cambridge, MA: MIT Press.

White, H. (1980). A heteroskedasticity-consistent covariance matrix estimator and a direct test for heteroskedasticity. *Econometrica, 48*(4), 817–838. doi:10.2307/1912934

Yildiz, M. (2007). E-government research: Reviewing the literature, limitations, and ways forward. *Government Information Quarterly, 24*(3), 646–665. doi:10.1016/j.giq.2007.01.002

Zhang, H., Xu, X., & Xiao, J. (2014). Diffusion of e-government: A literature review and directions for future directions. *Government Information Quarterly, 31*(4), 631–636. doi:10.1016/j.giq.2013.10.013

KEY TERMS AND DEFINITIONS

Digital Divide: A gap between different segments of society in terms of access to information and communication technologies.

E-Government: The online platforms, applications, and tools introduced by the government for provision of public services.

Gender Gap: A concept that refers to systematic differences between men and women, particularly in education, health, politics, and economic outcomes.

Marginal Effect: A measure which shows the effect of a change in an independent variable on predicted probability of the dependent variable on average, given everything else constant.

Probit Model: A non-linear regression model, estimated by maximum likelihood framework, where dependent variable takes only two values (i.e., zero or one).

Public Organization: An institution or entity, usually controlled by the government, which provides public services for the society.

Public Service: A service provided directly or indirectly by local or central government to its citizens.

Survey Data: A data set collected by means of systematic professional methods.

APPENDIX

Table 3. Description of variables

Variable	Description
E-Government Use	Measures if the individual used e-government tools for obtaining information or downloading forms or filling out forms in last 12 months. Yes=1 and No=0
Female	1=Female; 0=Male.
Age	Reported age by respondents, who are between 16 and 74 years old.
Education Level	No Diploma=0; Primary School Degree=1; Secondary School Degree=2; High School Degree=3; Associate Degree=4; Bachelor's Degree=5; Master's Degree=6; PhD Degree=7
Employed	1=Employed, 0=Otherwise
Household Income	Reported monthly household income by respondents (in thousand Turkish Liras).
Internet Usage Frequency	Internet usage frequency of participants in last three months. 1= Less than once a week; 2=At least once week; 3=Almost every day.

Source: TSI (2015, 2016).

Table 4. Descriptive statistics for survey of 2015

Variable	N	Mean	Standard Deviation	Min	Max
E-Government Use	11,381	0.532	0.498	0	1
Female	24,798	0.505	0.499	0	1
Age	24,798	40.362	15.31	16	74
Education Level	22,977	1.908	1.502	0	7
Employed	22,977	0.401	0.490	0	1
Household Income	24,798	2.020	1.794	0.001	30
Internet Usage Frequency	10,918	2.710	0.572	1	3

Source: TSI (2015, 2016).

Table 5. Descriptive statistics for survey of 2016

Variable	N	Mean	Standard Deviation	Min	Max
E-Government Use	13,789	0.614	0.486	0	1
Female	27,934	0.509	0.509	0	1
Age	27,934	40.907	15.52	16	74
Education Level	25,058	1.947	1.521	0	7
Employed	25,058	0.412	0.492	0	1
Household Income	27,934	2.407	2.301	0.001	70
Internet Usage Frequency	13,510	2.773	0.531	1	3

Source: TSI (2015, 2016).

Chapter 8
Gender Differences in ICT Studies:
A Study of Selected Public Secondary Schools in Ogun State, Nigeria

Tayo O. George
Covenant University, Nigeria

Anthony C. Onwumah
Covenant University, Nigeria

Michael O. Fagbohun
Covenant University, Nigeria

Mercy E. Adebayo
Covenant University, Nigeria

Olawale Yinusa Olonade
Covenant University, Nigeria

ABSTRACT

This study provides an empirical investigation of gender differences in ICT studies in selected public secondary schools. It describes gender differences in terms of students' attitude, perception, and choice of ICT subjects, parental influence, age, and religion. The study engages survey of selected public secondary schools in the region and in-depth interview of relevant stakeholders for the primary data. The study findings are anchored on existing literature, relevant theoretical positions, and data from statistical analyses. It concludes that equal opportunities in ICT studies for male and female students will empower all groups to contribute maximally to science and technology revolution for achieving needed economic and national development in the country.

DOI: 10.4018/978-1-5225-7068-4.ch008

INTRODUCTION

The dearth of female students in ICT-related studies is glaringly on the increase in many public institutions especially the secondary schools where basic infrastructure including electricity is lacking. One explanation for the obvious gender gap is as a result of gender inequality rather than lack of women's ability to acquire the requisite skills to function adequately within the sector (Odukoya, 2005). Another possible explanation lies in the fact that the significant others (family, schools, peers, etc) play a major role in influencing whether the young people decides to pursue STEM related studies or pursue a career in those domains or not (Zarrett, Malanchuk, Davis-Kean, & Eccles, 2006). A number of studies Eccles (1994), Zarrett et.al. (2006), Vekiri and Chronaki (2008), Lang (2012), Gras-Velazquez, Joyce, and Debry (2009), Sáinz et al. (2009), Yansen and Zukerfeld (2014), Yansen and Zukerfeld (2014), Trauth, Quesenberry, and Morgan (2004), Pechtelidis, Kosma, and Chronaki (2015), Pechtelidis, Kosma, and Chronaki (2015), Nelson (2014), Moakler and Kim (2014), Christoph et. al. (2015), Cheryan, Master, and Meltzoff (2015), Cheryan, Master and Meltzoff (2015), Cheryan, Master and Meltzoff (2015), Zagami et.al. (2015) and George and Suleiman (2015) have identified some social-cultural factors causing gender differences in ICTs studies.

This study is an investigation into the causes of gender differences in ICT studies at the secondary educational level where least attention of scholars and researchers in contemporary times have been focused.

BACKGROUND

The primary focus of this research is on gender differences among students of public or government owned secondary schools in Nigeria. Secondary education is a preparatory ground for higher education and ultimately the labour and the job market. Relevant foundation of ICT studies, skills and knowledge at this level will form a major basis for higher education (Universities, Polytechnics etc.) and ultimately employment in ICT domains and relevant fields. In today's 21st century, the demand for ICT professionals continues to rise, yet the availability of experts is insufficient to meet the rising demand. The insufficient number of women in technology and ICT-related subjects and studies has been the focus of interest of the scientific and educational communities during the last decades (Eccles, 2007; Cohoon & Asprey, 2006; Margolis & Fisher, 2002; Sáinz, 2007; Zarrett & Malanchuk, 2005). Previous studies by Development Information Network (DEVNET, 2005) include- Gender and Technology, ICTs as tools to challenge inequality and promote women's empowerment, Gender and ICT, Policy issues and Engendering the Information Society to mention a few- The way forward seem not to address the gender gap in ICT studies right from the Secondary school to the higher institutions of learning where manpower for ICT are produced. This missing link in the study of ICT at the public Secondary schools is what this study intends to fill. Thus, the study identifies and seeks to address the following research questions:

1. Are there gender differences in ICT studies in public secondary schools in Nigeria?
2. What are the causes of gender differences in ICT studies?
3. What are the means of bridging the gender gap in ICT Studies?

The Study attempts to achieve the following objectives:

1. Examine if gender differences in ICT studies exist in public secondary schools in Nigeria.
2. Identify the causes of gender differences in ICT studies.
3. To explore ways of bridging the gender gap on ICT studies.

Hypotheses of the Study

The following hypotheses stated in the alternate form were tested.

1. There is a significant relationship between gender differences and ICT studies.
2. There is a significant difference between Socio-cultural factors and gender differences in ICT studies.

MAIN FOCUS THE CHAPTER

Studies showed that in most developing nations, certain socio-cultural beliefs excluded female children from formal education and this created inequality in ICT studies. Webb and Miller (2015) opined that feminist viewpoints have acknowledged that female uses of technology were socially constructed. According to Sinha (2009), gender differences in formal education between females and males play an important communal part in how ICTs are appropriated along gender lines in developing countries. Filgona and Sababa (2017) asserted that by the standard of African societies have revealed that indomitable rules within the society provided what is female and what is male. The science biased subjects in many cultures are considered as masculine. That is why Skaalvik and Skaalvik (2004), reported that boys usually had higher expectations for outstanding and impressive performance in stereotypically masculine subjects like physical sciences, sports and mathematics than girls, whereas girls usually have higher expectations in oral skills than boys.

Ekine (2013) argued that the main reasons among the other causes of gender gap in the field of science socio-cultural bigotries in developing nations which believed that science was the field of males and not essential for girls' future lives. He also argued that girls were not as skillful as boys in science learning. Also sociocultural beliefs and cultural norms negatively influenced classroom practices and discouraged girl child's learning as well as their desire for science. In fact these practices favored males (Ekine, 2013). A school environment which tolerated and encouraged males and females made the girl child to develop interest in ICT. Female students growing up in a culture of all-ubiquitous technology, ICT offers new, and more thrilling and relevant, learning opportunities. If ICTs are not effectively integrated in teaching and learning, it may impede girl child interest in learning ICTs (Department of Education and Science, 2008). Alrasheedi (2009) also reported that socio-cultural factors influenced the adoption and use of ICT in schools, such as lack of understanding and training as well as cultural issues about gender. Kumari and Saraladevi (2012) submitted that it was the norm in some cultures to hold that girls do not have the capability to understand science's intricacies. It is crucial that students are treated equally in the classroom. This is important so that all students both male and female could have a profound grasp of all fields, particularly math and science.

Kiefer and Shih (2006) reported that women are more likely than boys to aspire to careers in health and biology-related careers. In contrast, men are more interested in pursuing scientific and technological studies and less interested in studies related to the provision of care and nurturance. It has long been argued that boys are more likely to have mathematical talent than girls while girls are more likely than boys to have communication skills, leading boys to do better in mathematics than girls, to develop high math ability, self-concepts, and to be more likely to enter math related technical fields (Skaalvik & Skaalvik, 2004). Research provides ample evidence that women consider themselves less competent in technology-related domains (despite their high performance in these domains) and that this belief can discourage them from participating in technology-related studies (Creamer, Lee, & Meszaros, 2006; Eccles, 2007). However, George and Suleiman (2015) opined that ICT is a vital tool for gender development. Women need exposure to the complex and often technical tools of ICT to access information and data needed for quality research. The influence of family, school, peers, mass media and immediate social environment shapes men and women's self-concept of their own abilities together with the value they attach to various subjects and academic disciplines (Eccles, 1994). Boys usually report higher expectations for success and abilities in stereotypically male domains (such as math, physical science and sports) than girls, while girls reported higher perceptions of their verbal skills than boys (Skaalvik & Skaalvik, 2004; Wigfield & Eccles, 2002).Empirical research demonstrates that women think that they are less competent than their male counterparts in computers (Sáinz, Fatsini, García, González, Meneses, Prat, & Solé, 2009; Zarrett & Malanchuk, 2005).

The Value Expectancy Theory was adopted to explain gender differences in ICT studies among public secondary schools. According to Hulleman, Barron, Kosovich and Lazowski (2014) Value Expectancy Theory (VET) emanated from expectancy-value models and psychological backgrounds that concentrated on cognizing elements that determined the conduct of individuals in a particular setting striving to attain a particular goal. The theory emphasized two important areas of motivation (expectancies and values) that are basic for both male and female students to be fully involved in ICT studies. The theory proposes that student's judgment to execute a certain task hinges on the perception that there are benefits in carrying out the task and conviction that they can succeed. There must be a high level expectancy of success by students Buabeng-Andoh (2014). Wentworth (2015) submitted that perceptions are mainly established on the student's analysis of his or her previous performance of ICT studies. The general feeling about previous proficiency is assumed to end in the expectation for future performance. Before any student either male or female can have a high expectancy for ICT studies, the student must feel competent in the area of ICT studies and science-oriented subjects and anticipate to perform well in the future, based on former performance (Wentworth, 2015). Expectancies are determined by student's interest, beliefs and judgments about their capabilities to perform a task, their self-perception, efficacy and self-concept of ability. In a situation where the female students begin to doubt her ability to cope with computer studies and related subjects, this is considered as an expectancy issue. Dlodlo (2009) inferred that customarily, girl children belief that tough tasks are considered a domain of the male species. Thus, psychologically girl children already have a barrier to taking up ICT studies and science-related subjects. This has made the majority of females not interested in studying ICT or pursuing a career in technology contrarily, the majority of male students are interested in ICT studies (Becta, 2008). The theory proposed that students must have the intention to engage in the ICT studies behavior and place value on the ICT studies tasks. Students need to be convinced and know the purpose and reason why they need to engage in ICT studies, that is, the need to have positive values for ICT studies. According to Hulleman et al. (2014), the extended components of the expectancy-value comprise the cultural setting, students' views of earlier engagements, students' self-concept, behaviors, objectives and perceptions of socializers, unique previous occurrences and expectations. All these are determinant of how female girl value ICT studies. Expectancy Value Theory (EVT) posits that socialization processes associated with socio-cultural settings introduce individual differences in motivational beliefs leading to differential performance. It identified how social-cultural and stereotype threat influence female students value for ICT studies. Female choices to study ICT and scientific studies are made based on stereotypes or rumors and not career prospects. This makes ICT studies less attractive to many female students and result in a gender difference or gap (Bøe & Henriksen, 2015).

METHODOLOGY

The research design adopted for this study was a survey using a structured questionnaire. This was informed by the scarcity of secondary data on gender and ICT studies in the country. The target populations for the study were male and female students of randomly selected public secondary schools (PSS) in Ota, Ogun State southwest Nigeria. Of the six (6) geo-political zones in the country, Ogun state has the highest number of public secondary schools and educational facilities yet it has not translated to the development of the state nor the educational sector. Male and female students in the Junior Secondary School (JSS 3) and the Senior School (SS3) were targeted for the study. Students in this category are selected for two reasons: external qualifying examinations are written at this level also, it is at this level of study that students make career choices for or against ICT studies. The authors ensured that both male and female students from different age brackets, religious affiliations and socio-economic backgrounds were adequately represented. A breakdown of the study population in the three secondary schools from where data was obtained is as follows; School A (2,083) School B (1,352) and School C (1,417) respectively. However, because students of the Public Secondary Schools in the region share a lot of characteristics, a sample size of 300 participants was used for this study. From School A (118), B (96) and C (86). Even though most of the students speak and write English very well, the researchers explained the various sections of the questionnaire to the students before administering. A total of 287 questionnaire were found useable for analysis representing 95.6percent response rate. A four (4) Likert Scale instrument comprising options ranging from (A= Agree SA = Strongly Agree, D= Disagree and SD=Strongly Disagree) was utilized to elicit responses from the target population on the main focus of the research questions. This method of data collection complemented other relevant archival materials from the print and electronic sources. Data collection from the survey questionnaire was analyzed by engaging relevant statistical tools (Mean and Standard Deviation and Statistical Packages for Social Sciences (SPSS 21.0) edition was utilized to arrive of the findings for the study. Conclusion and recommendations were made on the basis of the findings and its alignment with the stated research questions and study objectives.

Instrument of Data Collection

Survey questionnaire was the primary instrument of data collection. An 82-item questionnaire containing mainly closed ended questions using a four (4) Likert scale was adopted for the study. Section one examined the socio-demographic characteristics of the respondents. Section two focused on gender differences in ICT while section three was designed to elicit information on the causes of gender differences in ICT Studies. The last section was designed to obtain data on socio-cultural factors influencing ICT studies. The questionnaire was designed in a way to address the research questions, study objectives and the hypotheses stated for the study.

RESULTS AND DISCUSSION OF FINIDNGS

Hypothesis 1 - Hi: There is a significant relationship between gender differences and ICT studies.

Respondents were asked to indicate what kinds of things they do with computer and how often. The overall results on the kinds of things they used computer for are shown in Table 1. There is noticeable significant gender difference in use of computer by male and female respondents. Majority of the 80 (61.5%) male students indicates that they frequently use computer to play games, 71 (54.6%) regularly use computer to make films/animations, 68 (52.3%) use computer to write and as well 65 (50.0%) use

Table 1. Gender differences in Computer usage

Uses of Computer	Gender	Never Count (%)	Sometimes Count (%)	Frequently Count (%)	Regularly Count (%)	Total Count (%)
I draw	Male	21 (16.2)	36 (27.7)	10 (7.7)	**63 (48.5)**	130 (100.0)
	Female	95 (60.5)	35 (22.3)	10 (6.4)	17 (10.8)	157 (100.0)
I play game	Male	18 (13.8)	7 (5.4)	**80 (61.5)**	25 (19.2)	130 (100.0)
	Female	60 (38.2)	44 (28.0)	13 (8.3)	40 (25.5)	157 (100.0)
I search for info on the internet	Male	22 (16.9)	**62 (47.7)**	28 (21.5)	18 (13.8)	130 (100.0)
	Female	42 (26.8)	45 (28.7)	20 (12.7)	50 (31.8)	157 (100.0)
For educational software to learn new things	Male	39 (30.0)	14 (10.8)	35 (26.9)	42 (32.3)	130 (100.0)
	Female	56 (35.7)	35 (22.3)	25 (15.9)	41 (26.1)	157 (100.0)
I do programming	Male	69 (53.1)	14 (10.8)	34 (26.2)	13 (10.0)	130 (100.0)
	Female	97 (61.8)	32 (20.4)	15 (9.6	13 (8.3)	157 (100.0)
I use email	Male	24 (18.5)	16 (12.3)	27 (20.8	**63 (48.5)**	130 (100.0)
	Female	82 (52.2)	33 (21.0)	15 (9.6	27 (17.2)	157 (100.0)
I make films/animations on the computer	Male	17 (13.1)	13 (10.0)	29 (22.3	71 (54.6)	130 (100.0)
	Female	96 (61.1)	33 (21.0)	10 (6.4)	18 (11.5)	157 (100.0)
I create/record sound files on the computer	Male	69 (53.1)	32 (24.6)	17 (13.1)	12 (9.2)	130 (100.0)
	Female	103 (65.6)	28 (17.8)	11 (7.0)	15 (9.6)	157 (100.0)
I use the internet to revise for exams	Male	52 (40.0)	31 (23.8)	20 (15.4)	27 (20.8)	130 (100.0)
	Female	74 (47.1)	26 (16.6)	23 (14.6)	34 (21.7)	157 (100.0)
I use computer for writing	Male	26 (20.0)	18 (13.8)	**68 (52.3)**	18 (13.8)	130 (100.0)
	Female	81 (51.6)	30 (19.1)	19 (12.1)	27 (17.2)	157 (100.0)
I make/design things on the computer	Male	58 (44.6)	29 (22.3)	11 (8.5)	**32 (24.6)**	130 (100.0)
	Female	99 (63.1)	31 (19.7)	7 (4.5)	20 (12.7)	157 (100.0)

Source: Researchers' (Field work, 2018)

computer application to draw. It is clear that male students engage more in the use of computer than their female counterparts in the public Secondary schools sampled.

Causes of gender differences in ICT studies were examined using different parameters as shown in Tables 2-5.

Hypothesis 2 - HII: There is a significant difference between Socio-cultural factors and gender differences in ICT studies.

In Table 6, twenty-four questions relating to socio-cultural variables and gender differences in ICT were tested. The findings revealed that there is a significant difference between Socio-cultural factors and gender differences in ICT studies. Some respondents confirmed that boys know more than females in ICT. Female students are perceived as weak and not able to cope with the demand and rigor of ICT studies much less work in ICT sector. The study found that gender differences in ICT exist with the perception that boys excel more than girls in ICT and thus are unable to make the needed impacts in ICT like their male counterparts. While females are encouraged to stay within the house, assist with house chores and possibly get married to become good housewives and mothers, the boys are motivated to excel in ICT and related studies needed for societal development. The study found gaps in basic infrastructural notably, poor learning environment, dilapidated classrooms in virtually all the public secondary schools sampled. There were absence of computers in some of the schools visited. In cases where computers and computer laboratory exist, accessibility becomes a challenge for the students either male or female due to. Incessant power outage, poor infrastructural deficit and poor maintenance culture compounded the adoption and usage of ICT or studies by both males and females. Consequently ICT is hardly ever available in the public secondary schools sampled for this study. In the words of a female Principal in school A interviewed:

Table 2. Interest in Technology Studies and Gender Differences

Interest in Technology Studies	Female			Male		
	N	Mean	Std. Dev.	N	Mean	Std. Dev.
Working in technology would be interesting	157	3.37	.787	130	3.60	0.565
I will probably choose a job in technology	157	2.27	1.017	130	3.09	0.876
I would like a career in technology later on	157	2.29	.948	130	3.03	0.906
With a technological job your future is promised	157	2.77	1.067	130	3.30	0.784
If there was a school club about technology I would certainly join it	157	3.17	.849	130	3.35	0.794
I would rather not have technology lessons at school	157	2.63	1.040	130	2.19	1.005
I enjoy repairing things at home	157	2.06	1.048	130	3.31	0.922

Source: Researchers' (Field work, 2018)

Table 3. Confidence in ICT Studies and Gender Differences

Confidence in ICT Studies	Female			Male		
	N	Mean	Std. Dev.	N	Mean	Std. Dev.
I don't understand how some people seem to enjoy spending so much time on ICT Studies problems.	157	2.38	1.089	130	2.57	0.980
I do not have ICT Studies mind.	157	2.48	1.004	130	2.30	1.032
I find ICT Studies confusing.	157	2.45	1.016	130	2.27	1.010
I have never felt myself able to learn ICT Studies	157	2.57	0.982	130	2.35	0.970
I find many ICT Studies problems interesting and challenging.	157	2.12	0.996	130	2.07	0.982
I have never been very excited about ICT Studies	157	2.62	1.071	130	2.15	1.028
I have less trouble learning how to use a computer than I do learning other things.	157	2.19	1.020	130	2.15	1.096
When I have difficulties using a computer, I know I can handle them.	157	2.50	1.084	130	2.67	1.045
It takes me longer to understand computers than the average person.	157	2.34	1.011	130	2.71	0.976

Source: Researchers' (Field work, 2018)

Table 4. Self –Efficacy beliefs and Gender Difference in ICT Studies

Self-Efficacy Beliefs	Female			Male		
	N	Mean	Std. Dev.	N	Mean	Std. Dev.
I know enough about computers compared to other kids of my age.	157	2.46	0.874	130	3.15	0.919
In general I am good at computers.	157	2.94	0.782	130	3.05	1.056
I am confident that I can do well when I am doing something new on the computer.	157	2.68	0.949	130	2.98	1.184

Source: Researchers' (Field work, 2018)

Table 5. Perceived Peer Support and Gender Differences in ICT Studies

Perceived Peer Support	Female			Male		
	N	Mean	Std. Dev.	N	Mean	Std. Dev.
My friends are interested in computers.	157	3.06	0.938	130	3.38	0.638
When my friends and I get together, we enjoy doing things on the computer.	157	1.93	0.948	130	3.22	0.883
My friends and I like to help each other on the computer.	157	1.96	0.960	130	3.14	0.878
My friends and I enjoy talking about computers.	157	1.94	0.932	130	3.15	0.855

Source: Researchers' (Field work, 2018)

Table 6. Socio-Cultural factors influencing gender in ICT Studies

S/N	Socio-Cultural Impediments, Gender and ICT Studies	N	Maximum	Mean	Std. Dev.	Rank
1.	There is general view that female exposure to ICT affects their attitudes towards our culture	287	4	2.53	1.073	12th
2.	I believe that female do not need to go to learn anything about ICT	287	4	3.19	.923	4th
3.	Female need training, but only in ICT skills	287	4	2.73	1.021	7th
4.	It is enough for female to receive only basic formal education without any exposure to Computer Studies.	287	4	3.00	1.009	5th
5.	Cultural values have been affected female by exposure to ICT	287	4	2.71	.994	9th
6.	Female should be allowed to work but in only a few professions	287	4	2.84	1.073	6th
7.	Female should not be allowed to work with men	287	4	3.20	.900	3rd
8.	Female should not go out to work once she is married	287	4	3.28	.920	1st
9.	Female should remain within the four walls of the house	287	4	3.25	.975	2nd
10.	Many girls are not ambitious or interested in ICT studies because of societal, including parents and teachers expectations that their primary roles are to be wives and mothers	287	4	2.45	1.076	13th
11.	There is more employment and potential opportunity for studied ICTs compare to female	287	4	2.36	1.061	14th
12.	Boys know more about ICT than girls do	287	4	2.57	1.091	10th
13.	A female can very well have ICT job	287	4	1.55	.791	15th
14.	There is general perception that boys know more about ICT than girls do	287	4	2.51	1.103	12th
15.	There is general perception that females don't excel in male-dominant subjects like technology.	287	4	2.73	1.021	7th
16.	My parent belief that male have greater confidence in using technology for learning than female students.	287	4	3.00	1.009	5th
17.	A positive, supportive ICT culture exists throughout the school	287	4	2.71	.994	9th
18.	The school environment encourages students' independent ICT use by both teachers and students	287	4	2.84	1.073	6th
19.	Students have limited access to computers during school hours	287	4	3.20	.900	3rd
20.	The school does not have a computer laboratory to augment learning	287	4	3.28	.920	1st
21.	Computers are used reluctantly by teachers during lesson hour	287	4	3.25	.975	2nd
22.	ICT use outside normal teaching time is encouraged	287	4	2.45	1.076	12th
23.	The school is an ICT-friendly zone	287	4	2.36	1.061	14th
24.	ICT access is available during school time	287	4	2.57	1.091	10th

Source: Researchers' (Field work, 2018)

We lack basic facilities in this school. We have reported severally to the authorities but nothing was done about our ordeal. For instance, there is only one desktop computer in the entire school here in the Principal's office. At the moment, there is no light to power it except we buy fuel for the generator.

The above statement is very pathetic. If in a school of over two thousand population, only one desktop computer is available besides it is not optimally utilized due to power outage and absence of fuel to power the available generator. This is unacceptable in this era of ICT revolution. Hence, there is need for some level of attention by relevant stakeholders.

According to a middle aged female Vice-principal in School B:

We have computer a laboratory in this school donated by MTN telecommunications years ago. However, of the fifteen (15) computers, only Nine (9) are functional which is hardly enough for over 1,000 students. Because of irregular power supply we make arrangement to fuel the generator anytime the computer lab is to be engaged.

Further interaction of the researchers with students in school B revealed that, the available computers in the laboratory are not easily accessible except by due authorization of the Computer teacher and sometimes the school authorities. Even when accessible, too many students' especially interested male students are given the chance to engage the computers within limited time frame. Besides the challenges of power, and non-availability of adequate computer facilities to enhance usage and practical sessions for ICT/STEM related studies, the behavioral dispositions and attitudes of the female students to computer usage, adoption and studies was found to be low when compared with the male students. Findings from the questionnaire showed that more male students responded to the research questions in addition to showing interest in the research subject. A few of the female students declined from completing the questionnaire much less engaging in discussion around the research topic. The findings corroborate other studies in the field of computer science that more females hold negative attitude towards computer science related courses compared to their male counterparts (Sáinz, 2007). Cultural barriers and religious factor seemed to be obvious in school C which incidentally is populated by Muslims unlike school A and B populated by students from two dominant religions (Christianity and Islam).

CONCLUSION

The study examined gender differences in ICT studies in public secondary schools in Ota, Ogun State, Nigeria. Findings from the primary data showed the existence of gender differences in ICT studies in the schools sample. In spite of more female students enrollment in the public secondary schools studied, more male students were favorably disposed to ICT studies, computer and STEM. The study shows that boys more than girls were more likely to be encouraged to undertake STEM courses. In addition to the paucity of infrastructure (power, computer facilities), the study found out that more female students than males lack self-confidence and peer support in ICT studies. These negative attitudes towards computers deter women from pursuing computer-related studies and careers (Sáinz & López-Sáez, 2010). Young men are more likely than young women to receive more encouragement from significant others (parents, teachers, school advisors or peers) to pursue technology-related studies (Cussó, 2007). Not only is parental support influential for the ways in which young people use ICTs generally, but it has also been found to be crucial in the decision-making process of choosing studies and occupations and in shaping attitudes, habits and uses as revealed by findings from the Public Secondary schools sampled. Young men are more likely than young women to receive more encouragement from their parents to improve their knowledge about ICT (Vekiri & Chronaki, 2008).

RECOMMENDATIONS

Based on the findings of this study, the following recommendations are made:

1. There is need for a deliberate effort by the management of public secondary schools to introduce ICT and related studies in the school curriculum.
2. Both the provision of infrastructure, power and corresponding computer hard and soft ware should be given utmost priority by the relevant stakeholders. There is need for more budgetary allocation for education and schools to provide functional computer laboratories that can aid studies in ICTs and related subjects for needed societal transformation and development.
3. The need to reinforce the teaching of ICT and related courses in public secondary schools is highly recommended to bridge the gap between males and females in ICT studies thereby given more females opportunity and exposure to ICT related studies.
4. Bearing in mind that the male students are more exposed to ICTs, it is therefore imperative to give more encouragement and support their female counterparts.
5. Measures should be adopted to encourage female students to believe in themselves and in their abilities for ICT studies. ICT should not be seen as the exclusive preserve for the males.

FUTURE RESEARCH DIRECTION

The authors suggest the need for more in depth studies of the socio-cultural factors influencing gender differences in ICT adoption and usage with a view to increasing baseline data and literature in this area of scholarly research. The specific role of infrastructure and parental support for ICT studies should be engaged further for robust data in that area of scholarly research.

ACKNOWLEDGMENT

The authors acknowledge Covenant University Nigeria the home institution of the researchers for providing an enabling environment to carry out this study. The Covenant University Centre for Research Innovation and Discovery (CUCRID) is also acknowledged for promoting quality research. Our special thanks goes to the Principals of the Public Secondary Schools sampled and for additional data provided in terms oral interviews which complemented the data from the questionnaire. The authors are responsible for all errors and omissions in this study.

REFERENCES

Abedalaziz, N., Jamaluddin, S., & Leng, C. H. (2013). Measuring attitudes toward computer and internet usage among postgraduate students in Malaysia. *Turkish Online Journal of Educational Technology, 12*(2), 200–216.

Aesaert, K., & van Braak, J. (2015). Gender and socioeconomic related differences in performance based ICT competences. *Computers & Education, 84*, 8–25. doi:10.1016/j.compedu.2014.12.017

Aifan, H.A. (2016). Gender differences in terms of the experiences that Saudi Students have with social media technologies. *Global Advanced Research Journal of Educational Research and Review, 5*(5), 71-73,

Ainley, J., Fraillon, J., & Freeman, C. (2007). *National assessment program: ICT literacy years 6 & 10 report 2005*. MCEETYA.

Akinsowon, O. A., & Osisanwo, F. Y. (2014). Enhancing Interest in Sciences, Technology and Mathematics (STEM) for the Nigerian Female Folk. *International Journal of Information Science, 4*(1), 8–12. doi:10.5923/j.ijis.20140401.02

Alrasheedi, H. (2009). *Information and Communication Technology (ICT): Effects of Gender and Training among Kuwait Teachers* (PhD dissertation). Ohio University.

Amoo, S. A., Hambali., & M.A. & Amoo, A.O. (2013). Students' Learning Attitudes toward Computer Studies: A Study of SchoolNet, Nigeria. In *2nd International Conference on the Transformation of Public Examination*. University of Ibadan.

Atan, H., Azli, N., Rahman, Z., & Idrus, R. (2002). Computers in distance education: Gender differences in self-perceived computer competencies. *Journal of Educational Media, 27*(3), 123–135.

Baek, S.-G., Kim, D., Kim, M.-R., Kim, H. S., Yu, Y. L., Park, S.-H., . . . Kim, M. (2009). Assessing student ICT literacy on a national level. In T. Bastiaens, J. Dron, & C. Xin (Eds.), *Proceedings of e-learn: World conference on e-learning in corporate, government, healthcare, and higher education 2009* (pp. 2269-2275). Academic Press.

Baek, S. G., Kim, D. I., & Kim, M. R. (2009). The development of standardized ICT literacy assessment for secondary school student. *Asian Journal of Education, 10*(1), 175–198. doi:10.15753/aje.2009.10.1.008

Bain, C. D., & Rice, M. L. (2006). The Influence of Gender on Attitudes, Perceptions, and Uses of Technology. *Journal of Research on Technology in Education, 39*(2), 119–132. doi:10.1080/15391523.2006.10782476

Bandura, A., Barbaranelli, C., Caprana, C. V., & Pastorelli, C. (2001). Self-efficacy beliefs as shapers of children's aspirations and career trajectories. *Child Development, 72*(1), 187–206. doi:10.1111/1467-8624.00273 PMID:11280478

Barkatsas, A. N. (2012). Students' Attitudes, Engagement and Confidence in Mathematics and Statistics Learning: ICT, Gender, and Equity Dimensions. Academic Press.

Bøe, M. V., & Henriksen, E. K. (2015). Expectancy-Value Perspectives on Choice of Science and Technology Education in Late-Modern Societies. In Late-Modern Societies. In E. Henriksen, J. Dillon, & J. Ryder (Eds.), *Understanding Student Participation and Choice in Science and Technology Education*. Dordrecht: Springer.

Boneva, B., Kraut, R., & Frohlich, D. (2001). Using e-mail for personal relationships: The difference gender makes. *The American Behavioral Scientist, 45*(3), 530–549. doi:10.1177/00027640121957204

Brosnan, M. (1998). The role of psychological gender in the computer-related attitudes and attainments of primary school children (aged 6–11). *Computers & Education, 30*(3–4), 203–208. doi:10.1016/S0360-1315(97)00070-5

Buabeng-Andoh, C. (2014). Investigating students' pedagogical use of ICT in learning in Ghanaian secondary schools. *British Education Studies Association, 6*(2), 44–53.

Calvani, A., Fini, A., Ranieri, M., & Picci, P. (2012). Are young generations in secondary school digitally competent? A study on Italian teenagers. *Computers & Education, 58*(2), 797–807. doi:10.1016/j.compedu.2011.10.004

Cavas, B., Cavas, P., Karaoglan, B., & Kisla, T. (2009). A study on science teachers' attitudes toward information and communication technologies in Education. *TOJET*, (8), 2.

Cgggohoon, J. M., & Aspray, W. (2006). A critical review of the research on women's participation in postsecondary computing education. In *By the Numbers*. Boulder, CO: NCWIT. Retrieved November 7, 2017, from http://www.ncwit.org/resources/numbers

Cheryan, S., Master, A., & Meltzoff, A. (2015). Cultural stereotypes as gatekeepers: Increasing girls' interest in computer science and engineering by diversifying stereotypes. *Frontiers in Psychology*, 6. PMID:25717308

Christoph, G., Goldhammer, F., Zylka, J., & Hartig, J. (2015). Adolescents' computer performance: The role of self-concept and motivational aspects. *Computers & Education, 81*, 1–12. doi:10.1016/j.compedu.2014.09.004

Claro, M., Preiss, D. D., San Martín, E., Jara, I., Hinostroza, J. E., Valenzuela, S., ... Nussbaum, M. (2012). Assessment of 21st century ICT skills in Chile: Test design and results from high school level students. *Computers & Education, 59*(3), 1042–1053. doi:10.1016/j.compedu.2012.04.004

Claro, M., Preiss, D. D., San Martín, E., Jara, I., Hinostroza, J. E., Valenzuela, S., ... Nussbaum, M. (2012). Assessment of 21st century ICT skills in Chile: Test design and results from high school level students. *Computers & Education, 59*(3), 1042–1053. doi:10.1016/j.compedu.2012.04.004

Collis, B. A., & Williams, R. L. (1987). Differences in adolescents' attitudes toward computers and selected school subjects. *Journal of Educational Computing Research, 8*, 17–27.

Creamer, E. G., Lee, S., & Meszaros, P. S. (2006). *Factors Associated With Women's Interest In Computing Fields*. Research paper presented at the Association for the Study of Engineering Education (ASEE), Chicago, IL.

Cunningham, C. (2007). *Linking STEM and Communication Technology Research: A Research Agenda for Technology and Gender Equality. Paper presented at the annual meeting of the NCA 93rd Annual Convention*, Chicago, IL. Retrieved from http://www.allacademic.com/meta/p193877

Cussó, R. (2007). *Tecnologia: gènere i professió* [Technology: gender and profession]. Departament d'Educació de la Generalitat de Cataluña.

Cussó-Calabuig, R., Carrera Farran, X., & Bosch-Capblanch, X. (2017). Are boys and girls still digitally differentiated? The case of Catalonian teenagers. *Journal of Information Technology Education: Research, 16*, 411-435. https://repositori.udl.cat/bitstream/handle/10459.1/62324/026246.pdf?sequence=1 doi:Retrieved from

De Wit, K., Heerwegh, D., & Verhoeven, J. C. (2014). Can openness to ICT and scientific research predict the ICT skills and ICT use of bachelor's students? *Computers & Education*, *78*, 397–413. doi:10.1016/j.compedu.2014.07.003

Deloitte. (2016). *Women in STEM Technology, career pathways and the gender pay gap*. Deloitte.

Department of Education and Science. (2008). *ICT in Schools: Inspectorate Evaluation Studies*. Department of Education and Science.

Dettingen, G. (1995). Cross-cultural perspectives on self-efficacy. In A. Bandura (Ed.), *Self-efficacy in changing societies* (pp. 169–176). New York: Cambridge University Press. doi:10.1017/CBO9780511527692.007

Dlodlo, N. (2009). Access to ICT education for girls and women in rural South Africa: A case study. *Technology in Society*, *31*(2), 168–175. doi:10.1016/j.techsoc.2009.03.003

Doring, N., Hellwig, K., & Klimsa, P. (2005). Mobile communication among German youth. In K. Nyiri (Ed.), A sense of place: The global and the local in mobile communication (pp. 209-217). Vienna, Austria: Passagen Verlag.

Durndell, A., & Haag, Z. (2002). Computer self-efficacy, computer anxiety, attitudes towards the Internet and reported experience with the Internet, by gender, in an East European sample. *Computers in Human Behavior*, *18*(5), 521–535. doi:10.1016/S0747-5632(02)00006-7

Eccles, J. S. (1994). Understanding Women's Educational And Occupational Choices: Applying the Eccles et al. Model of Achievement-Related Choices. *Psychology of Women Quarterly*, *18*(4), 585–609. doi:10.1111/j.1471-6402.1994.tb01049.x

Eccles, J. S. (2007). Where Are All the Women? Gender Differences in Participation. In Why aren't more Women in science? Top researchers debate evidence. American Psychological Association.

Eccles, J. S., Adler, T. F., Futterman, R., Goff, S. B., Kaczala, C. M., & Meece, J. L. (1983). Expectancies, values and academic behaviours. In J. T. Spence (Ed.), *Achievement and achievement motivation* (pp. 75–146). San Francisco, CA: W. H. Freeman.

Eccles, J. S., & Wigfield, A. (2002). Motivational beliefs, values and goals. *Annual Review of Psychology*, *53*(1), 109–132. doi:10.1146/annurev.psych.53.100901.135153 PMID:11752481

Economides, A. A., & Grousopoulou, A. (2008). Use of mobile phones by male and female Greek students. *International Journal of Mobile Communications*, *6*(6), 729–749. doi:10.1504/IJMC.2008.019822

Else-Quest, N. M., Mineo, C. C., & Higgins, A. (2013). Maths and Sciences attitudes and achievement at the intersection of gender and ethnicity. *Psychology of Women Quarterly*, *37*(3), 293–309. doi:10.1177/0361684313480694

Fančovičová, J., & Prokop, P. (2008). Students' Attitudes toward Computer Use in Slovakia. *Eurasia Journal of Mathematics. Science & Technology Education*, *4*(3), 255–262.

Filgona, J., & Sababa, L. K. (2017). Effect of Gender on Senior Secondary School Students' Academic Achievement in Geography in Ganye Educational Zone, Nigeria. *European Journal of Education Studies*, *3*(4), 394–410.

Fomsi, E. F., & Orduah, S. E. (2017). Gender Differences in the Use of ICT among Teachers in Model Primary Schools in Rivers State, Nigeria. *Brock Journal of Education*, *5*(4), 88–94.

Fraillon, J., Ainley, J., Schulz, W., Friedman, T., & Gebhardt, E. (2014). *Preparing for life in a digital age - the IEA international computer and information literacy study international report.* Heidelberg, Germany: Springer International Publishing.

Fraillon, J., Ainley, J., Schulz, W., Friedman, T., & Gebhardt, E. (2014). *Preparing for life in a digital age – the IEA international computer and information literacy study, International Report.* Amsterdam: IEA.

Gebhardt, E., Fraillon, J., Ainley, J., & Schulz, W. (2016). Gender Differences In computer And Information Literacy and the Use of ICT. A thematic report from the IEA International Computer and Information Literacy Study. *IEA General Assembly Meeting*, *57*, 10–13.

George, T. O., Ahmadu, F. O., & Chukwuedozie, O. (2013). ICT and Secondary School Educational System in Nigeria: A Conceptual Review. In Panoply of Readings in Social Sciences Lessons for and from Nigeria. Covenant University.

George, T. O., & Barnabas, S. (2015), ICT and the Gender Question: Prospects and Challenges for the Knowledge Economy in the 21st Century. In *International conference on Africa development issues (CU-ICADI)*. Covenant University.

Ghavifekr, S., Kunjappan, T., Ramasamy, L., & Anthony, A. (2016). Teaching and Learning with ICT Tools: Issues and Challenges from Teachers' Perceptions. *Malaysian Online Journal of Educational Technology*, *4*(2), 28–57.

Gras-Velazquez, A., Joyce, A., & Debry, M. (2009). *Women and ICT: Why are girls still not attracted to ICT studies and careers?* European Schoolnet.

Gråstén, A. (2014). Students' physical activity, physical education enjoyment, and motivational determinants through a three-year school-initiated program (Dissertation). Jyväskylä: University of Jyväskylä.

Gråstén, A. (2016). Children's expectancy beliefs and subjective task values through two years of school-based program and associated links to physical education enjoyment and physical activity. *Journal of Sport and Health Science*, *5*(4), 500–508. doi:10.1016/j.jshs.2015.12.005

Gråstén, A., Watt, A., Hagger, M., Jaakkola, T., & Liukkonen, J. (2015). Secondary school students' physical activity participation across physical education classes—the expectancy–value theory approach. *Physics Education*, *72*, 340–358.

Gui, M., & Argentin, G. (2011). Digital skills of internet natives: Different forms of internet literacy in a random sample of northern Italian high school students. *New Media & Society*, *13*(6), 963–980. doi:10.1177/1461444810389751

Hafkin, N., & Taggart, N. (2001). *Gender, information technology, and developing countries: an analytic study for the Office of Women in Development Bureau for Global Programs, Field Support and Research, United States Agency for International Development (USAID).* Available at: http://www.usaid.gov/wid/pubs/hafnoph.pdf

Hakkarainena, K., IlomaÈki, L., Lipponena, L., Muukkonena, H., Rahikainenb, M., Tuominena, T., Lakkalaa, M., & Lehtinen, E. (2000). Students' skills and practices of using ICT: Results of a national assessment in Finland. *Computers & Education*, 34–117.

Hargittai, E., & Shafer, S. (2006). Differences in actual and perceived online skills: The role of gender. *Social Science Quarterly*, *87*(2), 432-448. . doi:10.1111/j.1540-6237.2006.00389.x

Hatlevik, O. E., & Christophersen, K. A. (2013). Digital competence at the beginning of upper secondary school: Identifying factors explaining digital inclusion. *Computers & Education*, *63*, 240–247. doi:10.1016/j.compedu.2012.11.015

Hatlevik, O. E., Scherer, R., & Christophersen, K. (2017). Moving beyond the study of gender differences: An analysis of measurement invariance and differential item functioning of an ICT literacy scale. *Computers & Education*, *113*, 280–293. doi:10.1016/j.compedu.2017.06.003

Hatlevik, O. V., Throndsen, I., Loi, M., & Gudmundsdottir, G. B. (2018). Students' ICT self-efficacy and computer and information literacy: Determinants and relationships. *Computers & Education*, *118*, 107–119. doi:10.1016/j.compedu.2017.11.011

Henriksen, E. K., Dillion, J., & Ryder, J. (Eds.). Understanding Student Participation and Choice in Science and Technology Education. Springer. DOI doi:10.1007/978-94-007-7793-4_2

Hill, O. W., Pettus, C., & Hedin, B. A. (1990). Three studies of factors affecting the attitudes of blacks and females toward the pursuit of science and science-related careers. *Journal of Research in Science Teaching*, *27*(4), 289–314. doi:10.1002/tea.3660270403

Hohlfeld, T. N., Ritzhaupt, A. D., & Barron, A. E. (2013). Are gender differences in perceived and demonstrated technology literacy significant? It depends on the model. *Educational Technology Research and Development*, *61*, 639-663. . doi:10.100711423-013-9304-7

Hulleman, C. S., Barron, K. E., Kosovich, J. J., & Lazowski, R. A. (2014). Current Theories, Constructs, and Interventions within an Expectancy-Value Framework. In Psychosocial skills and school systems in the Twenty-first century: Theory, research, and applications. Springer.

Jackson, L., Ervin, K., Gardner, P. D., & Schmitt, N. (2001). Gender and the Internet: Women communicating and men searching'. *Sex Roles*, *44*(5/6), 363–379. doi:10.1023/A:1010937901821

Jacobs, J. E., Lanza, S., Osgood, D. W., Eccles, J. S., & Wigfield, A. (2002). Changes in children's self-competence and values: Gender and domain differences across grade one through twelve. *Child Development, 73*(2), 509–527. doi:10.1111/1467-8624.00421 PMID:11949906

Jennings, S. E., & Onwuegbuzie, A. J. (2001). Computer attitudes as a function of age, gender, math attitude and developmental status. *Journal of Educational Computing Research, 25*(4), 367–384. doi:10.2190/WH2L-BBVB-DTPG-UG7R

Kayaoglu, N. M. (2012). Gender-Based Differences in Language Learning Strategies of Science Students. *J. Turkish Sci. Educ., 9*(2).

Kembler, S. (1996). Feminism, technology and Social representations. In J. Curran, D. Morley, & V. Walkerdine (Eds.), *Cultural Studies and Communications*. London: Arnold.

Kiefer, A., & Shih, M. (2006). Gender differences in persistence and attributions in stereotype relevant contexts. *Sex Roles, 54*(11-12), 859–868. doi:10.100711199-006-9051-x

Kiefer, A., & Shih, M. (2006). Gender differences in persistence and attributions in stereotype relevant contexts. *Sex Roles, 54*(11-12), 859–868. doi:10.100711199-006-9051-x

Kim, H.-S., Kil, H.-J., & Shin, A. (2014). An analysis of variables affecting the ICT literacy level of Korean elementary school students. *Computers & Education, 77*, 29–38. doi:10.1016/j.compedu.2014.04.009

Kim, J. M., & Lee, W. G. (2011). Meanings of criteria and norms: Analyses and comparisons of ICT literacy competencies of middle school students. *Computers & Education, 64*, 81–94. doi:10.1016/j.compedu.2012.12.018

Koch, S. C., Müller, S. M., & Sieverding, M. (2008). Women and computers. Effects of stereotype threat on attribution of failure. *Computers & Education, 51*(4), 1795-1803. doi:10.1016/j.compedu.2008.05.007

Kumari, S. N., & Saraladevi, K. (2012). Gender Differences in Attitude towards Science Teaching and Learning Styles among Adolescents. *International Journal of Science and Research, 3*(10), 50–58.

Langdon, G., McKittrick, D. B., Khan, B., & Doms, M. (2011). *STEM: Good jobs now and for the future*. U.S. Department of Commerce, Economics and Statistics Administration.

Laosethakul, K., & Leingpibul, T. (2010). Why females do not choose Computing: A lesson learned from China. *Multicultural Education & Technology Journal, 4*(3), 173–187. doi:10.1108/17504971011075174

Lau, W. W., & Yuen, A. Y. (2015). Factorial invariance across gender of a perceived ICT literacy scale. *Learning and Individual Differences, 41*, 79–85. doi:10.1016/j.lindif.2015.06.001

Li, N., & Kirkup, G. (2007). Gender and cultural differences in Internet use: A study of China and the UK. *Computers & Education, 48*(2), 301–317. doi:10.1016/j.compedu.2005.01.007

Lim, S., & Soon, C. (2010). The influence of social and cultural factors on mothers' domestication of household ICTs – Experiences of Chinese and Korean women. *Telematics and Informatics, 27*(3), 205–216. doi:10.1016/j.tele.2009.07.001

Litt, E. (2013). Measuring users' internet skills: A review of past assessments and a look toward the future. *New Media & Society, 15*(4), 612–630. doi:10.1177/1461444813475424

Luan, W. L., Aziz, S. A., Yunus, A. S., Sidek, Z., Bakar, K. A., Meseran, H., & Atan, A. (2005). Gender Differences in ICT Competencies among Academicians at Universiti Putra Malaysia. *Malaysian Online Journal of Instructional Technology, 2*(3), 62–69. Retrieved from http://pppjj.usm.my/mojit/articles/pdf/Dec05/08 - Gender_differences[1]-final.pdf

Major, D. A., Morganson, V. J., & Bolen, H. M. (2013). Predictors of occupational and organizational commitment in information technology: Exploring gender differences and similarities. *Journal of Business and Psychology, 28*(3), 301–304. doi:10.100710869-012-9282-5

Makrakis, V., & Sawada, T. (1996). Gender, computers and other school subjects among Japanese and Swedish students. *Computers & Education, 26*(4), 225–231. doi:10.1016/0360-1315(95)00085-2

Margolis, J., & Fisher, A. (2002). *Unlocking the clubhouse: Women in computing.* MIT Press.

Mceetya. (2007). *National assessment program e ICT literacy years 6 & 10, report 2005.* Carlton South: Ministerial council on education, employment, training and youth affairs. Retrieved from: http://www.nap.edu.au/verve/_resources/2005_ICTL_Public_Report_file_main.pdf

Meelissen, M. (2008). Computer attitudes and competencies among primary and secondary school students. In J. Voogt, & G. Knezek (Eds.), International handbook of information technology in primary and secondary education, part one (pp. 381–395). New York: Springer.

Meelissen, M. R. M., & Drent, M. (2008). Gender differences in computer attitudes: Does the school matter? *Computers in Human Behavior, 24*(3), 969–985. doi:10.1016/j.chb.2007.03.001

Meszaros, P. S., Soyoung, L., & Laughling, A. (2007). Information processing and IT career interest/choice among high school students. In Reconfiguring the firewall. Recruiting women to Information Technology across cultures and Continents (pp. 77-98). Wellesley, MA: A.K. Peters, Ltd.

Mitra, A., Willyard, J., Platt, C., & Parsons, M. (2005). Exploring Web usage and selection criteria among male and female students. *Journal of Computer-Mediated Communication, 10*(3), 00. doi:10.1111/j.1083-6101.2005.tb00258.x

Morris, D., & Trushell, J. (2014). Computer programming, ICT and gender in the classroom: A male-dominated domain or a female preserve? *Research in Teacher Education, 4*(1), 4–9.

Mumporeze, N., & Prieler, M. (2017). Gender digital divide in Rwanda: A qualitative analysis of socioeconomic factors. *Telematics and Informatics, 34*(7), 1285–1293. doi:10.1016/j.tele.2017.05.014

National Children's Bureau (NCB). (2015). *ICT & Me: A research study examining how young people's use of ICT and the amount of screen time impacts on GCSE attainment.* Retrieved from https://www.ncb.org.uk/sites/default/files/field/attachment/22%20ict_me.pdf

Nelson, B. (2014). The data on diversity. *Communications of the ACM, 57*(11), 86–95. doi:10.1145/2597886

Odukoya, A. (2005). *ICT & Women: Engendering the Information Society in Nigeria.* Lagos, Nigeria: DevNet.

Okunna, S. (2000). *Gender and Communication in Nigeria: Is this the Twenty First Century?* Paper presented at the 2000 Summit, Barcelona, Spain.

Olatokun, W. M. (2007). Availability, Accessibility and Use of ICTs by Nigerian Women Academics. *Malaysian Journal of Library and Information Science*, *12*(2), 13–33.

Ong, C. S., & Lai, J. Y. (2006). Gender differences in perceptions and relationships among dominants of e-learning acceptance. *Computers in Human Behavior*, *22*(5), 816–829. doi:10.1016/j.chb.2004.03.006

Ong, C. S., & Lai, J. Y. (2006). Gender differences in perceptions and relationships among dominants of e-learning acceptance. *Computers in Human Behavior*, *22*(5), 816–829. doi:10.1016/j.chb.2004.03.006

Oyelaran-Oyeyinka, B., & Adeya, C. (2004). Dynamics of adoption and usage of ICTs in African universities: A study of Kenya and Nigeria. *Technovation*, *24*(10), 841–851. doi:10.1016/S0166-4972(02)00170-0

Pechtelidis, Y., Kosma, Y., & Chronaki, A. (2015). Between a rock and a hard place: Women and computer technology. *Gender and Education*, *27*(2), 164–182. doi:10.1080/09540253.2015.1008421

Sáinz, M. (2007). *Aspectos psicosociales de las diferencias de género en actitudes hacialas nuevas tecnologías en adolescentes* [Psychosocial aspects of gender difference in gender attitudes towards new technologies among adolescents]. Retrieved from http://www.injuve.mtin.es/injuve/contenidos.item.action?id=1423691052&menuId=52682864

Sainz, M. (2011). Factors which influence girls' orientations to ICT subjects in schools. Evidence from Spain. *International Journal of Gender, Science and Technology*, *3*(2), 387–406.

Sainz, M., Fatsini, E., García, S., González, A., Meneses, J., Prat, P., & Solé, S. (2009). *¿Por qué las mujeres no eligen estudios TIC? La cañería que gotea en elcontexto de Cataluña?* [Why women do not pursue ICT-related studies The leaky pipeline in the context of Catalunya?]. Unpublished research report.

Sáinz, M., Fatsini, E., García, S., González, A., Meneses, N., Prat, P., & Solé, J. (2009) *¿Porqué las mujeres no eligen estudios TIC? La cañería que gotea en el contexto de Cataluña*. [Why women do not pursue ICT studies? The leaky pipeline in the context of Catalunya]. Research Report, unpublished.

Sanda, H. U., & Kurfi, M. H. (2013). Gender and Information Communication Technologies in Nigeria: Challenges and prospects. *Global Journal of Human Social Science Sociology and Culture*, *6*(13), 50–58.

Sangrà, A., & González-Sanmamed, M. (2010). The role of information and communication technologies in improving teaching and learning processes in primary and secondary schools. *Research in Learning Technology*, *18*(3), 207–220. doi:10.1080/09687769.2010.529108

Sarfo, F. K., Amartei, A. M., Adentwi, K. I., & Brefo, C. (2011). Technology and gender equity: Rural and urban students' attitudes towards information and communication technology. *Journal of Media and Communication Studies*, *3*(6), 221–230.

Saunders, B., & Quirke, P. (2002). Let my laptop lead the way: A Middle Eastern study. *Journal of Educational Technology & Society*, *5*(1), 1436–4522.

Schunk, D. H., Meece, J. L., & Pintrich, P. R. (2014). *Motivation in education: Theory, research, and applications* (4th ed.). Harlow: Pearson.

Shashaani, L., & Khalili, A. (2000). Gender and computers: Similarities and differences in Iranian college students' towards computers. *Computers & Education, 37*(3-4), 363–375. doi:10.1016/S0360-1315(01)00059-8

Shaw, L. H., & Gant, L. M. (2002). Users divided? Exploring the gender gap in Internet use. *Cyberpsychology & Behavior, 5*(6), 517–527. doi:10.1089/109493102321018150 PMID:12556114

Siddiq, F., Gochyyev, P., & Wilson, M. (2017). Learning in Digital Networks e ICT literacy: A novel assessment of students' 21st century skills. *Computers & Education, 109*, 11–37. doi:10.1016/j.compedu.2017.01.014

Sieverding, M., & Koch, S. C. (2009). (Self-)Evaluation of computer competence: How gender matters. *Computers & Education, 52*(3), 696-701. . doi:10.1016/j.compedu.2008.11.016

Sinha, C. (2009). Effects of Education and ICT Use on Gender Relations in Bhutan. *International Development Research Centre, 5*(3), 21–34.

Skaalvik, S., & Skaalvik, E. S. (2004). Gender Differences in Math And Verbal Self- Concept, Performance Expectations, and Motivation. *Sex Roles, 50*(3/4), 241–252. doi:10.1023/B:SERS.0000015555.40976.e6

Smith, B. N., & Necessary, J. R. (1996). Assessing the computer literacy of undergraduate college students. *Education, 117*(2), 188–193.

Tella, A., & Mutula, S. M. (2008). Gender Differences in Computer Literacy among Undergraduate Students at the University of Botswana: Implications for Library Use. *Malaysian Journal of Library and Information Science, 13*(1), 59–76.

Tømte, C. (2011). Challenging our views on ICT, gender and education. *Nordic Journal of Digital Literacy, 6*(SI), 309–325.

Trauth, E. M., Quesenberry, J. L., & Morgan, A. J. (2004). Understanding the underrepresentation of women in IT: toward a theory of individual differences. In *Proceedings of the 2004 SIGMIS conference on Computer personnel research: Careers, culture, and ethics in a networked environment*. ACM.

Tsai, P. S., Tsai, C. C., & Hwang, G. H. (2010). Elementary school students' attitudes and self-efficacy of using PDAs in a ubiquitous learning context. *Australasian Journal of Educational Technology, 26*(3), 297–308. doi:10.14742/ajet.1076

United Nations Educational, Scientific and Cultural Organization (UNESCO). (2017). *Cracking the code: Girls' and women's education in science, technology, engineering and mathematics (STEM)*. The United Nations Educational, Scientific and Cultural Organization. Retrieved from http://unesdoc.unesco.org/images/0025/002534/253479e.pdf

U.S. women surging online, closing gender gap, reshaping social landscape. (2000). *Media Report to Women, 28*(2), 1-2.

Van Deursen, A. (2012). Internet skill-related problems in accessing online health information. *International Journal of Medical Informatics, 81*(1), 61–72. doi:10.1016/j.ijmedinf.2011.10.005 PMID:22079240

Van Deursen, A., & Van Dijk, J. (2009). Improving digital skills for the use of online public information and services. *Government Information Quarterly*, *26*(2), 333–340. doi:10.1016/j.giq.2008.11.002

Van Deursen, A., Van Dijk, J., & Peters, O. (2011). Rethinking Internet skills. The contribution of gender, age, education, Internet experience, and hours online to medium- and content-related internet skills. *Poetics*, *39*(2), 125–144. doi:10.1016/j.poetic.2011.02.001

Vekiri, I. (2008). *The gender gap in attitudes and beliefs about ICT.* Paper prepared for the OECD Expert meeting on Gender, ICT and Education, Oslo, Norway.

Vekiri, I., & Chronaki, A. (2008). Gender issues in technology use: Perceived social support, computer self-efficacy and value beliefs, and computer use beyond school. *Computers & Education*, *51*(3), 1392–1404. doi:10.1016/j.compedu.2008.01.003

Vekiri, I., & Chronaki, A. (2008). Gender issues in technology use: Perceived social support, computer self-efficacy and value beliefs, and computer use beyond school. *Computers & Education*, *51*(3), 1392–1404. doi:10.1016/j.compedu.2008.01.003

Volman, M., & Van, E. E. (2001). Gender equity and information technology in education. The second decade. *Review of Educational Research*, *71*(4), 613–631. doi:10.3102/00346543071004613

Wajcman, J. (2006). Feminist perspectives on technology. In A. H. Teich (Ed.), *Technology and the Future* (pp. 67–79). Thomson Wardworth.

Webb, D.C. & Miller, S.B. (2015). *Gender Analysis of a Large Scale Survey of Middle Grades Students' Conceptions of Computer Science Education*. Academic Press.

Wentworth, B. (2015). *Using expectancy-value theory to predict intent to conform in Elementary school students* (MA thesis). Appalachian State University.

Wigfield, A., & Eccles, J. S. (2000). Expectancy–value theory of achievement motivation. *Contemporary Educational Psychology*, *25*(1), 68–81. doi:10.1006/ceps.1999.1015 PMID:10620382

Wigfield, A., & Eccles, J. S. (2002). The Development of Competence Beliefs, Expectancies For Success, And Achievement Values From Childhood Through Adolescence. In A. Wigfield & J.S. Eccles (Eds.), Development of achievement motivation. Academic Press.

Wigfield, A., & Eccles, J. S. (2002). The Development of Competence Beliefs, Expectancies for Success, And Achievement Values from Childhood Through adolescence. In A. Wigfield & J. S. Eccles (Eds.), *A Vol. in the educational psychology series. Development of achievement motivation* (pp. 91–120). San Diego, CA: Academic Press. doi:10.1016/B978-012750053-9/50006-1

Wilson, T. (2000). Web's gender shift more than a curiosity. *Internet Week*, *28*, 827.

Wong, K. C., & Cheung, W. K. (2013). Gender Differences in ICT Competency for University Students of Different Disciplines. *Journal of Communications and Information Sciences*, *3*(2). doi:10.4156/jcis.vol3.issue2.7

Xiang, P., McBride, R., Guan, J., & Solmon, M. (2003). Children's motivation in elementary physical education: An expectancy–value model of achievement choice. *Research Quarterly for Exercise and Sport*, *74*(1), 25–35. doi:10.1080/02701367.2003.10609061 PMID:12659473

Yang, J. H. (2012). Effects of high school ICT activities on students' digital literacy in Korea. *Journal of Educational Technology*, *28*(2), 347–369. doi:10.17232/KSET.28.2.347

Yansen, G., & Zukerfeld, M. (2014). Why Don't Women Program? Exploring Links between Gender, Technology and Software. *Science, Technology & Society*, *19*(3), 305–329. doi:10.1177/0971721814548111

Yau, H.K., & Cheng, A.L. (2012). Gender Difference of Confidence in Using Technology for Learning. *Journal of Technology Studies,* 74-79.

Yau, H. K., & Leung, Y. F. (2016). Gender Difference of Self-Efficacy and Attitudes Towards the Use of Technology in Learning in Hong Kong Higher Education. *Proceedings of the International Multi-Conference*. Retrieved from http://www.iaeng.org/publication/IMECS2016/IMECS2016_pp819-821.pdf

Yazilitas, D., Svensson, J., de Vries, G., & Saharso, S. (2013). Gendered study choice: A literature review. A review of theory and research into the unequal representation of male and female students in mathematics, science, and technology. *Educational Research and Evaluation*, *19*(6), 525–545. doi:10.1080/13803611.2013.803931

Yli-Piipari, S. (2013). The development of students' physical education motivation and physical activity: a 3.5-year longitudinal study across Grades 6 to 9 (Dissertation). Jyväskylä: University of Jyväskylä.

Zagami, J., Boden, M., Keane, T., Moreton, B., & Schulz, K. (2015). Girls and Computing: Female participation in computing in Schools, *Australian. Education and Computing*, *30*(2).

Zarrett, N. R., & Malanchuk, O. (2005). Who's computing? Gender and race differences in young adults' decisions to pursue an Information Technology career. *New Directions for Child and Adolescent Development*, *110*(110), 65–84. doi:10.1002/cd.150 PMID:16509540

Zarrett, N. R., & Malanchuk, O. (2005). Who is computing? Gender and race differences in young adults' decisions to pursue an information technology career. *New Directions for Child and Adolescent Development*, *110*(110), 65–84. doi:10.1002/cd.150 PMID:16509540

Zarrett, N. R., Malanchuk, O., Davis-Kean, P. E., & Eccles, J. S. (2006). Examining the gender gap in IT by race: young adults' decisions to pursue an IT career. In J. M. Cohoon & B. Aspray (Eds.), *Women and Information Technology: Research on the reasons for underrepresentation* (pp. 55–88). Cambridge, MA: MIT Press. doi:10.7551/mitpress/9780262033459.003.0002

Zarrett, N. R., Malanchuk, O., Davis-Kean, P. E., & Eccles, J. S. (2006). Examining the gender gap in IT by race: Young adults. Decisions to pursue an IT career. In B. Aspray & J. MacGrath Cohoon (Eds.), *Women and information technology: Research on the reasons for under- representation* (pp. 55–88). Cambridge, MA: MIT Press. doi:10.7551/mitpress/9780262033459.003.0002

Zhang, Y. X. (2002). Comparison of Internet attitudes between industrial employees and college students. *Cyberpsychology & Behavior*, *5*(2), 143–149. doi:10.1089/109493102753770534 PMID:12025881

Zhao, L., Lu, Y., Huang, W., & Wang, Q. (2010). Internet inequality: The relationship between high school students' Internet use in different locations and their Internet self-efficacy. *Computers & Education*, *55*(4), 1405–1423. doi:10.1016/j.compedu.2010.05.010

Zhong, Z. J. (2011). From access to usage: The divide of self-reported digital skills among adolescents. *Computers & Education*, *56*(3), 736–746. doi:10.1016/j.compedu.2010.10.016

Chapter 9
Sustainable Development With the Digitalization of Women:
Economic Empowerment, Information Technology, and Women

Tijen Över Özçelik
Sakarya University, Turkey

ABSTRACT

There is no single field that is unaffected by the developments experienced in information and communication technologies today. However, the questions, Have women been affected by these intensive technological developments and technology utilization—which are efficient in every field—as much as men have? If not, how may this be reversed? and how may technology be made effective in making women economic? arouse curiosity. Therefore, the study was shaped by answering these questions. Another reason why the study took these questions as the basis is that women and technology are of profound importance in the sustainable development and growth of societies. Women's efficient use of technology is a must to turn the changes and developments experienced in information and communication technologies into opportunities and to reach the standards of the information society. Women's economic empowerment and technology were examined, the importance of the subject was emphasized, and recommendations were made within the scope of the study.

INTRODUCTION

Sustainable growth and development are core objectives of all societies. Similarly, sustainable development; the ensuring of economic growth; the efficient use of scarce resources; and the increase in the technological capital and also goals are of importance for all societies. Attaining these goals would imply investing in the human resource. Therefore, if the human being is an indispensable element in economic development, it will be impossible to provide development without women. At this point, it is an undeniable fact that women, who make up about half of the world population, assume a significant role in economic growth and development as a human resource. In this context, women's empowerment should

DOI: 10.4018/978-1-5225-7068-4.ch009

be among the essential objectives of societies and intensive studies on the training of women and their participation in the labor force should be carried out. The low labor force participation of women, who are acknowledged as an important element of economic empowerment and sustainable development, particularly in developing countries is striking. Nevertheless, introducing women into the labor force and hence into the economy and further ensuring the improvement of their positions in the family are regarded as a gain for societies and as a requirement for economic development.

In the studies conducted by the United Nations Development Fund for Women (UNIFEM) and the World Bank, it is stated that the social gender inequalities in developing countries hinder economic growth and development. For instance, a report by the World Bank demonstrates that there is intensive poverty, slow economic growth, and low living standards in those countries where gender-based discrimination is experienced. The United Nations Development Program (UNDP) revealed that there was a very strong correlation among the gender empowerment measure, gender-related development indexes, and the Human Development Index (Doğan, 2014). As the countries achieved production-based growth and development in the aftermath of the industrial revolution process, the countries who are information societies based on Information and Communication Technologies (ICT) attain sustainable development and growth through the information they produce and technology-intensive activities. And the production processes in these information societies perform are more efficient than that of other societies. Therefore, empowering women technologically and enabling them to become entrepreneurs will provide the momentum for a country to become an information society. In the process attaining, sustainable development and economic empowerment nationwide, and on a global scale. If one desires to succeed in new business skills as well as in production and service with world standards, which are required for the technological advances and trends experienced, studies should be carried out for the social gender balance in the field of informatics, as in many fields.

Given the technological advances and trends experienced today, it is supposed that Industry 4.0 will be effective in shaping the future. Industry 4.0 refers to those production systems which are described as the smart factories of the future; which are able to communicate; which can act autonomously; which are product-based; and which have a smart network. The real and virtual worlds; the globalized fall in product life cycles; rapidly-developing embedded software; social networks and autonomous decision-making intersect within the scope of a concept known as the Internet of Things (IoT). And furthermore industries are now being digitized (Hozdić, 2015). In such a case, it is essential that enterprises, governments and individuals adapt to these technological advances and to the new jobs that will emerge, which they will need, and require new skills. To eliminate the skill gaps that will be experienced with respect to the new jobs, it becomes important to include women, who cannot be represented adequately within the scope of technology-related jobs; in employment by empowering them with technology in addition to preparing training programs according to these new jobs. Given that especially the gender difference will also have a positive impact on the provision of the required jobs, positions, occupations or specialties of the future, it is of great importance to deal with it under the leadership of experts as academics, international organizations, professional service firms, and the human resources managers of big organizations (Baller, 2016). Though women empowerment is regarded as a key component in reducing poverty, it should not be considered only as a development objective but also as an instrument which encourages growth and supports managementr (Globalization, Growth & Poverty., 2002).

The women in both developing and developed countries were emphasized in the study while particularly touching upon the importance of women in the empowerment of the economy. The differences in the use of technology by the women in developed countries, in their performance habits as compared with men, is naturally much smaller than that in developing countries. However, it is observed that the access to technology by the women in rural regions in developed countries to technology and their technology utilization pattern are also low, compared with cities. Thus, the studies on increasing the technology utilization by the women in developed countries and on attaching the importance to STEM-based (Science, Technology, Engineering, and Mathematics) education; the studies/projects on how women are introduced to technology and on how they are encouraged to use the technology in developing countries were examined and addressed. The reason why these two issues were addressed in the same pot was that the study was on a global scale and that technology utilization and women were considered significant components in sustainable development.

BACKGROUND

This section provides an overview of the concepts that will be discussed or mentioned in this chapter. These concepts include, women empowerment, social gender gap and social gender inequality.

Women Empowerment

The sentence "There is no instrument which is more effective for development than women's empowerment" emphasizes the importance of women empowerment. Women's empowerment is regarded as a driver for the flourishing of development and for the change of countries (Chairperson & K., 2005-2009). Whilst economic empowerment means creating markets for women, women's empowerment means enabling the competitiveness of women in these markets.

Women's economic empowerment is a driving force for not only social gender equality and human rights but also fighting poverty and economic growth. Studies indicates that when female employment increases, economies grow and companies which employ women in management ranks provide the shareholders with return of 34% as compared to those which employ fewer women. Studies also indicate that when the share of the household incomes managed by women increases, the amount of expenses useful to children also increases. . Even though women perform 66% of the studies in the world, they only earn 10% of the world income and spend 90% of this income of theirs for their families (Golla, 2011).

Empowerment should be understood as a multidimensional structure which performs transformative and comparative interventions in the sense of institutions, directives, and access to resources and which affects objectives. Women's economic empowerment is provided by two components, namely resources and institutions. The economic empowerment and success of a woman are related to the development of her abilities and her acquisition of the faculties of taking economic decisions and acting. These resources can be explained as the education, instruction, knowledge, and ability investments in human beings, financial support, and agricultural sources of income, etc. The economic empowerment, which is the next stage, is based on how to use these resources, their establishment as policies, and, briefly, setting up the rules of the game (Golla, 2011).

In their study, however, Taylor and Pereznieto (2014) obtained results on the fact that a structure integrated with life skills and education besides economic support (microloan support for female entrepreneurs) yielded the best results. They proved that while microloan programs alone had no impact on women; encouraging women towards vocational training and technology utilization made a significant contribution to the increase in their self-confidence and knowledge (Taylor, 2014).

Similarly, in Figure 1, Golla et al. (2011) state that economic advancement (through participation in economy and economic success), power and agency (based on determining and selecting the preferences by ensuring the controlling and sharing of resources) had an intrinsic relationship within economic empowerment. Both components, are also necessary in the improvement of the lives of women and their families. Participation in economy and success encourage the power and agency of women. If a woman is able to simultaneously use identification and selection of a preference when controlling and sharing a resource, she can have a better economic advantage.

The content and working principle of the mechanisms for women's economic empowerment are seen in Figure 1. The resources include intellectual capital, finance, networks, and physical assets; the rules encompass the roles, taboos and prohibitions depending on social gender as well as the cases and practices about whether women will be present in public areas, whether they will be able to have certain types of jobs or whether they will manage money; and the traditions include the laws and policies on economic systems, market structures, marriage, heredity, and education systems (Golla, 2011).

Social Gender Gap

Whilst the concept of 'gender' refers to the universal biological differences between women and men. The concepts of 'social gender/gender equality/gender gap', addressed within the scope of the study, define the social relationships between women and men and point to the variation of access to resources between men and women and how this relationship are formed socially. It is supposed that the social *gender* roles are dynamic and their contents vary by time and space. On the other hand, the *social gender gap*

Figure 1. The mechanism for women's economic empowerment
(Golla, 2011)

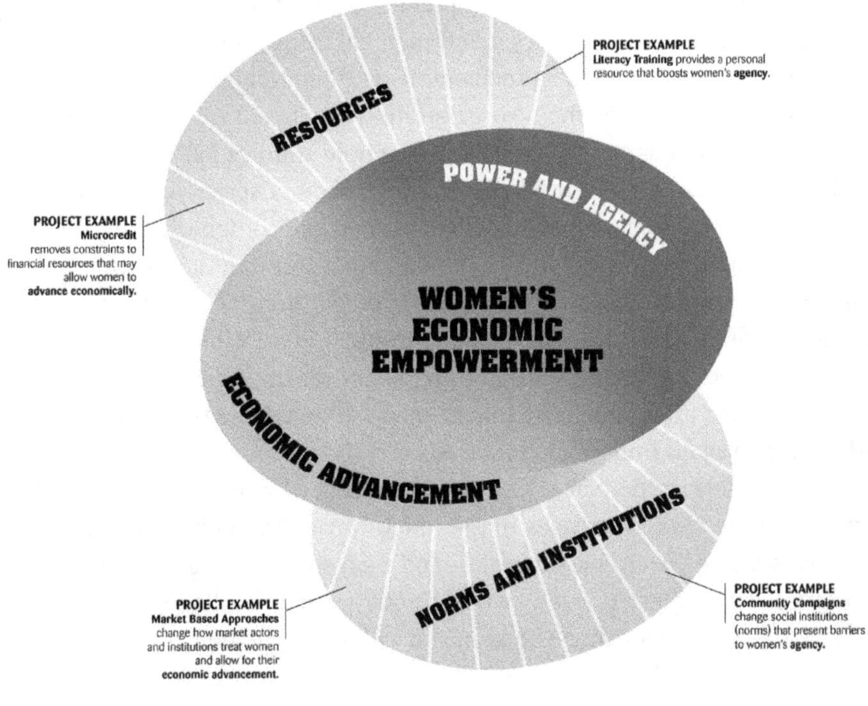

is based on the unequal power relationship where men are more dominant and women generally remain of secondary importance in many fields of life (e.g. education, access to job opportunities, technology utilization, wage determination, and health services) (Report, Equity and Development., 2006; Molina, 2015). Finally, when *social gender equality* is considered, the capacity of a person to be able to live the life he/she has chosen and not to experience deprivation should be understood as a fundamental right. And there should be equality for women or men in this sense as well.

Women Empowerment and Social Gender Equality

Social gender equality is essential as an instrument. This is because social gender equality contributes to economic productivity and sustainable development. This can be explained from different viewpoints such as:

- The view that *women's empowerment* and *social gender equality*, are effective for the attainment of the development goals is also acknowledged by the international development association. This view is acknowledged in the third and fifth points in the UN Millennium Development Goals (Report, Gender Equality and Development., 2012). These goals acknowledge that social gender equality strengthens economy, enhances its efficiency, and contributes to sustainable development in three ways.
    - The first one is based on the elimination of those cases which prevent women from accessing education, economic opportunities, and resources at the same rate as that of men. As a result of these gains a social competitive advantage can be obtained in the world which is now more competitive and globalized.
    - Secondly, positive contributions into many development outcomes, including those towards children, will be made through the improvement of the situations/statuses of women.
    - Thirdly, the way for sustainable development will be paved by increasing the power of agency in an environment where women and men have equal chances of decision-making and of shaping the policies as they become socially and politically active.
- The view that women also shape the next generation as a result of their empowerment and opportunities and that their greater control over the household sources has a positive impact on economic growth. This view has been verified. The findings from a series of countries (e.g. Bangladesh, Brazil, the Ivory Coast, Mexico, South Africa, and England) demonstrate that an increase in the share of household income controlled by women, either through their own earnings or cash transfers/microloans, has tilted the expenses in favor of children. The 10% increase of the average household income of the adult women in China resulted in a 1% increase in the survival rate of the girls and increased the number of school going years for both girls and boys. On the contrary, a similar rate of increase of income for Chinese men led to a decrease in the education and survival rate of girls. There was no impact on the boys.
- The view on public service delivery. The empowerment of women at the local level (through political quotas) in India led to increases in the rate of providing public services (services preferred by both women such as water and sanitation and men such as irrigation and school) and reduced the improprieties. The bribery given by women and men in the villages managed by women turned out to be 2.7% to 3.2% lower than those in the villages managed by men. The enhancement of

women's right to speak in the management of forests in India and Nepal provided significant improvements in the results of the forest conservation studies.

- The view on freedom of speech and political aspiration. The increase in the voices of women in the public domain brings advantages for not only women and children but also for men. In many rich countries, the greater participation of women in economic activity also brought about an increase in the representation of women in political leadership. This evolution initiated the reshaping of the social views about balancing business and family. It also resulted in the enactment of more family-friendly business and work related legislations. These gender-based differences are important in terms of, not only the, welfare of women but also a series of resulting positive outcomes for the families of these women and for the whole society in general (Report, Gender Equality and Development., 2012).

In the context of Turkey, as an institution which provides public employment services and carries out studies on social gender equality via various projects, the Turkish Employment Agency also plays a significant role in the personal empowerment of every woman. They do so by placing women in suitable and safe jobs thereby contributing to women' empowerment, the empowerment of their families (in this way, empowering the economy), and the realization of social development (Agency, Turkish employment, 2018).

In the context of the studies addressed above, the enhancement of the competences of women' and their empowerment depends heavily on technology and their participation in the labor force. This will yield significant results for both themselves and their own society. A summary of this section within a common framework is as follows:

- Employment of women enables them to gain economic independence and it enhances their ability in domestic decision-making processes. As such, one of the most important methods of providing social gender equality is the empowerment and employment of women.
- Employment of women is crucial for sustainable economic growth and balanced social development. One cannot expect any sound and productive growth from an economy in which women, who make up half of the total population at working age, are unable to participate actively.
- An increase in women's labor force participation is also of vital importance for a decrease in poverty. Employment of women means a higher income for the home and achieving better standards of living. As many international studies and experiences also show, poverty will diminish and the gross national product will increase as access to resources and economic equality are provided within the scope of social gender equality.

The existence of women in the social life, their strength and acquisition of a social status can only take place when they can equally access any type of resource and when they work (Ecevit, 2010).

GENDER GAP AND TECHNOLOGY

Every technological advancement often results in a revolution with respect to employees, machines, and work skill requirements. Whilst an order of organizational hierarchy was formed to facilitate fabrication in the first industrial revolution, the use of electricity, the increase in transportation and the communication networks gave rise to the birth to newer organizational orders in the second industrial revolution. This industrial revolution saw the emergence of newer occupations and the middle class. Electronification, Information Technologies (IT) and automatic production systems enabled service-based jobs in the period of the third industrial revolution. However in the fourth industrial revolution there is indication that many jobs will be more complicated, they will require complex competences, and enable automation as a result of emerging technology. This does not imply that people will be replaced at factories by robots. However, it does imply that some of the existing jobs which do and do not require non IT skills will disappear and that new forms of occupation will be based predominantly on IT. The newer jobs which will require IT skills will appear. Therefore women should be supported by balancing the gender inequality in order to manage this process more soundly (Schwab, 2017). There is further explanation on this in the next section.

A vision on how the 4th industrial revolution will impact the gender divide is presented in the World Economic Forum Report 2017. One of the most important inferences in the report is on how women, will be influenced by this revolution. While the rate of women working in the industries based on IT competences on the global scale is 26%, these employees are expected to fall to about 20% as a result of the increase in the jobs based on STEM skills. If this industrial trend continues and there is a failure in the transformation of women regarding their skillset (in the fields of IT and engineering/technological skills), women will be confronted with losing job opportunities of the future. Furthermore, it is quite clear that they will be negatively affected by the economic and social changes facilitated by the 4th industrial revolution.

Thus, by supporting women with IT and STEM education the future will be shaped. This is important in terms of the empowerment of both women and the society. Today, as every sector of the economy is intertwined with ICT, equipping every field from agriculture to automotive and from genetics to education with IT has stimulated some technology giants. These technology giant firms, i.e. Apple, Facebook, and Google are undertaking to improve or back-up the employment of women in the field of IT in the future. It is seen that the studies performed on the global scale often aim at women and IT for the present and for the next ten to fifteen years. While robotics, big data, digitization of industry and the Internet of things alter all sectors and the nature of all occupations, the dynamics of economic growth (Borthakur, 2016). These are technologies of the future.

The evaluation of the digital gap as the gender gap and the endeavors to develop strategies on this issue date back to the recent past. Having begun to flourish particularly in developed countries, these studies are supported by various action plans and strategies. Women in Global Science and Technology (WISAT/ http://wisat.org/who-we-are), an institution likely to be regarded as one of the firsts in this sense, has been operating in Canada since 2003. The institution regarded the gender difference in technology utilization as a problem which should be fought and they became an international non-profit institution to produce solutions to this end. Having stated that the countries will be devoid of the experiences, creativity, and perspective of women without the active participation of women in science and technology, the institution carries out efficient studies at the national, regional, and international levels.

The institution conducts studies in cooperation with many structures such as governments, the UN, donation institutions, foundations, research institutes, and Non-Governmental Organizations (NGO) and produces reports and publications on the global gender dimensions of IT. In their research they stated that women should be supported in scientific and technological studies for the development of countries. This institution also cooperates with the other international organizations which carry out studies that are similar to these.

Beside these organizations, one of the greatest international studies in this context was "the action plan to cover the digital gender gap" performed in collaboration with the world summit on 15 December 2015. The meeting took place with the cooperation of the International Telecommunications Union (ITU), Costa Rica, Sweden, Switzerland, Tunisia, The United States of America, and The United Nations Organization for Women, Microsoft, and Mozilla. Aiming to cover the social gender gap and at women's empowerment by 2030, the action plan presents critical studies to accelerate comprehensive and sustainable development.

Developing gender-sensitive strategies and policies, enabling women to access ICT; removing the barriers, and threats to access; developing practices and services to satisfy the needs of women,; developing the digital abilities of women; enabling women to be included in the decision-making processes by encouraging them towards the technology sector; and, in this context, the foundation and empowerment of multi-participant partnerships were taken as the bases for the plan. The plan was aimed towards making use of the transformative potential of ICT for women empowerment (Women's Empowerment in the Digital Age: Action Plan, 2015).

Besides the initiatives and studies by international organizations and NGO, the private companies operating in the field of ICT have studies on the digital gender divide. One of them, INTEL published a comprehensive report entitled 'Women and the Web, which contained micro- and macro assessments, data, and solution proposals on the digital divide experienced by women (http://www.intel.com/content/www/us/en/technology-in-education/women-in-the-web.html). Similarly, a Google initiative called Online Help for Women was designed to provide women with online training thereby promoting digital literacy in India. Thanks to this application, women are able to obtain assistance to help them with the utilization of the Internet, either by the help of a telephone or via the organization's website (https://www.hwgo.com/) (Akça, 2016).

Based on these visions, ideas and studies, both developing and developed countries should concentrate on further studies to overcome the gender gap. The dimensions of the gender gap experienced are explained below considering Global Gender Gap Report 2017 (Schwab, 2017).

Dimensions of the Gender Gap

The results for the components of the global gender gap are seen in Figure 4. In Global Gender Gap Report 2017, the gender gap between men and women was addressed in four basic categories and so as to determine the gender gap experienced on the global scale, the Gender Gap Index was calculated by using the *Economic Participation and Opportunity, Educational Attainment, Health and Survival,* and *Political Empowerment* data/sub-indexes and considering a total of 14 indicators.

- **Economic Participation and Opportunity Sub-Index:** It was calculated considering the data on the discrimination in participation in employment, wage discrimination, and the discrimination of promotion at work. *The discrimination in participation in employment* indicates the rate of participation in the labor force by. *Wage discrimination* refers to t income level earned by women and men (the difference in wages obtained for similar jobs). *The discrimination in promotion* refers to the differences in the rate of promotion between of women and men and the differences in the rates between the women and men working on technical issues (taking into consideration the statistical data about lawmakers, high-ranking authorities, and managers).

Figure 2. The global gender gap index
(Schwab, 2017)

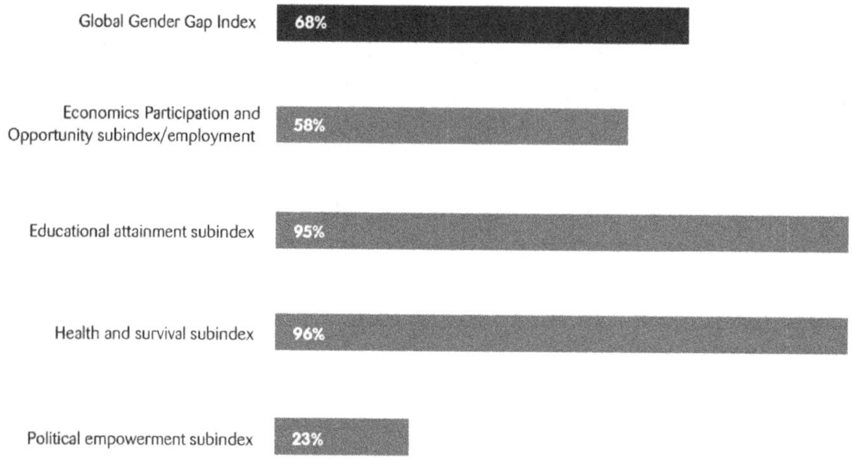

- **Educational Attainment Sub-Index:** It is based on the rate of literacy of women and men and the relative differences in the primary school, high school, and higher education they received.
- **Health and Survival Sub-Index:** It is the indicators of the sex ratio at birth (converted into the female/male value) and the ratio of the healthy life expectancy value for women to the healthy life expectancy value for men.
- **Political Empowerment Sub-Index:** The data about the female and male employees working in the political decision-making process were addressed in this sub-index

In the studies under examination, it is seen that the existing gender gap applies to not only employment but also all fields of life such as education, health, participation in politics, and decision-making. Prepared in cooperation of McKinsey & Company – one of the leading management consultancy companies of the world – and the Turkish Industry and Business Association (TUSIAD), the Women Matter 2016 Report for Turkey showcases interviews with the employees of 102 different big companies operating in 11 different sectors of Turkey. The report identified women's labor force participation rate as 30% and their rate of being in a leader position as 41% in Turkey. Moreover, according to the report, it was stated that the profitability rates of the companies with greater female labor force were higher than those of the other companies in their respective sectors. Furthermore the increase in the rate of female employees at the leadership level positively affected corporate performance as well. It was stated that in the event of an increase in women's labor force participation rate, social development, productivity and economic growth would also be positively affected by this increase and it was also stressed that Turkey, whose female participation rate remained below the general average among the countries of the Organization for Economic Co-operation and Development (OECD), would have great potential for increasing its Gross National Product in the event that it increased women's labor force participation rate (Devillard-Hoellinger, 2016).

WOMEN ECONOMIC EMPOWERMENT

This section provides an overview of women economic empowerment and how it enables women empowerment. Different topics are discussed in this section. These includes, Women empowerment and ICT adoption, ICT, women empowerment and economic growth and Digital comptence and women economic empowerment. In Table 1, economic empowerment is addressed within the scope of women's acquisition of economic freedom and empowerment in the below-defined issues. This is as a result of the support provided by various organizations and institutions to women with limited access to power and economic assets (Taylor, 2014).

If there are changes in the levels of these subjects mentioned in table 1, then sustainable economic empowerment and its sustainability. Such changes include self-respect, knowledge, an individual's ability, regulations and behaviors at the community and institution levels; and policies and laws in the context of the market and the value chain (Golla, 2011; Taylor, 2014). This has been proven by studies aimed not only at understanding whether women's access to incomes and assets increased but also to whether they became more empowered and whether they gained greater empowerment in other areas of life. . In these studies, economic empowerment depends on women's economic empowerment enabled both by technology and other resources they are provided with (such as support for entrepreneurship and training, access to information and communication technologies, and capacity building). In the next sub-section, the relationship between women empowerment and ICT adoption is discussed.

Women Empowerment and ICT Adoption

Women empowerment has become a central element in development policies in the recent years. The impact of women empowerment on economic development is within the scope of the Gender Action Plan that was launched in 2006 by the World Bank. Furthermore, the impact of women empowerment on development is within the scope of the United Nations Millennium Development Goals. Women empowerment also basically means reducing discrimination against women, along with having the above-mentioned economic freedoms. Discrimination is the inability to have adequate access to education and labor markets. In order to empower, the prevention of discrimination depends on the provision of positive feedback aimed at sustainable development (Doepke, 2011).

Table 1. Spheres of influence of power in economic empowerment

Influence of Power	Economic Empowerment
Power within	Knowledge, individual abilities, self-respect, belief/self-confidence in making changes in life, and learning skills concerning a job or required to work at an enterprise
Power to	To take decisions on home-related economic issues and to be in the market not only in the local sense but also on a regional basis.
Power over	Access to employment and income creation activities by controlling financial, physical, and knowledge-based assets.
Power with	The ability to work with others with respect to economic activity and right development.

Source: Özçelik (2018)

There is a relationship between women empowerment and the adoption of technology by women. This can be seen in the case of women engaged in the business world. As implied in the background section, the empowerment of women and the enhancement of their efficiency in the business world is an important factor in fighting poverty. This is because their efficiency in the business world influences their children, families and the society. The social and economic statuses of a mother has a direct correlation with the education, health, and welfare of her children, because the sustainability of a family is affected substantially by the increase in the family. The increase in the family income is influenced by the efficiency of the women in the business world. However this efficiency will be a result of her technology adoption. This is because, technology is a significant component of economic growth and sustainable development. At this very point, it becomes important that women adopt technology and be made economically active by the usage of ICT.

The usage of technology by women for their jobs compared to the average usage of technology by men in developed and developing countries lags by 50%. Studies have also shown that there were strong connections between the use of technology and economic growth. For instance, while there had been no economic growth in Malaysia and Thailand before investments into ICT between 1995 and 2000, increases by visible rates were achieved after the commencement of investments into ICT. As women are part of the labor force, they cannot afford to be left out in adopting ICT. This is because their adoption of ICT will result in overall economic growth. This is discussed more in the next sub-section. However in this context, women's economic empowerment driven by their adoption of ICT will result in efficient social life for women. This is an undeniable fact (OECD Horizontal, 2008).

ICT/ Women's Economic Empowerment/Economic Growth

Sustainable growth and development on the global and national scales are of vital importance for countries. Moreover, in order for growth and development to be sustainable, first of all, it is of great importance to empower women, who make up about 50% of the world population, to participate in the labor force. This is because empowering women to work by providing them with appropriate training and enabling the elevation of their level of participation in the social life are important factors in the economic and social development of countries. Thus, there is a need for awareness creation programs to education the women; develop labor policies for women, to facilitate their entry into labor markets. This will facilitate their individual and social empowerment, support female entrepreneurs, and strengthen employer and employee consciousness towards equal opportunities for women and men.

Sustainability of growth and development means development without disregarding the securing of the needs of future generations (Sorgner, 2017).The G20 countries, which comprise the developed and developing countries of the world make up about 66% of the world population and about 85% of global trade., They have conducted studies on how the digital revolution will influence social gender equality and on the utilization of new digital technologies in order to reduce the gender gaps in future (Sorgner, 2017). This shows the importance of technology utilization in the reduction of the gender gap. Therefore, ICT is in a key position in the empowerment of people and in combating poverty. Thus, how women might be empowered when they use ICT and how they could turn digitization into an opportunity is important and further supported by with some studies and projects (Obayelu, 2006).

However, the there is an ongoing search on how productivity enhancement, new forms of entrepreneurial innovations and new income generating opportunities determine how technology will empower women economic in developing countries. This search underlines the fact that investment in women and technology is key to economic development and growth. Furthermore, the usage of technology by women leads to women's economic empowerment. In developing countries, where gender discrimination in the usage of both traditional and modern technologies exist, women with very low income are employed to perform traditional agricultural jobs, while men uses and shapes agricultural technologies. It could be seen that these developing countries lag behind in economic growth compared to developed countries. In general, the gender discrimination in digital technologies is greater in the developing countries with low and middle incomes than in developed countries.

Therefore, it is important to find out how to root out the gender discrimination and the slow economic growth. In order to do so, there is a need for two basic transformations which should aim a eliminating the discrimination in both gender and technology. The first transformation is via women empowerment via ICT provision and adoption by women. For instance, the adoption of the Internet and ICT as a whole is quite effective on women's development of new careers. ICT is of profound importance towards women empowerment, especially in developing countries. The second transformation is the development of technological life cycles for both emerging technologies and the existing technologies in detail. This will result in requirement specifications which includes the needs of women. In this process, technology developers will enable women to adopt the technology, resulting in a greater penetration of the technology and further assess which technologies are effective in enabling the economic empowerment of women. The inclusion of women in the life cycle of a technology will not only enable women to develop with regards to technology, but also contribute to the reduction of technology and gender discrimination. This is because, currently, women are merely regarded as purchasers and users of technology in developing countries without being considered in the design and development of technology.

These transformations will be advantageous to women. This is because women often have limited time to investigate or try new technologies because of their engagement in the contribution to home economics and being engaged in housework. Women, are also generally restricted because technology is controlled by men. Also from the social perspective, women are deprived from using, hiring or purchasing new technologies. Due to these financial and traditional barriers, they are deprived of their economic advantage as well. These barriers can only be conquered through women's inclusion and the usage of, technology. Those women who are included in the life cycle of technology development may enhance their productivity and cause a positive chain reaction when they use technology and are included in economic activities. As women possess more income and resources they will gain self-confidence. In addition, their social empowerment and the resultant provision of better health and educational opportunities for their children will lead to the development of their families and the society in from an economic perspective (Gill, 2010)

The advantage is not only in how women adopt technology, but also in their level of involvement in the development of the technology. In the near future, 40-60% of the current spectrum of occupations will be encounter high risks due to digitization. As it seems now, men face the risk of losing their job than women. This is because, new technologies will alter the jobs of women less than that of men. This means that most jobs in health services or housekeeping performed by women may not be as automated as jobs performed by men, such as being a machine operator. However, the bad news is that if women become the minority in management and STEM-based occupations, there will have fewer probabilities that they will benefit from opportunities to be offered by new digital technologies. As a result, the gender gap will continue to exist (Sorgner, 2017).

Dıgıtal Competence /Women Economic Empowerment

A women's digitization skillset is also an important instrument that will enable her to become self-employed, backing up their ability as entrepreneurs, and, ensuring the women's economic empowerment. The digitization competences of women implies their authority over ICT, which fundamentally includes their utilization of the Internet, and their computer literacy. The digitization competence allows women to overcome the restrictions imposed on them in both developed and developing countries. Therefore, ICT reduces the importance of temporal and spatial restrictions women generally experience when earning an income and fulfilling their intra-family responsibilities. Furthermore, the anonymity of the Internet supports women to overcome the restrictions resulting from gender inequality. It also facilitates their access, and dissemination, information and ideas. For instance, women engaged in agriculture may effectively produce and sell their produce by accessing information on the weather forecast and the prices of the product in the market. Women producing handicrafts may earn an income by marketing them based on their acquired knowledge and by the means of e-trade. In addition, thanks to distance education, women in regions with intensive gender discrimination can also acquire knowledge online. These opportunities empower women economically, making them independent of men (Sorgner, 2017; Lal, 2011).

PRESENT STATUS OF THE GENDER DIVIDE

ICT Utilization by Gender

In addition, communication via the Internet helps women enhance their self-confidence and learn new role models. In Figure 2 below, it is seen that there is a noteworthy gap in women's Internet utilization in less developed countries and rural regions as compared to men. The differences in gender ICT utilization are provided in Figures 2 below. While differences in Internet utilization in the rural region, and urban are seen in Figure 2, the rate of utilization of the computer (by gender), Internet banking, and online shopping are seen in Figure 3. This gap is evident in Turkey, Saudi Arabia, Indonesia and Mexico and similarly indicating a very low level of ICT utilization in developing countries. The utilization rates are also quite high for Italy out of the developed countries. Nevertheless, this gap is small for Brazil and Korea. Naturally, Internet utilization is generally lower in rural areas than in urban areas and the utilization is higher for men compared with women (except for Australia, Brazil, and Russia). Similar results also apply to using a computer, Internet banking, and purchasing online, which are expressed with the other ICT utilization.

When Figures 2 and 3 are examined, it is discovered that the answer to the first question addressed in the study (Have women been affected by these intensive technological developments and technology utilization – which are efficient in every field – as much as men have?) is "No". For these values explicitly indicate that women have not been affected by the use of ICT (technology in the general sense) as much as men.

Figure 3. ICT utilization by women as compared to men, in percent, 2014/2015[a,b] Internet utilization (Sorgner, 2017)
a-Provisions according to availability, b- Gap: Ratio female/male

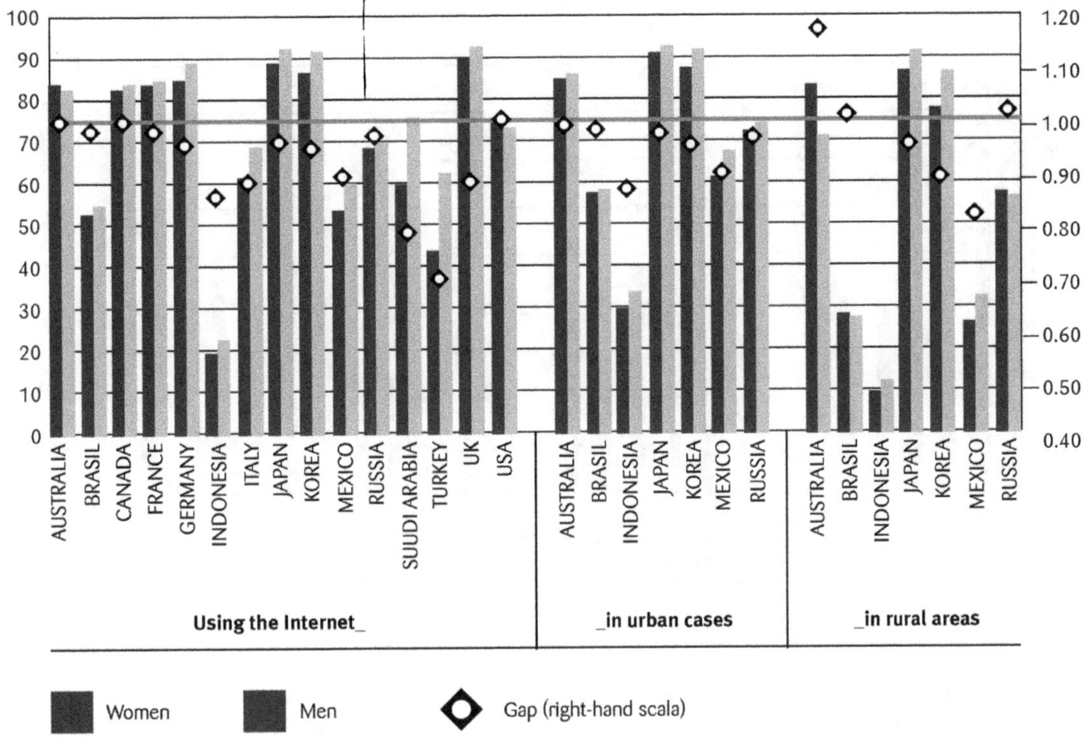

Mobile Phone Ownership by Gender

Mobile phones are observed to empower women in many aspects within the scope of digitization. In a study performed in developing countries, many women stated that mobile phone ownership enabled them to save money and time and it made them feel safer and more independent. Nevertheless, women own far less mobile phone far less than that of men. The divide still exists in India, where 36% of the population own a mobile phone. 43% of men own mobile phones compared to 28% of women. In summary, the gender gap in mobile telephone ownership in India and use is quite high. China has the largest mobile communication market in the world, the gender gap in this sense is observed to be rather low in China. The gender gap regarding telephone ownership is also rather small in Indonesia, which is another large mobile communication market in the world. Mexico and Turkey also show a low gender gap in this sense. Given their Internet utilization, it is observed that this gap has quite increased (Sorgner, 2017).

Female Unemployment

According to the data of 2016 by the Turkish Statistical Institute, the employment rate of women that constitute about half of the population (49.8%) is 27.5%. In summary, the percentage of women in the unemployed group is quite high. These statistical data reflect that the rate of women who produce value for the economy of the country is rather low. When the employment rates of the member countries to the

Figure 4. ICT utilization by women as compared to men, in percent, 2014/2015[a,b] Other ICT utilization (Sorgner, 2017)
a-Provisions according to availability, b- Gap: Ratio female/male

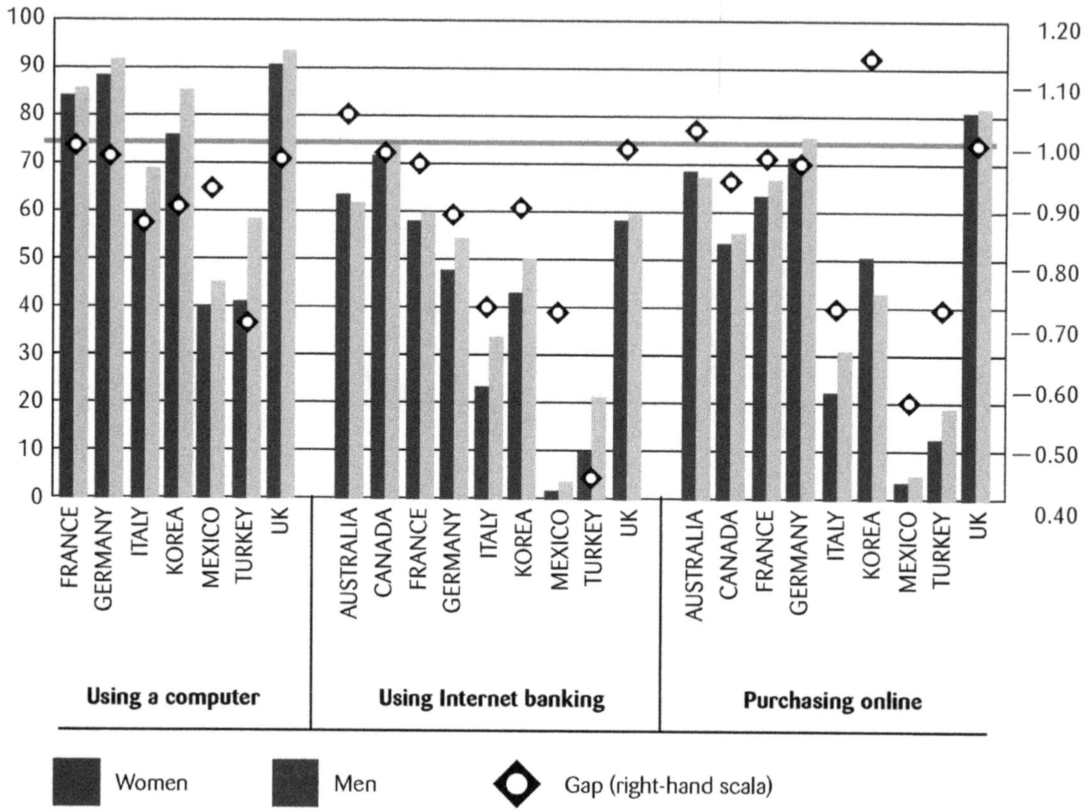

European Union are examined, it is seen that the country with the highest female employment was Sweden (80%), while the country with the lowest female employment was Greece (47.7%) in 2016. The average female employment was about 65.5% in the European Union. In light of these data, it is essential that women be included in the labor market and empowered by training them in the field of informatics with a direct relationship with every discipline within the career plans for the future (European Union, 2017).

Table 2. Selected indicators by gender, 2015 [%] (Agency, Turkish employment, 2018)

Selected Indicators	Total	Men	Women
Rate of the illiterate population (aged 25+)	5,4	1,8	9,0
Rate of the population that graduated from a graduate school or a faculty (aged 25+)	15,5	17,9	13,1
Employment rate (aged 15+)	46,0	65,0	27,5
Labor force participation rate (aged 15+)	51,3	71,6	31,5
Unemployment rate (aged 15+)	10,3	9,2	12,6
Youth unemployment rate (aged 15-24 years)	18,5	16,5	22,2

Source: Özçelik (2018)

PRESENT STATUS OF PROSPETIVE SOLUTIONS FOR THE GENDER DIVIDE

Social Gender Equality

Despite the inequalities with respect to having ICT, ICT is regarded as an essential instrument in social transformation and gender equality. For instance, tradeswomen can reach global markets by participating in e-trade activities thanks to the Internet. Through e-state applications, it may be possible for them to access some services for which they experience barriers in accessing. Thanks to the network of Women's Community-based Organizations (CBOs) within the scope of the project "The Inter-city Marketing Network of Women Entrepreneurs" for women in India, they can market their agricultural products to not only local but also neighboring markets. Moreover, both online and offline information tools assume significant roles regarding the dissemination of information on health. In this way, training on health and dissemination of information can be provided. In solving the crises experienced with regard to HIV/AIDS, solutions are produced again by using ICT. In this way, some advice and consultancy services are accessed without experiencing the fear of stigmatization. ICT is also used to back up women in issues such as e-training and the supporting of child development (Lal, 2011).

Quite considerable importance is attached to introducing women to technology and encouraging their technology utilization on a global scale. The Centre of Women in Technology in Bulgaria enable women to participate in the IT sector and to develop new projects in cooperation with other women in the development of technological and engineering studies. In the report on the studies carried out in 2008 by the Swedish International Cooperation Development Agency, especially the gap differences in IT utilization between women and men were mentioned and the studies carried out to overcome this were provided. For this purpose, 6 different projects were developed and evaluated within the scope of this report. Two of these projects were implemented in Bolivia, whereas the others were implemented in Kenya, India, Rwanda, and Vietnam. The projects are about women's empowerment by using ICT technologies, ecological sustainability, and the sharing of information in order for them to resist the violence they experience. Additionally, they provide online sales opportunities to the women who produce traditional baskets in Rwanda by using ICT technologies and they convey their traditional work to the people in different regions through communication technologies. Briefly, the report generally deals with the concept of gender in digital divide and women's empowerment with digital opportunities for a better life (Sretenova, 2010).

In summary, globally, ICT has changed the way people interact and access information, and opportunities that will enhance their economic and social lives (better health, developed governance, and developed education). These opportunities will lead to a decrease in the spatial and social isolation, especially that of women in rural regions. It will also enable them to be empowered which will positively affect their conscious decision-making processes, resulting in improvements in their lives and abilities. The study also qualifies as an answer to the questions "If women have not been affected by technology utilization as much as men have, how may this be reversed? And how may technology be made effective in making women economic?"

SOLUTIONS AND RECOMMENDATIONS

Whilst women globally make up 50% of the world population, they constitute only 37% of the gross national product and 39% of the global labor force. Hence, it might be stated that women constitute the majority of the globally unused labor force pool. Some 655 million fewer women than men are economically active in the global labor force. At the same time, women make up 50% of the graduates of higher education in the world, whereas only 25% of them work in the management rank. Owing to the aging population, the participation of more women in the labor force may be useful for the expansion of the labor force pool of the countries and the rise in their gross national products. For instance, it is predicted that the labor force in Russia will regress to 71 million from 76 million between 2014 and 2025 due to the aging population and that 240 million female employees will participate in the labor force on the global scale (It is assumed that the male participation rate does not decrease). In addition, the participation of fewer women within the STEM discipline in higher ranks will give rise to problems in scientific and technical fields (Desvaux, 2017).

Additionally, there is a greater need to deal with issues pertaining towards gender diversity (more employment of women). This need is necessary for combating the low growth rate on the global scale and the shortage of talented employees resulting from digitization. In the near future, enterprises will encounter the bottle neck in the recruitment of a lot of talented staff and decreasing labor force. Gender diversity (the increasing of female employment) may assume a key role for enterprises to cope with the shortage of working talents and for countries to provide the sustainable economic growth.

Briefly, it is considered a must to deal with four fundamental issues so as to reduce or eliminate the gender gap in both developed and developing countries.

- The first one is to eliminate the discrimination experienced, when women participate in employment, in the wage discrimination, and the discrimination of promotion at work.
- The second one is to increase the literacy rates, education levels, and computer literacy of women.
- The third one is to eliminate their shortcomings in health care delivery to women.
- The fourth one is to support them to work in political decision-making processes and in management ranks.

To realize these issues, it should be ensured that women be trained in tandem with emerging trends in sectors with high added value (such as informatics, engineering, and service) that their digital abilities be developed.

The sectors in which women are intensively employed (represented) and the sectors in which their employment is rather scarce (represented at a rather low level) are seen in Figure 5. As also understood from here, it is all but a must that women take part in the labor force with respect to STEM disciplines and ICT.

Regarding the employment of women, great duties fall particularly on governments to remove the barriers which discourage women from participating in business, e.g. in the improvement of the infrastructure of child care, making the tax systems supportive of women's participation in the labor force, and ensuring the issue of paid family leave as well as the elimination of a wide range of problems women are confronted with outside the workplace to enable their participation in economy (Desvaux, 2017; Türkiye Bilişim Derneği, 2018).

Figure 5. OECD: Women remain underrepresented in STEM disciplines
(Desvaux, 2017)

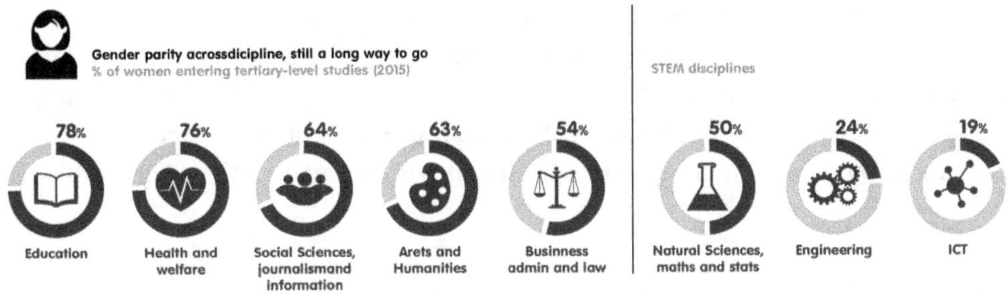

According to the World Economic Forum Report, the information sector will be confronted with a shortage of talented employees in the following years. The share of female graduates of engineering, computer, and informatics will be great in this shortage of talented employees. Thus, it is inevitable for the state institutions and organizations, NGOs and the private sector to carry out studies on women and young people in order to eliminate the shortage of talented employees.

When planning strategies about the economy of the future, dynamism and comprehensiveness should be prioritized. Importance should be attached to the possession of equal opportunities by everyone. It should be borne in mind that if women are not included in the process of shaping and benefiting from the opportunities, the loss will be global and that one will be devoid of the skills, ideas, and perspectives of critical importance in utilizing the new opportunities.

A period of transition from capitalism (capital economy) to talent economy is being experienced in the world. The criteria for capital economy are now being replaced by creativity and capability, which are regarded as the criteria for the talent economy. If women are not included, or do not participate, in the labor force pool in this process, gender discrimination will grow on the global scale and deprivation will occur in terms of women's capabilities and creative and innovative thoughts. The gender discrimination emphasized here is not a war of genders but is based on the determination of the roles of women in the development of the country and on women's empowerment (Schwab, 2017).

The studies suggest that the participation of women in the labor force on the global scale will:

- Provide an increase in economic growth in all countries;
- Provide a decrease in the number of people living in poverty and an increase in the rates of productivity in all countries;
- Provide the development of job performance and innovation;
- Provide an increase in cost-effective health services and social programs; and
- Enable state policies to better answer all citizens.

For this purpose, in state policies, the recommendation are as follows:

- The creation of family-friendly policies in order to ensure women's participation in the labor force;
- The creation of development support policies which increase the economic role of women;
- The increase in the status and income earning ability of women in the traditional business fields;
- Encouragement of women to pursue careers in the fields of science and technology;
- The provision of increased access to financial and support services for female entrepreneurs;
- Finding gender-specific approaches in health planning and treatments; and
- The determination of goals and objectives for female rulers and deputies (Türkiye Bilişim Derneği, 2018).

Through the cooperation of various institutions and organizations, women's greater utilization and use of technology should be turned into a social movement. To empower women by benefiting from the possibilities of the digital age, ICT should be utilized and it should be ensured that the social gender balance be established.

FUTURE RESEARCH DIRECTIONS

ICT enhances job performance and helps in reducing the high entry barrier to the business world for women. Therefore ICT literacy and the utilization of ICT are regarded as an essential instrument that will enable women to join the labor fource as well as for consolidate their positions and families. Increasing the ICT utilization by female entrepreneurs will enhance sustainable development and economic growth and the greater participation of women in the business world. It will also empower them and reduce social gender inequality, which will contribute to economic development. However, as also addressed in the sections above, the digital gap between women and men is quite clear. The studies based on this issue have been carried out since the early 2000s and it appears that they will keep maintaining their importance in the following years too (Kabeer, 2013).

Thus, it is of strategic importance that academics, developed countries, governments, the institutions involved in women's empowerment and the private sector go on jointly organize research studies and projects. These projects and studies should be on how female entrepreneurship should supported via ICT policies, products, and services in the future as well.

CONCLUSION

Those societies which aim at sustainable development and employment should determine strategies and policies particularly towards information- and technology-intensive activities. In addition to these strategies and policies, it is important to accurately train, direct, and manage the human resource that supports the activities. It should be kept in mind that enabling different sections of the society to make use of the opportunities provided by ICT and building an ecosystem which will provide development also to eliminate the gender-based gap and inequalities are the joint duties of governments, the private sector, and nongovernmental organizations.

As also seen from the reports and projects examined within the scope of the study, ICT have a significant role in economic development, fighting poverty, and women's empowerment. Moreover, it is important to encourage women to adopt STEM-based education and to increase their rate representation in technology-intensive sectors, especially in developed countries. This will result in dealing with the deficit of talented labor force, which is being experienced today and will be felt intensely in the near future. It will also result in the diminishing and elimination the gender divide. The point which should not be missed is the women with a key role in every case. It should be borne in mind that "Women's Empowerment with Technology Means Leaping Forward in Every Sense".

REFERENCES

Agency, Turkish employment. (2018). Retrieved May 27, 2018, from http://www.iskur.gov.tr/en-us/corporateprofile/institution.aspx

Akça, E. B. (2016). The Different Approaches to Digital Divide in the Concept of Gender Equality and It's Dimentions. Toplumsalcinsiyet eşitliği perspektifinden dijital bölünme ve farkli yaklaşimlar. doi:10.21645/intermedia.2017.16

Baller, S. D. (2016). *The Global Information Technology Report.* Innovating in the Digital Economy. Retrieved March 15, 2018, from http://www3.weforum.org/docs/GITR2016/WEF_GITR_Full_Report.pdf

Borthakur, A. C. (2016). *Women in STEM; Technology, career pathways and the gender pay gap.* London: Designed and produced by The Creative Studio at Deloitte. Retrieved February 15, 2018, from https://www.itu.int/en/ITU-D/Digital-Inclusion/Women-and-Girls/Girls-in-ICT-Portal/Documents/deloitte-uk-women-in-stem-pay-gap-2016.pdf

Chairperson, K. A. N. (2005-2009). *UN Gender Strategy Framework in the Philippines: Sustaining Women's Human Rights.* Makati City: Published by the United Nations System in The Philippines. Retrieved 6 11, 2018, from https://www.unicef.org/philippines/Gender_Strategy(1).pdf

Desvaux, G. D. S.-S. (2017). *Women Matter Time to accelerate. Ten years of insights into.* McKinsey & Company. Retrieved January 5, 2018, from https://www.mckinsey.com/global-themes/gender-equality

Devillard-Hoellinger, S. G. (2016). *Women Matter/Turkey's potential for the future: Women in Business.* Istanbul: McKinsey & Company and TUSIAD. Retrieved January 20, 2018, from http://www.mckinsey.com.tr/arastirma-ve-yayinlarimiz/McKinseyWomenMatterTurkiye2016RaporSonuclariSunumu.pdf

Doepke, M. T. (2011, April). *Does Female Empowerment Promote Economic Development?* Bonn, Germany: IZA Discussion Paper No. 5637. Retrieved January 10, 2018, from http://ftp.iza.org/dp5637.pdf

Doğan, B. B. (2014). Problems of Women Employment in TRC2 Region and Solution. *International Journal of Social and Economic Sciences, 4*(2), 91–106. Retrieved from http://dergipark.gov.tr/download/article-file/403287

Ecevit, Y. (2010). *İşgücü Piyasasında Toplumsal Cinsiyet Eşitliği El Kitabı.* Ankara: Pelin Ofset. Retrieved February 15, 2018, from https://statik.iskur.gov.tr/tr/proje_protokol/kad_ist_des_BC_kitapcik_18022010_sm.pdf

European Union. (2017). *Report on Equality Between Women and Men in the EU. European Union.* doi:10.2838/52591

Gender, science and technology/Report of the expert group meeting. (2010). Paris: United Nations Division for the Advancement of Women (DAW), part of UN Women with UNESCO. Retrieved from http://www.un.org/womenwatch/daw/egm/gst_2010/Final-Report-EGM-ST.pdf

Gill, K. B. (2010). *Bridging the Gender Divide.* Washington, DC: International Center for Research on Women. Retrieved January 7, 2018, from https://cleancookstoves.org/binary-data/RESOURCE/file/000/000/294-2.pdf

Globalization, Growth and Poverty. (2002). A World Bank Policy Research Report. New York: World Bank and Oxford University Press. Retrieved November 7, 2017, from http://documents.worldbank.org/curated/en/954071468778196576/pdf/multi0page.pdf

Golla, A. M. (2011). *Understanding and Measuring Women's Economic Empowerment: Defniton, Framework and Indicators.* Washington, DC: International Center for Research on Women. Retrieved November 25, 2017, from https://www.icrw.org/wp-content/uploads/2016/10/Understanding-measuring-womens-economic-empowerment.pdf

Hozdić, E. (2015). Smart Factory for Industry 4.0: A Review. *International Journal of Modern Manufacturing Technologies, 7*(1), 28–35. Retrieved from https://www.researchgate.net/publication/282791888_Smart_factory_for_industry_40_A_review

Kabeer, N. N. L. (2013, February 26). *Gender Equality and Economic Growth: Is there a Win-Win?* Retrieved June 12, 2018, from http://www.ids.ac.uk/publications: http://www.ids.ac.uk/files/dmfile/Wp417.pdf

Lal, B. S. (2011). Impact of Information and Communication Technologies on Women Empowerment in India. *Systemics, Cybernetics and Informatics, 9*(4), 17-23. Retrieved December 14, 2017, from http://www.iiisci.org/journal/CV$/sci/pdfs/QN001HZ.pdf

Molina, M. L. (2015). *Connecteted women- Accelerating the digital economy: Gender diversity in the telecommunications sector.* Retrieved 2018, from https://www.atkearney.com/documents/10192/5580445/Connected+Women+2015-WDReport.pdf/d3c08b0a-fab6-431c-80c0-0d332b9e882d

Obayelu, A. E. (2006). Analysis of the information and comminication technology for gender empowerment and sustainable poverty alleviation in Nigeria. International Journal of Education and Development using Information and Communication, 2(3), 45-69.

OECD Horizontal. (2008). *Gender and Sustainable Development: Maximising the Economic, Social and Environmental Role of Women.* Paris: Organisation for Economic Co-operation and Development. Retrieved December 17, 2017, from https://www.oecd.org/social/40881538.pdf

Report, W. D. (2006). *Equity and Development.* Washington, DC: The International Bank for Reconstruction and Development/The World Bank.

Report, W. D. (2012). *Gender Equality and Development.* Washington, DC: The International Bank for Reconstruction and Development/The World Bank. doi:10.1596/978-0-8213-8810-5

Schwab, F. (2017). *The Global Gender Gap Report.* Geneva: World Economic Forum.

Sorgner, A. B.-B. (2017). *The Effects of Digitalization on the Gender Equality in the G20 economies.* Kiel: Kiel Institute for the World Economy. Retrieved June 11, 2018, from https://economic-policy-forum.org/wp-content/uploads/2017/08/20170707_W20_Studie_v2.5.pdf

Sretenova, N. (2010, September 28). *What has Worked in Europe to Increase Women's Participation in Science and Technology.* Retrieved from http://www.un.org/womenwatch/daw/egm/gst_2010/: http://www.un.org/womenwatch/daw/egm/gst_2010/Stretenova-EP.11-EGM-ST.pdf

Taylor, G. a. (2014). *Review of evaluation approaches and methods used by interventions on women and girls' economic empowerment.* London: odi.org Publications. Retrieved July 6, 2017, from https://www.odi.org/publications/8275-review-evaluation-approaches-methods-used-by-interventions-women-girls-economic-empowerment

Türkiye Bilişim Derneği. (2018). *Değerlendirme Raporu.* Ankara: Türkiye Bilişim Derneği. Retrieved March 7, 2018, from http://www.tbd.org.tr/wp-content/uploads/2018/05/2017-degerlendirme-raporu.pdf

Women's Empowerment in the Digital Age: Action Plan. (2015, December 15). Retrieved from https://www.itu.int/en/action/gender-equality/Pages/women-empowerment.aspx: https://www.itu.int/en/action/gender-equality/Documents/GlobalPlatformReferences.pdf

Chapter 10
The Prospect of Post-Adoption Satisfaction and the Digital Gender Divide

Daniel Adjin
Ghana Technology University College, Ghana

Hannah Muat
University for Development Studies, Ghana

ABSTRACT

The discussion on the digital gender divide is often focused on the women who are yet to adopt ICT. The focus on women who adopt and reject ICT is rare. Women who adopt and reject ICT also account for women who do not access ICT. They often reject ICT because they are unsatisfied with the ICT technology or service adopted. To shed light on this discussion, a small scaled deductive exploratory research was conducted to understand the role of post-adoption satisfaction on the adoption of functionalities provided via mobile Facebook. The theoretical approach was the expectation and confirmation theory. The outcome indicated that post-adoption satisfaction did affect how much of the functionalities on mobile Facebook the female respondents were interested in exploring. Based on this outcome, this chapter presents a postulation in the form of a discussion to indicate that post-adoption satisfaction could be one of the reasons for the global digital gender divide.

INTRODUCTION

There is a lot of discussion and research on reasons why there is a digital gender divide. Often most of these reasons are reasons that prevent the disadvantaged gender from adopting Information and Communications Technologies and Services. In this chapter a different approach is adopted. This approach takes post-adoption satisfaction into consideration. It is understood that post-adoption satisfaction of a product, service or technology will obviously result in some degree of continued or discontinued usage (Oliver, 1980; Oliver, 1977). In the context of this book, it would imply that post-adoption satisfaction of certain ICTs could result in social inclusion and vice versa. This would be more so if the usage process

DOI: 10.4018/978-1-5225-7068-4.ch010

of the Information and Communication Technology (ICT) platform involves social, political or intellectual engagement. However, research into this topic with respect to the digital gender divide is rare. This is understandably so because of the pervasive nature of current ICTs in society. Which implies that if an ICT service is useful to a person, the person will adopt it. Hence research into the post-adoption behaviour of the user might be deemed irrelevant. In a scenario where there was no digital gender divide then such an argument would stand and research into the phenomena could be ignored.

But that is not the case. This is because, currently from a global perspective, women adopt less of ICT than men (See ITU, 2017). This is true in the adoption of the enabling ICT technologies, which are currently enabled by the Internet Protocol (IP); hence making the adoption of the Internet fundamental to the adoption of current and future ICT. However, the global Internet gender gap has not been decreasing but increasing. And from a global perspective more women adopt less of the Internet than men, resulting in a global Internet gender gap. The ITU reports that this global Internet Gender gap increased from 11% in 2013 to 12% in 2016 (ITU, 2016). The increase was attributed to the increasing internet gender gap in developing countries. The increase is also attributed to the low access to Internet networks in rural areas as well as a low number of women in cities adopting the existing Internet networks (see Williams, 2015; Kakar, Hausman, Thomas, & Denny-Brown, 2012). Another major reason is that developing countries are often laggards when it comes to adopting newer upgrades of IP networks and technologies. The existence of this global Internet gender gap implies that women, from a global perspective, also adopt less of ICT services than men. The protracted existence of this problem calls for a trouble shooting exercise that is different from the approaches adopted previously. This is why post-adoption satisfaction is examined to identify if it is one of the reasons for this problem.

This chapter sets the ball rolling from the context of Mobile Facebook adoption. The context was broad but later converged after receiving feedback from mostly developing countries. In this chapter the aim is to identifying how post-adoption satisfaction affects the gender divide. The guiding theory underpinning this exploration is the "Expectations and Confirmations Theory". The chapter is divided into the following sections. The background section presenting the concepts discussed in this chapter; the theoretical section describing the Expectations and Confirmations Theory; the methodology section; the results section; and the discussion and conclusion sections.

BACKGROUND

The background of this chapter is built on the following ideas. These are the possible correlation between satisfaction and ICT adoption; and the further correlation between Post-adoption satisfaction and the digital gender divide.

Satisfaction and ICT Adoption

The concept of satisfaction can be approached from two dimensions. The first dimension being economic satisfaction and the second dimension being social satisfaction. Economic satisfaction is a feeling a person derives from the use of a service or product based on the evaluation of his or her economic outcomes that emanate from factors such as sales volumes, margins and discounts (Geyskens & Steenkamp, 2000). Social satisfaction is a psychological feeling a person derives based on relationship outcomes that are fulfilling, gratifying and facile. In a nutshell, satisfaction could be described as an outcome of an evaluation of emotions resulting from an activity or a process (Clinton, Aigbavboa, & Wellington, 2013). In this chapter, the interest is on social satisfaction.

In contemporary times, ICT is not just an enabler of society, economy and culture; it is an integral part of society. It was difficult to imagine such a world, as we have now, back then in the 1980s. A world where ICT services control our electricity grid system, transportation (air, land and Sea), commerce, governance, health, education, our homes, entertainment and our social lives etc. If there is breakdown in any of these ICT systems today, most people would not know what to do with their lives. As a result there has been a lot of research on the ICT adoption in various sectors of the economy and parts of our lives (see examples (Sirirak, Islam, & Khang, 2011; Gayen & Roy, 2018; Jones, DeRuyter, Thompson, Norelli, & Morris, 2018, etc).

One of the reasons, why the integration of ICT into society is successful is because of the social and economic satisfaction derived as a result of improved performance in the delivery of services or assisted living services (see Attar & Sweis, 2010; Khojeh, Nor, & Aghakhani, 2010; Sirirak, Islam, & Khang, 2011, etc). Research indicates that the improved performance of an ICT will result in user satisfaction at the point of adoption and at the post-adoption stage (see Khalifa & Liu, 2003). Similarly, research indicates that satisfaction is the basis for the continued usage of ICTs (See Najmul Islam, 2011; Dong, Cheng, & Wu, 2014). This implies that an unsatisfied user could reject an ICT technology or service at the post-adoption stage. The rejection could range from a total withdrawal from the usage of ICT to the passive usage of ICT. Therefore, bases on the cited research, there is a plausible possible relationship between user satisfaction and ICT adoption. However in this chapter, the emphasis is not on the satisfaction felt from adoption but the continued satisfaction after adoption, which is the post-adoption satisfaction. Furthermore it is from the perspective of the female user.

Post-Adoption Satisfaction and the Gender Divide

As identified in the previous sub-section, there is a possible positive relationship between user satisfaction (social satisfaction) and the ICT adoption pattern. Furthermore, there was also a possible correlation between satisfaction, in this case post-adoption satisfaction and continued usage. From the perspective of the digital gender divide, one could assume that some female users are either passive users of ICT or those who have rejected ICT. This is because they were dissatisfied with the ICT they adopted. This could result in the digital gender divide.

Unfortunately, there is no research to back up such a claim. This is why there is an attempt to explore the claim in this chapter. But there are claims backed by research that are synonymously close to this claim. There is research on the relationship between satisfaction and continued usage of ICTs from a gender based perspective. In literature, the correlation between satisfaction and internet adoption by females in the United Arab Emirates is documented (see example Moussa & Seraphim, 2017) and the correlation between post-adoption satisfaction and continued usage of Social network services from a gender based perspective is documented (See Dong, Cheng, & Wu, 2014). Similarly, research actually indicates, that males and females do depend on satisfaction, for continued usage of ICTs (Khalifa & Liu, 2003). A Research with 75% of the respondent being women indicated that "post-adoption satisfaction had a significant impact on the interest on future mobile services" (Park, Snell, Ha, & Chung, 2011).

The difference between the research cited and the claim made in this section is that the works cited were not aimed at identifying or solving the gender divide. But based on the assertions identified in these sources among others, the assumption that the gender divide could also be the product of dissatisfied women who abandoned ICT. It can also be said that the satisfaction identified in the work cited is the post-adoption satisfaction. This is because from a marketing perspective consumer satisfaction is a product of post-choice evaluation (see Jiang, Klein, & Saunders, 2012).

Hence based on the analogy so-far, one could infer that there is a possible correlation between post-adoption satisfaction and the digital gender divide. However, such an inference could only hold credence if proven empirically to be true. Based on the background of this chapter, a theory that evaluates post-adoption satisfaction is used. This theory is discussed briefly in the next section.

EXPECTATIONS AND CONFIRMATION THEORY

The Expectations and Confirmation Theory (ECT) posits that the performance of a product in the market has a direct correlation with the confirmation and disconfirmation of the user's expectations and the user's perceived performance of the product (see Oliver, 1977; Oliver, 1980). The figurative representation of the model is seen in Figure 1. The theoretical basis is hinged on the R. Anderson's work on consumer dissatisfaction (see Oliver, 1977; Anderson, 1973). In his work, Anderson (1973) empirically proved that consumers are likely to reject a product when their threshold of trust is eroded by the "disparity between product claims and actual performance" (Anderson, 1973). Based on this foundation, Anderson explained users possess a cognitive expectation of the assumed performance of a product before they decide to adopt it (Oliver, 1977). If after purchasing the product, its performance is not what was expected, then the disconfirmation is negative (ibid). But if the product performance is what was expected then the disconfirmation is positive. Oliver (1977) extended this idea proposed by Anderson empirically by indicating that disconfirmation evaluation made by the user has an effect on consumer satisfaction. Therefore if the consumer is satisfied with the disconfirmation outcome, she might continue to use the product or buy more. Furthermore, Oliver (1977) also indicated that in a situation where the user has to repurchase the product or is purchasing the product based on positive ratings then, the perceived performance of the product is "*a positive function of expectation and disconfirmation, when other factors are held constant*" (Oliver, 1977).

This model was improved upon by Oliver in 1980, taking into considerations variables such as attitude and intention. However, Oliver (1980) argued that the measure of disconfirmation actually reveals if the user is satisfied or not without neglecting the impact of attitude and intention in his work. This theory has been improved upon over the years. The most popular variance of the model used in Information

Figure 1. Expectation and Confirmations Theory
Source: Oliver (1977)

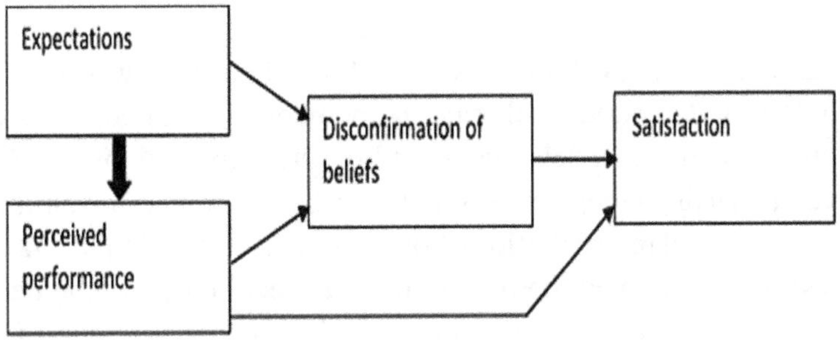

Systems (IS) research is the Expectation Confirmation Model by Bhattacherjee (see Bhattacherjee, 2001). The focus of this chapter is not on a particular information system but on ICT adoption as a whole. The information system mentioned here is used as a test case and not a case study. Based on this background the model by Oliver (1977) is adopted and used. Furthermore, as this chapter is not about marketing, the focus will not be not be about purchasing but adoption. This is because adoption, as a concept, is broader than "purchase" and it also encompasses "purchase".

Over the years this theory has been used widely to investigate post-adoption satisfaction in the field of marketing (see Tsao, 2013), Information systems (see Bhattacherjee, 2001; Khalifa & Liu, 2003); Consumer behaviour (see example Chou, Kiser, & Rodriguez, 2012) and a lot of other fields. In the interdisciplinary field of ICT, ECT has been used to investigate post-adoption satisfaction of users for various ICT systems, infrastructure and services (see Adjin & Williams, 2012; Mou, Shin, & Cohen, 2017). It has also been used to investigate sustained usage of Information systems (See example (Hossain & Quaddus, 2011). It has also been used to research into the sustained usage of online ICT services (see Chen, Carpenter, Li, Chen, & Hung, 2018; Lin, Wei, & Lekhawipat, 2018). It has been used to research on the level of satisfaction in service delivery after ICT was adopted see (Sirirak, Islam, & Khang, 2011).

In the context of this chapter, the ECT has been used to investigate the correlation between post-adoption satisfaction and continued usage of ICTs from not so strictly female standpoint. But one could extract results that are female related. An example is the work of Lin, Featherman and Sarker (2017). In their work they mention that females will be satisfied after adopting social networks if they find it useful to them and their privacy is assured. They also identified that they will only continue to use the network based on their reputation on the network, their sense of community identity on the network, how much they enjoy the network and their level of satisfaction (Lin, Featherman, & Sarker, 2017). Examples of other similar research includes the use of ECT to investigate the influence of enjoyment and subjective norms- which are identified as drivers of satisfaction – towards the continued usage of Facebook (see Mouakket, 2015). Another example which is not social media related is the use of ECT to investigate "the perceived enjoyment, perceived usefulness, satisfaction, and continuance intention to use digital textbooks in Korean middle school" (see Joo, Park, & Shin, 2017).

However, these forms of research are limited. Furthermore, it is difficult to locate a research that uses ECT or any of its contemporary variants to investigate the digital gender divide. However, the theory does hold promise for such a research; especially if the role of post-adoption satisfaction and the gender divide is to be determined. The theory is used in this chapter to investigate 12 female respondents from developing countries from different parts of the globe and their post-adoption satisfaction in the usage of Mobile Facebook. The outcome will be used to continue the discussion of the chapter.

METHODOLOGY

The empirical study was a deductive exploratory study. Mobile Facebook was used as the test case. Obviously because Facebook is an ICT service adopted by members of both gender groups. To conduct the exploratory study, a questionnaire was designed based on the Expectations and Confirmation Theory. 28 questions were developed using Google forms and distributed online. The online distribution was via Facebook chats, mass mailing and redistribution of the Google forms and links via colleagues. The questions elicited responses that highlighted the pre-adoption expectations and the perceived performance/possibilities of the services and functionalities provided by Mobile Facebook for social networking.

The respondents were further asked to provide their post-adoption disconfirmation evaluations of their expectations and perceived performance/possibilities of the services they adopted. Finally they were asked to indicate if they were generally satisfied with the usage of Mobile Facebook and how often they used Mobile Facebook.

13 female respondent provided feedback the time this chapter was written. 1 questionnaire was deemed invalid and rejected because it was submitted blank. 8 of the female respondents were from Ghana, 1 from Brazil and 1 from India. 3 of the female respondents did not indicate their country of residence, but 2 identified themselves as Asians and 1 as a black female. One of the respondents from Ghana uses Mobile Facebook for promoting her business. The respondent from Brazil does not use Mobile Facebook, but only Twitter and Linkedin. The other respondents use Mobile Facebook for leisure. Ultimately, data from only 12 female respondents could be used.

Since the initial responses were small in number and the survey is ongoing, responses from the respondents were analysed first using Google forms. The form was downloaded as a Comma Separated Value (CSV) file and filtered using Microsoft Excel. The outcome of the analysis is presented in the results section.

RESULTS

Five of the female respondents had their pre-adoption expectation fulfilled after adopting Mobile Facebook. Seven of the female respondents did not have their expectations fulfilled after adopting Mobile Facebook. The results from the female respondents are split into three sub-segments. Results and analysis of the five satisfied females are presented in sub-segment: 1.) Results for the 7 dissatisfied females are presented in sub-segment; 2.) The post-adoption pattern of both group of females is presented in sub-Segment; 3.) This section ends with a summary of the findings.

Segment 1: Results From the 5 Female Responders

As seen in the table above, 5 of the female respondents had a positive disconfirmation of their expectations after adopting Mobile Facebook. The profile of the respondents' is presented in the table below.

1. Result on Expectation and Disconfirmation of Expectation by the 5 Female Respondents

Their major expectation, except for female number 5 as seen in the table below was to socialize with old and new friends. Female number 5 could have had similar expectations. However, she indicated that she had no clear expectations but had a positive disconfirmation of her unclear expectation of Mobile Facebook.

2. Result on the Perceived Performance of Mobile Facebook

As a follow up from the ECT, the 5 respondents highlighted what they thought they will be able to do, when they adopt Mobile Facebook. The feedback is seen in the Figure 2 below.

Table 1. Profile of the 5 female respondents

	Age	Gender	Country of residence	Race	Do you own a mobile Phone	Is it a smart phone	What network do you use in accessing Mobile Facebook? (You can choose more than one option)	What type of mobile network does your mobile operator operate?
1	*NA	Female	India	Asian	Yes	Yes	Internet access (data package) on your mobile phone from your network provider	4G
2	26	Female	Ghana	Black	Yes	Yes	Internet access (data package) on your mobile phone from your network provider	4G
3	36	Female	Ghana	Black	Yes	Yes	Internet access (data package) on your mobile phone from your network provider; Public Wi-Fi Network	4G
4	22	Female	Ghana	Black	Yes	Yes	Internet access (data package) on your mobile phone from your network provider; Public Wi-Fi Network	3G
5	21	Female	Ghana	Black	Yes	Yes	Internet access (data package) on your mobile phone from your network provider	3G

*NA (No Answer)

Source: Field data (Williams, Adjin,& Muat, 2018)

Table 2. Expectation and disconfirmation of expectation by the 5 female respondents

	Gender	Country of Residence	Race	Expectation	Disconfirmation	
				What were your expectation when you subscribed to Facebook using your mobile phone?	Are all your expectations fulfilled?	If yes, which of them are fulfilled?
1	Female	India	Asian	Not many as such! Just to be in touch with friends.	Yes	I found all my friends
2	Female	Ghana	Black	Access to friends	Yes	I am able to upload profile pictures.
3	Female	Ghana	Black	Linking up with friends	Yes	I am able to link up with friends.
4	Female	Ghana	Black	Convenient access to friends	Yes	I now have easy access to friends on my phone without going to access Mobile Facebook at an Internet café.
5	Female	Ghana	Black	No clear expectation	Yes	I am just satisfied.

Source: Field data (Williams, Adjin, Muat (2018))

Figure 2. Perceived performance/possibilities of Mobile Facebook by the 5 female respondents
Source: Field data (Williams, Adjin, & Muat, 2018)

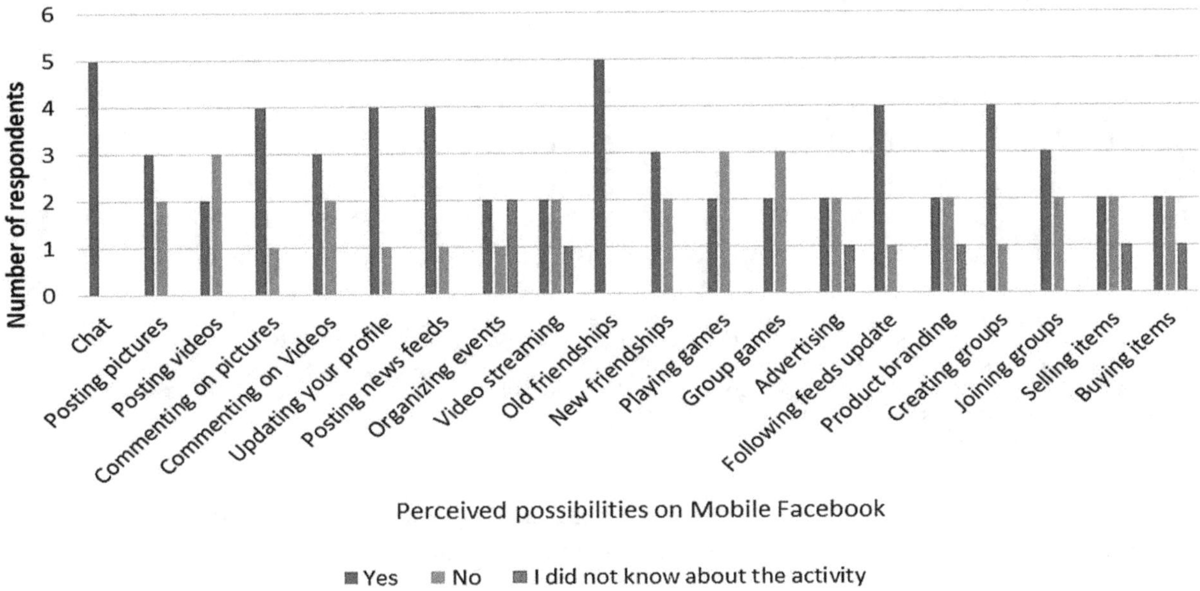

The most outstanding perceptions for them was the possibility to chat as well and to search for old friends online. Some of them did not know or perceive they could engage in activities such as posting pictures, posting videos, updating profile etc. Only 2 out of the 3 knew about the potential of using Mobile Facebook to advertise and promote their brand or even buy or sell items online. However, 2 of the respondents had no idea about the existence of certain functionalities, such as organizing events, video streaming, advertising possibilities, and product branding, buying and selling items online. That is indicated by "I do not know about the activity". While between 2 and 3 respondents knew of the functionalities but were not expecting it on Mobile Facebook. This is indicated by "No". "Yes" indicates that they were expecting to see and use the functionality on Mobile Facebook.

3. Result on the Disconfirmation of Perceived Performance of Mobile Facebook by the 5 Female Respondents

Based on their perceptions. After adopting Mobile Facebook, there was a positive disconfirmation for the perceived perception of the chat functionality and the searching for old friends by the 5 female respondents. Only one of them had a negative disconfirmation in the searching of old friends as seen in the figure below. Another negative disconfirmation is in the creation of groups and video streaming as seen in Figure 3. Furthermore, 4 respondents perceived they could create groups, but only 2 were satisfied with that process. However on an individual basis, each respondent had at least one disconfirmation related to these disconfirmations. But aside the disconfirmations, the post-adoption satisfaction of Mobile Facebook as seen in the figure below is also driven by the satisfaction in the use of functionalities they knew anything about before adopting Mobile Facebook.

Figure 3. Positive and negative disconfirmations of the perceived performance/possibilities on Mobile Facebook by the 5 female respondents
Source: Field data (Williams, Adjin, & Muat, 2018)

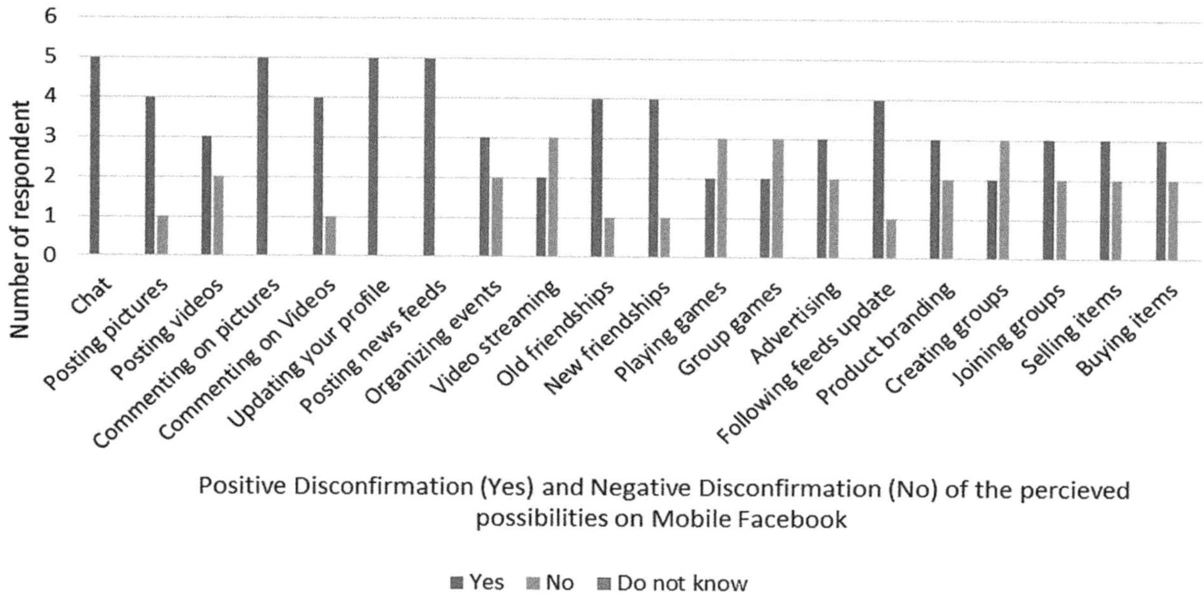

4. Conclusion on Segment 1

The 5 female respondent had a positive disconfirmation of their expectations. They also had positive disconfirmations for most of the perceived possibilities or perceived performance of Mobile Facebook. This implies that the respondents are generally satisfied with the Mobile Facebook platform.

Segment 2: Results From the 7 Female Responders

As seen in Table 3, 7 of the female respondents had negative disconfirmations of their expectations after adopting Mobile Facebook. The profile of the respondents is presented in the table below.

1. Result on the Expectation and Disconfirmation of Expectation of the 7 Female Respondents

As seen in the table below, only two of the 7 dissatisfied females had a clear expectation before adopting Mobile Facebook. 5 of the 7 female respondents had no clear expectations before adopting Mobile Facebook. However, none of them were satisfied. One female respondent with a clear expectation was dissatisfied because adverts were embedded in videos. The other female respondent found it difficult to access Facebook on her mobile device.

Two of the respondents had poor Quality of Experience (QoE) in the updating of pictures. And one of the female respondent had issues with the access network she subscribes to. Two of the respondents had no reason for their negative disconfirmation. Other reasons cited from the questionnaire response by

Table 3. Profile of the 7 female respondents

	Age	Gender	Country of Residence	Race	Do you own a mobile Phone	Is it a smart phone	What network do you use in accessing Facebook? (You can choose more than one option)	What type of mobile network does your mobile operator provide?
1	26	Female	Ghana	Black	Yes	Yes	Internet access (data package) on your mobile phone from your network provider	4G
2	*NA	Female	*NA	Black	Yes	Yes	Internet access (data package) on your mobile phone from your network provider	2G
3	27	Female	Ghana	Black	Yes	Yes	Internet access (data package) on your mobile phone from your network provider; Public Wi-Fi Network	4G
4	*NA	Female	*NA	Asian	Yes	No	Internet access (data package) on your mobile phone from your network provider	3G
5	*NA	Female	*NA	Asian	Yes	No	Internet access (data package) on your mobile phone from your network provider	3G
6	21	Female	Ghana	Black	Yes	Yes	Internet access (data package) on your mobile phone from your network provider	3G
7	21	Female	Ghana	Black	Yes	Yes	Internet access (data package) on your mobile phone from your network provider; Public Wi-Fi Network	3G

*NA (No Answer)
Source: Field data (Williams, Adjin, & Muat, 2018)

the unsatisfied respondents were, high consumption of data charges (respondents 1 and 4), High latency (respondent 3), and poor design of the functionalities (respondent 6).

2. Result on the Perceived Performance of Mobile Facebook of the 7 Female Respondents

As seen in Figure 4, 3 of the 7 female respondents could perceive some of the possibilities available on Mobile Facebook. Their response is "yes". Out of the 3 respondents, 2 of them were those with clear expectations. 2 of the respondents did not expect to find certain functionalities on Mobile Facebook. Their response was "no". But they knew about the functionalities. Unlike the first group of 5 female

Table 4. Expectation and disconfirmation of expectation of the 7 female respondents

	Gender	Country of Residence	Race	Expectation	Disconfirmation	
				What were your expectation when you subscribed to Facebook using your mobile phone?	**Are all your expectations fulfilled?**	**If no which of them are not fulfilled?**
1	Female	Ghana	Black	No expectation	No	*NA
2	Female		Black	No clear expectation	No	Poor Network
3	Female	Ghana	Black	Be able to view videos without ads because data is expensive	No	The videos are embedded with ads
4	Female	*NA	Asian	No clear expectation	No	Cannot Update pictures
5	Female	*NA	Asian	No clear expectation	No	Cannot Update pictures
6	Female	Ghana	Black	To make accessing easier	No	It is too much
7	Female	Ghana	Black	No expectation	No	*NA

*NA (No Answer)
Source: Field data (Williams, Adjin, & Muat, 2018)

responders, the idea of the 7 female respondents about the possibilities for social networking in general was limited. This limitation in idea affected their perceived performance of Mobile Facebook. As seen in the figure below, between 4 and 6 of the respondents were not aware of certain functionalities. Hence, they were not expecting these functionalities. Hence they chose the option tagged "I do not know". These group of responders could be tagged as the "explorers".

3. Result on the Disconfirmation of Perceived Performance of Mobile Facebook of the 7 Female Respondent

Based on their perception, only respondent 3 from Table 2 recorded a positive disconfirmation with respect to the chat, posting pictures, commenting on pictures, updating profile and posting news feeds. Respondent 3, 4 and 6 from Table 2 recorded most of the negative disconfirmations. It would be recalled that respondents 3 and 6 had clear expectations. Respondents, 1, 2, 5 and 7 had no disconfirmations to record as seen in Figure 5. They are likely to be active Mobile Facebook users that rarely or never contribute content due to poor network connectivity, but read feed contents provided by others on their own user feed page and not o the feed page of others. This results correlate with their dissatisfaction experience based on their expectations.

4. Conclusion on Segment 2

The 7 female respondents, recorded negative disconfirmations of their expectations. Although one of the respondent had some positive disconfirmation, she recorded a negative disconfirmation for all the other functionalities. The major problem with this group is that their poor access network robs them of the ability to actually explore Mobile Facebook, in the manner they would have loved to.

Figure 4. Perceived Performance possibilities with Mobile Facebook for the 7 female respondents
Source: Field data (Williams, Adjin, & Muat, 2018)

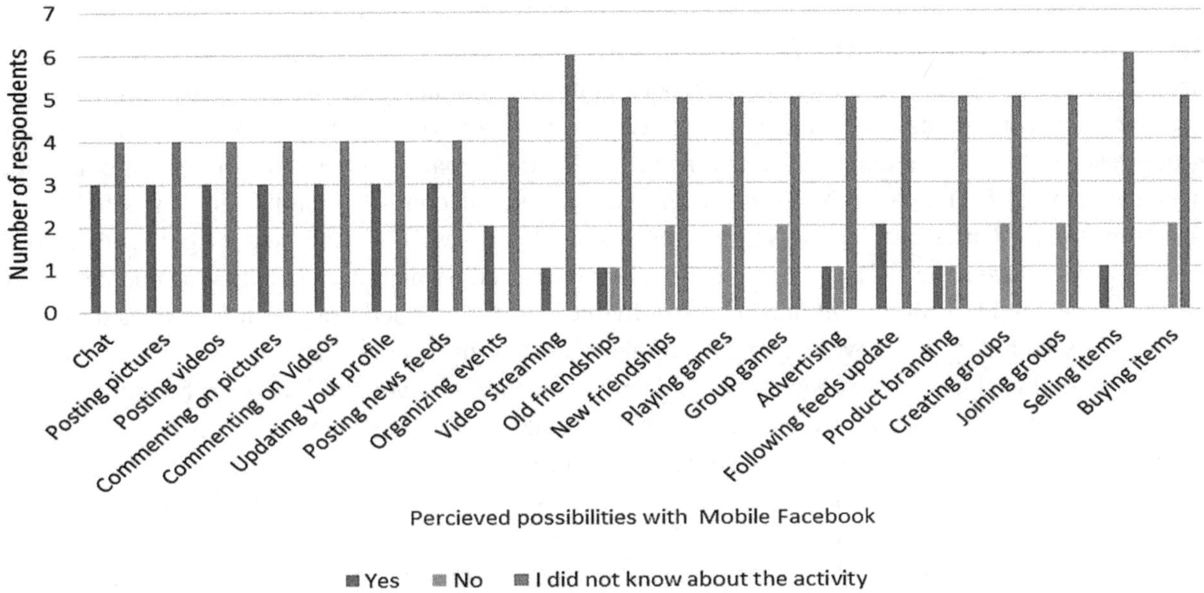

Figure 5. Positive and negative disconfirmations of the perceived performance/possibilities on Mobile Facebook by the 7 female respondents
Source: Field data (Williams, Adjin, & Muat, 2018)

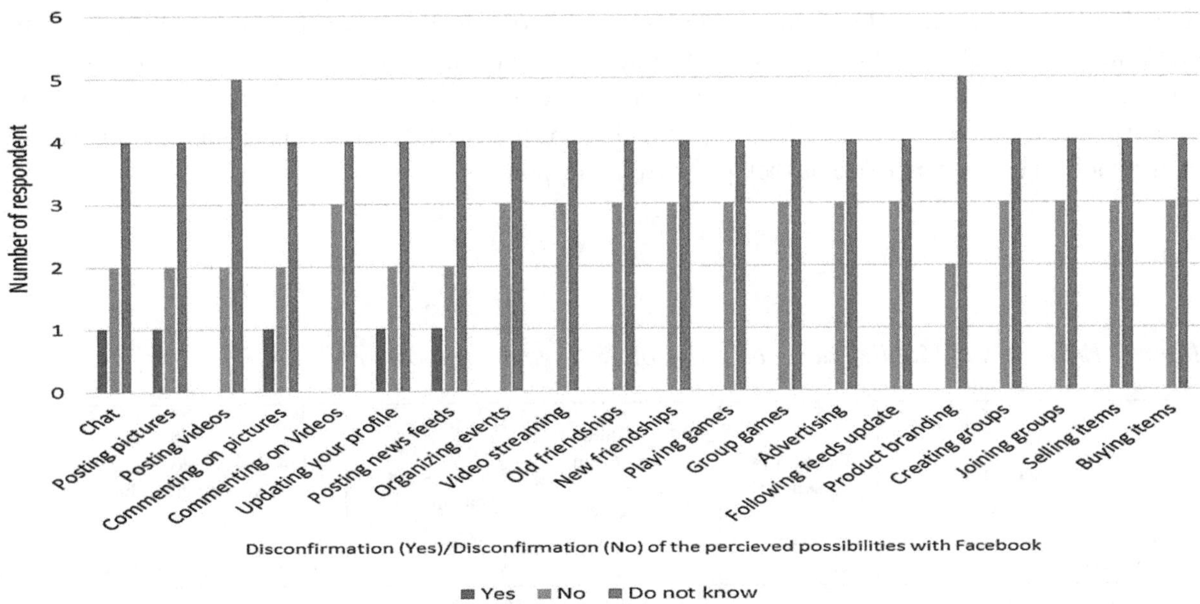

Segment 3: Post-Adoption Pattern of the Group of 5 and Group of 7 Respondents

Table 5 and 6 below showcases the frequency of usage of Mobile Facebook by the 5 and 7 female respondents respectively. The first finding worth reporting in this section is that the group of 5 who reported positive disconfirmations kept using Mobile Facebook as reported in Table 5. Female number 2 in the group has the longest continued usage of 10 years. While Female number 5 has the least continued usage of 3 months. That being because she adopted Mobile Facebook 3 months ago. It would be said that from the ECT perspective, that satisfaction will naturally result in continued usage. Furthermore, it would be said from the ECT perspective that a positive disconfirmation of expectation and perceived performance would result in continued usage. Obviously, the continued usage is for services they have adopted in which they did provide a positive or negative disconfirmation for.

The second finding worth reporting, in table 6, is that the 7 dissatisfied females who recorded majority of the disconfirmations also indicate sustained usage of Mobile Facebook. Respondents 2 and 6, who had clear expectations and recorded the most disconfirmations, actually use Mobile Facebook less frequently than other respondents that did not have clear expectations. It could be said that respondents in this group with a more frequent usage of Mobile Facebook use Mobile Facebook not because they are satisfied. But they do so either because of network effect or some other reason. However, table 6 also indicates that some of the 7 respondents might actually explore more of Mobile Facebook, if they were satisfied.

As seen in Tables 4, Respondents 2 and 7 in Table 4 could not respond. Respondent 4's response was no. Which implied that her usage pattern would not change even if she were satisfied. However, respondents 1, 3, 5 and 6 responded in the affirmative. This implies that respondents 1, 3, 5, and 6 might actually explore the possibilities on Mobile Facebook more, if they were satisfied after adopting the platform. If one could recall in segment 2 most of the respondents did not know about certain services offered by Mobile Facebook. They were assumed to be users who read their feeds only but do not contribute content. These were respondents 1, 2, 5 and 7. It is not clear if respondents 2 and 7 would change their mind if they were satisfied as they provided no response.

Table 5. Frequency of Mobile Facebook usage of the 5 female respondents

	Gender	Country of residence	If yes, how often do you use mobile Facebook?	How long have you accessed Facebook with your mobile phone?	How do you access Facebook on your mobile phone?
1	Female	India	Once a month	1 year	Facebook mobile website
2	Female	Ghana	Once a week	10 years	Facebook App
3	Female	Ghana	Every 1 hour	6 years	Facebook App
4	Female	Ghana	Once a week	6 years	Facebook App
5	Female	Ghana	Once a day	3 months	Facebook App.

Source: Field data (Williams, Adjin, Muat (2018))

Table 6. Frequency of Mobile Facebook usage of the 7 female respondents

	Gender	Country of Residence	If yes, how often do you use mobile Facebook?	How long have you accessed Facebook with your mobile phone?	How do you access Facebook on your mobile phone?	Does your lack of satisfaction affect your overall experience in the use of mobile Facebook?
1	Female	Ghana	Every 30 minutes	4 months	Facebook App	Yes
2	Female	*NA	Once a week	6 years	Facebook App	*NA
3	Female	Ghana	More than four times a day	5 years	Facebook App	Yes
4	Female	*NA	Once a day	*NA	Facebook App	No
5	Female	*NA	Once a day	*NA	Facebook App	Yes
6	Female	Ghana	Once in two weeks	5 years	Facebook App	Yes
7	Female	Ghana	Once in three weeks	4 years	Facebook App	*NA

*NA (No Answer)
Source: Field data (Williams, Adjin,& Muat, 2018)

Summary of Findings

The findings in segment 3 shed further light on the after effect of post-adoption satisfaction and dissatisfaction on the group of respondents. Especially for the second group of dissatisfied female users, some of them would explore Mobile Facebook more, if they were satisfied with the Quality of Service (QoS). The reason they have these low quality of experience are based on issues external to Facebook and issues related to the usability of Mobile Facebook.

One of the external reasons as mentioned by dissatisfied respondents, is the poor network connectivity. This degrades the quality of experience of the unsatisfied users. As seen in Table 1, the satisfied users all subscribe to 4G and 3G mobile networks and own smart phones. They do not face this issue. But on the contrary as seen in Table 3, respondent 2 subscribes to a 2G network. And she actually cites this as an issue. An issue that was surprising was high latency mentioned by respondent 3 of the 7 unsatisfied females. She is a 4G subscriber. However, the reason makes sense because in developing countries, mobile network operators do degrade their network delivery to 3G and sometimes 2G for 4G subscriber. So although she is a 4G subscriber, she might occasionally be receiving a 2G signal. This then results in her poor QoE on Mobile Facebook. For those respondent 1 and 4 who own smart phones and are connected to 3G and 4G networks respectively, their consumption charges for accessing Facebook is high. This might not be unrelated to problem of high latency as mentioned by respondent 3. This is because, the longer it takes to load a page, the more expensive it becomes. Naturally, the user will become impatient or like some of our respondents, stich to reading feeds. Another external issue not cited but could be a contributing factor is the use of feature phones by 2 of the unsatisfied respondents. Though they subscribe to 3G networks, the use of feature phones could prevent them from accessing the possibilities on Mobile Facebook. The problem respondent 6, from the unsatisfied group, faces is that of poor usability design of Mobile Facebook. She has a good 3G connectivity and a smart phone. But she cannot explore more functionalities due to the bad design. Her experience may not be decoupled from the external challenges mentioned earlier.

However, based on these findings, it is clear that post-adoption satisfaction/dissatisfaction is not stopping people from using Mobile Facebook. Rather those satisfied with Mobile Facebook seem to explore more of the platform as seen in segment 1. But those who are not satisfied are inhibited from exploring more of the platform. An interesting part of this result is that those who were not satisfied had other reasons which made them adopt a limited part of the platform. But assuming Mobile Facebook did not encourage sociability; furthermore, assuming Mobile Facebook was an ICT product or service that is exclusive to an individual; would post-adoption dissatisfaction result in a rejection? Based on this findings, the answer might be a "Yes". This is because if a person adopts a social network service, for which she is not satisfied with, for 6 years (such as respondent 2: see Table 6), then she may not be gaining satisfaction from the platform but the relationships of people she met on the platform. Else she is likely to reject the platform if she was not benefiting from some network effect provided by the Mobile Facebook platform.

DISCUSSION

The findings made in this chapter do not indicate a clear impact of post-adoption satisfaction on the gender divide. In a parallel study conducted for men, the pattern was similar. This indicates that there is no gender bias when it comes to post-adoption satisfaction. But if as mentioned in the introduction that men adopt more ICTs than women globally, including social media (Fatehkia, Kashyap, & Weber, 2018), then one cannot ignore the impact of post-adoption satisfaction on the gender divide.

However, based on the results it could be said that there could be some impact of post-adoption satisfaction on the gender divide. From the perspective of the respondents it is evident that post-adoption-satisfaction does affect how much of the Mobile Facebook platform, each respondent decide to access. The satisfied users adopted more functionalities on the platform than those who were not satisfied with the platform. Also evident was the fact that some of the unsatisfied users did indicate that they would like to explore the platform further if they were satisfied.

Although none of the female respondent who used Mobile Facebook as a whole, it was evident that such a scenario could occur. This is because individuals that adopt ICT as seen in the results and in some developing countries do so for personal usage (see Rowntree, 2018). Hence the QoS they receive from the network operator and the QoE they derive from the service being delivered is important. Therefore, if the user is unhappy with both forms of quality, they are likely to reject the network. An example can be found in a study conducted by Williams (2015), subscribers of an Internet Services provided by a Non-Governmental Organization in Ghana unsubscribed from the network when the QoS was poor (Williams, 2015). Therefore there is also that possibility that female users do reject ICT services of even Mobile Facebook because they are not satisfied.

If that were to be the case, then the digital gender divide would not only occur because of the low adoption of ICT by women, but also because some women might have unsubscribed from certain ICTs. It is difficult to make this assertion in the West because of the existence of varieties and use cases of ICTs which enable female adoption. As an example, females in some of the western countries are more likely to adopt ICTs before they get admitted into high schools. ICTs are integrated in the educational delivery process. On the contrary, most women in developing countries are likely to adopt ICTs when they can afford it. Very few women in developing countries are opportune to see, have the need for or use ICTs at an early age. However, when they do adopt ICTs it is mostly because they find it useful within their social context or in some cases economic context (e.g. mobile money). Otherwise, they might exhibit limited curiosity towards the ICT service. The curiosity fades once she cannot find the usefulness for it (see Williams, Siddi, & Kwofie, 2016). Such women are more likely to unsubscribe or not just use an ICT service granted to her by an NGO or International Donor Agency.

As such there is the need for more research. It is important to understand what constitute satisfaction with respect to ICT adoption for women. As mentioned in the section on ECT and in the result section, different women had different variables which would result in their satisfaction or made them unsatisfied respectively. In the result section, it could be seen that the problem was not just from Facebook alone rather it was mostly from the services delivered by the network operators. There could be lots of other variables out there that may be useful in understanding what would constitute satisfaction for an ICT network, service or and application. Furthermore, it is important to note that these variable could be moving targets because they would evolve as the ICT services evolve. This implies that such a research might continue for a long time if the digital gender divide is to be bridged globally. It is also important to develop frameworks on how this satisfaction can be measured? The starting point could be the ECT used in this chapter. However, the aspect of framework development is critical because measuring such satisfaction could lead to innovations that will result in a satisfying ICT service, where lots of women could be willing to adopt. Still, such frameworks would also have to evolve.

CONCLUSION

The chapter started out with the aim to understand how post-adoption satisfaction affects the digital gender divide, the direct impact could not be found based on the results analysed. However, there were indications from the unsatisfied respondents that they could not adopt most of the services on Mobile Facebook platform because they were unsatisfied with the service delivery. Service delivery was affected by poor QoS from the mobile network operator and, poor QoE in when users interact using the mobile Facebook platform.

However, this implies that post-adoption dissatisfaction does result in the restrictive use of ICTs by female users. Although the scenario would be the same for male users, more males use ICT globally than women. Hence if the problems with post-adoption satisfaction is solved for women, maybe the gender gap may experience a significant closure. This conceptual-proposition is solely based on the analysis of the empirical data gathered for this study.

REFERENCES

Adjin, D., & Williams, I. (2012). Comparative analysis between WiMAX and Fibre Optics Backhaul Network Depolyment in Developing countries- The case of Ghana. *29th World Wireless Research Forum Meeting*.

Aledhari, M., Aneja, N., Bashir, A. K., Bennett, R., Bielby, J., Hicks, H. A., . . . Wack, J. (2018, April). *Options and challenges in Providing Universal Access.* Retrieved from Internet Initiative IEEE: https://internetinitiative.ieee.org/images/files/resources/white_papers/OPTIONS-AND-CHALLENGES-IN-PROVIDING-UNIVERSAL-ACCESS-v180418.pdf

Alumanah, J. N. (2005). Access and use of information and communication technology for the African girl-child under cultural impediments. In *Proceedings of the international symposium on Women and ICT: creating global transformation.* Baltimore, MD: ACM.

Anderson, R. E. (1973). Consumer dissatisfaction: The effect of disconfirmed expectance on percieved product performance. *JMR, Journal of Marketing Research, 10*(1), 38–44. doi:10.2307/3149407

Attar, G. A., & Sweis, R. J. (2010). The relationship between information technology adoption and job satisfaction in contracting companies. *Adoption and Job Satisfaction in Contracting Companies, 15*, 44–63.

Awotwi, J. E. (2008). Lack of Eeual Access to ICTs by Women:an e-governance issue. In *ICEGOV '08: Proceedings of the 2nd international conference on Theory and practice of electronic governance.* ACM. 10.1145/1509096.1509190

Bhattacherjee, A. (2001). Understanding information systems continuance: An expectation-confirmation model. *MIS Quaterly, 25*(3), 351–370. doi:10.2307/3250921

Broadband Commission. (2017). *The state of Broadband: Broadband catalyzing sustainable development.* Broadband Commission.

Chen, X., Carpenter, D., Li, X., Chen, C., & Hung, S. (2018). Why do Individuals Continue Using Mobile Payments - A Qualitative Study in China. In *HICSS Conference.* University of Hawaii at Manoa. Retrieved 05 15, 2018, from https://scholarspace.manoa.hawaii.edu/handle/10125/50067

Chou, S. Y., Kiser, A. I., & Rodriguez, E. L. (2012). An expectation confirmation perspective of medical tourism. *Journal of Service Science Research, 4*(2), 299–318. doi:10.100712927-012-0012-3

Clinton, A. & Wellington. (2013). A Theoretical Framework of Users' satisfaction/Dissatisfaction Theories and models. *2nd International Conference on Arts, Behavioral Sciences and Economics Issues (ICABSEI'2013).*

Cohen, R. (2018). Afterword: Patterns of Inclusion and Exclusion in African Societies. In L. Landau (Ed.), *Forging African Communities.Global Diversities* (pp. 303–311). London: Palgrave Macmillan. doi:10.1057/978-1-137-58194-5_13

Conclaves, T. A., & Rosondo, D. (2016). New Communications Technologies: Women's Rights Violations, Limits on Freedom of Expression, and an Alternative ways to promote Human rights. In J. Wilson & N. D. Gapsiso (Eds.), *Overcoming gender inequalities through technology integration* (pp. 144–162). Hershey, PA: IGI.

Dong, T., Cheng, N., & Wu, Y. (2014). A study of the social networking website service in digital content industries: The Facebook case in Taiwan. *Computers in Human Behavior, 30*, 708–714. doi:10.1016/j.chb.2013.07.037

Europa. (2013). *What is Social Inclusion*. Retrieved from European Youth Portal: http://europa.eu/youth/sk/article/39/6145_en

Fatehkia, M., Kashyap, R., & Weber, I. (2018). Using Facebook ad Data to track the global digital gender gap. *World Development, 107*, 189–209. doi:10.1016/j.worlddev.2018.03.007

Gayen, A., & Roy, M. (2018). Exploring Impact of ICT Adoption on Business Performance outcome of Indian MSMES. *International Journal of Engineering Technology Science and Research, 5*(1), 1740-1744.

Geyskens, I., & Steenkamp, J. E. (2000). Economic and social Satisfaction:Measurement and Relevance to Marketing Channel Relationships. *Journal of Retailing, 76*(1), 11–32. doi:10.1016/S0022-4359(99)00021-4

Gillwald, A., Milek, A., & Stork, C. (2010). *Towards evidence -based ICT POlicy and Regulation:Gender Assessment of ICT Access and Usage in Africa*. Research ICT AFRICA.

Hafkin, N., & Huyer, S. (2007). Women and Gender in ICT statistics and Indicators for Development. *Information Technologies and International Development: Special Issue on Women's Empowerment and Information Society, 4*(2), 25–41. doi:10.1162/itid.2008.00006

Hilbert, M. (2011). Digital gender divide or technologically empowered women in developing countries? A typical case of lies, damned lies, and statistics. *Women's Studies International Forum, 34*(6), 479–489. doi:10.1016/j.wsif.2011.07.001

Hossain, M. A., & Quaddus, M. (2011). Expectation-Confirmation Theory in Information System Research: A review and Analysis. *Information Systems Theory*, 44-49.

ITU. (2013). *ICT Facts and Figures.* Geneva: ITU. Retrieved from https://www.itu.int/en/ITU-D/Statistics/Documents/facts/ICTFactsFigures2013-e.pdf

ITU. (2016). *ICT facts and figures 2016*. Retrieved 9 16, 2016, from ITU: http://www.itu.int/en/ITU-D/Statistics/Documents/facts/ICTFactsFigures2016.pdf

ITU. (2017). *ITU Facts and Figures 2017.* Geneva: ITU. Retrieved from https://www.itu.int/en/ITU-D/Statistics/Documents/facts/ICTFactsFigures2017.pdf

Jiang, J., Klein, G., & Saunders, C. (2012). Discrepancy theory models of satisfaction in IS research. *Information Systems Theory, 28*, 355-381. Retrieved from UQ Business School: https://www.business.uq.edu.au/sites/default/files/events/files/jjiang-paper.pdf

Jones, M. L., DeRuyter, F., Thompson, N. A., Norelli, J., & Morris, J. T. (2018). Survey of User Needs for ICT -- Community Living by People with Disabilities. *33rd Annual International Technology and Persons with Disabilities Conference Scientific/Research Proceedings.*

Joo, Y. J., Park, S., & Shin, E. K. (2017). Students' expectation, satisfaction, and continuance intention to use digital textbooks. *Computers in Human Behavior, 69*, 83–90. doi:10.1016/j.chb.2016.12.025

Kakar, Y. W., Hausman, V., Thomas, A., & Denny-Brown, C. (2012). *Women and the web.* Intel Corporation. Retrieved 08 5, 2018, from https://www.intel.com/content/dam/www/public/us/en/documents/pdf/women-and-the-web.pdf

Khalifa, M., & Liu, V. (2003). Determinants of Satisfaction at Different Adoption stages of Internet-Based Services. *Journal of the Association for Information Systems*, *4*(5), 206–232.

Khojeh, E., Nor, M. K., & Aghakhani, N. (2010). *Using ICT to improve customer satisfaction in small and medium sized construction companies: A study among malaysian construction SMEs. In 5th International Conference on Computer Sciences and Convergence Information Technology*. Seoul, South Korea: IEEE. Retrieved from https://ieeexplore.ieee.org/document/5711104/

Lareau, A., & Horvat, E. M. (1999). Moments of social inclusion and exclusion race, class and cultural capital in family- school relationships. *Sociology of Education*, *72*(1), 37–53. doi:10.2307/2673185

Lin, C., Wei, Y., & Lekhawipat, W. (2018). Time effect of disconfirmation on online shopping. *Behaviour & Information Technology*, 1.

Lin, X., Featherman, M., & Sarker, S. (2017). Understanding factors affecting users' socialnetworking site continuance: A gender difference perspective. *Information & Management*, *54*(3), 383–395. doi:10.1016/j.im.2016.09.004

Mou, J., Shin, D., & Cohen, J. (2017). Understanding trust and percieved usefulness in the consumer acceptance of an e-service: A longitudinal investigation. *Behaviour & Information Technology*, *36*(2), 125–139. doi:10.1080/0144929X.2016.1203024

Mouakket, S. (2015). Factors influencing continuance intention to use social network sites: The Facebook case. *Computers in Human Behavior*, *53*, 102–110. doi:10.1016/j.chb.2015.06.045

Moussa, B. H., & Seraphim, J. (2017). Digital gender divides and e-empowerment in the UAE: A critical perspective. *International Journal of Education and Development Using Information and Communication Technology*, *13*(3), 145–161.

Najmul Islam, A. K. (2011). Information Systems Post-Adoption Satisfaction And Dissatisfaction: A Study In The E-Learning Context. In *The Pacific Asia Conference on Information Systems (PACIS) Proceedings*. Brisbane: PAICS. Retrieved from http://aisel.aisnet.org/pacis2011/83/

Nungu, A., Brown, T., & Pehrson, B. (2011). Challenges in sustaining Municipal Broadband Networks in the Developing World. In *e-Technologies and Networks for Development* (p. 363). Heidelberg, Germany: Springer.

Oliver, R. L. (1977). Effect of Expectation and Disconfirmation on Post exposure product Evaluations:An Alternative Interpretation. *The Journal of Applied Psychology*, *62*(4), 480–486. doi:10.1037/0021-9010.62.4.480

Oliver, R. L. (1980). A Cognitive Model of the Antecedents and Consequences of Satisfaction Decisions. *JMR, Journal of Marketing Research*, *17*(4), 460. doi:10.2307/3150499

Park, J., Snell, W., Ha, S., & Chung, T. (2011). Consumers' Post-adoption of M-services: Interest in Future M-services Based on Consumer Evaluations of Current M-services. *Journal of Electronic Commerce Research*, *12*(13), 165–175. Retrieved from https://lib.dr.iastate.edu/cgi/viewcontent.cgi?article=1065&context=aeshm_pubs

Pocock, D. F. (1957). Inclusion and Exclusion:A process in the Caste System of Gujerat. *SouthWestern Journal of Anthropological Research, 13*(1), 19–31. doi:10.1086outjanth.13.1.3629155

Rebollo, M. A., & Vico, A. (2014). Perceived Social Support as a factor of rural Women'e Digital Inclusion in Online Social networks. *Media Education Research Journal, 43*(22), 173–180.

Rowntree, O. (2018). *Connected Woman: The mobile gender gap report.* GSMA.

Shen, C. Y., & Ge, J. (2005). Women and ICT: from the Chinese perspective. *Proceeding CWIT '05 Proceedings of the international symposium on Women and ICT: creating global transformation.* Baltimore, MD: ACM.

Shneiderman, B. (2000). Universal Usability: Pushing human-computer interaction research to empower every citizen. CS-TR-4043. *Communications of the ACM, 45*(3), 84–91. doi:10.1145/332833.332843

Sirirak, S., Islam, N., & Khang, D. B. (2011). Does ICT adoption enhance hotel performance? *Journal of Hospitality and Tourism Technology, 2*(1), 34–49. doi:10.1108/17579881111112403

Tsao, W. Y. (2013). Application of Expectation Confirmation Theory to Consumers' Impulsive Purchase Behavior for Products Promoted by Showgirls in Exhibits. *Journal of Promotion Management, 19*(3), 283–298. doi:10.1080/10496491.2013.770811

UN. (2016). *Leaving no one behind: The imperative of inclusive development.* New York: United Nations Economic and Social Affairs.

Williams, I. (2015). *Analysis of Public Private Interplay Frameworks in the Development of Rural Telecommunications Infrastructure: A Multi-Case Study.* Aalborg: Aalborg University Press.

Williams, I., Siddi, F., & Kwofie, B. (2016). Public Demand Aggregation as a means of Bridging the ICT Gender Divide. In J. Wilson & N. N. Gapsiso (Eds.), *Overcoming Gender Inequalities through technology Integration* (pp. 123–143). Hershey, PA: IGI Global. doi:10.4018/978-1-4666-9773-7.ch006

World Bank. (2018). *Social inclusion.* Retrieved from World Bank: http://www.worldbank.org/en/topic/social-inclusion

Chapter 11
Meeting Gender Gaps in Information and Communication Technology (ICT):
How Can Creativity Make a Difference?

Chunfang Zhou
Aalborg University, Denmark

ABSTRACT

This chapter will bridge theories such as ICT, creativity, learning, and gender in one framework, and particularly focuses on how to meet gender gaps in learning contexts by using ICT and the strategies of developing gender sensitive creativity training programs in developing contexts. In this sense, this chapter contributes to imply both how to encourage more women users and how women can better use ICT for developing contexts in the changes towards creative society. Accordingly, a review on developing ICT-supported educational programs in diverse contexts around the world will be firstly made, which highlights the strategy of learning though ICT is not a new initiative; however, why gender gaps in using ICT are still key issues? This drives this chapter to further discuss gender gaps in developing creativity by ICT from a psychological perspective. Finally, a series of strategies of developing gender sensitive creativity training programs will be discussed in order to facilitate the changes towards a creative society.

INTRODUCTION

The rapid development of Information and Communication Technologies (ICT) in the 21st century is demanding swift action to engage learners to participate in the mainstream of development. ICT encompasses a vast array of technologies that facilitate production, handling and processing of information, as well as technologies that enable the transfer and exchange of information and communication (Zhou, 2016). It has a broad scope of diverse technologies, including radio, television, as well as newer digital

DOI: 10.4018/978-1-5225-7068-4.ch011

technologies such as computers and the Internet (Tinio, 2003). Because of these multiple powers of processing and networking of information, ICTs have brought about a global socioeconomic paradigm shift which was not the case with earlier technologies such as radio and television (UNESCO, 2011). Now, access to ICT is considered necessary and fundamental for the socioeconomic development of a society (Zhou, 2016).

The resent research also shows that digital technologies have great potential to develop creativity (Loveless, 2007; Zhou, Chen, & Luo, 2013). Creativity in general has been understood as the generation of new and useful ideas (Amabile, 1996). A useful theoretical framework for recognizing and developing creativity can be described as an interaction between characteristics in people and communities, creative process, subject domains and wider social and cultural contexts. Thus, the affordances of ICT can also be part of this creative interaction as people exploit the distinctive features of ICT that enable digital technologies to act as tools in creative processes (Lovelss, Burton, & Turvey, 2006; Zhou, 2016). Meanwhile, the technological skills are important not only for children at schools but also for lifelong learning. The different levels of interaction and collaboration characteristics of new technologies facilitate personalization of learning paths. Learners become active stakeholders, who are empowered to shape their own learning spaces and resources and collaborative learning processes (Kampylis, Bocconi, & Punie, 2012; Zhou, 2016).

However, the integration of ICT in all aspects of life is recognized as a developed country. The birth and the growth of the Internet were in the United Sates, and this has led, in part, to large distortions in connectivity between the developed and developing nations. But the economics remains the obvious overarching reason for the continuation of the divide (ICT global). Thus, it requires more attention on issues of ICT should be paid to the developing contexts. For example, in relation to the discussion on learners' ICT literacy in Malaysia, Daud and Zakaria (2012) argued that Web 2.0 is an innovation in the application of Internet technology that enables users to be more creative, more involved, and easy to relate to each other. Furthermore, the country's education system should be able to provide the younger generation, who are able to face the possibilities for people facing the industry, global economic fluctuations, the influx of new technologies, the use of computers as a daily business need, and the wealth of information worldwide.

In particular to the literature on ICT in developing contexts, gender issues have been mentioned in recent studies (Purushothaman, 2013), especially from a creativity approach, for example, in Zhou and Purushothaman (2014). However, according to Stoltzfus and his colleagues (2011), the relationship between gender role and creativity is clearly influenced by gender. Future research design to identify personal characteristics, other than general role, that may explain gender differences in creativity, for example, self-esteem and self-image – would be most helpful in increasing the knowledge about how creativity is developed and expressed in men and women. Such information could potentially be valuable in the development of learning experiences designed to enhance creativity in women and men. This also directs for further research on women learners' psychological issues such as Technophobia, in experiences of using ICT related to creativity development. 'Technophobia' involves women's basic psychological issues including attitudes and confidence of approaching to new technologies; while 'self-efficacy' involves issues related to methods of using ICT. There are also other a series of factors discussed in the literature, such as beliefs, identity (Masunaga, 2011), and confidence (Drury, 2011), etc.

Following the above lines, this chapter will bridge theories such as ICT, creativity and gender in one framework, and particularly focuses on how to meet gender gaps in learning by ICT and the strategies of developing gender sensitive creativity training programmes. In other words, this chapter contributes to imply both 'how to encourage more women users' and 'how women can better use ICT' for developing contexts' in the changes towards creative society. In the following, a review on developing ICT-supported educational programmes in diverse contexts around the world will be firstly made, which highlights the strategy of learning though ICT is not a new initiative; however, why gender gaps are still key issues? This drives this chapter to further discuss gender gaps from a psychological perspective. Finally, a series of strategies of developing gender sensitive creativity training programmes will be discussed in order to meet the gender gaps of using ICT in the changes towards a creative society.

UNDERSTANDING THE CONTEXT: LEARNING BY ICT IS NOT NEW INNITIATE

The new technologies have the potential to fundamentally transform how and what learn throughout their lives. Just as the advances in biotechnologies made possible the "green revolution" in agriculture, new digital technologies make possible a "learning revolution" in education (Resnick, 2002). Generally, there are four ways ICTs can support the basic education: (1) supporting education in school; (2) providing non-formal education for out-of-school children and adults; (3) supporting pre-service distance education of teachers and their in-service professional development, and; (4) enhancing the management of schools (Wang & Zhou, 2013; Zhou, 2016).

Recently, ICT is thought much more than computers and the Internet or even telephony (Resnick, 2002). However, older technologies such as the telephone, radio and television, although now given less attention, have a longer and richer history as instructional tools. The use of computers and the internet is still in its infancy in developing countries due to limited infrastructure and the attendant high costs of access (Tinio, 2012). Thus, the potential of each technology varies according to how it is used. For example, radio and TV broadcasting can be used in direct class teaching, school broadcasting and general educational programming over community; computers and the Internet can be used in distance education; the Internet also provides Web-based collaboration tools, such as email, listservs, message boards, real-time chat and Web-based conferencing, etc. These tools connect learners to other learners, teachers, educators, scholars and researchers, scientists and artists, industry leaders and politicians – in short, to any individual with access to the Internet who can enrich the learning process (Tinio, 2012).

As mentioned, ICTs are potentially powerful tools for extending educational opportunities, both formal and non-formal, to previously underserved constituencies - scattered and rural populations, groups traditionally excluded from education due to cultural or social reasons such as ethnic minorities, girls and women, persons with disabilities, and the elderly, as well as all others who for reasons of cost or because of time constraints are unable to enroll on campus (Tinio, 2012). So many programmes of ICT-supported education have been developed in different countries that has been started from half century ago. The following shows some examples of different initiatives.

UKOU in the United Kingdom

The Open University of the United Kingdom (UKOU) established in 1969 as the first educational institution in the world wholly dedicated to open and distance learning, still relies heavily on print-based materials supplemented by radio, television and, in recent years, online programming (Tinio, 2012).

CCRTVU in China

The Chinese Central Radio and TV University (CCRTVU) has provided a wide range of TV-based training programmes through its network of provincial universities. CCRTVU has more than 80,000 hours of TV courses and education programmes on air. These programmes are developed in close co-operation with general universities. The best field teachers, experts of different disciplines and audio-visual professionals constitute the team to prepare educational materials. By the use of distance learning mode, China plans to expand the idea of the 'virtual classroom', breaking away from the constraint of learning place and time. The objective of the plan was also to combine TV technology, education programmes, revision of basic curriculum of schools and the whole process of teaching through distance education (Wang, & Zhou, 2013).

Programmes in the United States

The birth and the growth of the Internet were in the United States, and this has led, a great development of ICT-supported education programmes. Three examples are shown in the below:

- **Project CHILD (Computers Helping Instruction and Learning Development):** It is a computer-integrated instruction programme developed in 1988 by the University of Florida for grades K-5 (pre-school and primary school). The programme focuses on three subject areas – reading, writing and mathematics. Each Project CHILD classroom has a learning station with between three to six computers (Tinio, 2012).
- **E-Learning in MIT:** In April 2001, Massachusettes Institute of Technology (MIT) announced that learning materials and syllabi for all courses were being put on the Internet for anyone to use – recognizing the power of the Internet and that knowledge is for sharing. The recently developed Intelligent Computer-Assisted Instruction (ICAI) programmes are able to generate and solve problems, diagnose students' misconceptions, select appropriate teaching strategies and carry on dialogues with students based on in-depth studies by researchers on how people think, learn and solve problems (Sanyal, 2011).
- **GLOBE:** It is the most widely cited telecollaborative project. GLOBE stands for the Global Learning and Observations to Benefit the Environment. It is a U.S. Government-sponsored programme launched in 1994 that links primary and secondary students and teachers from over 10,000 schools in more than 95 countries to the scientific research community. GLOBE gives students the opportunity to take measurements of the atmosphere, water, soils, and land over at or near their schools, following strict protocols designed by GLOBE scientists (Sanyal, 2011; Wang & Zhou, 2013).

Telesecundaria in Mexico

In Mexico, Telesesundaria started as early as 1968 with its programme of transmitting live programmes through open public channels to television sets placed at distant classrooms where students of 7 to 9 grades (age 13-15) were learning in the presence of a teacher. By 1993 the programme reached 512,700 students in more than 9,000 schools. By 2004, there are around 1100,000 students have been enrolled in Telesecundaria. It is now an integrated and comprehensive programme providing a complete package of distance and in-person support to students and teachers (Sanyal, 2011).

SchoolNet in Thailand

In 1995, SchoolNet Thailand, a joint project of the National Electronic and Computer Technology Center (NECTEC) was started in Thailand. At present, SchoolNet Thailand boasts of approximately 4,000 schools in its network, with over 9000 of these with their own web pages in Thai. It expects to extend Internet service provision to the estimated 34,000 schools nationwide in the coming years and continue to lead in local content development in Thailand (Tinio, 2012).

NIIT in India

In India, the universities, the government agency (the Department of Electronics) and the National Council for Education, Research and Training and the private sector (including the private National Institute for Information Technology, NIIT) are working together to develop computer aided instructional material to be used for both distance and traditional learning programmes. NIIT works with various State governments in the area of IT education in schools. It provided computer training to 371 schools in the deep interiors of Tamil Nadu. It is also working with Karnataka Government to offer computer training to students of 700 government schools throughout the state with an ambitious target of reaching over 175,000 students every year (Sanyal, 2011).

VUTP in South Korean

The accelerated adoption of virtual education in South Korea was a result of deliberate planning by government. It began in 1998 with the launch of the Virtual University Trial Project (VUTP). With 65 universities and five companies participating, the VUTP was designed to: 1) create a cost-effective virtual education system without diminishing quality; 2) develop and implement Web-based or other types of distance education courses; 3) identify appropriate policies and standards for running a virtual university, and; 4) share experiences during the trial period (Tinio, 2012).

ProInfo in Brazil

The ProInfo programme is aimed at democratizing access to telematics, providing education for the exercise of basic rights and enabling educators to use new ICT. For this, master teachers are being trained at the universities for specialization courses and regular teachers are being trained in the Educational Technology Centres (NTEs). The Educational Technology Experimentation Centre (CETE) set up in the Ministry of Education is the central node of the ProInfo programme to facilitate all its actions (Sanyal, 2011).

Universitas Terbuka in Indonesia

Since its establishment in 1984 as the first distance and open learning institution in Indonesia, the Universitas Terbuka (Indonesian Open University) has made great strides in making higher education available to Indonesians. In its efforts to address issues of quality in instruction, it has recently introduced the use of the Internet and a combination of facsimile and Internet technologies for student tutorials in 40 of its more than 700 courses on offer. These electronic tutorials are a supplement to more traditional tutorial models – including face-to-face, regular mail, radio and television – already employed by the university (Tinio, 2012).

Learning Lab in Denmark

In Denmark, the Ministry of Education joined with the Ministry of Business and Industry to creative Learning Lab Denmark, a research lab that studies learning in all settings, in all stages of life. The Internet will open up new learning opportunities, enabling new types of 'knowledge-building communities' in which children (and adults) around the globe collaborate on projects and learn from one another (Resnick, 2002).

The above examples of programmes demonstrate diverse development of ICT-supported education systems. It is clear that for developing countries, ICTs have the potential for increasing access to and improving the relevance and quality of education. It thus represents a potentially equalizing strategy for developing countries (Resnick, 2002). However, the emergences of the era of new technologies such as the Internet and various applications have taken steps towards a new environmental challenge in the field of teaching, learning, and assessment (Daud & Zakaria, 2012). Broadly, this also brings a discussion on a change towards a creative society (Zhou, 2015).

THE COMING OF CREATIVE SOCIETY DRIVEN BY ICT

New technologies have the potential to fundamentally transform how and what people learn throughout their lives. Just as advances in biotechnologies led to the 'green revolution' in agriculture, new digital technologies can lead to a possible 'learning revolution' in education (Resnick, 2002). Technology is challenging the boundaries of the educational structures that have traditionally facilitated learning (Sam, Othman, & Nordin, 2005). What makes ICTs a significant component in today's system of learning is their capacity to support a wide range of learning activities (Tella, 2011). Mastering ICT skills can make a student competent and ready for the global workforce (Cradler, McNabb, Freeman, & Burchett, 2002). As Gauntlett (2011) suggested, education has become institutionalized in a system of schools where learning is a process directed by teachers, whose task is to transfer nuggets of knowledge into young people's minds.

Furthermore, we can see a growing engagement with a new learning culture mediated by ICT. This orientation rejects the passivity of learning, and seeks opportunities for creativity, social connections, and personal growth. Learning is encouraged by a 'hands-on' approach with a spirit of enquiry and questioning. In the years ahead, ICTs are bound to open up new learning opportunities and facilitate changes in the 'learning revolution'. More attention has been argued to focus on a new learning culture of learning afforded by technologies, where learners at the center of learning process, participating in ways that were not possible before. Flexibility, personalization and different learning styles can be combined; and learning cannot authentic, motivational and conceived as a social process, enabling peer-to-peer informal interactions that lead them to learn from each other (Kampylis, Bocconi, & Punie, 2012).

Therefore, 'creativity' has become the new key to learning activities that entail coming up with new and useful ideas (Zhou, 2016). In learning contexts, creativity offers opportunities to shape new knowledge. It can be viewed as a key driver for individual learners to engage in activities with their peers. Creativity is an inspirational force that generates new ideas or produces novel combinations of existing ideas that lead to further solutions or a deeper understanding of knowledge. Moreover, creativity is usually generated in collaborative contexts; it is situation-specific, and it can be understood to emerge within dynamic processes of co-construction. These processes will produce novel and appropriate ideas regarding the problems that are faced in collective learning endeavors (Zhou, 2012; Zhou, 2015). The proliferation of digital technologies has provided tools that can help learners to improve and reinvent themselves. There is no denying the fact that we live in a digital networked society where there is ever more dependence on newer ICTs (Fernandez-Villavicencio, 2010; Zhou, 2015).

As the literature (Gauntlett, 2011; Zhou, 2015) argued, we are on the cusp of change toward a 'creative society'. Even more than 10 years ago, Resnick (2002), pointed out, in the 1980s, information was the new king, which indicated that natural resources and manufacturing would no longer be the driving forces of economies and societies. It was in this period that we witnessed a transition from the 'Industrial Society' to 'Information Society'. In the 1990s, the 'Knowledge Society' was labeled as the characteristic of this society. People realized that information itself would not bring about any important change. Rather, it was the way in which people transformed information into knowledge and managed that knowledge, which would hold the key to this change. However, the 'Creative Society' is an improvement upon the shift in the focus from 'information' to 'knowledge'. It means that in future, our success will be based not on how much we know, but on our ability to think and act creatively.

The paradigm underpinning ICT-enabled innovation for learning entails a holistic transformational shift towards connecting learning organizations and process (i.e. connecting the realities of learner and their experience of community). However, in the changes towards developing ICT-based creative learning design in developing contexts, challenges exist both in technology and in the social sciences. For example, reducing the digital divide requires improvements across all the dimensions of ICT (dubbed the 4C framework): Computing, Connectivity, Content, and human Capacity (Wang, & Zhou, 2013):

- **Computing:** PCs are prohibitively expensive for most people, and shared access (e.g., community centers or cybercafés) becomes inevitable. PCs today are very difficult to use, and even "experts" spend a lot of time maintaining their machines, worrying about updates, security, compatibility of hardware, etc. As a complementary technology, non-PC devices are an important option, e.g., mobile phones.
- **Connectivity:** While mobile technology is improving worldwide, it remains expensive, limited in rural areas, and poor at proving data connectivity.
- **Content:** Meaningful content is lacking in many languages, and most content is not locally relevant. Today's systems tend to make people passive consumers of information, instead of enabling generation of local information. In addition, rich content demands multimedia (useful to overcome literacy issues), which, in turn, requires broadband connectivity.
- **(Human) Capacity:** Users need to be aware, literate, and innovative to harness the power of ICT. They also should be empowered to use ICT, both by society and by the state.

As mentioned previously, ICT usage does not occur in a vacuum, rather within social and cultural norms than also shape the digital divide between developed and developing contexts. ICT usage is based on policy and business models, especially regulation. Thus, in the long run, ICT must provide value and be sustainable from both a user and a provider perspective. Designers and developers of ICT could consider innovative ways to work with and develop understandings of the nature of digital technologies as both and a medium in creative process (Zhou, 2015). A creativity framework should underpin planning, practice, and evaluation. The framework should recognize the interaction between individuals and communities, processes, domains and fields, and the characteristics of imagination, fashioning, pursuing purpose, originality and value judgments (Loveless, 2007).

It should be noted that Internet has contributed to such a change towards a creative society. Out of all the information and communication technologies that we know of until now, few can match the global impact of Internet-based technologies that cut across a wide range of sectors and diverse socioeconomic groups (Hill, Wiley, Nelson, & Han, 2004). The rapid expansion of free electronic educational material on the Internet has given those fortunate enough to have access to it a new way of acquiring information (Hatakka & Lagsten, 2012). The Internet thus helps students to access information sources from various parts of the world and gives them the opportunity to choose instantaneously from an updated repository of materials (Kabilan & Rajab, 2010). The Internet has transformative powers in the development of educational organizations and for students in developing regions too (Hatakka & Lagsten, 2012).

However, like other ICTs, not all people are able to take advantage of the opportunities presented by the Internet, due to its uneven distribution across the world that leads to unequal access (UNESCO, 2011). This in turn brings uneven benefits to humanity (Moghaddam, 2010). Internet usage is distributed unequally, especially between developed and developing countries, and does not offer the same opportunities to everyone or every social group to the same extent (Pan, Yan, Jing, & Zheng, 2011; Walton, Yaaqoubi, & Kolko, 2012). This uneven distribution, or the separation between those who have access to digital information and communications technology and those who do not, and therefore are unable to participate in the information economy and reap the benefits of the opportunities provided by ICT is termed as the 'digital divide' (Qureshi, 2012). Some scholars use this term mainly to address the gap or difference in people's usage of the Internet (James, 2004). Internet usage is a fundamental aspect of digital divide. Since the Internet is an ICT tool, which has grown to touch all sectors, the digital divide is significantly about Internet usage in today's times.

GENDER GAPS IN ICT WITH CREATIVITY ISSUES

The development of different perspectives in describing creativity has been traced, from the concerns of 1950s to 1970s in areas of personality, cognition and the stimulation of creativity in individuals, to the awareness in the 1980s and 1990s of the influences of environments and social contexts on the creativity of individuals, groups and organizations (Loveless, 2007). According to the psychological studies (e.g. Amabile, 1996), creativity is a fundamental feature of human intelligence in general. It is grounded in everyday capacities such as the association of ideas, reminding, perception, analogical thinking, searching a structured problem-space, and reflective self-criticism (Boden, 1998). For example, Amabile (1996) has developed a social psychological and computational model of creativity, which includes three components within the individual: intrinsic motivation, domain-relevant knowledge, and creative skills, alongside a fourth environmental component encompassing the external setting, extrinsic motivation and rewards, social interactions, and time pressure. Accordingly, the literature shows creativity not only involves a cognitive dimension (the generation of new ideas) but also motivation and emotion, and is closely linked to cultural context and personality factors (Boden, 1998).

A number of observers of gender issues in creativity have offered rationales for social developmental influences that may negatively impact on the development of creativity in women (Stoltzfus, Leigh, Debra, & Elizabetht, 2011). The familial, economic and political practices are the main institutions thought which gender is enacted and patriarchy maintained, thus producing gender inequality (Negrey & Rausch, 2009). Many young women are expected to invest personal resources to meet social demands such as laying the foundation for establishing a family and initiating child rearing. The skills involved in pursuing these social role obligations may be inconsistent with the attributes that typify highly creative individuals. The highly affiliative interpersonal sensitivity and multitasking behaviors that contribute to successful achievement of conventional social role expectations for young women are incompatible with the single-minded absorption in one's work and unconventional, independent thinking that characterize highly creative personalities. In addition, the competing priorities stemming from feminine social role demands that are particularly salient during early adulthood that may limit the time and energy available to young women to pursue creative self-expression (Stoltzfus, Leigh, Debra, & Elizabetht, 2011).

Furthermore, the issues of women users of technology in creativity development have been discussed (Luo, Zhang, & Zhou, 2011). As suggested by Masunaga and Hitchock (2011), gender inequity has been especially prominent in traditionally male-dominant fields such as science, engineering, and technology, where females have received fewer resources and opportunities than have their male counterparts. In a study of females in the Purdue University students (Drury, 2011), it found a significant number of women: (a) experienced isolation in their technology-related classes; (b) felt uncomfortable asking professors for help outside of class; (c) believed men were treated more as equals by professors of technology courses, and; (d) felt marginalized when working with male classmates on group projects. The gender distinctions within organizations are embedded in the characteristics of the masculine-encoded structures and processes within which men and women are required to operate. To gain advantage, a woman may adopt masculine traits and styles, such as being more assertive, lowering the pitch of her voice, or dressing in a more being masculine manner. These points are in line with what has been discussed in an earlier study (Getzels & Csikszentmihalyi, 1976): the psychology of creative men is a feminine psychology and the psychology of creative women is a masculine psychology.

In a recent study, Zhou (2016) argued that creativity should be regarded as a literacy among software students in the context of ICT-enabled society innovation. In other words, digital literacy has become a prerequisite for students of this generation, especially after the shift from the 'Knowledge Society' to the 'Creative Society'. The global economy is transforming into an Internet economy (Ramayah, Jantan, & Ismail, 2003). If students are not able to analyze, interpret and create materials on the Web and in other digital environments, they may be incapable of functioning effectively in various social spheres as literate citizens (Hawisher, Selfe, Moraski, & Pearson, 2004). Therefore, educational strategies should provide platforms for the development of Internet skills required by 'Creative Society' (Purushothaman & Zhou, 2014). The analysis of the two-order factors that hamper women from using the Internet for learning has implications for strategies to improve women's education in developing contexts. We need a two-pronged approach to deal with barriers posed by the first-order factors caused by technical and economic issues, and the second-order factors that stem from socio-cultural mores.

RESPONDING TO CREATIVE SOCIETY: GENERAL STRAGIES

Preparing for technology deployment implies looking beyond the cognitive selling points of technology. Current practices in deploying information technology frequently focus on cognitive aspects by emphasizing how a new technology is a better choice than previous technologies, or how it will make a teacher's job easier. This strategy is logical and easy to implement; however, it is not sufficient. Evangelizing the benefits of a technology is only useful if the benefits are embraced by the environment (Straub, 2017). According to Wang and Zhou (2013), policymakers and planners, educators, education administrators and other stakeholders need to consider improvement of ICT-based educational systems in developing countries from the following aspects. The strategies put forward are specific to the ICT tool Internet (Purushothaman & Zhou, 2014).

Strategies for Education Policy and Planning

Attempts to enhance and reform education through ICT require clear and specific objectives, guidelines and time-bound targets, the mobilization of required resources, and political commitment at all levels to see the initiative through. The following are some essential elements of planning for ICT with a specific focus on the Internet:

1. A rigorous analysis of the present state of the educational system. ICT-based interventions using the Internet must take into account current institutional practices and arrangements. As Cook and his colleagues (2009) pointed out, concerns about the effectiveness of Internet-based learning have stimulated a growing body of research. In the first decade of the Internet's existence, 35 evaluative articles on Web-Based learning were published, whereas at least 32 were published in 2005 alone. A synthesis of this evidence could inform educators and learners about effective strategies for teaching and learning. Furthermore, when a new technology is introduced in the educational system, we have to consider its social or cultural implications, and possibilities of adoption. Thus, educational system can only lead students to superior levels in creative achievement through a self-evaluation of the culture in which the educational pedagogy is used, and the elements that are blocking the populace, as well as through the construction of a more fertile creative soil.
2. Policy decisions that give more priority to the provision of quality wireless and networking facilities in educational institutions that have no Internet and networking facilities. According to Lei and Zhao (2007), there are four categories of technology use: technology as media for inquiry, technology as media for communication, technology as media for construction, and technology as media for expression. However, in the case of Internet, quality is the key to realizing all kinds of technology uses. For example, when users' online experience is less gratifying because of slow connection speed they might go online less, and this will affect their information retrieval skills (Dimaggio, Hargittai, Celeste, & Shafer, 2004). Purushothaman's (2013) study on Internet usage among women students in a developing context found that slow speed of the Internet connections led to unpleasant and frustrating experiences that often-led women to stop using Internet. Poor quality net connections decrease women learners' motivation to engage in learning activities.
3. Piloting of an ICT-based model using the Internet. While emphasizing that the process of technology adoption by individuals takes time, Straub (2017) made the following points: (a) technology adoption is a complex, inherently social, developmental process; (b) individuals construct unique

(but malleable) perceptions of technology that influence the adoption process, and; (c) successful facilitation of technology adoption needs to address cognitive, emotional, and contextual concerns. Therefore, it is important to implement small-scale application of Internet before embarking on a comprehensive plan. In addition, the gender differences between cognitive styles, emotion and perceptions of technology will provide important references from the results of the pilot study.

Strategies for Issues of Infrastructure

A country's educational technology infrastructure depends on the national telecommunications and information infrastructure. Powerful broadband networks are crucial for gaining an edge in the knowledge economy, and countries should consider broadband networks part of the basic infrastructure (GITR, 2011). This is still a challenge for developing countries. Policy makers and planners must consider the following:

1. Are appropriate rooms or buildings available for providing computers with Internet connections in educational institutions? Space is an important issue in educational institutions in a developing context. Citing the educational changes in China, Zhou, Purushothaman and Rongbutsri (2013) pointed out how although creativity has been encouraged in higher education by the Ministry of Education of the People's Republic of China, there is a conflict between the limited classroom space and the huge number of students. It is also important to focus on reducing the gap in the student-to-computer ratio in accessing and using the Internet. Another basic requirement is the availability of uninterrupted electricity for providing Internet connectivity to institutions, which is often a big challenge in developing nations.
2. Specification of existing sources of financing and development of strategies for generating financial resources to provide networking and Internet facilities over the long term. Planners should consider cooperative innovation among various social groups such as educational institutions, government, and industry. The potential sources of financing and resources for the ICT use program include private donations, community support, membership fees, and public subsidies. Wang and Zhou (2013) cited Coca-Cola Company's ICT partnership with government, multilateral organizations, non-governmental organizations and educators in the Asia-Pacific in 1997 for the establishment of the first Coca-Cola Learning Center in Ho Chi Minh City, Vietnam. So far, Coca-Cola has expanded this approach to four other countries in the region – the Philippines, China, Malaysia and Australia – to bring e-learning opportunities and resources to tens of thousands of young people and their communities. Such cooperative innovation provides girls and boys with equal opportunities to use the Internet.

Strategies for Capacity Building

Various competencies must be developed throughout the educational system for making Internet usage successful in fostering the creativity of students. Teachers' professional development should focus on skills related to Internet-based technologies, Ideally, these skills should be addressed in pre-service teacher training and built upon in-service. Capacity building should start at the level of primary education so that students can become proficient when they reach higher classes. As suggested by and Purushothaman and Zhou (2014), coping with the complexity and adoption of new technologies necessities that teachers have a set of guiding principles. These principles include:

1. Negotiable expectations, clearly expressed, encourage deep approaches to learning.
2. Coherent knowledge structures (schema) facilitate purposeful and integrative learning.
3. Control creates commitment and encourages personal responsibility to monitor and manage meaningful approaches to learning.
4. Choice in content and process is a catalyst for spontaneous and creative learning experiences and outcomes while recognizing and valuing intuition and insight.
5. Critical discourse confirms understanding and diagnoses misconceptions.
6. Critical thinking must be modeled and rewarded.
7. Assessment must be congruent with expected learning outcomes.
8. Learning is confirmed through assessment.

Whether provided by in-school staff or external service providers, or both, technical support specialists are essential for the continued viability of Internet usage in institutions. As Zhou and Purushothaman (2015) emphasized, one kind of expertise can be defined with external aids that individuals use for their tasks, becoming part of their expertise. Expertise is not only shaped by the dynamic social context and artifacts in the setting, but also redefined by changes in the ways we do things. Thus, in the Internet-based learning environment, students are not replaced with computers, but empowered by them to make better use of their expertise. Technical support ensures that this process of learning expertise and building capability.

GENDER SENSITIVE CREATIVIEY DEVELOPMENT STRATEGIES

In order for women from developing countries to efficiently participate in this new information age, developing countries should focus on first-order as well as second-order factors that hamper the use of the Internet by women. Providing access to the Internet should not be limited to tackling first-order factors by providing infrastructure to bridge the divide. Attention needs to be paid to second-order factors, which hamper women from making use of available Internet facilities. More attention should be paid to women students in learning environment supported by ICT in developing contexts. Educational institutions should be aware of the gender differences in the usage of technologies in classrooms. The learning environments involving women users in a developing context should adopt a social embeddedness perspective that places emphasis on the cognitive and emotional capacities of the women participants, and focuses on what is meaningful and locally acceptable with regards to Internet usage (Zhou & Purushothaman, 2015; Purushothaman & Zhou, 2014)). Therefore, the following two strategies should be considered:

1. A design for teaching women to use the Internet for learning in a developing context, where gendered role definitions impact Internet use, should consider assigning a woman trainer or facilitator to make the participants feel more at ease. However, gender sensitivity should not be confined to providing a woman trainer, and care should also be taken to ensure that mobility and time constraints of the participants are also taken into consideration.
2. Some measures should also be taken to construct a learning environment in which women are able to express themselves freely and be more open to learning. It is worth considering trainings and workshops through educational institutions or Non-Governmental Organizations (NGOs) to

address the psychological barriers faced by women students. Motivational and inspirational talks from women from other walks of life making students aware of the importance of the Internet could also add value in a developing context.

There should be difference in approaches to providing assistance to women and men to support the learning processes using the Internet to foster their creativity. Huffaker and Calvert (2003) cited the example of the Game Design Project, in which children were asked to create their own video games in the programming language Logo. It was a six-month-long learning process. Results documented gender differences in the construction of video games. Although boys and girls built games that told stories, boys tended to construct action-adventure games based on the concept of Good versus Evil; in contrast, the games that girls created never presented evil themes, focusing instead on teaching or developing skills that reflected their personal interest. Most girls built their games in real-world settings, while most boys built fantasy worlds. Such differences imply that boys and girls need to be assisted differently, and this difference should be reflected in education plans and their implementation. As Luo and her colleagues (2011) pointed out in the context of mainland China, more attention should be paid to the creativity of women students than of the men students. They also called for helping women students face troubles positively with a humorous attitude besides stressing on the importance of constructing a relaxing social and cultural environment without rigid rules, in which women could have fun while learning.

As mentioned, we have addressed and should pay attention to the focus on a new learning culture of learning afforded by technologies, where learners at the center of learning process, participating in ways that were not possible before. Flexibility, personalization and different learning styles can be combined; and learning cannot authentic, motivational and conceived as a social process, enabling peer-to-peer informal interactions that lead them to learn from each other (Kampylis, Bocconi, & Punie, 2012). Thus, educational strategies should be both cultural-general and cultural-specific, as well as gender-general and gender-specific, in order to help learners in using the Internet to become a part of the "Creative Society".

CONCLUSION

Globalization and technological change bring the processes that have accelerated in tandem over past decade and have created a new global economy, which is powered by technology, fueled by information and driven by knowledge. ICTs are sparking a new entrepreneurial spirit, the creation of innovative products and services, and increased productivity in education systems. The lack of access to ICT for citizens in the developing countries reduces their chances of effectively participating in the experiences of creativity development in knowledge economy and reaping the benefits of the information revolution that can improve their overall life conditions. This chapter has particularly discussed the significances of a new focus on a creativity perspective to the issue of meeting gender gaps in using ICT and especially highlighted the roles of Internet in facilitating the changes towards the creative society. The issues involve different aspects of being socio-economical, socio-cultural, and psychological. From a general sense, future attention should be paid to the identification of stakeholders and harmonizing of efforts across different interest groups in the new learning communities. The challenge is to understand the emerging educational context and set up a creative learning environment that will facilitate the development of higher-order cognitive abilities and encourage these to thrive in the knowledge era. An Internet-savvy campus alone cannot facilitate the usage of Internet among women learners, it also requires cooperation among government, IT industries, educational administration as well as the society. Meanwhile, developing diverse gender sensitive creativity development programmes are necessary, which contribute to fill in the gender gaps of using ICT from a psychological perspective. This further facilitates women users to improve the knowledge and skills and overcome their technophobia and build self-efficacy beliefs. The designers of programmes accordingly should be thoughtful of how the women in group value the technology and how the women are encouraged to be more creative in and by using the technology.

REFERENCES

Amabile, T. M. (1996). *Creativity in Context*. Boulder, CO: Westview Press.

Boden, M. A. (2011). Creativity and artificial intelligence. *Artificial Intelligence*, *103*(1-2), 347–356. doi:10.1016/S0004-3702(98)00055-1

Cook, D. A., Levinson, A. J., Garside, S., Dupras, D. M., Erwin, P. J., & Montori, V. M. (2008). Internet-based learning in the health professions, a meta-analysis. *Journal of the American Medical Association*, *300*(10), 1181–1196. doi:10.1001/jama.300.10.1181 PMID:18780847

Cradler, J., McNabb, M., Freeman, M., & Burchett, R. (2002). How does technology influence student learning? *Learning and Leading with Technology*, *29*(8), 46–49.

Daud, M. Y., & Zakaria, E. (2012). Web 2.0 application to cultivate creativity in ICT literacy. *Procedia: Social and Behavioral Sciences*, *59*, 459–466. doi:10.1016/j.sbspro.2012.09.301

Dimaggio, P., Hargittai, E., Celeste, C., & Shafer, S. (2004). From unequal access to differentiated use: A literature review and agenda for research on digital inequality. In Social Inequality (pp. 355-400). New York: Russell Sage Foundation.

Drury, M. (2011). Women technology leaders: Gender issues in higher education information technology. *NASPA Journal About Women in Higher Education*, *4*(1), 96–123. doi:10.2202/1940-7890.1054

Fernandez-Villavicencio, N. G. (2010). Helping students become literate in a digital, networking-based society: A literature review and discussion. *The International Information & Library Review*, *42*(2), 124–136. doi:10.1080/10572317.2010.10762854

Gauntlett, D. (2011). *Making is Connecting, The Social Meaning of Creativity, from DIY and Knitting to Youtube and Web 2.0*. Polity Press.

Getzels, J. W., & Csikszentmihalyi, M. (1976). *The Creative Vision: A Longitudinal Study of Problem Finding in Art*. New York: Wiley.

GITR. (2011). *The global information technology report - Transformations 2.0*. Retrieved 17 June 2014, from http://www3.weforum.org/docs/WEF_GITR_Report_2011.pdf

Hatakka, M., & Lagsten, J. (2012). The capability approach as a tool for development evaluation – analyzing students' use of internet resources. *Information Technology for Development, 18*(1), 23–41. doi :10.1080/02681102.2011.617722

Hawisher, G. E., Selfe, C. L., Moraski, B., & Pearson, M. (2004). Becoming literate in the Information Age: Cultural ecologies and the literacies of technology. *College Composition and Communication, 55*(4), 642–692. doi:10.2307/4140666

Hill, J. R., Wiley, D., Nelson, L. M., & Han, S. (2004). Exploring research on Internet-based learning: From infrastructure to interactions. In D. H. Jonassen (Ed.), *Handbook of research on educational communications and technology* (pp. 433–460). Mahwah, NJ: Lawrence Erlbaum Associates.

Huffaker, D. A., & Calvert, S. L. (2003). The New science of learning: Active learning, metacognition, and transfer of knowledge in e-learning applications. *Journal of Educational Computing Research, 29*(3), 325–334. doi:10.2190/4T89-30W2-DHTM-RTQ2

James, J. (2004). Reconstruing the digital divide from the perspective of a large, poor, developing country. *Journal of Information Technology, 19*(3), 172–177. doi:10.1057/palgrave.jit.2000019

Kabilan, M., & Rajab, B. (2010). The utilization of the Internet by Palestinian English language teachers focusing on uses, practices and barriers and overall contribution to professional development. *International Journal of Education and Development Using ICT, 6*(3), 56-72.

Kampylis, P. G., Bocconi, S., & Punie, Y. (2012). *Towards a mapping framework of ICT-enabled innovation for learning*. Scientific and Policy Report by the Joint Research Centre of the European Commission.

Lei, J., & Zhou, Y. (2007). Technology uses and student achievement: A longitudinal study. *Computers & Education, 49*(2), 284–296. doi:10.1016/j.compedu.2005.06.013

Loveless, A. M. (2007). *Creativity, technology and learning – a review of recent literature* (No. 4 update). Retrieved from www. futurlab.org.dk/litereviews

Loveness, A., Burton, J., & Turvey, K. (2006). Developing conceptual frameworks for creativity, ICT and teacher education. *Thinking Skills and Creativity, 1*(1), 3–13. doi:10.1016/j.tsc.2005.07.001

Luo, L., Zhang, S., & Zhou, C. (2011). The comparisons of gender differences in playfulness, humor and creativity of postgraduate students between Mainland China and Taiwan. In *Proceedings of ECCIXII, 12th European Conference on Creativity and Innovation: The ultimate experience in collaboration* (pp. 470-491). University of the Algarve.

Masunaga, H., & Hitchock, M. A. (2011). How does gender interact with clinical teachers' perceptions of clinical teaching? NASPA. *Journal About Women in Higher Education, 4*(1), 50–72. doi:10.2202/1940-7890.1065

Moghaddam, G. G. (2010). Information technology and gender gap: Toward a global view. *The Electronic Library, 28*(5), 722–733. doi:10.1108/02640471011081997

Negrey, C., & Rausch, S. D. (2009). Creativity gaps and gender gaps: Women, men and place in the United States. *Gender, Place and Culture*, *16*(5), 517–533. doi:10.1080/09663690903148408

Nwagwu, E. W., Adekannbi, J., & Bello, O. (2009). Factors influencing use of the internet: A questionnaire survey of the students of University of Ibadan, Nigeria. *The Electronic Library*, *27*(4), 718–734. doi:10.1108/02640470910979651

Pan, Z., Yan, W., Jing, G., & Zheng, J. (2011). Exploring structured inequality in Internet use behavior. *Asian Journal of Communication*, *21*(2), 116–132. doi:10.1080/01292986.2010.543555

Purushothaman, A. (2013). *Empowering Women Through Learning To Use The Internet - An Ethnographic Action Research Project To Address The Second Order Digital Divide*. Aalborg University. Retrieved from http://vbn.aau.dk/files/195244502/Aparna_Thesis_VBN_Upload.pdf

Purushothaman, A., & Zhou, C. (2014). Change toward a Creative Society in Developing Contexts--Women's Barriers to Learning by Information and Communication Technology. *Gender, Technology and Development*, *18*(3), 363–386. doi:10.1177/0971852414544008

Qureshi, S. (2012). As the global digital divide narrows, who is being left behind? *Information Technology for Development*, *18*(4), 277–280. doi:10.1080/02681102.2012.730656

Ramayah, T., Jantan, M., & Ismail, N. (2003). *Impact of intrinsic and extrinsic motivation on Internet usage in Malaysia*. Presented at the 12th International Conference on Management of Technology, Nancy, France. Retrieved 17 June 2014, from http://www.ramayah.com/journalarticlespdf/impactofintrinsic.pdf

Resnick, M. (2002). Rethinking learning in the digital age. In G. Kirkman (Ed.), *The Global Information Technology Report: Readiness for the Networked Word*. Oxford, UK: Oxford University Press.

Sam, H. K., Othman, A. E. A., & Nordin, Z. S. (2005). Computer Self-Efficacy, Computer Anxiety, and Attitudes toward the Internet: A Study among Undergraduates in Unimas. *Journal of Educational Technology & Society*, *8*(4), 205–219.

Sanyal, B. C. (2001). *New functions of higher education and ICT to achieve education for all, in proceedings the Expert Roundtable on University and Technology-for-Literacy/Basic Education Partnership in Developing Countries*. International Institute for Educational Planning.

Stolzfus, G., Leigh, N. B., Debra, V., & Elizabetht, H. (2011). Gender, gender role and creativity. *Social Behavior and Personality*, *39*(3), 425–432. doi:10.2224bp.2011.39.3.425

Straub, E. T. (2017). *Understanding technology adoption: theory and future directions for informal learning*. Academic Press.

Tella, A. (2011). An assessment of mathematics teachers' Internet self-efficacy: Implications on teachers' delivery of mathematics instruction. *International Journal of Mathematical Education in Science and Technology*, *42*(2), 155–174. doi:10.1080/0020739X.2010.519798

TinioV. L. (2012). *ICT in Education*. Retrieved from http://139.179.20.111/egitim/eprimer-edu.pdf

Tongia, R., Subrahmanian, E., & Arunachalam, V. S. (2005). *ICT for Sustainable Development: Defining a Global Research Agenda*. Bangalore: Allied Publishers.

UNESCO. (2013). *Doubling digital opportunities: enhancing the inclusion of women & girls in the information society*. Retrieved from http://www.broadbandcommission.org/documents/working-groups/bb-doubling-digital-2013.pdf

Walton, R., Yaaqoubi, J., & Kolko, B. (2012). What's it for? Expectations of Internet value and usefulness in Central Asia. *Information Technologies and International Development*, *8*(3), 69–84.

Wang, F., & Zhou, C. (2013). A theoretical study on development of Information and Communication Technology (ICT)-supported education system. In *2013 10th International Conference on Fuzzy Systems and Knowledge Discovery (FSKD)*. Shenyang, China: IEEE Press.

Zhou, C. (2012). *Group Creativity Development in Engineering Education in Problem and Project-Based Learning (PBL) Environment*. Aalborg: akprint.

Zhou, C. (2016). Fostering Creative Problem Solvers in Higher Education: A Response to Complexity of Societies. In C. Zhou (Ed.), Handbook of Research on Creative Problem-Solving Skill Development in Higher Education (pp. 1-23). IGI global. Doi:10.4018/978-1-5225-0643-0.ch001

Zhou, C., Chen, H., & Luo, L. (2014). Students' Perceptions of Creativity in Learning Information Technology (IT) in Project Groups. *Computers in Human Behavior*, *41*, 454–463. doi:10.1016/j.chb.2014.09.058

Zhou, C., & Purushothaman, A. (2015). Improving Creativity in Collaborative Process: A Knowledge Model based on Communities of Practice in Organizational Learning Contexts. In J. Ogunleye (Ed.), *Research Papers on Knowledge, Innovation and Enterprise* (*Vol. 3*, pp. 57-68). 2015 KIE Conference Publications. KIE Conference Book Series.

Zhou, C., Purushothaman, A., & Rongbutsri, N. (2013). Facilitate Sustainability of Education by Problem-Based Learning (PBL) and Information and Communication Technology (ICT). *International Journal of Emerging Technologies in Learning*, *8*(6), 50–54. doi:10.3991/ijet.v8i6.3146

KEY TERMS AND DEFINITIONS

Creative Society: In the 1980s, information was the new king, which indicated that natural resources and manufacturing would no longer be the driving forces of economies and societies. It was in this period that we witnessed a transition from the "industrial society" to "information society." In the 1990s, the "knowledge society" was labeled as the characteristic of this society. People realized that information itself would not bring about any important change. Rather, it was the way in which people transformed information into knowledge and managed that knowledge, which would hold the key to this change. However, the "creative society" is an improvement upon the shift in the focus from "information" to "knowledge." It means that in future, our success will be based not on how much we know, but on our ability to think and act creatively.

Creativity: Generally, creativity involves the ability to offer new perspectives, generate novel and meaningful ideas, raise new questions, and come up with solutions to ill-defined problems. It has been demonstrated multiple manifestations of the conceptualization: personal cognitive and social or emotional processes, family aspects, education, characteristics of the domain and fields, social or cultural contextual aspects, as well as historical forces, event, and trends.

Information Communication Technology (ICT): ICT are a set of tools those include computer, internet, mobile phones, and diverse communication devices that contributes to education system and social learning system.

Learning: Learning is the act of gaining new knowledge, behaviors, skills, or ability. It may be regarded as a process, rather than a collection of factual and procedural knowledge. Human learning may occur as part of education, professional development, or training.

Chapter 12
Understanding the Reasons for Gender Difference in Online Information Processing of Consumers:
Based on Theories

Ceyda Tanrikulu
Adana Science and Technology University, Turkey

ABSTRACT

This chapter aims to provide proposals about understanding the gender difference in online information processing that have been developed based on the theories and the findings of the current research. Major findings in the literature indicate the gender difference in online information processing. This chapter can be used to help gain insight about the online consumer behavior based on gender approach by presenting theoretical perspective, providing basis for future research, enrich the understanding about gender differences in online information processing, and to give suggestion for implications requiring strategic decisions.

INTRODUCTION

Advancements in technology have been declared as the most dramatic forces in current highly competitive marketing environment (Kotler & Armstrong, 2016:108), which deeply encourages consumer behavioral alterations.

Although gender difference has decreased in consumer behavior thanks to technology, it has still been observed in online information processing of consumers. Therefore, gender is demonstrated as a significant variable in predicting and explaining the differences in information processing (Wang, Zhou, Jin, Fang, & Lee, 2017; Yasin, Yasin, Baghirov, Baghirov, Zhang, & Zhang, 2017; Zaharia, Kauke, & Hartung, 2017; Sin, 2016; Meyers-Levy & Loken, 2015; Bae & Lee, 2011; Halder, Ray, & Chakrabarty,

DOI: 10.4018/978-1-5225-7068-4.ch012

2010; Park, Yoon, & Lee, 2009; Kim, Lehto, & Morrison, 2007; Jackson, Ervin, Gardner, & Schmitt, 2001). More specifically, gender has been suggested as a useful influencing variable to comprehend cognitive and social background of information processing (Halder, Ray, & Chakrabarty, 2010). Furthermore, many academicians argue that gender should be considered in developing theory regarding the information processing (Lu & Hsiao, 2009:149) and information technology as well (Lin, Featherman, & Sarker, 2017; Gefen & Straub, 1997: 398).

In this book chapter, proposals about understanding the gender difference in online information processing have been developed based on the theories and the findings of the current research. This study is expected to help gaining insight about the online consumer behavior based on gender approach by presenting theoretical perspective, providing basis for future research, enrich the understanding about gender differences in online information processing, and to give suggestion for implications requiring strategic decisions. For the beginning, the theoretical infrastructure about the gender difference is given. This is followed by the gender difference theories in information processing, and then specifically the gender difference in online information processing. Finally, conclusions and implications are discussed.

GENERAL THEORIES ABOUT GENDER DIFFERENCE

Biological, psychological, and social literatures are suggested to explain the sex differences in behavior by many academicians (Meyers-Levy & Loken, 2015; Wood & Eagly, 2012; Eagly & Wood, 1991). In this section, the origin of gender difference is expounded based on the biological, psychological, and social theories.

Evolutionary theories are deemed as one of the explanatory theories that explain the root of the gender differences. It is claimed that males as hunters and female as gatherers in the ancestral past, naturally evolved sex-specific variation in personality traits. For instance, female engaged in nutrition and caution, whereas male took risk and were dominant in seeking. Inherent sex differences in personality traits have been indicated that it may become more likely to materialize as modern societies have transformed into being more egalitarian. In particular, cross-national research have demonstrated that compared to males across most nations, females have higher levels of neuroticism, extraversion, agreeableness, and conscientiousness as personality traits (Schmitt, Realo, Voracek, & Allik, 2008: 168-169). Another study in gender differences has illustrated that females determined themselves to be higher in neuroticism, agreeableness, warmth, and openness to feelings, whereas men identified themselves to be higher in assertiveness and openness to ideas (Costa, Terracciano, & McCrae, 2001: 322).

Evolutionary psychological theory and social psychological theory are considered as origin theories emphasizing the sex differences in human behavior. Evolutionary psychological theory indicates that females and males have sex-specific mechanisms, are psychologically different, and have tendency to possess different social roles. Thus, causation flows from evolutionary adaptations to psychological sex differences in this theory. Sex-specific evolved tendencies are approved as psychological propensities which are made through genetically mediated adaptation to primeval context. As to social psychological theory, causation flows from social structure to psychological sex differences. Females and males have different propensities to perform different social roles, and they become different psychologically through adaptation of these roles. Sex-specific dispositions are viewed as formed through accommodation to the contemporaneous sexual division of labor. Furthermore, division of labor in the given society is viewed as an engine of sex-specific behaviour, and also physical differences between females and males are accepted as one of the key influencer for role assignment which generate sexual division of labor and lead to psychological sex differences. These differences are in interaction with common beliefs in culture, social organization, and economic demand (Eagly & Wood, 1999: 408-409).

Social role theory is also viewed as an explanatory theory in understanding sex differences in human behavior. This theory suggests that sex differences are produced by the tendency to behave consistently with gender roles that common expectations about proper conduct which employ to people only depend on individuals' socially determined sex. Two dimensions are expected to be responsible for sex differences in behavior. In this regard, it is expected that females are communal (friendly, unselfish, concerned with others etc.) whereas males are agentic (independent, masterful, competent etc.). Shortly, having different social roles in society for females and males are believed to generate these expectations (Eagly & Wood, 1988: 4-5). In addition to these, societal expectations have effect on behavior via social rewards and punishment and generate gender differences. Thus gender roles, which are formed by shared belief in the given culture for females and males, guide behavior of sexes (Meyers-Levy & Boken, 2015: 131). Wood and Eagly (2012) have provided biosocial construction theory to explain the sex differences in behavior through biological attributes and social context. Biosocial construction theory claims that based on biological restrictions and local conditions, females and males divide labor, and they also adjust their behavior through the situations where they live. Through proximal social psychological and biological process, behavior is influenced by gender role expectations which are in harmony with the given culture.

Biology especially neurobiology still continues to provide new theoretical insights to the existence of gender related differences regarding the IT-related behavior (Riedl, Hubert, & Kenning, 2010; 398). The human brain consists of two hemispheres and each hemisphere (left for verbal abilities and right for spatial perception) specializes in different functions which refer to lateralization. For instance, for females, who have non-compartmentalizing brain, talking is deemed as an essential factor in information processing. Males' emotions can perform separately from other functions of their brain due to the fact that they are located in only right side of the brain, whereas females' brain switches hers emotions on while it operates other functions because of the fact that their emotions are located in two sides of it (Kim et al., 2007:425). Furthermore, mood may cause different information processing between genders. During sad mood, females have been investigated to utilize more detailed processing, whereas males have found to use disaction strategy to repair this (Meyers-Levy & Loken, 2015:136). Also, differences in brain lateralization between females and males give rise to different product evaluation and judgment process (Kim, Lehto, & Morrison, 2007:425). Different brain areas are activated during the evaluation processing among gender. There are differences between genders in patterns of activation in neural structures implicated in attention to emotional stimuli. For instance, female may use neural pathways differently from men during assessing ambiguous signals of social threat (McClure, Monk, Nelson, Zarahn, Leibenluft, Bilder,... & Pine, 2004:1054).

GENDER DIFFERENCE THEORIES IN INFORMATION PROCESSING

Human information processing is defined as a process that covers stages of acquiring, interpreting, manipulating, storing, retrieving, and classifying recorded information (Jansen, Moore, & Carman, 2013; Okazaki & Hirose,2009; Wilson, 2000). Several studies confirm that gender is one of the main influencer of information processing. This section presents the theories explaining the reasons of differences among the gender in information processing such as selectivity theory, self-concept orientation model, item-specific versus relational processing, and empathizing- systemizing theory.

Selectivity Theory

The selectivity theory has been provided by Meyers-Levy (1986), Meyers-Levy and Sternthal (1991), and Meyers-Levy and Maheswaran (1991) and explains the gender differences in information processing. Up to now, it has been employed in many research and so it is posited as an important milestones in gender research. This theory is claimed to sustain a unique viewpoint in gender differences due to the fact that it is asserted as a "homegrown theory" developed by consumer researchers, and it also provides no special assertion in regarding root of gender differences. As a mid-level theory, its major basis complies with agentic/communal role and socio-cultural viewpoints, hormone and brain activation, and evolutionary perspective in gender differences (Meyers-Levy & Loken, 2015:133-134).

This theory deems that females and males are different in performing strategies and having threshold for information processing. It also posits that females are comprehensive processors whereas males are selective processors (Meyers-Levy & Loken, 2015:133-134). Females' information processing frequently covers deeper elaboration of message content. Thus, this processing sometimes causes increased sensitivity to particular message claims in females. As to males, their processing is more likely to be conducted by overall message themes or schemas (Meyers-Levy & Maheswaran, 1991:68). Males processing bear on efficiency-striving heuristic instead of detailed message elaboration. Heuristic processing, which is used by males, refers to limited processing requiring little cognitive effort and capacity. Simply implicit rule, schemas or cognitive heuristic are used to make judgements and decision in the heuristic processing (Tsichla, Hatzithomas, & Boutsouki, 2016:567). Furthermore, Meyers-Levy and Sternthal (1991) have indicated that gender differences are observed during the usage of message cues and making judgement. Females have seemed to have a lower threshold for elaborating on message cues. They have also found to be using these cues more when they make a judgement about the products. Disposing of gender differences is more likely to occur in two conditions such that: first, when message cues have received slightly little attention which they are below males' and females' threshold for elaborating on message cues and second, when message cues have received very high amount of attention which both females' and males' threshold are exceeded (Meyers-Levy & Sternthal, 1991:93-94). It is mentioned that style of males' processing based seriously on right hemisphere so they have excellence nonverbal and visual spatial processing whereas, style of females' information processing is more integrated and verbal description may encourage more deeply processing and outstanding memory (Tsichla, Hatzithomas, & Boutsouki, 2016: 568).

Some important points draw attention related to this theory. It is argued that gender differences depend on conditions and will not always happen. However, gender differences should be found solely under the conditions where accessing target data is above females' threshold and below males' threshold because of the fact that gender differences derive from lower threshold of females for detecting and using target data. Furthermore, gender differences observed in comprehensiveness and heuristic ability are not evaluated as valuable. Detailed information processing which attributed to females does not always provide opportunities. Because, it also produces resource depletion, can be inefficient, and creates psychological cost for females (Meyers-Levy & Loken, 2015: 134). Moreover, the assertion that comprehensive processing attributed to females as a superior ability to provide better judgement as this theory claims, is criticized due to the fact that superior judgements are based on features of particular messages (Putrevu, 2001:8). Additionally, most of the research supporting it are also limited in scope and focus on gender differences in information processing, especially, related to complex stimuli about ads (McGivern, Huston, Byrd, King, Siegle, & Reilly, 1997; 324).

Self-Concept Orientation Model

Hupfer and Detlor (2006) make contribution to the field of gender differences in web information seeking behavior. They suggest self-concept model, adapted from selectivity model, which elucidate the relationship among gender, effort, and information content in web information seeking. This model defines these terms such that, *gender* is as a self-concept trait depending on individual differences and gender-related traits define interest in self-versus others orientation, *effort* means search frequency and *content* consists of twofold: its subject domain and its relevance for the individual. This model, which determines the gender based on individual differences, gives opportunity to measure the gender –related traits presenting the concern for self-versus for others.

Following suggestions are provided by Hupfer and Detlor (2006) in this model: "*1) self-orientation is associated with effort minimization and lower search frequency, regardless of the information's relevance for oneself or for others; 2) other-orientation is related to a more effortful search strategy and higher search frequency for both self- and other-relevant information; and 3) such patterns would be amplified when searching for other-relevant information.*" Frequency of search and behavioral indicator of strategy, selective or comprehensive, can be used as a helpful indicator of effort and search style. This model indicates that selective strategy may allocate information in a shorter time whereas comprehensive strategy may determine information which is ignored by speedy processing.

Brunel and Nelson (2000) argued that being female or male has a determinant role in evaluation of message. Moreover, that variation in world-views values could be used for elucidating these gendered differences. Gender differences have been observed in absolute and comparative judgements toward help-others and help-self appeals in their study. While females are found to respond more favorably to the help-others appeal, males are found to respond more favorably to the help-self one.

Item-Specific Versus Relational Processing

The selectivity theory claimed gender differences based on depth of processing whereas, item-specific versus relational processing as an alternative approach deem gender differences in style of processing (Putrevu, 2008: 64). Unlike selectivity theory, item-specific versus relational processing approach does not support the notion that one type of processing is superior to the other. It posits that both sexes have tendency to evaluate the different way of the given message and also superiority of processing style is related to features of messages such as nature of the stressed attributes (Putrevu, 2001:8). Item-specific/relational processing approach asserts that females and males differ in information processing and more specially, females use relational information processing while males use an item-specific information processing style (Putrevu, 2004:51; Putrevu, 2001:10). Hunt and Einstein (1981:497) define the relational processing as "*encoding of similarities among a class of events*" while item-specific as "*encoding of item-specific information*" or it is defined by Hunt and Seta (1984:454) as "*encoding of distinctive information for each event*".

Males, who have agentic goals and self-focused orientation, are more likely to concentrate on the messages affecting them directly. Thus, they give more importance to message attributes having the greatest personal impact. On the other hand, females, who have communal goals and relationship orientation, are more likely to focus on all features of messages and total impact of them. Females are also more likely to engage in decoding message attributes for determining their complicated intercommunion. It is claimed that item-specific processing clarifies that male uses plainly identifiable perceptual attributes while relational processing elucidates that females are more creative, associative, and imagery-laced comment. Furthermore, males are suggested to highly emphasize on self-generated information without considering social situation, whereas females are suggested to stress both self-generated and other-generated information in a given social environment (Putrevu, 2001:7).

Empathizing-Systemizing Theory

Empathizing-systemizing theory suggests that females are stronger empathizers, whereas males are stronger systemizers (Baron-Cohen, Knickmeyer, & Belmonte, 2005: 819). Empathizing is defined as:

the capacity to predict and to respond to the behavior of agents (usually people) by inferring their mental states and responding to these with an appropriate emotion

and systemizing is defined as

the capacity to predict and to respond to the behavior of nonagentive deterministic systems by analyzing input-operation-output relations and inferring the rules that govern such systems. (Baron-Cohen, Knickmeyer, & Belmonte, 2005)

The "typical female" and "typical male" brains are differently characterized in given literature. It is asserted that "typical female" brain shows superior empathizing over systemizing capabilities whereas "typical male" brain demonstrates the reverse pattern. Gender-related difference in empathizing and associated brain mechanism are also confirmed by neuroimage research (Schulte-Rüther, Markowitsch, Shah, Fink, & Piefke, 2008: 401). Furthermore, differences in empathy among gender are found to be consistent and stable across the lifespan (Christov-Moore, Simpson, Coudé, Grigaityte, Iacoboni, & Ferrari, 2014: 604).

Brain regions integrating information from multiple neural sources are activated by empathy. As to systemizing, it requires a narrow attentional focus to local information for understanding each part of a system (Baron-Cohen, Knickmeyer, & Belmonte, 2005, 821). Thus, based on this theory, during information process, brain structure used vary by sex, so that male use more cognitive brain structures while females use more affective structures. Moreover, emotion-related brain regions are more often used by females for social interaction duties, whereas brain regions related to cognitive information processing are more often activated by males (Riedl, Hubert, & Kenning, 2010; 398-403).

GENDER DIFFERENCE IN ONLINE INFORMATION PROCESSING

Many previous studies about the online information processing revealed the differences between genders (Zaharia, Kauke, & Hartung, 2017:143; Yasin, Yasin, Baghirov, Baghirov, Zhang, & Zhang, 2017:307; Goodrich, 2014; Kim, Kim, & Wise, 2014; Jansen, Moore, & Carman, 2013; Tsichla, Hatzithomas, & Boutsouki, 2016; Riedl, Hubert, & Kenning, 2010; Sun, Lim, Jiang, Peng, & Chen, 2010; Park, Yoon, & Lee, 2009; Kim, Lehto, & Morrison, 2007; Rodgers & Harris, 2003: 326).

Biological based differences strongly give rise to gender difference in online information processing. Brain activity for complex information processing has been observed to differ among genders (Qin, Shi, Ma, & Han, 2018:64). The inclination toward left-hemisphere processing is found to cause lower level emotional gratification for online shopping in females whereas, the proclivity for right hemisphere processing gives rise to higher level satisfaction in online shopping in males (Rodgers & Harris,2003: 325). As to information processing, in particular, neuroscience, which have up-to-date usage to determine individuals differences in online information processing (Lin, Cross, Jones, & Childers, 2018a:197), enables to identify the activated brain area, when a person engages in various trust-related activities or trust building stimuli. In this context, gender is determined as a moderator, and cognitive neuroscience is suggested as an empirical method for examining trust in order to enhance the understanding of nature, antecedents, and consequences of trust in online environments. Thus, one possible explanation of this suggestion is that trust and distrust are associated with activation of different brain areas (Gefen & Ridings, 2005:280-282). Furthermore, Riedl et al (2010) argue that gender differences exist when encoding trustworthiness of internet offerings and using brain areas. More specifically, female are found to activate more brain areas in making decision regarding the trust, which is accepted as a confirmation of the empathizing- systemizing theory.

Major findings of biological, more specifically neurological-based research have presented that due to the fact that difference in activated brain area during the information processing, females and males process not only offline information differently but also online information as well. Hence, following proposal can be presented:

Proposal 1: Biological-based difference can lead to gender difference in online information processing.

During the information processing, information acquiring is a field that gender- based differences are observed. A recent study in online information processing behavior has demonstrated that searching process vary by gender (Kim, Kim, & Wise, 2014: 819-820). The results revealed by this study suggest that female are more likely to engage in searching process and have more detailed visual information processing which is in accordance with Meyers-Levy's selectivity theory. Additionally, they are found to be better in short and long term memory for words and images, which is agreement with the previous findings indicating that females have superior recognition memory related to the their scanning behavior at encoding (Heisz, Pottruff, & Shore, 2013:1157). On the other hand, favorable findings for males have also presented in previous research. For instance, male students having medium level search task performance are found to engage in more search activities such as number of search, search queries and times (Zhou, 2014:174). In a previous study focused on middle school students having ages of 13 and 14 has also confirmed the gender differences in searching the web. The study has concluded that the performances of male students are better than girls not only on target-specific but also on target-related information measures (Roy & Chi, 2003: 335).

Gender-specific differences have been detected in several studies in information seeking behavior (Rowley, Johnson, & Sbaffi, 2017: 43; Hargittai & Shafer, 2014; Ek, 2013:741-742; Halder, Ray, & Chakrabarty, 2010; Atkinson, Saperstein, & Pleis, 2009). A previous study performed in students of elementary schools also demonstrate the gender differences in information seeking process on the web in a collaborative environment. It is reported that compared with girls groups, boys groups enter more searches and utilize less words during formulating queries at search engines, spend less time viewing pages, click more, demonstrate more page jumps per minute, gather information and record them more frequently. Gender differences are also identified for strategies of retrieving information from the web (Large, Beheshti, & Rahman, 2002:443). Halder et al. (2010) have also indicated that female are not only more interactive and better information seekers but also attach more importance to information and use more and wide range of information categories. Similarly, as to health-related issues, females are found to be more proactive, receive more information from wide range information resources and exhibit higher level personal information usage such as friends, family, and workmates. Compared to males, they are also found to obtain more information from health information research via internet, use internet more for both social motives and enjoyment during the health-related information searches (Bidmon & Terlutter, 2015) and especially, utilize physician-rating websites more (Terlutter & Bidmon, 2014). Such findings may help to demonstrate that the gender differences have key roles in the understanding of health information behaviour (Rowley, Johnson, & Sbaffi, 2017: 43; Ek, 2013:741-742) and using gender-specific models are suggested to explain the online health information seeking (Baumann, Czerwinski, & Reifegerste, 2017).

Gender groups seem to differ in perceived importance of online information and its source. Females have been found to pay more attention to hotel/apartment websites (Jacobsen & Munar, 2012:45). In a previous study, female has been found to like more information about the products and have less trust in information (Cyr & Bonanni, 2005: 573). During the process of decision making, females have been detected to consider a range of information source and more factors so they are less linear whereas males are found to be more systematic (Jansen, Moore, & Carman, 2013:300). It is also revealed that females search more product information and read more customer reviews and use assistant agent during online shopping. Therefore, they are accepted as more comprehensive processors than males (Park, Yoon, & Lee, 2009:364), which is in conformity with the selectivity model (Meyers-Levy 1989; Meyers-Levy & Maheswaran, 1991; Meyers-Levy & Sternthal, 1991). Although females give more importance to details, males are found to examine more pages in Google results than females when seeking information in a previous study (Lorigo, Pan, Hembrooke, Joachims, Granka, & Gay, 2006:1129).

Kim et al (2007) asserted the difference between the genders, particularly; they showed the gender difference regarding the attitude toward design and content of travel websites. They confirmed that females are more comprehensive and give more importance to details in external information in accordance with the selectivity theory. Therefore, extensive information content is a necessary criterion for female–based information processing. They also suggest marketing communication strategies which are gender-sensitive, for gaining competitive advantages in the current highly competitive online market. This suggestion is supported by current research indicating females are more affected from gender-specific online shop designs (Zaharia, Kauke, & Hartung, 2017:143). For instance, a website should emphasize the common themes for females, while it should stress the uniqueness of features for males (Kim, Lehto, & Morrison, 2007:431-432). In recent studies, information uniqueness is also emphasized to promote males' less effortful heuristic (Hwang & Lee, 2018:23) and encourage males' positive emotion which turns into a drive to share information (Wang, 2017:730). Thus, males tend to react more sensitively in information uniqueness through using IT. Thus, these findings support the item-specific processing style of males which asserts that males pay more attention to uniqueness and differential advantages in information processing (Putrevu, 2008.64; Putrevu, 2004:60: Putrevu, 2001:8).

Proposal 2: During the online information processing, females are likely to gather more information, use detailed information, use more evaluation criteria, so perform elaborative processing and are more self- and other oriented, whereas males are more likely to use heuristic cue, more engage in uniqueness of information and are more self- oriented.

Gender difference is also observed in evaluation of web advertising content. Sun et al. (2010) have examined the moderation effect of gender on evaluation process of web advertising by using a laboratory experiment. The authors emphasized the gender difference in interaction effect between informativeness and entertainment for web advertising; that is accepted as a cue for gender difference in information processing. Namely, during the evaluation process, the interaction of informativeness and entertainment effect is observed stronger for females than for males. In addition, they are found to put entertainment into consideration more than males and it has also been suggested that balance between the informativeness and entertainment must be provided when designing ads for females. As to males, informativeness is more significant so maximum informativeness is suggested for them in ads design process. Furthermore, more positive attitude is directed by informativeness for males and entertainment for females.

Regarding the web atmospherics, gender has been explored as a moderator in relationship between web atmospherics and virtual visitor's attitude toward both the brand and the websites in a recent study (Tsichla, Hatzithomas, & Boutsouki, 2016:577). More specially, male is likely to have more positive attitude toward the websites and brand in the presence of low task relevant whereas, female is more likely to have similar attitude toward the websites and brand both in the presence and absence of low task relevant cues. For males, as selective and heuristic processors, the stimuli that they are exposed to during the experiment are more reliable and used as an evaluation criteria. Their attitude toward brand is encouraged by providing the webpages with low relevant cues. For females, as comprehensive processors, put more variety of information-specific cues into consideration when making decisions so they take not only web atmosphere into account but also other stimuli apart from websites (past experience, word of mouth... etc.). The study also suggests that male-targeted web sites should include simple and single theme, and also low task relevant cues like music, graphs, pictures, and animations, while female-targeted websites should cover both low and high task relevant cues. Hence, the study is in agreement with the selectivity theory.

Gender differences are also investigated in online information sources. Compared to females, males are indicated to be more instrumental and extrinsically motivated for communication. This statement might be an explanation for higher level comfortability in males communicating and flirting through mobile chat services as a technological interface (Nysveen, Pedersen, & Thorbjørnsen, 2005: 253). A study in information behavior concerning Wikipedia as an information source has uncovered some gender differences (Lim & Kwon, 2010:219). This study has showed that male students use Wikipedia for the purposes of entertainment and idle reading more frequently, perceive less risk in exploring non-authoritative information source, have more self-confidence about the evaluating information quality and feel more positive emotion toward this information source.

A recent study confirming the gender difference indicates that differences appear among males and females in the preferences of information sources. Based on this study, female count upon internal sources like friends, whereas males rely external sources like blogs and Facebook to search for the information (Yasin, Yasin, Baghirov, Baghirov, Zhang, & Zhang, 2017:307). Online consumer reviews as an information source are identified to create fruitful information especially for the female consumers who believe in credibility of them more than male. Also, on the contrary to male consumers, negative review is perceived to be more diagnostic and beneficial by female consumers (Bae & Lee, 2011:211) and may be related to the fact that females recall more negative life events than males (Seidlitz & Diener, 1998:262). On the same manner, conflicting information is perceived to be more problematic by females when using social network sites (Sin, 2016). Female are also found to have higher level of information seeking anxiety, especially related to barriers of access and information resources (Erfanmanesh, 2016:8) which supports the previous finding that female are more anxious than male when using the internet (Jackson, 2001: 372).

It has been observed that some interesting distinctions occur between females and males in visuality issues in message (Hwang & Lee, 2018; Shaouf, Lü, & Li, 2016; Kim, Kim, & Wise, 2014; Cyr & Bonanni, 2005; Philip & Suri, 2004). Compared to males, females have reported that they interpret promotional emails with visual cues more favorably (Philip & Suri, 2004:364). As to visual attention that directly link to cognitive processing of shopping information provided by websites, a study using eye-tracking approach have confirmed that visual attention to product information is more likely to have influence on males' shopping attitude – cognitive, affective, and behavioral. In addition, compared to males', females' visual attention to AOIs have been found to be greater and more active, which confirm the selectivity theory indicating that females focus and engage in detailed information (Hwang & Lee, 2018: 22). In the same manner, the effects of visual features of web advertising on both attitude and intention to purchase have been investigated to be stronger for males. Thus, these findings, which corroborate selectivity theory, have suggested that web advertising should comprise visual elements and summary content for males and verbal advertisements and detailed content for females, to be attractive and stimulate the purchase (Shaouf, Lü, & Li, 2016:632).

Furthermore, gender differences have also been investigated in attitude towards information design and visual design. Female are found to be more attracted by colours on the site whereas males are found to be attracted by the interactive and 'flashy' aspects of the site (Cyr & Bonanni, 2005:576). Among the pupils, boys are found to enjoy animations, colours, and hyperlinks to pages with answers more than girls regarding Web-based science lesson (Leong & Hawamdeh, 1999). In a recent study confirming the selectivity theory, gender differences have explored in effecting factors that influence attitude toward online presentation which turns into purchase intention (Lin, Featherman, Brooks, & Hajli, 2018b;12). Gender as moderator has been found to have a critical role in effect of interactivity, vividness, and perceived risk on attitude and also effect of attitude on purchase intention in that study. More specially, interactivity, which is useful for making decision depending on specific information selected, has been found to have greater influence on males' attitude. Vividness, which convey the multiple information cue and quantity of information, and information diagnosity have been reported that have greater impact on attitude for females in that study. As to online advertising, Goodrich (2014) examined the gender differences in the processing of online advertising information in a recent research whose findings are consistent with the selectivity theory. The author has indicated that males put more both the graphical advertising stimuli and banner advertisement into consideration as a result of processing heuristically whereas female has greater female attention to other page elements due to comprehensive processing.

Considering the dominant findings, females and males are seem to be different in evaluation of message. They have different tendencies to take into account the message features due to having dissimilar processing style. Thus, following proposal can be offered:

Proposal 3: Males are likely to be attracted greater by messages that encourage their heuristic and selective processing, such as having summary content, graphical images, low task relevant cues, and interactivity. On the other hand, females are more likely to be attracted by messages that support their comprehensive processing, such as having detailed content, both low and high task relevant cues and vividness.

Significant gender variances are also demonstrated for perception of risk as a response about the information technology (Marriott & Williams, 2018; Hajli & Lin, 2016; Lin, Li, Califf, & Featherman, 2013a; Garbarino & Strahilevitz, 2004). In a recent study, for mobile shopping, females are found to attach more importance to overall risk, especially they perceived that psychological risk is at higher rate for them which encourage the overall risk significantly, whereas males perceive overall risk at lower level. In addition, it is observed that perceived risk is affected by trust which have a significant effect on intention (Marriott & Williams, 2018:142). Conversely, a study conducted on gender differences in Facebook usage has indicated that perceived risk has effect on males' Facebook continuance intention more than females (Lin, Li, Califf, & Featherman, 2013a; 697).

Gender differences in privacy concern is also investigated in various previous studies and they have indicated that females are found more to engage in privacy issues than males regarding the information sharing process in online environment (Hajli & Lin, 2016; Lin, Featherman, & Sarker, 2013b; Chai, Das, & Rao, 2011; Philips & Suri, 2004; Sheehan, 1999:34-35). Females has also been found to have more personal privacy concern in many information gathering situation and also, compared to males, they give incomplete information more often during registration for websites (Sheehan, 1999:34-35). In particular, perceived privacy risk during the information sharing on social media is observed to be stronger for females (Hajli & Lin, 2016:120; Lin, Featherman, & Sarker, 2013b:4). Gender has been determined as a moderator which influence both the perceived control and the perceived privacy risk on attitude toward information sharing through social media. Females have seem to give more importance on perceived control and perceived privacy risk during the process of sharing information on social media (Hajli & Lin, 2016:120). During this process, some distinctions regarding the influence of attitude and outcome expectations are also observed among males and females. It is indicated that the effects of both attitude and outcome expectation on sharing information are reported stronger for females than for males (Lin, Featherman, & Sarker, 2013b: 4). In the same manner, female bloggers are investigated to have more concern and their privacy concern is affected by trust more than males (Chai, Das, & Rao, 2011:332). Another study constructed on social network sites has also indicated that perceived privacy risk of females have stronger negative effect on their satisfaction than of males (Lin, Featherman, & Sarker, 2017: 392).

Credibility issue in online information processing is another difference field for gender groups. Many authors have deemed and emphasized that gender is a significant predictor for evaluation of credibility during this process (Embacher, McGloin, & Richards, 2017; Armstrong & McAdams, 2009; Flanagin & Metzger, 2003). Credibility evaluation may vary by gender so that males have perceived significantly higher rate credibility about both message and site (Flanagin & Metzger, 2003:694). As to effect of source sex on credibility perception, for females, information provided by male source is perceived more credible than that of female source in online setting. Thus, same-sex evaluation regarding the credibility in females may be harsher amongst them, which is explained with gender stereotypes and Goldberg paradigm indicating that females have prejudices about other females (Embacher, McGloin, & Richards, 2017: 13-15). In addition, a research examining credibility of informational blogs and gender has indicated that information perceived to be provided by male sources own more credibility perception than females' one. Therefore, gender is also deemed as a heuristic to evaluate information and also determine credibility (Armstrong & McAdams, 2009: 447). Thus, it can be concluded that gender play a key role in identifying source credibility.

Related to the evaluation of credibility of source, trusting information plays an important role. The effect of trust building information cues has been reported to vary depending on being female or male. Females, compared to males, are more affected by trust building information cues stressing communication, security, and functionality (Murphy & Tocher, 2011:32). Females may pay more intention to trust issues. Furthermore, gender is investigated as a moderator for trust building process in virtual communities. In this frame, it is offered to reach satisfactory trust that virtual communities should be customized to provide quality content for males and stimulate interaction and relationship buildings for females.

During the online information processing, female are more likely to perceive risk, engage in privacy concern and credibility of source. Thus, females is more likely to try to avoid risk and to be more risk averse. Considering with these, compared to males, female are have a tendency about the elaborate processing to cope with challenges originating from the nature of the internet online setting.

Proposal 4: Perceived risk, especially privacy risk, trust and credibility that mitigate the unfavorable results can be identified as stronger variables in identifying the females' online information processing.

Gender difference is also observed in sharing information on online social media (Geng, Zhang, Wei, & Feng, 2017; Wang, Zhou, Jin, Fang, & Lee, 2017; Hajli & Lin, 2016:120; Chen, Sin, Theng, & Lee, 2015; Lin, Featherman, & Sarker, 2013b). It is mentioned that females have higher level of tendency in sharing both information and misinformation through social media (Chen, Sin, Theng, & Lee, 2015:583). Furthermore, gender has been investigated as significant factor in detecting gender deception in online social media, especially, message recipient's gender may have an important role in identifying gender deception. Gender has also an effect on motivation to deceive. In addition to these, males are found to have higher level of self-efficacy beliefs in gender deception whereas, females are denoted that have a higher success rate in identifying gender deception (Ho, Lowry, Warkentin, Yang, & Hollister, 2017: 35). During the process of sharing information on social media, some distinctions regarding the influence of attitude and outcome expectations are also observed among males and females. It is indicated that the effects of both attitude and outcome expectation on sharing information are reported to be stronger for females than for males (Lin, Featherman, & Sarker, 2013b: 4). In addition, content of shared information through online media might also vary by gender. A recent study conducted for gender recognition of Twitter users by using texts and profile images has reported that males have tendency to make conversation regarding the sports (e.g., hashtags: nfl and nba) more frequently than females do, while females have tendency to talk about the subject of food and sensibility (e.g. hashtag: love) more frequently (Geng, Zhang, Wei, & Feng, 2017: 6).

The blogs as tools for satisfying needs of sharing personal information are preferred to many individuals regardless of gender. When it comes to participation on brand microblogs, gender is likely to give rise to differentiation among the consumers. Female gives more attention to partner quality and commitment, whereas male are more responsive to self-congruence and trust when the consumer decide to participate the microblogs (Zhang, Benyoucef, & Zhao, 2015:366). As to publishing decision, female appears to have more tendency to publish personal information on blogs (Lu & Hsiao 2009, 147). On the other hand, according to the Wang et al (2017), different from females, males have more tendency to share impulse-based information and to give information via microblogs under the crowding conditions. Furthermore, for blog-owned males, personal outcome expectations as extrinsic motivators are more important factors for publishing. The fact that males seem to be more pragmatic and have more attention for outcome during the technology usage, may provide an explanation for gender differences in publishing (Lu & Hsiao, 2009:149). Thus, the next proposal is that:

Proposal 5: Gender difference can be observed in publishing content via online communication tools.

Previous studies have argued that females use the online technology to become socialized consistent with the social theory (Wang, Zhou, Jin, Fang, & Lee, 2017; Goh & Sun, 2014; Philip & Suri, 2004: 360). Generally, gender difference is also observed regarding the effect of other peoples in technology adaptation. Compared to males, subjective norm, which refers to a degree that an individual believes that people who are important to her/him think she/he should perform the behavior in question, have stronger effect on behavioral intention of females (Venkatesh & Morris, 2000: 119-128).

Knowledge sharing behavior via blog, which is viewed as a type of online society, varies by gender due to the fact that social norms and societal expectation exist in the blogosphere that can be seen even in offline society. Compared to males, females bloggers' knowledge sharing behavior are affected by strength of social ties and reciprocity more than of males' (Chai, Das, & Rao, 2011:332). In addition, for females, self-expression is shown as the cause of higher level intention to publish on blogs that enable sharing personal information and opinions (Lu & Hsiao, 2009). For instance, female as a mother often use mommy blogs to share experiences, find audience and connect with others. They also get chance to gain and identify self-expression through these blogs as a helpful channels. Hence, it gives them digital opportunity to increase the level of socialization (Parmaksız, 2012: 123-130). Moreover, females use the virtual communities for the purpose of giving and getting social support (Gefen & Ridings, 2005:78). These findings also confirm that females frequently are found to have a higher level of empathy, social sensitivity, and emotion recognition features than males (Schulte-Rüther, 2008: 393). While female are found to value responsiveness of others to their posted online content, males are found to place greater importance to post content online which is proactive. Therefore, female are appeared to give online word of mouth more value based on receiving the response. Furthermore, receiving response regarding their posted online content may cause a great social presence for females (Awad & Rogowsky, 2008:114).

Previous studies also indicated that females value the recommendation of others as a useful information source with respect to males (Yasin, Yasin, Baghirov, Baghirov, Zhang, & Zhang, 2017:307; Bae & Lee, 2011:211; Garbarino & Strahilevitz, 2004:773) and engage more in transferring acquired information to others (Halder, Ray, & Chakrabarty, 2010). Female consumers most often use the recommendation of friends for evaluation of online behavior. For females, recommendation provided by a friend about the website is more likely to give rise to stronger increase for both willingness to buy and reduce the perceived risk that is at higher level for them, under the controlling for differences in Internet usage conditions (Garbarino & Strahilevitz, 2004:773). Online customer review as a consumer-centered information source has been found to stimulate females' memory, search and attitude for experience good, compared with celebrity endorsements (Wei & Lu, 2013:197).

The subject of the gender groups' difference in using internet for communication purposes is still unclear. A previous study indicated that females have more internet usage rate for interpersonal communication purposes while male have more usage for search purposes (Jackson, Ervin, Gardner, & Schmitt, 2001:374). Conversely, significant differences did not appear among the two gender groups for communication purposes in another study. It is claimed that relative to males, females are more likely to use shopping websites for gathering information (Wolin & Korgaonkar, 2003:382). Gender difference has also observed in using online services for interpersonal relationship. During the online transaction, online service offerings lead female more strongly than male. Also, female are revealed to appraise the online brand with taking their own objectives into account and put restrictions (Davis, Smith, & Lang, 2017:123). Interpersonal communication is accepted as one of the strongest predictor of females' extensive email usage. E-mail communication is also found as a helpful tool to cope with depression for females (Jackson, Ervin, Gardner, & Schmitt, 2001:374). Females are found to establish and sustain their interpersonal relationships by using email (Philip & Suri, 2004:364) and social media more than males (Wang, Zhou, Jin, Fang, & Lee, 2017) so perception in friendship value of social network sites seems to more stronger for them which confirm the females' communal interpersonal relationship features (Okazaki & Hurose, 2014: 723).

Considering the social role expectation and females having more relation centered orientation, females' information processing is formed by their superior features about the communal role, empathy, social sensitivity, emotion recognition, concern in social ties and reciprocity. Thus, they process information through social and interpersonal-based orientation in online setting.

Proposal 6: Females are likely to put more factors regarding the social and communal interpersonal relationships into consideration during the online information processing. In addition, their innate features that being associative and communal stimulate their processing.

Although many studies confirm the gender difference in online information processing, some of the studies in gender illustrate insignificant differences across the two sexes. Moreover, it is indicated that gender is alone insufficient to understand and explain the differences in information behavior (Hum, Chamberlin, Hambright, Portwood, Schat, & Bevan, 2011; Urquhart & Yeoman, 2010; Protopsaltis & Bouki, 2008; Hargittai, & Shafer, 2006). For instance, in a study analyzing the identity construction and gender in online social media by using Facebook profile photographs indicated that female and male Facebook users may have purpose for similar perceptions in forming their online identity via their profile pictures. They are also found equal in candidness and level of appropriateness that demonstrate the significance of personal online information for professional impressions (Hum, Chamberlin, Hambright, Portwood, Schat, & Bevan, 2011: 1831-1832). Notwithstanding, dominant findings in the literature have demonstrated the online information processing varies by gender.

CONCLUSION AND IMPLICATIONS

Gender differences in online information processing have been examined in this book chapter through especially not only consumer behavior but also biological, psychological, and social literatures. Also, some fruitful proposals have been developed by using previous findings and related theories. Major findings indicate that females and males demonstrate significant differences in online information processing.

This chapter also supports the notion that gender based segmentation is still acceptable and beneficial in current marketing environment for marketing communication. Dominant findings indicate that males and females use different information processing and response for the same message in online setting.

Like offline information processing, the origin of the differences in this processing root in biological, more specifically neurobiological, psychological and sociological based differences between two genders. In addition to these, antecedents that deprived from nature of online setting such as privacy concern can encourage the differences.

This study offers some important suggestions for both future search and implications. For future research, it suggests that the specific gender-based model should be generated for online information processing to gain deeper understanding about individual differences in online setting. Because of the dominant findings illustrating the gender difference, gender should be taken into account for examining the online consumer behaviour especially in their communication behaviour. Furthermore, gender can be used as a moderator and a control variable in future research examining relationship and interaction between other variables.

This study suggest the gender-based communications with consumers through implications of integrated marketing communications. These implications should enable to customize the information processing individually for both females and males. Marketing communication implications should encourage female consumers to process information with social and relational sensitivity, comprehensively, and in confidence that mitigate the perceived risk and privacy concerns. For females, favourable information, which has more detail, enables making comparison, supports females' communal role, gives rise to more effective online information processing. Thus, online information should consist of prevalent argument, emotions, recommendations of others that are specialist and with close relation, provide knowledge and more information, detailed content, verbal message, both low and high task relevant cues and vividness. As to male consumers, they should be encouraged by using implications to process information systematically, simply, and quickly. Successful communication with males as selective and heuristic processors requires the heuristic cue, summary content, visual and non-verbal message, simple but functional, unique, discriminative, and target specific information.

NOTE

The term "gender" is used to refer whether an individual is genetically and biologically male or female (Shaouf, Lü, & Li, 2016), and also gender and sex were used interchangeable in this book chapter.

REFERENCES

Armstrong, C. L., & McAdams, M. J. (2009). Blogs of information: How gender cues and individual motivations influence perceptions of credibility. *Journal of Computer-Mediated Communication, 14*(3), 435–456. doi:10.1111/j.1083-6101.2009.01448.x

Atkinson, N. L., Saperstein, S. L., & Pleis, J. (2009). Using the internet for health-related activities: Findings from a national probability sample. *Journal of Medical Internet Research, 11*(1), e4. doi:10.2196/jmir.1035 PMID:19275980

Awad, N. F., & Ragowsky, A. (2008). Establishing trust in electronic commerce through online word of mouth: An examination across genders. *Journal of Management Information Systems*, *24*(4), 101–121. doi:10.2753/MIS0742-1222240404

Bae, S., & Lee, T. (2011). Gender differences in consumers' perception of online consumer reviews. *Electronic Commerce Research*, *11*(2), 201–214. doi:10.100710660-010-9072-y

Baron-Cohen, S., Knickmeyer, R. C., & Belmonte, M. K. (2005). Sex differences in the brain: Implications for explaining autism. *Science*, *310*(5749), 819–823. doi:10.1126cience.1115455 PMID:16272115

Baumann, E., Czerwinski, F., & Reifegerste, D. (2017). Gender-specific determinants and patterns of online health information seeking: Results from a representative German health survey. *Journal of Medical Internet Research*, *19*(4), e92. doi:10.2196/jmir.6668 PMID:28377367

Bidmon, S., & Terlutter, R. (2015). Gender differences in searching for health information on the internet and the virtual patient-physician relationship in Germany: Exploratory results on how men and women differ and why. *Journal of Medical Internet Research*, *17*(6), e156. doi:10.2196/jmir.4127 PMID:26099325

Brunel, F. F., & Nelson, M. R. (2000). Explaining gendered responses to "help-self" and "help-others" charity ad appeals: The mediating role of world-views. *Journal of Advertising*, *29*(3), 15–28. doi:10.1080/00913367.2000.10673614

Chai, S., Das, S., & Rao, H. R. (2011). Factors affecting bloggers' knowledge sharing: An investigation across gender. *Journal of Management Information Systems*, *28*(3), 309–342. doi:10.2753/MIS0742-1222280309

Chen, X., Sin, S. C. J., Theng, Y. L., & Lee, C. S. (2015). Why students share misinformation on social media: Motivation, gender, and study-level differences. *Journal of Academic Librarianship*, *41*(5), 583–592. doi:10.1016/j.acalib.2015.07.003

Christov-Moore, L., Simpson, E. A., Coudé, G., Grigaityte, K., Iacoboni, M., & Ferrari, P. F. (2014). Empathy: Gender effects in brain and behavior. *Neuroscience and Biobehavioral Reviews*, *46*, 604–627. doi:10.1016/j.neubiorev.2014.09.001 PMID:25236781

Costa, P. T. Jr, Terracciano, A., & McCrae, R. R. (2001). Gender differences in personality traits across cultures: Robust and surprising findings. *Journal of Personality and Social Psychology*, *81*(2), 322–331. doi:10.1037/0022-3514.81.2.322 PMID:11519935

Cyr, D., & Bonanni, C. (2005). Gender and website design in e-business. *International Journal of Electronic Business*, *3*(6), 565–582. doi:10.1504/IJEB.2005.008536

Davis, R., Smith, S. D., & Lang, B. U. (2017). A comparison of online and offline gender and goal directed shopping online. *Journal of Retailing and Consumer Services*, *38*, 118–125. doi:10.1016/j.jretconser.2017.02.011

Eagly, A. H., & Wood, W. (1991). Explaining sex differences in social behavior: A meta-analytic perspective. *Personality and Social Psychology Bulletin*, *17*(3), 306–315. doi:10.1177/0146167291173011

Eagly, A. H., & Wood, W. (1999). The origins of sex differences in human behavior: Evolved dispositions versus social roles. *The American Psychologist*, *54*(6), 408–423. doi:10.1037/0003-066X.54.6.408

Ek, S. (2013). Gender differences in health information behaviour: A Finnish population-based survey. *Health Promotion International*, *30*(3), 736–745. doi:10.1093/heapro/dat063 PMID:23985248

Embacher, K., McGloin, R., & Richards, K. (2017). When Women Give Health Advice Online, Do We Listen? The Effect of Source Sex on Credibility and Likelihood to Use Online Health Advice. *Western Journal of Communication*, 1–18. doi:10.1080/10570314.2017.1367028

Erfanmanesh, M. (2016). Information seeking anxiety: Effects of gender, level of study and age. *Library Philosophy and Practice, 1*, 1-20.

Flanagin, A. J., & Metzger, M. J. (2003). The perceived credibility of personal Web page information as influenced by the sex of the source. *Computers in Human Behavior*, *19*(6), 683–701. doi:10.1016/S0747-5632(03)00021-9

Garbarino, E., & Strahilevitz, M. (2004). Gender differences in the perceived risk of buying online and the effects of receiving a site recommendation. *Journal of Business Research*, *57*(7), 768–775. doi:10.1016/S0148-2963(02)00363-6

Gefen, D., & Ridings, C. M. (2005). If you spoke as she does, sir, instead of the way you do: a sociolinguistics perspective of gender differences in virtual communities. *ACM SIGMIS Database: the DATABASE for Advances in Information Systems, 36*(2), 78-92.

Gefen, D., & Straub, D. W. (1997). Gender differences in the perception and use of e-mail: An extension to the technology acceptance model. *Management Information Systems Quarterly*, *21*(4), 389–400. doi:10.2307/249720

Geng, L., Zhang, K., Wei, X., & Feng, X. (2017, March). Soft Biometrics in Online Social Networks: A Case Study on Twitter User Gender Recognition. In Applications of Computer Vision Workshops (WACVW), 2017 IEEE Winter (pp. 1-8). IEEE.

Goh, T. T., & Sun, S. (2014). Exploring gender differences in Islamic mobile banking acceptance. *Electronic Commerce Research*, *14*(4), 435–458. doi:10.100710660-014-9150-7

Goodrich, K. (2014). The gender gap: Brain-processing differences between the sexes shape attitudes about online advertising. *Journal of Advertising Research*, *54*(1), 32–43. doi:10.2501/JAR-54-1-032-043

Hajli, N., & Lin, X. (2016). Exploring the security of information sharing on social networking sites: Thc role of perceived control of information. *Journal of Business Ethics*, *133*(1), 111–123. doi:10.100710551-014-2346-x

Halder, S., Ray, A., & Chakrabarty, P. K. (2010). Gender differences in information seeking behavior in three universities in West Bengal, India. *The International Information & Library Review*, *42*(4), 242–251. doi:10.1080/10572317.2010.10762869

Hallyburton, A., & Evarts, L. A. (2014). Gender and online health information seeking: A five survey meta-analysis. *Journal of Consumer Health on the Internet*, *18*(2), 128–142. doi:10.1080/15398285.2014.902268

Hargittai, E., & Shafer, S. (2006). Differences in actual and perceived online skills: The role of gender. *Social Science Quarterly*, *87*(2), 432–448. doi:10.1111/j.1540-6237.2006.00389.x

Heisz, J. J., Pottruff, M. M., & Shore, D. I. (2013). Females scan more than males: A potential mechanism for sex differences in recognition memory. *Psychological Science, 24*(7), 1157–1163. doi:10.1177/0956797612468281 PMID:23696202

Ho, S. M., Lowry, P. B., Warkentin, M., Yang, Y., & Hollister, J. M. (2017). Gender deception in asynchronous online communication: A path analysis. *Information Processing & Management, 53*(1), 21–41. doi:10.1016/j.ipm.2016.06.004

Hum, N. J., Chamberlin, P. E., Hambright, B. L., Portwood, A. C., Schat, A. C., & Bevan, J. L. (2011). A picture is worth a thousand words: A content analysis of Facebook profile photographs. *Computers in Human Behavior, 27*(5), 1828–1833. doi:10.1016/j.chb.2011.04.003

Hunt, R. R., & Einstein, G. O. (1981). Relational and item-specific information in memory. *Journal of Verbal Learning and Verbal Behavior, 20*(5), 497–514. doi:10.1016/S0022-5371(81)90138-9

Hunt, R. R., & Seta, C. E. (1984). Category size effects in recall: The roles of relational and individual item information. *Journal of Experimental Psychology. Learning, Memory, and Cognition, 10*(3), 454–464. doi:10.1037/0278-7393.10.3.454

Hwang, Y. M., & Lee, K. C. (2018). Using an Eye-Tracking Approach to Explore Gender Differences in Visual Attention and Shopping Attitudes in an Online Shopping Environment. *International Journal of Human-Computer Interaction, 34*(1), 15–24. doi:10.1080/10447318.2017.1314611

Jackson, L. A., Ervin, K. S., Gardner, P. D., & Schmitt, N. (2001). Gender and the Internet: Women communicating and men searching. *Sex Roles, 44*(5), 363–379. doi:10.1023/A:1010937901821

Jacobsen, J. K. S., & Munar, A. M. (2012). Tourist information search and destination choice in a digital age. *Tourism Management Perspectives, 1*, 39–47. doi:10.1016/j.tmp.2011.12.005

Jansen, B. J., Moore, K., & Carman, S. (2013). Evaluating the performance of demographic targeting using gender in sponsored search. *Information Processing & Management, 49*(1), 286–302. doi:10.1016/j.ipm.2012.06.001

Kim, D. Y., Lehto, X. Y., & Morrison, A. M. (2007). Gender differences in online travel information search: Implications for marketing communications on the internet. *Tourism Management, 28*(2), 423–433. doi:10.1016/j.tourman.2006.04.001

Kim, S. B., Kim, D. Y., & Wise, K. (2014). The effect of searching and surfing on recognition of destination images on Facebook pages. *Computers in Human Behavior, 30*, 813–823. doi:10.1016/j.chb.2013.07.010

Kotler, P., & Armstrong, G. (2016). *Principles of Marketing (16th Global Edition)*. Pearson.

Large, A., Beheshti, J., & Rahman, T. (2002). Gender differences in collaborative web searching behavior: An elementary school study. *Information Processing & Management, 38*(3), 427–443. doi:10.1016/S0306-4573(01)00034-6

Leong, S., & Hawamdeh, S. (1999). Gender and learning attitudes in using Web-based science lessons. *Information Research, 5*(1). Retrieved from http://www.informationr.net/ir/5-1/paper66.html

Lim, S., & Kwon, N. (2010). Gender differences in information behavior concerning Wikipedia, an unorthodox information source? *Library & Information Science Research, 32*(3), 212–220. doi:10.1016/j.lisr.2010.01.003

Lin, M. H. J., Cross, S. N., Jones, W., & Childers, T. L. (2018a). Online information processing of scent-related words and implications for decision making. In Analytics and Data Science (pp. 197-216). Springer.

Lin, X., Featherman, M., Brooks, S. L., & Hajli, N. (2018b). Exploring Gender Differences in Online Consumer Purchase Decision Making: An Online Product Presentation Perspective. *Information Systems Frontiers*, 1–15. doi:10.100710796-018-9831-1

Lin, X., Featherman, M., & Sarker, S. (2013b). Information Sharing in the Context of Social Media: An Application of the Theory of Reasoned Action and Social Capital Theory. *Proceedings of the 2013 AIS SIGHCI Workshop on HCI Research in MIS*, 1-5.

Lin, X., Featherman, M., & Sarker, S. (2017). Understanding factors affecting users' social networking site continuance: A gender difference perspective. *Information & Management, 54*(3), 383–395. doi:10.1016/j.im.2016.09.004

Lin, X., Li, Y., Califf, C. B., & Featherman, M. (2013a). Can social role theory explain gender differences in Facebook usage? In *System Sciences (HICSS), 2013 46th Hawaii International Conference on System Sciences* (pp. 690-699). IEEE.

Lorigo, L., Pan, B., Hembrooke, H., Joachims, T., Granka, L., & Gay, G. (2006). The influence of task and gender on search and evaluation behavior using Google. *Information Processing & Management, 42*(4), 1123–1131. doi:10.1016/j.ipm.2005.10.001

Lu, H. P., & Hsiao, K. L. (2009). Gender differences in reasons for frequent blog posting. *Online Information Review, 33*(1), 135–156. doi:10.1108/14684520910944436

Marriott, H. R., & Williams, M. D. (2018). Exploring consumers perceived risk and trust for mobile shopping: A theoretical framework and empirical study. *Journal of Retailing and Consumer Services, 42*, 133–146. doi:10.1016/j.jretconser.2018.01.017

McClure, E. B., Monk, C. S., Nelson, E. E., Zarahn, E., Leibenluft, E., Bilder, R. M., ... Pine, D. S. (2004). A developmental examination of gender differences in brain engagement during evaluation of threat. *Biological Psychiatry, 55*(11), 1047–1055. doi:10.1016/j.biopsych.2004.02.013 PMID:15158422

McGivern, R. F., Huston, J. P., Byrd, D., King, T., Siegle, G. J., & Reilly, J. (1997). Sex differences in visual recognition memory: Support for a sex-related difference in attention in adults and children. *Brain and Cognition, 34*(3), 323–336. doi:10.1006/brcg.1997.0872 PMID:9292185

Meyers-Levy, J., & Loken, B. (2015). Revisiting gender differences: What we know and what lies ahead. *Journal of Consumer Psychology, 25*(1), 129–149. doi:10.1016/j.jcps.2014.06.003

Meyers-Levy, J., & Maheswaran, D. (1991). Exploring differences in males' and females' processing strategies. *The Journal of Consumer Research, 18*(1), 63–70. doi:10.1086/209241

Meyers-Levy, J., & Sternthal, B. (1991). Gender differences in the use of message cues and judgments. *JMR, Journal of Marketing Research, 28*(1), 84–96. doi:10.2307/3172728

Murphy, G. B., & Tocher, N. (2011). Gender differences in the effectiveness of online trust building information cues: An empirical examination. *The Journal of High Technology Management Research*, *22*(1), 26–35. doi:10.1016/j.hitech.2011.03.004

Nysveen, H., Pedersen, P. E., & Thorbjørnsen, H. (2005). Explaining intention to use mobile chat services: Moderating effects of gender. *Journal of Consumer Marketing*, *22*(5), 247–256. doi:10.1108/07363760510611671

Okazaki, S., & Hirose, M. (2009). Does gender affect media choice in travel information search? On the use of mobile Internet. *Tourism Management*, *30*(6), 794–804. doi:10.1016/j.tourman.2008.12.012

Okazaki, S., Rubio, N., & Campo, S. (2014). Gossiping behavior on social networking sites: Does gender matter? *International Journal of Human-Computer Interaction*, *30*(9), 718–726. doi:10.1080/10447318.2014.907710

Park, J., Yoon, Y., & Lee, B. (2009). The effect of gender and product categories on consumer online information search. *Advances in Consumer Research. Association for Consumer Research (U. S.)*, *36*, 362–366.

Parmaksız, P. M. Y., & Melis, P. (2012). Digital opportunities for social transition: Blogosphere and motherhood in Turkey. *Fe Dergi*, *1*(1), 123–134. doi:10.1501/Fe0001_0000000069

Phillip, M. V., & Suri, R. (2004). Impact of gender differences on the evaluation of promotional emails. *Journal of Advertising Research*, *44*(4), 360–368. doi:10.1017/S0021849904040383

Protopsaltis, A., & Bouki, V. (2008, September). Gender and information processing in electronic age. In *Proceedings of the 26th annual ACM international conference on Design of communication* (pp. 131-138). ACM.

Putrevu, S. (2001). Exploring the origins and information processing differences between men and women: Implications for advertisers. *Academy of Marketing Science Review*, *2001*, 1–14. Retrieved from http://www.amsreview.org/articles/putrevu10-2001.pdf

Putrevu, S. (2004). Communicating with the sexes: Male and female responses to print advertisements. *Journal of Advertising*, *33*(3), 51–62. doi:10.1080/00913367.2004.10639168

Putrevu, S. (2008). Consumer responses toward sexual and nonsexual appeals: The influence of involvement, need for cognition (NFC), and gender. *Journal of Advertising*, *37*(2), 57–70. doi:10.2753/JOA0091-3367370205

Qin, J., Shi, Z., Ma, Y., & Han, S. (2018). Gender and neural substrates subserving implicit processing of death-related linguistic cues. *Cognitive Processing*, *19*(1), 63–71. doi:10.100710339-017-0847-0 PMID:29305759

Riedl, R., Hubert, M., & Kenning, P. (2010). Are there neural gender differences in online trust? An fMRI study on the perceived trustworthiness of eBay offers. *Management Information Systems Quarterly*, *34*(2), 397–428. doi:10.2307/20721434

Rodgers, S., & Harris, M. A. (2003). Gender and e-commerce: An exploratory study. *Journal of Advertising Research*, *43*(3), 322–329. doi:10.2501/JAR-43-3-322-329

Rodgers, S., & Harris, M. A. (2003). Gender and e-commerce: An exploratory study. *Journal of Advertising Research*, *43*(3), 322–329. doi:10.2501/JAR-43-3-322-329

Rowley, J., Johnson, F., & Sbaffi, L. (2017). Gender as an influencer of online health information-seeking and evaluation behavior. *Journal of the Association for Information Science and Technology*, *68*(1), 36–47. doi:10.1002/asi.23597

Roy, M., & Chi, M. T. (2003). Gender differences in patterns of searching the web. *Journal of Educational Computing Research*, *29*(3), 335–348. doi:10.2190/7BR8-VXA0-07A7-8AVN

Schmitt, D. P., Realo, A., Voracek, M., & Allik, J. (2008). Why can't a man be more like a woman? Sex differences in Big Five personality traits across 55 cultures. *Journal of Personality and Social Psychology*, *94*(1), 168–182. doi:10.1037/0022-3514.94.1.168 PMID:18179326

Schulte-Rüther, M., Markowitsch, H. J., Shah, N. J., Fink, G. R., & Piefke, M. (2008). Gender differences in brain networks supporting empathy. *NeuroImage*, *42*(1), 393–403. doi:10.1016/j.neuroimage.2008.04.180 PMID:18514546

Seidlitz, L., & Diener, E. (1998). Sex differences in the recall of affective experiences. *Journal of Personality and Social Psychology*, *74*(1), 262–271. doi:10.1037/0022-3514.74.1.262 PMID:9457787

Shaouf, A., Lü, K., & Li, X. (2016). The effect of web advertising visual design on online purchase intention: An examination across gender. *Computers in Human Behavior*, *60*, 622–634. doi:10.1016/j.chb.2016.02.090

Sheehan, K. B. (1999). An investigation of gender differences in online privacy concerns and resultant behaviors. *Journal of Interactive Marketing*, *13*(4), 24–38. doi:10.1002/(SICI)1520-6653(199923)13:4<24::AID-DIR3>3.0.CO;2-O

Sin, S. C. J. (2016). Social media and problematic everyday life information-seeking outcomes: Differences across use frequency, gender, and problem-solving styles. *Journal of the Association for Information Science and Technology*, *67*(8), 1793–1807. doi:10.1002/asi.23509

Sun, Y., Lim, K. H., Jiang, C., Peng, J. Z., & Chen, X. (2010). Do males and females think in the same way? An empirical investigation on the gender differences in Web advertising evaluation. *Computers in Human Behavior*, *26*(6), 1614–1624. doi:10.1016/j.chb.2010.06.009

Terlutter, R., Bidmon, S., & Röttl, J. (2014). Who uses physician-rating websites? Differences in sociodemographic variables, psychographic variables, and health status of users and nonusers of physician-rating websites. *Journal of Medical Internet Research*, *16*(3), e97. doi:10.2196/jmir.3145 PMID:24686918

Tsichla, E., Hatzithomas, L., & Boutsouki, C. (2016). Gender differences in the interpretation of web atmospherics: A selectivity hypothesis approach. *Journal of Marketing Communications*, *22*(6), 563–586. doi:10.1080/13527266.2014.903507

Venkatesh, V., & Morris, M. G. (2000). Why Don't Men Ever Stop to Ask for Directions? Gender, Social Influence, and Their Role in Technology Acceptance and Usage Behavior. *Management Information Systems Quarterly*, *24*(1), 115–139. doi:10.2307/3250981

Wang, C., Zhou, Z., Jin, X. L., Fang, Y., & Lee, M. K. (2017). The influence of affective cues on positive emotion in predicting instant information sharing on microblogs: Gender as a moderator. *Information Processing & Management, 53*(3), 721–734. doi:10.1016/j.ipm.2017.02.003

Wei, P. S., & Lu, H. P. (2013). An examination of the celebrity endorsements and online customer reviews influence female consumers' shopping behavior. *Computers in Human Behavior, 29*(1), 193–201. doi:10.1016/j.chb.2012.08.005

Wolin, L. D., & Korgaonkar, P. (2003). Web advertising: Gender differences in beliefs, attitudes and behavior. *Internet Research, 13*(5), 375–385. doi:10.1108/10662240310501658

Wood, W., & Eagly, A. H. (2012). Biosocial construction of sex differences and similarities in behavior. Advances in Experimental Social Psychology, 46, 55-123.

Yasin, B., Yasin, B., Baghirov, F., Baghirov, F., Zhang, Y., & Zhang, Y. (2017). The role of travel experience and gender on travel information source selection. *Journal of Hospitality and Tourism Technology, 8*(2), 296–310. doi:10.1108/JHTT-01-2017-0002

Zaharia, S., Kauke, D., & Hartung, E. (2017). Eye-Tracking Analysis of Gender-Specific Online Information Research and Buying Behavior. In *International Conference on HCI in Business, Government, and Organizations* (pp. 143-159). Springer.

Zhang, K. Z., Benyoucef, M., & Zhao, S. J. (2015). Consumer participation and gender differences on companies' microblogs: A brand attachment process perspective. *Computers in Human Behavior, 44*, 357–368. doi:10.1016/j.chb.2014.11.068

Zhou, M. (2014). Gender difference in web search perceptions and behavior: Does it vary by task performance? *Computers & Education, 78*, 174–184. doi:10.1016/j.compedu.2014.06.005

ADDITIONAL READING

Costa, J. A. (Ed.). (1994). *Gender issues and consumer behavior.* Sage Publications, Inc.

Eagly, A. H. (2013). *Sex differences in social behavior: A social-role interpretation.* Psychology Press. doi:10.4324/9780203781906

Fischer, E., & Arnold, S. J. (1994). Sex, gender identity, gender role attitudes, and consumer behavior. *Psychology and Marketing, 11*(2), 163–182. doi:10.1002/mar.4220110206

Kotler, P., Kartajaya, H., & Setiawan, I. (2016). *Marketing 4.0: Moving from traditional to digital.* John Wiley & Sons.

Otnes, C. C., & Zayer, L. T. (Eds.). (2012). *Gender, culture, and consumer behavior.* Taylor & Francis.

Whitley, B. E. Jr. (1997). Gender differences in computer-related attitudes and behavior: A meta-analysis. *Computers in Human Behavior, 13*(1), 1–22. doi:10.1016/S0747-5632(96)00026-X

Yin, C., Sun, Y., Fang, Y., & Lim, K. (2018). Exploring the dual-role of cognitive heuristics and the moderating effect of gender in microblog information credibility evaluation. *Information Technology & People*, *31*(3), 741–769. doi:10.1108/ITP-12-2016-0300

KEY TERMS AND DEFINITIONS

Gender Difference: Variance of behaviors and attitudes stemming from being female or male.

Perceived Risk: Perception about the possibility of a negative consequence or uncertainty related to any situation or incident.

Privacy Concern: Anxiety or sensitivity related to the loss of personal intimacy.

Social Role: Appropriate behavior of an individual in a given society.

Chapter 13
Internet Addiction and Fear of Missing Out:
The Gender Difference of Tertiary Students in Ghana

Joseph Kofi Wireko
Aalborg University, Denmark

ABSTRACT

Smartphones and the evolution of new ICTs have enabled people, especially the youth, to stay connected to their social and professional network. This has resulted in compulsive checking for status updates and messages, for fear of missing out (FOMO). FOMO, which is a form of internet addiction, has its downside among students. This chapter is an empirical study that seeks to examine the disruptive effect of FOMO on the academic performance of students. Four hundred twenty-two university students were surveyed on their use of internet (social media services) and its result on their academic activities. A Likert scale was used to measure their use of the internet (social media) and its relationship with their academic performance. Chi-square and factor analysis were conducted. The results showed that continuous use of internet had negative effect on students' academic performance and it affected the female students more than their male counterparts. Tertiary institutions should intensify guidance and counselling sessions for students in order to mitigate the negative effects of use of internet on students.

INTRODUCTION

The invention of Internet has brought various advantages and opportunities in almost every field. The Internet and social media have now taken major aspect of our daily life, especially in the area of education. The primary aim of Internet is sharing of information which is an important aspect in the educational sector. In recent times, people do not have to search for library and in books to get information, which was time-consuming and stressful. With a wealth of and abundant electronic library online, a click of the mouse button will download massive information and literature that will overwhelm you.

DOI: 10.4018/978-1-5225-7068-4.ch013

Several studies have been done to show the positive effect or impact of Internet (social media) on students. Barhoumi (2015), in a study, showed how the use of WhatsApp, a social media platform helped students to learn and interact in various contexts and thereby contributing to their academic work. In addition, some studies have also shown that the appropriate use of social media networks (Internet) can encourage students by providing an engaging forum through which they can explore their reflective practice and issues of professionalism and privacy (Brown, 2010). Other benefits such as online examination, teaching and learning materials (e-learning), research and many more provide endless opportunities to students and the academia in general. Apart from the use of Internet in education, students also benefit in using the Internet to shop online for everything they want without going outside to stores and super markets, play games and other entertainment to reduce academic pressure, look for jobs, conduct financial activities, check for bus schedules and book bus or transportation tickets online.

Notwithstanding these great advantages of the Internet to students, there are those who think that the Internet is rather disruptive and has the potential to cause harm in the very long term to the academic performance of students by making them addictive and dependent (Andreassen, Pallesen, & Griffiths, 2017; Alkhalaf, 2018). Some researchers have even identified Internet addiction (IA) as a significant public health threat and have recommended that Internet addiction is included in the Diagnostic and Statistical Manual of Mental Disorders (DSM) as a mental illness (Al-Hadrawi, 2018, Shao, Zheng, & Wang, 2018).

Although, Social media addiction is now observed to a greater extent among the younger generation, especially teenagers and the early adults in secondary and tertiary institutions, it is still not considered as a mental disorder that impairs students' academic performance (Al-Menayes, 2015). While, special clinics have been set up in most countries to deal with substance abuse, none have been established to deal with Internet addiction or abuse in African countries in general and Ghana in particular. For example, in South Korea, home of the world's most connected population, have since 2015 set up digital detox camps to treat thousands of children (Kim Se-jeong, 2015). It was not until 2016 that the first Internet addiction clinic in Africa was set up in Algeria to deal with the menace when the government saw it as a national problem (Djamila, 2016). To date, there is no known of such dedicated unit set up to deal with Internet addiction in Ghana.

Fear of missing out (FOMO), formerly known as "keeping up with the Joneses" is a psychological dependence on being online which could result in anxiety when one feels disconnected, thereby leading to a fear of missing out (Jonathan, 1998; Song, Larose, Eastin, & Lin, 2004). The word *addiction* is not only confined to substance abuse as "when talking about addiction, people usually think about tobacco, drugs, or alcohol dependency but also with the use of the Internet, especially the 'magic blue' of Facebook," For some users, going online is as important in their life as breathing, eating, or sleeping thus literally putting their life at risk (Djamila, 2016). It has been magnified by the new technology of Internet and of Facebook, Twitter, WhatsApp, Instagram, Telegram etc.

Internet addiction is considered as a pervasive apprehension that others might be having rewarding experiences from which one is absent (Przybylski, 2013). This social anxiety is characterized by a desire to stay continually connected with what others are doing (Walter, 2012). FOMO is also considered as a fear of regret which may lead to a compulsive concern that one might miss an opportunity for social interaction, a novel experience, a profitable investment, or other satisfying events (Wortham, 2011). As a consequence, FOMO is perceived to have negative influences on people's psychological health and well-being because it could contribute to people's negative mood and depressed feelings and by extension lead to lack of concentration or focus on studies (by students).

Internet addiction takes on different forms and is an important issue for diagnostic and preventive reasons. Fear of missing out (FOMO), is one of such forms by which students become addicted to the Internet. It is one of the criteria of classifying Internet use as destructive, threatening or asymptomatic and have been discussed in psychology and media pedagogy since Internet became prevalent. With the advent of technology, people's social and communicative experiences have been expanded from face-to-face to online. On one hand, modern technologies (e.g., mobile phones, smartphones) and social networking services_(e.g., Facebook, Twitter) provide a unique opportunity for people to be socially engaged with a reduced "cost of admission" (Przybylski, 2013).

It has been identified that FOMO serves as a motive for an increasing use of social media, which could distract people from learning in the classroom (Turkle, 2012). According to a survey conducted in the US and UK, the majority of adult Millennials (age between 18 and 34), over half of the respondents stated that they want to say yes to everything due to the fear of missing out; and hence they barely invest sufficient energy or time in delving into topics in their studies (Walter, 2012). Furthermore, unhealthy digital habits, such as constantly checking for emails and social media updates, could be developed and thus lead to insufficient engagement in academic activities.

FOMO involves anxiety and rapid, impulsive urge to use Internet (Social Media Networks-SMN in particular) when offline and it is connected with a strong need to stay online, receive media messages, passively or actively participate in information exchange through SNS, online games and other types of webpages and Internet services. Failure to respond to this need, in most cases evokes negative emotions. It usually begins with a pang of envy. Next comes the anxiety, the self-doubt, the gnawing sense of inadequacy. Finally, these feelings fizzle, leaving you full of bilious irritation (Anderson, 2011). What follows next is to resort to the Internet (Social Media Networks-SMN) to apprise oneself of various news, gossips, events etc.

Internet addiction is a very broad term covering several types of addictions mediated by electronic media. These addictions include, for example: shopping, virtual sex, games, social network services (SNS), smartphones, online gambling, cyber-relationships, file downloading — namely, e-services that provide positive stimulation for users (Kačániová & Bačíková, 2016; Mihajlov & Vejmelka, 2017).

Classic signs of Internet addiction include: constant thinking about online activities, even in situations that are not adequate; psychosomatic symptoms in case of withdrawal; prolonged time of engaging in online activities without reasonable need; struggling with self-control when it comes to time spent on the Internet; lack of interests in things outside the electronic network and limiting social interactions for the benefit of online activities; using Internet to forget about negative consequences in the real world (Medenica, Račić, & Joksimović, 2015). Thus, there is always a smart phone or device around to whisk you away into someone else's "reality", even when one is in class or lectures.

The menace and disruptive effects of Internet and in particular social media, have become so pervasive to the extent of threatening to undermine the huge benefits that the technology provides students. In Ghana and in most African countries where Internet access is a growing phenomenon, students and for that matter the youth have found themselves in the captive 'net' of the prolonged use of the Internet and are unable to extricate themselves and have become addictive to the extent of not only harming themselves academically but also in terms of health and finance.

Several research studies on the poor and deteriorating academic performances of Ghanaian students due to excessive and over use of internet have been reported in recent times. However, very few of these studies have been done to show the gender differences in the addictive condition of students. This research study seeks to answer the following two key questions; (1) are Ghanaian university students Internet usage addicted? and; (2) Which gender is at risk of Internet abuse (addicted)?

METHODS

There are different approaches to FOMO diagnosis. Abel, Buff, and Burr (2016) suggest measuring the phenomenon in terms of impulsive checking online and SNS resources in different situations while Przybylski et. al., (2013) locate FOMO more in the area of social behaviors, peer relationships and quality of such relations. Criteria for classifying Internet use as destructive, threatening or asymptomatic, have been discussed in psychology and media pedagogy since Internet became prevalent.

One of the most popular methods of measuring addiction is Internet Addiction Test (IAT) which contains characteristics of 20 most common symptoms of Internet abuse (Young, 2007). According to IAT, ways of using Internet can be classified into three categories: functional, at risk of abuse and abusive. This classification is also consistent with other typologies of three-phase mechanisms of development of Internet addiction (Augustynek, 2010). However, in recent times some researchers have claimed that the Internet per se is simply the *medium* and that people are in effect addicted to *processes* facilitated by the Internet (medium) and have proposed a more extensive model called the Internet Process Addiction Test (IPAT) to measure the processes to which individuals are addicted (Griffiths, 2000; Northrup, Lapierre, Kirk, & Rae, 2015).

Thus, from Young's (1998, 2007) model and other diverse contexts, the following four dimensions that manifest themselves across all instruments have developed into what is known as the IPAT framework (Widyanto & McMurran, (2004); Chang et al., (2008); Northrup et al., (2015):

1. **Excessive Use:** Compulsive Internet use and excessive online time-use;
2. **Withdrawal Symptoms:** Withdrawal symptoms including feelings such as depression and anger, given restricted Internet use;
3. **Tolerance:** The need for better equipment, increased internet use, and more applications/software;
4. **Negative Repercussions:** Internet use caused negative consequences in various aspects, including problematic performance in social, academic, or work domains.

However, it is to be noted that due to studies being conducted in divergent contexts, studies constantly modify scales for their own purposes, thereby imposing a further challenge to the standardization in assessing Internet addiction disorder but nonetheless all these studies contain the core IPAT components.

The FOMO journey starts at first by considering the Internet — as in case of non-addicts — as a source of information, entertainment, work, communication. The resources of the Internet are effectively utilized. In the second phase, users engage in excessive use of the Internet, not necessarily correlated with their real needs such as doing school assignments or work-related. The last stage involves the destructive behavior when addicted individuals limit or totally withdraw from their professional, family, social, leisure and academic activities in the case of students in order to use the Internet and network devices (Tomczyk, 2015).

Research Design

An exploratory descriptive correlational design was utilized to achieve the objectives of the current study. This research study was conducted in Accra at Ghana Technology University College (GTUC). The School has multicultural background with students coming from all over Ghana, and also including students from outside the country especially from the West African sub-region (ECOWAS). The choice of GTUC as a sample frame is based on the need to control for some factors such as socio-demographic characteristics; namely age, income and educational level. By choosing a university population, the respondents will exhibit similar levels of education, age, income and technology appreciation.

The sample design recruited for this research was a simple random sampling method. This was preferred because, it is able to provide an objective statistical inference for such academic research. The main requirement of random sampling is a sample frame, which was conveniently provided by the university community (students). A good sample frame should fulfil four basic requirements: (1) include all elements of sample; (2) no element of the sample is counted twice; (3) it is up to date, and; (4) and has a clear boundary (Saunders, Lewis, & Thornhill, 2007). All these conditions were present in the GTUC population.

The main data collection approach for this study is an email-based (online) survey of tertiary students. However, recognizing the fact that email responses could be low due to so many factors, paper-based survey was also developed along-side the online survey in order to improve the response rate. With the permission of the lecturer, students were approached to participate and respond to the questionnaire just before the start of their lectures. This time-location sample approach yielded very high response rate.

Research Tools and Procedure

To achieve the purpose of the study 3 main tools were used, it consisted the socio-demographic characteristics sheet of the participants that contains questions enquires about; age, academic year and stream; and number of hours spent on the Internet. The second part involved self-rated items. Each item was scored on a 5-point Likert scale with "0" meaning "Strongly Disagree" to "5" being "Strongly agree". The final part involved seeking students' perception on the effect of the Internet on their academic studies through a self-rated response also on a 5-point Likert scale ranging from Strongly Disagree to Strongly agree. The data was analyzed using the most recent SPSS version (Ver. 25). The collected data were coded; validated, cleaned and the missing data controlled before the analysis. Appropriate statistical tests such as, descriptive statistics (frequencies, percentages, and graphs) and the association among variables of the study with socio-demographic background by using the Spearman Rank Order Correlations were conducted. In order to achieve the objectives of this research and based on existing literature, the following hypothesis were formulated:

Hypothesis 1: There is a negative relationship between Internet addiction and academic performance of university students.

Hypothesis 2: There is a significant gender difference in the abuse of Internet usage (Internet addiction).

RESULTS

From the demographic profile, the respondents comprised of 65% males and 35% of females as shown in Table 1. It could be observed that male participation far outweighed the female counterpart. The reason being speculated by the researcher is that males were found to dominate the IT sector in Ghana and Ghana Technology University College where this research took place tend to attract the male sex as a natural order of admission towards the IT industry in the country.

Most of the respondents belong to the "15-29" and "30-39" age groups of about 86% and 10% respectively and thus constitute over 90% of respondents. These age groups of young adults present the best characteristics of profile for this research study. The rest of the age groups representing less than 10% are over 40 years who are special students (mature students) pursuing courses to bridge their educational qualification at their work places (Table 2).

All respondents are pursuing programs at the tertiary level, principally in an under graduate courses. Majority of respondents are students who are in the regular stream of morning session admission (82.5%) of the university and the rest enrolled in the evening and weekend streams. These students are at various levels or years in their undergraduate studies with a reasonable spread of 29.9%, 33%, 22.9%, 9.2% for levels 1,2,3, and 4 respectively. About 5% are mature students who are in special courses. The admission session mix is illustrated in Table 3.

Tables 4 and 5 illustrate the Internet behavior usage among the respondents. Based on the table, over 90% of respondents spend more than one hour on the Internet in a day when they accessed the Internet. About 58% spend between 1 to 3 hours, while about 23.7% spend six hours or more. Only a small number (6.4%) of the respondents spend less than an hour on the Internet in a day (Table 4).

When asked to indicate how often they connect to the Internet and the reason why they do so, about 74% who usually connect to the Internet three to over five times a day, do so for social media (i.e. non-academic activities) reasons while only 1.5% do so for academic reasons. About 10.9% of them who

Table 1. Gender of Respondents

	Male	Female	Total
Male	276	0	65.4%
Female	0	146	34.6%
Total	276	146	422

Table 2. Age group of Respondents

	Respondents	Percent
"15-29 years"	363	86.0%
30-39 years"	43	10.2%
40-49 years"	9	2.1%
"50-60 years"	7	1.7%
60 or more years"	0	0.0%
Total	422	100.0%

Table 3. Students School Session

	Morning	Evening	Weekend	Total	(%)
Level 1	121	3	2	126	29.9
Level 2	135	3	1	139	33.0
Level 3	73	2	22	97	22.9
Level 4	19	5	15	39	9.2
Others	-	14	7	21	5.0
Total	348	27	47	422	100
Percentage (%)	82.5%	6.4%	11.1%	100%	

Table 4. Hours Spent on Internet

Hours Spent on Internet	N	%
< 1hr	27	6.4%
1 hr	86	20.4%
2 hrs	108	25.6%
3 hrs	51	12.1%
4 hrs	23	5.5%
5 hrs	27	6.4%
6 hrs	44	10.4%
> 6 hrs	56	13.3%
N	422	100

accessed the Internet three to over times a day do so for other reasons or activities. Tables 5 illustrates the number of times and the reason why respondents connect to the Internet.

Probing further to find out if respondents feel competent in accessing the Internet, over half of them (52.3%) agreed that they are generally knowledgeable or skillful in using the Internet while about 20% of them doubted their skills and about one third (28.4%) generally disagreed that they have the needed skills and knowledge to access the Internet that will make them benefit (Table 6). In terms of the usefulness

Table 5. Internet Usage Behavior

No. Of Times	Time/Day on Social Media (Non-Academic)	Time/Day on Academic Activities	Time/Day on Other Activities
None	7.6%	78.4%	62.7%
One time	14.7%	14.7%	16.2%
Two times	4.7%	5.9%	10.2%
Three times	13.0%	0.5%	5.7%
Four times	22.5%	0.0%	2.6%
Five or more	38.2%	1.0%	2.6%

of the Internet, almost 70.5% considered the Internet to be useful in their academic studies as against 12.4% who disagreed. About 17.8% were not sure if the Internet is useful for them in their academic studies (Table 6). Regarding the means in accessing the Internet, almost 85.8% respondents agreed that they are able to access it easily, while 5.2% disagreed and 9% were neither agreed or disagreed (Table 6).

Table 7 shows that about 72.3% agreed they often neglect school work because of use of social media online, 16.4% disagreed and about 11% were not sure. In respect of un-intended stay online, about 43.8% agreed that they often found themselves using the Internet longer than they had intended, while 26.6% disagreed, about 31% were not sure if they did stay longer than intended when connected to the Internet. A good number of respondents, (about 70%) often found themselves thinking of what they might have missed in social media when they are away from the Internet or not connected (Table 7).

Only 14.2% disagreed that they worry about what happened on social media when they are not connected compared to 17% who neither agreed or disagreed (Table 7). About half of the respondents (49.4%) indicated that they did not find themselves cancelling meetings with friends because of their social media engagement online compared to 28% who were not sure and about 23.5% who often found themselves cancelling meetings with friends because of social media online. Regarding the effect of social media on academic studies, about 58.5% disagreed that their grades have deteriorated because of their pre-occupation with social media, 14% agreed that their grades have deteriorated and about 28% were not sure if their pre-occupation with social media usage has affected their grades.

DISCUSSION

The main objective of this study is to examine the relationship between Internet usage and its disruptive effect on academic performance of university students and also to identify which gender is most at risk. Based on the Internet Addiction (IA) typologies and framework by Young (2007) and Augustynek (2010) the Internet addiction items were grouped into three factors namely; functional, risk of abuse and abusive for analysis.

Factor 1: Functional Benefits of Internet Usage

1. To What extent would you agree that -Generally, you benefit from using the Internet (Fbenefits1)?

Table 6. Functional Benefits of Internet usage (Factor 1)

	Generally Benefiting From Using Internet	Generally Internet Is Useful for Academic Activities	Generally Ensure Access to Internet al times
Strongly Disagree	5.2%	1.9%	1.4%
Disagree	23.2%	10.5%	3.8%
Neither Agree or Disagree	19.7%	17.8%	9.0%
Agree	38.6%	42.5%	34.0%
Strongly Agree	13.7%	28.0%	51.8%

N=422

Table 7. Disruptive Effect of Internet on Academic Studies (%)

	Neglecting School Work Because of Social Media	Using Internet Longer Than Intended	Always Thinking of What Is Happening on Social Media When Away	Often Cancel Meeting With Friends Because of Social Media	My Grades Have Deteriorated Because of Social Media Usage
Strongly Disagree	5.7%	6.2%	5.2%	7.8%	13.8%
Disagree	10.7%	20.4%	9.0%	41.6%	44.7%
Neither Agree or Disagree	11.4%	30.6%	17.1%	28.0%	28.3%
Agree	48.6%	31.5%	53.7%	19.5%	11.4%
Strongly Agree	23.7%	12.3%	15.9%	4.0%	2.6%

2. To what extent would you agree that - Generally, the Internet could be useful in your academic activities (Fbenefits2)
3. To what extent would you agree that – Generally you would do all that can to ensure that you are able to access the Internet because of its benefits (Fbenefits3).

The relationship of these factors with Internet usage (Social Media) was examined using correlations between students' self-reported time spent on the Internet and the expected benefits or the disrupt effect on their studies. This was done by combining "agree" and "strongly agree" on the Likert scale responses to represent 'Yes' or confirmation to the questions regarding the benefits of the Internet to their activities. In respect of the functional benefits, the results in

From Table 8, an association between Internet addiction and academic performance was observed, (Fbenefits1: $\chi2(1)$ =.509, P=0.479; FBenefits2: $\chi2(1)$=.986, P=0.812 and Fbenefits3: $\chi2(1)$=.520, P=0.471). Since all p>0.05, we fail to reject hypothesis one. This means that students consider the use of Internet (and social media) to be detrimental to their academic studies. These findings are consistent with studies by Chou and Hsiao (2000), Frangos and Frangos, (2009) and Akhter (2013) who found out that excessive use of the Internet had a deteriorating effect on students in terms of their academic performance but when used judiciously, become a useful tool (Ibrahim et al. 2014 and Jumoke et al. 2015).

A correlation test was conducted to identify the strength and the direction of the relationship of the observations. A Pearson product-moment correlation coefficient was computed to assess the relationship between Internet access (usage/addiction) and functional benefits on academic performance. There was a negative correlation between the two variables of general benefits (Factor 1) of Internet access and academic performance, r = -0.061, n = 295, p = 0.292. Overall, there was a strong negative correlation between the use of Internet and academic performance. Thus, continuous use or excessive use (addiction or abuse) of the Internet were correlated with perceived negative academic performance of students.

Risk of Abuse

Following the Internet addiction framework or typologies by young (2007) and Augustynek (2010), this study further examined students on the factor of risk of abuse. Using similar wording for the typology that are indicative of activities or behavior that put them at risk, a cross tabulation analysis by way of chi-square was conducted to find out if there are any differences between the gender regarding risk of abuse of Internet usage.

Table 8. Chi-Square Tests Functional Benefits of Internet (Factor 1)

	Functional Benefits1	Functional Benefits2	Functional Benefits3
	Strongly Agree or Agree		
Pearson Chi-Square	.509	.986	.520
df	1	1	1
Asymptotic Significance (2-sided)	.476	.812	.471
Exact Sig. (2-sided)			
Exact Sig. (1-sided)			
N of Valid Cases	220	295	360

Table 9. Correlation Tests of Functional Benefits and -Risk of Abuse of Internet

		Fbenefits2 (Functional Benefits of Internet)	Factor2 (Risk of Abuse of Internet)
Fbenefits2 (Functional Benefits of Internet)	Pearson Correlation	1	-.061
	Sig. (2-tailed)		.292
	N	295	295
Factor2-(Risk of Abuse of Internet)	Pearson Correlation	-.061	1
	Sig. (2-tailed)	.292	
	N	295	422

Factor 2: Risk of Internet Abuse (Internet Over Use) Wording

1. On the average how many hours do you spend on the Internet in a day?
2. How often do you use the Internet in a day for Social Media (Non-Academic) activities?
3. How often do you use the Internet in a day for academic activities?

In general, about 70% (69.9%) of the students (most of them females) spend up to 4 hours every day on the Internet for various reasons including social media and academic reasons (Table 10).

The Chi-square result (Table 11) shows that there is a very strong evidence that students spend a lot of time on the Internet ($\chi 2(7) = 17.801$, P=0.013). In terms of gender differences on the number of hours student spend online about 56.1% of males compared to 71.3% of females spend up to 4 hours a day on the Internet. Thus females, once connected spend significantly more hours on the Internet. This shows that in terms of gender, females demonstrate behaviors that put them at risk of abuse compared to their male counterpart. This is consistent with a research study by Kasahara (2017) who found out that females were significantly more likely to post very often to Snapchat and be online than males.

Table 10. Gender and Risk Abuse of Internet

			Factor2-Risk								Total
			Less than Hour	1 Hour	2 Hours	3 Hours	4 Hours	5 Hours	6 Hours	More than 6 Hours	
Gender	Male	Count	16	46	79	36	14	45	16	24	276
		% within Gender	5.8%	16.7%	28.6%	13.0%	5.1%	16.3%	5.8%	8.7%	100.0%
	Female	Count	11	40	29	15	9	11	11	20	146
		% within Gender	7.5%	27.4%	19.9%	10.3%	6.2%	7.5%	7.5%	13.7%	100.0%
Total		Count	27	86	108	51	23	56	27	44	422
		% within Gender	6.4%	20.4%	25.6%	12.1%	5.5%	13.3%	6.4%	10.4%	100.0%

Table 11. Hours Spend on the Internet

Chi-Square Tests	Value	df	Asymptotic Significance (2-Sided)
Pearson Chi-Square	17.801[a]	7	.013
Likelihood Ratio	18.147	7	.011
Linear-by-Linear Association	.178	1	.673
N of Valid Cases	422		

a: 0 cells (0.0%) have expected count less than 5. The minimum expected count is 7.96

Abusive Stage of Internet Usage

The last phase of Internet Addiction (IA) is Internet usage abuse and was also based on the wording typologies of Young (2007 and Augustynek (2010) framework as shown in Factor 3 below.

Factor 3: Abusive State (Phase) of Wording of Internet Access and Social Media Addiction

1. I often find myself neglecting school work because of my usage of social media (FAbusive1)
2. I often find myself using the Internet longer than intended for social media (FAbusive2)
3. I often find myself thinking about what happened in social media when I am away from them (FAbusive3)
4. I often cancel meeting with my friends because of my occupation with social media (FAbusive4)
5. I think my school grades have deteriorated because of my pre-occupation with social media usage. (FAbusive5)

Combining students self-reported response of Ágree´ and ´Strongly agree´ on a five point-Likert scale, the students were of the view that they often find themselves neglecting school work (FAbusive1), thinking of social media when away from it (FAbusive3) and that their school grades have deteriorated due to pre-occupation with Social media or the Internet (FAbusive5). On these three elements of Internet addiction phase, both genders were unanimous in respect of the abusive status of their behavior which were detrimental to their studies (Table 12).

However, in respect of the numbers of hours spent on the Internet and avoiding meetings with friends because of pre-occupation with Internet or social media, some differences were observed between the two genders. While 99.2% of males reported that they often find themselves staying longer than intended on the Internet, all of the females (100%) reported stayed longer than they intended (FAbusive2).

About 98.5% of males compared to all (100%) of females also often found themselves cancelling meetings with friends because of their pre-occupation with social media or online activities (FAbusive4).

A chi-square analysis based on a two-tailed test was conducted to test if there is any association between the genders. As per Table 13, the results show that there are significant associations between spending longer time on the Internet and cancelling meetings due to pre-occupation with Internet ($\chi2(1)$ =.429, P=0.513 for FAbusive2 and $\chi2(1)$ =.467, P=0.494)

CONCLUSION, RECOMMENDATIONS, AND FURTHER RESEARCH

From above discussions, it is evidently clear that; Internet connectivity (and for that matter, Social Media) has been a necessary evil for students in tertiary institutions in Ghana. This is due to the fact that, access to the Internet can enhance the academic performance of students if used positively but when abused or used negatively could have disruptive effect or consequences on academic performances of students.

One of the key objectives of this paper was to investigate disruptive effect of continuous online presence (Internet access) on students´ academic activities and identify which gender is most at risk. The study found females to be more at risk compared to their male counterparts in respect of the disruptive effect on their academic studies. This state of Internet usage risk is alarming considering the fact that females constituted only half of the number of male respondents yet their (females) responses were strong enough to sway results onto their side regarding possible abuse of the Internet.

Table 12. Gender and Abusive stage of Internet usage

			FAbusive1	FAbusive2	FAbusive3	FAbusive4	FAbusive5
			Strongly Agree or Agree				
Gender	Male	Count	210	128	207	66	38
		% Within Gender	100%	99.2%%	100%	98.5%	100%%
	Female	Count	95	55	86	31	21
		% Within Gender	100%	100%	100%	100%	100%
Total		Count	305	183	293	97%	59
		% Within	100%	99.5%%	100%	99%	100%

Table 13. Chi-Square Tests of Hours spend on Internet and Meeting Schedules

	FAbusive2	FAbusive4
	Strongly Agree or Agree	Strongly Agree or Agree
Pearson Chi-Square	.429	.467
Df	1	1
Asymptotic Significance (2-sided)	.513	.494
Exact Sig. (2-sided)	0.000	0.000
Exact Sig. (1-sided)	0.000	0.000
N of Valid Cases	184	98

Note: 1. No statistics were computed for FAbusive1, FAbusive3 and FAbusive5 because they are constants.
2. Computed only for a 2x2 table
3. Based on a five-point Likert scale combining 'Strongly Agree' and 'Agree'

In concluding, based on the Internet Addiction framework (the Internet Addiction phase development typology), students from GTUC are at the advance risk stage of Internet addiction (abuse) notwithstanding the fact that they also considered access to the Internet as an enabler and beneficial to their academic studies.

Recommendations

It is recommended that:

- Management of Ghana Technology University College (GTUC) should intensify guidance and counselling sessions for students, especially the females, in order to mitigate the negative effects of use of Internet on students' academic achievements.
- Time management should be incorporated into the curriculum of tertiary institutions. This could include the use of use of special devices such as health wearables watches (if affordable) to monitor and provide timely notifications/alarm to the user (and his or her network) whenever there is a possible violation or time over-run.
- Unannounced quizzes should be conducted frequently by lecturers to compel students to learn and use time for productive academic activities.

Further Research Study

Additional studies on other tertiary institutions should provide further insights into the impact of Internet on the performance of tertiary students in Ghana. Although, framed within an academic context, the research can be extended to investigate the Internet abuse in other places such as at home, workplace, and various other settings, and as well as for a variety of different audiences such as teenagers, young adults, the elderly, or families in identifying possible FOMO presence.

REFERENCES

Abel, J. P., Buff, C. L., & Burr, S. A. (2016). Social media and the fear of missing out: Scale development and assessment. *Journal of Business & Economics Research*, *14*(1), 33. doi:10.19030/jber.v14i1.9554

Akhter, N. (2013, October 10). Relationship between Internet Addiction and Academic Performance among University. *Undergraduates in Academic Journals*, *8*(19), 1793–1796.

Al-Hadrawi. H. H., (2018). The Effect of Internet Addiction on the Academic Performance of Undergraduate Nursing Students, Dept. of Mental Health Nursing, College of Nursing, University of Babylon, Hillah City. *Iraq in Indian Journal of Public Health Research & Development*, *9*(5).

Al-Menayes, J. J. (2015). Dimensions of social media addiction among university students in Kuwait. *PBS*, *4*, 23–28. doi:10.11648/j.pbs.20150401.14

Alkhalaf, A. M. (2018). The impact of WhatsApp use on academic achievement among Saudi medical students. Medical Teacher, 1–5.

Anderson, H. (2011). Never heard of FOMO? You're so missing out. *The Guardian*. Retrieved from https://www.theguardian.com/commentisfree/2011/apr/17/hephzibah-anderson-fomo-new-acronym

Andreassen, C. S., Pallesen, S., & Griffiths, M. D. (2017). The relationship between addictive use of social media, narcissism, and self-esteem: Findings from a large national survey. *Addictive Behaviors*, *64*, 287–293. doi:10.1016/j.addbeh.2016.03.006 PMID:27072491

Augustynek, A. (2010). Computer addiction. Diagnosis, prevalence, therapy. Academic Press.

Barhoumi, C., (2015). The Effectiveness of WhatsApp Mobile Learning Activities Guided by Activity Theory on Students' Knowledge Management. *Contemporary Educational Technology*, *6*(3), 221-238.

Brown, A. D. (2010). Social media: A new frontier in reflective practice. *Medical Education*, *44*(8), 744–745. doi:10.1111/j.1365-2923.2010.03729.x PMID:20633213

Chang, M. K., & Man Law, S. P. (2008). Factor structure for Young's Internet Addiction Test: A Confirmatory study. *Computers in Human Behavior*, *24*(6), 2597–2619. doi:10.1016/j.chb.2008.03.001

Chou, C., & Hsiao, M. (2000). Internet addiction, usage, gratifications, and pleasure experience: The Taiwan College Student's case. *Comput. Educ*, *35*(1), 65–80. doi:10.1016/S0360-1315(00)00019-1

Djamila, O. K. (2016). *First internet addiction rehab clinic opens in Algeria.* Retrieved from https://www.aljazeera.com/news/2016/10/internet-addiction-rehab-clinic-opens-algeria-161009055354223.html

Frangos, C. C., & Frangos, C. C. (2009). Internet Dependence in College Students from Greece. *European Psychiatry*, *24*(Suppl 1), S419. doi:10.1016/S0924-9338(09)70652-2

Griffiths, M. (2000). Internet addiction-time to be taken seriously? *Addiction Research*, *8*(5), 413–418. doi:10.3109/16066350009005587

Ibrahim, J., Ros, R. C., Sulaiman, N. F., Nordin, R. C., & Yuan, L. Z. (2014). Positive impact of smart phone application: WhatsApp and Facebook for online business. *IJSTR*, *4*, 1–4.

Jonathan, K. J. (1998). Internet Addiction on Campus: The Vulnerability of College Students. *Cyberpsychology & Behavior*, *1*(1). doi:10.1089/cpb.1998.1.11

Jumoke, S., Oloruntoba, S. A., & Blessing, O. (2015). Analysis of mobile phone impact on student academic performance in tertiary institution. *IJAERT*, *5*, 361–367.

Kačániová, M. Z. B. (2016). Emotional aspects of Facebook textual posts a framework for marketing research. *European Journal of Science and Theology*, *12*(6).

Kasahara, G. M. (2017). *Gender Differences in Social Media Use and Cyberbullying in Belize.* All Theses, Dissertations, and Other Capstone Projects. 753. Retrieved from https://cornerstone.lib.mnsu.edu/etds/753

Kim, S. (2015). *14 out of 100 S. Korean teenagers addicted to Internet or smartphones.* Retrieved from http://www.koreatimesus.com/14-out-of-100-s-korean-teenagers-addicted-to-internet-or-smartphones/

Medenica, S., Račić, M., & Joksimović, V. (2015). Internet and computer addiction: "new age" disease of the 21st century. *Biomedical Research*, *9*(1). doi:10.7251/bii1501069m

Mihajlov, L., & Vejmelka, L. (2017). Internet addiction: A review of the first twenty years. *Psychiatria Danubina*, *29*(3), 260–272. doi:10.24869/psyd.2017.260 PMID:28949307

Northrup, J. C., Lapierre, C., Kirk, J., & Rae, C. (2015). The Internet Process Addiction Test: Screening for Addictions to Processes Facilitated by the Internet. *Behavioral Science*, *5*(3), 341–352. doi:10.3390/bs5030341 PMID:26226007

Przybylski, A. K., Murayama, K., DeHaan, C. R., & Gladwell, V. (2013, July). Motivational, emotional, and behavioral correlates of fear of missing out. *Computers in Human Behavior*, *29*(4), 1841–1848. doi:10.1016/j.chb.2013.02.014

Saunders, M., Lewis, P., & Thornhill, A. (2007). *Research Methods for Business Students.* Harlow, UK: Pearson Education.

Shao, Y., Zheng, T., & Wang, Y. (2018). Internet addiction detection rate among college students in the People's Republic of China: A meta-analysis in Child Adolescent *Psychiatry. Mental Health*, *12*, 25. PMID:29849754

Song, I., Larose, R., Eastin, M. S., & Lin, C. A. (2004). Internet Gratifications and Internet Addiction: On the Uses and Abuses of New Media. *Cyberpsychology & Behavior*, *7*(4), 384–394. doi:10.1089/cpb.2004.7.384 PMID:15331025

Tomczyk, T. (2015). Addiction to new media among youth — Attempt to characterize the phenomenon. *Debata Edukacyjna, 6.*

Turkle, S. (2012). *Alone together: Why we expect more from technology and less from each other.* New York: Basic Books.

Walter Thompson, J. (2012). *Fear of Missing Out (FOMO).* Retrieved from https://web.archive.org/web/20150626125816/http:/www.jwtintelligence.com/wp-content/uploads/2012/03/F_JWT_FOMO-update_3.21.12.pdf

Widyanto, L., & McMurran, M. (2004). The Psychometric Properties of the Internet Addiction Test. *Cyberpsychology & Behavior, 7*(4), 443–450. doi:10.1089/cpb.2004.7.443 PMID:15331031

Wortham, J. (2011). Feel like a wall flower? Maybe it's your Facebook wall. *The New York Times*. Retrieved from https://www.nytimes.com/2011/04/10/business/10ping.html

Young, K. S. (2007). Cognitive behavior therapy with internet addicts: Treatment outcomes and implications. *Cyberpsychology & Behavior, 10*(5), 671–679. doi:10.1089/cpb.2007.9971 PMID:17927535

Compilation of References

Abedalaziz, N., Jamaluddin, S., & Leng, C. H. (2013). Measuring attitudes toward computer and internet usage among postgraduate students in Malaysia. *Turkish Online Journal of Educational Technology, 12*(2), 200–216.

Abel, J. P., Buff, C. L., & Burr, S. A. (2016). Social media and the fear of missing out: Scale development and assessment. *Journal of Business & Economics Research, 14*(1), 33. doi:10.19030/jber.v14i1.9554

Accenture. (2018). *California Dreaming*. Retrieved from https://www.accenture.com/us-en/insight-outlook-california-dreaming-corporate-culture-silicon-valley

Adjin, D., & Williams, I. (2012). Comparative analysis between WiMAX and Fibre Optics Backhaul Network Depolyment in Developing countries- The case of Ghana. *29th World Wireless Research Forum Meeting.*

Aesaert, K., & van Braak, J. (2015). Gender and socioeconomic related differences in performance based ICT competences. *Computers & Education, 84*, 8–25. doi:10.1016/j.compedu.2014.12.017

Agency, Turkish employment. (2018). Retrieved May 27, 2018, from http://www.iskur.gov.tr/en-us/corporateprofile/institution.aspx

Aifan, H.A. (2016). Gender differences in terms of the experiences that Saudi Students have with social media technologies. *Global Advanced Research Journal of Educational Research and Review, 5*(5), 71-73,

Ainley, J., Fraillon, J., & Freeman, C. (2007). *National assessment program: ICT literacy years 6 & 10 report 2005.* MCEETYA.

Akça, E. B. (2016). The Different Approaches to Digital Divide in the Concept of Gender Equality and It's Dimentions. Toplumsalcinsiyet eşitliği perspektifinden dijital bölünme ve farkli yaklaşimlar. doi:10.21645/intermedia.2017.16

Akerlof, G. A., & Kranton, R. E. (2005). Identity and the economics of organizations. *The Journal of Economic Perspectives, 19*(1), 9–32. doi:10.1257/0895330053147930

Akhter, N. (2013, October 10). Relationship between Internet Addiction and Academic Performance among University. *Undergraduates in Academic Journals, 8*(19), 1793–1796.

Akinsowon, O. A., & Osisanwo, F. Y. (2014). Enhancing Interest in Sciences, Technology and Mathematics (STEM) for the Nigerian Female Folk. *International Journal of Information Science, 4*(1), 8–12. doi:10.5923/j.ijis.20140401.02

Akman, I., & Mishra, A. (2010). Gender, age and income differences in internet usage among employees in organizations. *Computers in Human Behavior, 26*(3), 482–490. doi:10.1016/j.chb.2009.12.007

Akman, I., Yazici, A., Mishra, A., & Arifoglu, A. (2005). E-Government: A global view and an empirical evaluation of some attributes of citizens. *Government Information Quarterly, 22*(2), 239–257. doi:10.1016/j.giq.2004.12.001

Ak, S., Koruklu, N., & Yilmaz, Y. (2013). A study on Turkish adolescent's Internet use: Possible predictors of Internet addiction. *Cyberpsychology, Behavior, and Social Networking, 16*(3), 205–209. doi:10.1089/cyber.2012.0255 PMID:23253206

Aledhari, M., Aneja, N., Bashir, A. K., Bennett, R., Bielby, J., Hicks, H. A., . . . Wack, J. (2018, April). *Options and challenges in Providing Universal Access.* Retrieved from Internet Initiative IEEE: https://internetinitiative.ieee.org/images/files/resources/white_papers/OPTIONS-AND-CHALLENGES-IN-PROVIDING-UNIVERSAL-ACCESS-v180418.pdf

Al-Hadrawi. H. H., (2018). The Effect of Internet Addiction on the Academic Performance of Undergraduate Nursing Students, Dept. of Mental Health Nursing, College of Nursing, University of Babylon, Hillah City. *Iraq in Indian Journal of Public Health Research & Development, 9*(5).

Alkhalaf, A. M. (2018). The impact of WhatsApp use on academic achievement among Saudi medical students. Medical Teacher, 1–5.

Al-Menayes, J. J. (2015). Dimensions of social media addiction among university students in Kuwait. *PBS, 4*, 23–28. doi:10.11648/j.pbs.20150401.14

Alrasheedi, H. (2009). *Information and Communication Technology (ICT): Effects of Gender and Training among Kuwait Teachers* (PhD dissertation). Ohio University.

Alumanah, J. N. (2005). Access and use of information and communication technology for the African girl-child under cultural impediments. In *Proceedings of the international symposium on Women and ICT: creating global transformation.* Baltimore, MD: ACM.

Alzouebi, K., & Isakovic, A. (2014). Exploring learner perspective of social Media in Higher Education in a UAE Context: Experience beyond Knowledge. *Global Education Journal, 2014*(2).

Amabile, T. M. (1996). *Creativity in Context.* Boulder, CO: Westview Press.

Ameera, V. U. (2017). Wails Unheard: The Women under Khap Panchayats. *Social Sciences International Research Journal, 3*(2), 156–158.

Amoo, S. A., Hambali., & M.A. & Amoo, A.O. (2013). Students' Learning Attitudes toward Computer Studies: A Study of SchoolNet, Nigeria. In *2nd International Conference on the Transformation of Public Examination.* University of Ibadan.

Andersen, M. S. (2018). *IT-branchen hungrer efter kvinder, men de kommer ikke af sig selv.* Retrieved from https://universe.ida.dk/artikel/it-branchen-hungrer-efter-kvinder-men-de-kommer-ikke-af-sig-selv-55868/

Anderson, H. (2011). Never heard of FOMO? You're so missing out. *The Guardian.* Retrieved from https://www.theguardian.com/commentisfree/2011/apr/17/hephzibah-anderson-fomo-new-acronym

Anderson, S. (2015). *India's Gender Digital Divide: Women and Politics on Twitter.* Retrieved December 31, 2017 from http://cf.orfonline.org/wp-content/uploads/2015/12/ORFIssueBrief_108.pdf

Anderson, R. E. (1973). Consumer dissatisfaction: The effect of disconfirmed expectance on percieved product performance. *JMR, Journal of Marketing Research, 10*(1), 38–44. doi:10.2307/3149407

Andreassen, C. S., Pallesen, S., & Griffiths, M. D. (2017). The relationship between addictive use of social media, narcissism, and self-esteem: Findings from a large national survey. *Addictive Behaviors, 64*, 287–293. doi:10.1016/j.addbeh.2016.03.006 PMID:27072491

Annabi, H., & Lebovitz, S. (2018). Improving the retention of women in the IT workforce: An investigation of gender diversity interventions in the USA. *Information Systems Journal*, 1–33. doi:10.1111/isj.12182

APA. (2018, June 22). *Personality*. Retrieved from American Psychological Association: http://www.apa.org/topics/personality/

Arends-Tóth, J., & van de Vijver, F. J. (2009). Cultural differences in family, marital, and gender-role values among immigrants and majority members in the Netherlands. *International Journal of Psychology*, *44*(3), 161–169. doi:10.1080/00207590701545676 PMID:22029491

Armstrong, C. L., & McAdams, M. J. (2009). Blogs of information: How gender cues and individual motivations influence perceptions of credibility. *Journal of Computer-Mediated Communication*, *14*(3), 435–456. doi:10.1111/j.1083-6101.2009.01448.x

Arun, S., Heeks, R., & Morgan, S. (2004). *ICT initiatives, women and work in developing countries: reinforcing or changing gender inequalities in South India?* Development Enformatics Working Paper Series No:20. Institute for Development Policy and Management.

Arun, S., & Arun, T. (2002). ICTs, gender, and development: Women in software production in Kerala. *Journal of International Development*, *14*(1), 39–50. doi:10.1002/jid.866

Arya, D. (2013, May 8). *Why Are Indian Women Being Attacked on Social Media?* Retrieved December 25, 2017 from http://www.bbc.com/news/world-asia-india-22378366

Ashcraft, C., McLain, B., & Eger, E. (2016). *Women in Tech: The Facts*. Retrieved from https://www.ncwit.org/sites/default/files/resources/womenintech_facts_fullreport_05132016.pdf

Atan, H., Azli, N., Rahman, Z., & Idrus, R. (2002). Computers in distance education: Gender differences in self-perceived computer competencies. *Journal of Educational Media*, *27*(3), 123–135.

Atik, H., & Altiparmak, A. (2011). Avrupa Birligi ve Turkiye'de Bilgi Sektorunun Istihdama Katkisi. *The Journal of Knowledge Economy & Knowledge Management*, *6*, 117–126.

Atkinson, A. B. (1998). Social Exclusion, poverty and unemployment. In B. A. Atkinson & J. Hills (Eds.), *Exclusion, Employment and Opportunity* (pp. 1–20). London, UK: Centre for Analysis of Social Exclusion, London School of Economics.

Atkinson, N. L., Saperstein, S. L., & Pleis, J. (2009). Using the internet for health-related activities: Findings from a national probability sample. *Journal of Medical Internet Research*, *11*(1), e4. doi:10.2196/jmir.1035 PMID:19275980

Attar, G. A., & Sweis, R. J. (2010). The relationship between information technology adoption and job satisfaction in contracting companies. *Adoption and Job Satisfaction in Contracting Companies*, *15*, 44–63.

Augustynek, A. (2010). Computer addiction. Diagnosis, prevalence, therapy. Academic Press.

Austen, S. (2004). Gender differences in academic rank in Australian universities. *Australian Bulletin of Labour*, *30*, 113–133.

Australian Bureau of Statistics. (2017). *Australian Demographic Statistics, Dec 2017*. Retrieved from http://www.abs.gov.au/AUSSTATS/abs@.nsf/mf/3101.0

Australian Government. (2018a). *Department of Education and Training Occupational Summary Sheets, 2331 Chemical and Materials Engineers*. Retrieved from https://docs.education.gov.au/system/files/doc/other/2331_chemical_and_materials_engineers.pdf

Australian Government. (2018b). *Department of Education and Training Occupational Summary Sheets, 2332 Civil Engineering Professionals*. Retrieved from https://docs.education.gov.au/system/files/doc/other/2332_civil_engineering_professionals_0.pdf

Australian Government. (2018c). *Department of Education and Training Occupational Summary Sheets, 2334 Electronics Engineers*. Retrieved from https://docs.education.gov.au/system/files/doc/other/2334_electronics_engineers.pdf

Australian Government. (2018d). *Department of Education and Training Occupational Summary Sheets, 2335 Industrial, Mechanical and Production Engineers*. Retrieved from https://docs.education.gov.au/system/files/doc/other/2335_industrial_mechanical_and_production_engineers.pdf

Australian Government. (2018e). *Department of Education and Training Occupational Summary Sheets, 2336 Electrical Engineers*. Retrieved from https://docs.education.gov.au/system/files/doc/other/2336_mining_engineers.pdf

Australian Government. (2018f). *Department of Education and Training Occupational Summary Sheets, 2336 Mining Engineers*. Retrieved from https://docs.education.gov.au/system/files/doc/other/2336_mining_engineers.pdf

Avramov, D. (2002). *People, demography and social exclusion*. Council of Europe.

Awad, N. F., & Ragowsky, A. (2008). Establishing trust in electronic commerce through online word of mouth: An examination across genders. *Journal of Management Information Systems*, *24*(4), 101–121. doi:10.2753/MIS0742-1222240404

Awotwi, J. E. (2008). Lack of Eeual Access to ICTs by Women:an e-governance issue. In *ICEGOV '08: Proceedings of the 2nd international conference on Theory and practice of electronic governance*. ACM. 10.1145/1509096.1509190

Aypay, A. (2010). Information and communication technology (ICT) usage and achievement of Turkish students in PISA 2006. *The Turkish Online Journal of Educational Technology*, *9*(2), 116–124.

Baek, S.-G., Kim, D., Kim, M.-R., Kim, H. S., Yu, Y. L., Park, S.-H., . . . Kim, M. (2009). Assessing student ICT literacy on a national level. In T. Bastiaens, J. Dron, & C. Xin (Eds.), *Proceedings of e-learn: World conference on e-learning in corporate, government, healthcare, and higher education 2009* (pp. 2269-2275). Academic Press.

Baek, S. G., Kim, D. I., & Kim, M. R. (2009). The development of standardized ICT literacy assessment for secondary school student. *Asian Journal of Education*, *10*(1), 175–198. doi:10.15753/aje.2009.10.1.008

Bae, S., & Lee, T. (2011). Gender differences in consumers' perception of online consumer reviews. *Electronic Commerce Research*, *11*(2), 201–214. doi:10.100710660-010-9072-y

Bain, C. D., & Rice, M. L. (2006). The Influence of Gender on Attitudes, Perceptions, and Uses of Technology. *Journal of Research on Technology in Education*, *39*(2), 119–132. doi:10.1080/15391523.2006.10782476

Balaban, U. (2014). Türkiye ve Avrupa Birliği'nde sosyal içerme uygulamaları: 2000'li yıllara ilişkin karşılaştırmalı bir değerlendirme. *Mülkiye Dergisi*, *38*(1), 103–149.

Baller, S. D. (2016). *The Global Information Technology Report*. Innovating in the Digital Economy. Retrieved March 15, 2018, from http://www3.weforum.org/docs/GITR2016/WEF_GITR_Full_Report.pdf

Banco Central de Chile. (2017). *Statistics Database: National Accounts*. Retrieved from http://si3.bcentral.cl/Siete/secure/cuadros/arboles.aspx

Bandura, A., Barbaranelli, C., Caprana, C. V., & Pastorelli, C. (2001). Self-efficacy beliefs as shapers of children's aspirations and career trajectories. *Child Development*, *72*(1), 187–206. doi:10.1111/1467-8624.00273 PMID:11280478

Barhoumi, C., (2015). The Effectiveness of WhatsApp Mobile Learning Activities Guided by Activity Theory on Students' Knowledge Management. *Contemporary Educational Technology*, *6*(3), 221-238.

Barkatsas, A. N. (2012). Students' Attitudes, Engagement and Confidence in Mathematics and Statistics Learning: ICT, Gender, and Equity Dimensions. Academic Press.

Baron-Cohen, S., Knickmeyer, R. C., & Belmonte, M. K. (2005). Sex differences in the brain: Implications for explaining autism. *Science, 310*(5749), 819–823. doi:10.1126cience.1115455 PMID:16272115

Baumann, E., Czerwinski, F., & Reifegerste, D. (2017). Gender-specific determinants and patterns of online health information seeking: Results from a representative German health survey. *Journal of Medical Internet Research, 19*(4), e92. doi:10.2196/jmir.6668 PMID:28377367

Beddoes, K. (2016). Selling Policy Short? Faculty Perspectives on the Role of Policy in Addressing Women's Underrepresentation in Engineering Education. *Studies in Higher Education, 43*(9), 1561–1572. doi:10.1080/03075079.2016.1266610

Behera, D. K. (2013). Dams, development and the exclusion of indigenous groups: a case from Odisha. In U. Skoda, K. B. Nielsen, & M. Q. Fibiger (Eds.), *Navigating social exclusion and inclusion in contemporary India and beyond: structures, agents, practices* (pp. 167–187). London, UK: Anthem Press.

Belanger, F., & Carter, L. (2008). Trust and risk in e-government adoption. *The Journal of Strategic Information Systems, 17*(2), 165–176. doi:10.1016/j.jsis.2007.12.002

Belanger, F., & Carter, L. (2009). The impact of the digital divide on e-government use. *Communications of the ACM, 52*(4), 132–135. doi:10.1145/1498765.1498801

Bellman, E., & Malhotra, A. (2016, October 13). *Why the Vast Majority of Women in India Will Never Own a Smartphone*. Retrieved January 1, 2018 from https://www.wsj.com/articles/why-the-vast-majority-of-women-in-india-will-never-own-a-smartphone-1476351001

Bhattacharya, A. (2016, September 7). *Facebook has a massive gender divide in India*. Retrieved January 1, 2018 from https://qz.com/775470/facebook-fb-has-a-massive-gender-divide-in-india/

Bhattacharya, A. (2017, April 26). *Rural Indian Women Are Lagging Far behind Their Urban Counterparts in Mobile Phone Usage*. Retrieved December 28, 2017 from https://qz.com/969565/rural-indian-women-are-lagging-far-behind-their-urban-counterparts-in-mobile-phone-usage/

Bhattacherjee, A. (2001). Understanding information systems continuance: An expectation-confirmation model. *MIS Quaterly, 25*(3), 351–370. doi:10.2307/3250921

Bidmon, S., & Terlutter, R. (2015). Gender differences in searching for health information on the internet and the virtual patient-physician relationship in Germany: Exploratory results on how men and women differ and why. *Journal of Medical Internet Research, 17*(6), e156. doi:10.2196/jmir.4127 PMID:26099325

Biery, M. E. (2017). *These Are The 10 Most Profitable Industries in 2017*. Retrieved from https://www.forbes.com/sites/sageworks/2017/08/06/these-are-the-10-most-profitable-industries/

Bilgel-Asici, T., & Kocak-Usluel, Y. (2013). Sayisal ucurumun universite ogrencilerinin demografik ozelliklerine gore incelenmesi. *Hacettepe Universitesi Egitim Fakultesi Dergisi, 44*, 73–84.

Bimber, B. (1999). The internet and citizen communication with government: Does the medium matter? *Political Communication, 16*(4), 409–428. doi:10.1080/105846099198569

Birru, M. S., Monaco, V. M., Charles, L., Drew, H., Njie, V., Bierria, T., ... Steinman, R. A. (2004). Internet Usage by Low-Literacy Adults Seeking Health Information: An Observational Analysis. *Journal of Medical Internet Research, 6*(3), e25. doi:10.2196/jmir.6.3.e25 PMID:15471751

Bivens, R., & Haimson, O. L. (2016). *Baking Gender Into Social Media Design: How Platforms Shape Categories for Users and Advertisers*. Retrieved from http://journals.sagepub.com/doi/pdf/10.1177/2056305116672486

Boden, M. A. (2011). Creativity and artificial intelligence. *Artificial Intelligence*, *103*(1-2), 347–356. doi:10.1016/S0004-3702(98)00055-1

Bøe, M. V., & Henriksen, E. K. (2015). Expectancy-Value Perspectives on Choice of Science and Technology Education in Late-Modern Societies. In Late-Modern Societies. In E. Henriksen, J. Dillon, & J. Ryder (Eds.), *Understanding Student Participation and Choice in Science and Technology Education*. Dordrecht: Springer.

Boneva, B., Kraut, R., & Frohlich, D. (2001). Using e-mail for personal relationships: The difference gender makes. *The American Behavioral Scientist*, *45*(3), 530–549. doi:10.1177/00027640121957204

Borthakur, A. C. (2016). *Women in STEM; Technology, career pathways and the gender pay gap*. London: Designed and produced by The Creative Studio at Deloitte. Retrieved February 15, 2018, from https://www.itu.int/en/ITU-D/Digital-Inclusion/Women-and-Girls/Girls-in-ICT-Portal/Documents/deloitte-uk-women-in-stem-pay-gap-2016.pdf

Bradford, L. (2018). *15 of the Most Powerful Women in Tech*. Retrieved October 3, 2018 from https://www.thebalancecareers.com/powerful-women-in-tech-2071172

Broadband Commission. (2017). *The state of Broadband: Broadband catalyzing sustainable development*. Broadband Commission.

Broadley, K. (2015). Entrenched gendered pathways in science, technology, engineering and mathematics: Engaging girls through collaborative career development. *Australian Journal of Career Development*, *24*(1), 27–38. doi:10.1177/1038416214559548

Brosnan, M. (1998). The role of psychological gender in the computer-related attitudes and attainments of primary school children (aged 6–11). *Computers & Education*, *30*(3–4), 203–208. doi:10.1016/S0360-1315(97)00070-5

Brown, A. D. (2010). Social media: A new frontier in reflective practice. *Medical Education*, *44*(8), 744–745. doi:10.1111/j.1365-2923.2010.03729.x PMID:20633213

Brunel, F. F., & Nelson, M. R. (2000). Explaining gendered responses to "help-self" and "help-others" charity ad appeals: The mediating role of world-views. *Journal of Advertising*, *29*(3), 15–28. doi:10.1080/00913367.2000.10673614

Buabeng-Andoh, C. (2014). Investigating students' pedagogical use of ICT in learning in Ghanaian secondary schools. *British Education Studies Association*, *6*(2), 44–53.

Bureau of Labor Statistics. (2011). *Educational Attainment of Women in the Labor Force, 1970–2010*. Retrieved September 25, 2018 from https://www.bls.gov/opub/ted/2011/ted_20111229.htm

Bureau of Labor Statistics. (2018). *Employed Persons by Detailed Occupation, Sex, Race, and Hispanic or Latino Ethnicity*. Retrieved from https://www.bls.gov/cps/cpsaat11.htm

Calvani, A., Fini, A., Ranieri, M., & Picci, P. (2012). Are young generations in secondary school digitally competent? A study on Italian teenagers. *Computers & Education*, *58*(2), 797–807. doi:10.1016/j.compedu.2011.10.004

Capano. (2010). *Social Networking Usage and Grades Among College students*. Whittemore School of Business and Economics. Retrieved from http://www.unh.edu/news/docs/UNHsocialmedia.pdf

Carmichael, S. G. (2015). *Why 'Network More' Is Bad Advice for Women*. Retrieved from https://hbr.org/2015/02/why-network-more-is-bad-advice-for-women

Carter, L., & Belanger, F. (2005). The utilization of e-government services: Citizen trust, innovation and acceptance factors. *Information Systems Journal*, *15*(1), 5–25. doi:10.1111/j.1365-2575.2005.00183.x

Cavas, B., Cavas, P., Karaoglan, B., & Kisla, T. (2009). A study on science teachers' attitudes toward information and communication technologies in Education. *TOJET*, (8), 2.

Cayhan, B. E. (2008). Implementing E-government in Turkey: A Comparison of Online Public Service Delivery in Turkey and the European Union. *The Electronic Journal on Information Systems in Developing Countries*, *35*(1), 1–11. doi:10.1002/j.1681-4835.2008.tb00245.x

Cech, E., Rubineau, B., Silbey, S., & Seron, C. (2011). Professional role confidence and gendered persistence in engineering. *American Sociological Review*, *76*(5), 641–666. doi:10.1177/0003122411420815

Center for Talent Innovation - Research & Insights. (n.d.). Accessed September 25, 2018, http://www.talentinnovation.org/publication.cfm?publication=1420

Cgggohoon, J. M., & Aspray, W. (2006). A critical review of the research on women's participation in postsecondary computing education. In *By the Numbers*. Boulder, CO: NCWIT. Retrieved November 7, 2017, from http://www.ncwit.org/resources/numbers

Chaffey, D. (2018, March 28). *Global social media research summary 2018*. Retrieved from Smart Insight: https://www.smartinsights.com/social-media-marketing/social-media-strategy/new-global-social-media-research/

Chairperson, K. A. N. (2005-2009). *UN Gender Strategy Framework in the Philippines: Sustaining Women's Human Rights*. Makati City: Published by the United Nations System in The Philippines. Retrieved 6 11, 2018, from https://www.unicef.org/philippines/Gender_Strategy(1).pdf

Chai, S., Das, S., & Rao, H. R. (2011). Factors affecting bloggers' knowledge sharing: An investigation across gender. *Journal of Management Information Systems*, *28*(3), 309–342. doi:10.2753/MIS0742-1222280309

Chang, E. (2018). *Brotopia: Breaking Up the Boys' Club of Silicon Valley*. New York, NY: Portfolio.

Chang, M. K., & Man Law, S. P. (2008). Factor structure for Young's Internet Addiction Test: A Confirmatory study. *Computers in Human Behavior*, *24*(6), 2597–2619. doi:10.1016/j.chb.2008.03.001

Chan, M. (2011). Shyness, sociability, and the role of media synchronicity in the use of computer-mediated communication for interpersonal communication. *Asian Journal of Psychology*, *14*(1), 84–90.

Chaturvedi, H. (2017, May 3). *Mathura Village to Fine Girls Using Cell Phones*. Retrieved December 24, 2017 from http://www.hindustantimes.com/india-news/mathura-village-to-fine-girls-using-cell-phones/story-6xmL3kYEKqEE-AFG0YNbp8M.html

Chaudhary, R., & Verick, S. (2014). *Female Labour Force Participation in India and Beyond*. Retrieved December 29, 2017 from http://www.ilo.org/wcmsp5/groups/public/@asia/@ro-bangkok/@sro-new_delhi/documents/publication/wcms_324621.pdf

Chauhan, A. (2016, February 19). *Panchayat Bans Mobile Phones Among Girls*. Retrieved December 24, 2017 from https://timesofindia.indiatimes.com/city/agra/Panchayat-bans-mobile-phones-among-girls/articleshow/51060339.cms

Cheek, J. M., & Buss, A. H. (1981). Shyness and Sociability. *Journal of Personality and Social Psychology*, *41*(2), 330–339. doi:10.1037/0022-3514.41.2.330

Chen, X., Carpenter, D., Li, X., Chen, C., & Hung, S. (2018). Why do Individuals Continue Using Mobile Payments - A Qualitative Study in China. In *HICSS Conference*. University of Hawaii at Manoa. Retrieved 05 15, 2018, from https://scholarspace.manoa.hawaii.edu/handle/10125/50067

Chen, X., Sin, S. C. J., Theng, Y. L., & Lee, C. S. (2015). Why students share misinformation on social media: Motivation, gender, and study-level differences. *Journal of Academic Librarianship*, *41*(5), 583–592. doi:10.1016/j.acalib.2015.07.003

Cherayi, S., & Jose, J. P. (2016). Empowerment and social inclusion of Muslim women: Towards a new conceptual model. *Journal of Rural Studies*, *45*, 243–251. doi:10.1016/j.jrurstud.2016.04.003

Cheryan, S., Master, A., & Meltzoff, A. (2015). Cultural stereotypes as gatekeepers: Increasing girls' interest in computer science and engineering by diversifying stereotypes. *Frontiers in Psychology*, 6. PMID:25717308

Chinn, M. D., & Fairlie, R. W. (2007). The determinants of the global digital divide: A cross-country analysis of computer and internet penetration. *Oxford Economic Papers*, *59*(1), 16–44. doi:10.1093/oep/gpl024

Chou, C., & Hsiao, M. (2000). Internet addiction, usage, gratifications, and pleasure experience: The Taiwan College Student's case. *Comput. Educ*, *35*(1), 65–80. doi:10.1016/S0360-1315(00)00019-1

Choudrie, J., & Dwivedi, Y. (2005). A survey of citizens' awareness and adoption of e-government initiatives, the 'Government Gateway': A United Kingdom perspective. eGovernment Workshop'05 (eGOV05).

Chou, S. Y., Kiser, A. I., & Rodriguez, E. L. (2012). An expectation confirmation perspective of medical tourism. *Journal of Service Science Research*, *4*(2), 299–318. doi:10.100712927-012-0012-3

Christoph, G., Goldhammer, F., Zylka, J., & Hartig, J. (2015). Adolescents' computer performance: The role of self-concept and motivational aspects. *Computers & Education*, *81*, 1–12. doi:10.1016/j.compedu.2014.09.004

Christov-Moore, L., Simpson, E. A., Coudé, G., Grigaityte, K., Iacoboni, M., & Ferrari, P. F. (2014). Empathy: Gender effects in brain and behavior. *Neuroscience and Biobehavioral Reviews*, *46*, 604–627. doi:10.1016/j.neubiorev.2014.09.001 PMID:25236781

Cipriano, A. (2008). Jerarquización Académica en Ingeniería, Pontificia Universidad Católica de Chile. *Theoria*, *17*(2), 15–25.

Clark, J., Codd, S. L., Des Jardins, A. C., Foreman, C. M., Gunnink, B. W., Plumb, C., & Stocker, K. R. (2015). *Peer Mentoring Program: Providing Early Intervention and Support to Improve Retention and Success of Women in Engineering, Computer Science, and Physics: American Society for Engineering Education.* Retrieved from https://www.asee.org/public/conferences/56/papers/12642/view

Claro, M., Preiss, D. D., San Martín, E., Jara, I., Hinostroza, J. E., Valenzuela, S., ... Nussbaum, M. (2012). Assessment of 21st century ICT skills in Chile: Test design and results from high school level students. *Computers & Education*, *59*(3), 1042–1053. doi:10.1016/j.compedu.2012.04.004

Clinton, A. & Wellington. (2013). A Theoretical Framework of Users' satisfaction/Dissatisfaction Theories and models. *2nd International Conference on Arts, Behavioral Sciences and Economics Issues (ICABSEI'2013).*

Cohen, R. (2018). Afterword: Patterns of Inclusion and Exclusion in African Societies. In L. Landau (Ed.), *Forging African Communities.Global Diversities* (pp. 303–311). London: Palgrave Macmillan. doi:10.1057/978-1-137-58194-5_13

Colesca, S. E., & Dobrica, L. (2008). Adoption and use of e-government services: The case of Romania. *Journal of Applied Research and Technology*, *6*(3), 204–217.

Collis, B. A., & Williams, R. L. (1987). Differences in adolescents' attitudes toward computers and selected school subjects. *Journal of Educational Computing Research*, *8*, 17–27.

CompTIA. (2018). *IT Industry Outlook 2018*. Retrieved from https://www.comptia.org/resources/it-industry-trends-analysis#section5

CompTIA. (n.d.). *Advancing Women in Technology*. Retrieved from https://www.comptia.org/communities/advancing-women-in-it

Comunidad Mujer. (2016). *Informe GET: Género, Educación y Trabajo. La brecha persistente. Primer estudio sobre la desigualdad de género en el ciclo de vida. Una revisión de los últimos 25 años*. Retrieved from http://www.informeget.cl/wp-content/uploads/2016/08/Informe-GET-Final.pdf

Comunidad Mujer. (2017). *Mujer y trabajo: Brecha de género en STEM, la ausencia de mujeres en Ingeniería y Matemáticas*. Retrieved from http://www.comunidadmujer.cl/biblioteca-publicaciones/wp-content/uploads/2017/12/BOLETIN-42-DIC-2017-url_vf.pdf

Conclaves, T. A., & Rosondo, D. (2016). New Communications Technologies: Women's Rights Violations, Limits on Freedom of Expression, and an Alternative ways to promote Human rights. In J. Wilson & N. D. Gapsiso (Eds.), *Overcoming gender inequalities through technology integration* (pp. 144–162). Hershey, PA: IGI.

Conexion Ingenieros. (2016). *Estudio de Sueldos de Ingenieros 2016 y Mercado Laboral*. Retrieved from http://conexioningenieros.com/wp-content/uploads/2016/11/Estudio-de-Sueldos-Conexi%C3%B3n-Ingenieros-2016.pdf

Conger, K. (2017). *Exclusive: Here's The Full 10-Page Anti-Diversity Screed Circulating Internally at Google* [Updated]. Retrieved September 25, 2018 from https://gizmodo.com/exclusive-heres-the-full-10-page-anti-diversity-screed-1797564320

Cook, D. A., Levinson, A. J., Garside, S., Dupras, D. M., Erwin, P. J., & Montori, V. M. (2008). Internet-based learning in the health professions, a meta-analysis. *Journal of the American Medical Association*, *300*(10), 1181–1196. doi:10.1001/jama.300.10.1181 PMID:18780847

Cooper, J. (2006). The digital divide: The special case of gender. *Journal of Computer Assisted Learning*, *22*(5), 320–334. doi:10.1111/j.1365-2729.2006.00185.x

Cooper, J., & Weaver, K. D. (2003). *Gender and computers: Understanding the digital divide*. Psychology Press.

Correa, T., Hinsley, A. M., Bachmann, I., & Gil de Zuniga, H. (2013). Personality and Social Media Use. In E. Li, S. Loh, C. Evans, & F. Lorenzi (Eds.), *Social Media to Engage Consumers* (pp. 41–61). Hershey, PA: IGI Global.

Costa, P. T. Jr, McCrae, R. R., & Dye, D. A. (1991). Facet Scales for Agreeableness and Conscientiousness: A Revision of the NEO Personality Inventory. *Personality and Individual Differences*, *12*(9), 887–898. doi:10.1016/0191-8869(91)90177-D

Costa, P. T. Jr, Terracciano, A., & McCrae, R. R. (2001). Gender differences in personality traits across cultures: Robust and surprising findings. *Journal of Personality and Social Psychology*, *81*(2), 322–331. doi:10.1037/0022-3514.81.2.322 PMID:11519935

Costa, P. T., & McCrae, R. R. (1980). Influence of Extraversion and Neuroticism of Subjective well-Being: Happy and Unhappy People. *Journal of Personality and Social Psychology*, *38*(4), 668–678. doi:10.1037/0022-3514.38.4.668 PMID:7381680

Council of Euproean Professional Informatics Societies. (n.d.). *Europe's Widening ICT Skills Gap*. Retrieved from https://www.cepis.org/media/CEPISe-CFBackgrounder1.pdf

Cradler, J., McNabb, M., Freeman, M., & Burchett, R. (2002). How does technology influence student learning? *Learning and Leading with Technology*, *29*(8), 46–49.

Creamer, E. G., Lee, S., & Meszaros, P. S. (2006). *Factors Associated With Women's Interest In Computing Fields*. Research paper presented at the Association for the Study of Engineering Education (ASEE), Chicago, IL.

Cunningham, C. (2007). *Linking STEM and Communication Technology Research: A Research Agenda for Technology and Gender Equality. Paper presented at the annual meeting of the NCA 93rd Annual Convention*, Chicago, IL. Retrieved from http://www.allacademic.com/meta/p193877

Cussó, R. (2007). *Tecnologia: gènere i professió* [Technology: gender and profession]. Departament d'Educació de la Generalitat de Cataluña.

Cussó-Calabuig, R., Carrera Farran, X., & Bosch-Capblanch, X. (2017). Are boys and girls still digitally differentiated? The case of Catalonian teenagers. *Journal of Information Technology Education: Research, 16*, 411-435. https://repositori.udl.cat/bitstream/handle/10459.1/62324/026246.pdf?sequence=1 doi:Retrieved from

Cyberstates. (n.d.). *Data Appendix*. Retrieved from https://www.cyberstates.org/

Cyr, D., & Bonanni, C. (2005). Gender and website design in e-business. *International Journal of Electronic Business*, *3*(6), 565–582. doi:10.1504/IJEB.2005.008536

Daly, M. (1989). *Women and poverty*. Dublin: Attic Press.

Damore, J. (2017). *Google's Ideological Echo Chamber*. Retrieved from https://assets.documentcloud.org/documents/3914586/Googles-Ideological-Echo-Chamber.pdf

Das, S., Jain-Chandra, S., Kochhar, K., & Kumar, N. (2015). *Women Workers in India: Why So Few Among So Many?* Retrieved December 29, 2017 from https://www.imf.org/external/pubs/ft/wp/2015/wp1555.pdf

Daud, M. Y., & Zakaria, E. (2012). Web 2.0 application to cultivate creativity in ICT literacy. *Procedia: Social and Behavioral Sciences*, *59*, 459–466. doi:10.1016/j.sbspro.2012.09.301

Dave, H. (2016, February 18). *Gujarat Village Bans Mobile Phones for Unmarried Women*. Retrieved December 24, 2017 from http://www.hindustantimes.com/india/gujarat-village-bans-mobile-phones-for-unmarried-women/story-iziKwjYckgmOOP8ZRBNn3K.html

Davis, F. (1985). *A technology Acceptance Model for emperically testing new end-user Information Systems: Theory and results*. Cambridge, MA: MIT Sloan School of Management.

Davis, R., Smith, S. D., & Lang, B. U. (2017). A comparison of online and offline gender and goal directed shopping online. *Journal of Retailing and Consumer Services*, *38*, 118–125. doi:10.1016/j.jretconser.2017.02.011

De Wit, K., Heerwegh, D., & Verhoeven, J. C. (2014). Can openness to ICT and scientific research predict the ICT skills and ICT use of bachelor's students? *Computers & Education*, *78*, 397–413. doi:10.1016/j.compedu.2014.07.003

Dedeoglu, S. (2009). Eşitlik mi ayrımcılık mı? Türkiye'de sosyal devlet, cinsiyet eşitliği politikaları ve kadın istihdamı. *Çalışma ve Toplum, 2*(21), 41-54.

Deloitte. (2012). *Information and Communication Technologies on the Road to 2023*. Uluslararasi Yatirimcilar Dernegi (YASED).

Deloitte. (2016). *Women in STEM Technology, career pathways and the gender pay gap*. Deloitte.

DeLong, T. J., Gabarro, J. J., & Lees, R. J. (2008). *Why Mentoring Matters in a Hypercompetitive World.* Retrieved from https://hbr.org/2008/01/why-mentoring-matters-in-a-hypercompetitive-world

Department of Education and Science. (2008). *ICT in Schools: Inspectorate Evaluation Studies.* Department of Education and Science.

Desvaux, G. D. S.-S. (2017). *Women Matter Time to accelerate. Ten years of insights into.* McKinsey & Company. Retrieved January 5, 2018, from https://www.mckinsey.com/global-themes/gender-equality

Dettingen, G. (1995). Cross-cultural perspectives on self-efficacy. In A. Bandura (Ed.), *Self-efficacy in changing societies* (pp. 169–176). New York: Cambridge University Press. doi:10.1017/CBO9780511527692.007

Devaraj, S., Easley, R. F., & Crant, J. M. (2008). ResearcResearch note—How Does Personality Matter? Relating the Five-Factor Model to Technology Acceptance and Use. *Information Systems Research, 19*(1), 93–105. doi:10.1287/isre.1070.0153

Devillard-Hoellinger, S. G. (2016). *Women Matter/Turkey's potential for the future: Women in Business.* Istanbul: McKinsey & Company and TUSIAD. Retrieved January 20, 2018, from http://www.mckinsey.com.tr/arastirma-ve-yayinlarimiz/McKinseyWomenMatterTurkiye2016RaporSonuclariSunumu.pdf

Dhillon, A. (2016, December 5). *Women Tap into New Roles as Mobile Internet Scheme Targets Rural India.* Retrieved June 20, 2018 from https://www.theguardian.com/global-development/2016/dec/05/india-women-mobile-internet-scheme-rural-digital-literacy

DigitalWatch Observatory. (2017). *Fighting Online Gender-based Violence Supports Freedom of Expression.* Retrieved January 20, 2018 from https://dig.watch/updates/fighting-online-gender-based-violence-supports-freedom-expression

Dimaggio, P., Hargittai, E., Celeste, C., & Shafer, S. (2004). From unequal access to differentiated use: A literature review and agenda for research on digital inequality. In Social Inequality (pp. 355-400). New York: Russell Sage Foundation.

Dimitrova, D. V., & Chen, Y. (2006). Profiling the adopters of e-government information and services: The influence of psychological characteristics, civicmindedness, and information channels. *Social Science Computer Review, 24*(2), 171–188. doi:10.1177/0894439305281517

Djamila, O. K. (2016). *First internet addiction rehab clinic opens in Algeria.* Retrieved from https://www.aljazeera.com/news/2016/10/internet-addiction-rehab-clinic-opens-algeria-161009055354223.html

Dlodlo, N. (2009). Access to ICT education for girls and women in rural South Africa: A case study. *Technology in Society, 31*(2), 168–175. doi:10.1016/j.techsoc.2009.03.003

Doepke, M. T. (2011, April). *Does Female Empowerment Promote Economic Development?* Bonn, Germany: IZA Discussion Paper No. 5637. Retrieved January 10, 2018, from http://ftp.iza.org/dp5637.pdf

Doğan, B. B. (2014). Problems of Women Employment in TRC2 Region and Solution. *International Journal of Social and Economic Sciences, 4*(2), 91–106. Retrieved from http://dergipark.gov.tr/download/article-file/403287

Dong, B., & Sivakumar, K. (2017). Customer participation in services: Domain, scope, and boundaries. *Journal of the Academy of Marketing Science, 45*(6), 944–965. doi:10.100711747-017-0524-y

Dong, T., Cheng, N., & Wu, Y. (2014). A study of the social networking website service in digital content industries: The Facebook case in Taiwan. *Computers in Human Behavior, 30,* 708–714. doi:10.1016/j.chb.2013.07.037

Doring, N., Hellwig, K., & Klimsa, P. (2005). Mobile communication among German youth. In K. Nyiri (Ed.), A sense of place: The global and the local in mobile communication (pp. 209-217). Vienna, Austria: Passagen Verlag.

Dreze, J., & Sen, A. (2002). *India: Development and Participation*. Oxford, UK: Oxford University Press. doi:10.1093/acprof:oso/9780199257492.001.0001

Drury, M. (2011). Women technology leaders: Gender issues in higher education information technology. *NASPA Journal About Women in Higher Education*, *4*(1), 96–123. doi:10.2202/1940-7890.1054

Dube, S., Dube, M., & Turan, A. (2015). Information technology in Turkey: Creating high-skill jobs along with more unemployed highly-educated workers? *Telecommunications Policy*, *39*(10), 811–829. doi:10.1016/j.telpol.2015.07.001

Durndell, A., & Haag, Z. (2002). Computer self-efficacy, computer anxiety, attitudes towards the Internet and reported experience with the Internet, by gender, in an East European sample. *Computers in Human Behavior*, *18*(5), 521–535. doi:10.1016/S0747-5632(02)00006-7

Dutt, B. (2017, May 12). *Let's Talk About Trolls: Online Abuse A Weapon to Silence Women*. Retrieved December 25, 2017 from http://www.hindustantimes.com/india-news/let-s-talk-about-trolls-trolling-is-a-weapon-to-silence-women-barkha-dutt/story-A9X3fAuRwZiwVrhYQnKbYL.html

Eagly, A. H., & Wood, W. (1991). Explaining sex differences in social behavior: A meta-analytic perspective. *Personality and Social Psychology Bulletin*, *17*(3), 306–315. doi:10.1177/0146167291173011

Eagly, A. H., & Wood, W. (1999). The origins of sex differences in human behavior: Evolved dispositions versus social roles. *The American Psychologist*, *54*(6), 408–423. doi:10.1037/0003-066X.54.6.408

Eccles, J. S. (2007). Where Are All the Women? Gender Differences in Participation. In Why aren't more Women in science? Top researchers debate evidence. American Psychological Association.

Eccles, J. S. (1994). Understanding Women's Educational And Occupational Choices: Applying the Eccles et al. Model of Achievement-Related Choices. *Psychology of Women Quarterly*, *18*(4), 585–609. doi:10.1111/j.1471-6402.1994.tb01049.x

Eccles, J. S., Adler, T. F., Futterman, R., Goff, S. B., Kaczala, C. M., & Meece, J. L. (1983). Expectancies, values and academic behaviours. In J. T. Spence (Ed.), *Achievement and achievement motivation* (pp. 75–146). San Francisco, CA: W. H. Freeman.

Eccles, J. S., & Wigfield, A. (2002). Motivational beliefs, values and goals. *Annual Review of Psychology*, *53*(1), 109–132. doi:10.1146/annurev.psych.53.100901.135153 PMID:11752481

Ecevit, Y. (2010). *İşgücü Piyasasında Toplumsal Cinsiyet Eşitliği El Kitabı*. Ankara: Pelin Ofset. Retrieved February 15, 2018, from https://statik.iskur.gov.tr/tr/proje_protokol/kad_ist_des_BC_kitapcik_18022010_sm.pdf

Economides, A. A., & Grousopoulou, A. (2008). Use of mobile phones by male and female Greek students. *International Journal of Mobile Communications*, *6*(6), 729–749. doi:10.1504/IJMC.2008.019822

Education Council. (2015). *National STEM School Strategy, 2016-2026: A comprehensive plan for Science, Technology, Engineering and Mathematics education for Australians*. Retrieved from http://www.educationcouncil.edu.au/site/DefaultSite/filesystem/documents/National STEM School Education Strategy.pdf

Edwards, D., Pearce, J., Perkins, K., & Brown, J. (2014). *Final Report, Focus Groups for the Engineering Workforce Study, ACER*. Retrieved from http://research.acer.edu.au.ezproxy.lib.monash.edu.au/cgi/viewcontent.cgi?article=1039&context=higher_education

e-Government Gateway of Turkey. (2018). Retrieved from: https://www.turkiye.gov.tr/

Ek, S. (2013). Gender differences in health information behaviour: A Finnish population-based survey. *Health Promotion International*, *30*(3), 736–745. doi:10.1093/heapro/dat063 PMID:23985248

Else-Quest, N. M., Mineo, C. C., & Higgins, A. (2013). Maths and Sciences attitudes and achievement at the intersection of gender and ethnicity. *Psychology of Women Quarterly*, *37*(3), 293–309. doi:10.1177/0361684313480694

Embacher, K., McGloin, R., & Richards, K. (2017). When Women Give Health Advice Online, Do We Listen? The Effect of Source Sex on Credibility and Likelihood to Use Online Health Advice. *Western Journal of Communication*, 1–18. doi:10.1080/10570314.2017.1367028

Emrich, C., Livingston, M. H., & Pruner, D. (2017). *Creating a Culture of Mentorship*. Retrieved September 25, 2018 from https://www.heidrick.com/Knowledge-Center/Publication/Creating_a_culture_of_mentorship

England, P. (1992). *Comparable Worth: Theories and Evidence* (1st ed.). New Brunswick, NJ: Aldine Transaction.

Erdogdu, F., & Erdogdu, E. (2015). The impact of access to ICT, student background and school/home environment on academic success of students in Turkey: An international comparative analysis. *Computers & Education*, *82*, 26–49. doi:10.1016/j.compedu.2014.10.023

Erfanmanesh, M. (2016). Information seeking anxiety: Effects of gender, level of study and age. *Library Philosophy and Practice, 1*, 1-20.

Europa. (2013). *What is Social Inclusion*. Retrieved from European Youth Portal: http://europa.eu/youth/sk/article/39/6145_en

European Comission. (2015). *Monitoring the Digital Economy & Society 2016 – 2021*. European Commission DG Communications Networks, Content & Technology. Retrieved from http://ec.europa.eu/eurostat/documents/341889/725524/Monitoring+the+Digital+Economy+%26+Society+2016-2021/7df02d85-698a-4a87-a6b1-7994df7fbeb7

European Commission (EC). (2003). *The Role of eGovernment for Europe's Future: COM (2003)567*. Brussels: European Commission.

European Commission (EC). (2017). eGovernment in Turkey. March 2017, Edition 3.00. European Commission.

European Commission. (2013, October 3). *Digital Agenda: Bringing more women into EU digital sector would bring €9 billion annual GDP boost, EU Study show*. Retrieved from European Commission: http://europa.eu/rapid/press-release_IP-13-905_en.htm

European Commission. (2014). *ICT TRENDS 2020 - Main Trends for Information and Communication Technologies (ICT) and their Implications for e-LEADERSHIP SKILLS*. Retrieved from http://eskills-lead.eu/fileadmin/lead/reports/lead_-_technology_trends_- _august_2014_rev_sep1.pdf

European Data Journalism Network. (2018). *The ICT Sector Is Booming. But Are Women Missing Out?* Retrieved from https://www.europeandatajournalism.eu/eng/News/Data-news/The-ICT-sector-is-booming.-But-are-women-missing-out

European Union. (2017). *Report on Equality Between Women and Men in the EU. European Union*. doi:10.2838/52591

Eurostat. (2008). *NACE Rev. 2. Statistical classificationof economic activities in the European Community: Methodologies and working papers*. Luxembourg: Eurostat.

Eurostat. (2018a). *Main features of the European Union – Labour Force Survey (EU-LFS) and scope of data*. Retrieved from http://ec.europa.eu/eurostat/web/lfs/overview)

Eurostat. (2018b). *Employment and activity by sex and age: annual data*. European Union Labor Force Survey (EU-LFS). Retrieved from http://appsso.eurostat.ec.europa.eu/nui/submitViewTableAction.do

Eurostat. (2018c). *Correspondence Tables: NACE Rev.2 – ISIC Rev.4.* Retrieved from http://ec.europa.eu/eurostat/ramon/relations/index.cfm?TargetUrl=LST_LINK&StrNomRelCode=NACE%20REV.%202%20-%20ISIC%20REV.%204&StrLanguageCode=EN

Eurostat. (2018d). *Employment by sex, age and detailed economic activity.* European Union Labor Force Survey (EU-LFS). Retrieved from http://appsso.eurostat.ec.europa.eu/nui/show.do?dataset=lfsq_egan22d&lang=en

Eurostat. (2018e). *Employed ICT specialists by sex.* European Union Labor Force Survey (EU-LFS). Retrieved from http://appsso.eurostat.ec.europa.eu/nui/show.do?dataset=isoc_sks_itsps&lang=en

Eurostat. (2018f). *ICT training Reference Metadata in Euro SDMX Metadata Structure.* European Union Labor Force Survey (EU-LFS). Retrieved from http://ec.europa.eu/eurostat/cache/metadata/en/isoc_skt_esms.htm

Eurostat. (2018g). *Employed persons with ICT education by sex.* European Union Labor Force Survey (EU-LFS). Retrieved from http://appsso.eurostat.ec.europa.eu/nui/show.do?dataset=isoc_ski_itsex&lang=en

Eurostat. (2018h). *ICT specialists in employment sex.* European Union Labor Force Survey (EU-LFS). Retrieved from http://ec.europa.eu/eurostat/statistics-explained/index.php/ICT_specialists_in_employment

Eurostats. (2018). *ICT specialists in employment.* European Commission. Retrieved from http://ec.europa.eu/eurostat/statistics-explained/index.php/ICT_specialists_in_employment

Fallows, J. (2013). *The 50 Greatest Breakthroughs Since the Wheel.* Retrieved from https://www.theatlantic.com/magazine/archive/2013/11/innovations-list/309536/

Fančovičová, J., & Prokop, P. (2008). Students' Attitudes toward Computer Use in Slovakia. *Eurasia Journal of Mathematics. Science & Technology Education, 4*(3), 255–262.

Farhadi, M., Ismail, R., & Fooladi, M. (2012). *Information and Communication Technology Use and Economic Growth.* Retrieved September 25, 2018 from https://www.ncbi.nlm.nih.gov/pmc/articles/PMC3495961/

Fatehkia, M., Kashyap, R., & Weber, I. (2018). Using Facebook ad Data to track the global digital gender gap. *World Development, 107*, 189–209. doi:10.1016/j.worlddev.2018.03.007

Fauville, G., Lantz-Andersson, A., & Säljö, R. (2014). ICT tools in environmental education: Reviewing two newcomers to schools. *Environmental Education Research, 20*(2), 248–283. doi:10.1080/13504622.2013.775220

Feldman, B. (2017). *Google Cancels Meeting on Memo After Employees Fear for Safety.* Retrieved from http://nymag.com/selectall/2017/08/google-cancels-meeting-on-bad-memo.html

Fernandez-Villavicencio, N. G. (2010). Helping students become literate in a digital, networking-based society: A literature review and discussion. *The International Information & Library Review, 42*(2), 124–136. doi:10.1080/10572317.2010.10762854

Ferrari, J. R., & Guerrero, M. (2018). My dad, the deacon:" Assessing the personality of married Catholic clergy fathers as predictor of number and gender of children. *Journal of Spirituality in Mental Health, 20*(2), 185–197. doi:10.1080/19349637.2017.1374113

Filgona, J., & Sababa, L. K. (2017). Effect of Gender on Senior Secondary School Students' Academic Achievement in Geography in Ganye Educational Zone, Nigeria. *European Journal of Education Studies, 3*(4), 394–410.

Financial Express Online. (2017, May 3). *Village Panchayat Bans Mobile Phones for Girls; Threatens to Impose Rs 2,100 Fine on Violators.* Retrieved December 24, 2017 from http://www.financialexpress.com/india-news/village-panchayat-bans-mobile-phones-for-girls-threatens-to-impose-rs-2100-fine-on-violators/652483/

Firstpost. (2012, December 3). *Bihar Panchayat's Diktat: Girls Using Mobiles to be Fined!* Retrieved December 24, 2017 from http://www.firstpost.com/india/bihar-panchayats-diktat-girls-using-mobiles-to-be-fined-543124.html

Flanagin, A. J., & Metzger, M. J. (2003). The perceived credibility of personal Web page information as influenced by the sex of the source. *Computers in Human Behavior*, *19*(6), 683–701. doi:10.1016/S0747-5632(03)00021-9

Flores, S. B. (2016). *¿Por qué las mujeres no quieren ser ingenieras? Caso: alumnas de Ingeniería de Tecnología Industrial en la UPCT.* UPCT. Retrieved from http://repositorio.upct.es/bitstream/handle/10317/5786/tfg-flo-por.pdf?sequence=1&isAllowed=y

Fomsi, E. F., & Orduah, S. E. (2017). Gender Differences in the Use of ICT among Teachers in Model Primary Schools in Rivers State, Nigeria. *Brock Journal of Education*, *5*(4), 88–94.

Food and Agriculture Organization of the United Nations. (2018). *Lightening the Load: Addressing Rural Women's Work Burden and Time Poverty*. Retrieved from http://www.fao.org/gender/insights/detail/en/c/424537/

Fraillon, J., Ainley, J., Schulz, W., Friedman, T., & Gebhardt, E. (2014). *Preparing for life in a digital age - the IEA international computer and information literacy study international report*. Heidelberg, Germany: Springer International Publishing.

Fraillon, J., Ainley, J., Schulz, W., Friedman, T., & Gebhardt, E. (2014). *Preparing for life in a digital age – the IEA international computer and information literacy study, International Report*. Amsterdam: IEA.

Francese, M. (2017, August). *Wage Determination, Modern Awards, and Salary Setting*. Paper session presented at the meeting of Work and Employment Relations, Melbourne, Australia.

Frangos, C. C., & Frangos, C. C. (2009). Internet Dependence in College Students from Greece. *European Psychiatry*, *24*(Suppl 1), S419. doi:10.1016/S0924-9338(09)70652-2

French-Davies, R. (2014). Is Chile a Model for Economic Development? Santiago de Chile: Departamento de Economía de la Universidad de Chile.

Fuciua, M., & Gorski, H. (2013). Marketing Research regarding the Usage of Online Social Networking Sites by High School Students. *Procedia Economics and Finance*, *6*, 482–490. doi:10.1016/S2212-5671(13)00166-4

Gallup, Inc., & International Labour Organization (2017). *Towards A Better Future for Women and Work: Voices of Women and Men*. Retrieved December 29, 2017 from http://www.ilo.org/wcmsp5/groups/public/---dgreports/---dcomm/---publ/documents/publication/wcms_546256.pdf

Garbarino, E., & Strahilevitz, M. (2004). Gender differences in the perceived risk of buying online and the effects of receiving a site recommendation. *Journal of Business Research*, *57*(7), 768–775. doi:10.1016/S0148-2963(02)00363-6

Gascoigne, C., Parry, E., & Buchanan, D. (2015). Extreme work, gendered work? How extreme jobs and the discourse of 'personal choice' perpetuate gender inequality. *Organization*, *22*(4), 457–475. doi:10.1177/1350508415572511

Gauld, R., Goldfinch, S., & Horsburgh, S. (2010). Do they want it? Do they use it? The 'Demand-Side'of e-Government in Australia and New Zealand. *Government Information Quarterly*, *27*(2), 177–186. doi:10.1016/j.giq.2009.12.002

Gauntlett, D. (2011). *Making is Connecting, The Social Meaning of Creativity, from DIY and Knitting to Youtube and Web 2.0*. Polity Press.

Gayen, A., & Roy, M. (2018). Exploring Impact of ICT Adoption on Business Performance outcome of Indian MSMES. *International Journal of Engineering Technology Science and Research*, *5*(1), 1740-1744.

Gebhardt, E., Fraillon, J., Ainley, J., & Schulz, W. (2016). Gender Differences In computer And Information Literacy and the Use of ICT. A thematic report from the IEA International Computer and Information Literacy Study. *IEA General Assembly Meeting*, *57*, 10–13.

Geek Feminism. (n.d.a). *List of Women Executives at Tech Companies*. Retrieved October 3, 2018 from http://geekfeminism.wikia.com/wiki/List_of_women_executives_at_tech_companies

Geek Feminism. (n.d.b). *Women on Boards of Directors of Tech Companies*. Retrieved October 3, 2018 from http://geekfeminism.wikia.com/wiki/Women_on_boards_of_directors_of_tech_companies

Gefen, D., & Ridings, C. M. (2005). If you spoke as she does, sir, instead of the way you do: a sociolinguistics perspective of gender differences in virtual communities. *ACM SIGMIS Database: the DATABASE for Advances in Information Systems, 36*(2), 78-92.

Gefen, D., & Straub, D. W. (1997). Gender differences in the perception and use of e-mail: An extension to the technology acceptance model. *Management Information Systems Quarterly*, *21*(4), 389–400. doi:10.2307/249720

Genc, Y., & Cat, G. (2013). Engellilerin istihdamı ve sosyal içerme ilişkisi. *Akademik İncelemeler Dergisi*, *8*(1), 363–393.

Gender, science and technology/Report of the expert group meeting. (2010). Paris: United Nations Division for the Advancement of Women (DAW), part of UN Women with UNESCO. Retrieved from http://www.un.org/womenwatch/daw/egm/gst_2010/Final-Report-EGM-ST.pdf

Geng, L., Zhang, K., Wei, X., & Feng, X. (2017, March). Soft Biometrics in Online Social Networks: A Case Study on Twitter User Gender Recognition. In Applications of Computer Vision Workshops (WACVW), 2017 IEEE Winter (pp. 1-8). IEEE.

George, T. O., & Barnabas, S. (2015), ICT and the Gender Question: Prospects and Challenges for the Knowledge Economy in the 21st Century. In *International conference on Africa development issues (CU-ICADI)*. Covenant University.

George, T. O., Ahmadu, F. O., & Chukwuedozie, O. (2013). ICT and Secondary School Educational System in Nigeria: A Conceptual Review. In Panoply of Readings in Social Sciences Lessons for and from Nigeria. Covenant University.

George, J. M., & Zhou, J. (2001). When openness to experience and conscientiousness are related to creative behavior: An interactional approach. *The Journal of Applied Psychology*, *86*(3), 513–524. doi:10.1037/0021-9010.86.3.513 PMID:11419810

Getzels, J. W., & Csikszentmihalyi, M. (1976). *The Creative Vision: A Longitudinal Study of Problem Finding in Art*. New York: Wiley.

Geyskens, I., & Steenkamp, J. E. (2000). Economic and social Satisfaction:Measurement and Relevance to Marketing Channel Relationships. *Journal of Retailing*, *76*(1), 11–32. doi:10.1016/S0022-4359(99)00021-4

Ghavifekr, S., Kunjappan, T., Ramasamy, L., & Anthony, A. (2016). Teaching and Learning with ICT Tools: Issues and Challenges from Teachers' Perceptions. *Malaysian Online Journal of Educational Technology*, *4*(2), 28–57.

Gill, K. B. (2010). *Bridging the Gender Divide*. Washington, DC: International Center for Research on Women. Retrieved January 7, 2018, from https://cleancookstoves.org/binary-data/RESOURCE/file/000/000/294-2.pdf

Gill, J., Sharp, R., Mills, J., & Franzway, S. (2008). I still wanna be an engineer! Women, education and the engineering profession. *European Journal of Engineering Education*, *33*(4), 391–402. doi:10.1080/03043790802253459

Gillwald, A., Milek, A., & Stork, C. (2010). *Towards evidence -based ICT POlicy and Regulation:Gender Assessment of ICT Access and Usage in Africa*. Research ICT AFRICA.

GITR. (2011). *The global information technology report - Transformations 2.0.* Retrieved 17 June 2014, from http://www3.weforum.org/docs/WEF_GITR_Report_2011.pdf

Glazer, N. (1988). *The Limits of Social Policy* (1st ed.). Cambridge, MA: Harvard University.

Global Engineering Deans Council (GEDC). (2017). *Global Engineering Deans Council Conference.* Niagara Falls, Canada: Author.

Globalization, Growth and Poverty. (2002). A World Bank Policy Research Report. New York: World Bank and Oxford University Press. Retrieved November 7, 2017, from http://documents.worldbank.org/curated/en/954071468778196576/pdf/multi0page.pdf

Godoy, L., & Mladinic, A. (2009). Estereotipos y roles de género en la evaluación laboral y personal de hombres y mujeres en cargos de dirección. *Psykhe (Santiago), 18*(2), 51–64. doi:10.4067/S0718-22282009000200004

Goh, T. T., & Sun, S. (2014). Exploring gender differences in Islamic mobile banking acceptance. *Electronic Commerce Research, 14*(4), 435–458. doi:10.100710660-014-9150-7

Goldfinch, S., Gauld, R., & Herbison, P. (2009). The participation divide? Political participation, trust in government, and e-government in Australia and New Zealand. *Australian Journal of Public Administration, 68*(3), 333–350. doi:10.1111/j.1467-8500.2009.00643.x

Golla, A. M. (2011). *Understanding and Measuring Women's Economic Empowerment: Defniton, Framework and Indicators.* Washington, DC: International Center for Research on Women. Retrieved November 25, 2017, from https://www.icrw.org/wp-content/uploads/2016/10/Understanding-measuring-womens-economic-empowerment.pdf

Gómez M, Roses S & Malaga P. S (2012). The Academic Use of Social Networks among University Students. *Comunicar Scientific Journal of Media Education, 38*(19), 131-138.

Gonzalez, A., Revelles, B., Almeda, E., Bosch, N. V., & García, J. (2016). Women in ICT: opportunities for their inclusion in an international labor market. *6th IFIP World Information Technology Forum (WITFOR), IFIP Advances in Information and Communication Technology AICT-481*, 171-177.

Goodrich, K. (2014). The gender gap: Brain-processing differences between the sexes shape attitudes about online advertising. *Journal of Advertising Research, 54*(1), 32–43. doi:10.2501/JAR-54-1-032-043

Google Diversity. (2017). *Google diversity annual report 2018.* Retrieved from https://diversity.google/annual-report

Government of Canada. (2014). *Harper Government Launches the Next Phase of Stop Hating Online to Combat Cyberbullying.* Retrieved January 3, 2018 from https://www.canada.ca/en/news/archive/2014/09/harper-government-launches-next-phase-stop-hating-online-combat-cyberbullying.html

Gram, C., Laaksonen, T., Ohlin, T., Lawson, H., Skår, R., & Stangegaard, O. (2005). History of the Nordic Computer Industry. In J. Bubenko, J. Impagliazzo, & A. Sølvberg (Eds.), *History of Nordic Computing. HiNC 2003. IFIP International Federation for Information Processing* (Vol. 174). Boston, MA: Springer.

Grameen Foundation. (2013). *Use of Mobile Financial Services Among Poor Women in Rural India and The Philippines.* Retrieved December 30, 2017 from https://www.gsma.com/mobilefordevelopment/wp-content/uploads/2014/07/Use-of-Mobile-Financial-Services-Among-Poor-Women-in-Rural-India-and-the-Philippines.pdf

Gråstén, A. (2014). Students' physical activity, physical education enjoyment, and motivational determinants through a three-year school-initiated program (Dissertation). Jyväskylä: University of Jyväskylä.

Gråstén, A. (2016). Children's expectancy beliefs and subjective task values through two years of school-based program and associated links to physical education enjoyment and physical activity. *Journal of Sport and Health Science*, *5*(4), 500–508. doi:10.1016/j.jshs.2015.12.005

Gråstén, A., Watt, A., Hagger, M., Jaakkola, T., & Liukkonen, J. (2015). Secondary school students' physical activity participation across physical education classes—the expectancy–value theory approach. *Physics Education*, *72*, 340–358.

Gras-Velazquez, A., Joyce, A., & Debry, M. (2009). *Women and ICT: Why are girls still not attracted to ICT studies and careers?* European Schoolnet.

Great Place to Work. (2017). *Best Workplaces for Women 2017*. Retrieved October 3, 2018 from https://www.greatplacetowork.com/best-workplaces/women/2017

Great Place to Work. (2018). *Best workplaces in Technology 2018*. Retrieved from https://www.greatplacetowork.com/best-workplaces/technology/2018?utm_source=online&utm_medium=press-release&utm_content=website&utm_campaign=2018-technology-list

Greene, H. (2016). *Job Skills Training to Empower Women in India*. Retrieved January 2, 2018 from http://www.readglobal.org/blog/161-job-skills-training

Griffith, E. (2018). *Everyone Hates Silicon Valley, Except Its imitators*. Retrieved from https://www.wired.com/story/everyone-hates-silicon-valley-except-its-imitators/

Griffiths, M. (2000). Internet addiction-time to be taken seriously? *Addiction Research*, *8*(5), 413–418. doi:10.3109/16066350009005587

GSMA. (2015a). *Accelerating Digital Literacy: Empowering Women to Use the Mobile Internet*. Retrieved January 1, 2018 from https://www.gsma.com/mobilefordevelopment/wp-content/uploads/2015/06/DigitalLiteracy_v6_WEB_Singles.pdf

GSMA. (2015b). *Bridging the Gender Gap: Mobile Access and Usage in Low- and Middle-Income Countries*. Retrieved December 27, 2017 from https://www.gsma.com/mobilefordevelopment/wp-content/uploads/2016/02/GSM0001_03232015_GSMAReport_NEWGRAYS-Web.pdf

Gui, M., & Argentin, G. (2011). Digital skills of internet natives: Different forms of internet literacy in a random sample of northern Italian high school students. *New Media & Society*, *13*(6), 963–980. doi:10.1177/1461444810389751

Gunawardena, C. (1997). Problems of Illiteracy in a Literate Developing Society: Sri Lanka. *International Review of Education*, *43*(5-6), 595–609. doi:10.1023/A:1003010726149

Gunduz, G. S. (2007). *Sosyal içerme politikalarının uygulanmasında kamu istihdam kurumlarının rolü (Yayınlanmamış uzmanlık tezi)*. Ankara: T.C. Çalışma ve Sosyal Güvenlik Bakanlığı, Türkiye İş Kurumu Genel Müdürlüğü.

Gupta, K. P., Singh, S., & Bhaskar, P. (2016). Citizen adoption of e-government: a literature review and conceptual framework. *Electronic Government, an International Journal*, *12*(2), 160-185.

Gurtoo, R. (2016). Khap Panchayats in Relation to Women's Human Rights: Indian Perspective. *Journal of Legal Studies and Research*, *2*(2), 46–59.

Gurumurthy, A., & Chami, N. (2014). *Digital Technologies and Gender Justice in India: An Analysis of Key Policy and Programming Concerns*. Retrieved December 30, 2017 from http://www.itforchange.net/sites/default/files/IT%20for%20Change%20-%20HLPC%20Submission%20-%2016%20April%202014-1.pdf

Hafkin, N., & Taggart, N. (2001). *Gender, information technology, and developing countries: an analytic study for the Office of Women in Development Bureau for Global Programs, Field Support and Research, United States Agency for International Development (USAID).* Available at: http://www.usaid.gov/wid/pubs/hafnoph.pdf

Hafkin, N., & Huyer, S. (2007). Women and Gender in ICT statistics and Indicators for Development. *Information Technologies and International Development: Special Issue on Women's Empowerment and Information Society*, *4*(2), 25–41. doi:10.1162/itid.2008.00006

Hajli, N., & Lin, X. (2016). Exploring the security of information sharing on social networking sites: The role of perceived control of information. *Journal of Business Ethics*, *133*(1), 111–123. doi:10.100710551-014-2346-x

Hakkarainena, K., IlomaÈki, L., Lipponena, L., Muukkonena, H., Rahikainenb, M., Tuominena, T., Lakkalaa, M., & Lehtinen, E. (2000). Students' skills and practices of using ICT: Results of a national assessment in Finland. *Computers & Education*, 34–117.

Halder, D., & Jaishankar, K. (2010). *Cyber Victimization in India: A Baseline Survey Report.* Retrieved December 25, 2017 from http://www.cybervictims.org/CCVCresearchreport2010.pdf

Halder, D., & Jaishankar, K. (2011). Cyber Gender Harassment and Secondary Victimization: A Comparative Analysis of the United States, the UK, and India. *Victims & Offenders*, *6*(4), 386–398. doi:10.1080/15564886.2011.607402

Halder, D., & Jaishankar, K. (2012). *Cyber Crime and the Victimization of Women: Laws, Rights, and Regulations.* Hershey, PA: IGI Global. doi:10.4018/978-1-60960-830-9

Halder, S., Ray, A., & Chakrabarty, P. K. (2010). Gender differences in information seeking behavior in three universities in West Bengal, India. *The International Information & Library Review*, *42*(4), 242–251. doi:10.1080/10572317.2010.10762869

Hallyburton, A., & Evarts, L. A. (2014). Gender and online health information seeking: A five survey meta-analysis. *Journal of Consumer Health on the Internet*, *18*(2), 128–142. doi:10.1080/15398285.2014.902268

Hamade, S. N. (2013). Perception and use of social networking sites among university students. *Library Review*, *62*(6/7), 388–397. doi:10.1108/LR-12-2012-0131

Hamat, A., Embi, M. A., & Hassan, H. A. (2012). The use of social networking sites among Malaysian university students. *International Education Studies*, *5*(3), 56–66. doi:10.5539/ies.v5n3p56

Hampson, S. E., Andrews, J. A., Barckley, M. P., & Peterson, M. (2007). Trait Stability and Continuity in Childhood: Relating Sociability and Hostility to the Five-Factor Model of Personality. *Journal of Research in Personality*, *41*(3), 507–523. doi:10.1016/j.jrp.2006.06.003 PMID:18488082

Harari, M. B., Thompson, H. A., & Viswesvaran, C. (2018). Extraversion and job satisfaction: The role of trait bandwidth and the moderating effect of status goal attainment. *Personality and Individual Differences*, *123*(1), 14–16. doi:10.1016/j.paid.2017.10.041

Harcar, T., & Yucelt, U. (2012). American Consumer's Attitudes Towards Different Airline Companies Channels: A Comparison of Transaction Methods. *Recista De Turismoy Patrimonio Cultural*, *10*(2), 59–68. doi:10.25145/j.pasos.2012.10.027

Hargittai, E., & Shafer, S. (2006). Differences in actual and perceived online skills: The role of gender. *Social Science Quarterly*, *87*(2), 432-448. . doi:10.1111/j.1540-6237.2006.00389.x

Haseloff, A. M. (2005). Cybercafes and Their Potential as Community Development Tools in India. *The Journal of Community Informatics*, *1*(3). Retrieved from http://ci-journal.net/index.php/ciej/article/view/226/181

Hatakka, M., & Lagsten, J. (2012). The capability approach as a tool for development evaluation – analyzing students' use of internet resources. *Information Technology for Development, 18*(1), 23–41. doi:10.1080/02681102.2011.617722

Hatlevik, O. E., & Christophersen, K. A. (2013). Digital competence at the beginning of upper secondary school: Identifying factors explaining digital inclusion. *Computers & Education, 63*, 240–247. doi:10.1016/j.compedu.2012.11.015

Hatlevik, O. E., Scherer, R., & Christophersen, K. (2017). Moving beyond the study of gender differences: An analysis of measurement invariance and differential item functioning of an ICT literacy scale. *Computers & Education, 113*, 280–293. doi:10.1016/j.compedu.2017.06.003

Hatlevik, O. V., Throndsen, I., Loi, M., & Gudmundsdottir, G. B. (2018). Students' ICT self-efficacy and computer and information literacy: Determinants and relationships. *Computers & Education, 118*, 107–119. doi:10.1016/j.compedu.2017.11.011

Hawisher, G. E., Selfe, C. L., Moraski, B., & Pearson, M. (2004). Becoming literate in the Information Age: Cultural ecologies and the literacies of technology. *College Composition and Communication, 55*(4), 642–692. doi:10.2307/4140666

Healy, J. (2015). The Australian labour market in 2014: Still ill? *The Journal of Industrial Relations, 57*(3), 348–365. doi:10.1177/0022185615571981

Heaverlo, C. A. (2011). *'STEM Development: A Study of 6th-12th Grade Girls' Interest in Mathematics and Science'* (Graduate Theses and Dissertations). Iowa State University. Retrieved from www://lib.dr.iastate.edu/etd/10056

Heisz, J. J., Pottruff, M. M., & Shore, D. I. (2013). Females scan more than males: A potential mechanism for sex differences in recognition memory. *Psychological Science, 24*(7), 1157–1163. doi:10.1177/0956797612468281 PMID:23696202

Helbig, N., Gil-García, J. R., & Ferro, E. (2009). Understanding the complexity of electronic government: Implications from the digital divide literature. *Government Information Quarterly, 26*(1), 89–97. doi:10.1016/j.giq.2008.05.004

Helmers, C. (1980). *The Era of the off-the-shelf personal computers (Byte Magazine)*. Retrieved from Archive.org: https://archive.org/stream/byte-magazine-1980-01#page/n7/mode/2up

Henriksen, E. K., Dillion, J., & Ryder, J. (Eds.). Understanding Student Participation and Choice in Science and Technology Education. Springer. DOI doi:10.1007/978-94-007-7793-4_2

Hepburn, A. (2003). Feminist critics: hetrosexism and lesbian and gay psychology. An introduction to critical social psychology. Thousand Oaks, CA: Sage.

Hilbert, M. (2011). Digital gender divide or technologically empowered women in developing countries? A typical case of lies, damned lies, and statistics. *Women's Studies International Forum, 34*(6), 479–489. doi:10.1016/j.wsif.2011.07.001

Hill, C. (2018). *Solving the Equation: The Variables for Women's Success in Engineering and Computing*. Retrieved from https://www.aauw.org/research/solving-the-equation/

Hill, J. R., Wiley, D., Nelson, L. M., & Han, S. (2004). Exploring research on Internet-based learning: From infrastructure to interactions. In D. H. Jonassen (Ed.), *Handbook of research on educational communications and technology* (pp. 433–460). Mahwah, NJ: Lawrence Erlbaum Associates.

Hill, O. W., Pettus, C., & Hedin, B. A. (1990). Three studies of factors affecting the attitudes of blacks and females toward the pursuit of science and science-related careers. *Journal of Research in Science Teaching, 27*(4), 289–314. doi:10.1002/tea.3660270403

Hindustan Times. (2017, May 12). *Gurmehar Kaur Deletes Her Facebook Account.* Retrieved December 25, 2017 from http://www.hindustantimes.com/delhi-news/gurmehar-kaur-deletes-her-facebook-account/story-dnLz9leGiQ2gWm-F9YGrwEM.html

Hitschfeld, K. N., & Martinez, S. (2016). *En búsqueda de la equidad de género en ingeniería: Estudio de la participación femenina en la FCFM y los 40 cupos de equidad. Conversatorio: "Más emprendedoras de alto impacto para Chile".* Girls In Tech. Retrieved from http://www.girlsintechchile.com/wp-content/uploads/2016/08/Conversatorio2016.pdf

Hodgkinson, L. (2000). Is technology masculine? Theorising the absence of women. In *Technology to Society, IEEE International Symposium on Technology and Society* (pp. 121-126). Rome, Italy: IEEE.

Hoerning, C. (1940). *Preparación de los ingenieros y la admiración de empresas industriales y comerciales.* Paper presented at the Anales del Instituto de Ingenieros de Chile.

Hofstede Insights. (2018). *Country Comparison - Denmark.* Retrieved October 3, 2018 from https://www.hofstede-insights.com/country-comparison/Denmark

Hofstede Insights. (n.d.). *Country Comparison USA.* Retrieved October 3, 2018 from https://www.hofstede-insights.com/country-comparison/USA

Hohlfeld, T. N., Ritzhaupt, A. D., & Barron, A. E. (2013). Are gender differences in perceived and demonstrated technology literacy significant? It depends on the model. *Educational Technology Research and Development, 61*, 639-663. . doi:10.100711423-013-9304-7

Ho, S. M., Lowry, P. B., Warkentin, M., Yang, Y., & Hollister, J. M. (2017). Gender deception in asynchronous online communication: A path analysis. *Information Processing & Management, 53*(1), 21–41. doi:10.1016/j.ipm.2016.06.004

Hossain, M. A., & Quaddus, M. (2011). Expectation-Confirmation Theory in Information System Research: A review and Analysis. *Information Systems Theory*, 44-49.

Howell, B. (2017). *Can Smart Policies Alter the Lot of Women in the ICT Workforce?* Retrieved from http://www.aei.org/publication/can-smart-policies-alter-lot-women-ict-workforce/

Hozdić, E. (2015). Smart Factory for Industry 4.0: A Review. *International Journal of Modern Manufacturing Technologies, 7*(1), 28–35. Retrieved from https://www.researchgate.net/publication/282791888_Smart_factory_for_industry_40_A_review

Huffaker, D. A., & Calvert, S. L. (2003). The New science of learning: Active learning, metacognition, and transfer of knowledge in e-learning applications. *Journal of Educational Computing Research, 29*(3), 325–334. doi:10.2190/4T89-30W2-DHTM-RTQ2

Hughes, D. J., Rowe, M., Batey, M., & Lee, A. (2012). A tale of two sites: Twitter vs Facebook and the personality indicators of scial media usage. *Computers in Human Behavior, 28*(2), 561–569. doi:10.1016/j.chb.2011.11.001

Hulleman, C. S., Barron, K. E., Kosovich, J. J., & Lazowski, R. A. (2014). Current Theories, Constructs, and Interventions within an Expectancy-Value Framework. In Psychosocial skills and school systems in the Twenty-first century: Theory, research, and applications. Springer.

Hum, N. J., Chamberlin, P. E., Hambright, B. L., Portwood, A. C., Schat, A. C., & Bevan, J. L. (2011). A picture is worth a thousand words: A content analysis of Facebook profile photographs. *Computers in Human Behavior, 27*(5), 1828–1833. doi:10.1016/j.chb.2011.04.003

Hung, S. Y., Chang, C. M., & Yu, T. J. (2006). Determinants of user acceptance of the e-Government services: The case of online tax filing and payment system. *Government Information Quarterly, 23*(1), 97–122. doi:10.1016/j.giq.2005.11.005

Hunt, R. R., & Einstein, G. O. (1981). Relational and item-specific information in memory. *Journal of Verbal Learning and Verbal Behavior, 20*(5), 497–514. doi:10.1016/S0022-5371(81)90138-9

Hunt, R. R., & Seta, C. E. (1984). Category size effects in recall: The roles of relational and individual item information. *Journal of Experimental Psychology. Learning, Memory, and Cognition, 10*(3), 454–464. doi:10.1037/0278-7393.10.3.454

Huppatz, K., & Goodwin, S. (2013). Masculinised jobs, feminised jobs and men's 'gender capital' experiences: Understanding occupational segregation in Australia. *Journal of Sociology (Melbourne, Vic.), 49*(2-3), 291–308. doi:10.1177/1440783313481743

Huyer, S., & Mitter, S. (2003). Poverty reduction, gender, equality and the knowledge society: Digital exclusion or digital opportunity? In *ICTs, Globalisation and Poverty Reduction: Gender Dimensions of the Knowledge Society.* Retrieved from http://unpan1.un.org/intradoc/groups/public/documents/unpan/unpan037351.pdf

Hwang, Y. M., & Lee, K. C. (2018). Using an Eye-Tracking Approach to Explore Gender Differences in Visual Attention and Shopping Attitudes in an Online Shopping Environment. *International Journal of Human-Computer Interaction, 34*(1), 15–24. doi:10.1080/10447318.2017.1314611

IBM. (2018). *The birth of the IBM PC.* Retrieved from IBM: https://www-03.ibm.com/ibm/history/exhibits/pc25/pc25_birth.html

Ibrahim, J., Ros, R. C., Sulaiman, N. F., Nordin, R. C., & Yuan, L. Z. (2014). Positive impact of smart phone application: WhatsApp and Facebook for online business. *IJSTR, 4*, 1–4.

Iglesias Rodríguez, A., García Riaza, B., & Sánchez Gómez, M. C. (2017). Collaborative learning and mobile devices: An educational experience in Primary Education. *Computers in Human Behavior*, 72664–72677. doi:10.1016/j.chb.2016.07.019

Ilie, V., Van Slyke, C., Green, G., & Hao, L. (2005). Gender differences in perceptions and use of communication technologies: A diffusion of innovation approach. *Information Resources Management Journal, 18*(3), 13–31. doi:10.4018/irmj.2005070102

Ilomaki, L. (2011). Does Gender Have a Role in ICT Among Finnish Teachers and Students? *Scandinavian Journal of Educational Research, 55*(3), 325–340. doi:10.1080/00313831.2011.576910

Instituto Nacional de Estadísticas de Chile (INE). (2017). *Compendio Estadístico.* Retrieved from http://www.censo2017.cl/descargas/home/sintesis-de-resultados-censo2017.pdf

Intel Corporation and Dalberg Global Development Advisors. (2012). *Women and the Web.* Retrieved December 26, 2017 from https://www.intel.com/content/www/us/en/technology-in-education/women-in-the-web.html

International Labour Organization (ILO). (2012). *International Standard Classification of Occupations (ISCO-08): Structure, Group Definitions and Correspondence Tables.* Geneva: International Labour Organization.

International Labour Organization Country Office for India. (2017). *India Labour Market Update.* Retrieved December 29, 2017 from http://www.ilo.org/wcmsp5/groups/public/---asia/---ro-bangkok/---sro-new_delhi/documents/publication/wcms_568701.pdf

International Telecommunication Union (ITU). (2017). *ICT Facts and Figures 2016 Report.* ITU.

International Telecommunication Union. (n.d.). *Measuring the Information Society Report 2017.* Retrieved from https://www.itu.int/pub/D-IND-ICTOI

Invest Siophia. (2017). *ICT Sector in Bulgaria Is The Best Performing Industry - 600% Income Growth for 10 Years.* Retrieved from http://investsofia.com/en/it-sector-in-bulgaria-is-the-best-performing-industry-600-income-growth-for-10-years/

Isaacson, P. (1978). Personal Computing Position paper. *ACM SIGPC, 1*(2), 5–9. doi:10.1145/1164917.1164919

ISACA. (n.d.). *2017 Women In Technology Survey: Breaking Down Gender Barriers to Build the Future Tech Workforce.* Retrieved from http://www.isaca.org/info/2017-women-in-technology-survey/index.html

ITU. (2013). *ICT Facts and Figures.* Geneva: ITU. Retrieved from https://www.itu.int/en/ITU-D/Statistics/Documents/facts/ICTFactsFigures2013-e.pdf

ITU. (2016). *ICT facts and figures 2016.* Retrieved 9 16, 2016, from ITU: http://www.itu.int/en/ITU-D/Statistics/Documents/facts/ICTFactsFigures2016.pdf

ITU. (2017). *ITU Facts and Figures 2017.* Geneva: ITU. Retrieved from https://www.itu.int/en/ITU-D/Statistics/Documents/facts/ICTFactsFigures2017.pdf

Jackson, L., Ervin, K., Gardner, P. D., & Schmitt, N. (2001). Gender and the Internet: Women communicating and men searching'. *Sex Roles, 44*(5/6), 363–379. doi:10.1023/A:1010937901821

Jacobsen, J. K. S., & Munar, A. M. (2012). Tourist information search and destination choice in a digital age. *Tourism Management Perspectives, 1*, 39–47. doi:10.1016/j.tmp.2011.12.005

Jacobs, J. E., Lanza, S., Osgood, D. W., Eccles, J. S., & Wigfield, A. (2002). Changes in children's self-competence and values: Gender and domain differences across grade one through twelve. *Child Development, 73*(2), 509–527. doi:10.1111/1467-8624.00421 PMID:11949906

James, J. (2004). Reconstruing the digital divide from the perspective of a large, poor, developing country. *Journal of Information Technology, 19*(3), 172–177. doi:10.1057/palgrave.jit.2000019

Jansen, B. J., Moore, K., & Carman, S. (2013). Evaluating the performance of demographic targeting using gender in sponsored search. *Information Processing & Management, 49*(1), 286–302. doi:10.1016/j.ipm.2012.06.001

Jennings, S. E., & Onwuegbuzie, A. J. (2001). Computer attitudes as a function of age, gender, math attitude and developmental status. *Journal of Educational Computing Research, 25*(4), 367–384. doi:10.2190/WH2L-BBVB-DTPG-UG7R

Jiang, J., Klein, G., & Saunders, C. (2012). Discrepancy theory models of satisfaction in IS research. *Information Systems Theory, 28*, 355-381. Retrieved from UQ Business School: https://www.business.uq.edu.au/sites/default/files/events/files/jjiang-paper.pdf

Jonathan, K. J. (1998). Internet Addiction on Campus: The Vulnerability of College Students. *Cyberpsychology & Behavior, 1*(1). doi:10.1089/cpb.1998.1.11

Jones, M. (2017). *Why Can't Companies Get Mentorship Programs Right?* Retrieved from https://www.theatlantic.com/business/archive/2017/06/corporate-mentorship-programs/528927/

Jones, M. L., DeRuyter, F., Thompson, N. A., Norelli, J., & Morris, J. T. (2018). Survey of User Needs for ICT -- Community Living by People with Disabilities. *33rd Annual International Technology and Persons with Disabilities Conference Scientific/Research Proceedings.*

Joo, Y. J., Park, S., & Shin, E. K. (2017). Students' expectation, satisfaction, and continuance intention to use digital textbooks. *Computers in Human Behavior, 69*, 83–90. doi:10.1016/j.chb.2016.12.025

Jumoke, S., Oloruntoba, S. A., & Blessing, O. (2015). Analysis of mobile phone impact on student academic performance in tertiary institution. *IJAERT*, *5*, 361–367.

Junglas, I. A., Johnson, N. A., & Spitzmuller, C. (2008). Personality traits and concern for privacy: An empirical study in the context of location-based services. *European Journal of Information Systems*, *17*(4), 387–402. doi:10.1057/ejis.2008.29

K2 Space. (n.d.). *The History of Office Design*. Retrieved October 3, 2018 from https://k2space.co.uk/knowledge/history-of-office-design/

Kabeer, N. N. L. (2013, February 26). *Gender Equality and Economic Growth: Is there a Win-Win?* Retrieved June 12, 2018, from http://www.ids.ac.uk/publications: http://www.ids.ac.uk/files/dmfile/Wp417.pdf

Kabilan, M., & Rajab, B. (2010). The utilization of the Internet by Palestinian English language teachers focusing on uses, practices and barriers and overall contribution to professional development. *International Journal of Education and Development Using ICT*, *6*(3), 56-72.

Kablan, S., Oulaı, A., & Elliott, E. (2015). Legal aspects of accessibility and usability of online public services in Quebec and Canada. *Electronic Commerce Research*, *15*(3), 387–406. doi:10.100710660-015-9186-3

Kačániová, M. Z. B. (2016). Emotional aspects of Facebook textual posts a framework for marketing research. *European Journal of Science and Theology*, *12*(6).

Kachhwaha, K. (2011). Khap Adjudication in India: Honouring the Culture with Crimes. *International Journal of Criminal Justice Sciences*, *6*(1&2), 297–308.

Kakar, Y. W., Hausman, V., Thomas, A., & Denny-Brown, C. (2012). *Women and the web*. Intel Corporation. Retrieved 08 5, 2018, from https://www.intel.com/content/dam/www/public/us/en/documents/pdf/women-and-the-web.pdf

Kampylis, P. G., Bocconi, S., & Punie, Y. (2012). *Towards a mapping framework of ICT-enabled innovation for learning*. Scientific and Policy Report by the Joint Research Centre of the European Commission.

Kapur, S., & Murthi, M. (2009). *Literacy in India*. Retrieved December 31, 2017 from http://www.bbk.ac.uk/ems/faculty/kapur/personal/literacy

Karakaya Polat, R. (2012). Digital exclusion in Turkey: A policy perspective. *Government Information Quarterly*, *29*(4), 589–596. doi:10.1016/j.giq.2012.03.002

Kasahara, G. M. (2017). *Gender Differences in Social Media Use and Cyberbullying in Belize*. All Theses, Dissertations, and Other Capstone Projects. 753. Retrieved from https://cornerstone.lib.mnsu.edu/etds/753

Katiyar, S. P. (2016). Gender Disparity in Literacy in India. *Social Change*, *46*(1), 46–69. doi:10.1177/0049085715618558

Kaushik, D. (2017, February 23). *Why are the number of female Facebook users more than male users even if total male users of the internet are more than female?* Retrieved from Quora: https://www.quora.com/Why-are-the-number-of-female-Facebook-users-more-than-male-users-even-if-total-male-users-of-the-internet-are-more-than-female

Kayaoglu, N. M. (2012). Gender-Based Differences in Language Learning Strategies of Science Students. *J. Turkish Sci. Educ.*, *9*(2).

Kay, C. K. (1972). A personal Computer for Children of all Ages. In ACM '72 proceedings of the ACM annual conference (vol. 1). Boston: ACM.

Kay, C. K. (1972). A personal Computer for Children of all Ages. In ACM '72 proceedings of the ACM annual conference (Vol. 1). Boston: ACM.

Kelan, E. K. (2008). Emotions in a rational profession: The gendering of skills in ICT work. *Gender, Work and Organization, 15*(1), 49–71.

Kembler, S. (1996). Feminism, technology and Social representations. In J. Curran, D. Morley, & V. Walkerdine (Eds.), *Cultural Studies and Communications*. London: Arnold.

Khalifa, M., & Liu, V. (2003). Determinants of Satisfaction at Different Adoption stages of Internet-Based Services. *Journal of the Association for Information Systems, 4*(5), 206–232.

Khan, Z. (2017). *The Internet is Bad for Indian Women*. Retrieved June 20, 2018 from https://internetdemocracy.in/media/the-internet-is-bad-for-indian-women/

Khojeh, E., Nor, M. K., & Aghakhani, N. (2010). *Using ICT to improve customer satisfaction in small and medium sized construction companies: A study among malaysian construction SMEs. In 5th International Conference on Computer Sciences and Convergence Information Technology*. Seoul, South Korea: IEEE. Retrieved from https://ieeexplore.ieee.org/document/5711104/

Kibernum. (2011). *Sólo el 10% de los estudiantes son mujeres: ¿Por qué no ingresan más mujeres a estudiar carreras informáticas?* Retrieved from http://www.kibernum.com/noticias/solo-el-10-de-los-estudiantes-son-mujeres-por-que-no-ingresan-mas-mujeres-a-estudiar-carreras-informaticas/

Kiefer, A., & Shih, M. (2006). Gender differences in persistence and attributions in stereotype relevant contexts. *Sex Roles, 54*(11-12), 859–868. doi:10.100711199-006-9051-x

Kilic, A. (2008). The gender dimension of social policy reform in Turkey: Towards equal citizenship. *Social Policy and Administration, 42*(5), 487–503. doi:10.1111/j.1467-9515.2008.00620.x

Kilinc-Savrul, A., & Kilic, A. (2011). Küreselleşme sürecinde bilişim sektörünün Türkiye ve Avrupa Birliği ülkelerinin ekonomileri üzerindeki etkileri. *İstanbul Üniversitesi İktisat Fakültesi Mecmuası, 61*(2), 257-289.

Kim, S. (2015). *14 out of 100 S. Korean teenagers addicted to Internet or smartphones*. Retrieved from http://www.koreatimesus.com/14-out-of-100-s-korean-teenagers-addicted-to-internet-or-smartphones/

Kim, D. Y., Lehto, X. Y., & Morrison, A. M. (2007). Gender differences in online travel information search: Implications for marketing communications on the internet. *Tourism Management, 28*(2), 423–433. doi:10.1016/j.tourman.2006.04.001

Kim, H.-S., Kil, H.-J., & Shin, A. (2014). An analysis of variables affecting the ICT literacy level of Korean elementary school students. *Computers & Education, 77*, 29–38. doi:10.1016/j.compedu.2014.04.009

Kim, J. M., & Lee, W. G. (2011). Meanings of criteria and norms: Analyses and comparisons of ICT literacy competencies of middle school students. *Computers & Education, 64*, 81–94. doi:10.1016/j.compedu.2012.12.018

Kim, S. B., Kim, D. Y., & Wise, K. (2014). The effect of searching and surfing on recognition of destination images on Facebook pages. *Computers in Human Behavior, 30*, 813–823. doi:10.1016/j.chb.2013.07.010

Koch, S. C., Müller, S. M., & Sieverding, M. (2008). Women and computers. Effects of stereotype threat on attribution of failure. *Computers & Education, 51*(4), 1795-1803. doi:10.1016/j.compedu.2008.05.007

Konrad, A. M., Waryszak, R., & Hartmann, L. (1997). What do managers like to do? Comparing women and men in Australia and the US. *Australian Journal of Management, 22*(1), 71–97. doi:10.1177/031289629702200104

Koppi, T., Sheard, J., Naghdy, F., Edwards, S. L., & Brookes, W. (2010). Towards a gender inclusive information and communications technology curriculum: A perspective from graduates in the workforce. *Computer Science Education, 20*(4), 265–282. doi:10.1080/08993408.2010.527686

Koren, M. (2018). *One Wikipedia Page Is a Metaphor for the Nobel Prize's Record With Women*. Retrieved from https://www.theatlantic.com/science/archive/2018/10/nobel-prize-physics-donna-strickland-gerard-mourou-arthur-ashkin/571909/

Kotler, P., & Armstrong, G. (2016). *Principles of Marketing (16th Global Edition)*. Pearson.

Kovacs, A., Padte, R. K., & Shobha, S. V. (2013). *'Don't Let It Stand!' An Exploratory Study of Women and Verbal Online Abuse in India*. Retrieved December 25, 2017 from https://internetdemocracy.in/wp-content/uploads/2013/12/Internet-Democracy-Project-Women-and-Online-Abuse.pdf

Krishnani, R. (2015). Indian Women: No Friends Online. *World Policy Journal*, *32*(2), 85–91. doi:10.1177/0740277515591546

Kumari, S. N., & Saraladevi, K. (2012). Gender Differences in Attitude towards Science Teaching and Learning Styles among Adolescents. *International Journal of Science and Research*, *3*(10), 50–58.

Kurfali, M., Arifoglu, A., Tokdemir, G., & Pacin, Y. (2017). Adoption of e-government services in Turkey. *Computers in Human Behavior*, *66*, 168–178. doi:10.1016/j.chb.2016.09.041

Laher, S. (2013). Understanding the Five-Factor Model and Five-Factor Theory through a South African cultural lens. *South African journal of psychology = Suid-Afrikaanse tydskrif vir sielkunde*, *43*(2), 208-221.

Lal, B. S. (2011). Impact of Information and Communication Technologies on Women Empowerment in India. *Systemics, Cybernetics and Informatics*, *9*(4), 17-23. Retrieved December 14, 2017, from http://www.iiisci.org/journal/CV$/sci/pdfs/QN001HZ.pdf

Lang, A., & Craig, C. (2010). International collaboration for women in IT: How to avoid reinventing the wheel. *Information in Motion: The Journal Issues in Informing Science and Information Technology*, *7*, 329.

Langdon, G., McKittrick, D. B., Khan, B., & Doms, M. (2011). *STEM: Good jobs now and for the future*. U.S. Department of Commerce, Economics and Statistics Administration.

Laosethakul, K., & Leingpibul, T. (2010). Why females do not choose Computing: A lesson learned from China. *Multicultural Education & Technology Journal*, *4*(3), 173–187. doi:10.1108/17504971011075174

Laouchez, J. M., Penk, W., Binvel, Y., Guarino, A., & Franzino, M. (2018). *The $8.5 Trillion Talent Shortage*. Retrieved from https://www.kornferry.com/institute/talent-crunch-future-of-work

Lareau, A., & Horvat, E. M. (1999). Moments of social inclusion and exclusion race, class and cultural capital in family- school relationships. *Sociology of Education*, *72*(1), 37–53. doi:10.2307/2673185

Large, A., Beheshti, J., & Rahman, T. (2002). Gender differences in collaborative web searching behavior: An elementary school study. *Information Processing & Management*, *38*(3), 427–443. doi:10.1016/S0306-4573(01)00034-6

Lau, W. W., & Yuen, A. Y. (2015). Factorial invariance across gender of a perceived ICT literacy scale. *Learning and Individual Differences*, *41*, 79–85. doi:10.1016/j.lindif.2015.06.001

Layton, R., & Kane, J. (2017). *Alternative Approaches to Broadband Policy: Lessons on Deregulation from Denmark*. Retrieved from https://www.mercatus.org/publications/broadband-policy-deregulation-denmark

Lee, D. (2009). *The Impact of Mobile Phones on the Status of Women in India*. Retrieved January 21, 2018 from https://pdfs.semanticscholar.org/e9fc/09860814f607f84c2f33b4db274dc48435dc.pdf

Lei, J., & Zhou, Y. (2007). Technology uses and student achievement: A longitudinal study. *Computers & Education*, *49*(2), 284–296. doi:10.1016/j.compedu.2005.06.013

Leong, S., & Hawamdeh, S. (1999). Gender and learning attitudes in using Web-based science lessons. *Information Research, 5*(1). Retrieved from http://www.informationr.net/ir/5-1/paper66.html

Leung, L., & Wei, R. (1998). The gratifications of pager use: Sociability, information- seeking, entertainment, utility, and fashion and status. *Telematics and Informatics, 15*(4), 253–264. doi:10.1016/S0736-5853(98)00016-1

Levanon, A., England, P., & Allison, P. (2009). Occupational Feminization and Pay: Assessing Causal Dynamics Using 1950–2000 U.S. Census Data. *Social Forces, 88*(2), 865–891. doi:10.1353of.0.0264

Lewis, K. (2016, February 22). *Girls and Unmarried Women in India Banned from Using Mobile Phones to Prevent 'Disturbance in Society'*. Retrieved December 24, 2017 from http://www.independent.co.uk/news/world/asia/girls-and-unmarried-women-in-india-forbidden-from-using-mobile-phones-to-prevent-disturbance-in-a6888911.html

Lim, S., & Kwon, N. (2010). Gender differences in information behavior concerning Wikipedia, an unorthodox information source? *Library & Information Science Research, 32*(3), 212–220. doi:10.1016/j.lisr.2010.01.003

Lim, S., & Soon, C. (2010). The influence of social and cultural factors on mothers' domestication of household ICTs – Experiences of Chinese and Korean women. *Telematics and Informatics, 27*(3), 205–216. doi:10.1016/j.tele.2009.07.001

Lin, M. H. J., Cross, S. N., Jones, W., & Childers, T. L. (2018a). Online information processing of scent-related words and implications for decision making. In Analytics and Data Science (pp. 197-216). Springer.

Lin, X., Li, Y., Califf, C. B., & Featherman, M. (2013a). Can social role theory explain gender differences in Facebook usage? In *System Sciences (HICSS), 2013 46th Hawaii International Conference on System Sciences* (pp. 690-699). IEEE.

Li, N., & Kirkup, G. (2007). Gender and cultural differences in Internet use: A study of China and the UK. *Computers & Education, 48*(2), 301–317. doi:10.1016/j.compedu.2005.01.007

Lin, C., Wei, Y., & Lekhawipat, W. (2018). Time effect of disconfirmation on online shopping. *Behaviour & Information Technology*, 1.

Lin, X., Featherman, M., Brooks, S. L., & Hajli, N. (2018b). Exploring Gender Differences in Online Consumer Purchase Decision Making: An Online Product Presentation Perspective. *Information Systems Frontiers*, 1–15. doi:10.100710796-018-9831-1

Lin, X., Featherman, M., & Sarker, S. (2013b). Information Sharing in the Context of Social Media: An Application of the Theory of Reasoned Action and Social Capital Theory. *Proceedings of the 2013 AIS SIGHCI Workshop on HCI Research in MIS*, 1-5.

Lin, X., Featherman, M., & Sarker, S. (2017). Understanding factors affecting users' socialnetworking site continuance: A gender difference perspective. *Information & Management, 54*(3), 383–395. doi:10.1016/j.im.2016.09.004

Litt, E. (2013). Measuring users' internet skills: A review of past assessments and a look toward the future. *New Media & Society, 15*(4), 612–630. doi:10.1177/1461444813475424

Lorigo, L., Pan, B., Hembrooke, H., Joachims, T., Granka, L., & Gay, G. (2006). The influence of task and gender on search and evaluation behavior using Google. *Information Processing & Management, 42*(4), 1123–1131. doi:10.1016/j.ipm.2005.10.001

Loveless, A. M. (2007). *Creativity, technology and learning – a review of recent literature* (No. 4 update). Retrieved from www. futurlab.org.dk/litereviews

Loveness, A., Burton, J., & Turvey, K. (2006). Developing conceptual frameworks for creativity, ICT and teacher education. *Thinking Skills and Creativity, 1*(1), 3–13. doi:10.1016/j.tsc.2005.07.001

Luan, W. L., Aziz, S. A., Yunus, A. S., Sidek, Z., Bakar, K. A., Meseran, H., & Atan, A. (2005). Gender Differences in ICT Competencies among Academicians at Universiti Putra Malaysia. *Malaysian Online Journal of Instructional Technology, 2*(3), 62–69. Retrieved from http://pppjj.usm.my/mojit/articles/pdf/Dec05/08 - Gender_differences[1]-final.pdf

Lu, H. P., & Hsiao, K. L. (2009). Gender differences in reasons for frequent blog posting. *Online Information Review, 33*(1), 135–156. doi:10.1108/14684520910944436

Luo, L., Zhang, S., & Zhou, C. (2011). The comparisons of gender differences in playfulness, humor and creativity of postgraduate students between Mainland China and Taiwan. In *Proceedings of ECCIXII, 12th European Conference on Creativity and Innovation: The ultimate experience in collaboration* (pp. 470-491). University of the Algarve.

Major, D. A., Morganson, V. J., & Bolen, H. M. (2013). Predictors of occupational and organizational commitment in information technology: Exploring gender differences and similarities. *Journal of Business and Psychology, 28*(3), 301–304. doi:10.100710869-012-9282-5

Makrakis, V., & Sawada, T. (1996). Gender, computers and other school subjects among Japanese and Swedish students. *Computers & Education, 26*(4), 225–231. doi:10.1016/0360-1315(95)00085-2

Male Champions of Change Institute. (2018). *About the Male Champions of Change: A Strategy Focused on Gender Equality*. Retrieved from http://malechampionsofchange.com/about-us/

Malhotra, A., Kanesathasan, A., & Patel, P. (2012). *Connectivity: How Mobile Phones, Computers and the Internet Can Catalyze Women's Entrepreneurship. India: A Case Study*. Retrieved December 30, 2017 from https://www.icrw.org/wp-content/uploads/2016/10/Connectivity-how-mobile-phones-computers-and-the-internet-can-catalyze-womens-entrepreneurship.pdf

Manjunatha, S. (2013). The Usage of Social Networking sites Among the College Students in India, *International Research. Journal of Social Sciences, 2*(5), 15–21.

Margolis, J., & Fisher, A. (2002). *Unlocking the clubhouse: Women in computing*. MIT Press.

Marriott, H. R., & Williams, M. D. (2018). Exploring consumers perceived risk and trust for mobile shopping: A theoretical framework and empirical study. *Journal of Retailing and Consumer Services, 42*, 133–146. doi:10.1016/j.jretconser.2018.01.017

Masunaga, H., & Hitchock, M. A. (2011). How does gender interact with clinical teachers' perceptions of clinical teaching? NASPA. *Journal About Women in Higher Education, 4*(1), 50–72. doi:10.2202/1940-7890.1065

Mauro, A. (2004). *Trayectorias Laborales en el Sector Financiero. Recorridos de las Mujeres*. Unidad Mujer y Desarrollo. Retrieved from https://books.google.com.au/books?id=bdkXxgx0kncC&pg=PA49&lpg=PA49&dq=trayectoria+laboral+de+la+mujer+ingeniero+en+chile&source=bl&ots=bwZU-gk4V4&sig=RFV2AIf00JM09RCmPFF2jVNoS6o&hl=es-419&sa=X&ved=0ahUKEwiWppLB0tnZAhVDwrwKHd82CxcQ6AEIcTAL-v=onepage&q&f=false

Mayes, R., & Pini, B. (2014). The Australian mining industry and the ideal mining woman: Mobilizing a public business case for gender equality. *The Journal of Industrial Relations, 56*(4), 527–546. doi:10.1177/0022185613514206

McClure, E. B., Monk, C. S., Nelson, E. E., Zarahn, E., Leibenluft, E., Bilder, R. M., ... Pine, D. S. (2004). A developmental examination of gender differences in brain engagement during evaluation of threat. *Biological Psychiatry, 55*(11), 1047–1055. doi:10.1016/j.biopsych.2004.02.013 PMID:15158422

McCrae, R. R., & Costa, P. T. (1997). Conceptions and correlates of openness to experience. In R. Hogan, J. Johnson, & S. Briggs (Eds.), Handbook on Personality Psychology (pp. 825-847). Academic Press.

McCrae, R. R. (1994). Openness to Experience: Expanding the boundaries of Factor V. *European Journal of Personality*, *8*(4), 251–272. doi:10.1002/per.2410080404

McCrae, R. R., & John, O. P. (1992). An introduction to the Five-Factor Model and its applications. *Journal of Personality*, *60*(2), 175–216. doi:10.1111/j.1467-6494.1992.tb00970.x PMID:1635039

McDonald, S. (2011). What You Know or Who You Know? Occupation-Specific Work Experience and Job Matching through Social Networks. *Social Science Research*, *40*(6), 1664–1675. doi:10.1016/j.ssresearch.2011.06.003

Mceetya. (2007). *National assessment program e ICT literacy years 6 & 10, report 2005*. Carlton South: Ministerial council on education, employment, training and youth affairs. Retrieved from: http://www.nap.edu.au/verve/_resources/2005_ICTL_Public_Report_file_main.pdf

McGivern, R. F., Huston, J. P., Byrd, D., King, T., Siegle, G. J., & Reilly, J. (1997). Sex differences in visual recognition memory: Support for a sex-related difference in attention in adults and children. *Brain and Cognition*, *34*(3), 323–336. doi:10.1006/brcg.1997.0872 PMID:9292185

McGregor, J., Davies, S. G., Giddings, L. S., & Pringle, J. (2017). Pursuing equal pay: The perspectives of female engineers and potential policy interventions. *The Journal of Industrial Relations*, *59*(1), 3–21. doi:10.1177/0022185616659677

McNeal, R. S., Hale, K., & Dotterweich, L. (2008). Citizen-government interaction and the internet: Expectations and accomplishments in contact, quality, and trust. *Journal of Information Technology & Politics*, *5*(2), 213–229. doi:10.1080/19331680802298298

Medenica, S., Račić, M., & Joksimović, V. (2015). Internet and computer addiction: "new age" disease of the 21st century. *Biomedical Research*, *9*(1). doi:10.7251/bii1501069m

Meelissen, M. (2008). Computer attitudes and competencies among primary and secondary school students. In J. Voogt, & G. Knezek (Eds.), International handbook of information technology in primary and secondary education, part one (pp. 381–395). New York: Springer.

Meelissen, M. R. M., & Drent, M. (2008). Gender differences in computer attitudes: Does the school matter? *Computers in Human Behavior*, *24*(3), 969–985. doi:10.1016/j.chb.2007.03.001

Meller, P. (2010). Perspectiva histórica de la discriminación femenina a nivel profesional. In *Carreras universitarias. Rentabilidad, selectividad y discriminación.* Santiago de Chile: UQBAR-editores.

Mendel, T., Puddephatt, A., Wagner, B., Hawtin, D., & Torres, N. (2012). *Global Survey on Internet Privacy and Freedom of Expression.* Retrieved January 3, 2018 from http://unesdoc.unesco.org/images/0021/002182/218273e.pdf

Mendonça, S., Crespo, N., & Simões, N. (2015). Inequality in the network society: An integrated approach to ICT access, basic skills, and complex capabilities. *Telecommunications Policy*, *39*(3/4), 192–207. doi:10.1016/j.telpol.2014.12.010

Meszaros, P. S., Soyoung, L., & Laughling, A. (2007). Information processing and IT career interest/choice among high school students. In Reconfiguring the firewall. Recruiting women to Information Technology across cultures and Continents (pp. 77-98). Wellesley, MA: A.K. Peters, Ltd.

Meyers, E. M., Erickson, I., & Small, R. V. (2013). Digital Literacy and Informal Learning Environments: An Introduction. *Learning, Media and Technology*, *38*(4), 355–367. doi:10.1080/17439884.2013.783597

Meyers-Levy, J., & Loken, B. (2015). Revisiting gender differences: What we know and what lies ahead. *Journal of Consumer Psychology*, *25*(1), 129–149. doi:10.1016/j.jcps.2014.06.003

Meyers-Levy, J., & Maheswaran, D. (1991). Exploring differences in males' and females' processing strategies. *The Journal of Consumer Research, 18*(1), 63–70. doi:10.1086/209241

Meyers-Levy, J., & Sternthal, B. (1991). Gender differences in the use of message cues and judgments. *JMR, Journal of Marketing Research, 28*(1), 84–96. doi:10.2307/3172728

Mihajlov, L., & Vejmelka, L. (2017). Internet addiction: A review of the first twenty years. *Psychiatria Danubina, 29*(3), 260–272. doi:10.24869/psyd.2017.260 PMID:28949307

Mills, J. E. (2011). Reflections on the past, present and future of women in engineering. *Australasian Journal of Engineering Education, 17*(3), 139–146. doi:10.1080/22054952.2011.11464065

Ministry of Electronics & Information Technology. (2017). *About Digital India: Introduction*. Retrieved December 13, 2017 from http://www.digitalindia.gov.in/content/introduction

Ministry of Health and Family Welfare. (2017). *National Family Health Survey 4: 2015-16*. Retrieved December 28, 2017 from http://rchiips.org/nfhs/pdf/NFHS4/India.pdf

Ministry of Statistics and Programme Implementation. (2017). *Women and Men in India-2016*. Retrieved December 29, 2017 from http://www.mospi.gov.in/publication/women-and-men-india-2016

Minton-Eversole, T. (2010). *Mentoring: Make It Pay*. Retrieved from https://www.shrm.org/resourcesandtools/hr-topics/organizational-and-employee-development/pages/makementoringpay.aspx

Mitra, A., Willyard, J., Platt, C., & Parsons, M. (2005). Exploring Web usage and selection criteria among male and female students. *Journal of Computer-Mediated Communication, 10*(3), 00. doi:10.1111/j.1083-6101.2005.tb00258.x

Moghaddam, G. G. (2009). Information technology and gender gap: Toward a global view. *The Electronic Library, 28*(5), 722–773. doi:10.1108/02640471011081997

Molina, M. L. (2015). *Connecteted women- Accelerating the digital economy: Gender diversity in the telecommunications sector.* Retrieved 2018, from https://www.atkearney.com/documents/10192/5580445/Connected+Women+2015-WDReport.pdf/d3c08b0a-fab6-431c-80c0-0d332b9e882d

Monash University. (2017). *Women's Mentoring Program*. Retrieved from https://www.monash.edu/gender-equity/programs/mentoring

Monash University. (2018). *Severe shortage of mining engineers looming*. Retrieved from https://www.monash.edu/engineering/about-us/news-events/latest-news/articles/2018/severe-shortage-of-mining-engineers-looming2

Montagnier, P., & van Welsum, D. (2006). ICTs and gender: Evidence from OECD and non-OECD countries. *UNCTAD Expert Meeting*. In *Support of the Implementation and Follow-Up of WSIS: Using ICTs to Achieve Growth and Development. Jointly organized by UNCTAD*, OECD and ILO.

Moore, K., Griffiths, M., Richardson, H., & Adam, A. (2008). Gendered futures? Women, the ICT workplace and stories of the future. *Gender, Work and Organization, 15*(5), 523–542. doi:10.1111/j.1468-0432.2008.00416.x

Moreno, R. R., Molina, C. M., Figueroa, J. C. S., & Moreno, M. R. (2013). Gender and E-government adoption in Spain. *International Journal of Electronic Government Research, 9*(3), 23–42. doi:10.4018/jegr.2013070102

Morris, D., & Trushell, J. (2014). Computer programming, ICT and gender in the classroom: A male-dominated domain or a female preserve? *Research in Teacher Education, 4*(1), 4–9.

Morris, M. G., Venkatesh, V., & Ackerman, P. L. (2005). Gender and age differences in employee decisions about new technology: An extension to the theory of planned behavior. *IEEE Transactions on Engineering Management*, *52*(1), 69–84. doi:10.1109/TEM.2004.839967

Mouakket, S. (2015). Factors influencing continuance intention to use social network sites: The Facebook case. *Computers in Human Behavior*, *53*, 102–110. doi:10.1016/j.chb.2015.06.045

Mou, J., Shin, D., & Cohen, J. (2017). Understanding trust and percieved usefulness in the consumer acceptance of an e-service: A longitudinal investigation. *Behaviour & Information Technology*, *36*(2), 125–139. doi:10.1080/0144929X.2016.1203024

Moussa, B. H., & Seraphim, J. (2017). Digital gender divides and e-empowerment in the UAE: A critical perspective. *International Journal of Education and Development Using Information and Communication Technology*, *13*(3), 145–161.

Mridha, M., Erlandsson, B. E., Islam, M., & Sultana, N. (2016). To improve rural health care and patient safety by empowering the health workers utilizing the modern medical devices and ICT tools. *Annual Global Healthcare Conference*, 1-4.

Mukerji, M. (2008). Telecentres in Rural India: Emergence and A Typology. *The Electronic Journal on Information Systems in Developing Countries*, *35*(5), 1–13. doi:10.1002/j.1681-4835.2008.tb00242.x

Mumporeze, N., & Prieler, M. (2017). Gender digital divide in Rwanda: A qualitative analysis of socioeconomic factors. *Telematics and Informatics*, *34*(7), 1285–1293. doi:10.1016/j.tele.2017.05.014

Murphy, G. B., & Tocher, N. (2011). Gender differences in the effectiveness of online trust building information cues: An empirical examination. *The Journal of High Technology Management Research*, *22*(1), 26–35. doi:10.1016/j.hitech.2011.03.004

Nair, N. (2010). Women's Education in India: A Situational Analysis. *IMJ*, *1*(4), 100–114. PMID:20486309

Najmul Islam, A. K. (2011). Information Systems Post-Adoption Satisfaction And Dissatisfaction: A Study In The E-Learning Context. In *The Pacific Asia Conference on Information Systems (PACIS) Proceedings*. Brisbane: PAICS. Retrieved from http://aisel.aisnet.org/pacis2011/83/

Nam, T. (2014). Determining the type of e-government use. *Government Information Quarterly*, *31*(2), 211–220. doi:10.1016/j.giq.2013.09.006

Narula, R., & Zanfei, A. (2006). *Globalization of Innovation: The Role of Multinational Enterprises*. The Oxford Handbook of Innovation. doi:10.1093/oxfordhb/9780199286805.003.0012

Nasdaq. (n.d.). *Technology Companies*. Retrieved September 25, 2018 from https://www.nasdaq.com/screening/companies-by industry.aspx?industry=Technology&sortname=marketcap&sorttype=1

National Center For Women and Information Technology. (2014). *What Is the Impact of Gender Diversity on Technology Business Performance? Research Summary*. Retrieved from https://www.ncwit.org/sites/default/files/resources/impactgenderdiversitytechbusinessperformance_print.pdf

National Children's Bureau (NCB). (2015). *ICT & Me: A research study examining how young people's use of ICT and the amount of screen time impacts on GCSE attainment*. Retrieved from https://www.ncb.org.uk/sites/default/files/field/attachment/22%20ict_me.pdf

National Post. (n.d.). *Who is Donna Strickland and Why is She One of the Few Women to Win a Nobel Prize?* Retrieved from https://nationalpost.com/news/world/donna-strickland-nobel-prize

Neely, C. (2018, Jan 29). *Japan's Top Social Media Networks in 2018*. Retrieved from Humble Bunny: http://www.humblebunny.com/japans-top-social-media-networks-2018/

Negrey, C., & Rausch, S. D. (2009). Creativity gaps and gender gaps: Women, men and place in the United States. *Gender, Place and Culture*, *16*(5), 517–533. doi:10.1080/09663690903148408

Nelson, B. (2014). The data on diversity. *Communications of the ACM*, *57*(11), 86–95. doi:10.1145/2597886

Norris, P. (2001). *Digital divide: Civic engagement, information poverty, and the Internet worldwide*. Cambridge University Press. doi:10.1017/CBO9781139164887

Northrup, J. C., Lapierre, C., Kirk, J., & Rae, C. (2015). The Internet Process Addiction Test: Screening for Addictions to Processes Facilitated by the Internet. *Behavioral Science*, *5*(3), 341–352. doi:10.3390/bs5030341 PMID:26226007

Nov, O., & Ye, C. (2008). Personality and Technology Acceptance: Personal Innovativeness in IT, Openness and Resistance to Change. In *Proceedings of the 41st Annual Hawaii International Conference on System Sciences (HICSS 2008) 7-10 Jan. 2008*. Waikoloa, HI: IEEE. 10.1109/HICSS.2008.348

Nungu, A., Brown, T., & Pehrson, B. (2011). Challenges in sustaining Municipal Broadband Networks in the Developing World. In *e-Technologies and Networks for Development* (p. 363). Heidelberg, Germany: Springer.

Nwagwu, E. W., Adekannbi, J., & Bello, O. (2009). Factors influencing use of the internet: A questionnaire survey of the students of University of Ibadan, Nigeria. *The Electronic Library*, *27*(4), 718–734. doi:10.1108/02640470910979651

Nysveen, H., Pedersen, P. E., & Thorbjørnsen, H. (2005). Explaining intention to use mobile chat services: Moderating effects of gender. *Journal of Consumer Marketing*, *22*(5), 247–256. doi:10.1108/07363760510611671

Obayelu, A. E. (2006). Analysis of the information and comminication technology for gender empowerment and sustainable poverty alleviation in Nigeria. International Journal of Education and Development using Information and Communication, 2(3), 45-69.

Odukoya, A. (2005). *ICT & Women: Engendering the Information Society in Nigeria*. Lagos, Nigeria: DevNet.

OECD Horizontal. (2008). *Gender and Sustainable Development: Maximising the Economic, Social and Environmental Role of Women*. Paris: Organisation for Economic Co-operation and Development. Retrieved December 17, 2017, from https://www.oecd.org/social/40881538.pdf

OECD. (n.d.). *Where Are Tomorrow's Female Scientists?* Retrieved October 3, 2018 from http://www.oecd.org/gender/data/wherearetomorrowsfemalescientists.htm

Okazaki, S., & Hirose, M. (2009). Does gender affect media choice in travel information search? On the use of mobile Internet. *Tourism Management*, *30*(6), 794–804. doi:10.1016/j.tourman.2008.12.012

Okazaki, S., Rubio, N., & Campo, S. (2014). Gossiping behavior on social networking sites: Does gender matter? *International Journal of Human-Computer Interaction*, *30*(9), 718–726. doi:10.1080/10447318.2014.907710

Okunna, S. (2000). *Gender and Communication in Nigeria: Is this the Twenty First Century?* Paper presented at the 2000 Summit, Barcelona, Spain.

Olatokun, W. M. (2007). Availability, Accessibility and Use of ICTs by Nigerian Women Academics. *Malaysian Journal of Library and Information Science*, *12*(2), 13–33.

Oliver, R. L. (1977). Effect of Expectation and Disconfirmation on Post exposure product Evaluations:An Alternative Interpretation. *The Journal of Applied Psychology*, *62*(4), 480–486. doi:10.1037/0021-9010.62.4.480

Oliver, R. L. (1980). A Cognitive Model of the Antecedents and Consequences of Satisfaction Decisions. *JMR, Journal of Marketing Research*, *17*(4), 460. doi:10.2307/3150499

Ong, C. S., & Lai, J. Y. (2006). Gender differences in perceptions and relationships among dominants of e-learning acceptance. *Computers in Human Behavior*, *22*(5), 816–829. doi:10.1016/j.chb.2004.03.006

Organisation for Economic Cooperation and Development (OECD). (2006). *Classifying Information and Communication Technology (ICT) Services*. Paris: OECD Publishing.

Organisation for Economic Cooperation and Development (OECD). (2007). *Measuring the Impacts of ICT Using Official Statistics*. Paris: OECD Publishing.

Organisation for Economic Cooperation and Development (OECD). (2011). *OECD Guide to Measuring the Information Society 2011*. Paris: OECD Publishing. doi:10.1787/10.1787/9789264113541-e

Organisation for Economic Cooperation and Development (OECD). (2018a). *Education and training: Enrolment by field*. Retrieved from http://stats.oecd.org/Index.aspx?DataSetCode=EDU_ENRL_FIELD

Organisation for Economic Cooperation and Development (OECD). (2018b). *Labour force participation rate*. Retrieved from https://data.oecd.org/emp/labour-force-participation-rate.htm

Organisation for Economic Cooperation and Development. (2004). *Information Technology Outlook 2004*. Paris: OECD Publishing.

Organisation for Economic Co-operation Development (OECD). (2003). *The e-Government Imperative*. OECD e-Government Studies.

Organization For Economic Co-Operation and Development. (1997). *National Innovation Systems*. Retrieved from https://www.oecd.org/science/inno/2101733.pdf

Orser, B., Riding, A., & Stanley, J. (2012). Perceived career challenges and response strategies of women in the advanced technology sector. *Entrepreneurship and Regional Development*, *24*(1-2), 73–93. doi:10.1080/08985626.2012.637355

Oxoby, R. (2009). Understanding social inclusion, social cohesion, and social capital. *International Journal of Social Economics*, *36*(12), 1133–1152. doi:10.1108/03068290910996963

Oyelaran-Oyeyinka, B., & Adeya, C. (2004). Dynamics of adoption and usage of ICTs in African universities: A study of Kenya and Nigeria. *Technovation*, *24*(10), 841–851. doi:10.1016/S0166-4972(02)00170-0

Padte, R. K. (2012). *Section 66A, Sexual Harassment and Women's Rights*. Retrieved January 3, 2018 from https://internetdemocracy.in/2012/12/section-66a-sexual-harassment-and-womens-rights-2/

Padte, R. K., & Kovacs, A. (2013). *Keeping Women Safe? Gender, Online Harassment and Indian Law*. Retrieved January 3, 2018 from https://internetdemocracy.in/reports/keeping-women-safe-gender-online-harassment-and-indian-law/

Palmero Hinojosa, M. G., & Guzman, M. G. (2015). Application deployment on mobile devices as a useful tool for self-learning in health doctors in training in secondary hospital. *International Journal of Integrated Care*, 1565–1568.

Palvia, P., Baqir, N., & Nemati, H. (2018). ICT for socio-economic development: A citizens' perspective. *Information & Management*, *55*(2), 160–176. doi:10.1016/j.im.2017.05.003

Pan, Z., Yan, W., Jing, G., & Zheng, J. (2011). Exploring structured inequality in Internet use behavior. *Asian Journal of Communication*, *21*(2), 116–132. doi:10.1080/01292986.2010.543555

Parbat, K. (2016, June 8). *Google, Tata Trusts launch 'Internet Sathi' in West Bengal to Empower Rural Women*. Retrieved June 20, 2018 from https://economictimes.indiatimes.com/tech/internet/google-tata-trusts-launch-internet-sathi-in-west-bengal-to-empower-rural-women/articleshow/52651338.cms

Parihar, J. (2017). How Digital India Minimised the Great Gender Divide? *IOSR Journal Of Humanities And Social Science*, *22*(11), 29-33.

Park, J., Snell, W., Ha, S., & Chung, T. (2011). Consumers' Post-adoption of M-services: Interest in Future M-services Based on Consumer Evaluations of Current M-services. *Journal of Electronic Commerce Research*, *12*(13), 165–175. Retrieved from https://lib.dr.iastate.edu/cgi/viewcontent.cgi?article=1065&context=aeshm_pubs

Park, J., Yoon, Y., & Lee, B. (2009). The effect of gender and product categories on consumer online information search. *Advances in Consumer Research. Association for Consumer Research (U. S.)*, *36*, 362–366.

Parmaksız, P. M. Y., & Melis, P. (2012). Digital opportunities for social transition: Blogosphere and motherhood in Turkey. *Fe Dergi*, *1*(1), 123–134. doi:10.1501/Fe0001_0000000069

Parrado Herrera, E. (2017). *Can behavioural science 'nudge' Chilean women towards equality?* World Economic Forum. Retrieved from https://www.weforum.org/agenda/2017/11/chile-women-equality-nudge-gender-gap-report-2017/.Harvard

Pascual, C. (2017). *Q&A: 3 questions for Chile's minister of gender equity. Devex Inside Development/Gender Equality/ Interviewer: K.* Rogers.

Pechtelidis, Y., Kosma, Y., & Chronaki, A. (2015). Between a rock and a hard place: Women and computer technology. *Gender and Education*, *27*(2), 164–182. doi:10.1080/09540253.2015.1008421

Pew Research Center. (2018, February 5). *Social Media Fact Sheet*. Retrieved from Pew Research Center: http://www.pewinternet.org/fact-sheet/social-media/

Pew Research. (2017). *Pew Global*. Retrieved from Gender divide on social media use tilts toward men in developing economies, women in advanced economies: http://www.pewglobal.org/2018/06/19/3-social-network-adoption-varies-widely-by-country/pg_2018-06-19_global-tech_3-03/

Phillip, M. V., & Suri, R. (2004). Impact of gender differences on the evaluation of promotional emails. *Journal of Advertising Research*, *44*(4), 360–368. doi:10.1017/S0021849904040383

Plan International. (2018, April 26). *Digital empowerment of girls*. Retrieved from Plan International: https://plan-international.org/sites/default/files/digital_empowerment_of_girls_-_briefing_paper_26_april_2018_-_final.pdf

Pocock, B. (1998). All change, still gendered: The Australian labour market in the 1990s. *The Journal of Industrial Relations*, *40*(4), 580–604. doi:10.1177/002218569804000405

Pocock, D. F. (1957). Inclusion and Exclusion:A process in the Caste System of Gujerat. *SouthWestern Journal of Anthropological Research*, *13*(1), 19–31. doi:10.1086outjanth.13.1.3629155

Poushter, J., Bishop, C., & Chwe, H. (2018, June 19). *Social network adoption varies widely by country*. Retrieved from Pew Research Center: http://www.pewglobal.org/2018/06/19/3-social-network-adoption-varies-widely-by-country/

Power, M. (2004, Spring). Gender and Chile's split culture. *Harvard Review of Latin America*.

Professionals Australia. (2014). *Women in IT scholarship – Continuing Professional Development as a way to help address barriers to advancement*. Retrieved from http://www.professionalsaustralia.org.au/support/career-progression/scholarships/-tab-1433426140677-3-5

Protopsaltis, A., & Bouki, V. (2008, September). Gender and information processing in electronic age. In *Proceedings of the 26th annual ACM international conference on Design of communication* (pp. 131-138). ACM.

Przybylski, A. K., Murayama, K., DeHaan, C. R., & Gladwell, V. (2013, July). Motivational, emotional, and behavioral correlates of fear of missing out. *Computers in Human Behavior*, *29*(4), 1841–1848. doi:10.1016/j.chb.2013.02.014

Puri, I. K. (2017). *Why Engineering Schools Globally Need More Creative Women*. Retrieved from http://theconversation.com/au

Purnell, N. (2016, October 3). *How Google's Bicycle-Riding Internet Tutors Are Getting Rural Indian Women Online*. Retrieved June 20, 2018 from https://blogs.wsj.com/indiarealtime/2016/10/03/how-googles-bicycle-riding-internet-tutors-are-getting-rural-indian-women-online/

Purushothaman, A. (2013). *Empowering Women Through Learning To Use The Internet - An Ethnographic Action Research Project To Address The Second Order Digital Divide*. Aalborg University. Retrieved from http://vbn.aau.dk/files/195244502/Aparna_Thesis_VBN_Upload.pdf

Purushothaman, A., & Zhou, C. (2014). Change toward a Creative Society in Developing Contexts--Women's Barriers to Learning by Information and Communication Technology. *Gender, Technology and Development*, *18*(3), 363–386. doi:10.1177/0971852414544008

Putrevu, S. (2001). Exploring the origins and information processing differences between men and women: Implications for advertisers. *Academy of Marketing Science Review*, *2001*, 1–14. Retrieved from http://www.amsreview.org/articles/putrevu10-2001.pdf

Putrevu, S. (2004). Communicating with the sexes: Male and female responses to print advertisements. *Journal of Advertising*, *33*(3), 51–62. doi:10.1080/00913367.2004.10639168

Putrevu, S. (2008). Consumer responses toward sexual and nonsexual appeals: The influence of involvement, need for cognition (NFC), and gender. *Journal of Advertising*, *37*(2), 57–70. doi:10.2753/JOA0091-3367370205

Qin, J., Shi, Z., Ma, Y., & Han, S. (2018). Gender and neural substrates subserving implicit processing of death-related linguistic cues. *Cognitive Processing*, *19*(1), 63–71. doi:10.100710339-017-0847-0 PMID:29305759

Qureshi, S. (2012). As the global digital divide narrows, who is being left behind? *Information Technology for Development*, *18*(4), 277–280. doi:10.1080/02681102.2012.730656

Radu, S. (2018). *These Are the 5 Best Countries for Women*. Retrieved from https://www.usnews.com/news/best-countries/best-women

Rajpurohit, G. S., & Kaur, A. (2017). An Appraisal of Khap Panchayat: Issues and Concerns. *International Journal of Science and Research*, *6*(4), 290–295.

Rajpurohit, G. S., & Prakash, A. (2015). Khap Panchayat in India: Legitimacy, Reality and Reforms. *International Journal of Allied Practice. Research and Review*, *2*(3), 81–90.

Ramayah, T., Jantan, M., & Ismail, N. (2003). *Impact of intrinsic and extrinsic motivation on Internet usage in Malaysia*. Presented at the 12th International Conference on Management of Technology, Nancy, France. Retrieved 17 June 2014, from http://www.ramayah.com/journalarticlespdf/impactofintrinsic.pdf

Rana, N. P., Dwivedi, Y. K., & Williams, M. D. (2015). A meta-analysis of existing research on citizen adoption of e-government. *Information Systems Frontiers*, *17*(3), 547–563. doi:10.100710796-013-9431-z

Randstad. (2017). *Diversidad en ingeniería en 2017*. Retrieved from https://www.randstad.cl/tendencias360/archivo/diversidad-en-ingenieria-en-2017_1365/

Rebollo, M. A., & Vico, A. (2014). Perceived Social Support as a factor of rural Women'e Digital Inclusion in Online Social networks. *Media Education Research Journal*, *43*(22), 173–180.

Reddick, C. G. (2005). Citizen interaction with e-government: From the streets to servers? *Government Information Quarterly*, *22*(1), 38–57. doi:10.1016/j.giq.2004.10.003

Report, W. D. (2006). *Equity and Development*. Washington, DC: The International Bank for Reconstruction and Development/The World Bank.

Report, W. D. (2012). *Gender Equality and Development*. Washington, DC: The International Bank for Reconstruction and Development/The World Bank. doi:10.1596/978-0-8213-8810-5

Resnick, M. (2002). Rethinking learning in the digital age. In G. Kirkman (Ed.), *The Global Information Technology Report: Readiness for the Networked Word*. Oxford, UK: Oxford University Press.

Rets Information. (n.d.). *Bekendtgørelse af lov om ligestilling af kvinder og mænd*. Retrieved from https://www.retsinformation.dk/forms/r0710.aspx?id=160578

Riedl, R., Hubert, M., & Kenning, P. (2010). Are there neural gender differences in online trust? An fMRI study on the perceived trustworthiness of eBay offers. *Management Information Systems Quarterly*, *34*(2), 397–428. doi:10.2307/20721434

Rincon, P. (2018). *First Woman Physics Nobel Winner in 55 Years*. Retrieved from https://www.bbc.com/news/science-environment-45655151

Roberts, P., & Ayre, M. (2002). Did she jump or was she pushed? A study of women's retention in the engineering workforce. *International Journal of Engineering Education*, *18*(4), 415–421.

Rodgers, S., & Harris, M. A. (2003). Gender and e-commerce: An exploratory study. *Journal of Advertising Research*, *43*(3), 322–329. doi:10.2501/JAR-43-3-322-329

Rodrigues, G., Sarabdeen, J., & Balasubramanian, S. (2016). Factors that influence consumer adoption of e-government services in the UAE: A UTAUT model perspective. *Journal of Internet Commerce*, *15*(1), 18–39. doi:10.1080/15332861.2015.1121460

Roelofsen, P. (2002). The impact of office environments on employee performance: The design of the workplace as a strategy for productivity enhancement. *Journal of Facilities Management*, *1*(3), 247-264.

Rogers, E. M. (2003). *Diffusion of Innovations* (5th ed.). New York, NY: Simon and Schuster.

Rogers, E. M. (2003). *Diffusion of innovations* (5th ed.). New York: Free Press.

Ross, M. S., & Godwin, A. (2016). *Engineering Identity Implications on the Retention of Black Women in the Engineering Industry*. Retrieved from https://peer.asee.org/engineering-identity-implications-on-the-retention-of-black-women-in-the-engineering-industry

Ross, C., Orr, E. S., Sisic, M., Arseneault, J. M., Simmering, M. G., & Orr, R. R. (2009). Personality and mtivation associated with Facebook use. *Computers in Human Behavior*, *25*(2), 578–586. doi:10.1016/j.chb.2008.12.024

Rowley, J., Johnson, F., & Sbaffi, L. (2017). Gender as an influencer of online health information-seeking and evaluation behavior. *Journal of the Association for Information Science and Technology*, *68*(1), 36–47. doi:10.1002/asi.23597

Rowntree, O. (2018). *Connected Woman: The mobile gender gap report*. GSMA.

Roy, P. K. (2012 November 6). *Why Was An Indian Man Held for Sending A Tweet?* Retrieved January 3, 2018 from http://www.bbc.com/news/world-asia-india-20202275

Roy, M., & Chi, M. T. (2003). Gender differences in patterns of searching the web. *Journal of Educational Computing Research, 29*(3), 335–348. doi:10.2190/7BR8-VXA0-07A7-8AVN

Sadiq, S., & Khan, A. (2015). Khap Panchayats in India: Precepts and Practices. *International Journal of Current Research, 7*(1), 11753–11757.

SageWorks. (2017). *Most Profitable Industries over Past Year.* Retrieved from https://www.sageworks.com/most-profitable-industries-over-past-year/

Saha, T., & Srivastava, A. (2014). Indian Women at Risk in the Cyber Space: A Conceptual Model of Reasons of Victimization. *International Journal of Cyber Criminology, 8*(1), 57–67.

Sáinz, M. (2007). *Aspectos psicosociales de las diferencias de género en actitudes hacialas nuevas tecnologías en adolescentes* [Psychosocial aspects of gender difference in gender attitudes towards new technologies among adolescents]. Retrieved from http://www.injuve.mtin.es/injuve/contenidos.item.action?id=1423691052&menuId=52682864

Sainz, M., Fatsini, E., García, S., González, A., Meneses, J., Prat, P., & Solé, S. (2009). *¿Por qué las mujeres no eligen estudios TIC? La cañería que gotea en elcontexto de Cataluña?* [Why women do not pursue ICT-related studies The leaky pipeline in the context of Catalunya?]. Unpublished research report.

Sáinz, M., Fatsini, E., García, S., González, A., Meneses, N., Prat, P., & Solé, J. (2009) *¿Porqué las mujeres no eligen estudios TIC? La cañería que gotea en el contexto de Cataluña.* [Why women do not pursue ICT studies? The leaky pipeline in the context of Catalunya]. Research Report, unpublished.

Sainz, M. (2011). Factors which influence girls' orientations to ICT subjects in schools. Evidence from Spain. *International Journal of Gender, Science and Technology, 3*(2), 387–406.

Salehan, M., Kim, D. J., & Kim, C. (2017). Use of Online Social Networking Services from a Theoretical Perspective of the Motivation Participation-Performance Framework. *Journal of the Association for Information Systems, 18*(2), 141–172. doi:10.17705/1jais.00449

Salignac, F., Galea, N., & Powell, A. (2017). Institutional entrepreneurs driving change: The case of gender equality in the Australian construction industry. *Australian Journal of Management, 43*(1), 152–169. doi:10.1177/0312896217705179

Sam, H. K., Othman, A. E. A., & Nordin, Z. S. (2005). Computer Self-Efficacy, Computer Anxiety, and Attitudes toward the Internet: A Study among Undergraduates in Unimas. *Journal of Educational Technology & Society, 8*(4), 205–219.

Sanchez-Franco, M. J. (2006). Exploring the influence of gender on the web usage via partial least squares. *Behaviour & Information Technology, 25*(1), 19–36. doi:10.1080/01449290500124536

Sanda, H. U., & Kurfi, M. H. (2013). Gender and Information Communication Technologies in Nigeria: Challenges and prospects. *Global Journal of Human Social Science Sociology and Culture, 6*(13), 50–58.

Sandemose , A. (1936). A Fugitive Crosses His Tracks [En flyktning krysser sitt spor]. New York, NY: Alfred A. Knopf.

Sangrà, A., & González-Sanmamed, M. (2010). The role of information and communication technologies in improving teaching and learning processes in primary and secondary schools. *Research in Learning Technology, 18*(3), 207–220. doi:10.1080/09687769.2010.529108

Sanyal, B. C. (2001). *New functions of higher education and ICT to achieve education for all, in proceedings the Expert Roundtable on University and Technology-for-Literacy/Basic Education Partnership in Developing Countries*. International Institute for Educational Planning.

Sarabdeen, J., & Rodrigues, G. (2010). Gender differences in e-government adoption in Dubai. *The Business Review, Cambridge*, *16*(2), 120–126.

Sarfo, F. K., Amartei, A. M., Adentwi, K. I., & Brefo, C. (2011). Technology and gender equity: Rural and urban students' attitudes towards information and communication technology. *Journal of Media and Communication Studies*, *3*(6), 221–230.

Saunders, B., & Quirke, P. (2002). Let my laptop lead the way: A Middle Eastern study. *Journal of Educational Technology & Society*, *5*(1), 1436–4522.

Saunders, M., Lewis, P., & Thornhill, A. (2007). *Research Methods for Business Students*. Harlow, UK: Pearson Education.

Schmitt, D. P., Realo, A., Voracek, M., & Allik, J. (2008). Why can't a man be more like a woman? Sex differences in Big Five personality traits across 55 cultures. *Journal of Personality and Social Psychology*, *94*(1), 168–182. doi:10.1037/0022-3514.94.1.168 PMID:18179326

Schulte-Rüther, M., Markowitsch, H. J., Shah, N. J., Fink, G. R., & Piefke, M. (2008). Gender differences in brain networks supporting empathy. *NeuroImage*, *42*(1), 393–403. doi:10.1016/j.neuroimage.2008.04.180 PMID:18514546

Schunk, D. H., Meece, J. L., & Pintrich, P. R. (2014). *Motivation in education: Theory, research, and applications* (4th ed.). Harlow: Pearson.

Schwab, F. (2017). *The Global Gender Gap Report*. Geneva: World Economic Forum.

Science Daily. (2009). *Fridges And Washing Machines Liberated Women, Study Suggests*. Retrieved from 1. https://www.accenture.com/us-en/insight-outlook-california-dreaming-corporate-culture-silicon-valley

Seidlitz, L., & Diener, E. (1998). Sex differences in the recall of affective experiences. *Journal of Personality and Social Psychology*, *74*(1), 262–271. doi:10.1037/0022-3514.74.1.262 PMID:9457787

Seidman, G. (2013). Self-presentation and belonging on Facebook: How personality influences social media use and motivations. *Personality and Individual Differences*, *54*(3), 402–407. doi:10.1016/j.paid.2012.10.009

Seron, C., Silbey, S. S., Cech, E., & Rubineau, B. (2016). Persistence is cultural: Professional socialization and the reproduction of sex segregation. *Work and Occupations*, *43*(2), 178–214. doi:10.1177/0730888415618728

Sevillano-García, M. L., & Vázquez-Cano, E. (2015). The Impact of Digital Mobile Devices in Higher Education. *Journal of Educational Technology & Society*, *18*(1), 106–118.

Shaouf, A., Lü, K., & Li, X. (2016). The effect of web advertising visual design on online purchase intention: An examination across gender. *Computers in Human Behavior*, *60*, 622–634. doi:10.1016/j.chb.2016.02.090

Shao, Y., Zheng, T., & Wang, Y. (2018). Internet addiction detection rate among college students in the People's Republic of China: A meta-analysis in Child Adolescent *Psychiatry. Mental Health*, *12*, 25. PMID:29849754

Sharma, M. (2016, July 31). *20 Years On: India's Cyber Cafes Disappearing as Pocket Internet Takes Over*. Retrieved December 28, 2017 from http://www.hindustantimes.com/india-news/20-years-on-india-s-cyber-cafes-disappearing-as-pocket-internet-takes-over/story-vszaWMYND6Mm2lqOxkx5SK.html

Sharma, S. K. (2015). Adoption of e-government services: The role of service quality dimensions and demographic variables. *Transforming Government: People. Process and Policy*, *9*(2), 207–222.

Shashaani, L., & Khalili, A. (2000). Gender and computers: Similarities and differences in Iranian college students' towards computers. *Computers & Education, 37*(3-4), 363–375. doi:10.1016/S0360-1315(01)00059-8

Shaw, L. H., & Gant, L. M. (2002). Users divided? Exploring the gender gap in Internet use. *Cyberpsychology & Behavior, 5*(6), 517–527. doi:10.1089/109493102321018150 PMID:12556114

Sheehan, K. B. (1999). An investigation of gender differences in online privacy concerns and resultant behaviors. *Journal of Interactive Marketing, 13*(4), 24–38. doi:10.1002/(SICI)1520-6653(199923)13:4<24::AID-DIR3>3.0.CO;2-O

Shen, C. Y., & Ge, J. (2005). Women and ICT: from the Chinese perspective. *Proceeding CWIT '05 Proceedings of the international symposium on Women and ICT: creating global transformation.* Baltimore, MD: ACM.

Shneiderman, B. (2000). Universal Usability: Pushing human-computer interaction research to empower every citizen. CS-TR-4043. *Communications of the ACM, 45*(3), 84–91. doi:10.1145/332833.332843

Shu, C. (2018). *Former Software Engineer Accuses Uber of 'Degrading Conduct' toward Women in New Lawsuit.* Retrieved October 3, 2018 from http://social.techcrunch.com/2018/05/21/former-software-engineer-accuses-uber-of-degrading-conduct-toward-women-in-new-lawsuit/

Siddiq, F., Gochyyev, P., & Wilson, M. (2017). Learning in Digital Networks e ICT literacy: A novel assessment of students' 21st century skills. *Computers & Education, 109*, 11–37. doi:10.1016/j.compedu.2017.01.014

Sieverding, M., & Koch, S. C. (2009). (Self-)Evaluation of computer competence: How gender matters. *Computers & Education, 52*(3), 696-701. . doi:10.1016/j.compedu.2008.11.016

Singh, M. (2014, October 13). *64% of Urban Indian Women Busy with Housework, Study Reveals.* Retrieved December 28, 2017 from https://timesofindia.indiatimes.com/india/64-of-urban-Indian-women-busy-with-housework-study-reveals/articleshow/44796358.cms

Singh, S., & Pawar, G. S. (2016). Khap Panchayat: Analysis in Light of Jurisprudence. *Bharati Law Review, 5*(3), 240–251.

Sinha, C. (2009). Effects of Education and ICT Use on Gender Relations in Bhutan. *International Development Research Centre, 5*(3), 21–34.

Sin, S. C. J. (2016). Social media and problematic everyday life information-seeking outcomes: Differences across use frequency, gender, and problem-solving styles. *Journal of the Association for Information Science and Technology, 67*(8), 1793–1807. doi:10.1002/asi.23509

Sipior, J. C., Ward, B. T., & Connolly, R. (2011). The digital divide and t-government in the United States: Using the technology acceptance model to understand usage. *European Journal of Information Systems, 20*(3), 308–326. doi:10.1057/ejis.2010.64

Sirirak, S., Islam, N., & Khang, D. B. (2011). Does ICT adoption enhance hotel performance? *Journal of Hospitality and Tourism Technology, 2*(1), 34–49. doi:10.1108/17579881111112403

Skaalvik, S., & Skaalvik, E. S. (2004). Gender Differences in Math And Verbal Self- Concept, Performance Expectations, and Motivation. *Sex Roles, 50*(3/4), 241–252. doi:10.1023/B:SERS.0000015555.40976.e6

Smith, T. W., & Son, J. (2014). *Measuring Occupational Prestige on the 2012 General Social Survey.* Retrieved from http://gss.norc.org/Documents/reports/methodological-reports/MR122%20Occupational%20Prestige.pdf

Smith, B. N., & Necessary, J. R. (1996). Assessing the computer literacy of undergraduate college students. *Education, 117*(2), 188–193.

Snizek, W. E., & Neil, C. C. (1992). Job characteristics, gender stereotypes and perceived gender discrimination in the workplace. *Organization Studies*, *13*(3), 403–427. doi:10.1177/017084069201300305

Sommers, C. H. (2015). *The Gender Gap: What the World Economic Forum Got Wrong*. Retrieved from http://www.aei.org/multimedia/the-gender-gap-what-the-world-economic-forum-got-wrong/

Song, I., Larose, R., Eastin, M. S., & Lin, C. A. (2004). Internet Gratifications and Internet Addiction: On the Uses and Abuses of New Media. *Cyberpsychology & Behavior*, *7*(4), 384–394. doi:10.1089/cpb.2004.7.384 PMID:15331025

Sorgner, A. B.-B. (2017). *The Effects of Digitalization on the Gender Equality in the G20 economies*. Kiel: Kiel Institute for the World Economy. Retrieved June 11, 2018, from https://economic-policy-forum.org/wp-content/uploads/2017/08/20170707_W20_Studie_v2.5.pdf

Soto, J. A. F., Etchegaray, M. V. S., Guzmán, S. A. C., Soto, P. A. G., & Calderón. (2016). *Mujeres Ingeniería UC y más Mujeres para la Ingeniería y las Ciencias de la U. de Chile: Una Mirada al Impulso del Acceso, Experiencia y Permanencia de las Mujeres en las Carreras Ingenieriles y Científicas en Chile* (Magíster en Gestión de Obras Públicas). Universidad de Chile, Santiago de Chile.

Sretenova, N. (2010, September 28). *What has Worked in Europe to Increase Women's Participation in Science and Technology*. Retrieved from http://www.un.org/womenwatch/daw/egm/gst_2010/: http://www.un.org/womenwatch/daw/egm/gst_2010/Stretenova-EP.11-EGM-ST.pdf

Statista. (2018). *Forecast of the Internet User Penetration Rate in Bulgaria from 2015-2020*. Retrieved from https://www.statista.com/statistics/567448/predicted-internet-user-penetration-rate-in-bulgaria/

Statista. (2018a). *Distribution of Facebook users worldwide as of April 2018, by age and gender*. Retrieved from Statista: https://www.statista.com/statistics/376128/facebook-global-user-age-distribution/

Statista. (2018b, March). *Percentage distribution of Facebook users in Spain in 2017, by gender*. Retrieved from Statista: https://www.statista.com/statistics/774511/distribution-by-gender-from-the-users-from-facebook-in-spain/

Statista. (2018c, January). *Share of users of selected social networks in the United Kingdom (UK) in January 2018, by gender*. Retrieved from Statista: https://www.statista.com/statistics/611848/penetration-of-social-networks-in-the-united-kingdom-by-gender/

Statistical Office of the European Communities (EUROSTAT). (2018). *Eurostat Information Society Indicators*. Luxembourg: Eurostat.

Stolzfus, G., Leigh, N. B., Debra, V., & Elizabetht, H. (2011). Gender, gender role and creativity. *Social Behavior and Personality*, *39*(3), 425–432. doi:10.2224bp.2011.39.3.425

Strachan, G. (2010). Still working for the man? Women's employment experiences in Australia since 1950. *The Australian Journal of Social Issues*, *45*(1), 117–130. doi:10.1002/j.1839-4655.2010.tb00167.x

Straub, E. T. (2017). *Understanding technology adoption: theory and future directions for informal learning*. Academic Press.

Strickland, P., & Dent, J. (2017). *Online Harassment and Cyber Bullying*. Retrieved January 20, 2018 from http://www.parliament.uk/commons-library

Subramanian, S. (2017, May 29). *Why Are There So Few Women on the Internet in India?* Retrieved December 25, 2017 from http://www.hindustantimes.com/opinion/locating-gender-in-the-digital-divide/story-zt10VjNAwnOqcChjkYCLfN.html

Sunita, & Yudhvir. (2013). Khap Panchayat: Changing Perspectives. *Asian Journal of Multidimensional Research*, *2*(7), 14-20.

Sun, Y., Lim, K. H., Jiang, C., Peng, J. Z., & Chen, X. (2010). Do males and females think in the same way? An empirical investigation on the gender differences in Web advertising evaluation. *Computers in Human Behavior*, *26*(6), 1614–1624. doi:10.1016/j.chb.2010.06.009

Surie, M. D. (2016). *Where Are India's Working Women?* Retrieved December 29, 2017 from https://asiafoundation.org/2016/03/09/where-are-indias-working-women/

Surman, M., Gardner, C., & Ascher, D. (2014). Local Content, Smartphones, and Digital Inclusion. *Innovations: Technology, Governance, Globalization*, *9*(3-4), 63–74. doi:10.1162/inov_a_00217

Svendsen, G. B., Johnsen, J. K., Almås-Sørensen, L., & Vittersø, J. (2011). Personality and technology acceptance: The influence of personality factors on the core constructs of the Technology Acceptance Model. *Behaviour & Information Technology*, *32*(4), 323–334. doi:10.1080/0144929X.2011.553740

Taddeo, M., & Floridi, L. (2016). The Debate on the Moral Responsibilities of Online Service Providers. *Science and Engineering Ethics*, *22*(6), 1575–1603. doi:10.100711948-015-9734-1 PMID:26613596

Tahiroglu, A. Y., Celik, G. G., Uzel, M., Ozcan, N., & Avci, A. (2008). Internet use among Turkish adolescents. *Cyberpsychology & Behavior*, *11*(5), 537–543. doi:10.1089/cpb.2007.0165 PMID:18785800

Taipale, S. (2013). The use of e-government services and the Internet: The role of sociodemographic, economic and geographical predictors. *Telecommunications Policy*, *37*(4), 413–422. doi:10.1016/j.telpol.2012.05.005

Tariq, M., & Syed, J. (2017). Intersectionality at work: South Asian muslim women's experiences of employment and leadership in the United Kingdom. *Sex Roles*, *77*(7-8), 510–522. doi:10.100711199-017-0741-3 PMID:28979062

Taylor, G. a. (2014). *Review of evaluation approaches and methods used by interventions on women and girls' economic empowerment.* London: odi.org Publications. Retrieved July 6, 2017, from https://www.odi.org/publications/8275-review-evaluation-approaches-methods-used-by-interventions-women-girls-economic-empowerment

Tella, A. (2011). An assessment of mathematics teachers' Internet self-efficacy: Implications on teachers' delivery of mathematics instruction. *International Journal of Mathematical Education in Science and Technology*, *42*(2), 155–174. doi:10.1080/0020739X.2010.519798

Tella, A., & Mutula, S. M. (2008). Gender Differences in Computer Literacy among Undergraduate Students at the University of Botswana: Implications for Library Use. *Malaysian Journal of Library and Information Science*, *13*(1), 59–76.

Terlutter, R., Bidmon, S., & Röttl, J. (2014). Who uses physician-rating websites? Differences in sociodemographic variables, psychographic variables, and health status of users and nonusers of physician-rating websites. *Journal of Medical Internet Research*, *16*(3), e97. doi:10.2196/jmir.3145 PMID:24686918

Tezgel, O., & Gokbayrak, S. (2013). The effects of gender inequalities in the labor market and the social security system on women's social inclusion in Turkey. *Is. Guc Industrial Relations and Human Resources Journal*, *15*(4), 39–59. doi:10.4026/1303-2860.2013.0236.x

Thakur, R., Sinha, A. K., & Pathak, R. K. (2015). *Khap* Panchayats in Transition with Contemporary Times: An Anthropological Evaluation. *South Asian Anthropologist*, *15*(1), 9–14.

Tham, J., & Ahmed, N. (2011). The Usage and Implications of Social Networking Sites: A Survey of College Students. *Journal of Interpersonal. Intercultural and Mass Communication*, *2*(1), 1–11.

The Express Tribute. (2017, May 3). *Indian Village Bans Women from Using Mobile Phones*. Retrieved December 24, 2017 from https://tribune.com.pk/story/1399963/indian-village-bans-women-using-mobile-phones/

The Global Economy. (2018). *Female Labor Force Participation by Country, around the World*. Retrieved from https://www.theglobaleconomy.com/rankings/Female_labor_force_participation/

The GSMA Development Fund, The Cherie Blair Foundation for Women, & Vital Wave Consulting. (2010). *Women & Mobile: A Global Opportunity A Study on the Mobile Phone Gender Gap in Low and Middle-Income Countries*. Retrieved December 28, 2017 from http://www.cherieblairfoundation.org/wp-content/uploads/2012/07/women_and_mobile_a_global_opportunity.pdf

The Hindu. (2017, May 3). *₹2,100 Fine on Women Using Mobile Phones in Public in U.P. Village*. Retrieved December 24, 2017 from http://www.thehindu.com/news/national/2100-rupees-fine-on-women-using-mobile-phones-in-public-in-up-village/article18377318.ece

The Indian Express. (2015, May 26). *Almost Half of Indian Women Find No Reason to Use Internet, Says Google*. Retrieved June 20, 2018 from https://indianexpress.com/article/technology/technology-others/49-indian-women-find-no-reason-to-use-internet-google/

The International Center for Research on Women. (2010). *Bridging the Gender Divide: How Technology Can Advance Women Economically*. Retrieved January 1, 2018 from https://www.icrw.org/wp-content/uploads/2016/10/Bridging-the-Gender-Divide-How-Technology-can-Advance-Women-Economically.pdf

The Nobel Prize. (2018). *The Nobel Prize in Physics 2018*. Retrieved from https://www.nobelprize.org/prizes/physics/2018/summary/

The United Nations Broadband Commission for Digital Development. (2015). *Cyber Violence Against Women and Girls: A World-wide Wake-up Call*. Retrieved January 3, 2018 from http://www.unesco.org/fileadmin/MULTIMEDIA/HQ/CI/CI/images/wsis/GenderReport2015FINAL.pdf

Thorpe, D., & Delaney, B. (2014). *Enhancing the role of women in engineering*. Paper presented at the 25th Annual Conference of the Australasian Association for Engineering Education: Engineering the Knowledge Economy: Collaboration, Engagement & Employability.

TinioV. L. (2012). *ICT in Education*. Retrieved from http://139.179.20.111/egitim/eprimer-edu.pdf

Tomczyk, T. (2015). Addiction to new media among youth — Attempt to characterize the phenomenon. *Debata Edukacyjna*, *6*.

Tømte, C. (2011). Challenging our views on ICT, gender and education. *Nordic Journal of Digital Literacy*, *6*(SI), 309–325.

Tongia, R., Subrahmanian, E., & Arunachalam, V. S. (2005). *ICT for Sustainable Development: Defining a Global Research Agenda*. Bangalore: Allied Publishers.

Torenli, N. (2006). The ‘other’ faces of digital exclusion: ICT gender divides in the broader community. *European Journal of Communication*, *21*(4), 435–455. doi:10.1177/0267323106070010

Torenli, N. (2010). The potential of ICT to generate ‘solidaristic’ practices among women home-based workers in Turkey. *New Technology, Work and Employment*, *25*(1), 49–62. doi:10.1111/j.1468-005X.2009.00238.x

Trauth, E. M., Quesenberry, J. L., & Morgan, A. J. (2004). Understanding the underrepresentation of women in IT: toward a theory of individual differences. In *Proceedings of the 2004 SIGMIS conference on Computer personnel research: Careers, culture, and ethics in a networked environment*. ACM.

Trauth, E. M., Nielsen, S. H., & von Hellens, L. A. (2003). Explaining the IT gender gap: Australian stories for the new millennium. *Journal of Research and Practice in IT, 35*(1), 7–20.

Tsai, P. S., Tsai, C. C., & Hwang, G. H. (2010). Elementary school students' attitudes and self-efficacy of using PDAs in a ubiquitous learning context. *Australasian Journal of Educational Technology, 26*(3), 297–308. doi:10.14742/ajet.1076

Tsao, W. Y. (2013). Application of Expectation Confirmation Theory to Consumers' Impulsive Purchase Behavior for Products Promoted by Showgirls in Exhibits. *Journal of Promotion Management, 19*(3), 283–298. doi:10.1080/10496491.2013.770811

Tshin, E. Y. H., Tanakinja, G. H., & Sondoh, S. L. (2014). The Key Dimensions of Online Service Quality: A Study of Consumer Perceptions. *The IUP. Journal of Marketing Management, 13*(2).

Tsichla, E., Hatzithomas, L., & Boutsouki, C. (2016). Gender differences in the interpretation of web atmospherics: A selectivity hypothesis approach. *Journal of Marketing Communications, 22*(6), 563–586. doi:10.1080/13527266.2014.903507

Turkish Statistical Institute (TSI). (2015). *Information and Communication Technology (ICT) Usage Survey on Households and Individuals, 2015*. TSI.

Turkish Statistical Institute (TSI). (2016). *Information and Communication Technology (ICT) Usage Survey on Households and Individuals, 2016*. TSI.

Turkish Statistical Institute (TurkStat). (2018). *Labour force statistics*. Retrieved from https://biruni.tuik.gov.tr/medas/?kn=72&locale=en

Türkiye Bilişim Derneği. (2018). *Değerlendirme Raporu*. Ankara: Türkiye Bilişim Derneği. Retrieved March 7, 2018, from http://www.tbd.org.tr/wp-content/uploads/2018/05/2017-degerlendirme-raporu.pdf

Turkle, S. (2012). *Alone together: Why we expect more from technology and less from each other*. New York: Basic Books.

Tuurosong, D., & Faisal, M. A. (2014). The Social Media Scourge among University Students: A Study of the University for Development Studies. *Ghana J. Asian Dev. Studium (Roma), 3*(2).

U.S. women surging online, closing gender gap, reshaping social landscape. (2000). *Media Report to Women, 28*(2), 1-2.

UN. (2016). *Leaving no one behind: The imperative of inclusive development*. New York: United Nations Economic and Social Affairs.

Undurraga, T. (2015). Neoliberalism in Argentina and Chile: Common antecedents, divergent paths. *Revista de Sociologia e Politica, 23*(55), 11–34. doi:10.1590/1678-987315235502

UNESCO. (2006). *Education for All Global Monitoring Report*. Retrieved December 31, 2017 from http://www.unesco.org/education/GMR2006/full/chapt6_eng.pdf

UNESCO. (2013). *Doubling digital opportunities: enhancing the inclusion of women & girls in the information society*. Retrieved from http://www.broadbandcommission.org/documents/working-groups/bb-doubling-digital-2013.pdf

UNESCO. (2015). *Mobile Phones & Literacy: Empowerment in Women's Hands - A Cross-Case Analysis of Nine Experiences*. Retrieved January 21, 2018 from http://unesdoc.unesco.org/images/0023/002343/234325E.pdf

Ungerleider, N. (2013). *What It Really Takes To Succeed In Silicon Valley: Money And Status*. Retrieved from https://www.fastcompany.com/3017402/what-it-really-takes-to-succeed-in-silicon-valley-money-and-status

UNICEF. (2017). *The State of the World's Children 2017: Children in a Digital World.* Retrieved December 13, 2017 from https://www.unicef.org/publications/index_101992.html

United Nations (UN). (2002). *Information and Communication technologies and their impact on and use as an instrument for the advancement and empowerment of women* (Report of the Expert Group Meeting Seoul, Republic of Korea, 11 – 14 November 2002). United Nations Division for the Advancement of Women (UN DAW), Department of Economic and Social Affairs. Retrieved from http://www.un.org/womenwatch/daw/egm/ict2002/reports/EGMFinalReport.pdf

United Nations (UN). (2008). *International Standard Industrial Classification (ISIC) of All Economic Activities Revision 4*. New York: United Nations Department of Economic and Social Affairs Statistics Division.

United Nations (UN). (2016). *United Nations e-Government survey 2016. E-government in support of sustainable development*. New York: Department of Economic and Social Affairs, United Nations.

United Nations Conference on Trade and Development (UNCTAD). (2015). *Global assessment of sex-disaggregated ICT employment statistics: Data availability and challenges on measurement and compilation.* UNCTAD Technical Notes on ICT for Development No.4. United Nations.

United Nations Development Programme. (2012). *Mobile Technologies and Empowerment: Enhancing Human Development through Participation and Innovation.* Retrieved January 1, 2018 from http://www.undp.org/content/dam/undp/library/Democratic%20Governance/Access%20to%20Information%20and%20E-governance/Mobile%20Technologies%20and%20Empowerment_EN.pdf

United Nations Educational, Scientific and Cultural Organization (UNESCO). (2006). *International Standard Classification of Education (ISCED) 1997.* UNESCO Institute for Statistics.

United Nations Educational, Scientific and Cultural Organization (UNESCO). (2012). *International Standard Classification of Education ISCED 2011.* Montreal, Canada: UNESCO Institute for Statistics.

United Nations Educational, Scientific and Cultural Organization (UNESCO). (2017). *Cracking the code: Girls' and women's education in science, technology, engineering and mathematics (STEM).* The United Nations Educational, Scientific and Cultural Organization. Retrieved from http://unesdoc.unesco.org/images/0025/002534/253479e.pdf

United Nations Population Fund. (2014). *The Human Rights-Based Approach.* Retrieved December 13, 2017 from http://www.unfpa.org/human-rights-based-approach

United Nations. (2005). *Gender Equality and Empowerment of Women through ICT.* Retrieved January 2, 2018 from http://www.un.org/womenwatch/daw/public/w2000-09.05-ict-e.pdf

United Nations. (2015). *Universal Declaration of Human Rights.* Retrieved from http://www.un.org/en/universal-declaration-human-rights/

University Rankings Australia. (2018). *Male-Female Ratios by University.* Retrieved from http://www.universityrankings.com.au/gender-balance-ratio.html

Urbina, A. U., & Abe, N. (2017). Citizen-centric Perspective on the Adoption of E-Government in the Philippines. *Electronic. Journal of E-Government, 15*(2).

Van Deursen, A. (2012). Internet skill-related problems in accessing online health information. *International Journal of Medical Informatics, 81*(1), 61–72. doi:10.1016/j.ijmedinf.2011.10.005 PMID:22079240

Van Deursen, A., & Van Dijk, J. (2009). Improving digital skills for the use of online public information and services. *Government Information Quarterly, 26*(2), 333–340. doi:10.1016/j.giq.2008.11.002

Van Deursen, A., Van Dijk, J., & Peters, O. (2011). Rethinking Internet skills. The contribution of gender, age, education, Internet experience, and hours online to medium- and content-related internet skills. *Poetics*, *39*(2), 125–144. doi:10.1016/j.poetic.2011.02.001

Van Dijk, J. (2004). Digital Media. In J. D. H. Downing, D. McQuail, P. Schlesinger, & E. Wartella (Eds.), *The SAGE Handbook of Media Studies* (pp. 145–164). Thousand Oaks, CA: SAGE. doi:10.4135/9781412976077.n8

Van Dijk, J. (2005). *The deepening divide: Inequality in the information society*. London: Sage.

Van Dijk, J., & Hacker, K. (2003). The digital divide as a complex and dynamic phenomenon. *The Information Society*, *19*(4), 315–326. doi:10.1080/01972240309487

Varma, R. (2010). Computing Self-Efficacy Among Women in India. *Journal of Women and Minorities in Science and Engineering*, *16*(3), 257–274. doi:10.1615/JWomenMinorScienEng.v16.i3.40

Vatchkov, P. (n.d.). *Bulgarian Software Industry*. Retrieved from http://www.daits.government.bg/gallery/BSI/BulgarianSoftwareIndustry.pdf

Vekiri, I. (2008). *The gender gap in attitudes and beliefs about ICT.* Paper prepared for the OECD Expert meeting on Gender, ICT and Education, Oslo, Norway.

Vekiri, I., & Chronaki, A. (2008). Gender issues in technology use: Perceived social support, computer self-efficacy and value beliefs, and computer use beyond school. *Computers & Education*, *51*(3), 1392–1404. doi:10.1016/j.compedu.2008.01.003

Velasco, S. (2017). *Male Nurses? Female Firefighters? Yes, as Career Boundaries Erode*. Retrieved from https://www.csmonitor.com/Business/2017/0713/Male-nurses-Female-firefighters-Yes-as-career-boundaries-erode

Venkatesh, V., & Morris, M. G. (2000). Why Don't Men Ever Stop to Ask for Directions? Gender, Social Influence, and Their Role in Technology Acceptance and Usage Behavior. *Management Information Systems Quarterly*, *24*(1), 115–139. doi:10.2307/3250981

Venkatesh, V., Sykes, T. A., & Venkatraman, S. (2014). Understanding e-Government portal use in rural India: Role of demographic and personality characteristics. *Information Systems Journal*, *24*(3), 249–269. doi:10.1111/isj.12008

Vodanovich, S., Urquhart, C., & Shakir, M. (2010). Same but different: understanding women's experience of ICT in the UAE. *The Electronic Journal on Information Systems in Developing Countries*. Retrieved from https://onlinelibrary.wiley.com/doi/abs/10.1002/j.1681-4835.2010.tb00286.x

Volman, M., & Van, E. E. (2001). Gender equity and information technology in education. The second decade. *Review of Educational Research*, *71*(4), 613–631. doi:10.3102/00346543071004613

Voutinioti, A. (2013). Determinants of user adoption of e-government services in Greece and the role of citizen service centres. *Procedia Technology*, *8*, 238–244. doi:10.1016/j.protcy.2013.11.033

Vrasidas, C., Zembylas, M., Evagorou, M., Avraamidou, L., & Aravi, C. (2007). ICT as a Tool for Environmental Education, Peace, and Reconciliation. *Educational Media International*, *44*(2), 129–140. doi:10.1080/09523980701295125

Wachter-Boettcher, S., & Emmes, A. (2017). *Technically Wrong: Sexist Apps, Biased Algorithms, and Other Threats of Toxic Tech, Unabridged edition*. Prince Frederick, MD: HighBridge Audio.

Wajcman, J. (2004). *Echnofeminism*. Malden, MA: Polity.

Wajcman, J. (2006). Feminist perspectives on technology. In A. H. Teich (Ed.), *Technology and the Future* (pp. 67–79). Thomson Wardworth.

Walia, S. (2016, March 3). *From Rape Threats to Twitter Trolls: Being A Woman Journalist in India is Tough*. Retrieved December 25, 2017 from https://qz.com/629423/from-rape-threats-to-twitter-trolls-being-a-woman-journalist-in-india-is-tough/

WalterThompson, J. (2012). *Fear of Missing Out (FOMO)*. Retrieved from https://web.archive.org/web/20150626125816/http:/www.jwtintelligence.com/wp-content/uploads/2012/03/F_JWT_FOMO-update_3.21.12.pdf

Walton, R., Yaaqoubi, J., & Kolko, B. (2012). What's it for? Expectations of Internet value and usefulness in Central Asia. *Information Technologies and International Development*, *8*(3), 69–84.

Wang, F., & Zhou, C. (2013). A theoretical study on development of Information and Communication Technology (ICT)-supported education system. In *2013 10th International Conference on Fuzzy Systems and Knowledge Discovery (FSKD)*. Shenyang, China: IEEE Press.

Wanga, J. (2016, July 3). *Men and women who operate without mobile phones*. Retrieved from Daily Nation: https://www.nation.co.ke/lifestyle/lifestyle/1214-3277376-76g2y0/index.html

Wang, C., Zhou, Z., Jin, X. L., Fang, Y., & Lee, M. K. (2017). The influence of affective cues on positive emotion in predicting instant information sharing on microblogs: Gender as a moderator. *Information Processing & Management*, *53*(3), 721–734. doi:10.1016/j.ipm.2017.02.003

Wanpena, S. (2013). The Relationship between Learning Styles and the Social Network Use of Tertiary Level Students. *Procedia: Social and Behavioral Sciences*, *88*, 334–339. doi:10.1016/j.sbspro.2013.08.514

Warschauer, M. (2003). *Technology and social inclusion: Rethinking the digital divide*. Cambridge, MA: MIT Press.

Watts, J. H. (2009). 'Allowed into a man's world' meanings of work–life balance: Perspectives of women civil engineers as 'minority' workers in construction. *Gender, Work and Organization*, *16*(1), 37–57. doi:10.1111/j.1468-0432.2007.00352.x

Webb, D.C. & Miller, S.B. (2015). *Gender Analysis of a Large Scale Survey of Middle Grades Students' Conceptions of Computer Science Education*. Academic Press.

Weber, L. (2018). *White Men Challenge Workplace Diversity Efforts*. Retrieved from https://www.wsj.com/articles/white-men-challenge-workplace-diversity-efforts-1521036001

Wei, P. S., & Lu, H. P. (2013). An examination of the celebrity endorsements and online customer reviews influence female consumers' shopping behavior. *Computers in Human Behavior*, *29*(1), 193–201. doi:10.1016/j.chb.2012.08.005

Weiss, C., Parkinson, D., & Duncan, A. (2015). Living longer on less: Women, paid work, and superannuation in Victoria, Australia. *SAGE Open*, *5*(3). doi:10.1177/2158244015597966

Wentworth, B. (2015). *Using expectancy-value theory to predict intent to conform in Elementary school students* (MA thesis). Appalachian State University.

WES. (2018, January). *Statistics on women in Engineering*. Retrieved from Womwn in Engineering Statistics: https://www.wes.org.uk/sites/default/files/2018-01/Women%20in%20Engineering%20Statistics%20-%20January%202018%20-%20created%20by%20Sarah%20Peers_0.pdf

Whaite, E. O., Shensa, A., Sidani, J. E., Colditz, J. B., & Primack, B. A. (2018). Social media use, personality characteristics, and social isolation among young adults in the United States. *Personality and Individual Differences*, *124*(1), 45–50. doi:10.1016/j.paid.2017.10.030

White, H. (1980). A heteroskedasticity-consistent covariance matrix estimator and a direct test for heteroskedasticity. *Econometrica*, *48*(4), 817–838. doi:10.2307/1912934

White, K., & Özkanlı, Ö. (2010). A comparative study of perceptions of gender and leadership in Australian and Turkish universities. *Journal of Higher Education Policy and Management*, *33*(1), 3–16. doi:10.1080/1360080X.2011.536976

Widyanto, L., & McMurran, M. (2004). The Psychometric Properties of the Internet Addiction Test. *Cyberpsychology & Behavior*, *7*(4), 443–450. doi:10.1089/cpb.2004.7.443 PMID:15331031

Wigfield, A., & Eccles, J. S. (2002). The Development of Competence Beliefs, Expectancies For Success, And Achievement Values From Childhood Through Adolescence. In A. Wigfield & J.S. Eccles (Eds.), Development of achievement motivation. Academic Press.

Wigfield, A., & Eccles, J. S. (2000). Expectancy–value theory of achievement motivation. *Contemporary Educational Psychology*, *25*(1), 68–81. doi:10.1006/ceps.1999.1015 PMID:10620382

Wigfield, A., & Eccles, J. S. (2002). The Development of Competence Beliefs, Expectancies for Success, And Achievement Values from Childhood Through adolescence. In A. Wigfield & J. S. Eccles (Eds.), *A Vol. in the educational psychology series. Development of achievement motivation* (pp. 91–120). San Diego, CA: Academic Press. doi:10.1016/B978-012750053-9/50006-1

Wikipedia. (n.d.a). *Talk: Donna Strickland*. Retrieved from https://en.wikipedia.org/wiki/Talk:Donna_Strickland#Coverage_of_Wikipedia's_anti-woman_bias

Wikipedia. (n.d.b). *Criticism of Wikipedia*. Retrieved from https://en.wikipedia.org/wiki/Criticism_of_Wikipedia

Williams, I. (2015). *Analysis of Public Private Interplay Frameworks in the Development of Rural Telecommunications Infrastructure: A Multi-Case Study*. Aalborg: Aalborg University Press.

Williams, I. (2016). Co-Financing of Bottom-Up Approaches towards Broadband Infrastructure Development: A New Opportunity for Universal Service Funding. *Journal of NBICT*, *1*, 39–64.

Williams, I., Siddi, F., & Kwofie, B. (2016). Public Demand Aggregation as a means of Bridging the ICT Gender Divide. In J. Wilson & N. N. Gapsiso (Eds.), *Overcoming Gender Inequalities through technology Integration* (pp. 123–143). Hershey, PA: IGI Global. doi:10.4018/978-1-4666-9773-7.ch006

Wilson, T. (2000). Web's gender shift more than a curiosity. *Internet Week*, *28*, 827.

Wiseman, A. W., Al-bakr, F., Davidson, P. M., & Bruce, E. (2018). Using technology to break gender barriers: Gender differences in teachers' information and communication technology use in Saudi Arabian classrooms. *Compare: A Journal of Comparative Education*, *48*(2), 224–243. doi:10.1080/03057925.2017.1301200

Wolin, L. D., & Korgaonkar, P. (2003). Web advertising: Gender differences in beliefs, attitudes and behavior. *Internet Research*, *13*(5), 375–385. doi:10.1108/10662240310501658

Women Centre of Peel. (2018). *IT Computer Training*. Retrieved January 2, 2017 from http://www.womencentreofpeel.org/it-computer-training/

Women's Empowerment in the Digital Age: Action Plan. (2015, December 15). Retrieved from https://www.itu.int/en/action/gender-equality/Pages/women-empowerment.aspx: https://www.itu.int/en/action/gender-equality/Documents/GlobalPlatformReferences.pdf

Wong, K. C., & Cheung, W. K. (2013). Gender Differences in ICT Competency for University Students of Different Disciplines. *Journal of Communications and Information Sciences*, *3*(2). doi:10.4156/jcis.vol3.issue2.7

Wood, W., & Eagly, A. H. (2012). Biosocial construction of sex differences and similarities in behavior. Advances in Experimental Social Psychology, 46, 55-123.

Workplace Gender Equality Agency (WGEA). (2018a). *2017-2018 WGEA EOCGE citation holders by industry*. Retrieved from https://www.wgea.gov.au/sites/default/files/WGEA-Employer-of-Choice-citation-holders-by-industry-2017-18.pdf

Workplace Gender Equality Agency (WGEA). (2018b). *Our Role*. Retrieved from https://www.wgea.gov.au/about-wgea/our-role-0

Workplace Gender Equality Agency (WGEA). (2018c). *Relevant Employers*. Retrieved from https://www.wgea.gov.au/who-needs-report/relevant-employers

World Bank. (2018). *Social inclusion*. Retrieved from World Bank: http://www.worldbank.org/en/topic/social-inclusion

World Economic Forum. (2016). *The Global Gender Gap Report 2016*. Retrieved December 29, 2017 from http://www3.weforum.org/docs/GGGR16/WEF_Global_Gender_Gap_Report_2016.pdf

World Economic Forum. (2017). *The Global Gender Gap Report 2017*. Retrieved December 29, 2017 from http://www3.weforum.org/docs/WEF_GGGR_2017.pdf

Wortham, J. (2011). Feel like a wall flower? Maybe it's your Facebook wall. *The New York Times*. Retrieved from https://www.nytimes.com/2011/04/10/business/10ping.html

Xiang, P., McBride, R., Guan, J., & Solmon, M. (2003). Children's motivation in elementary physical education: An expectancy–value model of achievement choice. *Research Quarterly for Exercise and Sport*, *74*(1), 25–35. doi:10.1080/02701367.2003.10609061 PMID:12659473

Yang, J. H. (2012). Effects of high school ICT activities on students' digital literacy in Korea. *Journal of Educational Technology*, *28*(2), 347–369. doi:10.17232/KSET.28.2.347

Yansen, G., & Zukerfeld, M. (2014). Why Don't Women Program? Exploring Links between Gender, Technology and Software. *Science, Technology & Society*, *19*(3), 305–329. doi:10.1177/0971721814548111

Yasin, B., Yasin, B., Baghirov, F., Baghirov, F., Zhang, Y., & Zhang, Y. (2017). The role of travel experience and gender on travel information source selection. *Journal of Hospitality and Tourism Technology*, *8*(2), 296–310. doi:10.1108/JHTT-01-2017-0002

Yau, H. K., & Leung, Y. F. (2016). Gender Difference of Self-Efficacy and Attitudes Towards the Use of Technology in Learning in Hong Kong Higher Education. *Proceedings of the International MultiConference*. Retrieved from http://www.iaeng.org/publication/IMECS2016/IMECS2016_pp819-821.pdf

Yau, H.K., & Cheng, A.L. (2012). Gender Difference of Confidence in Using Technology for Learning. *Journal of Technology Studies,* 74-79.

Yazilitas, D., Svensson, J., de Vries, G., & Saharso, S. (2013). Gendered study choice: A literature review. A review of theory and research into the unequal representation of male and female students in mathematics, science, and technology. *Educational Research and Evaluation*, *19*(6), 525–545. doi:10.1080/13803611.2013.803931

Yeganehfar, M., Zarei, A., Isfandyari-Mogghadam, A. R., & Famil-Rouhani, A. A. (2018). Justice in technology policy: A systematic review of gender divide literature and the marginal contribution of women on ICT. *Journal of Information, Communication and Ethics in Society*. doi:10.1108/JICES-06-2017-0038

Yildiz, M. (2007). E-government research: Reviewing the literature, limitations, and ways forward. *Government Information Quarterly*, *24*(3), 646–665. doi:10.1016/j.giq.2007.01.002

Yildiz, M. (2010). Digital divide in Turkey: A general assessment. In E. Ferro, Y. K. Dwivedi, J. R. Gil-Garcia, & M. D. Williams (Eds.), *Handbook of research on overcoming digital divides: Constructing an equitable and competitive information society* (pp. I75–I89). Hershey, PA: IGI Global. doi:10.4018/978-1-60566-699-0.ch005

Yli-Piipari, S. (2013). The development of students' physical education motivation and physical activity: a 3.5-year longitudinal study across Grades 6 to 9 (Dissertation). Jyväskylä: University of Jyväskylä.

York, A. (2017, March 6). *Social Media Demographics to Inform a Better Segmentation Strategy.* Retrieved from Sprout Social: https://sproutsocial.com/insights/new-social-media-demographics/

Young, K. S. (2007). Cognitive behavior therapy with internet addicts: Treatment outcomes and implications. *Cyberpsychology & Behavior, 10*(5), 671–679. doi:10.1089/cpb.2007.9971 PMID:17927535

Zagami, J., Boden, M., Keane, T., Moreton, B., & Schulz, K. (2015). Girls and Computing: Female participation in computing in Schools, *Australian. Education and Computing, 30*(2).

Zaharia, S., Kauke, D., & Hartung, E. (2017). Eye-Tracking Analysis of Gender-Specific Online Information Research and Buying Behavior. In *International Conference on HCI in Business, Government, and Organizations* (pp. 143-159). Springer.

Zarrett, N. R., & Malanchuk, O. (2005). Who's computing? Gender and race differences in young adults' decisions to pursue an Information Technology career. *New Directions for Child and Adolescent Development, 110*(110), 65–84. doi:10.1002/cd.150 PMID:16509540

Zarrett, N. R., Malanchuk, O., Davis-Kean, P. E., & Eccles, J. S. (2006). Examining the gender gap in IT by race: young adults' decisions to pursue an IT career. In J. M. Cohoon & B. Aspray (Eds.), *Women and Information Technology: Research on the reasons for underrepresentation* (pp. 55–88). Cambridge, MA: MIT Press. doi:10.7551/mitpress/9780262033459.003.0002

Zhang, H., Xu, X., & Xiao, J. (2014). Diffusion of e-government: A literature review and directions for future directions. *Government Information Quarterly, 31*(4), 631–636. doi:10.1016/j.giq.2013.10.013

Zhang, K. Z., Benyoucef, M., & Zhao, S. J. (2015). Consumer participation and gender differences on companies' microblogs: A brand attachment process perspective. *Computers in Human Behavior, 44*, 357–368. doi:10.1016/j.chb.2014.11.068

Zhang, Y. X. (2002). Comparison of Internet attitudes between industrial employees and college students. *Cyberpsychology & Behavior, 5*(2), 143–149. doi:10.1089/109493102753770534 PMID:12025881

Zhao, L., Lu, Y., Huang, W., & Wang, Q. (2010). Internet inequality: The relationship between high school students' Internet use in different locations and their Internet self-efficacy. *Computers & Education, 55*(4), 1405–1423. doi:10.1016/j.compedu.2010.05.010

Zhong, Z. J. (2011). From access to usage: The divide of self-reported digital skills among adolescents. *Computers & Education, 56*(3), 736–746. doi:10.1016/j.compedu.2010.10.016

Zhou, C. (2012). *Group Creativity Development in Engineering Education in Problem and Project-Based Learning (PBL) Environment.* Aalborg: akprint.

Zhou, C. (2016). Fostering Creative Problem Solvers in Higher Education: A Response to Complexity of Societies. In C. Zhou (Ed.), Handbook of Research on Creative Problem-Solving Skill Development in Higher Education (pp. 1-23). IGI global. Doi:10.4018/978-1-5225-0643-0.ch001

Zhou, C., & Purushothaman, A. (2015). Improving Creativity in Collaborative Process: A Knowledge Model based on Communities of Practice in Organizational Learning Contexts. In J. Ogunleye (Ed.), *Research Papers on Knowledge, Innovation and Enterprise* (*Vol. 3*, pp. 57-68). 2015 KIE Conference Publications. KIE Conference Book Series.

Zhou, C., Chen, H., & Luo, L. (2014). Students' Perceptions of Creativity in Learning Information Technology (IT) in Project Groups. *Computers in Human Behavior*, *41*, 454–463. doi:10.1016/j.chb.2014.09.058

Zhou, C., Purushothaman, A., & Rongbutsri, N. (2013). Facilitate Sustainability of Education by Problem-Based Learning (PBL) and Information and Communication Technology (ICT). *International Journal of Emerging Technologies in Learning*, *8*(6), 50–54. doi:10.3991/ijet.v8i6.3146

Zhou, M. (2014). Gender difference in web search perceptions and behavior: Does it vary by task performance? *Computers & Education*, *78*, 174–184. doi:10.1016/j.compedu.2014.06.005

Zolkepli, I. A., & Kamarulzaman, Y. (2011). Understanding Social Media Adoption: The Role of Perceived Media Needs And Technology Characteristics. *World Journal of Social Sciences*, *1*(1), 188–199.

Zurer, R. (2018). *Diversity Is For White Men Too. Here's How — and Why It Matters*. Retrieved from https://consciouscompanymedia.com/workplace-culture/diversity-inclusion/diversity-is-for-white-men-too/

About the Contributors

Idongesit Williams is a Post-Doctoral Researcher and Lecturer at Center for Communication, Media and Information Technologies (CMI), Aalborg University Copenhagen. He teaches Internet Economics and Governance. He holds a Bachelor in Physics, a Master degree in Information and Communications Technologies and a Ph.D. He is a specialist in telecommunications and Internet policy. In addition to his specialization, he has since 2010 researched into issues pertaining to Knowledge Management, Organizational Learning, Public-Private Partnerships, gender divide, socioeconomic and socio-technical issues surrounding Information and Communications Technologies. He is also involves in EU projects focused on the Digitization and Business development and he has also consulted for companies. He has authored and co-authored more than 40 research publications, including journal papers, books, book chapters, conference papers and magazine articles. He is the co-editor of the following books, The African Mobile Story, and the Handbook on ICT for developing countries:5G perspectives. Evaluating mobile richness in organizational learning, to mention a few.

Olga Millward is a PhD fellow at Aalborg University Copenhagen and holds a master degree in law. She is an experienced lawyer, specialising in ICT and telecommunications law as well as in other more general legal subjects. The title of her study is "Legal and political challenges and solutions to ICT deployments for development of the Digital society in Ukraine". As part of interdisciplinary research, she also analyses policy and strategy development for implementation of e-government platform (e-services) and smart urban digital solutions for sustainable living environment taking recent world best practices and particularly those developed within Danish Smart City concept and real life cases as models of possible adaption or replication. She is an external lecturer at Erhvervsakademi Zealand Denmark on the following legal subjects: IT contract, copyright protection of software, legal aspects of Open Source Software in commercial projects.

Roslyn Layton is an international expert in evidence-based policy for information & communications technology (ICT) industries. She is a Visiting Researcher at the Center for Communication, Media, and Information Technologies (CMI) at Aalborg University and a Visiting Scholar at the American Enterprise Institute. She holds a PhD from the Doctoral School of Engineering and Science at Aalborg University in Denmark. Her doctoral thesis investigated the empirical outcome of net neutrality policy across 53 countries, using data science and business economics to measure the impact of different types of rules on the level of mobile app innovation. She holds an MBA from the Rotterdam School of Management where she was awarded the Wall Street Journal Europe Women in Business Scholarship and an undergraduate degree from the School of International Service at the American University in Washington

D.C. with a focus on economics and Japanese studies. Roslyn writes on technology policy for Forbes, US News and World Report, and AEIdeas. Prior to academe, she worked in the information technology (IT) industry and financial industry. She was a business development executive for TCS Innovation Labs in Hyderabad, India focusing on bioinformatics, algorithmic finance, and e-security. She managed a leading digital advertising agency with the Coremetrics IBM analytics platform serving 2000 companies from San Mateo, CA. As a financial advisor at Piper Jaffray, she worked with non-profit organizations on fund development and endowment management. Roslyn serves on the Program Committee of the Telecom Policy Research Conference.

* * *

Mercy Adebayo is a Doctoral candidate in the Department of Sociology at Covenant University, Nigeria.

Andrea Diaz is a Civil Industrial Engineer who studied and worked in Chile. She is currently undertaking a Masters in Business Information Systems at Monash University, Melbourne, Australia, and is interested in how women engineers construct their careers and the differences and similarities experienced by women engineers in Chile and Australia.

Michael Fagbohun is a passionate professional librarian. He is a Technical Services Librarian, Centre for Learning Resources. Experienced Librarian with a demonstrated history of working in the different libraries. He has strong education professional skilled in research, digital library, lifelong learning and ICT studies.

Tayo O. George (PhD) is an Associate Professor of Gender and Development Studies at Covenant University, Nigeria. She has published widely in the area of gender, development, women empowerment, education and Capacity building. She currently teaches Sociology course:, social inequality, stratification, mobility, gender issues and studies in leadership and Africa's Development.

Selda Gorkey, Ph.D., is an assistant professor at Istanbul Kultur University, Turkey. She holds a Ph.D. degree in Economics from Istanbul University, Turkey. In her doctoral dissertation, she has empirically analyzed the impact of international technology diffusion channels on manufacturing industry's total-factor productivity in emerging countries within the EU and in Turkey. Her main research areas include; development economics, economics of technological change, economics of gender, human capital and education.

Marjorie Jerrard is a Senior Lecturer in the Monash Business School, Victoria, Australia, and researches in the areas of industrial relations, trade unions, gender diversity-related issues, and the meat processing/packing industry (Australia, New Zealand, Britain, and the US), with a recent focus on migrant workers in that industry.

Tekin Kose got his PhD in Economics from University of Pittsburgh. His research areas include experimental economics, applied microeconomics and international economics. He has published in Journal of Balkan and Near Eastern Studies, International Journal of Behavioral Accounting and Finance and International Journal of Pluralism and Economics Education. He is currently an Assistant Professor in TED University, Department of Economics, Ankara, Turkey.

Sabrina Ching Yuen Luk is Assistant Professor in Public Policy and Global Affairs, Nanyang Technological University (NTU), Singapore. She was awarded her PhD from the Department of Political Science and International Studies, University of Birmingham, the United Kingdom, and her MPhil and Bachelor of Social Science (First Class Honours) from the Department of Government and Public Administration, the Chinese University of Hong Kong.

Hannah Muat holds an MA in Leadership and Development and works as an administrator at the University for Development studies, Ghana. Her research interests focus on the experiences of students and the changing nature of higher education. She employs critical theories of education and qualitative methodologies to explore issues of gender, access and equity in higher education. Her previous research has focused on the girl child education. Currently, her research emphasizes on transnational education and internationalization in higher education. Specifically, she explores mobility among students and brings to the fore the motivations for seeking cross border education.

Olawale Olonade is a Research Fellow in the Department of Sociology at Covenant University, Nigeria.

Anthony O. Onwumah (PhD) is a Senior Lecturer in the Department of Sociology at Covenant University Nigeria where he teaches social anthropology, medical sociology and cultural studies.

Tijen Över Özçelik is an Assistant Professor for Industrial Engineering at Sakarya University, Engineering Faculty, Department of Industrial Engineering, Sakarya, Turkey. She graduated from faculty of engineering, metallurgical engineering department, at İstanbul Tech. University in 1987. She worked as a quality controller engineering in Lucas Industries Plc. between the years of 1987-1989. She received her MBA degree at the Institute of Natural Sciences, in Metallurgical Engineering discipline in 1999. And than she worked as a research assistant in the department of informatics, Sakarya University between 1999-2006. She got her PhD degree from Sakarya University at the Department of Industrial Engineering by thesis about Information Requirements Determination. Her current research interests include lean production, system development, system requirements determination, management information systems, innovation and technology management, electronic government and Industry 4.0. Dr. Över Özçelik has been working as a member of Sakarya University Women Research Center since 2011.

Ceyda Tanrikulu received her BS, MS, and PhD degrees in business administration from University of Cukurova. Her PhD studies focused on consumer behaviour. She is now an associate professor in the Department of International Business and Finance in Adana Science and Technology University. Her research areas are consumer behavior and sales management. Her publications have appeared in SSCI and internationally indexed journals.

Fred Totimeh is a Lecturer at Pentecost University College, Ghana, with over twenty years industry experience as an IT Manager with Ghana Prisons Service and a Programmer at the Office of the President. He holds Masters Degree in Information Technology from Sikkim Manipal University. He also holds a Bsc. in Computer Science degree and Postgraduate Certificate in Business Administration.

Joseph Kofi Wireko is a Lecturer at the Ghana Technology University College (GTUC), Ghana and a Ph.D. fellow at Center for Communications Media and Information Technologies (CMI), Aalborg University-Copenhagen, Denmark.

Winfred Yaokumah is the Dean of the Faculty of Engineering, Science and Computing at the Pentecost University College, Accra, Ghana. He holds a PhD in Information Technology with specialization in Information Assurance and Security. He has published extensively in several international journals, including the Information Management & Computer Security, International Journal of Technology Diffusion, Journal of Information Technology Research, International Journal of Information Systems and Social Change, International Journal of IT/Business Alignment and Governance, and the International Journal of Information Systems in the Service Sector. His research interest includes information security, e-services, IT governance, cloud computing, technology diffusion, information security governance, and IT leadership.

Chunfang Zhou, Ph.D., is an associate professor in Department of Planning at Aalborg University, Denmark. Chunfang locates her research in the area of Science, Technology and Society (STS), with a particular focus on creativity study and its relations to technology design, user-driven innovation, group collaboration, engineering practice and education, organisational learning, Problem-Based Learning (PBL), sustainability, and Information Communication Technology (ICT). She recently has contributed to a cross-cultural study on comparison of creativity among young engineers between Denmark and China. She was the editor of the Handbook of Research on Creative Problem-solving Skill Development in Higher Education, published in 2016, by IGI Global. She is currently one in editorial team in series Arts, Creativities and Learning Environments in Global Perspectives, with publisher Brill/Sense.

Index

www.ingramcontent.com/pod-product-compliance
Lightning Source LLC
LaVergne TN
LVHW060420300926
849162LV00006B/1479